"We are in debt to Colin Kruse for his patient and meticulous study of the Greek text of Second Corinthians, which will be of inestimable value for those who teach from this epistle. Instead of trawling through many books, much of what is needed is here between the covers of one book. This is a remarkable achievement that will bless congregations for years to come. All praise for the vision of the series editors."

—Paul Barnett, lecturer emeritus, Moore Theological College, Sydney, New South Wales, Australia

"The series design—providing grammatical analysis pertinent to interpretation and relevant further reading—is enacted in an exemplary way in this volume. The brief and accurate overviews of interpretive cruxes are particularly impressive. Any exegete who goes to this volume first, will save themselves much time in finding and following the mountain of other works to be read."

—David Instone-Brewer, senior research fellow in Rabbinics and the New Testament, Tyndale House, Cambridge, UK

"Colin Kruse's volume on 2 Corinthians is a worthy addition to the Exegetical Guide to the Greek New Testament series. This series is notable for its attention to the details of the Greek text, making it especially valuable for students of Greek. Kruse's 2 Corinthians goes considerably beyond Greek details, however, providing a very useful guide to the meaning of the text. Because the commentary is relatively uncluttered with references to secondary sources, this interpretive guidance is easily followed. This volume should be used by anyone working with the Greek text of 2 Corinthians."

—Douglas Moo, Wessner Chair of Biblical Studies, Wheaton College, and chair, Committee on Bible Translation

The Exegetical Guide to the Greek New Testament

Volumes Available

Matthew	Charles L. Quarles
Luke	Alan J. Thompson
John	Murray J. Harris
Romans	John D. Harvey
2 Corinthians	Colin G. Kruse
Ephesians	Benjamin L. Merkle
Philippians	Joseph H. Hellerman
Colossians, Philemon	Murray J. Harris
Hebrews	Dana M. Harris
James	Chris A. Vlachos
1 Peter	Greg W. Forbes

Forthcoming Volumes

Mark	Joel F. Williams
Acts	L. Scott Kellum
1 Corinthians	Jay E. Smith
Galatians	David A. Croteau
1–2 Thessalonians	David W. Chapman
1–2 Timothy, Titus	Ray Van Neste
2 Peter, Jude	Terry L. Wilder
1–3 John	Robert L. Plummer
Revelation	Alexander Stewart

EXEGETICAL
GUIDE TO THE GREEK
NEW TESTAMENT

2 CORINTHIANS

Colin G. Kruse

EXEGETICAL
GUIDE TO THE GREEK
NEW TESTAMENT

2 CORINTHIANS

Andreas J. Köstenberger
Robert W. Yarbrough

GENERAL EDITORS

Nashville, Tennessee

Exegetical Guide to the Greek New Testament: 2 Corinthians
Copyright © 2020 by Colin G. Kruse
Published by B&H Academic
Nashville, Tennessee
All rights reserved.

ISBN: 978-1-4627-4396-4

Dewey Decimal Classification: 227.3
Subject Heading: BIBLE. N.T. 2 CORINTHIANS—STUDY AND TEACHING /
BIBLE. N.T.—CRITICISM

Printed in the United States of America
1 2 3 4 5 6 7 8 9 10 VP 25 24 23 22 21 20

To my colleague,
Greg W. Forbes,
from whom I have learned much
about New Testament Greek

Contents

Acknowledgments   xix

Publisher's Preface   xxi

General Introduction to the EGGNT Series   xxiii

Abbreviations   xxvii

2 CORINTHIANS

Introduction   3
  Author   3
  Date and Provenance   3
  Occasion and Purpose   4
  Structure   4
  Outline   5
  Recommended Commentaries   6

I. Paul's Response to a Crisis Resolved (1:1–9:15)   7

  A. Preface (1:1–11)   7

    1. The Address and Greeting (1:1–2)   7

  For Further Study   9
    1. Apostleship in the NT (1:1)   9
    2. Christology (1:1)   10
    3. The Will of God (1:1)   10
    4. The Church (1:1)   10
    5. Ancient Letters (1:1–2)   10
    6. Greetings and Benedictions (1:2)   11
    7. Fatherhood of God (1:2)   11

  Homiletical Suggestions   11
    The Church of God (1:1–2)   11

    2. The Benediction (1:3–11)   11

      a. Paul Blesses God and Expresses His Hope for His Readers (1:3–7)   11
      b. Paul's Troubles in Asia (1:8–11)   17

  For Further Study   21
    8. Mercy (οἰκτιρμός) (1:3)   21
    9. Comfort (παράκλησις) (1:3)   22
    10. Affliction/Suffering (θλῖψις/πάθημα) (1:4–7)   22

11. Participation/Sharing (κοινωνία) (1:7)   22
12. Affliction in Asia (1:8)   22
13. Trust in God (1:9)   22
14. The Sentence of Death (ἀπόκριμα) (1:9)   22

Homiletical Suggestions   23
  God Comforts His People (1:3–7)   23
  The Discipline of Affliction (1:8–11)   23

B. The Body of the Response (1:12–7:16)   24

  1. Personal Defense (1:12–24)   24

    a. General Defense of Integrity (1:12–14)   24
    b. Defense of Changed Travel Plans (1:15–22)   28
    c. Paul Calls upon God as His Witness (1:23–24)   35

For Further Study   37
  15. Conscience (συνείδησις) (1:12)   37
  16. The Day of the Lord (1:14)   37
  17. Paul's Travels (1:15–16)   37
  18. Down Payment of the Spirit (ἀρραβών) (1:21–22)   37
  19. God as Witness (μάρτυς) (1:23)   37

Homiletical Suggestions   38
  Paul Asks for Understanding (1:12–14)   38
  Paul Explains His Actions and Why He Can Be Trusted (1:15–22)   38
  Real Concern for Those to Whom We Minister (1:23–24)   38

  2. The "Severe Letter": Its Purpose and Aftermath (2:1–13)   39

    a. The Purpose of the "Severe Letter" (2:1–4)   39
    b. Forgiveness for the Offender (2:5–11)   43
    c. Waiting for Titus (2:12–13)   47

For Further Study   49
  20. Paul's Painful Visit (2:1–2)   49
  21. The "Severe Letter" (2:3–4)   49
  22. The Offender and His Offense (2:5)   49
  23. Punishment—Judicial as Well as Remedial (2:6–8)   49
  24. Satan's Schemes (2:11)   49
  25. Troas (2:12–13)   49
  26. Titus (2:13)   49

Homiletical Suggestions   50
  Paul Seeks to Avoid Pain and Causing Pain (2:1–4)   50
  The Crucial Importance of Forgiveness (2:5–11)   50
  Open Doors but No Peace of Mind (2:12–13)   50

  3. Competency in Ministry (2:14–4:6)   51

    a. Led in Triumph (2:14–17)   51

For Further Study   56

  27. Led in Triumph (2:14)   56
  28. Aroma/Fragrance of Christ (2:15)   56
  29. Sufficiency for Apostolic Ministry (2:16)   56
  30. Marketing the Word of God (2:17)   56

Homiletical Suggestions   57
    Led in Triumph (2:14–17)   57

        1. God spreads abroad the knowledge of his Son as we share the gospel
          message (v. 14).   57
        2. When the message is accepted, it leads to life, but when rejected, it
          leads to death (v 15).   57
        3. The question of adequacy for such a ministry (v. 16)   57
        4. The crucial importance of integrity in ministry, avoiding the
          temptation to regard it as a means of profit (v. 17)   57

    b. Letters of Recommendation (3:1–3)   58
    c. Ministers of the New Covenant (3:4–6)   61

For Further Study   64

    31. Letters of Recommendation (3:1–3)   64
    32. Self-Commendation (3:1)   64
    33. Competency for Ministry (3:4–5)   64
    34. Ministry/διαχονία (3:6)   64
    35. A New Covenant (3:6)   65
    36. Letter and Spirit (3:6)   65

Homiletical Suggestions   65
    Authentication of Ministry (3:1–3)   65
    Competency for Ministry (3:4–6)   65

    d. The Greater Glory of New Covenant Ministry (3:7–11)   67
    e. The Greater Boldness of New Covenant Ministers (3:12–18)   71

For Further Study   78
    37. Glory (3:7–11)   78
    38. Veiled and Unveiled Faces (3:12–16)   79
    39. Use of Scripture (3:14–16)   79
    40. Covenant (3:14)   79
    41. The Law and the Spirit (3:15–18)   79
    42. The Spirit Transformation (3:18)   80

Homiletical Suggestions   80
    New Covenant Ministry (3:7–11)   80
    New Covenant Ministers (3:12–18)   80

    f. The Conduct of Paul's Ministry (4:1–6)   81

For Further Study   88
    43. Ministry (4:1)   88
    44. Mercy (4:1)   88
    45. Conscience (4:2)   88
    46. The God of This World (4:4)   89
    47. The Knowledge of God's Glory in the Face of Christ (4:6)   89

Homiletical Suggestions   89
    How to Conduct the Glorious Ministry of the Gospel (4:1–6)   89

    4. Present Suffering and Future Glory (4:7–5:10)   90

    a. Treasure in Jars of Clay (4:7–15)   90
    b. We Do Not Give Up (4:16–18)   97

For Further Study   100
        48. Catalogue of Afflictions (4:8–12)   100
        49. Death and Life (4:10)   101
        50. Believing and Speaking (4:13)   101
        51. Future Hope/Resurrection (4:14)   101

Homiletical Suggestions   101
        Treasure in Jars of Clay (4:7–15)   101
        Why We Do Not Lose Heart (4:16–18)   101
            c. The Heavenly Dwelling (5:1–10)   103

For Further Study   112
        52. Personal Eschatology (5:1–8)   112
        53. General (5:1–10)   112
        54. An Eternal Dwelling in the Heavens (5:1)   112
        55. Pledge or Down Payment (Ἀρραβών) (5:5)   112
        56. At Home in the Body, Away from the Lord (5:6–9)   113
        57. Appearing before the Judgment Seat of Christ (5:10)   113

Homiletical Suggestions   113
        The Christian Hope (5:1–5)   113
        Living "Away from the Lord" (5:6–10)   113

    5. The Ministry of Reconciliation (5:11–21)   114

        a. Defense of His Ministry (5:11–15)   114
        b. God's Reconciling Act in Christ (5:16–21)   119

For Further Study   126
        58. Self-Commendation (5:11–12)   126
        59. Paul's Ecstasy or Madness? (5:13)   126
        60. Christ Died for All (5:14–15)   126
        61. The Compelling Love of Christ (5:14)   126
        62. Paul's Knowledge of Christ (5:16)   126
        63. A New Creation (5:17)   127
        64. Reconciliation (5:18–19)   127
        65. Paul as Ambassador (5:20)   127
        66. Made to Be Sin and Becoming the Righteousness of God (5:21)   127

Homiletical Suggestions   127
        Setting the Record Straight (5:11–15)   127
        Reconciliation and Its Implications (5:16–21)   127

    6. Reconciliation Practiced (6:1–7:4)   128

        a. An Appeal for Reconciliation (6:1–13)   128

For Further Study   135
        67. Now Is the Day of Salvation (6:2–3)   135
        68. Self-Commendation (6:4)   135
        69. Paul's Hardship Lists (6:4–5)   135

Homiletical Suggestions   135
        Paul's Appeal (6:1–2)   135
        Giving No Offense (6:3–10)   135
        Frank and Openhearted Communication (6:11–13)   135

b. A Call for Holy Living (6:14–7:1)   136
c. A Further Appeal for Reconciliation (7:2–4)   141

For Further Study   143
70. Understanding 2 Cor 6:14–7:1   143
71. Unequally Yoked Together (6:14)   144
72. Belial (6:15)   144
73. Paul's Use of Scripture (6:16–18)   144
74. Dying and Living (7:3)   144

Homiletical Suggestions   144
Paul's Exhortation (6:14–15a)   144
The Promises of God (6:16–18)   144
Paul's Appeal (7:1–4)   145

7. Paul's Joy after a Crisis Resolved (7:5–16)   146

a. Paul's Relief When Titus Arrived (7:5–7)   146
b. The "Severe Letter" and Its Effects (7:8–13a)   149
c. Titus's Happiness and Affection for the Corinthians (7:13b–16) 155

For Further Study   158
75. Comfort (7:6–7)   158
76. Titus (7:6)   158
77. Repentance (7:9–10)   158
78. Discipline (7:11)   159
79. The Offender (7:12)   159

Homiletical Suggestions   159
Paul's Anxiety and Comfort (7:5–7)   159
Regrets Giving Way to Joy (7:8–11)   159
Godly Motivation (7:12)   159
Risk-Taking for the Greater Good (7:14)   159
The Importance of Affirmation (7:16)   159

C. The Matter of the Collection (8:1–9:15)   160

1. The Example of the Macedonians (8:1–6)   160
2. Paul Exhorts the Corinthians to Finish What They Began (8:7–15) 165
3. Commendation of Those Who Will Receive the Collection (8:16–24) 171

For Further Study   178
80. The Collection (8:1–24)   178
81. Κοινωνία (8:4)   178
82. Paul and Persuasion (8:7–15)   179
83. Financial Integrity (8:18–23)   179
84. The Glory of Christ (8:23)   179
85. Boasting and Joy (8:24)   179

Homiletical Suggestions   179
The Power of a Godly Example (8:1–6)   179
Motivation for and Practical Advice Regarding Christian Giving (8:7–15) 179
Ensuring the Administration of Aid Is above Reproach (8:16–24) 180

4. Be Prepared and Avoid Humiliation (9:1–5)   181
5. An Exhortation to Be Generous (9:6–15)   186

For Further Study   193
    86. The Collection (9:1–13)   193
    87. Paul and Persuasion (9:1–14)   194
    88. Boasting and Joy (9:3–4)   194
    89. Financial Integrity (9:5)   194
    90. Word Studies   194

Homiletical Suggestions   194
    Practical Incentives (9:1–5)   194
    Theological Incentives (9:6–11)   195
    Practical Outcomes (9:12–14)   195
    God's Indescribable Gift (9:15)   195

II. Paul Responds to a New Crisis (10:1–13:14)   196

  A. Paul's Exercise of Apostolic Authority (10:1–18)   196

    1. Paul Responds to Criticisms (10:1–11)   197
    2. Boasting within Proper Limits (10:12–18)   206

For Further Study   212
    91. Appeal by the Meekness and Gentleness of Christ (10:1)   212
    92. Military Metaphors (10:3–6)   212
    93. Ministry Rights and κανών (10:13–15)   213
    94. Boasting and Self-Commendation (10:12–18)   213
    95. Paul's Use of the OT (10:17–18)   213

Homiletical Suggestions   213
    Christian "Warfare" (10:2–6)   213
    The Purpose of Ministry: To Build People Up, Not Tear Them Down
    (10:8–11)   214
    Boasting within Appropriate Limits (10:12–18)   214

  B. A Plea for Tolerance and Condemnation of the Opponents (11:1–15)   215

    1. The Corinthians' Gullibility (11:1–6)   215
    2. The Matter of Financial Remuneration (11:7–15)   221

For Further Study   227
    96. Paul's Appeal and the Betrothal Image (11:2–3)   227
    97. Another Jesus, a Different Spirit, and Another Gospel (11:4)   227
    98. Boasting and Foolishness (11:5–6)   228
    99. Paul's Financial Policy (11:7–12)   228
    100. False Apostles, Servants of Satan (11:13–15)   228

Homiletical Suggestions   228
    Concern for Converts (11:1–6)   228
    Responding to Criticism (11:5–11)   228
    Straight Talk (11:12–15)   229

  C. The Fool's Speech (11:16–12:13)   230

    1. Accept Me as a Fool (11:16–21a)   230
    2. Paul's Jewish Ancestry (11:21b–22)   234
    3. A Better Servant of Christ (11:23–33)   236

For Further Study   243
    101. Boasting and Foolishness (11:1–20)   243

102. False Apostles, Servants of Satan (11:20)   243
103. Hardships (11:23–29)   243
104. Ethnarch of Aretas (11:32)   244

Homiletical Suggestions   244
Speaking Foolishly (11:16–21a)   244
Speaking Foolishly of Ancestral Pride (11:21b–22)   244
Speaking Foolishly of External Sources of Suffering (11:23–26)   244
Speaking Foolishly of Self-Imposed Privation and Anxiety (11:27–29)   244
Speaking Foolishly of the Ignominy of His First Experience of Persecution
(11:30–33)   244

4. Visions and Revelations (12:1–10)   245
5. Signs of an Apostle (12:11–13)   253

For Further Study   256
105. Visions and Revelation (12:1–4)   256
106. Human Weakness and the Power of God (12:5, 9–10)   257
107. Paul's Thorn in the Flesh (12:7–8)   257
108. The Signs of an Apostle (12:11–13)   257
109. False Apostles, Servants of Satan (12:11)   257

Homiletical Suggestions   257
Boasting about Visions and Revelations (12:1–6)   257
Paul's Thorn in the Flesh (12:7–10)   258
Paul Is in No Way Inferior to the "Super Apostles" (12:11–13)   258

D. Paul's Planned Third Visit (12:14–13:10)   259

1. Paul Refuses to Burden the Corinthians (12:14–18)   259
2. The Real Purpose of Paul's Fool's Speech (12:19–21)   263

For Further Study   266
110. Paul's Self-Understanding (12:14–15)   266
111. Paul's Opponents and the Corinthian Church (12:14–17)   266
112. Paul's Financial Integrity (12:14–18)   267
113. Paul's Fellow Workers (12:17–18)   267

Homiletical Suggestions   267
Financial Integrity (12:14–18)   267
Building Up People Is the Goal of Ministry (12:19–21)   267

3. Paul Threatens Strong Action on His Third Visit (13:1–10)   268

E. Conclusion (13:11–13)   276

1. Final Exhortations (13:11–12)   276

For Further Study   277
114. Two or Three Witnesses (13:1)   277
115. Weakness and Power (13:3–4)   277
116. Perseverance (13:5)   278

Homiletical Suggestions   278
Responding to Criticisms (13:1–4)   278
Testing Oneself to Ensure the Authenticity of Christian Experience
(13:5–8)   278

Exhortations and Encouragements (13:11–12)   278
2. Benediction (13:13)   279
For Further Study   280
   117. Benedictions and Doxologies (13:13)   280
   118. Fellowship (13:13)   280
Homiletical Suggestions   280
   A Trinitarian Benediction, Invoking Grace, Love, and Fellowship (13:13)   280

Exegetical Outline   281

Grammar Index   283

Scripture Index   285

Acknowledgments

I am grateful to the editors, Andreas J. Köstenberger and Robert W. Yarbrough, for their kind invitation to contribute the volume on 2 Corinthians to the Exegetical Guide to the Greek New Testament series (EGGNT).

I also want to acknowledge and express my thanks to InterVarsity Press for permission to use and adapt some material from my recently revised commentary on 2 Corinthians for the Tyndale New Testament Commentary series in the production of this volume for the EGGNT series.

It is my hope and prayer that this guide will assist readers of the Greek New Testament to understand better the original language of Paul's Second Letter to the Corinthians and, in so doing, to appreciate the incredible grace of the God whom he served.

Publisher's Preface

It is with great excitement that we publish this volume of the Exegetical Guide to the Greek New Testament series. When the founding editor, Dr. Murray J. Harris, came to us seeking a new publishing partner, we gratefully accepted the offer. With the help of the coeditor, Andreas J. Köstenberger, we spent several years working together to acquire all of the authors we needed to complete the series. By God's grace we succeeded and contracted the last author in 2011. Originally working with another publishing house, Murray's efforts spanned more than twenty years. As God would have it, shortly after the final author was contracted, Murray decided God wanted him to withdraw as coeditor of the series. God made clear to him that he must devote his full attention to taking care of his wife, who faces the daily challenges caused by multiple sclerosis.

Over the course of many years, God has used Murray to teach his students how to properly exegete the Scriptures. He is an exceptional scholar and professor. But even more importantly, Murray is a man dedicated to serving Christ. His greatest joy is to respond in faithful obedience when his Master calls. "There can be no higher and more ennobling privilege than to have the Lord of the universe as one's Owner and Master and to be his accredited representative on earth."[1] Murray has once again heeded the call of his Master.

It is our privilege to dedicate the Exegetical Guide to the Greek New Testament series to Dr. Murray J. Harris. We pray that our readers will continue the work he started.

B&H Academic

---

1. Murray J. Harris, *Slave of Christ: A New Testament Metaphor for Total Devotion to Christ* (Downers Grove, IL: InterVarsity Press, 1999), 155.

General Introduction to the EGGNT Series

Studying the New Testament in the original Greek has become easier in recent years. Beginning students will work their way through an introductory grammar or other text, but then what? Grappling with difficult verb forms, rare vocabulary, and grammatical irregularities remains a formidable task for those who would advance beyond the initial stages of learning Greek to master the interpretive process. Intermediate grammars and grammatical analyses can help, but such tools, for all their value, still often operate at a distance from the Greek text itself, and analyses are often too brief to be genuinely helpful.

The Exegetical Guide to the Greek New Testament (EGGNT) aims to close the gap between the Greek text and the available tools. Each EGGNT volume aims to provide all the necessary information for understanding the Greek text and, in addition, includes homiletical helps and suggestions for further study. The EGGNT is not a full-scale commentary. Nevertheless, these guides will make interpreting a given New Testament book easier, in particular for those who are hard-pressed for time and yet want to preach or teach with accuracy and authority.

In terms of layout, each volume begins with a brief introduction to the particular book (including such matters as authorship, date, etc.), a basic outline, and a list of recommended commentaries. At the end of each volume, you will find a comprehensive exegetical outline of the book. The body of each volume is devoted to paragraph-by-paragraph exegesis of the text. The treatment of each paragraph includes:

1. The Greek text of the passage, phrase by phrase, from the fifth edition of the United Bible Societies' *Greek New Testament* (UBS[5]).[1]
2. A structural analysis of the passage. Typically, verbal discussion of the structure of a given unit is followed by a diagram, whereby the verbal discussion serves to explain the diagram and the diagram serves to provide a visual aid illumining the structural discussion. While there is no one correct or standard

---

1. The English translation from the Christian Standard Bible (CSB) has been added below each Greek phrase to help readers form a bridge between the Greek text and the following analysis. Please note that the CSB uses bold text for OT quotations.

way to diagram Greek sentences, the following format is typically followed in EGGNT volumes:

a. The original Greek word order is maintained.

b. When Greek words are omitted, this is indicated by ellipses (. . .).

c. The diagramming method, moving from left to right, is predicated on the following. In clauses with a finite verb, the default order is typically verb-subject-object. In verbless clauses or clauses with nonfinite verb forms, the default order is typically subject-(verb)-object. Departures from these default orders are understood to be pragmatically motivated (e.g., contrast, emphasis, etc.).

d. Indents are used to indicate subordination (e.g., in the case of dependent clauses).

e. Retaining original word order, modifiers are centered above or below the word they modify (e.g., a prepositional phrase in relation to the verb).

f. Where a given sentence or clause spans multiple lines of text, drawn lines are used, such as where a relative pronoun introduces a relative clause (often shifting emphasis).

g. Underline is used to indicate imperatives; dotted underline is used to indicate repetition (the same word or cognate used multiple times in a given unit); the symbol ⁞ may be used where an article is separated from a noun or participle by interjected material (such as a prepositional phrase).

h. In shorter letters diagrams are normally provided for every unit; in longer letters and Revelation, ellipses may be used to show less detail in diagramming (keeping larger blocks together on the same line) in order to focus primarily on the larger structure of a given unit; in the Gospels and Acts, detailed diagrams will usually not be provided, though less detailed diagrams may be used to illustrate important or more complex structural aspects of a given passage.

3. A discussion of each phrase of the passage with discussion of relevant vocabulary, significant textual variants, and detailed grammatical analysis, including parsing. When more than one solution is given for a particular exegetical issue, the author's own preference is indicated by an asterisk (*). When no preference is expressed, the options are judged to be evenly balanced, or it is assumed that the text is intentionally ambiguous. When a particular verb form may be parsed in more than one way, only the parsing appropriate in the specific context is supplied; but where there is difference of opinion among grammarians or commentators, both possibilities are given and the matter is discussed.

4. Various translations of significant words or phrases.

5. A list of suggested topics for further study with bibliography for each topic. An asterisk (*) in one of the "For Further Study" bibliographies draws

   attention to a discussion of the particular topic that is recommended as a
   useful introduction to the issues involved.
6. Homiletical suggestions designed to help the preacher or teacher move from
   the Greek text to a sermon outline that reflects careful exegesis. The first
   suggestion for a particular paragraph of the text is always more exegetical
   than homiletical and consists of an outline of the entire paragraph. These
   detailed outlines of each paragraph build on the general outline proposed for
   the whole book and, if placed side by side, form a comprehensive exegetical
   outline of the book. All outlines are intended to serve as a basis for sermon
   preparation and should be adapted to the needs of a particular audience.[2]

The EGGNT volumes will serve a variety of readers. Those reading the Greek text
for the first time may be content with the assistance with vocabulary, parsing, and
translation. Readers with some experience in Greek may want to skip or skim these
sections and focus attention on the discussions of grammar. More advanced students
may choose to pursue the topics and references to technical works under "For Further
Study," while pastors may be more interested in the movement from grammatical
analysis to sermon outline. Teachers may appreciate having a resource that frees them
to focus on exegetical details and theological matters.

The editors are pleased to present you with the individual installments of the
EGGNT. We are grateful for each of the contributors who has labored long and hard
over each phrase in the Greek New Testament. Together we share the conviction that
"all Scripture is inspired by God and is profitable for teaching, for rebuking, for correcting, for training in righteousness" (2 Tim 3:16 CSB) and echo Paul's words to
Timothy: "Be diligent to present yourself to God as one approved, a worker who
doesn't need to be ashamed, correctly teaching the word of truth" (2 Tim 2:15 CSB).

Thanks to Michael Naylor, who served as assistant editor for this volume.

Andreas J. Köstenberger

Robert W. Yarbrough

---

2. As a Bible publisher, B&H Publishing follows the "Colorado Springs Guidelines for Translation of
Gender-Related Language in Scripture." As an academic book publisher, B&H Academic asks that authors
conform their manuscripts (including EGGNT exegetical outlines in English) to the B&H Academic style
guide, which affirms the use of singular "he/his/him" as generic examples encompassing both genders.
However, in their discussion of the Greek text, EGGNT authors have the freedom to analyze the text and
reach their own conclusions regarding whether specific Greek words are gender specific or gender inclusive.

Abbreviations

For abbreviations used in discussion of text-critical matters, the reader should refer to the abbreviations listed in the Introduction to the United Bible Societies' *Greek New Testament*.

*   indicates the reading of the original hand of a manuscript as opposed to subsequent correctors of the manuscript, *or*

indicates the writer's own preference when more than one solution is given for a particular exegetical problem, *or*

in the "For Further Study" bibliographies, indicates a discussion of the particular topic that is recommended as a useful introduction to the issues involved

§, §§   paragraph, paragraphs

Books of the Old Testament

Gen	Genesis	Song	Song of Songs (Canticles)
Exod	Exodus	Isa	Isaiah
Lev	Leviticus	Jer	Jeremiah
Num	Numbers	Lam	Lamentations
Deut	Deuteronomy	Ezek	Ezekiel
Josh	Joshua	Dan	Daniel
Judg	Judges	Hos	Hosea
Ruth	Ruth	Joel	Joel
1–2 Sam	1–2 Samuel	Amos	Amos
1–2 Kgs	1–2 Kings	Obad	Obadiah
1–2 Chr	1–2 Chronicles	Jonah	Jonah
Ezra	Ezra	Mic	Micah
Neh	Nehemiah	Nah	Nahum
Esth	Esther	Hab	Habakkuk
Job	Job	Zeph	Zephaniah
Ps(s)	Psalm(s)	Hag	Haggai
Prov	Proverbs	Zech	Zechariah
Eccl	Ecclesiastes	Mal	Malachi

Books of the New Testament

Matt	Matthew	1–2 Thess	1–2 Thessalonians
Mark	Mark	1–2 Tim	1–2 Timothy
Luke	Luke	Titus	Titus
John	John	Phlm	Philemon
Acts	Acts	Heb	Hebrews
Rom	Romans	Jas	James
1–2 Cor	1–2 Corinthians	1–2 Pet	1–2 Peter
Gal	Galatians	1–3 John	1–3 John
Eph	Ephesians	Jude	Jude
Phil	Philippians	Rev	Revelation
Col	Colossians		

Dead Sea Scrolls

1QM	War Scroll
1QS	Rule of the Community
CD	Damascus Document

General Abbreviations

AB	Anchor Bible
ABD	The Anchor Bible Dictionary, 6 vols., ed. D. N. Freedman (New York: Doubleday, 1992)
ABR	Australian Biblical Review
abs.	absolute(ly)
acc.	accusative
act.	active (voice)
adj.	adjective, adjectival(ly)
adv.	adverb, adverbial(ly)
Allo	E. B. Allo, Saint Paul: seconde épître aux Corinthiens, Etudes biblique (Paris: Gabalda, 1956)
ANRW	Austieg und Niedergang der romischen Welt
AsJT	Asia Journal of Theology
anar.	anarthrous
aor.	aorist
advers.	adversative
apod.	apodosis
appos.	apposition, appositional
Aram.	Aramaic, Aramaism
art.	(definite) article, articular

attrib.	attributive(ly)
ACCSC	Gerald Bray, ed., *Ancient Christian Commentary on Scripture: New Testament VII 1-2 Corinthians* (InterVarsity Press: Downers Grove, Illinois, 1999)
AUSS	*Andrews University Seminary Studies*
BA	Biblical Archaeologist
Barnett	P. Barnett, *The Second Epistle to the Corinthians*, NICNT (Grand Rapids: Eerdmans, 1997)
Barrett	C. K. Barrett, *The Second Epistle to the Corinthians* (London: A. & C. Black, 1973)
Betz	H. D. Betz, *2 Corinthians 8 and 9,* Hermeneia (Philadelphia: Fortress, 1985)
BBR	*Bulletin for Biblical Research*
BDAG	*A Greek-English Lexicon of the New Testament and Other Early Christian Literature*, rev. and ed. F. W. Danker (Chicago/London: University of Chicago, 2000), based on W. Bauer's *Griechisch- deutsches Wörterbuch* (6th ed.) and on previous English ed. W. F. Arndt, F. W. Gingrich, and F. W. Danker. References to BDAG are by page number and quadrant on the page, *a* indicating the upper half and *b* the lower half of the left-hand column, and *c* and *d* the upper and lower halves of the right-hand column. With the use of dark type, biblical references are now clearly visible within each subsection.
BDF	F. Blass and A. Debrunner, *A Greek Grammar of the New Testament and Other Early Christian Literature*, trans. and rev. R. W. Funk (Chicago: University of Chicago Press, 1961)
Beale and Carson	G. K. Beale and D. A. Carson, eds., *Commentary on the New Testament Use of the Old Testament* (Grand Rapids: Baker, 2007)
Best	E. Best, *One Body in Christ: A Study in the Relationship of the Church to Christ in the Epistles of the Apostle Paul* (London: SPCK, 1975)
BGk.	Biblical Greek (i.e., LXX and NT Greek)
Bib	*Biblica*
BibInt	*Biblical Interpretation*
BJRL	*Bulletin of the John Rylands University Library of Manchester*
BR	*Biblical Research*
BRev	*Bible Review*

Bray	G. Bray, ed. *Ancient Christian Commentary on Scripture: New Testament VII 1–2 Corinthians* (InterVarsity Press: Downers Grove, Illinois, 1999)
Bruce	F. F. Bruce, *1 and 2 Corinthians*, NCBC (London: Marshall Morgan & Scott, 1971)
BSac	*Bibliotheca Sacra*
BT	*Bible Translator*
BTB	*Biblical Theology Bulletin*
Bultmann	R. Bultmann, *The Second Letter to the Corinthians*. ET by R. A. Harrisville (Minneapolis: Augsburg, 1985)
Burton	E. de W. Burton, *Syntax of the Moods and Tenses in New Testament Greek*, 3rd ed. (Edinburgh: T&T Clark, 1898)
Calvin	J. Calvin, *The Second Epistle of Paul the Apostle to the Corinthians and the Epistles to Timothy, Titus and Philemon* (Grand Rapids: Eerdmans, 1980)
Campbell	C. R. Campbell, *Basics of Verbal Aspect in Biblical Greek* (Grand Rapids: Zondervan, 2008)
Carson	D. A. Carson, *From Triumphalism to Maturity: An Exposition of 2 Corinthians 10–13* (Grand Rapids: Baker, 1984)
CBQ	*Catholic Biblical Quarterly*
CEV	Contemporary English Version (1995)
cf.	*confer* (Lat.), compare
ChicStud	Chicago Studies
ch(s).	chapter(s)
comp.	comparative, comparison
cond.	condition(al)
conj.	conjunctive, conjunction
contemp.	contemporaneous
Conybeare and Stock	E. C. Conybeare and G. Stock, *Grammar of Septuagint Greek* (Grand Rapids: Baker, 2001)
cstr.	construction, construe(d)
CSB	Christian Standard Bible
CTJ	*Calvin Theological Journal*
CTM	Concordia Theological Monthly
CTR	*Criswell Theological Review*
CurTM	*Currents in Theology and Missions*
dat.	dative
dbl.	double

def.	definite
delib.	deliberative
dem.	demonstrative
Denney	J. Denney, *The Death of Christ* (London: Tyndale, 1951)
dep.	deponent
DJG	*Dictionary of Jesus and the Gospels*, 2nd ed, ed. J. B. Green, J. K. Brown, and N. Perrin (Downers Grove, IL: InterVarsity, 2013)
DLNT	*Dictionary of the Later New Testament and Its Developments*, ed. R. P. Martin and P. H. Davids (Leicester / Downers Grove, IL: InterVarsity, 1997)
DNTB	*Dictionary of New Testament Background*, ed. C. A. Evans and S. E. Porter (Leicester / Downers Grove, IL: InterVarsity, 2000)
DPL	*Dictionary of Paul and His Letters*, ed. G. F. Hawthrone, R. P. Martin, and D. G. Reid (Downers Grove, IL: InterVarsity, 1993)
dimin.	diminutive
dir.	direct
EDNT	*Exegetical Dictionary of the New Testament*, 3 vols., ed. H. Balz and G. Schneider (Grand Rapids: Eerdmans, 1990–93)
ed(s).	edited by, edition(s), editor(s)
Egan	R. P. Egan, "Lexical Evidence on Two Pauline Passages," *NovT* 19 (1977): 34–62.
e.g.	*exempli gratia* (Lat.), for example
Eng.	English
epex.	epexegetic, epexegetical(ly)
esp.	especially
ESV	English Standard Version (2011)
et al.	*et alii* (Lat.), and others
etym.	etymology (etymological)
Eusebius, *History*	Eusebius, *Ecclesiastical History*
EvQ	*Evangelical Quarterly*
EVV	English versions of the Bible
ExpTim	*Expository Times*
f(f).	and the following (verse[s] or page[s])
Fanning	Buist Fanning, *Verbal Aspect in New Testament Greek* (Oxford: Oxford University Press, 1991)

fem.	feminine
fig.	figurative(ly)
Forbes	G. Forbes, *New Testament Greek: An Introductory Grammar* (self-published)
FS	Festschrift
fr.	from
Furnish	V. P. Furnish, *II Corinthians* AB 32a (New York: Doubleday, 1984)
fut.	future
gen.	genitive
Gk.	Greek
G. B. Winer	G. B. Winer, *A Greek Grammar of the New Testament* (Andover, MA: Codman, 1825)
Geneva	Geneva Bible (1599)
Gildersleeve	B. L. Gildersleeve, *A Syntax of Classical Greek from Homer to Demosthenes* (New York: American Book Company, 1900)
GJ	*Grace Journal*
GNB	Good News Bible
Gos. Pet.	Gospel of Peter
Greg.	*Gregorianum*
Hafemann	S. J. Hafemann, *2 Corinthians,* NIVAC (Grand Rapids: Zondervan, 2000)
Harris, *Prepositions*	M. J. Harris, *Prepositions and Theology in the Greek New Testament* (Grand Rapids: Zondervan, 2012)
Harris	M. J. Harris, *The Second Epistle to the Corinthians: A Commentary on the Greek Text*, NIGTC (Grand Rapids: Eerdmans, 2005)
Heb.	Hebrew, Hebraism
Héring	J. Héring, *The Second Epistle of St. Paul to the Corinthians* (London: Epworth, 1967)
HTB	Histoire du text biblique
HTR	*Harvard Theological Review*
HUT	*Hermeneutische Untersuchungen zur Theologie*
IBS	*Irish Biblical Studies*
ICC	International Critical Commentary
IDBSup	*Interpreter's Dictionary of the Bible (Supplement Volume)*
i.e.	*id est* (Lat.), that is
impers.	impersonal

impf.	imperfect (tense)
impv.	imperative (mood), imperatival(ly)
incl.	including
indecl.	indeclinable
indef.	indefinite
indic.	indicative (mood)
indir.	indirect
inf.	infinitive
ingr.	ingressive
instr.	instrument, instrumental(ly)
intrans.	intransitive(ly)
Int	*Interpretation*
interr.	interrogative
iter.	iterative
ITQ	*Irish Theological Quarterly*
JBL	*Journal of Biblical Literature*
JETS	*Journal of the Evangelical Theological Society*
JJS	*Journal of Jewish Studies*
Jos. *Ant.*	Josephus, *Jewish Antiquities*
JSNT	*Journal for the Study of the New Testament*
JSNTSup	*Journal for the Study of the New Testament Supplements*
JTS	*Journal of Theological Studies*
KJ21	21st Century King James Version
KJV	King James Version (= "Authorized Version") (1611)
Kruse	C. G. Kruse, *2 Corinthians: An Introduction and Commentary. Revised Edition,* TNTC 8 (Nottingham/Downers Grove: IVP, 2015)
LEB	Lexham English Bible
Levinsohn	S. Levinsohn, *Discourse Features of New Testament Greek*, 2nd ed. (Dallas: SIL International, 2000)
lit.	literal(ly)
LN	J. P. Louw and E. A. Nida, eds., *Introduction and Domains*, vol. 1 of *Greek-English Lexicon of the New Testament Based on Semantic Domains* (New York: United Bible Societies, 1988)
locat.	locative
LS	*Louvain Studies*

LouvStud	*Louvain Studies*
LSJ	H. G. Liddell and R. Scott, *Greek-English Lexicon* (Oxford: Clarendon, 1996)
LTJ	*Lutheran Theological Journal*
LXX	Septuagint (= Greek Old Testament)
Macc	Maccabees
Martin	R. P. Martin, *2 Corinthi*ans, WBC 40 (Waco: Word, 1986)
masc.	masculine
McKay	K. L. McKay, *A New Syntax of the Verb in New Testament Greek: An Aspectual Approach* (New York: Peter Lang, 1994)
Metzger	B. M. Metzger, *A Textual Commentary on the Greek New Testament* (Stuttgart: Deutsche Bibelgesellschaft / New York: United Bible Societies, 1994; original ed. of 1971 based on UBS[3])
mg.	margin
MH	J. H. Moulton and W. F. Howard, *Accidence and Word-Formation*, vol. 2 of *A Grammar of New Testament Greek*, ed. J. H. Moulton (Edinburgh: T&T Clark, 1939)
mid.	middle
mng.	meaning
Moule	C. F. D. Moule, *An Idiom Book of New Testament Greek*, 2nd ed. (Cambridge: CUP, 1960)
Moulton	J. H. Moulton, *A Grammar of New Testament Greek*, vol. 1: *Prolegomena* 3rd ed. (Edinburgh: Clark, 1908)
ms(s).	manuscript(s)
MSG	The Message
MT	Masoretic Text
n.	note
NA28	*Novum Testamentum Graece*, Nestle-Aland, 28th ed.
NAB	New American Bible
NASB	New American Standard Bible (1995)
NB	Nota Bene (Latin: Note Well)
NCBC	New Century Bible Commentary
NDBT	*New Dictionary of Biblical Theology*, ed. T. D. Alexander and B. S. Rosner (Downers Grove, IL: InterVarsity, 2000)
NEASB	*Near Eastern Archaeological Society Bulletin*
NEB	New English Bible (1970)

neg.	negative, negation
Neot	*Neotestamentica*
NET	New English Translation Bible (2005)
NETS	New English Translations of the Septuagint (2007)
neut.	neuter
New Docs	*New Documents Illustrating Early Christianity*, ed. G. H. R. Horsely and S. R. Llewelyn (Macquarie University, 1981-2002)
NICNT	New International Commentary on the New Testament
NIDNTT	*The New International Dictionary of New Testament Theology*, 3 vols., ed. C. Brown (Grand Rapids: Zondervan, 1975–78)
NIDNTTE	*New International Dictionary of New Testament Theology and Exegesis*, 5 vols., ed. M. Silva (Grand Rapids: Zondervan, 2014)
NIGTC	New International Greek Testament Commentary
NIV	New International Version (2011)
NIVAC	NIV Application Commentary
NJB	New Jerusalem Bible (1985)
NKJV	New King James Version
NLT	New Living Translation (1996)
nom.	nominative
NovT	*Novum Testamentum*
NovTSup	Novum Testamentum Supplements
NRSV	New Revised Standard Version (1990)
NSBT	New Studies in Biblical Theology
NT	New Testament
NTS	*New Testament Studies*
obj.	object(ive)
orig.	origin, original(ly)
OT	Old Testament
p(p).	page(s)
pass.	passive
periph.	periphrastic
pers.	person(al)
pf.	perfect
PIBA	Proceedings of the Irish Biblical Association
pl.	plural

pluperf.	pluperfect, pluperfective
PNTC	Pillar New Testament Commentary
Porter, *Idioms*	S. E. Porter, *Idioms of the Greek New Testament* (Sheffield: JSOT, 1992)
Porter, *VA*	S. E. Porter, *Verbal Aspect in the Greek of the New Testament, with Reference to Tense and Mood*, Studies in Biblical Greek 1 (New York: Peter Lang, 1989)
poss.	possessive, possession
pred.	predicate, predicative
pref.	prefix
prep.	preposition(al)
pres.	present
prob.	probably
prog.	progressive
pron.	pronoun
prot.	protasis
PRS	*Perspectives in Religious Studies*
ptc.	participle, participial(ly)
R	A. T. Robertson, *A Grammar of the Greek New Testament in the Light of Historical Research*, 4th ed. (Nashville: Broadman, 1934)
RB	Revue Biblique
rdg(s).	(textual) reading(s)
REB	Revised English Bible (1990)
ref.	reference
refl.	reflexive
rel.	relative
rev.	revised, revision
RevExp	*Review and Expositor*
ResQ	*Restoration Quarterly*
RHPR	*Revue d'histoire et de philosophie religieuses*
R-P	M. Robinson and W. Pierpont, *The New Testament in the Original Greek* (Southborough, MA: Chilton, 2005)
RSV	Revised Standard Version (1952)
RTR	*Reformed Theological Review*
Runge	S. E. Runge, *Discourse Grammar of the Greek New Testament: A Practical Introduction for Teaching and Exegesis* (Peabody, MA: Hendrickson, 2010)

SBLMS	*Society of Biblical Literature Monograph Series*
SBLSP	*Society of Biblical Literature Seminar Papers*
SBJT	*Southern Baptist Journal of Theology*
SE	*Studia Evangelica*
Seifrid	M. A. Seifrid, *The Second Letter to the Corinthians*, PNTC (Grand Rapids: Eerdmans, 2014)
Sem.	Semitic, Semitism
sg.	singular
sim.	similar(ly)
Sir	Sirach/Ecclesiasticus
SJT	*Scottish Journal of Theology*
Smyth	H. W. Smyth, *Greek Grammar* (Boston: Harvard University Press, 1984)
SNTSMS	Society for New Testament Studies Monograph Series
ST	*Studia Theologica*
subj.	subject(ive)
subjunc.	subjunctive
subord.	subordinate, subordination
subst.	substantive, substantival(ly)
superl.	superlative
SwJT	*Southwestern Journal of Theology*
TCNT	Twentieth Century Bible
TDNT	*Theological Dictionary of the New Testament*, 9 vols., ed. G. Kittel and G. Friedrich, trans. G. W. Bromiley (Grand Rapids: Eerdmans, 1964–74)
temp.	temporal(ly)
Thayer	J. H. Thayer, *Greek-English Lexicon of the New Testament* (New York: American Book Company, 1889)
Thrall 1, 2	M. E. Thrall, *The Second Epistle to the Corinthians*, ICC, vols. 1 and 2 (Edinburgh: T & T Clark, 1994, 2000)
Thucydides	*Historicus History of the Peloponnesian War*
TJ	*Trinity Journal*
TLG	Thesaurus Linguae Graecae
TMSJ	*The Master Seminary Journal*
TNTC 8	Tyndale New Testament Commentary 8
tr.	translate(d), translator(s), translation(s)
TSK	*Theologische Studien und Kritiken*

TS	*Theological Studies*
Turner, *Grammatical*	N. Turner, *Grammatical Insights into the New Testament* (Edinburgh: T&T Clark, 1965)
Turner, *Style*	N. Turner, *Style*, vol. 4 of *A Grammar of New Testament Greek*, ed. J. H. Moulton (Edinburgh: T&T Clark, 1976)
Turner, *Syntax*	N. Turner, *Syntax*, vol. 3 of *A Grammar of New Testament Greek*, ed. J. H. Moulton (Edinburgh: T&T Clark, 1978)
TynBul	*Tyndale Bulletin*
TZ	Theologische Zeitschrift
UBS[5]	*The Greek New Testament*, ed. B. Aland, K. Aland, J. Karavidopoulos, C. M. Martini, and B. M. Metzger, 5th rev. ed. (Stuttgart: Deutsche Bibelgesellschaft/New York: United Bible Societies, 2014)
UBS Journal	*Union Biblical Seminary Journal*
v(v).	verse(s)
var.	variant (form or reading)
vb(s).	verb(s)
VE	*Vox Evangelica*
voc.	vocative
vol(s).	volume(s)
Wallace	Daniel B. Wallace, *Greek Grammar Beyond the Basics: An Exegetical Syntax of the New Testament* (Grand Rapids: Zondervan, 1996)
WBC	Word Biblical Commentary
W. E. Jelf	W. E. Jelf, *A Grammar of the Greek Language* (London: Parker, 1881)
Wis	Wisdom of Solomon
WTJ	*Westminster Theological Journal*
WUNT	Wissenschaftliche Untersuchungen zum Neuen Testament
WW	*Word and World*
YLT	Young's Literal Translation
Z	M. Zerwick, *Biblical Greek Illustrated by Examples*, trans. J. Smith (Rome: Pontifical Biblical Institute, 1963)
ZG	M. Zerwick, *A Grammatical Analysis of the New Testament*, trans. Mary Grosvenor (Roma: Pontificao Instituto Biblico, 1988)
ZNW	*Zeitschrift* für die *neutestamentliche Wissenschaft und die Kunde der* älteren *Kirche*
ZWT	Zeischrift fur wissenschaftliche Theologie

2 CORINTHIANS

Introduction

AUTHOR

Paul identifies himself as the author of this letter and as "an apostle of Christ Jesus by God's will." While this ascription is generally universally accepted, some have questioned whether 6:14–7:1 is an original part of the letter and whether it might be a later interpolation either by Paul himself or even some other person. However, interpolation theories raise greater problems than they solve, for it is extremely difficult to explain, on those theories, why anyone would introduce such a passage at this place. If it is not a later interpolation, we have two tasks before us: to understand the message of 6:14–7:1 itself, and to relate it somehow to the rest of the letter, especially its immediate context. These issues are discussed in commentaries recommended for further reading.

DATE AND PROVENANCE

Assigning dates to the various points in Paul's career and to the time of writing of his letters is fraught with difficulties. In the case of his relationship with the Corinthians, we do have a couple of possible reference points that may help. First, Acts 18:2 tells us that when Paul arrived in Corinth on his first visit "he found a Jew named Aquila, a native of Pontus, who had recently come from Italy with his wife Priscilla because Claudius had ordered all the Jews to leave Rome." This edict of Claudius is generally held to have been promulgated in AD 49. Second, in Acts 18:12–17 we read that during Paul's first visit to Corinth, he was brought before Gallio, the proconsul of Achaia. Fragments of an inscription found during excavations at Delphi contain a reproduction of a letter from the emperor Claudius from which it can be inferred that Gallio held office in Corinth from the spring of AD 51 to the spring of AD 52. However, a statement made by Seneca, the Stoic philosopher and brother of Gallio, informs us that Gallio did not complete his term of office, and it is therefore impossible to date Paul's encounter with him in the latter part of his term. It must have taken place then between July and October AD 51.

Working from these reference points and taking note of the information provided about Paul's movements in the Acts of the Apostles (and assuming that this is essentially compatible with what may be inferred from Paul's letters), the following chronology for Paul's contacts with the Corinthians can be suggested. He arrived in Corinth for his first visit in early AD 50. After spending eighteen months there, he was arraigned before Gallio (latter half of AD 51). He stayed on in Corinth "for some time" after the arraignment (Acts 18:18), then sailed for Antioch. After spending "some time" there (v. 18:23), Paul traveled through Galatia to Ephesus, where he spent two years and three months (AD 52–55). After leaving Corinth, and quite possibly during his stay in Ephesus, the apostle wrote the "previous letter" to the Corinthians. Toward the end of his time in Ephesus (AD 55), he wrote 1 Corinthians, made the "painful visit" (2 Cor 2:1), and wrote the "severe letter." Paul then left Ephesus, traveling via Troas to Macedonia, where he met Titus, and from there he wrote 2 Corinthians (AD 56). He then made his third visit to Corinth and spent three months in Greece before setting out with the collection to Jerusalem, hoping to arrive there in time for Pentecost AD 57.

OCCASION AND PURPOSE

Paul wrote 2 Corinthians from Macedonia around AD 56, having received news from Titus that the Corinthians had responded positively to his "severe letter," and had disciplined the offender who had attacked their apostle when he made his "painful visit" to them. He wanted to deal with criticisms of himself that had been aired in Corinth (1:12–24). The offender had apparently repented of his actions, so another reason Paul wrote was to call upon the Corinthians to forgive and reinstate him "so that we may not be taken advantage of by Satan" (2:1–13). Having done this, Paul was able to urge the Corinthians to carry out their previous intention to contribute to the collection for the poor believers in Jerusalem (chs. 8–9). At the same time, or as a follow up, in chs. 10–13 Paul wrote to defend himself against a frontal attack on his ministry being made by "false apostles" who had infiltrated the Christian community in Corinth (11:1, 13). The letter ends without any indication whether this defense was successful. However, Paul's Letter to the Romans, written shortly after 2 Corinthians, indicates that the Corinthians had contributed to the collection he was organizing for the believers in Jerusalem, not something they would have wanted to do if they still believed the slanderous charges the false apostles made against him.

STRUCTURE

As reflected in the following outline, 2 Corinthians consists of two major parts: Paul's response to a crisis already resolved by the time of writing (1:1–9:15), and his response to a new crisis (10:1–13:13). The first major part includes the preface (1:1–11), the body of the response (1:12–7:16), and advice about the collection for the poor saints in Jerusalem (8:1–9:15). The second major part includes a description of Paul's exercise of apostolic authority (10:1–18), his pleas for tolerance on the part of his readers and the condemnation of his opponents (11:1–15), the so-called fool's speech (11:16–12:13), information relating to his planned third visit (12:14–13:10), and the letter conclusion (13:11–13).

OUTLINE

I. Paul's Response to a Crisis Resolved (1:1–9:15)
   A. Preface (1:1–11)
      1. The Address and Greeting (1:1–2)
      2. The Benediction (1:3–11)
         a. Paul Blesses God and Expresses His Hope for His Readers (1:3–7)
         b. Paul's Troubles in Asia (1:8–11)
   B. The Body of the Response (1:12–7:16)
      1. Personal Defense (1:12–24)
         a. General Defense of Integrity (1:12–14)
         b. Defense of Changed Travel Plans (1:15–22)
         c. Paul Calls upon God as His Witness (1:23–25)
      2. The "Severe Letter": Its Purpose and Aftermath (2:1–13)
         a. The Purpose of the "Severe Letter" (2:1–4)
         b. Forgiveness for the Offender (2:5–11)
         c. Waiting for Titus (2:12–13)
      3. Competency in Ministry (2:14–4:6)
         a. Led in Triumph (2:14–17)
         b. Letters of Recommendation (3:1–3)
         c. Ministers of the New Covenant (3:4–6)
         d. The Greater Glory of New Covenant Ministry (3:7–11)
         e. The Greater Boldness of New Covenant Ministers (3:12–18)
         f. The Conduct of Paul's Ministry (4:1–6)
      4. Present Suffering and Future Glory (4:7–5:10)
         a. Treasure in Jars of Clay (4:7–15)
         b. We Do Not Give Up (4:16–18)
         c. The Heavenly Dwelling (5:1–10)
      5. The Ministry of Reconciliation (5:11–21)
         a. Defense of His Ministry (5:11–15)
         b. God's Reconciling Act in Christ (5:16–21)
      6. Reconciliation Practiced (6:1–7:4)
         a. An Appeal for Reconciliation (6:1–13)
         b. A Call for Holy Living (6:14–7:1)
         c. A Further Appeal for Reconciliation (7:2–4)
      7. Paul's Joy after a Crisis Resolved (7:5–16)
         a. Paul's Relief When Titus Arrived (7:5–7)
         b. The "Severe Letter" and Its Effects (7:8–13a)
         c. Titus's Happiness and Affection for the Corinthians (7:13b–16)
   C. The Matter of the Collection (8:1–9:15)
      1. The Example of the Macedonians (8:1–6)
      2. Paul Exhorts the Corinthians to Finish What They Began (8:7–15)
      3. Commendation of Those Who Will Receive the Collection (8:16–24)
      4. Be Prepared and Avoid Humiliation (9:1–5)

     5. An Exhortation to Be Generous (9:6–15)
II. Paul Responds to a New Crisis (10:1–13:14)
   A. Paul's Exercise of Apostolic Authority (10:1–18)
     1. Paul Responds to Criticisms (10:1–11)
     2. Boasting within Proper Limits (10:12–18)
   B. A Plea for Tolerance and Condemnation of the Opponents (11:1–15)
     1. The Corinthians' Gullibility (11:1–6)
     2. The Matter of Financial Remuneration (11:7–15)
   C. The Fool's Speech (11:16–12:13)
     1. Accept Me as a Fool (11:16–21a)
     2. Paul's Jewish Ancestry (11:21b–22)
     3. A Better Servant of Christ (11:23–33)
     4. Visions and Revelations (12:1–10)
     5. Signs of an Apostle (12:11–13)
   D. Paul's Planned Third Visit (12:14–13:10)
     1. Paul Refuses to Burden the Corinthians (12:14–18)
     2. The Real Purpose of Paul's Fool's Speech (12:19–21)
     3. Paul Threatens Strong Action on His Third Visit (13:1–10)
   E. Conclusion (13:11–13)
     1. Final Exhortations (13:11–12)
     2. Benediction (13:13)

RECOMMENDED COMMENTARIES

Barnett, P. *The Second Epistle to the Corinthians*. New International Commentary on the New Testament. Grand Rapids: Eerdmans, 1997.

Hafemann, S. J. *2 Corinthians*. NIV Application Commentary. Grand Rapids: Zondervan, 2000.

Harris, M. J. *The Second Epistle to the Corinthians: A Commentary on the Greek Text*. New International Greek Testament Commentary. Grand Rapids: Eerdmans, 2005.

Kruse, C. G. *2 Corinthians: An Introduction and Commentary*. Rev. ed. Tyndale New Testament Commentary 8. Nottingham/Downers Grove: IVP, 2015.

Seifrid, M. A. *The Second Letter to the Corinthians*. Pillar New Testament Commentary. Grand Rapids: Eerdmans, 2014.

Thrall, M. E. *The Second Epistle to the Corinthians*. International Critical Commentary. Vols. 1 and 2. Edinburgh: T & T Clark, 1994, 2000.

Harris and Thrall provide thorough and detailed commentary on the Greek text, Barnett and Seifrid give less comment on the Greek text but provide strong theological commentary on the English text, Hafemann offers applications of the text, and Kruse's recent commentary provides a user-friendly introduction and commentary on the text.

I. Paul's Response to a Crisis Resolved (1:1–9:15)

A. PREFACE (1:1–11)

1. The Address and Greeting (1:1–2)

STRUCTURE

Paul's opening words follow the formula found at the beginning of many ancient Greek letters: A to B, greeting. But he has expanded it with words that emphasize his apostolic authority (which had been called into question at Corinth), and by the inclusion of specifically Christian sentiments dominated by references to God: "by the will of God," "the church of God," and "God our Father."

In verse 1 Paul introduces himself as an apostle of Christ Jesus by the will of God, and his colleague, Timothy, whom he associates with himself in the writing of this letter, which is addressed to the church in Corinth and believers throughout the province of Achaia.

Verse 2 completes the greeting by invoking grace and peace from God our Father and the Lord Jesus Christ.

1 Παῦλος
    ἀπόστολος Χριστοῦ Ἰησοῦ
        διὰ θελήματος θεοῦ
    καὶ Τιμόθεος
    ὁ ἀδελφὸς   τῇ ἐκκλησίᾳ τοῦ θεοῦ
                          τῇ οὔσῃ ἐν Κορίνθῳ
                              σὺν τοῖς ἁγίοις πᾶσιν
                                  τοῖς οὖσιν ἐν ὅλῃ τῇ Ἀχαΐᾳ,
2 χάρις ὑμῖν καὶ εἰρήνη
        ἀπὸ θεοῦ πατρὸς ἡμῶν
        καὶ κυρίου Ἰησοῦ Χριστοῦ.

VERSE 1

Παῦλος ἀπόστολος Χριστοῦ Ἰησοῦ διὰ θελήματος θεοῦ καὶ Τιμόθεος ὁ ἀδελφός
Paul, an apostle of Christ Jesus by God's will, and Timothy our brother:

The names Παῦλος and Τιμόθεος are both anar., being proper names, and nom. abs. because they are not the subj. of a verb.

Ἀπόστολος is in the nom. case, being in appos. to Παῦλος, describing his status, and is anar. because Paul is not the only apostle of Christ. In the NT ἀπόστολος is used variously of (1) the Twelve appointed by Christ during his earthly ministry (Matt 10:2; Acts 1:2; 1 Cor 15:7); (2) Paul, appointed in a special appearance of the risen Christ (1 Cor 9:1); (3) James, the brother of the Lord (Gal 1:19) and Andronicus and Junia (Rom 16:7); and (4) messengers sent by the churches (2 Cor 8:17–18; Phil 2:25).

Χριστοῦ Ἰησοῦ is either gen. of possession ("belonging to Christ Jesus") or subj. gen. ("sent by Christ Jesus"). The phrase Χριστοῦ Ἰησοῦ is found only here in 2 Corinthians. Elsewhere in this letter the apostle uses Ἰησοῦ Χριστοῦ (1:2, 3; 4:6; 8:9; 13:3), and this is the rdg. of most later manuscripts. However, Χριστοῦ Ἰησοῦ is the rdg. of the earlier and better manuscripts, incl. $\mathfrak{P}^{46}$ ℵ B M, whose mng. is "Messiah Jesus." The later adoption of Ἰησοῦ Χριστοῦ reflects a time when the two words were joined to form a proper name (cf. Harris 129).

Διὰ θελήματος θεοῦ is a gen. prep. phrase that qualifies ἀπόστολος, indicating the means by which Paul was appointed as an apostle. The gen. θεοῦ may be either poss. ("God's will") or subj. ("God willing it"). Θελήματος is an anar. noun as often, but not always, in prep. phrases.

Ὁ ἀδελφός is nom. case, in appos. to Τιμόθεος, and further identifies him as "the brother" (a fellow Christian). Having the art. suggests that Τιμόθεος was well-known. CSB renders ὁ ἀδελφός as "our brother," a way of indicating he was well-known as a fellow member of the Christian community (cf. BDAG 18a).

τῇ ἐκκλησίᾳ τοῦ θεοῦ τῇ οὔσῃ ἐν Κορίνθῳ σὺν τοῖς ἁγίοις πᾶσιν τοῖς οὖσιν ἐν ὅλῃ τῇ Ἀχαΐᾳ,
To the church of God at Corinth, with all the saints who are throughout Achaia.

Ἐκκλησίᾳ, dat. sg. fem. ἐκκλησία, -ας, ἡ, "assembly, church." Τῇ ἐκκλησίᾳ is a dat. prep. phrase indicating to whom the letter is addressed. Here ἐκκλησίᾳ denotes a congregation "as the totality of Christians living and meeting in a particular location or larger geographical area, but not necessarily limited to one meeting place" (BDAG 304a). The poss. gen. τοῦ θεοῦ qualifies τῇ ἐκκλησίᾳ indicating the church belongs to God. Τῇ οὔσῃ ἐν Κορίνθῳ is a dat. attrib. ptc. phrase, modifying τῇ ἐκκλησίᾳ, locating the church in Corinth. Οὔσῃ, dat. sg. fem. of pres. act. ptc. of εἰμί, "be."

Σὺν τοῖς ἁγίοις πᾶσιν is a dat. prep. phrase further describing the addressees as incl. "all the saints." The adj. ἅγιος -ία, -ον, "saints, holy ones," refers to Christians consecrated to God (BDAG 11c). Οὖσιν, dat. pl. masc. of pres. act. ptc. of εἰμί, "be." Τοῖς οὖσιν ἐν ὅλῃ τῇ Ἀχαΐᾳ is an attrib. ptc. phrase qualifying "all the saints" by incl. all those in the wider Achaian province.

VERSE 2

χάρις ὑμῖν καὶ εἰρήνη ἀπὸ θεοῦ πατρὸς ἡμῶν καὶ κυρίου Ἰησοῦ Χριστοῦ.
Grace to you and peace from God our Father and the Lord Jesus Christ.

Χάρις and εἰρήνη are nom. abs. nouns requiring an optative form (the mood of possibility, used to express prayers, wishes, and benedictions [as here]) of the verb εἰμί to complete the sense ("Grace and peace *be to you*"). In this case the verb is unstated. The standard Gk. greeting was simply χαίρειν (cf. Acts 15:23; 23:26; Jas 1:1; 2 John 11), but Paul replaces it with the uniquely Christian expression χάρις ("grace") and εἰρήνη ("peace" [Heb. šālôm]). In Paul's letters God's grace is linked with God's love in sending his Son to effect salvation for humanity (Rom 8:32; 2 Cor 8:9), and then with his ongoing acts of loving provision (Rom 8:32). The peace Paul invokes is the subjective sense of peace and well-being that rests upon the objective peace with God won through Christ's death (Eph 2:13–18).

Θεοῦ following ἀπό is a gen. of source, indicating that God is the source of the grace and peace Paul invokes for his readers. Πατρὸς ἡμῶν stands in appos. to θεοῦ, further defining God as the Father and the source of the blessing invoked. Πατρός, gen. sg. masc. πατήρ, πατρός, ὁ, "father."

Καὶ κυρίου Ἰησοῦ Χριστοῦ complements this, closely associating Jesus with the Father as the source of the blessing invoked. Harris, *Prepositions*, 62: "The single ἀπό standing before both personal names points to the unity and singularity of the source. God the Father and the Lord Jesus Christ jointly form a single source of divine grace, mercy, and peace." Barnett 63: "Paul does use *kyrios* to identify Jesus with Yahweh, as may be seen in the way he applies to Jesus a number of texts from the LXX that refer to Kyrios = Yahweh."

FOR FURTHER STUDY

1. Apostleship in the NT (1:1)

Agnew, F. "The Origin of the NT Apostle-Concept: A Review of Research." *JBL* 105 (1986): 75–96.

———. "On the Origin of the Term, Apostolos," *CBQ* 38 (1976): 49–53.

*Barnett, P. W. *DPL* 45–51.

Barrett, C. K. *The Signs of an Apostle*. Philadelphia: Fortress, 1972.

Giles, K. *Patterns of Ministry among the First Christians*. Melbourne: Collins Dove, 1989.

Herron, R. W. "The Origin of the New Testament Apostolate." *WTJ* 45 (1983): 101–31.

Kirk, J. A. "Apostleship since Rengstorf: Towards a Synthesis." *NTS* 21 (1974–75): 249–64.

Kruse, C. G. *New Testament Foundations for Ministry*. London: Marshall, Morgan & Scott, 1983.

————. *DLNT* 76–82.

Lightfoot, J. B. "The Name and Office of an Apostle." In *Saint Paul's Epistle to the Galatians*. London: MacMillan, 1921. See pp. 92–101.

Rengstorf, K. H. *TDNT* 1.407–447.

Schmithals, W. *The Office of Apostle in the Early Church*. Nashville: Abingdon, 1969.

Schnabel, E. J. *DJG* 34–45.

Schnackenburg, R. "Apostles before and during Paul's Time." In *Apostolic History and the Gospel*. Edited by W. W. Gasque and R. P. Martin. Grand Rapids: Eerdmans, 1970. See pp. 287–303.

Silva, Moisés. *NIDNTTE* 1.365–76.

2. Christology (1:1)

Bowman, R. M., Jr., and J. E. Komoszewski. *Putting Jesus in His Place: The Case for the Deity of Christ*. Grand Rapids: Kregel, 2007.

Dunn, J. D. G. *Christology in the Making: A New Testament Inquiry into the Origins of the Doctrine of the Incarnation*. 2nd. ed. Grand Rapids/Cambridge, UK: Eerdmans, 1996.

*Harris, M. J. *Jesus as God: The New Testament Use of* Theos *in Reference to Christ*. Grand Rapids: Baker, 1992.

Hurtado, L. W. *DLNT* 170–84.

————. *Lord Jesus Christ: Devotion to Jesus in Earliest Christianity*. Grand Rapids: Eerdmans, 2003.

Kim, Seyoon. *The Origin of Paul's Gospel*. Tübingen: Mohr, 1984.

Longenecker, Richard N., ed. *Contours of Christology in the New Testament*. Grand Rapids: Eerdmans, 2005.

Moule, C. F. D. *The Origin of Christianity*. New York: Cambridge University Press, 1977.

Witherington, B., III. *DPL* 100–15.

3. The Will of God (1:1)

Schrenk, G. *TDNT* 3.52–62.
*Silva, Moisés, ed. *NIDNTTE* 2.426–30.

4. The Church (1:1)

Banks, R. *Paul's Idea of Community: The Early House Churches in Their Historical Setting*. Rev. ed. Grand Rapids: Baker, 1994. See pp. 1–81.

Bowers, P. "Church and Mission in Paul." *JSNT* 44 (1991): 89–111.

Coenen, L. *NIDNTT* 1.298–302.

Ladd, G. E. *A Theology of the New Testament*. Grand Rapids: Eerdmans, 1974. See pp. 531–49.

Ridderbos, H. *Paul: An Outline of His Theology*. Grand Rapids: Eerdmans, 1975. See pp. 327–95.

Kruse, C. G. *New Testament Foundations for Ministry*. London: MMS, 1983. See pp. 116–17, 130–31, 152–56, 169–73.

O'Brien, P. T. *DPL* 123–31.

5. Ancient Letters (1:1–2)

Doty, W. G. *Letters in Primitive Christianity*. Philadelphia: Fortress, 1973.

Klauck, H-J, and D. P. Bailey, *Ancient Letters and the New Testament: A Guide to Context and Exegesis*. Waco: Baylor University Press, 2006.

Morello, R., and A. D. Morrison. *Ancient Letters: Classical and Late Antique Epistolography*. Oxford: Oxford University Press, 2007.

O'Brien, P. T. *DPL* 550–53.

*Richards, E. R. *Paul and First-Century Letter Writing: Secretaries, Composition and Collection*. Downers Grove, IL: InterVarsity, 2004.

Stowers, S. K. *Letter Writing in Greco-Roman Antiquity*. Philadelphia: Westminster, 1986.

*Weima, J. A. D. *DNTB* 640–44.

6. Greetings and Benedictions (1:2)

Llewelyn, S. R. "Greeting as a New Testament Form." *JBL* 87 (1986): 418–26.

Mullins, T. Y. "Benediction as a NT Form." *AUSS* 15 (1977): 59–64.

*O'Brien, P. T. *DPL* 68–71.

Westermann, C. *Blessing in the Bible and the Life of the Church*. Philadelphia: Fortress, 1978.

7. Fatherhood of God (1:2)

Guthrie, D., and R. P. Martin. *DPL* 345–69. See pp. 357–58.

*Stein, R. H. *The Method and Message of Jesus' Teaching*. Rev. ed. Louisville: Westminster John Knox, 1994. See pp. 82–89.

Thompson, M. M. "'Mercy upon All': God as Father in the Epistle to the Romans." In *Romans and the People of God*. Edited by Sven Soderlund and N. T. Wright. Grand Rapids: Eerdmans, 1999. See pp. 203–16.

———. *The Promise of the Father: Jesus and God in the New Testament*. Louisville: Westminster John Knox, 2000. See pp. 87–115.

HOMILETICAL SUGGESTIONS

The Church of God (1:1–2)

1. Apostles as the foundation of the church (v. 1a, cf. Eph 2:20)
2. The nature and makeup of the local church (v. 1b., cf. 1 Cor 1:26–31)
3. The grace and peace of God extended to the church (v. 2, cf. Rom 8:31–39)

2. The Benediction (1:3–11)

a. Paul Blesses God and Expresses His Hope for His Readers (1:3–7)

STRUCTURE

In ancient Greek letters, a thanksgiving section followed the introductory greeting. This usually included a short expression of praise and prayerful concern or thanksgiving for the recipients. Paul's letters usually begin in the same way. However, 2 Corinthians is unusual in that what follows the greeting is a benediction in which he blesses God, not for grace evident in the lives of his readers, as is the case in most of his other letters, but for the comfort he and his colleagues have experienced amid great affliction. Paul tells his readers that these afflictions are for their comfort and salvation, and he hopes that as they share in sufferings, they will share in the comfort he and his colleagues have experienced as well.

In verses 3–4 Paul praises God, who comforts him in all his afflictions, so that he can in turn comfort others experiencing affliction with the comfort he himself has experienced from God. In Christ comfort also overflows to him. In verses 6–7 the apostle explains that his affliction is for the comfort and salvation of his readers, which they will experience as they undergo similar afflictions, and his firm hope is that as they share the sufferings [of Christ] they will also share comfort [through Christ].

3   Εὐλογητὸς ὁ θεὸς
            καὶ πατὴρ
                   τοῦ κυρίου ἡμῶν Ἰησοῦ Χριστοῦ,
            ὁ πατὴρ τῶν οἰκτιρμῶν
            καὶ θεὸς πάσης παρακλήσεως,
4   ὁ παρακαλῶν ἡμᾶς
                   ἐπὶ πάσῃ τῇ θλίψει ἡμῶν
                   εἰς τὸ δύνασθαι ἡμᾶς παρακαλεῖν τοὺς ἐν πάσῃ θλίψει
                                  διὰ τῆς παρακλήσεως
                                         ἧς παρακαλούμεθα αὐτοὶ
                                                ὑπὸ τοῦ θεοῦ.
5   ὅτι καθὼς περισσεύει τὰ παθήματα τοῦ Χριστοῦ εἰς ἡμᾶς,
            οὕτως διὰ τοῦ Χριστοῦ περισσεύει καὶ ἡ παράκλησις ἡμῶν.
6   εἴτε δὲ θλιβόμεθα,
                   ὑπὲρ τῆς ὑμῶν παρακλήσεως καὶ σωτηρίας·
      εἴτε παρακαλούμεθα,
                   ὑπὲρ τῆς ὑμῶν παρακλήσεως
                          τῆς ἐνεργουμένης
                                 ἐν ὑπομονῇ τῶν αὐτῶν παθημάτων
                                         ὧν καὶ ἡμεῖς πάσχομεν.
7   καὶ ἡ ἐλπὶς ἡμῶν βεβαία ὑπὲρ ὑμῶν
                   εἰδότες ὅτι ὡς κοινωνοί ἐστε τῶν παθημάτων,
                                 οὕτως καὶ τῆς παρακλήσεως.

VERSE 3

Εὐλογητὸς ὁ θεὸς καὶ πατὴρ τοῦ κυρίου ἡμῶν Ἰησοῦ Χριστοῦ,
Blessed be the God and Father of our Lord Jesus Christ,

Εὐλογητός, "blessed, praised" (BDAG 408c), is a pred. verbal adj. placed at the beginning of the sentence, as it is the main point of the prayer wish (cf. Eph 1:3; 1 Pet 1:3). A form of the verb εἰμί is implied, either the opt. (εἴη, "may God be blessed") or an impv. (ἔστω, "let God be blessed") or an indic. (ἔστιν, "blessed is God") (R 396, 945, 1133).

Ὁ θεὸς καὶ πατήρ is an example of the Granville-Sharpe rule: where two subj. nom. sg. personal non-proper nouns are linked by καί and governed by one art., the second noun refers to the same person as the first (R 785; Wallace 274, 277). Barnett 69: "It is probable that 'the God and Father of our Lord Jesus Christ' is to be understood as 'God, even the Father, that is, as Paul's gloss on the synagogue benediction of God (cf. 11:31; Rom 15:6)."

Τοῦ κυρίου ἡμῶν Ἰησοῦ Χριστοῦ is a gen. of relationship expressing God's fatherly relationship to Jesus. Κυρίου ἡμῶν is also a gen. of relationship, expressing believers' subord. to Jesus Christ as Lord.

God, who in OT times was known as the God of Abraham, Isaac, and Jacob, is now more perfectly revealed as "the God and Father of our Lord Jesus Christ" (cf. Gal 4:4). As it stands, this description of God is ambiguous and could be taken to mean that he is not only the Father of our Lord Jesus Christ but also his God, indicating that the Lord Jesus Christ was in no way independent of God the Father. To remove the ambiguity Paul could have written "God and the Father (ὁ θεὸς καὶ ὁ πατήρ) of our Lord Jesus Christ." In his incarnate state Christ spoke of God as "my God" (cf. Matt 27:46; John 20:17). All this suggests, as Harris 142 notes, "a duality of relation" between the Father and the Son.

ὁ πατὴρ τῶν οἰκτιρμῶν καὶ θεὸς πάσης παρακλήσεως,
the Father of mercies and the God of all comfort.

Ὁ πατὴρ τῶν οἰκτιρμῶν stands in appos. to and further defines ὁ θεὸς καὶ πατήρ. Οἰκτιρμῶν, gen. pl. masc. οἰκτιρμός, -οῦ, ὁ, "mercies, compassions," an obj. gen. ("God who shows mercy").

Καὶ θεὸς πάσης παρακλήσεως also stands in appos. to and defines further ὁ θεὸς καὶ πατήρ. The mercies (or, "compassion" in the NIV) of God are frequently celebrated and invoked in the OT (e.g., Neh 9:19; Ps 51:1; Isa 63:7; Dan 9:9; Wis 9:1). Paul's appreciation of the mercies of God had been deepened by his understanding of God's saving action in Christ (Rom 12:1 uses the expression "the mercies of God" to denote the great saving acts of God in Christ as described in Romans 1–11).

Παρακλήσεως, gen. sg. fem. παράκλησις, -εως, ἡ, "comfort, consolation," obj. gen. (God who "comforts" his people). The word παράκλησις is used by Luke in his Gospel when describing those who, like the aged Simeon, were "looking forward to Israel's consolation" (Luke 2:25). The consolation expected was the deliverance which God would provide through the coming of the Messiah. For Paul, the messianic age had already begun, albeit while the present age was still running its course, and it is the overlapping of the ages that accounts for the surprising coincidence of affliction and consolation of which he speaks in the present passage. The final consolation of the children of God awaits the day of the revelation of Jesus Christ in glory. But because the messianic age has been inaugurated by Jesus, Israel's Messiah, at his first coming, believers experience comfort in the present time as a foretaste of that final consolation.

VERSE 4

ὁ παρακαλῶν ἡμᾶς ἐπὶ πάσῃ τῇ θλίψει ἡμῶν
He comforts us in all our affliction,

Παρακαλῶν, nom. sg. masc. of pres. act. ptc. of παρακαλέω, "comfort." Ὁ παρακαλῶν ἡμᾶς is a nom. attrib. ptc. clause describing God as the one who also "comforts us." Ἐπί with the dat. πάσῃ τῇ θλίψει is spatial, indicating the place/situation in which God's comfort is expressed: "in all our affliction." Πάσῃ τῇ θλίψει ἡμῶν (BDF §275[3]): "all tribulations actually encountered [by Paul]."

εἰς τὸ δύνασθαι ἡμᾶς παρακαλεῖν τοὺς ἐν πάσῃ θλίψει
so that we may be able to comfort those who are in any kind of affliction,

Εἰς τὸ δύνασθαι ἡμᾶς is an art. inf. cstr. comprising the prep. εἰς with the acc. neut. art. τό, the pres. mid. inf. δύνασθαι, and the acc. subj. ἡμᾶς, expressing purpose, i.e., "to enable us."
Παρακαλεῖν τοὺς ἐν πάσῃ θλίψει: the inf. παρακαλεῖν stands in complementary relationship with δύνασθαι, i.e., expressing what Paul is enabled by God to do: "to comfort those who are in any kind of affliction." The phrase τοὺς ἐν πάσῃ θλίψει is the object of the inf. παρακαλεῖν, in which the dat. prep. phrase ἐν πάσῃ θλίψει describes the cond. of those to be comforted ("in any kind of affliction" [cf. R 772]). BDF §275(3): "in any situation which may be encountered."

διὰ τῆς παρακλήσεως ἧς παρακαλούμεθα αὐτοὶ ὑπὸ τοῦ θεοῦ.
through the comfort we ourselves receive from God.

Διά with gen. τῆς παρακλήσεως ("through the comfort") indicates the means by which Paul is able to comfort others. Παρακαλούμεθα, 1st pl. pres. mid. indic. of παρακαλέω, "comfort."
Ἧς παρακαλούμεθα αὐτοὶ ὑπὸ τοῦ θεοῦ is an attrib. clause qualifying τῆς παρακλήσεως, indicating the source of the comfort that enables Paul to comfort others. Ἧς is an instance of an acc. pron. attracted into the gen. (R 716). Αὐτοί, nom. pl. masc. standing in the pred. position, functions as an emphasizing pron. "ourselves." Ὑπό with gen. τοῦ θεοῦ indicates the "agent" ("God") by whom Paul was comforted.

VERSE 5

ὅτι καθὼς περισσεύει τὰ παθήματα τοῦ Χριστοῦ εἰς ἡμᾶς,
For just as the sufferings of Christ overflow to us,

Ὅτι, or "for," is a subord. conj. loosely connecting what follows with what precedes (BDAG 732c; BDF §456; R 962f.) and explains why he is able to comfort others (cf. Barnett 74). Καθώς . . . functions as an adv. of comp.: "just as . . ." (BDAG 493c–d).

Παθήματα, nom. pl. neut. πάθημα, -ατος, τό "sufferings," takes a sg. verb περισσεύει (3rd sg. pres. act. indic. of περισσεύω, "overflow"). Τὰ παθήματα τοῦ Χριστοῦ, denoting Christ's sufferings shared by Paul or believers, has been variously interpreted: (a) Paul experienced suffering in his apostolic work just as Christ did in his work as Messiah (Denney 82); (b) the sufferings experienced by Christ are extended so as to reach and be shared by others (Barrett 61); (c) sharing the sufferings of Christ is an allusion to Christian baptism (Thrall 1:107–10); (d) the sufferings of Christ experienced by believers are no special sufferings, but those experienced by humankind in general; however Christians experience and understand them in a new way (Bultmann 24); (e) Paul's Jewish contemporaries expected the messianic age to be preceded and ushered in by a period of suffering. These were known as the messianic woes or birth pangs of the Messiah/Christ (Best 131–36); (f) "Christ, who suffered personally on the cross, continues to suffer in his people" while the old age lasts (Bruce 178, Harris 146, cf. Acts 9:4–5).

Evaluating the various suggestions: the view that to share the sufferings of Christ is related to Christian baptism has found few supporters. Bultmann's suggestion that it refers to humankind's experience in general lacks cogency in the light of the lists of afflictions in 2 Corinthians, all of which are related to Paul's ministry as an apostle. More likely is the suggestion that the sufferings of Christ refer to afflictions Paul endured in the course of his apostolic ministry. It is also possible that while Christians suffer for the sake of Christ, he at the same time suffers in his people (cf. Acts 9:4–5), or that united with Christ, they too fulfill the role of the Suffering Servant and share his afflictions (cf. Col 1:24–25). Seifrid 26: "Paul inverts the tradition that later appears in the rabbinic expectation of the 'travails of the Messiah' (heblē shel meshiah). These were the times of suffering that were expected to precede the coming of the Messiah, and from which one hoped to be spared. Paul speaks instead of Christ's sufferings, in which he shares as an apostle, and which belong to all Christians."

Εἰς, prep. with acc. ἡμᾶς denotes movement towards, here referring to the sufferings of Christ that overflow "to us."

οὕτως διὰ τοῦ Χριστοῦ περισσεύει καὶ ἡ παράκλησις ἡμῶν.
so also through Christ our comfort overflows.

Οὕτως completes the comp. begun by καθώς . . . ("Just as the sufferings of Christ overflow to us, so also through Christ our comfort overflows"). Διά is a prep. with gen. τοῦ Χριστοῦ indicating the means by which God brings comfort: "through Christ." Παράκλησις see note on v. 3 above. Περισσεύει, 3rd sg. pres. act. indic. of περισσεύω, "abound." ZG 532: "exceed the measure, be without measure."

VERSE 6

εἴτε δὲ θλιβόμεθα, ὑπὲρ τῆς ὑμῶν παρακλήσεως καὶ σωτηρίας·
If we are afflicted, it is for your comfort and salvation.

Εἴτε . . . εἴτε. . . . The combination of subord. conj. εἴτε ("if") found here "does not introduce mutually exclusive alternatives but rather successive experiences" (Harris 147). So: "If we are afflicted. . . . If we are comforted. . . ." Θλιβόμεθα, 1st pl. pres. pass. indic. of θλίβω, "afflict." For the afflictions experienced by Paul in his apostolic ministry, see 4:7–12; 11:23–29. Ὑπέρ is a prep. with gen. meaning "on behalf of, for the benefit of." Moule 65.ii.b: "with a view to." R 632: "the object at which one is aiming," in this case for the Corinthians' "comfort and salvation." Τῆς ὑμῶν παρακλήσεως καὶ σωτηρίας is an instance of two things "treated as one for the purpose in hand, and hence use only one article" (R 787). Clearly ὑμῶν is an obj. gen. relating to the comfort received, not a subj. gen. denoting comfort bestowed by the Corinthians. The comfort they received through Paul's ministry includes both the firstfruits of salvation experienced in the present and their final salvation on the last day. Σωτηρίας, gen. sg. fem. σωτηρία, -ας, ἡ "salvation."

εἴτε παρακαλούμεθα, ὑπὲρ τῆς ὑμῶν παρακλήσεως
If we are comforted, it is for your comfort,

Εἴτε . . . εἴτε. . . . See comment above. Παρακαλούμεθα, 1st pl. pres. mid. indic. of παρακαλέω, "comfort." Παρακλήσεως, gen. sg. fem. παράκλησις, -εως, ἡ, "comfort, consolation." See notes on ὑπέρ and ὑμῶν above. It was not only through Paul's willingness to endure afflictions while preaching the gospel in Corinth that comfort came to the Corinthians, but also through the comfort the apostle himself received in the midst of afflictions that enabled him to comfort them.

τῆς ἐνεργουμένης ἐν ὑπομονῇ τῶν αὐτῶν παθημάτων ὧν καὶ ἡμεῖς πάσχομεν.
which produces in you patient endurance of the same sufferings that we suffer.

A rel. clause qualifying παρακλήσεως: "[comfort] which produces . . .").
Ἐνεργουμένης, gen. sg. fem. of pres. mid. ptc. of ἐνεργέω, "work." BDAG 335b: "intrans. 'work', 'be at work', 'be active', 'operate', 'be effective.'" Τῆς ἐνεργουμένης has been variously translated: "which produces" (CSB, NIV); "which [or, that] you experience" (NRSV, ESV, NET); "which is effective" (NASB); "that functions in [the act of] enduring" (BDAG 335c). The essential choice is between comfort that produces endurance of sufferings (so, e.g., Barnett 77; Harris 148; Seifrid 28) or comfort experienced in the midst of sufferings. Παθημάτων gen. pl. neut. from πάθημα, -ατος, τό, "suffering." In the attrib. position αὐτῶν functions as an identical adj.: "the same sufferings." Πάσχομεν, 1st pl. pres. act. indic. of πάσχω, "suffer." Ὧν καὶ ἡμεῖς πάσχομεν is a rel. clause ("that we also suffer") qualifying τῶν αὐτῶν παθημάτων, i.e., Paul identifies the Corinthians' sufferings with his own. We can only guess in what way the sufferings of the Corinthians might have been similar to Paul's. It is unlikely that they were like those experienced by Paul in the course of his apostolic mission (cf. 4:7–12; 11:23–29). Allo 10 suggests they were simply the conflicts among families and relatives, the painful problems and the small everyday vexations that living out the gospel would give rise to in the midst of a town submerged in paganism and

licentiousness. If so, Paul recognizes that, in such afflictions, the Corinthians may be said to be sharing the sufferings of Christ (cf. v. 5; Phil 1:29–30).

For reasons for not adopting the rdg. of some mss. that omit ὧν καὶ ἡμεῖς πάσχομεν. καὶ ἡ ἐλπὶς ἡμῶν βεβαία ὑπὲρ ὑμῶν εἰδότες ὅτι ὡς κοινωνοί ἐστε τῶν παθημάτων in vv. 6–7, see Metzger 505–6.

VERSE 7

καὶ ἡ ἐλπὶς ἡμῶν βεβαία ὑπὲρ ὑμῶν
And our hope for you is firm,

᾽Ελπίς, nom. sg. fem. of ἐλπίς, -ίδος, ἡ, "hope." Βεβαία, nom. sg. fem. adj. of βέβαιος, -α, -ον, "firm, unshaken." Cf. BDAG 172c: "our expectation [of things to be fulfilled] for you is not misplaced." Ὑπέρ is a prep. with gen. ὑμῶν: "for you."

εἰδότες ὅτι ὡς κοινωνοί ἐστε τῶν παθημάτων, οὕτως καὶ τῆς παρακλήσεως.
because we know that as you share in the sufferings, so you will also share in the comfort.

Εἰδότες, nom. pl. masc. of perf. act. ptc. of οἶδα "know," a causal adv. ptc.: "because we know. . . ." Ὡς, a conj., introduces a comp. completed by οὕτως (dem. adv.: "as . . . so . . ."). Ὡς κοινωνοί ἐστε τῶν παθημάτων, lit. means "as you are partakers of the sufferings" (CSB: "as you share in the sufferings"). As the Corinthians share in the sufferings, so surely they will also share in the comfort. Κοινωνοί, nom. pl. masc. κοινωνός, -οῦ, ὁ "partaker."

b. Paul's Troubles in Asia (1:8–11)

STRUCTURE

Paul informs his readers of the troubles he experienced in the province of Asia, an experience that was still very fresh in his memory. We lack sufficient information for a positive identification of what those Asian troubles were. Several suggestions have been made, of which Jewish opposition stirred up against the apostle in Ephesus commends itself the most.

Vv. 8–9a describe the intensity of this suffering and its effect on Paul; v. 9b indicates the purpose/result of the sufferings—that he should not trust in himself, but in God, who raises the dead. V. 10 further describes God as the one who delivered Paul from so terrible a death, and as the one whom he trusts will deliver him again. V. 11 connects the prayers of his readers for him with an expected future deliverance by God, deliverance that, in answer to their prayers, will result in many giving thanks to God.

8   Οὐ γὰρ θέλομεν ὑμᾶς ἀγνοεῖν, ἀδελφοί,
                        ὑπὲρ τῆς θλίψεως ἡμῶν
                        τῆς γενομένης ἐν τῇ Ἀσίᾳ,

ὅτι καθ᾽ ὑπερβολὴν ὑπὲρ δύναμιν ἐβαρήθημεν
        ὥστε ἐξαπορηθῆναι ἡμᾶς καὶ τοῦ ζῆν·
9   ἀλλ᾽ αὐτοὶ ἐν ἑαυτοῖς τὸ ἀπόκριμα τοῦ θανάτου ἐσχήκαμεν,
        ἵνα μὴ πεποιθότες ὦμεν ἐφ᾽ ἑαυτοῖς
            ἀλλ᾽ ἐπὶ τῷ θεῷ
                τῷ ἐγείροντι τοὺς νεκρούς·
10   ὃς ἐκ τηλικούτου θανάτου ἐρρύσατο ἡμᾶς καὶ ῥύσεται,
                    εἰς ὃν ἠλπίκαμεν [ὅτι] καὶ ἔτι ῥύσεται,
11   συνυπουργούντων καὶ ὑμῶν ὑπὲρ ἡμῶν
        τῇ δεήσει,
            ἵνα ἐκ πολλῶν προσώπων τὸ εἰς ἡμᾶς χάρισμα διὰ πολλῶν εὐχαριστηθῇ
                                                        ὑπὲρ ἡμῶν.

VERSE 8

Οὐ γὰρ θέλομεν ὑμᾶς ἀγνοεῖν, ἀδελφοί, ὑπὲρ τῆς θλίψεως ἡμῶν τῆς γενομένης ἐν τῇ
Ἀσίᾳ,
We don't want you to be unaware, brothers and sisters, of our affliction that took place
in Asia.

Γάρ "serves as an explanatory bridge from the general reference to 'all our afflictions' in the benediction (v. 4) to the specific 'our affliction in Asia' in this present
passage" (Barnett 82). Ἀγνοεῖν, pres. act. inf. ἀγνοέω, "know," stands in complementary reln. with θέλομεν (1st pl. pres. act. indic. of θέλω, "want"), "We do not want you
to be unaware." Ὑμᾶς, acc. subj. of inf. ἀγνοεῖν. Ἀδελφοί, voc. pl. masc. ἀδελφός, -οῦ,
ὁ, "brother."

Ὑπέρ with gen. here means "concerning, about" (Moule 65.5c). Θλίψεως, gen. sg.
fem. θλῖψις, -εως, ἡ, "affliction." Τῆς γενομένης ἐν τῇ Ἀσίᾳ ("that took place in Asia")
is a rel. ptc. clause qualifying θλίψεως. Γενομένης, gen. sg. fem. of aor. mid. ptc. of
γίνομαι, "be, take place." Numerous attempts have been made to identify Paul's troubles in Asia: (1) imminent danger of drowning implied in 2 Cor 11:25; (2) a grave
illness; (3) fighting with "wild beasts in Ephesus," mentioned in 1 Cor 15:32; (4)
exposure to "such a deadly a peril" during an Ephesian imprisonment; (5) the tumult
in Ephesus following the charges brought against Paul by the guild of silversmiths (cf.
Acts 19:23–41). For a fuller discussion of possible identifications and an evaluation of
the likelihood of each of them, see Harris 166–72; Kruse 94–96.

ὅτι καθ᾽ ὑπερβολὴν ὑπὲρ δύναμιν ἐβαρήθημεν
We were completely overwhelmed—beyond our strength—

Harris 153 notes that there is no other instance in the Pauline letters "where ἀγνοεῖν
is modified by two qualifiers such as ὑπέρ and ὅτι. These considerations suggest that
only the ὅτι clause defines the content of ἀγνοεῖν." The ὅτι clause explains the nature of
the "affliction" (θλίψεως) of which Paul does not want the Corinthians to be unaware.

Ὑπερβολήν, acc. sg. fem. ὑπερβολή, -ῆς, ἡ, "excess, exceeding quality." BDAG 1032c–d: "state of exceeding to an extraordinary degree on a scale of extent." Καθ' ὑπερβολήν, BDAG 1032d: "to an extraordinary degree, beyond measure, utterly." Καθ' ὑπερβολὴν ὑπὲρ δύναμιν ἐβαρήθημεν: "We were completely overwhelmed—beyond our strength." Cf. BDAG 166d: "we were burdened altogether beyond our strength (= 'the load was so heavy we did not have the strength to keep going . . .')." Ὑπέρ is a prep. with acc. δύναμιν, "above, beyond." NIV: "far beyond our ability to endure." Δύναμιν, acc. sg. fem. of δύναμις, -εως, ἡ, "power, strength." Ἐβαρήθημεν, 1st pl. aor. pass. indic. of βαρέω, "burden, overwhelm."

ὥστε ἐξαπορηθῆναι ἡμᾶς καὶ τοῦ ζῆν·
so that we even despaired of life itself.

Ὥστε with inf. ἐξαπορηθῆναι indicates the result of Paul's affliction: "so that we despaired." Ἐξαπορηθῆναι, aor. pass. inf. of ἐξαπορέω, "be in despair," takes the gen. in respect of which it occurs (τοῦ ζῆν "of life"); cf. BDAG 345c. Ἡμᾶς, acc. subj. of the inf. ἐξαπορηθῆναι. Ζῆν, pres. act inf. of ζάω, "live." Τοῦ ζῆν, a gen. art. inf., explains of what Paul despaired: separation from life. Καί is intensive: "even . . . of life itself," lit. "even of living."

VERSE 9

ἀλλ' αὐτοὶ ἐν ἑαυτοῖς τὸ ἀπόκριμα τοῦ θανάτου ἐσχήκαμεν,
Indeed, we felt that we had received [in ourselves] the sentence of death,

Ἀλλ' is rhetorically ascensive ("indeed") (BDAG 45c). Αὐτοί, nom. pl. masc. of αὐτός in pred. position, functions as a verbal intensifier of the refl. ἑαυτοῖς, "we ourselves . . ." (BDF §283.4): "The strengthening of the refl. with αὐτός, frequent in Attic, appears only in scattered instances." Cf. 10:12. Ἑαυτοῖς, dat. 3rd pl. masc. refl. pron., ἑαυτοῦ, -ῆς, -οῦ. Ἐσχήκαμεν, 1st pl. perf. act. indic. of ἔχω, "have." The traditional understanding of the perf. tense, a past event with a present effect, seems appropriate here (cf. Seifrid 36–37). Ἀπόκριμα τοῦ θανάτου: Harris 155 states, "There is no doubt that τοῦ θανάτου is an epexegetic genitive; the ἀπόκριμα was 'death'." Ἀπόκριμα, acc. sg. neut. ἀπόκριμα, -ατος, τό, "sentence, answer," is a hapax legomenon in the NT, and not found in the LXX. The statement αὐτοὶ ἐν ἑαυτοῖς τὸ ἀπόκριμα τοῦ θανάτου ἐσχήκαμεν is difficult to interpret. Two factors are determinative: the mng. of the Greek word translated "sentence" (ἀπόκριμα), and the significance of the words "in ourselves" (ἐν ἑαυτοῖς). Paul's reference to having received the sentence "in ourselves" suggests that a subjective experience was involved. It was not so much a verdict pronounced by some external authority, but rather a perception in the heart and mind of the apostle himself. It follows then that the "sentence" (ἀπόκριμα) was prob. not one pronounced by some magistrate. It was more likely either the conclusion reached by Paul himself as he realized the dire straits he was in (so most commentators), or possibly the "answer" (ἀπόκριμα can mean either "answer" or "verdict") given by God to the apostle's prayer about this situation. Hemer, "A Note," 103–7, argues that "there is no ground in contemporary usage for seeing a judicial metaphor here"; rather, ἀπόκριμα is best understood as an "answer" given by God to a petition made by the apostle. In any case, Paul was in a hopeless situation, and humanly speaking, there was no escape. Barnett 85 disagrees: "ἀπόκριμα . . . is to be taken as 'official report' (so BAGD)."

ἵνα μὴ πεποιθότες ὦμεν ἐφ᾽ ἑαυτοῖς
so that we would not trust in ourselves

A neg. purpose clause. Πεποιθότες, nom. pl. masc. of pf. act. ptc. of πείθω, "trust," with ὦμεν (1st pl. pres. subjunc. of εἰμί) a periph. pf. subjunc. following ἵνα expresses purpose "so that we would not trust." The prep. ἐφ᾽ (contracted form of ἐπί) with dat. ἑαυτοῖς indicates that upon which Paul's trust is not to be placed, i.e., "ourselves."

ἀλλ᾽ ἐπὶ τῷ θεῷ τῷ ἐγείροντι τοὺς νεκρούς·
but in God who raises the dead.

Ἀλλ᾽ advers. introduces a positive alternative: "[not in ourselves] but in God. . . ." Ἐπί with dat. τῷ θεῷ indicates upon whom Paul's trust is to be placed, i.e., "God." Τῷ ἐγείροντι τοὺς νεκρούς is a rel. ptc. clause qualifying τῷ θεῷ ("[God] who raises the dead"). Ἐγείροντι, dat. sg. masc. of pres. act. ptc. of ἐγείρω, "raise." The ptc. is atemporal, describing a permanent attribute of God (Harris 157).

VERSE 10

ὃς ἐκ τηλικούτου θανάτου ἐρρύσατο ἡμᾶς καὶ ῥύσεται,
He has delivered us from such a terrible death, and he will deliver us.

A rel. clause further qualifies τῷ θεῷ, describing him as the one who not only raises the dead, but who also has delivered and will deliver the apostle again. Ἐκ τηλικούτου θανάτου, a gen. prep. phrase (ἐκ with gen.), describes from what God delivers Paul ("from such a terrible death"). Τηλικούτου, gen. sg. masc. dem. pron. τηλικοῦτος, -αύτη, -οῦτο, "such, so great." Most mss. support the sg. θανάτου; however, the oldest known ms., 𝔓⁴⁶, has the plural θανάτων. Cf. discussion in Metzger 506. Ἐρρύσατο, 3rd sg. aor. mid. indic. of ῥύομαι, "deliver." Ῥύσεται, 3rd sg. fut. mid. indic. of ῥύομαι, "deliver." Some later mss. have the pres. ῥύεται ("delivers") instead of the fut. ῥύσεται ("will deliver"), though the latter has the support of the earliest and best mss., incl. 𝔓⁴⁶ ℵ B C; see discussion in Metzger 506.

εἰς ὃν ἠλπίκαμεν [ὅτι] καὶ ἔτι ῥύσεται,
We have put our hope in him that he will deliver us again

Εἰς is a prep. with acc ὃν ἠλπίκαμεν, indicating on whom Paul put his hope. Ὅν, acc. sg. masc. rel. pron. ὅς, refers back to τῷ θεῷ: "On him [God] we have set our hope"

(NIV). Ἠλπίκαμεν, 1st pl. act. indic. pf. of ἐλπίζω, "hope." According to the verbal aspect theory, the use of the perf. tense here indicates Paul's present state of mind (cf. Porter, *Idioms*, 40). According to the traditional view, the perf. indicates a present state of affairs resulting from a past action. [Ὅτι] καὶ ἔτι ῥύσεται 𝔓⁴⁶ B D* omit ὅτι (see discussion in Metzger 506–7), ἡμᾶς as obj. understood. Ῥύσεται, 3rd sg. fut. mid. indic. ῥύομαι, "deliver."

VERSE 11

συνυπουργούντων καὶ ὑμῶν ὑπὲρ ἡμῶν τῇ δεήσει,
while you join in helping us by your prayers.

Συνυπουργούντων, gen. pl. masc. of pres. act. ptc. of συνυπουργέω, "help," with ὑμῶν (2nd plur. gen. σύ) forms the gen. abs. const. συνυπουργούντων . . . ὑμῶν, used to denote a change of subject from that of the main verb—i.e., an action taking place while Paul set his hope on God. Δεήσει, dat. sg. fem. δέησις, -εως, ἡ, "prayer."

ἵνα ἐκ πολλῶν προσώπων τὸ εἰς ἡμᾶς χάρισμα διὰ πολλῶν εὐχαριστηθῇ ὑπὲρ ἡμῶν.
Then many will give thanks on our behalf for the gift that came to us through the prayers of many.

Moule 108: "If διὰ πολλῶν goes with εὐχαριστηθῇ as = *may be thanked for by many*, then ἐκ πολλῶν is redundant; but if διὰ πολλῶν goes with τὸ εἰς ἡμᾶς χάρισμα as = *the gift which reached us by the agency of many*, then strict grammar requires a second article—τὸ εἰς ἡμᾶς χάρισμα τὸ διὰ πολλῶν." Ἵνα with εὐχαριστηθῇ (3rd sg. aor. pass subjunc. of εὐχαριστέω, "give thanks") expresses the result of Paul's converts' prayers: thanksgiving [to God] because of his gracious favour granted to Paul. Cf. BDF (§312[2]) for the passive with an intransitive verb. Ἐκ is a prep. with gen. πολλῶν προσώπων, lit. "from many faces," where the part ("faces") stands for the whole ("many people"), though it has also been suggested that it denotes "faces upturned in prayer." Προσώπων, gen. pl. neut. πρόσωπον, -ου, τό, "face." Τὸ εἰς ἡμᾶς χάρισμα ("the gracious favor granted us"), acc. of respect. Διὰ πολλῶν appears to be redundant following ἐκ πολλῶν προσώπων, the ἐκ and διά phrases referring to the same agents (cf. Harris 162: "We need not identify the 'many' who render thanks totally with the 'many' who intercede for Paul's deliverance, but presumably the overlap would be considerable"). Ὑπέρ is a prep. with gen. ἡμῶν denoting for whom thanksgiving is made ("on our behalf"). Some mss. have ὑμῶν instead of ἡμῶν, but this is unintelligible in context. See discussion in Metzger 507.

FOR FURTHER STUDY

8. Mercy (οἰκτιρμός) (1:3)
Esser, H. H. *NIDNTT* 2.593–601.

Morris, L. *DPL* 601–2.

9. Comfort (παράκλησις) (1:3)

Braumann, G. *NIDNTT* 1.567–71. See p. 571.
Schmitz, O. S. G. *TDNT* 5.773–99.

10. Affliction/Suffering (θλῖψις/πάθημα) (1:4–7)

Ahern, B. M. "The Fellowship of His Sufferings (Phil 3:10): A Study of St. Paul's Doctrine on Christian Suffering." *CBQ* 22 (1960): 1–32.
Hafemann, S. J. *DPL* 919–21.
———. *Suffering and Ministry in the Spirit: Paul's Defense of His Ministry in II Corinthians 2:14–3:3.* Grand Rapids: Eerdmans, 1990.
Kruse, C. G. *DPL* 18–20.
———. *DNTB* 775–78.
———. "The Price Paid for a Ministry among Gentiles: Paul's Persecution at the Hands of the Jews." Pages 260–272 in *Worship, Theology and Ministry in the Early Church: Essays in honor of Ralph P. Martin.* Edited by M. J. Wilkins and T. Paige. JSNTSup 87. Sheffield: Sheffield Academic Press, 1992.

11. Participation/Sharing (κοινωνία) (1:7)

Hauck, F. *TDNT* 3.797–809.
O'Brien, P. T. *DPL* 293–95.

12. Affliction in Asia (1:8)

Harris, M. J. "Excursus: Paul's Affliction in Asia. (2 Cor. 1:8–11): The Personal Background to 2 Corinthians." In *The Second Epistle to the Corinthians.* NIGTC. Grand Rapids: Eerdmans, 2005. See pp. 164–82.
Kruse, C. G. "Additional Note: Paul's Troubles in the Province of Asia." In *2 Corinthians: An Introduction and Commentary.* TNTC 8. Nottingham/Downers Grove: IVP, 2015. See pp. 94–96.
Yates, R. J. "Paul's Affliction in Asia: 2 Corinthians 1:8." *EvQ* 53 (1981): 241–45.

13. Trust in God (1:9)

Young, N. M. "'. . . To Make Us Rely Not on Ourselves but on God Who Raises the Dead.' 2 Cor 1,9b as the Heart of Paul's Theology." Pages 384–98 in *Die Mitte des Neuen Testament.* Edited by U. Luz and H. Weder. Göttingen: Vandenhoeck and Ruprecht, 1983.

14. The Sentence of Death (ἀπόκριμα) (1:9)

Büchsel, F. *TDNT* 3.945–46.
Hemer, C. J. "A Note on 2 Corinthians 1:9." *TynBul* 23 (1972): 103–7.

HOMILETICAL SUGGESTIONS

God Comforts His People (1:3–7)

1. God is the Father of mercies and all comfort (vv. 3–4)
2. God comforts us so that we are able to comfort others (v. 4)
3. The privilege of sharing Christ's sufferings (v. 5)
4. Both our afflictions and comfort enable us to comfort others (v. 6–7)

The Discipline of Affliction (1:8–11)

1. Afflictions teach us to rely not on ourselves but on God (vv. 8–9)
2. God's deliverance experienced provides hope for future deliverance (v. 10)
3. The role of prayer in bringing God's comfort to others in their afflictions (vv. 10–11)

B. THE BODY OF THE RESPONSE (1:12–7:16)

1. Personal Defense (1:12–24)

Paul was aware of criticisms of his character and actions entertained by some in Corinth. So, even while responding to the good news Titus brought regarding changes for the better there, he felt it necessary to defend his personal integrity before dealing with matters related to the "severe letter," the reinstatement of the offender, and the nature of his apostolic ministry. In this section, then, he defends his integrity in general terms (1:12–14) and then specifically in relation to changes to his travel plans and saying one thing and mng. another in his letters (1:15–22), before calling upon God as witness to his truthfulness (1:23–24).

a. General Defense of Integrity (1:12–14)

Paul concluded the previous section (1:3–11) with a request for prayer. It may be that the general defense of his integrity in 1:12–14 is intended as a justification of this request, but it is more likely that it looks forward and paves the way for the specific defense of his integrity in relation to his travel plans and the writing of the "severe letter" in 1:15–2:4.

STRUCTURE

12 Ἡ γὰρ καύχησις ἡμῶν αὕτη ἐστίν,
      τὸ μαρτύριον τῆς συνειδήσεως ἡμῶν,
            ὅτι ἐν ἁπλότητι καὶ εἰλικρινείᾳ τοῦ θεοῦ,
            [καὶ] οὐκ ἐν σοφίᾳ σαρκικῇ
                  ἀλλ᾽ ἐν χάριτι θεοῦ,
            ἀνεστράφημεν ἐν τῷ κόσμῳ,
                  περισσοτέρως δὲ πρὸς ὑμᾶς.
13 οὐ γὰρ ἄλλα γράφομεν ὑμῖν
            ἀλλ᾽ ἢ ἃ ἀναγινώσκετε
                  ἢ καὶ ἐπιγινώσκετε·
                        ἐλπίζω δὲ ὅτι ἕως τέλους ἐπιγνώσεσθε,
14   καθὼς καὶ ἐπέγνωτε ἡμᾶς ἀπὸ μέρους,
                              ὅτι καύχημα ὑμῶν ἐσμεν
                              καθάπερ καὶ ὑμεῖς ἡμῶν
                                    ἐν τῇ ἡμέρᾳ τοῦ κυρίου [ἡμῶν] Ἰησοῦ.

VERSE 12

Ἡ γὰρ καύχησις ἡμῶν αὕτη ἐστίν, τὸ μαρτύριον τῆς συνειδήσεως ἡμῶν,
Indeed, this is our boast: The testimony of our conscience

Γάρ, a conj., may function either to introduce the reason for Paul's confidence in the Corinthians' willingness to pray for him (v. 11) or more likely as a loose connector with what precedes (cf. Harris 184; Z §473). Καύχησις, nom. sg. fem. καύχησις, -εως, ἡ, "boast." BDAG 537b: "object of boasting, reason for boasting." Καύχησις is pred. nom. with ἐστίν. Paul uses the concept of boasting more than any other New Testament writer. Essentially to boast means to take pride in something or someone, and in Paul's writings it is used both negatively and positively. Used negatively it refers to an unwarranted pride in one's own merits; used positively it denotes legitimate pride based on what God has done and enabled one to do (cf. Rom 15:17–19). Αὕτη, nom. sg. fem. pron. "this," agreeing with pred. nom. καύχησις.

Μαρτύριον, nom. sg. neut. μαρτύριον, -ου, τό, "testimony." BDAG 619b: "a statement that is brought out as testimony." Συνειδήσεως, gen. sg. fem. συνείδησις, -εως, ἡ, "conscience." The word συνείδησις is found more often in the Pauline corpus than in the rest of the books of the NT put together. Unlike the Stoics, Paul did not regard conscience as the voice of God within, nor did he restrict its function to a person's past acts (usually the bad ones), as was the case in the secular Greek world of his day. For Paul conscience is a human faculty whereby people either approve or disapprove of their actions (whether already performed or only intended) and those of others. The conscience is not to be equated with the voice of God or even the moral law; rather, it is a human faculty that adjudicates upon human action in the light of the highest standard a person perceives. Seeing that all of human nature has been affected by sin, both a person's perception of the standard of action required and the function of the conscience itself (as a constituent part of human nature) are also affected by sin. For this reason conscience can never be accorded the position of ultimate judge of one's behavior. It is possible that the conscience may excuse one for that which God will not excuse, and conversely it is equally possible that conscience may condemn a person for that which God allows. The final judgment, therefore, belongs only to God (cf. 1 Cor 4:2–5). Nevertheless, to reject the voice of conscience is to court spiritual disaster (cf. 1 Tim 1:19). We cannot reject the voice of conscience with impunity, but we can modify the highest standard to which it relates by gaining for ourselves a greater understanding of the truth.

ὅτι ἐν ἁπλότητι καὶ εἰλικρινείᾳ τοῦ θεοῦ, [καὶ] οὐκ ἐν σοφίᾳ σαρκικῇ ἀλλ' ἐν χάριτι θεοῦ, ἀνεστράφημεν ἐν τῷ κόσμῳ,
that we have conducted ourselves in the world . . . with godly sincerity and purity, not by human wisdom but by God's grace.

This ὅτι clause explains the positive content of the testimony of Paul's conscience: that he has conducted himself in a godly manner. Ἐν ἁπλότητι καὶ εἰλικρινείᾳ τοῦ θεοῦ, adv. prep. phrase (ἐν with dat.) explains the way Paul conducted himself: "with godly sincerity and purity." Ἁπλότητι, dat. sg. fem. ἁπλότης,- ητος, ἡ, "sincerity." BDAG 104a: "personal integrity expressed in word or action (cp. our colloq. 'what you see is what you get') simplicity, sincerity, uprightness, frankness." Some early mss., incl. 𝔓⁴⁶, read ἁγιότητι ("holiness") instead of ἁπλότητι ("sincerity"); however, ἁπλότητι fits the context better, and ἁγιότητι is not found elsewhere in Paul's letters (cf. Metzger 507). Harris 183 prefers ἁγιότητι. Εἰλικρινείᾳ, dat. sg. fem. εἰλικρίνεια, -ας, ἡ, "purity." BDAG 282c: "the quality or state of being free of dissimulation, sincerity, purity of motive." Τοῦ θεοῦ, attrib. gen. "godly [sincerity and purity]."

Ἀνεστράφημεν, 1st pl. aor. pass. indic. of ἀναστρέφω, "conduct oneself, behave." BDAG 72d: "to conduct oneself in terms of certain principles, act, behave, conduct oneself, live." Employed here with several uses of the prep. ἐν with different mngs. to explain the various aspects of his behavior: ἐν ἁπλότητι καὶ εἰλικρινείᾳ ("with godly sincerity and purity"), οὐκ ἐν σοφίᾳ σαρκικῇ ("not by human wisdom"), ἀλλ' ἐν χάριτι θεοῦ ("but by God's grace"), and ἐν τῷ κόσμῳ ("in the world"). Οὐκ ἐν σοφίᾳ σαρκικῇ, the neg. content of the testimony of Paul's conscience, that he has not conducted himself "by human wisdom." Σοφίᾳ, dat. sg. fem. σοφία, -ας, ἡ, "wisdom." Seifrid 50: "This single reference to "wisdom" in Second Corinthians displays the link between its theme and Paul's opening attack on human wisdom in 1 Cor 1–2, a wisdom that has been revealed as foolishness by the 'word of the cross' (1 Cor 1:18)." Σαρκικῇ, adj. dat. sg. σαρκικός, -ή, -όν, "human, worldly." Harris 186: "because σάρξ is the seat of sin (Rom. 7:17–18, 23, 25), in Paul's usage σαρκικός sometimes gains the pejorative sense of 'guided by sinful passions' (1 Cor 3:3 twice)."

περισσοτέρως δὲ πρὸς ὑμᾶς.
and especially toward you,

Περισσοτέρως, comp. adv. mng. "especially, even more so." Πρός is a prep. with acc. ὑμᾶς, "toward you." We can only guess the reason Paul was so careful in Corinth. Perhaps the Corinthians were more critical than most of the behavior of itinerants (whose methods were not always exemplary) and Paul wanted it to be abundantly clear that as a messenger of the gospel, he renounced all such questionable methods.

VERSE 13

οὐ γὰρ ἄλλα γράφομεν ὑμῖν ἀλλ' ἢ ἃ ἀναγινώσκετε ἢ καὶ ἐπιγινώσκετε
For we are writing nothing to you other than what you can read and also understand.

Γάρ connects what follows with what precedes (the godly way Paul conducts his ministry) and indicates that it will also relate to his conduct toward the Corinthians (the straightforward nature of what he writes in his letters); cf. Barnett 96. Ἄλλα, acc. neut. pl. adj. ἄλλος, -η, -ον, "other." Γράφομεν, 1st pl. pres. act. indic. of γράφω, "write." Ὑμῖν, dat. pl. indirect object of γράφομεν, "(we are writing) *to you.*"

Ἀλλ', conj. ἀλλά, "but." R 1187: "ἄλλα—ὑμῖν ἀλλ' ἤ, a sort of pleonastic use of ἀλλά. This is a classical idiom." Ἤ, particle, "than." Ἀλλ' ἤ. CSB: "other than." Ἅ, pron. acc. pl. neut. rel. pron. ὅς, ἥ, ὅ, "what." Ἀναγινώσκετε, 2nd pl. pres. act. indic. of ἀναγινώσκω, "read." Cf. Moule 89: "J. H. Kennedy argued interestingly, if not convincingly, for interpreting the ἀνα- in II Cor. i. 13, iii. 2 as an intensive making the verb mean admit or acknowledge." Ἐπιγινώσκετε, 2nd pl. pres. act. indic. of ἐπιγινώσκω, "understand, recognize." Ἃ ἀναγινώσκετε ἢ καὶ ἐπιγινώσκετε, ZG 535: "what you read and what is familiar to you (= you recognize)." Barnett 96–97: "Paul connects similar sounding words *anaginōskete* and *epiginōskete* (cf. 'comprehend' and 'apprehend' as a partial analogy in English), as a rhetorical device. If the first, 'read,' applies to the hearing of what is read aloud to the gathered congregation, the second, 'understand,' applies to its acceptance and implementation."

ἐλπίζω δὲ ὅτι ἕως τέλους ἐπιγνώσεσθε,
I hope you will understand completely—

Ἐλπίζω, 1st sg. pres. act indic., "hope." Ὅτι, conj. introducing direct discourse "that," expresses the content of Paul's hope. Ἕως, conj. with gen. τέλους, "to the end." R 643: "In ἕως τέλους (2 Cor 1:13), the phrase is almost adverbial." Harris 188: "In conjunction with ἀπὸ μέρους ('partially') [v. 14a], the phrase ἕως τέλους means 'fully,' not 'to the end' (of the age/of your lives)." Contra BDAG 998c: "to the end=until the Parousia." Τέλους, gen. sg. neut. τέλος, ους, τό, "end, goal." Ἐπιγνώσεσθε, 2nd pl. fut. mid. indic. of ἐπιγινώσκω, "understand, recognize." Harris 188: "a punctiliar rather than a linear future: 'you will come to understand (fully),' rather than 'you will continue to recognize (to the end).'"

VERSE 14

καθὼς καὶ ἐπέγνωτε ἡμᾶς ἀπὸ μέρους,
just as you have partially understood us—

Καθώς, the comp. conj. "just as," introduces a comp. with what precedes. Ἐπέγνωτε, 2nd pl. aor. act. indic. of ἐπιγινώσκω, "know." Ἀπό is a prep. with μέρους, "in part." Paul's wish is that they will understand completely, just as they have understood in part. CSB: "just as you have partially understood us." Barnett 97: "There may be a double entendre here. 'Understand fully' can mean both 'in full' (i.e., as distinct from 'in part') and in 'the day of the Lord Jesus' (at the 'end') as distinct from at present ('now')." Μέρους, gen. sg. neut. μέρος, -ους, τό, "part."

ὅτι καύχημα ὑμῶν ἐσμεν καθάπερ καὶ ὑμεῖς ἡμῶν
that we are your reason for pride, just as you also are ours

This expresses what Paul hopes the Corinthians will understand completely: "that we are your reason for pride, just as you also are ours." Ὅτι, conj., "that," introduces direct discourse. Καύχημα, nom. sg. neut. καύχημα, -ατος, τό, "reason for pride or boasting." It is difficult to distinguish the mng. of καύχημα from that of καύχησις (v. 12), for in context both seem to refer to the ground or reason for boasting. Ἐσμεν, 1st pl. pres. indic. of εἰμί, "be." Καθάπερ, coord. conj. "just as." Καθάπερ καὶ ὑμεῖς ἡμῶν, "just as you also are ours."

ἐν τῇ ἡμέρᾳ τοῦ κυρίου [ἡμῶν] Ἰησοῦ.
in the day of our Lord Jesus.

The external evidence for and against the inclusion of ἡμῶν make it difficult to decide the preferable rdg.; however, "longer readings that involve the sacred names are suspect as scribal expansions" (Metzger 507). Ἐν with dat. τῇ ἡμέρᾳ (dat. sg. fem. ἡμέρα, -ας, ἡ, "day") indicates the day on which Paul hopes the Corinthians will completely understand that he is their true ground of boasting as they are his. "The day of our Lord Jesus" is the day of his parousia; cf. 1 Thess 5:2; 2 Pet 3:10, 12. Barnett 98: "The 'day of the Lord Jesus' is the occasion of the general resurrection (4:14) and the universal judgment (5:10), and issues in the union between the heavenly Lord and his betrothed, the church (11:2)."

b. Defense of Changed Travel Plans (1:15–22)

From the general defense of his integrity in vv. 12–14, Paul now turns to address the specific matter of changes to his travel plans, which the Corinthians took as evidence of fickleness in his dealings with them.

STRUCTURE

15   Καὶ ταύτῃ τῇ πεποιθήσει
ἐβουλόμην πρότερον πρὸς ὑμᾶς ἐλθεῖν,
        ἵνα δευτέραν χάριν σχῆτε,
16   καὶ δι' ὑμῶν διελθεῖν εἰς Μακεδονίαν
        καὶ πάλιν ἀπὸ Μακεδονίας ἐλθεῖν πρὸς ὑμᾶς
        καὶ ὑφ' ὑμῶν προπεμφθῆναι εἰς τὴν Ἰουδαίαν.
17 τοῦτο οὖν βουλόμενος
        μήτι ἄρα τῇ ἐλαφρίᾳ ἐχρησάμην;
    ἢ ἃ βουλεύομαι κατὰ σάρκα βουλεύομαι,
        ἵνα ᾖ παρ' ἐμοὶ τὸ ναὶ ναὶ
            καὶ τὸ οὒ οὔ;
18 πιστὸς δὲ ὁ θεὸς
        ὅτι ὁ λόγος ἡμῶν
            ὁ πρὸς ὑμᾶς οὐκ ἔστιν ναὶ
                καὶ οὔ.
19 ὁ τοῦ θεοῦ γὰρ υἱὸς
            Ἰησοῦς Χριστὸς
                ὁ ἐν ὑμῖν δι' ἡμῶν κηρυχθείς,
                        δι' ἐμοῦ καὶ Σιλουανοῦ καὶ
                            Τιμοθέου,

        οὐκ ἐγένετο Ναὶ καὶ Οὒ
        ἀλλὰ Ναὶ ἐν αὐτῷ γέγονεν.
20 ὅσαι γὰρ ἐπαγγελίαι θεοῦ,
        ἐν αὐτῷ τὸ Ναί·

διὸ καὶ δι' αὐτοῦ τὸ Ἀμὴν τῷ θεῷ πρὸς δόξαν δι' ἡμῶν.
21 ὁ δὲ
        βεβαιῶν ἡμᾶς
                σὺν ὑμῖν
                εἰς Χριστὸν
            καὶ χρίσας ἡμᾶς
    θεός,
22 ὁ καὶ σφραγισάμενος ἡμᾶς
    καὶ δοὺς τὸν ἀρραβῶνα τοῦ πνεύματος
                ἐν ταῖς καρδίαις ἡμῶν.

VERSE 15

Καὶ ταύτῃ τῇ πεποιθήσει
Because of this confidence,

Dat. of cause: "Because of this confidence" (Wallace 151: "with this confidence"). Paul's confidence that the Corinthians will be proud of their apostle was the reason he made his plans to visit them. Ταύτῃ, dat. sg. fem. pron. οὗτος, αὕτη, τοῦτο, "this." Πεποιθήσει, dat. sg. fem. πεποίθησις, -εως, ἡ, "confidence."

ἐβουλόμην πρότερον πρὸς ὑμᾶς ἐλθεῖν,
I planned to come to you first,

Ἐβουλόμην, 1st sg. impf. mid. indic. of βούλομαι, "plan a course of action" (BDAG 182c). The impf. depicts Paul's motivation as an unfolding/ongoing past action. Πρότερον adv. "first," denotes something taking place in former times (BDAG 888d). Πρός is a prep. with acc. ὑμᾶς "to/toward you." Ἐλθεῖν, aor. act. inf. of ἔρχομαι, "come." Stands in complementary reln. with ἐβουλόμην.

ἵνα δευτέραν χάριν σχῆτε,
so that you could have a second benefit,

Ἵνα with subjunc. σχῆτε indicates the purpose of Paul's desire to come to the Corinthians again: that they "might benefit twice" (cf. v. 16). Σχῆτε 2nd pl. aor. act. subjunc. of ἔχω, "have." Harris 192: "ἔχω is ingressive (or inceptive) in sense, 'come to have,' thus 'obtain,' 'acquire,' 'receive.'" Δευτέραν acc. sg. fem. adj. δεύτερος, -α, -ον, "second." Χάριν acc. sg. fem. χάρις, -ιτος, ἡ, "benefit, gift." Δευτέραν χάριν. ZG 536: "a double pleasure."

VERSE 16

καὶ δι᾽ ὑμῶν διελθεῖν εἰς Μακεδονίαν
and to visit you on my way to Macedonia,

Δι᾽ (contraction of διά) is a prep. with gen. ὑμῶν, lit. "via you." Διελθεῖν, aor. act. inf. of διέρχομαι, "go through," also stands in complementary reln. with ἐβουλόμην (cf. v. 15). Εἰς is a prep. with acc. Μακεδονίαν (Μακεδονία, -ας, ἡ), "to Macedonia."

καὶ πάλιν ἀπὸ Μακεδονίας ἐλθεῖν πρὸς ὑμᾶς
and then come to you again from Macedonia

Πάλιν, adv. "again." Ἀπό is a prep. with gen. Μακεδονίας, "from Macedonia." Ἐλθεῖν, aor. act. inf. of ἔρχομαι, "come," also stands in complementary reln. with ἐβουλόμην (cf. v. 15). Πρός is a prep. with acc. ὑμᾶς, "to/toward you." Ὑμᾶς, 2nd pl. acc. σύ, "you."

καὶ ὑφ᾽ ὑμῶν προπεμφθῆναι εἰς τὴν Ἰουδαίαν.
and be helped by you on my journey to Judea.

This was also part of Paul's desire (ἐβουλόμην, cf. v. 15) in visiting the Corinthians again: that they might help him on his journey to Judea. Ὑφ᾽(contraction of ὑπό) is a prep. with gen. ὑμῶν "by you." Προπεμφθῆναι aor. pass. inf. of προπέμπω "help on a journey." BDAG 873d: "assist someone in making a journey, send on one's way with food, money, by arranging for companions, means of travel, etc." Εἰς is a prep. with acc. τὴν Ἰουδαίαν "to Judea." Τὴν Ἰουδαίαν, (BDF §261[4]): "Many names of countries regularly take the article as a result of their original use as adjectives." Harris 194: "The particular prepositions used in the sequence πρὸς ὑμᾶς . . . εἰς Μακεδονίαν . . . πρὸς ὑμᾶς . . . εἰς τὴν Ἰουδαίαν in vv. 15–16 illustrate the general rule in NT Greek that in expressing the idea of direction, πρός is used with personal objects and εἰς with impersonal."

VERSE 17

τοῦτο οὖν βουλόμενος μήτι ἄρα τῇ ἐλαφρίᾳ ἐχρησάμην;
Now when I planned this, was I of two minds?

Τοῦτο οὖν βουλόμενος is an adv. ptc. phrase depicting ongoing action taking place at the same time as that of the main verb (ἐχρησάμην) "while I was planning." CSB: "when I planned this." Οὖν is an inferential conj. CSB: "now." Βουλόμενος, nom. sg. masc. of pres. mid. ptc. of βούλομαι. BDAG 182c: "plan a course of action." Μήτι ἄρα τῇ ἐλαφρίᾳ ἐχρησάμην, a question expecting a neg. response: "was I making use of vacillation?" CSB: "Was I of two minds?" Μήτι is a marker inviting a neg. response. Ἄρα is a conj. mng. "then, therefore." Ἐλαφρίᾳ, dat. sg. fem. ἐλαφρία, -ας, ἡ, "vacillation." ZG 536: "irresponsibility." Harris 196: "ἐλαφρία is a hapax legomenon in the

Greek Bible and is not found in Greek writers before the Christian era." Ἐχρησάμην, 1st sg. aor. mid. indic. of χράομαι, "make use of."

ἤ ἃ βουλεύομαι κατὰ σάρκα βουλεύομαι
Or what I plan, do I plan in a purely human way

Another question expecting a neg. response: "or what I plan, do I plan in a purely human way?" Ἤ, particle mng. "or." When used with double questions, at the beginning of one question it has reference to an implied alternative (R 1177). Harris 196: "The particle ἤ does not introduce a generalized restatement of the first rhetorical question, as though v. 17b stood in synonymous parallelism with v. 17a. Rather it introduces an additional and more general accusation made against Paul (μήτι is understood), one perhaps prompted by the further alterations to his projected itinerary." Βουλεύομαι, 1st sg. pres. mid. indic. of βούλομαι. BDAG 182c: "plan a course of action." Κατά is a prep. with acc. σάρκα, lit. "according to [the] flesh." CSB: "in a purely human way." Harris, *Prepositions*, 149: "impulsively." Σάρκα, acc. sg. fem. σάρξ, σαρκός, ἡ, "flesh."

Ἵνα ᾖ παρ᾿ ἐμοὶ τὸ Ναὶ ναὶ καὶ τὸ Οὒ οὔ;
so that I say "Yes, yes"and "No, no" at the same time?

Completes Paul's question expecting a neg. answer, rejecting any duplicity on his part: lit. "so that there exists with me 'Yes, yes' and 'No, no'?" Paul denies saying one thing while intending another. Wallace 237: "the 'yes' should be 'yes' and the 'no' [should be] 'no' with me." ZG 536: "shilly-shallying." Barnett 102: "In other words, while his words at the time were 'Yes, yes' ('I am coming back soon'), he really meant 'No, no' ('I am not coming back until much later')." Ἵνα with subjunc. ᾖ introduces the intended result of Paul's presumed vacillating, something that he denies. Ἦ, 3rd sg. pres. subjunc. of εἰμί, "be, exist." Παρ᾿ (contraction of παρά) is a prep. with dat. ἐμοὶ, "with me." Ἐμοί, dat. 1st sg. pron., "me." Ναί, particle "yes." Οὔ, particle "no."

VERSE 18

πιστὸς δὲ ὁ θεὸς ὅτι ὁ λόγος ἡμῶν ὁ πρὸς ὑμᾶς οὐκ ἔστιν Ναὶ καὶ Οὔ.
As God is faithful, our message to you is not "Yes and no."

At this point Paul moves from particular issues addressed in vv. 15–17 to theological truths that undergird his mission in vv. 18–22, before returning to the particular issues once more in vv. 23–24. Cf. Harris 198. Paul appeals to the faithfulness of God as a guarantee for the integrity of his message. Πιστὸς δὲ ὁ θεός functions as an oath formula, "as God is faithful"—a form of εἰμί to be supplied. Πιστός, nom. sg. masc. adj. πιστός, -ή, -όν, "faithful, reliable."

Ὅτι, the conj. "that," introduces the content of Paul's claim to integrity: "our message to you is not 'Yes and no.'" Ὁ πρὸς ὑμᾶς is a prep. rel. phrase qualifying ὁ λόγος ἡμῶν, lit. "[our word] which [is] to you." CSB: "our message to you." Harris 199: The meaning of ὁ λόγος cannot be restricted to the initial proclamation of the gospel at Corinth (cf. v. 19) but presumably includes not only the preaching and teaching of Paul and others at Corinth but also Paul's letter to the Corinthians—that is, all his spoken and written words, his language, not simply 'the word of the gospel.'" Οὐκ ἔστιν Ναὶ καὶ Οὔ, Paul denies saying one thing while mng. another.

VERSE 19

ὁ τοῦ θεοῦ γὰρ υἱὸς Ἰησοῦς Χριστός
For the Son of God, Jesus Christ,

Paul appeals to the character of Jesus Christ, whom he preached among the Corinthians, as he asserts the integrity of his own ministry. Τοῦ θεοῦ, gen. of relationship. Regarding the unusual placement of γάρ as the fourth word here (cf. BDF §574[2]): "ὁ τοῦ θεοῦ γὰρ υἱὸς . . . gives more emphasis to θεοῦ than ὁ γὰρ τ. Θ. υἱὸς." Ἰησοῦς Χριστός stands in appos. to ὁ τοῦ θεοῦ . . . υἱός.

ὁ ἐν ὑμῖν δι' ἡμῶν κηρυχθείς, δι' ἐμοῦ καὶ Σιλουανοῦ καὶ Τιμοθέου,
whom we proclaimed among you—Silvanus, Timothy, and I—

Rel. clause describing Jesus Christ as the one proclaimed by Paul and his colleagues among the Corinthians. [Ἰησοῦς Χριστὸς] ὁ . . . δι' ἡμῶν κηρυχθείς, "[Jesus Christ] who . . . was proclaimed by us." Cf. Wallace 433–34: "The subject of a passive verb receives the action that is expressed by διά + genitive. Here, the agent named is intermediate, not ultimate." Ἐν is a prep. with dat. ὑμῖν, "among you." Δι' is a prep. with gen. ἡμῶν, lit. "through us." Harris 200: "We might have expected Paul to write ὁ . . . ὑφ' ἡμῶν κηρυχθείς. His choice of διά rather than ὑπό highlights the intermediary or secondary role of the preacher, just as Rom. 10:14–17 focuses on the indispensable or primary role of the preacher." Κηρυχθείς, nom. sg. masc. of aor. pass. ptc. of κηρύσσω, "proclaim." Δι' ἐμοῦ καὶ Σιλουανοῦ καὶ Τιμοθέου stands in appos. to δι' ἡμῶν.

οὐκ ἐγένετο Ναὶ καὶ Οὔ ἀλλὰ Ναὶ ἐν αὐτῷ γέγονεν.
did not become "Yes and no." On the contrary, in him it is always "Yes."

Οὐκ ἐγένετο Ναὶ καὶ Οὔ, Paul denies any duplicity in their proclamation (cf. vv. 17–18). Ἐγένετο, 3rd sg. aor. mid. indic. of γίνομαι, "become." The aor. represents action as a completed whole, and in the indic. here refers to proclamation in the past (cf. Seifrid 61). Ἀλλὰ Ναὶ ἐν αὐτῷ γέγονεν, Paul affirms the positive nature of their proclamation: "On the contrary, in him it is always 'Yes.'" Harris 201: "His point is that the life of Jesus Christ did not turn out to be . . . an ambiguous blend of affirmation and denial with regard to God's promises." Ἐν is a prep. with dat. αὐτῷ, "in him," i.e., "in Christ." Γέγονεν, 3rd sg. perf. act. indic. of γίνομαι, "become." The traditional understanding of the perf. (a past event with ongoing consequences) does not suit here; it is better to adopt the verbal aspect defn. of the perf. a present state of affairs (cf.

Porter, *Idioms* 40), yielding, "in him it is always 'Yes,'" as in CSB. Barnett 105: "We infer, then, that Paul's kerygmatic 'word' and his personal 'word' are inseparable; both express the faithfulness of God, whose minister Paul is."

VERSE 20

ὅσαι γὰρ ἐπαγγελίαι θεοῦ, ἐν αὐτῷ τὸ Ναί·
For every one of God's promises is "Yes" in him.

῞Οσαι, nom. pl. fem. pron. ὅσος, -η, -ον, "as many as." CSB: "every one." Ἐπαγγελίαι, nom. pl. fem. ἐπαγγελία, -ας, ἡ, "promise." Ἐστιν needs to be supplied: "For every one of God's promises *is* 'Yes' in him."

διὸ καὶ δι' αὐτοῦ τὸ Ἀμὴν τῷ θεῷ πρὸς δόξαν δι' ἡμῶν.
Therefore, through him we also say "Amen" to the glory of God.

Lit. "Therefore also through him the Amen to God for glory through us." The Greek underlying this sentence is difficult to translate and interpret accurately, although its general thrust is clear enough. It may reflect the worship of the early church in which ascriptions of praise to God were offered "through him" (Christ) by members of the Christian community and confirmed by their "Amen," implying assent (cf. Seifrid 64). A similar form is found in many of the ascriptions of praise elsewhere in the New Testament (e.g., Rom 1:25; 9:5; 11:36; 15:33; 16:27; Gal 1:5; Eph 3:21; Phil 4:20; 1 Tim 1:17; 6:16; 2 Tim 4:18; Heb 13:21; 1 Pet 4:11; 5:11; 2 Pet 3:18 [NIV]; Jude 25; Rev 1:6; 7:12), a fact that confirms the use of "Amen" in this way in the early church. However, the immediate context (especially v. 19) suggests that the "we" by whom the "Amen" is spoken here refers to Paul and his missionary colleagues. Cf. CSB: "Therefore, through him we also say 'Amen' to the glory of God;" NIV: "And so through him the 'Amen' is spoken by us to the glory of God;" NRSV: "For this reason it is through him that we say the 'Amen,' to the glory of God." ZG 536: "Therefore through him also the Amen from us to God for his glory." Harris 202–3: "For this reason it is through Christ also that our 'Amen' ascends to God for his glory through us." Διό, conj. "therefore." Δι' αὐτοῦ and δι' ἡμῶν are instances of the use of the prep. διά, with the gen. indicating in the first case the means ("through him") and in the second the agency ("by us," NIV) by which the "Amen" is uttered to the glory of God. Ἀμήν, emphatic particle, "Amen." Δόξαν, acc. sg. fem. δόξα, -ης, ἡ, "glory."

VERSE 21

ὁ δὲ βεβαιῶν ἡμᾶς σὺν ὑμῖν εἰς Χριστὸν καὶ χρίσας ἡμᾶς θεός,
Now it is God who strengthens us together with you in Christ, and who has anointed us.

Lit. "Now he who strengthens us with you in Christ and anointed us [is] God." Ὁ δὲ βεβαιῶν ἡμᾶς . . . καὶ χρίσας ἡμᾶς is a ptc. clause describing God as the one who strengthens and anoints us. Βεβαιῶν, nom. sg. masc. of pres. act. ptc. of βεβαιόω, "strengthen, establish." βεβαιόω is used in a legal sense in the papyri of a guarantee given that certain commitments will be carried out. In the NT it is used in connection with the proclamation of the gospel, which is "confirmed" by miraculous signs or the bestowal of spiritual gifts (Mark 16:20; 1 Cor 1:6). When used of human beings it indicates their strengthening or establishing so that they exhibit certain characteristics. For example, in 1 Cor 1:8 Paul writes of believers being kept firm so as to be blameless in the day of the Lord. Here he argues that God has made him stand firm to be trust-worthy. Εἰς Χριστόν. Harris 205: "On linguistic grounds it is preferable to classify εἰς as referential ('with respect/reference to'), rather than taking εἰς Χριστὸν as equivalent to ἐν Χριστῷ, since, although εἰς and ἐν share some common territory in Hellenistic Greek, Paul is not prone to confuse them. But either way, the resulting sense of εἰς Χριστὸν is 'in our union with Christ.'"

Χρίσας, nom. sg. masc. of aor. act. ptc. of χρίω, "anoint." Anointing was used in com-missioning rites in the OT (cf. Exod 28:41; 1 Sam 15:1; 1 Kings 19:16). References to anointing in the NT are found in Luke 4:18; Acts 4:27; 10:38; Heb 1:9 (using the verb χρίω); and in 1 John 2:20, 27 (twice) (using the noun χρῖσμα). In the Lucan texts it twice refers explicitly to anointing with the Spirit, and arguably it is implied in the third, and it refers to the anointing of the Spirit in 1 John as well. Given the empha-sis on the Spirit in the present context, it is best to see here also a reference to being anointed with the Spirit.

VERSE 22

ὁ καὶ σφραγισάμενος ἡμᾶς καὶ δοὺς τὸν ἀρραβῶνα τοῦ πνεύματος ἐν ταῖς καρδίαις ἡμῶν. He has also put his seal on us and given us the Spirit in our hearts as a down payment.

Ὁ καὶ σφραγισάμενος ἡμᾶς, "who also sealed us," refers to God's activity (cf. v. 21). Σφραγισάμενος, nom. sg. masc. of aor. mid. ptc. of σφραγίζω, "seal," a word used in commercial documents found among the papyri of the sealing of letters and sacks so that nobody can tamper with the contents. Used figuratively in the NT, it means to keep secret or stamp with a mark of identification or ownership (cf. Rev 7:3–8). In Ephesians Paul speaks of Christians being "sealed with the promised Holy Spirit" (1:13, cf. 4:30), something that occurs at conversion as people are baptized (cf. Acts 2:38), and this is its mng. here also.

Καὶ δοὺς τὸν ἀρραβῶνα τοῦ πνεύματος, "and has given us the down payment of the Spirit," again referring to God's activity (cf. v. 21). Δούς, nom. sg. masc. of aor. act. ptc. of δίδωμι, "give." Ἀρραβῶνα, acc. sg. masc. ἀρραβών, -ῶνος, ὁ: a commercial term Paul applied figuratively to the Spirit, whom God has given him and to whose presence he appeals as a guarantee of his apostolic integrity. It is generally regarded as a "down payment" made by a purchaser to a seller as a guarantee that the full purchase price will be paid at the proper time. So, e.g., BDAG 134c: "payment of part of a purchase price in advance, first installment, deposit, down payment, pledge." But cf. Yon-Gyong Kwon, "*Arrabōn* as Pledge in Second Corinthians," *NTS* 54 (2008) 525–41, who rejects the idea that ἀρραβών means "deposit" in the sense of a partial payment now, the balance of which will be paid later. He argues that here Paul appeals to the Spirit simply as God's pledge of his apostolicity. Τοῦ πνεύματος, gen. of appos., "a down payment which is the Spirit." Cf. Wallace 98, Z §45. Ἐν ταῖς καρδίαις ἡμῶν, a prep. adv. phrase indicating the place in which the Spirit was given, "in our hearts." Ἐν, a prep. with dat. ταῖς καρδίαις, indicates location. Harris, *Prepositions*, 121: "Where ἐν follows δίδωμι . . . ἐν is pregnant . . . presupposing εἰς, with the emphasis not on the direction of the giving but on the final location of the gift."

In relation to the tenses of the four participles in vv. 21–22, the first (βεβαιῶν) is pres., the second, third, and fourth (χρίσας, σφραγισάμενος, δούς) are all aor., suggesting that the first relates to the ongoing experience of the believers, and the others to their initial conversion-initiation experience.

c. Paul Calls upon God as His Witness (1:23–24)

Beginning with an oath, "I call on God as a witness, on my life," Paul asserts the purity of his motives and insists that changes to his travel plans were made bearing in mind the feelings of the Corinthians, something he needed to emphasize because his motives had been called into question.

STRUCTURE

23 Ἐγὼ δὲ μάρτυρα τὸν θεὸν ἐπικαλοῦμαι
              ἐπὶ τὴν ἐμὴν ψυχήν,
     ὅτι   φειδόμενος ὑμῶν
          οὐκέτι ἦλθον εἰς Κόρινθον.
24 οὐχ ὅτι κυριεύομεν ὑμῶν τῆς πίστεως
     ἀλλὰ συνεργοί ἐσμεν τῆς χαρᾶς ὑμῶν·
τῇ γὰρ πίστει ἑστήκατε.

VERSE 23

Ἐγὼ δὲ μάρτυρα τὸν θεὸν ἐπικαλοῦμαι ἐπὶ τὴν ἐμὴν ψυχήν,
I call on God as a witness, on my life,

Μάρτυρα, acc. sg. masc. μάρτυς, μάρτυρος, ὁ, "witness." Ἐπικαλοῦμαι, 1st sg. pres. mid. indic. of ἐπικαλέω, "call on." Harris 212: "In the middle voice ἐπικαλέομαι τινα means 'I appeal to someone in my favor.'" Ἐπί, a prep. with acc. τὴν ἐμὴν ψυχήν, is used to indicate that for which Paul calls on God's testimony (R 601–2). The expression ἐπὶ τὴν ἐμὴν ψυχήν may be taken as part of an imprecatory oath whereby Paul calls upon God as witness against him if he is not speaking the truth, and as it were, stakes his life on it. This is the way Paul calls upon God as his witness in the four other places in his letters that he does so (cf. Rom 1:9; Phil 1:8; 1 Thess 2:5, 10), and the way it was used in Greco-Roman tradition and in the literature of the Hellenistic and Roman period (cf. Novenson, "God Is Witness," 355–75). ZG 536: "over my life, i.e. I stake my life on it." BDAG 1099c: "Paul calls God as a witness against his soul; if he is lying, he will forfeit his salvation." Moule 185: "It is clear that soul would be a far too theological rendering. In II Cor.1.23 . . . ψυχήν looks like . . . on my life."

ὅτι φειδόμενος ὑμῶν οὐκέτι ἦλθον εἰς Κόρινθον.
that it was to spare you that I did not come to Corinth.

This ὅτι clause provides the assertion for which Paul calls upon God as witness, i.e., "that it was to spare you that I did not come to Corinth." Φειδόμενος, nom. sg. masc. of pres. mid. ptc. of φείδομαι, "spare," with the gen. of those spared (ὑμῶν). Οὐκέτι, adv. "no more." BDAG 736a: "up to a point." Ἦλθον, 1st sg. aor. act. indic. of ἔρχομαι, "come."

VERSE 24

οὐχ ὅτι κυριεύομεν ὑμῶν τῆς πίστεως
I do not mean that we lord it over your faith,

Οὐχ ὅτι . . . ἀλλ᾽ expresses "sharp antithesis" (R 1166). Lest the Corinthians conclude from Paul's reference to sparing them (v. 23) that he exercised some form of spiritual tyranny over them, he adds, "I do not mean that we lord it over your faith." Κυριεύομεν, 1st pl. pres. act. indic. of κυριεύω, "rule over, lord over," with gen. of those ruled over (ὑμῶν). Verbs of ruling take the gen. (cf. R 510). Τῆς πίστεως, gen. of reference: "we do not exercise lordship over you in the matter of your faith."

ἀλλὰ συνεργοί ἐσμεν τῆς χαρᾶς ὑμῶν·
but we are workers with you for your joy,

Paul insists that his role is not to lord it over people but to work for their joy. Ἀλλά, coord. advers. conj. "but, on the contrary." Συνεργοί, nom. pl. masc. adj. συνεργός, -όν, "helping," as subst. "helper, fellow-worker." Χαρᾶς, obj. gen. sg. fem. χαρά, -ᾶς, ἡ, "joy." Ὑμῶν, poss. gen. "your [joy]." The CSB translation (like many other English translations) implies that Paul works with the Corinthians for their joy, but this is unlikely, as nowhere else does he speak of his converts as his fellow-workers. Another possibility is that he speaks of being a fellow-worker with God (so, e.g., Seifrid 71), but there is little in the immediate context to support that. It is prob. best to see here a reference to Paul's missionary colleagues, Silas and Timothy, to whom he refers in v. 19.

τῇ γὰρ πίστει ἐστήκατε.
because you stand firm in your faith.

Γάρ, "because," introduces a clause explaining the reason Paul does not "lord it over" his converts' faith: τῇ . . . πίστει ἐστήκατε, "by faith you stand" (CSB: "you stand firm in your faith"). Τῇ . . . πίστει, dat. of means. Ἐστήκατε, 2nd pl. perf. act. indic. of ἵστημι, "stand, stand firm." The traditional understanding of the perf. depicting a past event with ongoing consequences does not suit here. It is better to adopt the verbal aspect defn. of the perf. depicting a present state of affairs (cf. Porter, *Idioms* 40; Wallace 574–76).

FOR FURTHER STUDY

15. Conscience (συνείδησις) (1:12)

Eckstein, H. J. *Der Begriff Syneidesis bei Paulus*. WUNT 2/10. Tübingen: Mohr Siebeck, 1983.
Gundry-Volf, J. M. *DPL* 153–56.
Marietta, D. E. "Conscience in Greek Stoicism." *Numen* 17 (1970): 176–87.
Maurer, C. *TDNT* 6.898–919.
Sevenster, J. N. *Paul and Seneca*. NovTSup 4. Leiden: Brill, 1961. See pp. 84–102.
Thrall, M. E. "The Pauline Use of SYNEIDHSIS." *NTS* 14 (1967–68): 118–25.

16. The Day of the Lord (1:14)

Kreitzer, L. J. *DPL* 253–69. See pp. 259–62.

17. Paul's Travels (1:15–16)

Alexander, L. C. A. *DPL* 115–23. See pp. 116–19.
Fee, G. D. "CHARIS in 2 Corinthians 1:15: Apostolic Parousia and Paul-Corinth Chronology." *NTS* 24 (1977–78): 533–38.
Jewett, R. *A Chronology of Paul's Life*. Philadelphia: Fortress, 1979.

18. Down Payment of the Spirit (ἀρραβών) (1:21–22)

Kwon, Yon-Gyong. "*Arrabōn* as Pledge in Second Corinthians." *NTS* 54 (2008): 525–41.
Paige, T. *DPL* 404–13. See p. 411.

19. God as Witness (μάρτυς) (1:23)

Novenson, M. V. "'God Is Witness': A Classical Rhetorical Idiom in Its Pauline Usage." *NovT* 52 (2012): 355–75.
Trites, A. A. *DPL* 973–75.

HOMILETICAL SUGGESTIONS

Paul Asks for Understanding (1:12–14)

1. The need for a clear conscience (v. 12a)
2. Crucial importance of godly conduct (v. 12b)
3. Transparency in communication (v. 13)
4. An eye to approval in the day of the Lord (v. 14)

Paul Explains His Actions and Why He Can Be Trusted (1:15–22)

1. The importance of "setting the record straight" (vv. 15–17)
2. Ministering in a way that is consistent with the message proclaimed (vv. 18–20)
3. It is God who enables authentic ministry (vv. 21–22)

Real Concern for Those to Whom We Minister (1:23–24)

1. Concern for those we serve (v. 23)
2. The aim of ministry: to work with people for their joy (v. 24)

2. The "Severe Letter": Its Purpose and Aftermath (2:1–13)

Paul explains how troubled in mind he was when writing the "severe letter" urging the Corinthians to take disciplinary action against the offender (vv.1–4). He describes how news of their positive actions triggered relief but also concern that Satan might gain the advantage if the offender were to be overwhelmed by excessive sorrow. So he urges the Corinthians to reaffirm their love to the now presumably repentant offender (vv. 5–8). He minimizes for their sakes the wrong he personally had suffered at the hands of the offender so that they will know they have his full support in reinstating the one who had hurt him (v. 10), and by so doing deny Satan an opportunity to take advantage of them (v. 11). In vv. 12–13 Paul describes the unsettled state of mind he experienced when he did not find Titus in Troas as planned, and therefore left behind great opportunities for preaching the gospel and departed for Macedonia, hoping to meet Titus there (vv. 12–13).

a. The Purpose of the "Severe Letter" (2:1–4)

STRUCTURE

1 ἔκρινα γὰρ ἐμαυτῷ τοῦτο
    τὸ μὴ πάλιν ἐν <u>λύπῃ</u> πρὸς ὑμᾶς ἐλθεῖν.
2   εἰ γὰρ ἐγὼ <u>λυπῶ</u> ὑμᾶς,
καὶ τίς ὁ εὐφραίνων με
  εἰ μὴ ὁ <u>λυπούμενος</u> ἐξ ἐμοῦ;
3 καὶ <u>ἔγραψα</u> τοῦτο αὐτό,
    ἵνα μὴ   ἐλθὼν
    <u>λύπην</u> σχῶ ἀφ' ὧν ἔδει με χαίρειν,
    πεποιθὼς ἐπὶ πάντας ὑμᾶς
    ὅτι ἡ ἐμὴ χαρὰ πάντων ὑμῶν ἐστιν.
4   ἐκ γὰρ πολλῆς θλίψεως καὶ συνοχῆς καρδίας
<u>ἔγραψα</u> ὑμῖν
  διὰ πολλῶν δακρύων,
  οὐχ ἵνα <u>λυπηθῆτε</u>
  ἀλλὰ τὴν ἀγάπην ἵνα γνῶτε
    ἣν ἔχω περισσοτέρως εἰς ὑμᾶς.

VERSE 1

ἔκρινα γὰρ ἐμαυτῷ τοῦτο
In fact, I made up my mind about this:

Lit. "I decided this with myself." Ἔκρινα, 1st sg. aor. act. indic. of κρίνω, "judge." BDAG 568a–b: "come to a conclusion after a cognitive process, reach a decision." Ἐμαυτῷ, dat. 1st sg. masc. refl. pron. ἐμαυτοῦ, -ῆς, "myself." CSB: with ἔκρινα: "I made up my mind." Cf. R 538–39 regarding the personal aspect of the dative case here.

τὸ μὴ πάλιν ἐν λύπῃ πρὸς ὑμᾶς ἐλθεῖν.
I would not come to you on another painful visit.

This explains what Paul made up his mind not to do: "come to you on another pain-ful visit." The art. inf. τὸ . . . ἐλθεῖν, stands in apposition to τοῦτο. Cf. R 700. Ἐλθεῖν, aor. act. inf. of ἔρχομαι, "come." Πάλιν, adv. "again." Ἐν is a prep. with dat. λύπῃ, lit. "with pain," i.e., to make another painful visit. Λύπῃ, dat. sg. fem. λύπη, -ης, ἡ, "pain." Πρός is a prep. with acc. ὑμᾶς, lit. "to you."

VERSE 2

εἰ γὰρ ἐγὼ λυπῶ ὑμᾶς,
For if I cause you pain,

Prot. of first-class cond. sentence formed by εἰ with indic., assuming a situation for the sake of argument. Ἐγώ, nom. 1st sg. pron. used emphatically. Λυπῶ, 1st sg. pres. act. indic. of λυπέω, "cause pain, grieve." Ὑμᾶς, acc. 2nd pl. σύ, "you," direct obj. of λυπῶ.

καὶ τίς ὁ εὐφραίνων με
then who will cheer me

Apod. of first-class cond. sentence stating the consequence of the assumed situa-tion, in this case in the form of a question, lit. "and who is the one who cheers me?" (BDF §442[8]): "καί is to be understood differently when the apod. is a question . . . 'who then' (under the circumstances set forth in the apododis)." R 1182: "Sometimes καί begins a sentence when the connection is with an unexpressed idea." Τίς, nom. sg. masc. interog. pron. τίς, τί, "who." Ὁ εὐφραίνων, "the one who makes glad." Εὐφραίνων, nom. sg. masc. of pres. act. ptc. of εὐφραίνω, "make glad." Με, acc. 1st sg. pron. ἐγώ, "me," direct obj. of ὁ εὐφραίνων.

εἰ μὴ ὁ λυπούμενος ἐξ ἐμοῦ;
other than the one being hurt by me?

Answers question, "who is there to make me glad?": only "the one being hurt by me." Cf. Harris 217: "the successive singulars τίς, ὁ εὐφραίνων and ὁ λυπούμενος indicate that the Corinthians as a community are in view in the apod., so that εἰ μὴ ὁ λυπούμενος has the sense 'except (you,) the people who are pained.'" So, too, Barnett 117. Εἰ, subord. conj. "if" with neg. particle μή: "except," cf. BDAG 278d. Ὁ λυπούμενος, adj. ptc. phrase, lit. "the one being hurt." Λυπούμενος, nom. sg. masc. of pres. pass. ptc. of λυπέω, "cause pain, grieve." Ἐξ is a prep. with gen. ἐμοῦ, lit. "from me." Ἐμοῦ, gen. 1st sg. pron. ἐγώ.

VERSE 3

καὶ ἔγραψα τοῦτο αὐτό,
I wrote this very thing

Refers to the "severe letter." Harris 218: "Paul here states an additional (καί) purpose in writing the 'severe letter': he wished to shield not only the Corinthians (1:23; 2:1–2) but also himself from further pain." Ἔγραψα, 1st sg. aor. act. indic. γράφω, "write." Τοῦτο, acc. sg. neut. pron. οὗτος, αὕτη, τοῦτο, "this." Αὐτό, acc. sg. neut. emphatic pers. pron. αὐτός, -ή, -ό in pred. position: "this *very* thing." Cf. BDAG 153a; BDF (§290[4]): "Paul frequently has αὐτὸ τοῦτο 'just this (and nothing else)'; he also uses it adverbially (§160)='for this very reason' (2 C 2:3)." R 686: "In Ac. 24:15, the classical idiom αὐτοὶ οὗτοι occurs . . . The other order is found in ἔγραψα τοῦτο αὐτό (2 Cor. 2:3)." R 699, 705: "In 2 Cor 2:3, ἔγραψα τοῦτο αὐτό, ἵνα, we probably have the direct accusative, though τοῦτο αὐτό could be adverbial accusative, 'for this very reason.'"

ἵνα μὴ ἐλθὼν λύπην σχῶ ἀφ᾽ ὧν ἔδει με χαίρειν,
so that when I came I wouldn't have pain from those who ought to give me joy,

Lit. "in order that I might not have pain from those who should make me rejoice." Ἵνα, conj. with σχῶ (1st sg. aor. act. subjunc. of ἔχω, "have"), expresses purpose. Ἐλθών, nom. sg. masc. of aor. act. ptc. of ἔρχομαι, "come": "when I came." Ἀφ᾽ (contraction of ἀπό), prep. with gen. ὧν, "from whom." R 706: "suppressed antecedent." Harris 219: "ἀφ᾽ ὧν is elliptical, standing for ἀπό ἐκείνων ἀφ᾽ ὧν ('by those by whom')." CSB: "from those who." Ὧν, gen. pl. masc. ὅς, ἥ, ὅ, "who." R 706: "suppressed antecedent." Harris 219: "ἀφ᾽ ὧν is elliptical, standing for ἀπό ἐκείνων ἀφ᾽ ὧν ('by those by whom')." CSB: "from those who." Ἔδει, 3rd sg. impf. act. indic. of δεῖ, "it is necessary." R 886: "Verbs of propriety, possibility, obligation or necessity are also used in the imperfect when the obligation, etc., is not lived up to, had not been met." Χαίρειν, pres. act. inf. of χαίρω, "rejoice," stands in complementary relationship with ἔδει, i.e., expressing what Paul thought the Corinthians ought to have done: "made me rejoice." Barnett 118: "in these verses Paul gives his *purpose* in (v. 3) and *reason* (v. 4) for writing."

πεποιθὼς ἐπὶ πάντας ὑμᾶς ὅτι ἡ ἐμὴ χαρὰ πάντων ὑμῶν ἐστιν.
because I am confident about all of you that my joy will also be yours.

Πεποιθώς, nom. sg. masc. of pf. act. ptc. of πείθω, "be confident." Wallace 631: an adv. pf. ptc. The pf. depicts Paul's state of mind and relates to the main verb ἔγραψα, "and I wrote this very thing . . . being confident. . . ." Cf. ZG 537: "pf. (w. pres. mng.) . . . *relying on, trusting in you all that my joy is (that) of all of you.*" CSB: "because I am confident." Harris 220: "Although πεποιθώς is a perfect with a present mng., this participle here relates to past time (ἔγραψα) 'I felt sure of all of you.'" Ἐπί is a prep. with acc. πάντας ὑμᾶς, "about all of you."

Ὅτι, conj. "that," introduces the content of Paul's confidence about the Corinthians: ἡ ἐμὴ χαρὰ πάντων ὑμῶν ἐστιν. CSB: "my joy will be yours also"; NIV: "you would all share my joy"; NRSV: "my joy would be the joy of all of you." Ἐμή, nom. sg. fem. poss. pron. ἐμός, -ή, -όν, "my." Χαρά, nom. sg. fem. χαρά, -ᾶς, ἡ, "joy."

VERSE 4

ἐκ γὰρ πολλῆς θλίψεως καὶ συνοχῆς καρδίας ἔγραψα ὑμῖν διὰ πολλῶν δακρύων,
For I wrote to you with many tears out of an extremely troubled and anguished heart—

Harris 220–21: "γάρ is not strongly causal here; it simply introduces a restatement of the fact that Paul avoided a painful visit by writing a letter (2:32)." Barnett 118 says here Paul gives his reason for writing, having stated his purpose for doing so in v. 3. Ἐκ, prep. with gen. πολλῆς θλίψεως καὶ συνοχῆς καρδίας. Paul depicts his frame of mind (when he wrote). NIV: "out of great distress and anguish of heart." R 598 describes the use of ἐκ here as denoting "the idea of origin or source." Harris 221: "ἐκ describes the origin and διά the circumstances of the painful letter." Θλίψεως, gen. sg. fem. θλῖψις, -εως, ἡ, "affliction." BDAG 457d: "trouble and anguish of heart." Συνοχῆς, gen. sg. fem. συνοχή, -ῆς, ἡ, "distress." BDAG 974b: "a state of distress that involves a high degree of anxiety, distress, dismay, anguish." Ἔγραψα, 1st sg. aor. act. indic. of γράφω, "write." Refers to the writing of the "severe letter." Διά, prep. with gen. πολλῶν δακρύων, depicting attendant circumstances: "*with many tears*" (BDAG 224d). Cf. ZG 537; Moule 57; Z §114. Δακρύων, gen. pl. neut. δάκρυον, -ου, τό "teardrop."

οὐχ ἵνα λυπηθῆτε ἀλλὰ τὴν ἀγάπην ἵνα γνῶτε ἣν ἔχω περισσοτέρως εἰς ὑμᾶς.
not to cause you pain, but that you should know the abundant love I have for you.

In v. 3, employing a ἵνα with subjunc. cstr., Paul stated positively his reason for writing: "so that when I came I wouldn't have pain from those who ought to give me joy." In v. 4 he employs two such cstrs., the first to insist that it was not his purpose in writing: "not to cause you pain," the second to affirm that his purpose was rather "that you should know the abundant love I have for you." Ἵνα with subjunc. λυπηθῆτε (2nd pl. aor. pass. subjunc. of λυπέω, "grieve") expresses purpose: lit. "in order that you might not be caused pain."

Ἀλλά, conj. BDAG 44c–d: "after a negative . . . on the contrary, but, yet, rather." Ἀγάπην acc. sg. fem. ἀγάπη, -ης, ἡ, "love," dir. obj. of γνῶτε. Ἵνα with subjunc. γνῶτε (2nd pl. aor. act. subj. of γινώσκω, "know") expresses purpose: lit. "so that you should know." Placing τὴν ἀγάπην before ἵνα γνῶτε is an example of prolepsis. R 423: "Prolepsis is not uncommon where either the substantive is placed out of its right place before the conjunction in a subordinate clause like τὴν ἀγάπην ἵνα γνῶτε." Harris 221: "Not only the absolute οὐχ . . . ἀλλά but also the irregular and therefore emphatic position of τὴν ἀγάπην before ἵνα draw attention to the fact of Paul's love, just as the adverb περισσοτέρως highlights the quality of that love." Ἥν ἔχω περισσοτέρως εἰς ὑμᾶς, a relative clause explaining the love the apostle wants the

Corinthians to know about. Ἥν, acc. sg. fem. rel. pron. (ὅς, ἥ, ὅ, "which"), agrees with its antecedent, ἀγάπην. Ἔχω, 1st sg. pres. act. indic., "have." Περισσοτέρως, comp. adv. "even more so." CSB: "abundant." BDAG 806b: "especially, elative." Εἰς, prep. with acc. ὑμᾶς, "for you."

b. Forgiveness for the Offender (2:5–11)

STRUCTURE

5   Εἰ δέ τις λελύπηκεν,
οὐκ ἐμὲ λελύπηκεν,
ἀλλ' ἀπὸ μέρους,
    ἵνα μὴ ἐπιβαρῶ,
        πάντας ὑμᾶς.
6   ἱκανὸν τῷ τοιούτῳ
ἡ ἐπιτιμία αὕτη
ἡ ὑπὸ τῶν πλειόνων,
7   ὥστε τοὐναντίον μᾶλλον ὑμᾶς χαρίσασθαι καὶ παρακαλέσαι,
        μή πως τῇ περισσοτέρᾳ λύπῃ καταποθῇ ὁ τοιοῦτος.
8   διὸ παρακαλῶ ὑμᾶς κυρῶσαι εἰς αὐτὸν ἀγάπην·
9   εἰς τοῦτο
γὰρ καὶ ἔγραψα,
        ἵνα γνῶ τὴν δοκιμὴν ὑμῶν,
        εἰ εἰς πάντα ὑπήκοοί ἐστε.
10   ᾧ δέ τι χαρίζεσθε, κἀγώ·
κἀὶ γὰρ ἐγὼ   ὃ κεχάρισμαι,
        εἴ τι κεχάρισμαι,
            δι' ὑμᾶς
        ἐν προσώπῳ Χριστοῦ,
11   ἵνα μὴ πλεονεκτηθῶμεν ὑπὸ τοῦ Σατανᾶ·
        οὐ γὰρ αὐτοῦ τὰ νοήματα ἀγνοοῦμεν.

VERSE 5

Εἰ δέ τις λελύπηκεν,
If anyone has caused pain,

The prot. of a first-class cond. sentence, εἰ + indic. stating a true hypothesis: "If anyone has caused harm." Cf. R 1007–08. Εἰ, conj. "if," BDAG 277b: "marker of a condition, existing in fact or hypothetical." Λελύπηκεν, 3rd sg. pf. act. indic. of λυπέω, "cause pain."

οὐκ ἐμὲ λελύπηκεν,
he has caused pain not so much to me

The apod. of the first-class cond. sentence: "he has not caused pain to me . . ." Ἐμέ, acc. 1st sg. pron. ἐγώ, "I, me." Λελύπηκεν, see above.

ἀλλ᾽ ἀπὸ μέρους, ἵνα μὴ ἐπιβαρῶ, πάντας ὑμᾶς.
but to some degree—not to exaggerate—to all of you.

Ἀλλ᾽ (contraction of ἀλλά), advers. particle "but." Ἀπό, prep. with gen. μέρους, "in part." BDAG 633d: "in some degree." Μέρους, gen. sg. neut. μέρος, -ους, τό, "part." Ἵνα μὴ ἐπιβαρῶ. Ἵνα with subjunc. expresses purpose (neg. with μή). BDAG 368b: "'in order not to heap up too great a burden of words' = in order not to say too much." CSB: "not to exaggerate." Ἐπιβαρῶ, 1st sg. pres. act. subjunc. of ἐπιβαρέω, "be a burden." Πάντας ὑμᾶς, acc. direct obj. of λελύπηκεν. Πάντας, acc. pl. masc. adj. πᾶς, πᾶσα, πᾶν, "all." Ὑμᾶς, acc. 2nd pl. pron. σύ, "you."

VERSE 6

ἱκανὸν τῷ τοιούτῳ ἡ ἐπιτιμία αὕτη ἡ ὑπὸ τῶν πλειόνων,
This punishment by the majority is sufficient for that person.

Ἱκανὸν, nom. sg. neut. adj. ἱκανός, -ή, -όν, "sufficient." Harris 228: "The neuter ἱκανόν is not a case of incongruence in gender, grammatical discord between subject (ἡ ἐπιτιμία) and predicate, as Turner (311) alleges. Rather, ἱκανόν is a substantival use of the neuter adjective." Τοιούτῳ, dat. sg. masc. pron. τοιοῦτος, -αύτη, -οῦτον, "such, such a one." Τῷ τοιούτῳ, dat. phrase, lit. "for such a one." CSB: "for that person." Ἐπιτιμία, nom. sg. fem. ἐπιτιμία, -ας, ἡ "punishment," a word used only here in the NT, but in extrabiblical writings it is used of the imposition of either legal penalties or commercial sanctions. Its use here approximates to the former sense and suggests that the congregation had acted formally and judicially against the offender, possibly by excluding him from their gatherings. Αὕτη, nom. sg. fem. pron. οὗτος, αὕτη, τοῦτο, "this." Ὑπό, prep. with gen. τῶν πλειόνων, "by the majority." Πλειόνων, gen. pl. masc. comp. adj. πολύς, πολλή, πολύ, with art. τῶν, subst. "the majority." Its use here might imply there was a minority who did not approve of the punishment to be meted out, or alternatively it may refer more generally to the whole congregation (minus the offender), in which case the punishment of the offending member would have been determined by a unanimous decision of the whole congregation, not simply by the majority of them. In whatever way the punishment was decided and carried out, Paul was now convinced that it was enough.

VERSE 7

ὥστε τοὐναντίον μᾶλλον ὑμᾶς χαρίσασθαι καὶ παρακαλέσαι,
As a result, you should instead forgive and comfort him.

Τοὐναντίον (= τὸ ἐναντίον), adv. "instead." BDAG 330d: "on the other hand." Ὥστε with inf. χαρίσασθαι καὶ παρακαλέσαι expresses result. Cf. R 1090. Μᾶλλον, adv. "rather." Ὑμᾶς, 2nd pl. acc. σύ, subject of the inf. χαρίσασθαι καὶ παρακαλέσαι. Χαρίσασθαι, aor. mid. inf. of χαρίζομαι, "forgive." Παρακαλέσαι, aor. act. inf. of παρακαλέω, "comfort." Moule 144: "There seems to be a tendency, sometimes, to ellipsis in the use of ὥστε . . . II Cor. ii. 6, 7 ἱκανὸν τῷ τοιούτῳ ἡ ἐπιτιμία αὕτη . . . ὥστε τοὐναντίον μᾶλλον ὑμᾶς [δεῖν] χαρίσασθαι. . . ."

μή πως τῇ περισσοτέρᾳ λύπῃ καταποθῇ ὁ τοιοῦτος.
Otherwise, he may be overwhelmed by excessive grief.

Μή πως with subjunc., "lest." ZG 537: "so that . . . not"; BDAG 901d: "marker of a negative perspective expressing misgiving, frequently rendered lest"; Harris 229: "lest perhaps." Τῇ περισσοτέρᾳ λύπῃ, dat. adv. phrase "by excessive grief," expresses agency. Περισσοτέρᾳ, dat. sg. comp. adj. περισσός, -ή, -όν, "excessive," qualifying λύπη. Λύπῃ, dat. sg. fem. λύπη, -ης, ἡ, "grief, sorrow." Καταποθῇ, 3rd sg. aor. pass. subjunc. of καταπίνω, "swallow, overwhelm," following μή πως: "otherwise, he may be overwhelmed. . . ." Τοιοῦτος, nom. sg. masc. adj. τοιοῦτος, -αύτη, -οῦτον, "of such a kind." BDAG 1009c–d: "being like some prs." With masc. art. ὁ "such a man." Translated as "he" by CSB, NIV, NRSV.

VERSE 8

διὸ παρακαλῶ ὑμᾶς κυρῶσαι εἰς αὐτὸν ἀγάπην·
Therefore I urge you to reaffirm your love to him.

In light of the danger that the offender, once disciplined and presumably now repentant, could be overwhelmed with excessive sorrow, Paul calls upon the Corinthians to reaffirm their love for him. Διό, conj. (infer.) "so, therefore." Παρακαλῶ, 1st sg. pres. act. indic. of παρακαλέω, "urge, exhort." Ὑμᾶς, acc. 2nd pl. pron. σύ, "you," direct obj. of παρακαλῶ. Κυρῶσαι, aor. act. inf. of κυρόω, "reaffirm." BDAG 579c: "decide in favor of." Κυρόω was used in the papyri to denote confirmation of a sale or ratification of an appointment. It is used in Gal 3:15 of the ratification of a covenant. The reaffirmation of love for which Paul calls, then, appears to be a formal act by the congregation, in the same way that the imposition of punishment in the first place appears to have been formal and judicial. Paul's desire to see the repentant offender reinstated is a reminder that church discipline is intended not only as a punishment but also to be remedial. Εἰς, prep. with acc. αὐτόν, "to him," indir. obj. of κυρῶσαι. Ἀγάπην, acc. sg. fem. ἀγάπη, -ης, ἡ, "love," dir. obj. of inf. κυρῶσαι.

VERSE 9

εἰς τοῦτο γὰρ καὶ ἔγραψα,
I wrote for this purpose:

Εἰς, prep. with acc. sg. neut. dem. pron. οὗτος, αὕτη, τοῦτο, "for this [reason]."
Harris 230–31: "anticipates the epexegetic ἵνα, 'for this (purpose, namely) that,' and
introduces the third purpose of the 'severe letter,' which was to test the Corinthians'
obedience." Ἔγραψα, 1st sg. aor. act. indic. of γράφω, "write."

ἵνα γνῶ τὴν δοκιμὴν ὑμῶν, εἰ εἰς πάντα ὑπήκοοί ἐστε.
to test your character to see if you are obedient in everything.

Ἵνα with subjunc. γνῶ (1st sg. aor. act. subjunc. of γινώσκω, "know") expresses purpose, lit. "that I might know." Δοκιμήν, acc. sg. fem. δοκιμή -ῆς, ἡ, "proof, character,"
with γινώσκω, "test character." Cf. NIV: "to see if you would stand the test."
Εἰ, conj. "if, whether." Εἰς, prep. with acc. πάντα, "in everything." Πάντα, acc. pl.
neut. πᾶς, πᾶσα, πᾶν, "all, everything." Ὑπήκοοι, nom. pl. masc. adj. ὑπήκοος, -ον,
"obedient." What Paul expected was not obedience to him pers., but obedience to him
as an apostle of Christ. This did not mean he wished to "lord it over" their faith, but as
he wrote earlier, he was working for their joy (1:24).

VERSE 10

ᾧ δέ τι χαρίζεσθε, κἀγώ·
Anyone you forgive, I do too.

Lit. "and to whom you forgive anything, I also [forgive]." Moule 130: "II Cor. ii. 10
ᾧ δέ τι χαρίζεσθε, κἀγώ (for ἐκείνου ᾧ χαρίζεσθε τι καὶ ἐγὼ χαρίζομαι αὐτό)." Ὧι, dat.
sg. masc. rel. pron. ὅς, ἥ, ὅ, "who." Τι, acc. sg. neut. indef. pron. τις, τι, "anything."
Χαρίζεσθε, 2nd pl. pres. mid. indic. of χαρίζομαι, "forgive, favor." Seifrid 78–79: "The
word that Paul uses here for 'forgiveness' (charizomai) is significant. In place of the
more frequent term aphiēmi, which communicates forgiveness through the metaphor
of release, charizomai normally signifies 'giving,' the free giving of gifts. Κἀγώ (contraction of καὶ ἐγώ), "and I."

καὶ γὰρ ἐγὼ ὃ κεχάρισμαι, εἴ τι κεχάρισμαι, δι' ὑμᾶς ἐν προσώπῳ Χριστοῦ,
For what I have forgiven—if I have forgiven anything—it is for your benefit in the
presence of Christ,

Κεχάρισμαι, 1st sg. pf. mid. indic. of χαρίζομαι, "forgive, favor." Εἴ τι, "if anything."
Δι', prep. with ὑμᾶς, "for your sake." CSB: "it is for your benefit." Ἐν, prep. with dat.
προσώπῳ, "in the presence (of Christ)." The expression ἐν προσώπῳ Χριστοῦ (lit. "in
[the] face of Christ") is difficult, and it could be construed in a number of ways. It

could be taken as an oath formula, in which case Paul would be saying, "As I stand in the sight of Christ, I have forgiven the offense." Alternatively, it could mean his forgiveness has the approval of Christ. In this case the translation would run, "What I have forgiven has been forgiven in the sight of Christ, who looks down with approval." Finally, the expression could reflect the fact that at the time of writing the apostle had not had opportunity to express his forgiveness face-to-face with the offender, but nevertheless he had already forgiven him "in the sight of Christ."

VERSE 11

ἵνα μὴ πλεονεκτηθῶμεν ὑπὸ τοῦ Σατανᾶ·
so that we may not be taken advantage of by Satan.

Ἵνα with subjunc. πλεονεκτηθῶμεν (neg. by μή) expresses purpose. Πλεονεκτηθῶμεν, 1st pl. aor. pass. subjunc. of πλεονεκτέω, "take advantage of, outwit." Πλεονεκτέω is found in four other places in the NT—all in Paul's letters (2 Cor 7:2; 12:17, 18; 1 Thess 4:6). The other uses in 2 Cor (and arguably so for that in 1 Thess) denote taking advantage of people in the sense of defrauding them of something that belongs to them. It seems likely, therefore, that what Paul has in mind in this verse is that Satan might take advantage of the situation and defraud the congregation of one of its members permanently. Ὑπό, prep. with gen. τοῦ Σατανᾶ, expresses agency "by Satan." Σατανᾶ, gen. sg. proper noun Σατανᾶς, -ᾶ, ὁ, "Satan (Heb. adversary)."

οὐ γὰρ αὐτοῦ τὰ νοήματα ἀγνοοῦμεν.
For we are not ignorant of his schemes.

Νοήματα, acc. pl. neut. νόημα, -ατος, τό, "designs, schemes." Ἀγνοοῦμεν, 1st pl. pres. act. indic. of ἀγνοέω, "be ignorant."

c. Waiting for Titus (2:12–13)

STRUCTURE

12   Ἐλθὼν δὲ εἰς τὴν Τρῳάδα
              εἰς τὸ εὐαγγέλιον τοῦ Χριστοῦ
              καὶ θύρας μοι ἀνεῳγμένης ἐν κυρίῳ,
13   οὐκ ἔσχηκα ἄνεσιν τῷ πνεύματί μου
              τῷ μὴ εὑρεῖν με Τίτον τὸν ἀδελφόν μου,
              ἀλλ’ ἀποταξάμενος αὐτοῖς
       ἐξῆλθον εἰς Μακεδονίαν.

VERSE 12

Ἐλθὼν δὲ εἰς τὴν Τρῳάδα εἰς τὸ εὐαγγέλιον τοῦ Χριστοῦ
When I came to Troas to preach the gospel of Christ,

Ἐλθών, nom. sg. masc. of aor. act. ptc. of ἔρχομαι, "come." Εἰς, prep. with acc. Τρῳάδα indicates motion toward Troas. Τρῳάδα, acc. sg. fem. Τρῳάς, -άδος, ἡ, "Troas." Εἰς, prep. with acc. τὸ εὐαγγέλιον, "to preach the gospel." R 595: εἰς "suggests the purpose of his coming." Εὐαγγέλιον, acc. sg. neut. εὐαγγέλιον, -ου, τό, "gospel." Τοῦ Χριστοῦ, descriptive gen., "(the gospel) about Christ."

καὶ θύρας μοι ἀνεῳγμένης ἐν κυρίῳ,
even though the Lord opened a door for me,

Θύρας . . . ἀνεῳγμένης, descriptive gen. depicting circumstances in force at the time of the main verb, ἔσχηκα (v. 13a): "When I came to Troas . . . and a door was opened . . . I had no rest . . ." Cf. R 513. Θύρας, gen. sg. fem. θύρα, -ας, ἡ, "door." Ἀνεῳγμένης, gen. sg. fem. of pf. pass. ptc. of ἀνοίγω, "open." Harris 237: "As a perfect participle, ἀνεῳγμένης probably means not 'was opened' (as if it were a narrative or aoristic perfect) but 'stood open.'" Ἐν, prep. with dat. κυρίῳ, "in the Lord." NRSV: "a door was opened for me in the Lord." Κυρίῳ, dat. sg. masc. κύριος, -ου, ὁ, "Lord."

VERSE 13

οὐκ ἔσχηκα ἄνεσιν τῷ πνεύματί μου
I had no rest in my spirit

Ἔσχηκα, 1st sg. pf. act. indic. of ἔχω, "have." The pf. is used to depict Paul's state of mind: "I had no rest in my spirit." Ἄνεσιν, acc. sg. fem. ἄνεσις, -εως, ἡ, "rest, relief." In this case relief from his anxiety arising from failure to meet Titus and receive news of the Corinthians' response to the "severe letter" is meant. Τῷ πνεύματί, dat. of respect, "no rest *in my spirit.*"

τῷ μὴ εὑρεῖν με Τίτον τὸν ἀδελφόν μου,
because I did not find my brother Titus.

Dat. art. inf. clause explaining the cause of Paul's unrest of spirit. Cf. Moule 44. R. 765, 966, 1061 depicts the dat. as instr. Harris 239: "This is the only NT instance of an articular infinitive in the dative case without a preposition." Εὑρεῖν, aor. act. inf. of εὑρίσκω, "find." Με, acc. 1st sg. pron. ἐγώ "I," acc, subj. of inf. εὑρεῖν. Τὸν ἀδελφόν μου stands in appos. to Τίτον.

ἀλλ᾽ ἀποταξάμενος αὐτοῖς ἐξῆλθον εἰς Μακεδονίαν.
Instead, I said good-bye to them and left for Macedonia.

Lit. "but saying good-bye to them, I left for Macedonia." Ἀποταξάμενος, nom. sg. masc. of aor. mid. ptc. of ἀποτάσσω, "leave, say good-bye, say farewell." Takes dat. of those bidden farewell. Αὐτοῖς, dat. 3rd pl. masc. αὐτός, -ή, -ό, "them." Ἐξῆλθον, 1st sg. aor. act. indic. of ἐξέρχομαι, "go, leave." Εἰς, prep. with acc. Μακεδονίαν, "to/for Macedonia." The narrative, broken off here, is continued in 7:5 ff.

FOR FURTHER STUDY

20. Paul's Painful Visit (2:1–2)

Batey, R. "Paul's Interaction with the Corinthians." *JBL* 84 (1966): 139–146.

21. The "Severe Letter" (2:3–4)

Kruse, C. G. 2 *Corinthians: An Introduction and Commentary*. TNTC 8. Nottingham/ Downers Grove: IVP, 2015. See pages 38–40.

Stegman, T. D. "Reading *Egrapsa* in 2 Corinthians 2:9 as an Epistolary Aorist." *NovT* 54 (2012): 50–67.

22. The Offender and His Offense (2:5)

Barrett, C. K. "Paul's Opponents in II Corinthians." *NTS* 17 (1971): 233–254.

Kruse, C. G. "The Offender and the Offence in 2 Corinthians 2:5 and 7:12." *EvQ* 60 (1988): 129–139.

———. "The Relationship between the Opposition to Paul Reflected in 2 Corinthians 1-7 and 10-13." *EvQ* 61 (1989): 195–202.

23. Punishment—Judicial as Well as Remedial (2:6–8)

Schmidt, T. E. *DPL* 214–218.

Stauffer, E. *TDNT* 2.623–627.

24. Satan's Schemes (2:11)

Reid, D. C. *DPL* 862–7.

Twelftree, G. H. *NDBT* 796–802.

25. Troas (2:12–13)

Burdick, D. W. "With Paul in the Troad." *NEASB* n.s. 12 (1978): 31–65.

Hemer, C. J. "Alexandria Troas." *TynB* 26 (1975): 79–112.

Perriman, A. C. "Between Troas and Macedonia: 2 Cor 2:13–14." *ExpTim* 101/2 (1989): 39–41.

26. Titus (2:13)

Barrett, C. K. "Titus." In *Neotestamentica et Semitica. Studies in Honour of Matthew Black*. Edited by E. E. Ellis and M. Wilcox. Edinburgh: T&T Clark, 1969. See pp. 1–14. Reprinted in his *Essays on Paul*. London: SPCK, 1982. See pp. 118–31.

Mitchell, M. M. "NT Envoys in the Context of Greco-Roman Diplomatic and Epistolary Conventions: The Example of Timothy and Titus." *JBL* 111 (1992): 641–62.

HOMILETICAL SUGGESTIONS

1. The purpose of the "severe letter" (2:1–4)
2. Forgiveness for the offender (2:5–11)
3. Waiting for Titus (2:12–13)

Paul Seeks to Avoid Pain and Causing Pain (2:1–4)

1. A practical decision made to avoid a painful situation (v. 1)
2. Acknowledgment of grief caused and experienced (v. 2)
3. Sometimes it's necessary to write a difficult letter (vv. 3–4)
4. In the midst of difficulties, it's good to express confidence in people (v. 3)

The Crucial Importance of Forgiveness (2:5–11)

1. Recognizing the reality of the hurt (v. 5)
2. Discipline is sometimes necessary (v. 6)
3. Discipline is remedial—restoration follows repentance (vv. 7–8)
4. The call for discipline—a test of obedience (v. 9)
5. The one hurt makes the first step in showing forgiveness (v. 10)
6. Refusing to forgive makes people vulnerable in the face of Satan's schemes (v. 11)

Open Doors but No Peace of Mind (2:12–13)

1. The Lord opens doors for preaching the gospel (v. 12)
2. Even Christian leaders can't take up some opportunities due to lack of peace of mind (v. 13)

3. Competency in Ministry (2:14–4:6)

Paul's description of events in the previous passage concluded with the information that he did not meet up with Titus in Troas as he expected. It breaks off at that point and is only resumed in 7:5ff. There intervenes a long digression to balance what could be taken as a rather depressing account of his ministry. He has spoken of affliction in Asia, criticisms of his integrity, the pain experienced in Corinth because of the offender, and his inability to settle to missionary work in Troas. As if to balance this somewhat depressing account, in 2:14–4:6 Paul strikes a positive note, describing how God always and in every place enables him to carry on an effective ministry despite many difficulties (2:14–17). He follows this up with an assertion that he does not need to bear letters of recommendation to Corinth because the very existence of the church there constitutes a "letter" from Christ validating his ministry (3:1–3). Then he acknowledges that his competency for ministry comes from God, who has made him an able minister of the new covenant (3:4–6). Next he compares the greater glory of apostolic ministry under the new covenant with the lesser glory of the ministry of Moses under the old covenant (3:7–18). The section concludes with a description of the way Paul conducted his ministry (4:1–6).

a. Led in Triumph (2:14–17)

In these verses Paul uses the imagery of a triumphal procession accorded a victorious Roman general to depict his apostolic ministry. The general led his army through the streets of Rome up to the Capitoline Hill, exhibiting the spoils and captives of war. During the procession incense was burned to the gods, and the aroma wafted over the spectators as well as those in the procession. For those celebrating the victory, the aroma had pleasant associations, but for the vanquished the associations were far from pleasant.

STRUCTURE

14   Τῷ δὲ θεῷ
     χάρις
       Τῷ πάντοτε θριαμβεύοντι ἡμᾶς
              ἐν τῷ Χριστῷ
         καὶ   τὴν ὀσμὴν τῆς γνώσεως αὐτοῦ
         φανεροῦντι
            δι' ἡμῶν
            ἐν παντὶ τόπῳ·
15   ὅτι Χριστοῦ εὐωδία ἐσμὲν τῷ θεῷ
          ἐν τοῖς σῳζομένοις
          καὶ ἐν τοῖς ἀπολλυμένοις,
16   οἷς μὲν ὀσμὴ ἐκ θανάτου εἰς θάνατον,
             οἷς δὲ ὀσμὴ ἐκ ζωῆς εἰς ζωήν.
     καὶ πρὸς ταῦτα τίς ἱκανός;
17   οὐ γάρ ἐσμεν

ὡς οἱ πολλοὶ
    καπηλεύοντες τὸν λόγον τοῦ θεοῦ,
ἀλλ᾽ ὡς   ἐξ εἰλικρινείας,
ἀλλ᾽ ὡς   ἐκ θεοῦ
    κατέναντι θεοῦ
    ἐν Χριστῷ
λαλοῦμεν.

VERSE 14

Τῷ δὲ θεῷ χάρις
But thanks be to God,

A thanksgiving period, "But thanks be to God." Δέ, conj. "but," adversative, introduces positive comments to balance the rather depressing accounts that precede. Τ ῷ
. . . θεῷ, dat. indir. obj. of implied verb "be." Χάρις, nom. sg. fem. χάρις, -ιτος, ἡ,
"thanks." BDAG 1080c: "response to generosity or beneficence, thanks, gratitude."

τῷ πάντοτε θριαμβεύοντι ἡμᾶς ἐν τῷ Χριστῷ
who always leads us in Christ's triumphal procession

Dat. rel clause qualifying θεῷ. Πάντοτε, adv. "always." Θριαμβεύοντι, dat. sg. masc.
of pres. act. ptc. of θριαμβεύω, a verb found only twice in the NT, here and in Col 2:15,
and not at all in the LXX. It is found a number of times in extrabiblical writings (see
LSJ 806, BDAG 459bc). Six major interpretations of θριαμβεύω followed by an accusative object (as here in 2:14) have been suggested: (a) To lead someone as a captive in
a triumphal procession. This has the best lexical support; is the rendering of the NIV,
NEB and GNB; and is adopted by a number of modern interpreters. (b) To lead victorious soldiers in a triumphal procession. This does not have lexical support in extrabiblical texts. It is the interpretation underlying the JB translation, and the choice of
Calvin, Allo, Héring, Barrett, and Bruce. (c) To cause someone to triumph. This is the
rendering of the KJV, but it has no lexical support and has been abandoned by modern
interpreters. (d) To triumph over someone. This is the mng. it has in Col 2:15, the only
other place it is found in the New Testament: "He disarmed the rulers and authorities
and disgraced them publicly; he triumphed over [θριαμβεύσας] them in him." (e) To
expose to shame. In this case the idea of the triumphal procession is submerged and
θριαμβεύω is a metaphor denoting low esteem. (f) To put someone on show or display.
This view has been recently advanced by R. P. Egan. He rejects any association of
θριαμβεύω with the Roman triumphal procession, arguing instead that Paul wishes to
stress the idea of openness or visibility by the use of the verb.

Of these interpretations, to lead someone as a captive in a triumphal procession
is preferred by the majority of more recent commentators, though it does not fit that
well into its context in 2:14–17, where Paul appears to be striking a positive note. For
this reason some modern interpreters have preferred to interpret θριαμβεύω to mean

lead victorious soldiers in triumphal procession, despite its lack of lexical support. Alternatively, if we allow Col 2:15 to inform our interpretation, we could say that Paul depicts himself as one who has been defeated by God and made a captive. Now God leads him as a willing captive "in Christ's triumphal procession" and "spreads the aroma of the knowledge of him in every place." Cf. BDAG 459bc; ZG 538; Harris 242–45. Hafemann 107–9 concludes his discussion of the use of the term: "Paul's point is that, as the one 'being led in triumph,' God is leading him to his death." So, too, Seifrid 84.

Ἡμᾶς, acc. 1st pl. pron. ἐγώ, "us," dir. obj. of θριαμβεύοντι. Ἐν, prep. with dat. τῷ Χριστῷ, "in Christ." Harris 246: "With θριαμβεύοντι referring to τῷ θεῷ, it seems more appropriate to regard the triumph as God's, with ἐν τῷ Χριστῷ meaning 'through (our union with) Christ' or 'in the cause of Christ,' rather than to take ἐν τῷ Χριστῷ as an equivalent to ἐν τῷ θριάμβῳ τοῦ Χριστοῦ, 'in Christ's triumphal procession' (NEB, REB)."

καὶ τὴν ὀσμὴν τῆς γνώσεως αὐτοῦ φανεροῦντι δι᾽ ἡμῶν ἐν παντὶ τόπῳ·
and through us spreads the aroma of the knowledge of him in every place.

Dat. rel. clause further qualifying θεῷ. Ὀσμήν, acc. sg. fem. ὀσμή, -ῆς, ἡ, "fragrance, aroma, stench," dir. obj. of φανεροῦντι. Τῆς γνώσεως αὐτοῦ. Harris 246–47: "With regard to the two genitives that follow τὴν ὀσμήν, the first (τῆς γνώσεως) could be subjective ('the fragrance that comes from knowing him,' NRSV) but is most likely epexegetic ('that sweet incense, the knowledge of him,' Weymouth). The second genitive (αὐτοῦ) is clearly objective ('the knowledge of him,' 'knowing him') but could refer to God or to Christ." Γνώσεως, gen. sg. fem. γνῶσις, -εως, ἡ, "knowledge," qualifying ὀσμήν, "aroma of the knowledge. . . ." Αὐτοῦ, "of him," qualifying τῆς γνώσεως. Φανεροῦντι, dat. sg. masc. of pres. act. ptc. of φανερόω, "spread." BDAG 1048c: "make known." Harris 246: "φανεροῦντι is coordinate with θριαμβεύοντι, both being present participles describing God's continuous action." Δι᾽ ἡμῶν ἐν παντὶ τόπῳ, adv. phrase modifying τὴν ὀσμὴν τῆς γνώσεως αὐτοῦ φανεροῦντι, "through us [spreads the aroma of the knowledge of him] in every place." Barnett 149 fn. 17: "The phrase ἐν παντὶ τόπῳ specifies that in each place Paul goes, he spreads the fragrance of the knowledge of Christ." Δι᾽ ἡμῶν, gen. instr. phrase, "through us." Ἐν παντὶ τόπῳ, dat. adv. phrase, "in every place." Παντί, dat. sg. masc. adj. πᾶς, πᾶσα, πᾶν, "every." Τόπῳ dat. sg. masc. τόπος, -ου, ὁ, "place."

VERSE 15

ὅτι Χριστοῦ εὐωδία ἐσμὲν τῷ θεῷ
For to God we are the fragrance of Christ

Ὅτι, conj. "for, because," introduces a clause that explains how the fragrance of the knowledge of Christ spreading through Paul and his colleagues (δι᾽ ἡμῶν) affects their hearers. Χριστοῦ, gen. sg. qualifying εὐωδία, "[fragrance] of Christ." If Χριστοῦ is a subj. gen., it would refer to the fragrance Christ offers to God (NEB); if possessive it would refer to Paul and his colleagues as Christ's fragrance ascending to God; cf. Harris 248. Εὐωδία, nom. sg. fem. εὐωδία, -ας, ἡ, "aroma, fragrance," pred. nom. of ἐσμέν. Unlike ὀσμή, which may denote either a pleasant or unpleasant odor, εὐωδία always denotes a pleasant odor. Cf. Seifrid 90: "Paul splits the usual biblical idiom 'fragrant odor' (LXX osmē euōdias) into its two distinct terms, 'odor' (vv. 14,16) and 'fragrance' (v. 15). This allows him to speak—in warning to the Corinthians—of the twofold effect of his being paraded in God's triumph." Ἐσμέν, 1st pl. pres. indic. of εἰμί, "be." Τῷ θεῷ, dat. prep. phrase, "to God," indicating for whom the aroma is primarily intended (as in the Roman procession, the incense was offered to the gods). Cf. Harris 249: "τῷ θεῷ is locative. . . . But it could also be classified as a dative of advantage, 'for God's sake' (NAB), 'to/for God's glory.'"

ἐν τοῖς σῳζομένοις καὶ ἐν τοῖς ἀπολλυμένοις.
among those who are being saved and among those who are perishing.

Prep. phrase (ἐν with dat.) indicating among whom the aroma is also having its effect. Σῳζομένοις, dat. pl. masc. of pres. pass. ptc. of σῴζω, "save." Ἀπολλυμένοις, dat. pl. masc. of pres. pass. ptc. of ἀπόλλυμι, "perish." BDAG 116a–b: τοῖς ἀπολλυμένοις "those who are lost." Because, for Paul, salvation is both a present reality and a future hope, for "those who are being saved" it may be understood as a present experience, and sim. "those who are perishing" denotes a present reality, as Harris 249 says, "in the sense of being spiritually dead (Eph. 2:1) and under God's wrath (Rom 1:18)."

VERSE 16

οἷς μὲν ὀσμὴ ἐκ θανάτου εἰς θάνατον,
To some we are an aroma of death leading to death,

Harris 251: "a deadly stench that leads to death." Οἷς . . . οἷς, BDAG 727d: "the one . . . the other." Οἷς, dat. pl. masc. rel. pron. ὅς, ἥ, ὅ, "to the one." Ὀσμή, nom. sg. fem. ὀσμή, -ῆς, ἡ, "aroma, fragrance." Harris 252: "the ὀσμή is either the gospel as proclaimed by the apostles or the apostles themselves as proclaimers. Either way, the messengers and the message are indistinguishable." Ἐκ, prep. with gen. θανάτου, "from death." Cf. Harris, *Prepositions*, 109: "ἐκ expresses a result or effect: 'leading to/resulting in [death or life].'" Εἰς, prep. with acc. θάνατον, "to death."

οἷς δὲ ὀσμὴ ἐκ ζωῆς εἰς ζωήν.
but to others, an aroma of life leading to life.

Harris 251: "a vitalizing fragrance that leads to life." Οἷς, dat. pl. masc. rel. pron. ὅς, ἥ, ὅ, "to the other." Ὀσμή, see above. Ἐκ, prep. with ζωῆς, "from life." ζωῆς, gen. sg. fem. ζωή, -ῆς, ἡ, "life." Εἰς, prep. with acc. ζωήν, "to life."

καὶ πρὸς ταῦτα τίς ἱκανός;
Who is adequate for these things?

A question asked in light of the weighty responsibility of preaching the gospel. Cf. Exod 4:10, where Moses, in response to God's call, says he is not sufficient (LXX ἱκανός) for the task to which he is being called. Hafemann 113: "By alluding to Moses' call, Paul's point is that, as in the case of Moses, God is the one who has made Paul sufficient for his ministry." Πρός, prep. with acc. ταῦτα, "for these things." R 626: "Adjectives may have πρός in this general sense of fitness, like . . . ἱκανός." Τίς, nom. sg. masc. pron. τίς, τί, "who." Ἱκανός, nom. sg. masc. adj. ἱκανός, -ή, -όν, "adequate, sufficient." BDAG 472c: "pert. to meeting a standard, fit, appropriate, competent, qualified, able, w. the connotation worthy, good enough."

VERSE 17

οὐ γάρ ἐσμεν ὡς οἱ πολλοὶ καπηλεύοντες τὸν λόγον τοῦ θεοῦ,
For we do not market the word of God for profit like so many.

Paul explains the reason for his sense of inadequacy. Ἐσμέν . . . καπηλεύοντες, a periph. present. Cf. Moule, 17; Wallace 647–48; R 881. Ἐσμέν, 1st pl. pres. indic. of εἰμί, "be."

Ὡς, comp. particle, "like." Πολλοί, nom. pl. masc. adj. πολύς, πολλή, πολύ, "many." Harris 254: "When πολλοί is articular, it may mean either 'the many' or 'the majority.' If, as here, the context suggests disapproval, 'most people' or 'the crowd' is an appropriate translation." Καπηλεύοντες, nom. pl. masc. of pres. act. ptc. of καπηλεύω, "market for profit." BDAG 508a: "trade in, peddle, huckster." καπηλεύω is found only here in the NT, though the cognate noun, κάπηλος ("merchant"), is found twice in the LXX (Isa 1:22; Sir 26:29). Because of the tricks of petty traders, who would adulterate their wine with water or use false weights, καπηλεύω came to have neg. connotations. Paul's mng. here, then, is that he felt the burden of responsibility of gospel preaching so heavily because he refused to tamper with God's word (cf. 4:2) and remove its offense so that, like others, he might peddle it for personal gain by making it more pleasant to his hearers. The term was used by Plato in his criticisms of the Sophists (*Protagoras* 311b–311e); cf. Seifrid 94.

ἀλλ' ὡς ἐξ εἰλικρινείας, ἀλλ' ὡς ἐκ θεοῦ κατέναντι θεοῦ ἐν Χριστῷ λαλοῦμεν.
On the contrary, we speak with sincerity in Christ, as from God and before God.

Contrary to the practice of those who adulterate the gospel for personal gain, Paul spoke with sincerity, and as one aware that he was sent from God, carried out his ministry before God, and spoke in Christ. Ἀλλ' (contraction of ἀλλά), a strong advers. coord. conj. "but," introducing a contrast between the way Paul conducts his ministry and the way adopted by many others. Ὡς, particle "as," BDAG 1104d: "marker introducing the perspective from which a pers., thing, or activity is viewed or understood as to character, function, or role, *as.*" Ἐξ, prep. with gen. εἰλικρινείας, BDAG 282c: "out of pure motives." Εἰλικρινείας, gen. sg. fem. εἰλικρίνεια, -ας, ἡ, "sincerity." Ἀλλ'. Barnett 156, fn. 49: "the repetition of ἀλλά is ascensive, 'but . . . indeed . . .'. Ἐκ, prep. with gen. θεοῦ, "from God." Κατέναντι, prep. with gen. θεοῦ, "before God." Κατέναντι, BDAG 530d: "in the sight of someone." Cf. R 644; Harris, *Prepositions*, 247. Ἐν Χριστῷ λαλοῦμεν, "in Christ we speak." Harris 256 suggests this could mean either "as taught by Christ," or "in the name of Christ." Λαλοῦμεν, 1st pl. pres. act. indic. of λαλέω, "speak."

FOR FURTHER STUDY

27. Led in Triumph (2:14)

Breytenbach, C. "Paul's Proclamation and God's 'Thriambos' (Notes on 2 Corinthians 2:14–16b)." *Neot* 24 (1990): 257–71.

Duff, P. B. "Metaphor, Motif, and Meaning: The Rhetorical Strategy Behind the Image 'Led in Triumph' in 2 Cor 2:14." *CBQ* 53 (1991): 79–82.

Egan, R. P. "Lexical Evidence on Two Pauline Passages." *NovT* 19 (1977): 34–62.

Hafemann, S. J. *Suffering and Ministry in the Spirit.* Grand Rapids: Eerdmans, 1990. See pages 16–34.

Marshall, P. "A Metaphor of Social Shame: ΘΡΙΑΜΒΕΥΕΙΝ in 2 Cor. 2:14." *NovT* 25 (1983): 302–17.

Scott, J. M. "The Triumph of God in 2 Cor 2.14: Additional Evidence of Merkabah Mysticism in Paul." *NTS* 42 (1996): 206–81.

Williamson, L. "Led in Triumph. Paul's Use of *Thriambeuō*." *Int* 22 (1968): 317–32.

Yates, R. "Colossians 2.15: Christ Triumphant." *NTS* 37 (2004): 537–91.

28. Aroma/Fragrance of Christ (2:15)

Carrez, M. "Odeur de Mort, Odeur de Vie (à propos de 2 Co 2, 16)." *RHPR* 64 (1984): 135–42.

Kurek-Chomycz, D. A. "Scenting the Aroma of Christ: 2 Cor. 2:15–6 in Origen's Interpretation." Pages 275–79 in *Studia Patristica.* Edited by Jane Baun et al. Vol. 44 of *Archaeologica, Arts, Iconographica; Tools; Historica; Biblica; Theologica, Philosophica, Ethica.* Louvain: Peeters, 2010.

Lambrecht, J. "The Defeated Paul, Aroma of Christ: An Exegetical Study of 2 Corinthians 2:14–16b." *LS* 20 (1995): 170–86.

Novick, T. "Peddling Scents: Merchandise and Meaning in 2 Corinthians 2:14–17." *JBL* 130 (2011): 543–49.

Thurston, B. B. "2 Corinthians 2:14–16a: Christ's Incense." *ResQ* 29 (1987): 65–69.

29. Sufficiency for Apostolic Ministry (2:16)

Fallon, F. T. "Self's Sufficiency or God's Sufficiency: 2 Corinthians 2:16." *HTR* 76 (1983): 369–74.

30. Marketing the Word of God (2:17)

Windisch, H. *TDNT* 3.603–5.

HOMILETICAL SUGGESTIONS

Led in Triumph (2:14–17)

1. God spreads abroad the knowledge of his Son as we share the gospel message (v. 14).
2. When the message is accepted, it leads to life, but when rejected, it leads to death (v 15).
3. The question of adequacy for such a ministry (v. 16).
4. The crucial importance of integrity in ministry, avoiding the temptation to regard it as a means of profit (v. 17).

b. Letters of Recommendation (3:1–3)

Paul claims—in the case of the Corinthians, at least—he did not need to produce a letter of recommendation for them or to receive one from them. It is not that he disapproved of letters of recommendation, but as founding apostle of the Corinthian church, he needed no such letter to prove the authenticity of his apostleship to that church. Also the fact that he planted the church in Corinth can be seen by others as proof of his apostleship, so he does not need a letter of recommendation from them either.

STRUCTURE

1   Ἀρχόμεθα πάλιν ἑαυτοὺς συνιστάνειν;
   ἢ μὴ χρήζομεν ὥς τινες συστατικῶν ἐπιστολῶν
                πρὸς ὑμᾶς
                ἢ ἐξ ὑμῶν;
2   ἡ ἐπιστολὴ ἡμῶν ὑμεῖς ἐστε,
        ἐγγεγραμμένη
           ἐν ταῖς καρδίαις ἡμῶν,
        γινωσκομένη
        καὶ ἀναγινωσκομένη
        ὑπὸ πάντων ἀνθρώπων,
3   φανερούμενοι ὅτι ἐστὲ ἐπιστολὴ Χριστοῦ
           διακονηθεῖσα ὑφ’ ἡμῶν,
           ἐγγεγραμμένη οὐ μέλανι
              ἀλλὰ πνεύματι θεοῦ ζῶντος,
              οὐκ ἐν πλαξὶν
                λιθίναις
              ἀλλ’ ἐν πλαξὶν καρδίαις
              σαρκίναις.

VERSE 1

Ἀρχόμεθα πάλιν ἑαυτοὺς συνιστάνειν;
Are we beginning to commend ourselves again?

The punctuation, but not the form, depicts this sentence as a question (Moule 158). R 1175 cites it as an instance where "it is a matter of doubt whether a sentence is interrogative or declarative." Harris 258 says, "It is possible to regard this as an 'open question' with no formal indication of the answer anticipated and only the context making it clear what answer is expected. However, because the second question in this verse begins with ἤ ("or") and expects a negative response (μή), there are both formal and contextual reasons for expecting a 'No.'"

Barnett 162 n. 15: "It is not certain whether πάλιν is connected with ἀρχόμεθα or with συνιστάνειν. Either way the πάλιν tells us that Paul is here responding to the criticism of self-commendation." Ἀρχόμεθα, 1st pl. pres. mid. act. of ἄρχω, "begin."

Πάλιν, adv. "again." Ἑαυτούς, acc. pl. masc. refl. pron. ἑαυτοῦ, -ῆς, -οῦ, "ourselves." Συνιστάνειν, pres. act inf. of συνίστημι, "commend." The phrase ἑαυτόν συνιστάνειν has a pejorative sense here, as it does in 3:1; 5:12; 10:12, 18, but in the form συνιστάνειν ἑαυτόν, it is used in a positive sense in 4:2; 6:4; cf. 7:11; 10:13–18 (Harris 259).

ἢ μὴ χρῄζομεν ὥς τινες συστατικῶν ἐπιστολῶν πρὸς ὑμᾶς ἢ ἐξ ὑμῶν;
Or do we need, like some, letters of recommendation to you or from you?

Μή, neg. particle, used in questions expecting a neg. response. Χρῄζομεν, 1st pl. pres. act. indic. of χρῄζω (χράομαι), "(have) need (of)." Τινες, nom. pl. masc. pron. τις, τι, "some, certain ones." When referring to "some people" Paul would have had in mind the "many" of 2:17, the false apostles who were already making their presence felt in Corinth. Συστατικῶν, gen. pl. fem. adj. συστατικός, -ή, -όν, "commendatory." Ἐπιστολῶν, gen. pl. fem. ἐπιστολή, -ῆς, ἡ, "letter, epistle." Ἐξ, prep. with ὑμῶν, "from you." Paul's denial of his need for commendatory letters *from* the Corinthians suggests that his opponents were requesting such letters to commend them to other churches, prob. those founded by Paul (Barnett 163).

VERSE 2

ἡ ἐπιστολὴ ἡμῶν ὑμεῖς ἐστε, ἐγγεγραμμένη ἐν ταῖς καρδίαις ἡμῶν
You yourselves are our letter, written on our hearts, known and read by everyone.

Ἐγγεγραμμένη, nom. sg. fem. of pf. pass. ptc. of ἐγγράφω, "write, inscribe." BDAG 270d–271a: "write down, inscribe." R 559–60 cites this as an instance of ἐν repeated after a composite verb, ἐγγεγραμμένη. Ἐν, prep. with locat. dat. ταῖς καρδίαις ἡμῶν, "on our hearts." Καρδίαις, dat. pl. fem. καρδία, -ας, ἡ, "heart." Ἡμῶν (*"our* hearts") has the strongest manuscript support (𝔓⁴⁶ A B C D F G Ψ 075ˢᵘᵖᵖ 0150 0243 6 81 104 256 263 365 424 459 1241 1319 1573 1739 1859 1962 2127 2200 2464 *Byz* [K L P] *Lect* itar, b, d, f, g, o vg syrᵖ, h copˢᵃ, ᵇᵒ arm eth geo slav Chrysostom Cyril; Ambrosiaster Jerome Pelagius) and is adopted in the CSB, ESV, NIV, NRSV, and by Barnett 164; Harris 261; Seifrid 111; Hafemann 116. The sense, then, is of a "letter" written on the heart of Paul, consisting presumably of the knowledge of what God had done in the lives of the Corinthians through his preaching of the gospel. To knowledge of this fact Paul could appeal whenever his credentials were called into question. Other ancient manuscripts support the rdg. ὑμῶν (*"your* hearts") (ℵ 33 436 1175 1881 1912 ℓ 593 ℓ 1441 BJ), for which a strong case may be made because it fits well in the context. Earlier in this verse Paul says "*you yourselves* are our letter," and in the following verse he says "*you* are a letter from Christ, the result of our ministry" (NIV). It was through Paul's ministry that Christ constituted to the Corinthians a letter of recommendation for him.

γινωσκομένη καὶ ἀναγινωσκομένη ὑπὸ πάντων ἀνθρώπων,
known and read by everyone.

Γινωσκομένη καὶ ἀναγινωσκομένη, an instance of *annominatio*, the recurrence of words of similar sense and sound (R 1201). Γινωσκομένη, nom. sg. fem. of pres. pass. ptc. of γινώσκω, "know." Ἀναγινωσκομένη, nom. sg. fem. of pres. pass. ptc. of ἀναγινώσκω, "read." Ὑπό, prep. with gen. πάντων ἀνθρώπων "by everyone," lit. "by all men."

VERSE 3

φανερούμενοι ὅτι ἐστὲ ἐπιστολὴ Χριστοῦ διακονηθεῖσα ὑφ᾽ ἡμῶν,
You show that you are Christ's letter, delivered by us,

Φανερούμενοι ὅτι ἐστὲ ἐπιστολὴ Χριστοῦ, an example of a "personal construction" of which "the Greeks were more fond . . . than we English are" (R 658). Φανερούμενοι, nom. pl. masc. of pres. mid. ptc. of φανερόω, "show, make known, reveal." The mid. has the sense of "you show that you are." It could be read as pass., in which case it would mean "you are shown to be," or as causal, "for you are shown to be" (cf. Harris 263).
Ὅτι is the conj. "that," an instance of a "declarative ὅτι" here following φανερούμενοι (R 1034). Ἐστὲ ἐπιστολὴ Χριστοῦ, R 404 notes that "it is not necessary . . . that a predicate substantive should agree in number with the subject." The gen. has been variously construed, as a poss. gen. "Christ's letter" (CSB), gen. of source "from Christ" (NIV, ESV), subj. gen. "that Christ wrote" (Harris 263). Cf. Seifrid 113: "The genitive relation in the first instance is probably that of possession, as in Paul's preceding reference to the Corinthians as 'our letter.' Yet the idea of Christ's authorship is also surely present: the Corinthians are 'Christ's letter, communicated . . . by the apostle.'" Διακονηθεῖσα, nom. sg. fem. of aor. pass. ptc. of διακονέω, "serve, deliver." Ὑφ᾽ (contraction of ὑπό), prep. with ἡμῶν, "by us." Ἡμῶν, gen. 1st pl. ἐγώ. Διακονηθεῖσα ὑφ᾽ ἡμῶν has been variously translated: "delivered by us" (CSB), "the result of our ministry" (NIV), "prepared by us" (NRSV), "we transcribed" (Harris 263), "ministered by us" (Barnett 167).

ἐγγεγραμμένη οὐ μέλανι ἀλλὰ πνεύματι θεοῦ ζῶντος,
not written with ink but with the Spirit of the living God—

Ἐγγεγραμμένη, nom. sg. fem. of pf. pass. ptc. of γράφω, "write." Μέλανι, dat. sg. neut. μέλαν, -ανος, τό, "ink," dat. of means "with ink." Πνεύματι, dat. sg. neut. πνεῦμα, -ατος, τό, "Spirit," dat. of means "with the Spirit." Θεοῦ, descriptive gen. "(Spirit) of God." Ζῶντος, gen. sg. masc. of pres. act. ptc. of ζάω, "live," descriptive gen. "living (God)." Cf. Josh 3:10; 1 Sam 17:26, 36; Jer 10:10; Acts 14:15; 1 Thess 1:9. Within a metaphor of letter writing (as here) where an author and a scribe are envisaged, Paul describes a "living letter" dictated by Christ and "inscribed" in the Corinthians' hearts through his preaching of the gospel. He takes the analogy one step further when he says this scribal work was "not written with ink but with the Spirit of the living God."

His ministry was empowered by the Spirit of God, and any changes wrought in the lives of his hearers were effected by the Spirit (cf. Rom 15:17–19; 1 Cor 2:4–5).

οὐκ ἐν πλαξὶν λιθίναις ἀλλ᾽ ἐν πλαξὶν καρδίαις σαρκίναις.
not on tablets of stone but on tablets of human hearts.

Ἐν, prep. with locat. dat. πλαξὶν, "on tablets." Πλαξὶν, dat. pl. fem. πλάξ, πλακός, ἡ, "tablet." Λιθίναις, dat. pl. fem. adj. λίθινος, -ίνη, -ον, "made of stone." Καρδίαις, dat. pl. fem. καρδία, -ας, ἡ, "heart." Σαρκίναις, dat. pl. fem. adj. σάρκινος, -η, -ον, "fleshly, human." BDF (§113[2]): "made of flesh." Ἐν πλαξὶν καρδίαις σαρκίναις, "on tablets of human hearts." "Tablets of stone" is an allusion to the law written in stone at Mount Sinai (Exod 31:18). But "Christ's letter" is not written on stone, as was the law of Moses, but on human hearts. Here the allusion is to the prophetic description of the new covenant under which God would write his law on human hearts (cf. Jer 31:31–34; Ezek 36:24–32), which paves the way for Paul's description of himself as a minister of the new covenant (vv. 4–6) and for an extended comparison and contrast of ministries under the old and new covenants (vv. 7–18).

c. Ministers of the New Covenant (3:4–6)

Here Paul answers the question he asked in 2:16, "Who is equal to such a task?" by showing that his competence as a minister of the new covenant comes from God. In the process he picks up and expands the allusion to Jer 31:31 in v. 3 and by so doing introduces the contrast between ministries under the old and new covenants that he will develop in vv. 7–18.

STRUCTURE

4   Πεποίθησιν δὲ τοιαύτην ἔχομεν
                        διὰ τοῦ Χριστοῦ
                        πρὸς τὸν θεόν.
5   οὐχ ὅτι ἀφ᾽ ἑαυτῶν ἱκανοί ἐσμεν λογίσασθαί τι ὡς ἐξ ἑαυτῶν,
      ἀλλ᾽ ἡ ἱκανότης ἡμῶν ἐκ τοῦ θεοῦ,
6   ὃς καὶ ἱκάνωσεν ἡμᾶς διακόνους καινῆς διαθήκης,
                                    οὐ γράμματος
                                    ἀλλὰ πνεύματος·
                                        τὸ γὰρ γράμμα ἀποκτέννει,
                                        τὸ δὲ πνεῦμα ζῳοποιεῖ.

VERSE 4

Πεποίθησιν δὲ τοιαύτην ἔχομεν διὰ τοῦ Χριστοῦ πρὸς τὸν θεόν.
Such is the confidence we have through Christ before God.

Πεποίθησιν, acc. sg. fem. πεποίθησις -εως, ἡ, "confidence." Τοιαύτην, acc. sg. fem. adj. τοιοῦτος, -αύτη, -οῦτον, "such, of such a kind." Ἔχομεν, 1st pl. pres. act. indic. of ἔχω, "have." Διά, prep. with gen. τοῦ Χριστοῦ, "through Christ." Πρός, prep. with acc. τὸν θεόν, "before God." Harris 267: "The prepositional phrase πρὸς τὸν θεόν may mean 'toward God,' 'before God,' or 'in regard to God' (TCNT). All of Christian existence is 'in relation to' God 'through' Christ."

VERSE 5

οὐχ ὅτι ἀφ᾽ ἑαυτῶν ἱκανοί ἐσμεν λογίσασθαί τι ὡς ἐξ ἑαυτῶν,
It is not that we are competent in ourselves to claim anything as coming from ourselves,

Paul insists that his competence in ministry comes from God, and in so doing answers the question he raised in 2:16: "Who is adequate for these things?" His denial of self-sufficiency does not reflect an exaggerated humility, but rather a sober recognition of the facts of the matter. Spiritual ministry can be accomplished only by the power of God at work in the minister and released through the preaching of the gospel (cf. Rom 15:17–19; 1 Cor 1:18–2:5). Ἀφ᾽ (contraction of ἀπό), prep. with ἑαυτῶν, "from ourselves." Z §209: "The third-person form of the reflexive (ἑαυτῶν) often takes the place of the first or second person forms in the singular, and always does so in the plural . . . e.g. 2 Cor 3,5 «not that we are capable of thinking something of ourselves (ἀφ᾽ ἑαυτῶν) as from ourselves (ὡς ἐξ ἑαυτῶν).»" Ἑαυτῶν, gen. 3rd pl. masc. ἑαυτοῦ, -ῆς, -οῦ, "ourselves." Ἱκανοί, nom. pl. masc. adj. ἱκανός, -ή, -όν, "sufficient, competent." ZG 539: "here adequate, qualified." Cf. LXX Exod 4:10, where Moses, in response to God's call, says οὐχ ἱκανός εἰμι. Harris 267: "As in the case of οὐχ ὅτι in 1:24, Paul is correcting a possible misinterpretation of his previous statement . . . his confidence before God should not be taken to imply self-confidence, far less any independence of God." Λογίσασθαί, aor. mid. inf. of λογίζομαι, "claim." BDAG 598a: "to hold a view about someth., think, believe, be of the opinion." ZG 539: "reckon, put down to one's account." Ἐξ, prep. with ἑαυτῶν, "from ourselves." Harris 268 notes three main ways of understanding λογίσασθαί τι ὡς ἐξ ἑαυτῶν: "(1) Paul is rejecting any fitness for wise thinking that is independent of God . . . (2) Paul is disclaiming any ability to form an accurate assessment of the results of his ministry . . . (3) Paul is disowning any qualification to claim credit for himself for an aspect of his ministry." The third of these interpretations is adopted by most translations and commentators.

ἀλλ᾽ ἡ ἱκανότης ἡμῶν ἐκ τοῦ θεοῦ,
but our adequacy is from God.

Ἱκανότης, nom. sg. fem. ἱκανότης, -ητος, ἡ. BDAG 473a: "state of being qualified or adequate for someth., fitness, capability, qualification." Harris 269: "As in 2:17, the ἱκανότης is general. The qualification that God gave Paul and his apostolic colleagues was the giftedness and motivation to fulfill their apostolic mission, to serve as God's agents under the new covenant (v. 6)." Ἐκ, prep. with gen. of source τοῦ θεοῦ "from God."

VERSE 6

ὃς καὶ ἱκάνωσεν ἡμᾶς διακόνους καινῆς διαθήκης, οὐ γράμματος ἀλλὰ πνεύματος·
He has made us competent to be ministers of a new covenant, not of the letter, but of the Spirit.

Ὅς, nom. 3rd sg. masc. rel. pron. ὅς, ἥ, ὅ, "who," referring to God. Harris 270: "Καί may strengthen the rel. ὅς ('it is he who . . .'), emphasize the verb ἱκάνωσεν ('who has indeed qualified us . . .), or even point to a further divine qualification ('who also . . .')." Ἱκάνωσεν, 3rd sg. aor. act. indic. of ἱκανόω, "make able, competent, sufficient." Here with the double acc. ἡμᾶς διακόνους, lit. "make competent us ministers" (cf. R 480). Ἡμᾶς, acc. pl. masc. ἐγώ, "us," obj. of ἱκάνωσεν. Διακόνους, acc. pl. masc. διάκονος, -ου, ὁ, "minister, servant," also obj. of ἱκάνωσεν. Καινῆς, gen. sg. fem. adj. καινός, -ή, -όν, "new," qualifying διαθήκης. Διαθήκης, gen. sg. fem. διαθήκη, -ης, ἡ, "covenant." Καινῆς διαθήκης, "new covenant." This expression is found in only one other place in Paul's writings, in 1 Cor 11:25, where it forms part of the Lord's Supper tradition which Paul received ("This cup is the new covenant in my blood," cf. Luke 22:20). Both Jesus's words of institution and Paul's reference to the new covenant indicate that the prophecy of Jer 31:31 has been fulfilled. Both Jesus's words of institution, which Paul quotes in 1 Cor 11:25, and the exposition of Jer 31:31 in Heb 9:15–28 make it clear it was the death of Christ that established the new covenant. Hafemann 129: "As William Lane has observed, 'Paul's pastoral response to the disruptive situation in Corinth' entailed 'an appeal to the New Covenant and the administration of its provisions.' Like an Old Testament prophet, called to be a 'messenger of the covenant lawsuit of God,' Paul was called to proclaim the 'divine complaint against the rebellious Corinthians and to call them back to the stipulations of the covenant'" (W. L. Lane, "Covenant: The Key to Paul's Conflict with Corinth." TynBul 33 (1982): 6, 10).

Οὐ γράμματος ἀλλὰ πνεύματος. This has been interpreted as a ministry that does not focus on the literal mng. of the OT ("letter") but on its real underlying intention ("spirit"). But this fails to recognize that in this chapter Paul uses "letter" and "Spirit" to characterize the law of Moses ("chiseled in letters on stones," v. 7) and the Holy Spirit (v. 8), which are the primary features of ministry under the old and new covenants respectively. Οὐ γράμματος, "not of (the) letter," qualifying διαθήκης. Γράμματος, gen. sg. neut. γράμμα, -ατος, τό, "letter." Πνεύματος, gen. sg. neut. πνεῦμα, -ατος, τό, "of (the) Spirit," qualifying διαθήκης.

τὸ γὰρ γράμμα ἀποκτέννει, τὸ δὲ πνεῦμα ζωοποιεῖ.
For the letter kills, but the Spirit gives life.

How can Paul say that the "letter"—i.e., the law of Moses—kills? There is nothing wrong with the law—elsewhere he insists that the law is holy, righteous, good, and spiritual (Rom 7:12, 14). But he also says it is powerless to curb human sin (Rom 8:3) or to bring life and be a means to establish righteousness (Gal 3:21). Instead it pronounces God's judgement upon sinners and therefore brings death (Rom 7:10). So a ministry of the "letter" is a ministry of death. The Spirit, on the other hand, "gives life" and does what the law could never do, that is, bring about the fulfilment of its own demands (Rom 8:2–4). It is a ministry of the new covenant under which sins are forgiven and remembered no more and God's law is written on people's hearts (cf. Jer 31:31–34; Ezek 36:25–27). It is a ministry of the new covenant under which people are motivated and enabled by the Spirit to overcome their sinful tendencies and live lives pleasing to God (Rom 7:4, 6), the final outcome of which is eternal life (Gal 6:8). Γράμμα, nom. sg. neut. γράμμα, -ατος, τό, "letter," subj. of ἀποκτέννει. Ἀποκτέννει, 3rd sg. pres. act. indic. of ἀποκτείνω, "kill," used gnomicly here to depict what is always the case. Πνεῦμα, nom. sg. neut. πνεῦμα, -ατος, τό, "Spirit," subj. of ζωοποιεῖ. Ζωοποιεῖ, 3rd sg. pres. act. indic. ζωοποιέω, "give life, make alive," also used gnomicly to depict what is always the case. The references to "the letter kills" and "the Spirit gives life" prepare the way for the contrast between ministries under old and new covenants that follows in 3:8–18. BDF (§488[1.d]) cites vv. 5–10 as an instance of *paronomasia*: "Paul loves to dwell on an idea or word without giving it different meanings and without reintroducing it too quickly, yet with some artistry and reflection . . . 2 C 3:5ff. first ἱκανοί . . . ἱκανότη . . . ἱκάνωσεν, then γράμμα three times . . . likewise πνεῦμα . . . ; διάκονος once in 6, διακονία four times 7ff.; δόξα eight times 7–11 and in addition οὐ δεδόξασται τὸ δεδοξασμένον 10."

FOR FURTHER STUDY

31. Letters of Recommendation (3:1–3)

Baird, W. R. "Letters of Recommendation: A Study of II Cor. 3:1–3." *JBL* 80 (1961): 166–72.
Keyes, C. W. "The Greek Letter of Introduction." *AJP* 56 (1935): 28–44.
Kim, S. H. *Form and Structure of the Familiar Greek Letter of Recommendation.* SLBDS 4. Missoula: Scholars, 1972.

32. Self-Commendation (3:1)

Hafemann, S. J. "'Self-Commendation' and Apostolic Legitimacy in 2 Corinthians: A Pauline Dialectic?" *NTS* (1990–91): 61–68.
Kasch, W. *TDNT* 7.896–98.

33. Competency for Ministry (3:4–5)

Provence, T. E. "Who Is Sufficient for These Things." *NovT* 24 (1982): 54–81.

34. Ministry/διακονία (3:6)

Collins, J. N. *Diakonia: Reinterpretation of Ancient Sources.* New York: Oxford University Press, 1990. See pp. 195–215.

Kruse, C. G. *DPL* 602–8.
———. *DPL* 869–71.

35. A New Covenant (3:6)

Campbell, W. S. *DPL* 179–83.
Lane, W. "Covenant: The Key to Paul's Conflict with Corinth." *TynBul* 33 (1982): 3–29.
Seifrid, M. A. "Excursus: Paul's Understanding of 'Covenant.'" Pages 123–27 in *The Second Letter to the Corinthians*. PNTC. Grand Rapids: Eerdmans, 2014.

36. Letter and Spirit (3:6)

Chau, W.-S. *The Letter and the Spirit: A History of Interpretation from Origen to Luther.* New York: Lang, 1995.
Cohen, B. "A Note on Letter and Spirit in the New Testament." *HTR* 47 (1954): 197–203.
Fee, G. D. *God's Empowering Presence: The Holy Spirit in the Letters of Paul.* Peabody, MA: Hendrickson, 1994. See pages 302–8.
Hafemann, S. J. *Paul, Moses, and the History of Israel: The Letter/Spirit Contrast and the Argument from Scripture in 2 Corinthians 3.* Peabody, MA: Hendrickson, 1996.
Käsemann, E. "The Spirit and the Letter." Pages 138–66 in *Perspectives on Paul.* Philadelphia: Fortress, 1971.
Murphy-O'Connor, J. "A Ministry beyond the Letter (2 Cor 3:1–6)." Pages 25–45 in *Keys to Second Corinthians: Revisiting the Major Issues.* Oxford: Oxford University Press, 2010.
Schweizer, E. *TDNT* 6 398–445.
Seifrid, M. A. "Excursus: The Letter and the Spirit in Recent Interpretation." Pages 130–50 in *The Second Letter to the Corinthians*. PNTC. Grand Rapids: Eerdmans, 2014.
Westerholm, S. "Letter and Spirit: The Foundation of Pauline Ethics." *NTS* 30 (1984): 229–48.

HOMILETICAL SUGGESTIONS

Authentication of Ministry (3:1–3)

1. The authenticity of one's ministry is not established by self-commendation (3:1a)
2. The authenticity of one's ministry is not established by letters of recommendation from others (3:1b)
3. The fruit of one's ministry in people's lives attests its authenticity (3:2)
4. Christ himself produces this fruit though the ministry of his servants who are empowered by the Holy Spirit (3:3)

Competency for Ministry (3:4–6)

1. Competence for new covenant ministry does not come from ministers of the gospel themselves (3:4–5a)
2. God makes his servants competent for new covenant ministry (3:5b)

3. New covenant ministry is one of the Spirit, who gives life, not the letter of the law, which kills (3:6)

d. The Greater Glory of New Covenant Ministry (3:7–11)

Having contrasted the new covenant "of the Spirit" with the old covenant "of the letter" in 3:6, Paul further contrasts them in 3:7–18 in two stages. In this section, vv. 7–11, he does so by an exposition of Exod 34:29–32. In the following section, vv. 12–18, he will do so by an exposition of Exod 34:33–35. His primary purpose in doing all this is to demonstrate the greater glory of the new covenant under which he was privileged to minister as an apostle and so explain why, despite so many difficulties, he does not lose heart (cf. 4:1).

STRUCTURE

7 Εἰ δὲ ἡ διακονία   ἐγενήθη ἐν δόξῃ,
        τοῦ θανάτου
        ἐν γράμμασιν
        ἐντετυπωμένη λίθοις
        ὥστε μὴ δύνασθαι ἀτενίσαι τοὺς υἱοὺς Ἰσραὴλ
                εἰς τὸ πρόσωπον Μωϋσέως
                διὰ τὴν δόξαν τοῦ προσώπου αὐτοῦ
                        τὴν καταργουμένην,
8 πῶς οὐχὶ μᾶλλον ἡ διακονία τοῦ πνεύματος ἔσται ἐν δόξῃ;
9   εἰ γὰρ τῇ διακονίᾳ τῆς κατακρίσεως δόξα,
        πολλῷ μᾶλλον περισσεύει ἡ διακονία τῆς δικαιοσύνης δόξῃ.
10 καὶ γὰρ οὐ δεδόξασται τὸ δεδοξασμένον
        ἐν τούτῳ τῷ μέρει εἵνεκεν τῆς ὑπερβαλλούσης δόξης.
11   εἰ γὰρ τὸ καταργούμενον διὰ δόξης,
        πολλῷ μᾶλλον τὸ μένον ἐν δόξῃ.

Harris 279–80: "The most notable feature is the series of three carefully structured contrasts, perhaps prompted by the antithesis in 3:6b.

vv. 7–8	Εἰ δὲ . . . πῶς οὐχὶ μᾶλλον
v. 9	εἰ γὰρ . . . πολλῷ μᾶλλον
v. 11	εἰ γὰρ . . . πολλῷ μᾶλλον . . .

These three qal wāḥômer contrasts are related to some ten antitheses found in vv. 3:1–11.

v. 3	μέλανι	πνεύματι
	πλαξὶν λιθίναις	λαξὶν καρδίαις σαρκίναις
v. 6	τῆς παλαιᾶς διαθήκης (v. 14)	καινῆς διαθήκης
	γράμματος	πνεύματος
	γράμμα	πνεῦμα
	ἀποκτέννει	ζωοποιεῖ
v. 7	ἡ διακονία τοῦ θανάτου	ἡ διακονία τοῦ πνεύματος (v. 8)
	ἣν δόξαν . . . τὴν καταργουμένην	τῆς ὑπερβαλλούσης δόξης (v. 10)

v. 9 τῇ διακονίᾳ τῆς κατακρίσεως   ἡ διακονία τῆς δικαιοσύνης
v. 11 τὸ καταργούμενον   τὸ μένον."

VERSE 7

Εἰ δὲ ἡ διακονία τοῦ θανάτου ἐν γράμμασιν ἐντετυπωμένη λίθοις ἐγενήθη ἐν δόξῃ,
Now if the ministry that brought death, chiseled in letters on stones, came with glory,

This is the prot. of the long cond. sentence (vv. 7–8). Εἰ with ἐγενήθη in the prot.
indicates a first-class cond. sentence in which "the protasis postulates a certain situation, while the apod. states the consequence of such a situation" (Forbes 153). Ἐγενήθη,
3rd sg. aor. pass. indic. of γίνομαι, "become." Διακονία, nom. sg. fem. διακονία, -ας,
ἡ, "ministry, dispensation," subj. of pass. ptc. ἐντετυπωμένη. Harris 281: "διακονία
denotes the whole system of the Mosaic Law, along with its agents; personal and
impersonal elements are blended in one." Θανάτου, gen. sg. masc. θάνατος, -ου, ὁ,
"death." Either obj. gen. "that brings death" (CSB) or adj. gen. "one that deals in death"
(Furnish 202). Cf. Seifrid 151: "As Paul's language makes clear, the Law itself brings
death, and not merely Moses' deficient administration of it. The 'mission of death'
is engraved—ineffaceably—with letters in stones (*diakonia . . . entetypōmenē*). The
very content of the Law, its requirements and threats, appears here as 'the *diakonia* of
death.'" Ἐν, prep. with dat. of means γράμμασιν, "in letters." Γράμμασιν, dat. pl. neut.
γράμμα, -ατος, τό, "letter." Ἐντετυπωμένη, nom. sg. fem. of pf. pass. ptc. of ἐντυπόω,
"engrave." Λίθοις, dat. pl. masc. λίθος, -ου, ὁ, "stone," dat. of location. Ἐγενήθη, 3rd
sg. aor. pass. indic. of γίνομαι, "be, come to be." Moule 15: "the Aorist ἐγενήθη in v.
7 is strictly appropriate—of glory which is *past*; and the perfect οὐ δεδόξασται in v.
10 is its strictly correct correlative—of a glory which *no longer exists* because it is
superseded." Barnett 182, n. 20: "The historic gift of the Law is implied by the aorist
ἐγενήθη ἐν δόξῃ." Ἐν with δόξῃ (dat. sg. fem. δόξα, -ης, ἡ), dat. of attendant circumstances "in/with glory."

ὥστε μὴ δύνασθαι ἀτενίσαι τοὺς υἱοὺς Ἰσραὴλ εἰς τὸ πρόσωπον Μωϋσέως
so that the Israelites were not able to gaze steadily at Moses's face

Ὥστε, with inf. δύνασθαι, expresses result. Δύνασθαι, pres. mid. inf. of δύναμαι,"be
able." Ἀτενίσαι, aor. act. inf. of ἀτενίζω, "look steadily, gaze." A constative aorist
depicting an action as a whole, even though here it encompasses "the repeated inability
of the Israelites to keep their gaze focused on the shining brilliance (δόξα) of Moses'
face" (Harris 283). Cf. Seifrid 254: "The sense of the verb is that of 'looking intentionally' and not that of 'prolonging one's gaze,' although, of course, duration may be
incidental to such a beholding." Υἱούς, acc. pl. masc. υἱός, -οῦ, ὁ, "son," acc. subj. of
mid. inf. δύνασθαι. Ἰσραήλ, gen. sg. masc. proper noun, "Israel," descriptive gen. "sons
of Israel." Εἰς, prep with acc. τὸ πρόσωπον, denotes movement (of the gaze) toward
(Moses's) face. Πρόσωπον, acc. sg. neut. πρόσωπον, -ου, τό, "face." Μωϋσέως, gen. sg.
masc. proper noun Μωϋσῆς, "Moses," descriptive gen. "face *of Moses.*"

διὰ τὴν δόξαν τοῦ προσώπου αὐτοῦ τὴν καταργουμένην,
because of its glory, which was set aside,

Διά, with acc. τὴν δόξαν (acc. sg. fem. δόξα, -ης, ἡ) "because of the glory." Τοῦ προσώπου αὐτοῦ, poss. gen. "glory *of his face*." Καταργουμένην, acc. sg. fem. of pres. mid. ptc. of καταργέω, which has been variously translated: "set aside" (CSB, NRSV), "transitory" (NIV), "brought to an end" (ESV), "annulled" (Darby), "fading" (NASB, NLT), "made ineffective, inoperative" (NET, Hafemann 147), "vanishing" (Weymouth), "do away with" (Schreiner 155), and "invalidated" (Furnish 203). Τὴν καταργουμένην, BDAG 526a: "Subst . . . *what is transitory*." Implying the obsolescence of (the ministry of) the old covenant, cf. Barnett 181. Harris 285: "since the verb καταργέομαι appears as a neuter substantival participle in vv. 11 and 13 in reference to the era and order of the old covenant, it is relatively insignificant that Paul attaches the participle καταργουμένη to δόξα, not διακονία. The glory on Moses' face symbolizes the whole Mosaic dispensation, including its διαθήκη and διακονία."

VERSE 8

πῶς οὐχὶ μᾶλλον ἡ διακονία τοῦ πνεύματος ἔσται ἐν δόξῃ;
how will the ministry of the Spirit not be more glorious?

This clause is the apod. (in the form of a question) of the long cond. sentence (vv. 7–8) and completes the argument from the lesser to the greater (*qal wahomer*) begun in v. 7. Πῶς is the interr. particle "how?" Οὐχί is the strengthened form of neg. particle οὐ. Μᾶλλον, adv. "rather." Διακονία, nom. sg. fem. διακονία, -ας, ἡ, "ministry." Τοῦ πνεύματος, descriptive or adj. gen. "ministry *of the Spirit*," a ministry marked by the activity of the Spirit. Cf. Z §38. Ἔσται, 3rd sg. fut. act. indic. of εἰμί, "be." A logical rather than a temp. future (Harris 286). Ἐν, prep. with dat. δόξῃ, "in glory," signifying attendant circumstances. Δόξῃ, dat. sg. fem. δόξα, -ης, ἡ, "glory."

VERSE 9

This verse restates the comparison of ministries under the old and new covenant that is found in vv. 7–8, though the comparison is now stated in terms of ministries of condemnation and righteousness rather than of ministries of death and life.

εἰ γὰρ τῇ διακονίᾳ τῆς κατακρίσεως δόξα,
For if the ministry that brought condemnation had glory,

This clause functions as the prot. of a cond. sentence. Διακονίᾳ, dat. sg. fem. διακονία, -ας, ἡ, "ministry." One would normally expect the nom. case (διακονία) here, and there is some external evidence for this. However, cf. Metzger 509: "A majority of the committee, impressed by the weight of the external evidence supporting τῇ διακονίᾳ was inclined to regard the nominative as due to scribal assimilation to the preceding (and following) διακονία." Harris 287 says the dat. "may be classified as a dative of possession, a locative dative, or a dative of respect," and adopting the locative offers this translation: "For if there was glory *in the dispensation* that brought condemnation . . ." (italics added). Cf. Furnish 204: "with the ministry." Κατακρίσεως, gen. sg. fem. κατάκρισις, -εως, ἡ, "condemnation."

πολλῷ μᾶλλον περισσεύει ἡ διακονία τῆς δικαιοσύνης δόξῃ.
the ministry that brings righteousness overflows with even more glory.

This clause is the apod. of the cond. sentence begun in v. 9a. Πολλῷ μᾶλλον, BDAG 849a–b: *"much more, to a much greater degree."* Πολλῷ, dat. sg. neut. adj. πολύς, πολλή, πολύ, "much." Μᾶλλον, adv. "rather, more." Περισσεύει, 3rd sg. pres. act. indic. of περισσεύω, *"exceed, abound."* Τῆς δικαιοσύνης, obj. gen. "(ministry) that brings righteousness," i.e., justification, not condemnation, and leading to righteousness of life. Δικαιοσύνης, gen. sg. fem. δικαιοσύνη, -ης, ἡ, "righteousness." Δόξῃ, dat. sg. fem. δόξα, -ης, ἡ, "glory," "with glory" (cf. BDF §172).

VERSE 10

καὶ γὰρ οὐ δεδόξασται τὸ δεδοξασμένον
In fact, what had been glorious is not glorious now

Paul's point is that, compared with the greater glory of ministry under the new covenant, ministry under the old covenant appears to have no glory at all. Καὶ γάρ, intensive, "for indeed." CSB: "in fact." BDAG 496b: *"for even. . . ."* Οὐ δεδόξασται, "is not glorified." Δεδόξασται, 3rd sg. pf. pass. indic. of δοξάζω, "glorify." Τὸ δεδοξασμένον, "what had been glorified." R 1109: "The substantive use of the participle is a classic idiom." Seifrid 151: "This designation denotes that the apostle is not referring to the law (which in Greek is masculine), or to the glory of the old covenant itself (which in Greek is feminine), or even to the ministry of the glory as such (also feminine). Instead, the abstract or collective use of the neuter indicates that Paul's reference is the ministry of the old covenant as a whole, especially its theological purpose (v. 9a), results (v. 7), and function (v. 6b)." Cf. Furnish 204: "The neuter (substantive) participle *what has had splendor* stands for ministry and the covenant of Moses." Δεδοξασμένον, nom. sg. neut. of pf. pass. ptc. of δοξάζω, "glorify."

ἐν τούτῳ τῷ μέρει εἵνεκεν τῆς ὑπερβαλλούσης δόξης.
by comparison because of the glory that surpasses it.

Ἐν τούτῳ τῷ μέρει, "in this respect," cf. BDAG 633c: *"in this case, in this matter,"* CSB: "by comparison." Μέρει, dat. sg. neut. μέρος, -ους, τό, "part." BDAG 633c: "matter, affair." Εἵνεκεν, improper prep. with gen. "because of." Τῆς ὑπερβαλλούσης δόξης, "the surpassing glory." Ὑπερβαλλούσης, gen. sg. fem. of pres. act. ptc. of ὑπερβάλλω, "surpass," attrib. ptc. describing δόξα.

VERSE 11

εἰ γὰρ τὸ καταργούμενον διὰ δόξης, πολλῷ μᾶλλον τὸ μένον ἐν δόξῃ.
For if what was set aside was glorious, what endures will be even more glorious.

Τὸ καταργούμενον, ptc. phrase "what was set aside/transitory," referring to minis-try under the old covenant, and by implication the old covenant itself. Furnish 205: "In v. 7 the attributive participle *tēn katagoumenēn* (feminine) described the *splendor of [Moses'] face as being annulled.* Here, however, the neuter participle must be interpreted more generally (and in accord with the neuter substantive participle in v. 10 . . .) as applying to the entire ministry of the old covenant symbolized by Moses." Καταργούμενον, nom. sg. neut. of pres. pass. ptc. καταργέω, "set aside, pass away." Διά, prep. with gen. δόξης, "(came) through glory." R 583 gen. of means; ZG 540 gen. of attendant circumstances. Moule 58: "II Cor. iii.11 διὰ δόξης, practically = *glorious*" (cf. ibid, ἐν δόξῃ). Δόξης, gen. sg. fem. δόξα, -ης, ἡ, "glory."

Πολλῷ μᾶλλον, BDAG 849a–b: "*much more, to a much greater degree.*" Πολλῷ, dat. sg. neut. adj. πολύς, πολλή, πολύ, "much." Μᾶλλον, adv. "rather, more." Τὸ μένον, ptc. phrase "what endures," referring to ministry under the new covenant, and by implication the new covenant itself. BDAG 631d: "*what is permanent . . .* opp. τὸ καταργούμενον." Μένον, nom. sg. neut. of pres. act. ptc. of μένω, "remain, endure." Ἐν, prep. with dat. δόξῃ, "in glory," describing attendant circumstances. Some form of the verb εἰμί is understood, either the logical fut. ἔσται (as in v. 8) or the pres. ἐστίν. Δόξῃ, dat. sg. fem. δόξα, -ης, ἡ, "glory." Seifrid 160 distinguishes the sense of the two expres-sions, διὰ δόξης and ἐν δόξῃ: "That which has been abrogated came about 'through glory.' That which abides does so 'in glory.' Although there was divine glory to Moses' mission of death, that glory did not properly belong to it but only came *through* it. It was thus an 'alien' glory. In contrast, the abiding ministry of the Spirit and righteous-ness remains enveloped *in* the bright, divine glory that properly belongs to it."

e. The Greater Boldness of New Covenant Ministers (3:12–18)

Verses 12–18 are an exposition of Exod 34:33–35, which tells how Moses veiled his face after communicating God's law to the Israelites so that they would not see "the end of the glory of what was being set aside" (v. 13). In his exposition Paul stresses two matters: (1) the boldness with which he conducts his own ministry in contrast to the lack of boldness of Moses, who covered his face with a veil, and (2) believers, who with "unveiled faces" behold the glory of the Lord in the face of Christ, in contrast to his Jewish contemporaries, over whose hearts a veil lies whenever they hear the law of Moses read.

STRUCTURE

12   Ἔχοντες οὖν τοιαύτην ἐλπίδα
     πολλῇ παρρησίᾳ χρώμεθα

13   καὶ οὐ καθάπερ Μωϋσῆς ἐτίθει <u>κάλυμμα</u> ἐπὶ τὸ πρόσωπον
                               αὐτοῦ

                                              πρὸς τὸ μὴ ἀτενίσαι τοὺς υἱοὺς
                                              Ἰσραὴλ
                                                      εἰς τὸ τέλος
                                                      τοῦ καταργουμένου.

14   ἀλλ᾽ ἐπωρώθη τὰ νοήματα αὐτῶν.
                          ἄχρι γὰρ τῆς σήμερον ἡμέρας
     τὸ αὐτὸ <u>κάλυμμα</u>
                          ἐπὶ τῇ ἀναγνώσει τῆς παλαιᾶς διαθήκης
                          μένει
     μὴ <u>ἀνακαλυπτόμενον</u>
                     ὅτι ἐν Χριστῷ καταργεῖται·
15   ἀλλ᾽   ἕως σήμερον ἡνίκα ἂν ἀναγινώσκηται Μωϋσῆς,
              <u>κάλυμμα</u>   ἐπὶ τὴν καρδίαν αὐτῶν
                         κεῖται·
16   ἡνίκα δὲ ἐὰν ἐπιστρέψῃ πρὸς κύριον,
     περιαιρεῖται τὸ <u>κάλυμμα</u>.
17   ὁ δὲ κύριος τὸ <u>πνεῦμά</u> ἐστιν
            οὗ δὲ τὸ <u>πνεῦμα</u> κυρίου,
     ἐλευθερία.
18   ἡμεῖς δὲ πάντες
                                        <u>ἀνακεκαλυμμένῳ</u> προσώπῳ
                     τὴν δόξαν κυρίου κατοπτριζόμενοι
                     τὴν αὐτὴν εἰκόνα μεταμορφούμεθα
                                    ἀπὸ δόξης
                                    εἰς δόξαν
     καθάπερ ἀπὸ κυρίου <u>πνεύματος</u>.

VERSE 12

Ἔχοντες οὖν τοιαύτην ἐλπίδα πολλῇ παρρησίᾳ χρώμεθα
Since, then, we have such a hope, we act with great boldness.

Ἔχοντες, nom. pl. masc. of pres. act. ptc. of ἔχω, "have." Οὖν, inferential conj. mng. "therefore," looking back to vv. 7–11. Τοιαύτην, acc. sg. fem. pron. τοιοῦτος, αὕτη, οὗτον, "such, such as this." Ἐλπίδα, acc. sg. fem. ἐλπίς, -ίδος, ἡ, "hope," obj. of ἔχοντες. Τοιαύτην ἐλπίδα alludes to v. 11, the glory of what endures. Πολλῇ παρρησίᾳ, R 532: dat. of means. Harris 295: "With the same phrase . . . occurring in 7:4, where the 'confident frankness' is directed πρὸς ὑμᾶς (cf. Phlm. 8) it is likely that Paul's relation to other people is principally in mind, whether the Corinthians as representative of all his converts, his opponents at Corinth and elsewhere, or those to whom he proclaimed the gospel." Πολλῇ, dat. sg. fem. adj. πολύς, πολλή, πολύ, "great, much." Παρρησίᾳ, dat. sg. fem. παρρησία, -ας, ἡ, "boldness, confidence." Χρώμεθα, 1st pl. pres. mid. indic. of χράομαι, "act, use." Harris 295: "Although χρώμεθα could be a hortatory subjunctive ('let us act'), the parallel in 4:1 (ἔχοντες τὴν διακονίαν ταύτην . . . οὐκ ἐγκακοῦμεν) shows that Paul is making an affirmation, not giving an exhortation."

VERSE 13

καὶ οὐ καθάπερ Μωϋσῆς ἐτίθει κάλυμμα ἐπὶ τὸ πρόσωπον αὐτοῦ
We are not like Moses, who used to put a veil over his face

Οὐ καθάπερ Μωϋσῆς, (BDF §482): "Abbreviation is probably . . . to be assumed for the main clause in comparisons: 2 C 3:13 καὶ οὐ ('we do not do . . .') καθάπερ Μωϋσῆς etc." R 1159: "In comparative clauses with the indicative the negative comes outside in the principal sentence, since comparison is usually made with a positive note. So οὐ καθάπερ (2 Cor 3:13)." Καθάπερ, conj. "as, like." Ἐτίθει, 3rd sg. act. impf. indic. τίθημι, "put," impf. indicating linear action (cf. R 883). Κάλυμμα, acc. sg. neut. κάλυμμα, -ατος, τό, "veil," direct object of ἐτίθει. Ἐπί, prep. with acc. τὸ πρόσωπον, "over/upon the face." Πρόσωπον, acc. sg. neut. πρόσωπον, -ου, τό, "face."

πρὸς τὸ μὴ ἀτενίσαι τοὺς υἱοὺς Ἰσραὴλ εἰς τὸ τέλος τοῦ καταργουμένου.
to prevent the Israelites from gazing steadily until the end of the glory of what was being set aside,

Πρός, with the acc. (negated) articular inf. τὸ μὴ ἀτενίσαι expressing (neg.) purpose "to prevent the sons of Israel from gazing. . . ." Cf. R 1003, 1075. Harris 297 suggests the reason Moses veiled his face was "to prevent the people from being preoccupied with what they saw, from gazing in amazement, as opposed to giving attention to what they had heard." Ἀτενίσαι, aor. act. inf. ἀτενίζω, "look steadily, gaze." See comments on v. 7. Τοὺς υἱοὺς Ἰσραήλ, acc. subj. of inf. of ἀτενίσαι. Ἰσραήλ, gen. sg. masc. proper noun Ἰσραήλ, ὁ, gen. of relationship. Εἰς, prep. with acc. τὸ τέλος, "(gazing) at the end." Cf. ZG 540: *up to the end*, i.e. the parousia." Τὸ τέλος τοῦ καταργουμένου (gen. sg. neut. of pres. mid. ptc. of καταργέω, "set aside, pass away"): BDAG 998a: *"The end of the fading (splendor)."* Τέλος, -ους, τό, "end," may be construed as either "terminus" or "goal." Some scholars argue for the latter (e.g., Seifrid 164; Hafemann 155; Thrall 1:257), while others argue the former is required by the flow of Paul's thought here (e.g., Furnish 207; Barrett 119; Bultmann 85). Τοῦ καταργουμένου, neut. subst. ptc. καταργέω, "what is passing away/annulled." There are differences of opinion whether this should be understood as "fading" (e.g., Harris 299–300) or "annulled" (e.g., Furnish 207; Hafemann 164). See comment on v. 7. Καταργουμένου.

VERSE 14

ἀλλ᾽ ἐπωρώθη τὰ νοήματα αὐτῶν.
but their minds were hardened.

The purpose of these words appears to be to correct any impression that Moses was to blame for the Israelites' inability to behold the glory of the old covenant reflected in his face. He may have veiled his face, but it was the Israelites' minds that were dull (cf. Ps 95:8; Heb 3:8, 15; 4:7, wherein "hearts" is used instead of "minds"). Cf. Furnish 207. Ἀλλ᾽ (contraction of ἀλλά), conj. "but." Furnish 207: "The Greek *alla* should be regarded as a true adversative. As such it introduces a clarification, and, in a sense, a correction of the preceding reference to Moses' veiling himself before the Israelites: not that Moses sought to deceive; rather, their own minds were hardened.'" Cf. Barnett 192 n. 18: "However, the point of ἀλλά is to contrast those like Paul who now 'have such a hope' and are 'very open' (v. 12), i.e., 'unveiled' (v. 18), with those who remain blinded, without hope under the old covenant (v. 13)." Ἐπωρώθη, 3rd sg. aor. pass. indic. of πωρόω, "harden." Barnett 193 n. 19 describes it as an ingressive aorist: "became hardened." Harris 301: "ἐπωρώθη ('were hardened') may be a 'theological passive' with God as the implied agent (cf. Deut 29:4), but an element of human agency need not be excluded." Νοήματα, nom. pl. neut. νόημα, -ατος, τό, "mind," subj. of pass. verb ἐπωρώθη.

ἄχρι γὰρ τῆς σήμερον ἡμέρας τὸ αὐτὸ κάλυμμα ἐπὶ τῇ ἀναγνώσει τῆς παλαιᾶς διαθήκης μένει,
For to this day, at the reading of the old covenant, the same veil remains;

Ἄχρι γὰρ τῆς σήμερον ἡμέρας, NRSV: "Indeed, to this very day." Ἄχρι, prep. with gen. ἡμέρας, "until (this) day." Ἡμέρας, gen. sg. fem. ἡμέρα, -ας, ἡ, "day." Σήμερον, adv. "today." Τὸ αὐτὸ κάλυμμα, "the same veil"; αὐτό standing in the attrib. position functions adjectivally, mng. "the same." Κάλυμμα, nom. sg. neut. κάλυμμα, -ατος, τό, "veil, covering," subj. of μένει. Ἐπί, with dat. τῇ ἀναγνώσει, "upon/at the time of the reading." Harris 302: "If ἐπί is rendered 'upon (the reading),' the implication is that three veils are mentioned in this paragraph—a literal one over Moses' face (v. 13), a metaphorical one over the old covenant (= Scripture) when it is read (v. 14), and a metaphorical one over the hearts of Paul's Jewish contemporaries (v. 15)." Ἀναγνώσει, dat. sg. fem. ἀνάγνωσις, -εως, ἡ, BDAG 61c: "the process of reading." Παλαιᾶς διαθήκης, an expression found only here in the NT. It stands in contrast to καινῆς διαθήκης (v. 6), an expression Paul received as part of the Last Supper tradition (1 Cor 11:25). Παλαιᾶς, gen. sg. fem. adj. παλαιός, -ά, -όν, "old," BDAG 751c: "of long ago." Διαθήκης, gen. sg. fem. διαθήκη, -ης, ἡ, "covenant." Μένει, 3rd sg. pres. act. indic. of μένω, "remain."

μὴ ἀνακαλυπτόμενον ὅτι ἐν Χριστῷ καταργεῖται·
it is not lifted, because it is set aside only in Christ.

NIV: "It has not been removed, because only in Christ is it taken away"; NRSV: "that same veil is still there, since only in Christ is it set aside"; ESV: "that same veil remains unlifted, because only through Christ is it taken away."
Ἀνακαλυπτόμενον, nom. sg. neut. of pres. pass. ptc. of ἀνακαλύπτω, "lifted/removed." Barnett 193 n. 21 lists three options for the translation of ἀνακαλυπτόμενον:

"(1) '. . . the same veil remains unlifted, [the veil] *which* is abolished in Christ . . .
(2) 'the same veil remains; it is not revealed *that* it (the old covenant) is abolished
in Christ' . . . (3) 'the same veil . . . remains unlifted *because* [it is] in Christ that [it
is] abolished,'" and opts for the third option. Similarly, ZG 540 notes that some treat
"ἀνακαλυπτόμενον as nom. abs. μὴ ἀνακ. ὅτι ἐν Χριστῷ καταργεῖται '(the fact) not
having been revealed that in Christ (the old dispensation) is done away.'" Similarly,
Seifrid 169–70: The grammatical subject of the neuter, passive participle *mē anakalyptomenon* is not 'the veil' (*to kalymma*) but the following nominal clause (revealed that
. . . [*hoti*]), as is regularly the case after passive verbs of saying, communication, or
revelation. The last clause of v. 14 thus should be read: 'it not having been revealed [or
uncovered] that in Christ it [namely, the old covenant] is done away with.'"

Ἐν, with dat. Χριστῷ, "in Christ." Καταργεῖται, 3rd sg. pass. pres. indic. of καταργέω,
"remove, take away," possibly referring to the veil, but cf. Seifrid 170–71, who argues
that it refers to the old covenant, and summarizes his view: "The negated particle *mē
anakalyptomenon*, 'it not being uncovered,' serves as an adverbial modifier, interpreting the figure of the veil that lies on the reading of the old covenant. God has not (yet!)
uncovered (or revealed) to 'the sons of Israel' that the old covenant has been abrogated
in Christ."

VERSE 15

ἀλλ᾽ ἕως σήμερον ἡνίκα ἂν ἀναγινώσκηται Μωϋσῆς, κάλυμμα ἐπὶ τὴν καρδίαν αὐτῶν
κεῖται·
Yet still today, whenever Moses is read, a veil lies over their hearts,

Ἀλλ᾽ (contraction of ἀλλά) is the conj. "but," Furnish 210: "Indeed." Ἕως, adv.
"until." BDAG 423c: "w. adv. of time . . . ἕ. σήμερον [until today]." Σήμερον, adv.
"today." Ἡνίκα, particle denoting time "when," with ἂν, "whenever." BDF (§455[1])
classifies ἡνίκα as a temporal conj. "which strictly refers to an hour or season of the
year." Ἄν BDAG 56b: "A particle peculiar to Gk. (Hom.+) denoting *aspect of contingency,* incapable of translation by a single English word; it denotes that the action of
the verb is dependent on some circumstance or cond.; the effect of ἄν upon the meaning
of its clause depends on the mood and tense/aspect [here pres. subjunc.] of the verb w.
which it is used." Ἀναγινώσκηται, 3rd sg. pres. pass. subjunc. of ἀναγινώσκω, "read."
Μωϋσῆς, nom. sg. masc. proper noun "Moses," subj. of pass. verb ἀναγινώσκηται.
Μωϋσῆς here stands for the "Book of Moses" (cf. 2 Chr 25:4; Neh 13:1; Mark 12:26;
Acts 15:21).

Κάλυμμα, nom. sg. neut. κάλυμμα, -ατος, τό, "veil, covering," subj. of κεῖται. Ἐπί,
with acc. τὴν καρδίαν (αὐτῶν) "over/upon (their) heart(s)." Cf. R. 600–2. Καρδίαν,
acc. sg. fem. καρδία, -ας, ἡ, "heart." Κεῖται, 3rd sg. pres. mid. indic. of κεῖμαι, "lie
down."

VERSE 16

ἡνίκα δὲ ἐὰν ἐπιστρέψῃ πρὸς κύριον, περιαιρεῖται τὸ κάλυμμα.
but whenever a person turns to the Lord, the veil is removed.

Ἡνίκα, particle denoting time "when," with ἐάν, "whenever." R. 300 describes ἡνίκα as an adv. of time. Ἐπιστρέψῃ, 3rd sg. aor. act. subjunc. following ἐάν, ἐπιστρέφω, "turn, return." Comparing v. 16 with the text of Exod 34:34a, Harris 307 comments: "Whereas the imperfect εἰσεπορεύετο [of Exod 34:34a] depicts repeated entry (into 'the tent of meeting') in the past on the part of one person (Moses), the aorist ἐπιστρέψῃ signifies a single turning to the Lord in the future on the part of many persons. The change from εἰσπορεύεσθαι to ἐπιστρέφειν πρός was doubtless prompted by Paul's desire to express spiritual rather than physical movement." ZG 540: "in Ex 34:34 ref. Moses, but here the text is referred to the people of Israel as a whole; in Paul's mind Moses is a type prefiguring what is to come." The implied subj. of ἐπιστρέψῃ is best understood in light of v. 18 (ἡμεῖς . . . πάντες) to refer to any and all people who turn to the Lord, "apostles and non-apostles, Jews and non-Jews" (Harris 308). Πρός, prep. with acc. κύριον, "to the Lord," is best understood in the light of the allusion to Exod 34:34a, to mean turning to Yahweh (e.g., Furnish 211; Harris 308; Hafemann 160). Cf. Barnett 198–99: "Although 'Lord' is here frequently taken to mean Yahweh, as in the OT passage referred to, Paul's words in v. 14, 'because in Christ [the veil] is abolished' give a christological identification of the 'Lord' in this verse."

Περιαιρεῖται, 3rd sg. pres. pass. indic. of περιαιρέω, "take away, remove," the pass. voice implying the veil is removed by Yahweh. Κάλυμμα, nom. sg. neut. κάλυμμα, -ατος, τό, "veil, covering," subj. of pass. verb περιαιρεῖται.

VERSE 17

ὁ δὲ κύριος τὸ πνεῦμά ἐστιν· οὗ δὲ τὸ πνεῦμα κυρίου, ἐλευθερία.
Now the Lord is the Spirit, and where the Spirit of the Lord is, there is freedom.

Ὁ δὲ κύριος τὸ πνεῦμά ἐστιν is not to be taken as a comprehensive one-to-one identi-fication equating the Lord (God in his trinitarian fullness) with the Spirit (third pers. of the Trinity), but rather as a way of saying that under the new covenant people experi-ence/relate to the Lord/Yahweh as the Holy Spirit. Cf. Harris 312. Contra Barnett 202: "Since 'the Lord' to whom one 'turns' is 'the Lord Jesus Christ,' it must mean that 'the Spirit of the Lord' is his 'Spirit,' who must in turn be identified with 'the Spirit of the living God' referred to earlier in the chapter (v3). The Spirit of Christ is the Spirit of God (see Rom 8:9, 10)." Cf. Z §169: "In the much discussed text 2 Cor 3,17: ὁ δὲ Κύριος τὸ πνεῦμά ἐστιν, it would seem from the context that ὁ Κύριος means God, for verse 17 explains (δέ, cf. 467) verse 16, where the LXX is cited concerning the «con-version (of the Jews) to the Lord (πρὸς Κύριον)»."

Οὗ δὲ τὸ πνεῦμα κυρίου, ἐλευθερία.This statement must be understood within the overall context of chap. 3, where the new covenant of the Spirit is contrasted with the old covenant of the law. Under the new covenant where the Spirit is the operative power there is freedom. Under the old covenant, where the law reigns, there is bondage. The best commentary on this freedom is Gal 3:23–25, where the apostle describes the Jewish people as those "confined under the law," the law being their "guardian until Christ," but once they come to faith in Christ, they are no longer under the law's guardianship. Cf. Hafemann 161: "In our present passage, this positive result is a freedom *for* an obedience to the law that flows from the power of the Spirit as promised by Jeremiah and Ezekiel (2 Cor 3:3, 6)." Metzger 509: "In order to provide a correlative for οὗ ['where'] the Textus Receptus . . . inserts ἐκεῖ ['there'] before ἐλευθερία. The shorter reading is decisively supported by 𝔓⁴⁶ ℵ* A B C D* 33 424ᶜ 1912 itʳ syrᵖ copᵇᵒ; furthermore, the use of ἐκεῖ to balance οὗ is apparently not in Paul's style (cf. Rom 4:15; 5:20)." Ἐλευθερία, nom. sg. fem. ἐλευθερία, -ας, ἡ, "freedom."

VERSE 18

ἡμεῖς δὲ πάντες ἀνακεκαλυμμένῳ προσώπῳ τὴν δόξαν κυρίου κατοπτριζόμενοι
We all, with unveiled faces, are looking as in a mirror at the glory of the Lord

Ἀνακεκαλυμμένῳ, dat. sg. neut. of pf. pass. ptc. of ἀνακαλύπτω, "unveil, uncover," qualifying προσώπῳ. Harris 313: "The perfect participle ἀνακεκαλυμμένῳ stresses the permanence and irreversibility of their unveiled state." Προσώπῳ, dat. sg. neut. πρόσωπον, -ου, τό, "face." Ἀνακεκαλυμμένῳ προσώπῳ, descriptive dat., cf. R 891: "with unveiled face." Cf. ZG 540: "dat. of manner." Δόξαν, acc. sg. fem. δόξα, -ης, ἡ, "glory," direct obj. of κατοπτριζόμενοι. Τὴν δόξαν κυρίου refers to the glory of God/Yahweh, which in 4:6 Paul describes as "God's glory in the face of Jesus Christ." Cf. John 14:9b: "The one who has seen me has seen the Father. How can you say, 'Show us the Father'?" Κατοπτριζόμενοι, nom. pl. masc. of pres. mid. ptc. of κατοπτρίζω, "behold," BDAG 535b: "look at someth. as in a mirror, contemplate someth." The middle form of the verb *katoptrizō* generally means "to behold oneself or something as in a mirror," although there is evidence that it could also be used to mean "to reflect as in a mirror." However, the idea of beholding fits the context better. In Exod 34:33–35, which forms the basis of Paul's exposition, we are told that it was when Moses went in before the Lord that his face was unveiled, and at that time he was beholding, rather than reflecting, the glory of the Lord. Further, Paul's idea of being changed into his likeness from one degree of glory to another (v. 18b) is better understood to occur while believers are beholding rather than reflecting the glory of God. Cf. R 810: "κατοπτριζόμενοι . . . is probably 'beholding for ourselves in a mirror.'"

τὴν αὐτὴν εἰκόνα μεταμορφούμεθα ἀπὸ δόξης εἰς δόξαν
and are being transformed into the same image from glory to glory;

BDF (§159[4]) lists τὴν αὐτὴν εἰκόνα μεταμορφούμεθα as an instance of the acc. with the pass. and translates it as "into the same form." Harris 315: "In the active voice μεταμορφόω is followed by two accusatives, τινά τι, 'transform someone into something'; in the passive, the accusative of the thing is retained—here τὴν αὐτὴν εἰκόνα." Τὴν αὐτὴν εἰκόνα. Standing in the attrib. position, αὐτήν functions adjectivally mng. "the same." Εἰκόνα, acc. sg. fem. εἰκών, -όνος, ἡ, "image." Μεταμορφούμεθα, 1st pl. pres. mid. indic. μεταμορφόω, "transform, change." Barnett 207: "Significantly, the verbs, 'behold' and 'transformed' are both present tense, suggesting that the second occurs at the same time as—and as the result of—the first. As we behold, so we are transformed." Ἀπό, prep. with gen. δόξης, "from glory." Εἰς, prep. with acc. δόξαν, "to glory." Ἀπὸ δόξης εἰς δόξαν. Harris, Prepositions, 64–65: "The progressive nature of the Christian's present transformation is expressed by the phrase ἀπὸ δόξης εἰς δόξαν. . . . If the two prepositions [ἀπό and εἰς] together express the nature or direction of the μεταμόφωσις, the meaning will be 'with ever-increasing glory' (NIV, REB), or 'from one degree of glory to another (RSV, NRSV)." But cf. Barnett 208 n. 52: "The phrase ἀπὸ δόξης εἰς δόξαν is idiomatic for glory 'seen' initially in the world, within history, in and through the gospel, in relationship with that 'glory' which will be revealed eschatologically and which will be infinite and eternal."

καθάπερ ἀπὸ κυρίου πνεύματος.
this is from the Lord who is the Spirit.

NIV: "which comes from the Lord, who is the Spirit." ZG 541: "from the Lord (who is) the Spirit . . . also possible, from the Spirit of the Lord." But see BDF (§474[4]) where a rule that an attrib. gen. comes first is cited, and offers the translation of ἀπὸ κυρίου πνεύματος as "from the Spirit of the Lord." Cf. R 503: "In 2 Cor. 3:18, ἀπὸ κυρίου πνεύματος, it is not clear whether κυρίου is genitive or is the ablative in apposition with πνεύματος." But cf. Harris, Prepositions, 44: "If a preposition is followed by two anar. substantives both in the genitive case, the preposition always seems to qualify the former . . . Thus in 2C 3:18 ἀπὸ κυρίου πνεύματος is unlikely to mean 'by the Spirit of the Lord' . . . but rather means 'by the Lord [= Yahweh, 2C 3:16-17] who is [now experienced as] the Spirit.'"

Καθάπερ, conj. "as." Ἀπό, prep. with gen. sg. masc. κυρίου, "from the Lord," denoting agent (R 820). Harris 318: "If our interpretation of v. 17a is correct—'Now this "Lord" (= "Yahweh" in Exod. 34:34) is in the present era experienced as the Holy Spirit'—v. 18c may be seen as an abbreviated restatement of this: 'the Lord (= Yahweh), who is (now experienced as) the Spirit.'"

FOR FURTHER STUDY

37. Glory (3:7–11)

Baker, W. R. "Did the Glory of Moses' Face Fade? A Reexamination of Katargeō in 2 Corinthians 3:7–18." BBR 10 (2000): 1–15.

Belleville, L. L. *Reflections of Glory: Paul's Polemical Use of the Moses-Doxa Tradition in 2 Corinthians 3.1–18.* JSNTSup 52. Sheffield: JSOT Press, 1991.

Byrne, Brendan, "'Glory' as Apostolic Credibility in 2 Corinthians 2:14–4:18." *ABR* 66 (2018): 13-30.

Fitzmyer, J. A. "Glory Reflected on the Face of Christ (2 Cor 3:7–4:6) and a Palestinian Jewish Motif." *TZ* 42 (1981): 630–44. Reprinted in *According to Paul: Studies in the Theology of the Apostle*, 64–79. New York: Paulist, 1993.

Gaffin, R. B. *DPL* 348–50.

Hickling, C. J. A. "The Sequence of Thought in II Corinthians, Chapter Three." *NTS* 21 (1974–75): 380–95.

Wright, N. T. "Reflected Glory: 2 Corinthians 3:18." Pages 139–150 in *The Glory of Christ in the New Testament* (in memory of G. B. Caird). Edited by L. D. Hurst and N. T. Wright. Oxford: Oxford University Press, 1987.

38. Veiled and Unveiled Faces (3:12–16)

Garrett, D. A. "Veiled Hearts: The Translation and Interpretation of 2 Corinthians 3." *JETS* 53 (2010): 729–72.

Hafemann, S. J. "The Glory and Veil of Moses in 2 Cor 3:7–14: An Example of Paul's Contextual Exegesis of the OT—A Proposal." *HBT* 14 (1992): 31-49.

Stockhausen, C. K. *Moses' Veil and the Glory of the New Covenant: The Exegetical Substructure of II Cor. 3:1–4:6.* Analecta Biblica 116. Rome: Editrice Pontifico, Instituto Biblica, 1989.

van Unnik, W. C. "'With Unveiled Face,' an Exegesis of 2 Corinthians iii 12–18." *NovT* 6 (1963): 153–69.

39. Use of Scripture (3:14–16)

Dumbrell, W. J. "Paul's Use of Exodus 34 in 2 Corinthians 3." Pages 179–194 in *God Who is Rich in Mercy: Essays Presented to Dr. D. B. Knox.* Edited by Peter T. O'Brien and David G. Peterson. Grand Rapids: Baker, 1986.

Hanson, A. T. "Midrash in II Corinthians 3: A Reconsideration." *JSNT* 9 (1980): 2–23.

Hays, R. B. *Echoes of Scripture in the Letters of Paul.* New Haven: Yale University, 1989. See pp. 122–53.

Silva, M. *DPL* 630–42.

Sloan, R. B. "2 Corinthians 2:14-4:6 and 'New Covenant Hermeneutics'—A Response to Richard Hays." *BBR* (1995): 129–54.

40. Covenant (3:14)

Campbell, W. S. *DPL* 179–83.

Willimson, P. R. *NDBT* 419–29.

Wright, N. T. *The Climax of the Covenant: Christ and the Law in Pauline Theology.* Edinburgh: T&T Clark, 1991. See pp. 175–92.

41. The Law and the Spirit (3:15–18)

Grindheim, S. "The Law Kills but the Gospel Gives Life: The Letter-Spirit Dualism in 2 Corinthians 3.5–18." *JSNT* 84 (2001): 97–115.

Kruse, C. G. *NDBT* 629–36.

———. "Paul, the Law and the Spirit." Pages 109–30 in *Paul and his Theology*. Pauline
Studies 3. Edited by S. E. Porter. Leiden: Brill, 2006.

Westerholm, S. *Israel's Law and the Church's Faith: Paul and his Recent Interpreters*.
Grand Rapids: Eerdmans, 1988.

42. The Spirit Transformation (3:18)

Duff, P. B. "Transformed 'From Glory to Glory': Paul's Appeal to the Experience of His
Readers in 2 Corinthians 3:18." *JBL* 127 (2008): 759–80.

Dunn, J. D. G. "2 Corinthians III.17—'The Lord Is the Spirit.'" *JTS* n.s. 21 (1970):
309–20.

Fee, G. D. *God's Empowering Presence: The Holy Spirit in the Letters of Paul*. Peabody:
Hendrickson, 1994.

Moule, C. F. D. "2 Cor 3:18b." *Essays in New Testament Interpretation*, 227–34.
Cambridge: Cambridge University Press, 1982.

HOMILETICAL SUGGESTIONS

New Covenant Ministry (3:7–11)

1. A ministry of the Spirit, not of death (vv. 7–8)
2. A ministry of righteousness, not condemnation (v. 9)
3. A ministry that endures and is not put aside (v. 11)

New Covenant Ministers (3:12–18)

1. They act with boldness and transparency (vv. 12–13)
2. Through their preaching the Lord removes the veil preventing people from
   seeing his glory (vv. 14–16)
3. With their converts they are transformed as they behold the glory of the Lord
   (vv. 17–18)

f. The Conduct of Paul's Ministry (4:1–6)

In 3:7–18 Paul describes the glory of the ministry entrusted to him. It was a ministry of the Spirit, which brings life, righteousness, and transformation of character to those who believe the gospel. In 4:1–6 he tells how, in the light of the great privilege of participating in such a ministry, he conducted himself and proclaimed the gospel. He also tells why the minds of some were still blinded to his gospel, and he concludes by explaining the content of his gospel—Jesus Christ as Lord—and by affirming that the glory of God shines in the face of the Christ he proclaims.

STRUCTURE

1   Διὰ τοῦτο,

               ἔχοντες τὴν διακονίαν ταύτην
                   καθὼς ἠλεήθημεν,
          οὐκ ἐγκακοῦμεν

2   ἀλλ' ἀπειπάμεθα τὰ κρυπτὰ τῆς αἰσχύνης,
               μὴ περιπατοῦντες ἐν πανουργίᾳ
               μηδὲ δολοῦντες τὸν λόγον τοῦ θεοῦ
               ἀλλὰ   τῇ φανερώσει τῆς ἀληθείας
                συνιστάνοντες ἑαυτοὺς
                    πρὸς πᾶσαν συνείδησιν ἀνθρώπων
                    ἐνώπιον τοῦ θεοῦ.

3   εἰ δὲ καὶ ἔστιν <u>κεκαλυμμένον</u> τὸ εὐαγγέλιον ἡμῶν,
         ἐν τοῖς ἀπολλυμένοις
    ἐστὶν <u>κεκαλυμμένον</u>,

4   ἐν οἷς
    ὁ θεὸς τοῦ αἰῶνος τούτου ἐτύφλωσεν τὰ νοήματα
                         τῶν ἀπίστων
                   εἰς τὸ μὴ αὐγάσαι τὸν <u>φωτισμὸν</u>
                        τοῦ εὐαγγελίου
                        τῆς δόξης
                        τοῦ Χριστοῦ,

         ——————————————
         ὅς ἐστιν εἰκὼν τοῦ θεοῦ.

5   οὐ γὰρ ἑαυτοὺς κηρύσσομεν
    ἀλλ'   Ἰησοῦν Χριστὸν κύριον,
         ἑαυτοὺς δὲ δούλους ὑμῶν διὰ Ἰησοῦν

6   ὅτι ὁ θεὸς ὁ εἰπών,
               Ἐκ σκότους <u>φῶς</u> λάμψει,
       ὃς ἔλαμψεν
            ἐν ταῖς καρδίαις ἡμῶν
            πρὸς <u>φωτισμὸν</u> τῆς γνώσεως τῆς δόξης τοῦ θεοῦ
            ἐν προσώπῳ [Ἰησοῦ] Χριστοῦ.

VERSE 1

Διὰ τοῦτο, ἔχοντες τὴν διακονίαν ταύτην καθὼς ἠλεήθημεν, οὐκ ἐγκακοῦμεν
Therefore, since we have this ministry because we were shown mercy, we do not give up.

Διά, prep. with acc. τοῦτο, "because of this, therefore." Ἔχοντες, nom. pl. masc. of pres. act. ptc. of ἔχω, "have." Διακονίαν, acc. sg. fem. διακονία, -ας, ἡ, "ministry," obj. of ἔχοντες. Καθώς, causal conj. "because, in so far as." Ἠλεήθημεν, 1st pl. aor. pass. indic. of ἐλεέω, "show mercy." The apostle was very conscious that his participation in this ministry was only "because we were shown mercy," for he never forgot he was formerly a persecutor of the church of God (cf. 1 Cor 15:9–10; 1 Tim 1:12–16). Ἐγκακοῦμεν, 1st pl. pres. act. indic. of ἐγκακέω, "give up, become discouraged." This verb is found in four other places in Paul's letters (4:16; Gal 6:9; Eph 3:13; 2 Thess 3:13) and once in Luke 18:1. In each case the context indicates that the translation "lose heart" (ESV, NIV) or "give up" is appropriate. So, alternative translations such as "behave badly," appropriate in some extrabiblical texts, should not be adopted here (but cf. Seifrid 190, who interprets it as "moral failure"). Harris 323: "ἐγκακέω basically means 'behave badly,' especially in a cowardly (κακός) fashion or in reference to a culpable omission. It is a small step to the two NT meanings: 'become weary,' . . . 'lose heart'. That is, weariness and despair that lead to slackening of effort or neglect of duty are ways of 'conducting oneself remissly.'"

VERSE 2

In this verse Paul explains how he conducts his apostolic ministry, first negatively, by spelling out practices he rejects, then positively by emphasizing the godly practices he adopts.

ἀλλ᾽ ἀπειπάμεθα τὰ κρυπτὰ τῆς αἰσχύνης,
Instead, we have renounced secret and shameful things,

This is the first of the practices he rejects. Ἀπειπάμεθα, 1st pl. aor. mid. indic. of ἀπεῖπον, "renounce." The mid. conveys the sense of renouncing "for myself," cf. R 810. Harris 324: "The aorist ἀπειπάμεθα . . . is timeless: there was no time when it was not true that he had refused to adopt tactics unworthy of his calling." τὰ κρυπτὰ τῆς αἰσχύνης has been variously translated: e.g., CSB "secret and shameful things," NRSV "the shameful things that one hides," NIV "secret and shameful ways," ESV "disgraceful, underhanded ways." Harris 324 includes the following construals of the gen. αἰσχύνης in this phrase: epexegetical "the secrecy that means shame," possessive "the secretive practices of disgraceful conduct," and subjective "the secrecy prompted by shame," before opting for "underhand and disgraceful ways." Κρυπτά, acc. pl. neut. subst. adj. κρυπτός, -ή, -όν with article, "the hidden/secret things." Αἰσχύνης, gen. sg.

fem. αἰσχύνη, -ης, ἡ, "shame," descriptive gen. qualifying τὰ κρυπτά: "the secret things of shame," which are described in the following clause.

μὴ περιπατοῦντες ἐν πανουργίᾳ μηδὲ δολοῦντες τὸν λόγον τοῦ θεοῦ
not acting deceitfully or distorting the word of God,

This is the second of the practices Paul rejects. Περιπατοῦντες, nom. pl. masc. of pres. act. ptc. of περιπατέω, "walk, act, conduct oneself." Ἐν, with dat. πανουργίᾳ, "with deceit, deceitfully." Cf. 11:3: ὁ ὄφις ἐξηπάτησεν Εὕαν ἐν τῇ πανουργίᾳ αὐτοῦ ("the serpent deceived Eve by his cunning"). Cf. 12:16–18, where the apostle insists that he did not deceive the Corinthians in the matter of the collection in order to line his own pockets. Πανουργίᾳ, dat. sg. fem. πανουργία, -ας, ἡ, "deceit, cunning, craftiness. Δολοῦντες, nom. pl. masc. of pres. act. ptc. of δολόω, "distort, falsify," a verb found only here in the NT. Its use in the papyri in relation to the dilution of wine suggests that Paul had in mind the corruption of the word of God by mingling it with alien ideas (cf. 2:17). Τὸν λόγον, obj. of ptc. δολοῦντες. Τοῦ θεοῦ either subj gen. ("the word spoken by God") or possessive gen. ("God's word").

ἀλλὰ τῇ φανερώσει τῆς ἀληθείας
but . . . by an open display of the truth.

Here Paul states his positive practice, the opposite to distorting the truth; "an open display of the truth." Τῇ φανερώσει τῆς ἀληθείας, an instr. dat. phrase. BDAG 1049a: "[by] the open proclamation of the truth." Φανερώσει, dat. sg. fem. φανέρωσις, -εως, ἡ, "disclosure," BDAG 1049a: "open proclamation." Ἀληθείας, obj. gen. sg. fem. ἀλήθεια, -ας, ἡ, "truth."

συνιστάνοντες ἑαυτοὺς πρὸς πᾶσαν συνείδησιν ἀνθρώπων ἐνώπιον τοῦ θεοῦ.
commending ourselves before God to everyone's conscience

Here he further explains his approach to ministry. Συνιστάνοντες, nom. pl. masc. of pres. act. ptc. of συνίστημι, "commend." Barnett 215 n. 25: "The participle συνιστάνοντες is in consequence of the instrumental τῇ φανερώσει τῆς ἀληθείας. The manifestation of the truth in his life serves to commend him to the consciences of others (cf. 5:11)." Ἑαυτούς, acc. 1st pl. masc. refl. pron. ἑαυτοῦ, -ῆς, -οῦ, "ourselves," obj. of ptc. συνιστάνοντες. Πρός, prep. with acc. πᾶσαν συνείδησιν, "to every conscience." Πᾶσαν συνείδησιν, R 771: "In the singular πᾶς may be used without the article in the sense of 'every.'" So . . . πᾶσαν συνείδησιν ἀνθρώπων (2 Cor. 4:2). Συνείδησιν, acc. sg. fem. συνείδησις, -εως, ἡ, "conscience." See note on 1:12 for a comment on the mng. of συνείδησις. Ἀνθρώπων, possessive gen. pl. masc. ἄνθρωπος, -ου, ὁ, "man, human being." BDAG 81a–b: "a person of either sex." By the straightforward nature of his ministry, Paul invites the approval of everyone, convinced that when they judge him in the light of their own consciences, they will acknowledge that he has acted with integrity. Ἐνώπιον, prep. with gen. τοῦ θεοῦ, "before, in the sight of God." Paul, while concerned that the conduct of his ministry should commend itself to people's consciences, was concerned ultimately to minister in a way that finds God's approval. Comparing the placement of ἑαυτοὺς in 3:1 with that used in 4:2, Hafemann 176 n. 2 says this: "In the former, negative case it precedes the verb (*heautous synistanein*), in the latter it follows it (*synistanein heautous*)." Cf. comment on 3:1.

VERSE 3

εἰ δὲ καὶ ἔστιν κεκαλυμμένον τὸ εὐαγγέλιον ἡμῶν,
But if our gospel is veiled,

This is the prot. of a first-class cond. sentence (εἰ + indic. in the prot.), which assumes a situation is correct for the sake of argument (Forbes 153). Εἰ δὲ καί, Harris 326: "yet in fact." Barnett 215 n. 30: "A concessive construction" (i.e., "But even if . . ."). Ἔστιν κεκαλυμμένον periphrastic, pf. cstr. (pres. tense of εἰμί with pf. ptc.) emphasizing a present state of affairs. Cf. Moule 18. Harris 327: "'veiledness,' alludes to the use of κάλυμμα in 3:14–16." Κεκαλυμμένον, nom. sg. neut. of pf. pass. ptc. of καλύπτω, "veil, conceal." Εὐαγγέλιον, nom. sg. neut. "gospel, good news." Ἡμῶν subj. gen. 1st pl. masc. "the good news we proclaim." NLT: "The Good News we preach."

ἐν τοῖς ἀπολλυμένοις ἐστὶν κεκαλυμμένον,
it is veiled to those who are perishing.

This is the apod. of the cond. sentence. If Paul had been criticized because his gospel was hidden/veiled to many of his own people (cf. Acts 13:44–45; 17:5–9; 18:5–6, 12–31; 19:8–9), his response was that its hiddenness was due, not to deficiencies in his ministry, but to the cond. of the hearers: it is veiled only "to those who are perishing," cf. 1 Cor 1:18–25. Ἐν, prep. with dat. τοῖς ἀπολλυμένοις, "*to* those who are perishing (BDF §220[1])," or "*among* those who are perishing" (Barnett 217). Ἀπολλυμένοις, dat. pl. masc. of pres. mid. ptc. of ἀπόλλυμι, "perish." Ἐστὶν κεκαλυμμένον, see above.

VERSE 4

ἐν οἷς ὁ θεὸς τοῦ αἰῶνος τούτου ἐτύφλωσεν τὰ νοήματα τῶν ἀπίστων
In their case, the god of this age has blinded the minds of the unbelievers

Ἐν, prep. with dat. οἷς, lit. "in whom." ZG 541: "in whose case." Refers back to τοῖς ἀπολλυμένοις in v. 3, and "may be epexegetic ('to those who are perishing . . . that is, to those . . .') or resumptive ('in whose case . . .')," so, too, Harris 327. Ὁ θεὸς τοῦ αἰῶνος τούτου = Satan. Τοῦ αἰῶνος τούτου, obj. gen. "the one exercising power over this age." "This age" refers to the present age as opposed to "the coming age." Αἰῶνος, gen. sg. masc. αἰών, -ῶνος, ὁ; BDAG 32c: "the present age." Ἐτύφλωσεν, 3rd sg. aor. act. indic. of τυφλόω, "make blind." In 3:14–16 Paul spoke of the veil over the minds of his Jewish contemporaries, which prevented them from understanding their own

Scriptures. Here it is implied that Satan was involved in veiling the minds not only of Jewish people but of all unbelievers. Hafemann 177: "People are not blinded because they choose to renounce the gospel; rather, they choose to renounce the gospel because they are blind. And they are not blind because they choose to be so, but because Satan has made them so." Νοήματα, acc. pl. neut. νόημα, -ατος, τό, "mind, thought." Τῶν ἀπίστων, poss. gen. "minds of the unbelievers" = "the unbelievers' minds." Ἀπίστων, gen. pl. masc. subst. adj. ἄπιστος, -ον, "unbelieving (people)."

εἰς τὸ μὴ αὐγάσαι τὸν φωτισμὸν τοῦ εὐαγγελίου τῆς δόξης τοῦ Χριστοῦ, ὅς ἐστιν εἰκὼν τοῦ θεοῦ.
to keep them from seeing the light of the gospel of the glory of Christ, who is the image of God.

There is no equivalent to "them" in the Greek text, it being appropriately added by the CSB translators as an implied reference back to τῶν ἀπίστων earlier in the verse. Εἰς τὸ μὴ αὐγάσαι τὸν φωτισμὸν τοῦ εὐαγγελίου. Cf. Moule 143 fn. 2: "Note that in II Cor. iv.4 a real 'infatuation' such as prevents people seeing and accepting the truth is spoken of, and there a construction is used which is ambiguous, and might even, considered from the point of view of strict syntax, be either final [purpose] or consecutive [result]." When Paul says the god of this age prevents unbelievers (implied) from seeing the light of the gospel, he means that when they hear the gospel, they do not appreciate its truth. Jesus made a sim. point when, explaining the parable of the sower, he said of the seed that fell on the path: "Those along the path are the ones who hear, and then the devil comes and takes away the word from their hearts, so that they may not believe and be saved" (Luke 8:12 NIV). Εἰς, prep. with negated articular inf. τὸ μὴ αὐγάσαι, "to keep (unbelievers) from seeing." Αὐγάσαι, aor. act. inf. of αὐγάζω, "see." Φωτισμόν, acc. sing. masc. φωτισμός, -οῦ, ὁ, "light," obj. of αὐγάσαι. Τὸν φωτισμὸν τοῦ εὐαγγελίου τῆς δόξης τοῦ Χριστοῦ, R 503 says this is an example of a "Concatenation of Genitives. Two or more genitives may be used together . . . 2 Cor. 4:4." Cf. BDF (§168[2]): "Generally one genitive is dependent on another, whereby an author, particularly Paul, occasionally produces quite cumbersome accumulation of genitives; to facilitate clarity in such cases, the governing genitive must always precede the dependent genitive . . . : 2 C 4:4 τὸν φωτισμὸν τοῦ εὐαγγελίου ('the light emanating from the Gospel') τῆς δόξης (content) τοῦ Χριστοῦ." Z §47: "Where, as often happens in Paul, several genitives follow one another, each commonly depends upon the preceding one, e.g. 2 Cor 4,4 τὸν φωτισμὸν τοῦ εὐαγγελίου τῆς δόξης (objective genitive) τοῦ Χριστοῦ." Τοῦ εὐαγγελίου adj. gen. of source "light of the gospel." Εὐαγγελίου, see comments on v. 3. Τῆς δόξης, Harris 330: "probably a genitive of content ('the gospel that contains the glory'), or an objective genitive ('the gospel that displays the glory')." Τοῦ Χριστοῦ, poss. gen. "belonging to Christ."

Ὅς ἐστιν εἰκὼν τοῦ θεοῦ, rel. clause "who is the image of God," qualifying τοῦ Χριστοῦ. There may be allusions here to the creation of mankind in Gen 1:26 ("Then God said, 'Let us make mankind in our image, in our likeness,'" NIV) and to Wis 7:26 (NRSV), where Wisdom is personified and her glories celebrated: "For she is a reflection of eternal light, a spotless mirror of the working of God, and an image of his goodness" (Wis 7:26 NRSV). Bringing the two possible allusions together, it has been suggested that for Paul Christ is the image of God after the fashion of Adam as far as his humanity is concerned, and after the fashion of Wisdom as far as his transcendence is concerned. Εἰκών, nom. sg. fem. εἰκών, -όνος, ἡ, "image." Cf. Phil 2:6; Col 1:15. Τοῦ θεοῦ, descriptive gen. sg. masc. qualifying εἰκών.

VERSE 5

This verse could be understood as either apologetic or polemic, possibly even both. It would be apologetic if Paul is responding to criticism that in his preaching he puts himself forward, i.e., that he is more concerned about drawing attention to his own importance as an apostle than about proclaiming the gospel. It would be polemic if Paul is implying that, unlike others who do put themselves forward in their preaching, he preaches the lordship of Christ. Barrett 134 comments: "It would be hard to describe the Christian ministry more comprehensively in so few words."

οὐ γὰρ ἑαυτοὺς κηρύσσομεν ἀλλ' Ἰησοῦν Χριστὸν κύριον,
For we are not proclaiming ourselves but Jesus Christ as Lord,

Οὐ . . . ἀλλά indicates a sharp antithesis (R 1187). Γάρ, explanatory conj. Harris 331: "He may wish to prevent anyone from concluding that 'our gospel' (v. 3) meant 'the gospel about us.' But far more probably his train of thought is this: 'If the gospel proclaims the glory of Christ (v. 4b) and we preach the gospel (v. 3), that means we proclaim the glory of Christ, that is, Jesus Christ as Lord, Jesus Christ as risen and glorified.'" Ἰησοῦν Χριστὸν κύριον: a concise statement of the content of Paul's proclamation. Ἑαυτούς, acc. 3rd pl. masc. refl. pron. ἑαυτοῦ, -ῆς, -οῦ, "ourselves," dir. obj. of κηρύσσομεν. Κηρύσσομεν, 1st pl. pres. act. indic. of κηρύσσω, "preach, proclaim." Ἀλλ' (contraction of ἀλλά), adversative conj., "but, on the contrary."

Ἰησοῦν Χριστὸν κύριον, double acc. (Ἰησοῦν Χριστὸν and κύριον) dir. obj. of an implied κηρύσσομεν. Harris 331–32: "The word order (Ἰησοῦν Χριστὸν κύριον not κύριον Ἰησοῦν Χριστὸν) and the parallel expression that follows (ἑαυτοὺς . . . δούλους, which can only mean 'ourselves as slaves') show that κύριον is predicative, 'Jesus Christ as Lord.'" Metzger 509–10: "Good representatives of both the Alexandrian and the Western texts . . . join in support of the reading Ἰησοῦν [acc.]. An early variant reading, Ἰησοῦ [gen.], also makes good sense, but is slightly less well supported. . . . The other readings, which involve the word 'Christ,' are obviously secondary."

ἑαυτοὺς δὲ δούλους ὑμῶν διὰ Ἰησοῦν.
and ourselves as your servants for Jesus's sake.

Ἑαυτούς . . . δούλους is a double acc. dir. obj. of an implied κηρύσσομεν. Ἑαυτούς, see above. Δούλους, acc. pl. masc. δοῦλος, -ου, ὁ, "servant, slave." Διά, prep. with acc. Ἰησοῦν, "for Jesus's sake." Contrary to any idea that in his preaching he promoted his own authority and importance, Paul says he regards himself as the servant/slave of those to whom he preaches. But this must not be misunderstood to mean that they are his masters any more than he is theirs (cf. 1:24). Paul acknowledges only one Master, and it is in obedience to him that he serves his converts—"διὰ Ἰησοῦν, for Jesus' sake." Cf. Seifrid 199: "The concluding causal clause, *dia Iēsoun*, might be taken retrospectively [on account of Jesus] . . . or prospectively ('for Jesus' sake') . . . The former reading is more likely, since in v. 1, and again in the following explanatory statement in v. 6, Paul describes himself in a passive role."

VERSE 6

This verse very possibly reflects Paul's encounter with the risen Christ on the Damascus Road (cf. Acts 9:3–6; 22:6–11; 26:12–18).

ὅτι ὁ θεὸς ὁ εἰπών, Ἐκ σκότους φῶς λάμψει,
For God who said, "Let light shine out of darkness,"

Ὅτι is the conj. "because, for," introducing a sentence in which Paul describes his motivation for preaching Jesus Christ as Lord, and himself as a servant/slave for the Corinthians; i.e., he has received a revelation from God of the glory of Christ and feels under obligation to and has the privilege of sharing this with others. Ὁ θεὸς ὁ εἰπών is a ptc. phrase (with the ptc. in the attrib. position), "the God who said." R 764: "The article with the participle is very common as the equivalent of a relative clause." Εἰπών, nom. sg. masc. of aor. act. ptc. of λέγω, "say."

Ἐκ is a prep. with gen. σκότους "out of darkness." Σκότους, gen. sg. neut. σκότος, -ους, τό, "darkness." Λάμψει, 3rd sg. fut. act. indic. intrans. of λάμπω, "shine." The CSB construes the fut. λάμψει as an impv., "Let light shine" (legitimate as the fut. functions this way frequently in the NT). Cf. BDAG 586a: "Of the light that shone forth at creation by God's command." However, construing it as a simple fut. is also possible, in which case it could allude to the prophecy concerning the land of Zebulun and Naphtali in Isa 9:2: "The people walking in darkness have seen a great light; a light has dawned on those living in the land of darkness." This text is taken up and applied to the ministry of Jesus in Matt 4:15–16 and Luke 1:79.

ὃς ἔλαμψεν ἐν ταῖς καρδίαις ἡμῶν
has shone in our hearts

Rel. clause further qualifying ὁ θεός: "who has shone in our hearts." Ἔλαμψεν, 3rd sg. aor. act. indic. intrans. of λάμπω, "shine." Ἐν, prep. with dat. ταῖς καρδίαις: "in the (our) hearts," locat. indicating where the light shone. Καρδίαις, dat. pl. fem. καρδία, -ας, ἡ, "heart."

πρὸς φωτισμὸν τῆς γνώσεως τῆς δόξης τοῦ θεοῦ ἐν προσώπῳ [Ἰησοῦ] Χριστοῦ.
to give the light of the knowledge of God's glory in the face of Jesus Christ.

Πρός is a prep. with acc. φωτισμόν stating purpose: "give light." Φωτισμόν, acc. sg. masc. φωτισμός, -οῦ, ὁ, "light, enlightenment, bringing to light"; cf. BDAG 1074d. Τῆς γνώσεως, gen. of source ("light coming from knowledge"), or possibly obj. gen. ("light producing knowledge"); cf. Harris 335. Τῆς δόξης, obj. gen. ("light revealing the glory"). Τοῦ θεοῦ, poss. gen. ("the glory belonging to God"). Ἐν is a prep. with dat. προσώπῳ "in (the) face." Moule 184: "in translating ἐν προσώπῳ the problem arises when to take it literally: in II Cor. ii.10 it seems only to mean in the presence of, but in II Cor. iv.6 it may mean literally in the face (countenance) or person." Προσώπῳ, dat. sg. neut. πρόσωπον, -ου, τό, "face." [Ἰησοῦ] Χριστοῦ, Metzger 510: "There are three variants: (a) Ἰησοῦ Χριστοῦ . . . (b) Χριστοῦ . . . and (c) Χριστοῦ Ἰησοῦ . . . On the basis of what was regarded as superior external support a majority of the Committee preferred the reading Ἰησοῦ Χριστοῦ. At the same time, in view of the evidence supporting the shorter reading, it was decided to enclose Ἰησοῦ within square brackets." Barnett 224: "There is an outward as well as an inward aspect here. Outwardly, on the way to Damascus, Paul saw 'the glory of God in the face of Christ'; inwardly, and as consequence, 'God has shone in our hearts' (cf. 'God revealed his son in me'—Gal 1:16)."

FOR FURTHER STUDY

43. Ministry (4:1)

Cranfield, C. E. B. "Minister and Congregation in the Light of II Corinthians 4:5–7: An Exposition." *Int* 19 (1965): 163–67.

Hanson, A. T. *The Pioneer Ministry.* London: SCM, 1967. See pp. 72–75.

Kruse. C. G. *DPL* 602–8.

———. *New Testament Models for Ministry: Jesus and Paul.* Nashville: Thomas Nelson, 1985.

———. *DPL* 869–71.

44. Mercy (4:1)

Bultmann, R. *TDNT* 2.477–487.

Esser, H. H. *NIDNTT* 2.593–601.

Grundmann, W. *TDNT* 3.486.

Morris, L. *DPL* 601–602.

45. Conscience (4:2)

Eckstein, H.- J. *Der Begriff Syneidesis bei Paulus.* WUNT 2/10. Tübingen: Mohr Siebeck, 1983.

Gundry-Volf, J. M. *DPL* 153–56.

Marietta, D. E. "Conscience in Greek Stoicism." *Numen* 17 (1970): 176–87.

Maurer, C. *TDNT* 7.898–919.

Sevenster, J. N. *Paul and Seneca.* NovTSup 4. Leiden: Brill, 1961. See pp. 84–102.

Thrall, M. E. "The Pauline Use of SYNEIDHSIS." *NTS* 14 (1967–68): 118–25.

46. The God of This World (4:4)

Garrett, S. R. "The God of This World and the Affliction of Paul: 2 Cor. 4:1–12." In *Greeks, Romans, and Christians: Essays in Honor of Abraham J. Malherbe*, edited by D. L. Balch, et. al., 99–117. Minneapolis: Fortress, 1990.

Stockhausen, C. K. *Moses' Veil and the Glory of the New Covenant: The Exegetical Substructure of II Cor. 3:1–4:6.* Analecta Biblica 116. Rome: Editrice Pontifico, Instituto Biblica, 1989.

Uddin, M. "Paul, the Devil and 'Unbelief' in Israel (with Particular Reference to 2 Corinthians 3–4 and Romans 9–11)." *TynB* 50 (1999): 265–80.

47. The Knowledge of God's Glory in the Face of Christ (4:6)

Fitzmyer, J. A. "Glory Reflected on the Face of Christ (2 Cor 3:7–4:6) and a Palestinian Jewish Motif." *TZ* 42 (1981): 630–44. Reprinted in *According to Paul: Studies in the Theology of the Apostle*, 64–79. New York: Paulist, 1993.

Kim, S. *The Origin of Paul's Gospel.* WUNT 2. Reihe. Vol. 4. Tübingen: J. C. Mohr (Paul Siebeck), 1981. See pp. 6–13, 137–268.

HOMILETICAL SUGGESTIONS

How to Conduct the Glorious Ministry of the Gospel (4:1–6)

1. A ministry based on the experience of the mercy of God (v. 1).
2. Integrity in ministry (v. 2)
3. Spiritual blindness and the god of this age (vv. 3–4a)
4. The glorious light of the gospel (v. 4b)
5. The importance of proclaiming Christ and not promoting ourselves (v. 5)
6. God's "creative" act in giving people the light of his glory in the face of Christ (v. 6)

4. Present Suffering and Future Glory (4:7–5:10)

Having spoken of the glorious ministry in which he was privileged to participate in 3:1–4:7, and especially the light of the glory of God that has shone in his heart in 4:6, here in 4:7–5:10 Paul explains that he experiences all this in the context of suffering and weakness, but with the prospect of future glory.

a. Treasure in Jars of Clay (4:7–15)

He states this as a general principle in 4:7, illustrates it in 4:8–9, restates it as a principle in 4:10–12, and adds that despite all the difficulties, he continues to operate in a "spirit of faith" in 4:13–15.

STRUCTURE

7   Ἔχομεν δὲ τὸν θησαυρὸν τοῦτον
            ἐν ὀστρακίνοις σκεύεσιν,
                    ἵνα ἡ ὑπερβολὴ τῆς δυνάμεως ᾖ τοῦ θεοῦ
                                    καὶ μὴ ἐξ ἡμῶν·
8   ἐν παντὶ
        θλιβόμενοι   ἀλλ' οὐ στενοχωρούμενοι,
        ἀπορούμενοι   ἀλλ' οὐκ ἐξαπορούμενοι,
9   διωκόμενοι   ἀλλ' οὐκ ἐγκαταλειπόμενοι,
        καταβαλλόμενοι ἀλλ' οὐκ ἀπολλύμενοι,
10   πάντοτε τὴν νέκρωσιν τοῦ Ἰησοῦ
                 ἐν τῷ σώματι
        περιφέροντες,
                 ἵνα καὶ ἡ ζωὴ τοῦ Ἰησοῦ ἐν τῷ σώματι ἡμῶν φανερωθῇ.
11 ἀεὶ γὰρ ἡμεῖς οἱ ζῶντες   εἰς θάνατον
                            παραδιδόμεθα
                                    διὰ Ἰησοῦν,
                 ἵνα καὶ ἡ ζωὴ τοῦ Ἰησοῦ φανερωθῇ
                                    ἐν τῇ θνητῇ σαρκὶ ἡμῶν.
12   ὥστε ὁ θάνατος ἐν ἡμῖν ἐνεργεῖται,
                 ἡ δὲ ζωὴ ἐν ὑμῖν.
13   ἔχοντες δὲ τὸ αὐτὸ πνεῦμα τῆς πίστεως
                         κατὰ τὸ γεγραμμένον,
                                    Ἐπίστευσα, διὸ ἐλάλησα,
        καὶ ἡμεῖς πιστεύομεν,
        διὸ καὶ λαλοῦμεν,
14   εἰδότες
                 ὅτι ὁ ἐγείρας τὸν κύριον Ἰησοῦν
                         καὶ ἡμᾶς σὺν Ἰησοῦ ἐγερεῖ
                         καὶ παραστήσει σὺν ὑμῖν.
15 τὰ γὰρ πάντα δι' ὑμᾶς,
        ἵνα ἡ χάρις πλεονάσασα

διὰ τῶν πλειόνων
τὴν εὐχαριστίαν περισσεύσῃ
εἰς τὴν δόξαν τοῦ θεοῦ.

VERSE 7

Ἔχομεν δὲ τὸν θησαυρὸν τοῦτον ἐν ὀστρακίνοις σκεύεσιν,
Now we have this treasure in clay jars,

Ἔχομεν, 1st pl. pres. act. indic. of ἔχω, "have." Δέ either serves as a simple transition or perhaps denotes the contrast between "the light of the knowledge of God's glory in the face of Jesus Christ" that has shone in believers' hearts (v. 6) and the "clay jars" in which it is manifest. Θησαυρόν, acc. sg. masc. θησαυρός, -οῦ, ὁ, "treasure," referring to the light of the knowledge of God's glory (v. 6). Ἐν is a prep. with dat. σκεύεσιν, "in jars." Σκεύεσιν, dat. pl. neut. σκεῦος, -ους, τό, "jar." Ὀστρακίνοις, dat. pl. neut. adj. ὀστράκινος, -η, -ον, "made of clay," qualifying σκεύεσιν. Clay jars were found in virtually every home in the ancient Middle East. They were inexpensive and easily broken, and once broken, they had to be discarded. They were thus cheap and of little intrinsic value. Paul may have had in mind the small earthenware oil lamps sold so cheaply in the marketplaces. If so, "the light of the knowledge of God's glory in the face of Christ" (v. 6) would be the treasure, while the apostles in their frailty would be the earthenware lamps from whom the light was made to shine in the world. Seifrid 205: "The 'earthen vessel' that bears the treasure is the *whole* of Paul's bodily life. The 'body' is not merely an external, dispensable part of him."

ἵνα ἡ ὑπερβολὴ τῆς δυνάμεως ᾖ τοῦ θεοῦ καὶ μὴ ἐξ ἡμῶν·
so that this extraordinary power may be from God and not from us.

This is prob. a purpose clause indicating why the treasure of "the light of the knowledge of God's glory in the face of Jesus Christ" is entrusted to human vessels "made of clay." It has positive and negative elements: "from God" and "not from us." Ἵνα with subjunc. ᾖ (3rd sg. pres. subjunc. of εἰμί) expresses purpose: "may be." Alternatively it could express result: "is." Ὑπερβολή, nom. sg. fem. ὑπερβολή, -ῆς, ἡ, BDAG 1032d: "extraordinary quality." Ἡ ὑπερβολὴ τῆς δυνάμεως, lit. "the extraordinary quality of the power." NIV: "this all-surpassing power." Δυνάμεως, gen. sg. fem. δύναμις, -εως, ἡ, "power" descriptive gen. Τοῦ θεοῦ, gen. of source. Cf. R 497 (514), where it is classified as a predicate (ablative) gen. of origin following the copulative ᾖ. Ἐξ is a prep. with gen. ἡμῶν, gen. of source "from us." Μή is a neg. particle negating an implied subjunc. ᾖ (καὶ μὴ [ᾖ] ἐξ ἡμῶν).

VERSE 8

The general principle enunciated in v. 7 is illustrated in vv. 8–9 by "four balanced antitheses" (Harris 342). These reflect the vulnerability of Paul and his coworkers on the one hand and the power of God, which sustains them, on the other. Harris 342–43 notes, "Although participles are generally negated by μή in NT Greek, here four occurrences of οὐ are found. This apparent irregularity may be explained in two ways: οὐ is negating a single concept, and examples of οὐ with a participle in the papyri reflect 'the lingering consciousness that the proper negative for a statement of a downright fact is οὐ.'"

ἐν παντὶ θλιβόμενοι ἀλλ᾽ οὐ στενοχωρούμενοι,
We are afflicted in every way but not crushed;

Ἐν is a prep. with the dat. παντί, "in every way." Θλιβόμενοι, nom. pl. masc. of pres. pass. ptc. of θλίβω, "afflict, hard press." Οὐ στενοχωρούμενοι, the ptc. is negated with οὐ, not μή, which is unusual, though οὐ is found about twenty times with the participle in the NT (cf. BDF §430[3], Moule 105). Στενοχωρούμενοι, nom. pl. masc. of pres. pass. ptc. of στενοχωρέω, "crush, distress." The ptc. θλιβόμενοι and στενοχωρούμενοι are sim. in mng., but in this context the latter clearly represents an intensification of the experience of affliction referred to in the former. Paul's point is that while God allows him to be hard-pressed, by his power at work in his life God saves him from being completely crushed.

ἀπορούμενοι ἀλλ᾽ οὐκ ἐξαπορούμενοι,
we are perplexed but not in despair;

This an example of paronomasia, the recurrence of the same word or word stem in close proximity, in this case to make a contrast; cf. BDF (§488[1.b]). Ἀπορούμενοι, nom. pl. masc. of pres. mid. ptc. of ἀπορέω, "be perplexed, bewildered." Ἐξαπορούμενοι, nom. pl. masc. of pres. mid. ptc. of ἐξαπορέω, "be in despair, at a loss." The ptc. ἐξαπορούμενοι is a compound form and expresses an intensification of ἀπορούμενοι. Paul's point again is that while he is often perplexed, because of God's power at work in his life he does not succumb to despair. Commenting on the apparent contradiction between this statement and Paul's reference to despairing of life itself in 1:8, Thrall 1:327–28 suggests that he may have learned from the past experience referred to in 1:8 not to despair completely (as he says in 1:9: "this happened that we might not rely on ourselves but on God," NIV).

VERSE 9

διωκόμενοι ἀλλ᾽ οὐκ ἐγκαταλειπόμενοι,
we are persecuted but not abandoned;

Διωκόμενοι, nom. pl. masc. of pres. pass. ptc. of διώκω, "persecute." Ἐγκαταλειπόμενοι, nom. pl. masc. of pres. pass. ptc. of ἐγκαταλείπω, "abandon," BDAG 273b: "forsake, abandon, desert." The verb ἐγκαταλείπω is used by Paul of Demas, who abandoned Paul when he was in prison (2 Tim 4:10) and of those who abandoned him at his first defense before Caesar (2 Tim 4:16). It is also the word Jesus used when abandoned by God on the cross (Matt 26:46). Paul's point is that while he was often persecuted in the course of his ministry, he was never abandoned by God.

καταβαλλόμενοι ἀλλ᾿ οὐκ ἀπολλύμενοι,
we are struck down but not destroyed.

Καταβαλλόμενοι, nom. pl. masc. of pres. pass. ptc. of καταβάλλω, "strike down." Harris 344: "καταβάλλω was a technical term in wrestling ('throw down'), in boxing ('knock down') and in battle ('strike down')." Ἀπολλύμενοι, nom. pl. masc. of pres. mid. ptc. of ἀπόλλυμι, "destroy." The allusion here may be a military one—a soldier struck down but not killed by his opponent.

VERSE 10

πάντοτε τὴν νέκρωσιν τοῦ Ἰησοῦ ἐν τῷ σώματι περιφέροντες,
We always carry the death of Jesus in our body,

Πάντοτε is the adv. "always." Νέκρωσιν, acc. sg. fem. νέκρωσις, -εως, ἡ, "death," dir. obj. of ptc. περιφέροντες. BDAG 668c–d: "death as process, *death, putting to death.*" Seifrid 207: "The term *nekrōsis* is best translated 'deadness,' expressing an enduring state, rather than as 'death' (ESV, NIV, NRSV), which might be taken to signify merely a past event." Ἐν with locat. dat. τῷ σώματι indicating where "the death of Jesus" is experienced. Σώματι, dat. sg. neut. σῶμα, -ατος, τό, "body." Περιφέροντες, nom. pl. masc. of pres. act. ptc. of περιφέρω, "carry about." BDAG 808a: "*carry about, carry here and there.*" Harris 346: "Like the participles in vv. 8–9, περιφέροντες should be treated as asyntactically independent, functioning as an indicative."

The death/dying of Jesus is best understood as all his afflictions that culminated in his death. In like manner Paul's carrying around the death/dying of Jesus may be understood as all his apostolic sufferings that would culminate in his martyrdom. Thrall 1:332–34 lists three interpretations of how Paul carried the death of Jesus in his body: "(i) Paul suffers as Jesus suffered . . . (ii) At baptism the believer is united with the death of Christ . . . (iii) the νέκρωσις of Jesus may be primarily revelational. The apostolate is the earthly manifestation of the gospel, and apostolic suffering plays a part in this." Thrall says the third of these makes the best sense.

ἵνα καὶ ἡ ζωὴ τοῦ Ἰησοῦ ἐν τῷ σώματι ἡμῶν φανερωθῇ.
so that the life of Jesus may also be displayed in our body.

Ἵνα with subjunc. φανερωθῇ expresses purpose. Ζωή, nom. sg. fem. ζωή, -ῆς, ἡ, "life." Σώματι, see above. Φανερωθῇ, 3rd sg. aor. pass. indic. of φανερόω, "display, reveal, make known." Harris 346–47: "ἡ ζωὴ τοῦ Ἰησοῦ refers to the immortal life of the risen Jesus, not the earthly life of the historical Jesus. It is both the life that belongs

to Jesus (possessive genitive) by virtue of his resurrection (Rom. 6:9–10) and the life
that is imparted by Jesus (subjective genitive) through his Spirit (3:6; Rom. 8:2)."

VERSE 11

ἀεὶ γὰρ ἡμεῖς οἱ ζῶντες εἰς θάνατον παραδιδόμεθα διὰ Ἰησοῦν,
For we who live are always being given over to death for Jesus's sake,

This verse is essentially an unpacking of the antithesis found in v. 10, the substitution of θάνατον and σαρκί in v. 11 for νέκρωσιν and σώματι in v. 10 being stylistic
rather than substantial. So, then, "being given over to death for Jesus's sake" (v. 11)
is equivalent to "carry the death of Jesus in our body" (v. 10), and "so that Jesus's life
may also be displayed in our mortal flesh" (v. 11) parallels "so that the life of Jesus
may also be displayed in our body" (v. 10). It also expresses the purpose for which "the
death of Jesus" is carried about in the apostle's "body"—that Jesus's life may also be
displayed in his body.
Ἀεί is the adv. "always," sim. to πάντοτε in v. 10. Ἡμεῖς οἱ ζῶντες means "we who
live" or "while we live." Ζῶντες, nom. pl. masc. of pres. act. ptc. of ζάω, "live." Εἰς
with acc. θάνατον, "to death." Παραδιδόμεθα, 1st pl. pres. pass. indic. of παραδίδωμι,
"give over, hand over [here, to death]," used by Jesus in Mark 9:31 and 10:33 of his
being handed over to death. Διά with acc. Ἰησοῦν, "for Jesus' sake," cf. BDAG 225c.

ἵνα καὶ ἡ ζωὴ τοῦ Ἰησοῦ φανερωθῇ ἐν τῇ θνητῇ σαρκὶ ἡμῶν.
so that Jesus's life may also be displayed in our mortal flesh.

This clause explains the purpose for which the apostle is "being given over to death
for Jesus's sake," and repeats what is found in v. 10b. Ἵνα with subjunc. φανερωθῇ
expresses purpose "so that (Jesus's life) may be displayed." Φανερωθῇ, see note on v.
10b. Ἐν is a prep. with dat. τῇ θνητῇ σαρκί, "in [our] mortal flesh"; cf. ἐν τῷ σώματι
ἡμῶν in v. 10. Θνητῇ, dat. sg. fem. adj. θνητός, -ή, -όν, "mortal, subject to death."
Σαρκί, dat. sg. fem. σάρξ, σαρκός, ἡ, "flesh." Harris 349: "Paul evidently saw a parallelism between Jesus' life of suffering and his own. This would account for three
distinctive features of vv. 10–11: his use of νέκρωσις ('dying') rather than θάνατος
('death,' v. 10a), his choice of the evocative verb παραδίδωμι, and the four uses of the
simple name Ἰησοῦς."

VERSE 12

ὥστε ὁ θάνατος ἐν ἡμῖν ἐνεργεῖται, ἡ δὲ ζωὴ ἐν ὑμῖν.
So then, death is at work in us, but life in you.

This clause explains in general terms the result of "being given over to death for
Jesus's sake so that Jesus's life may be displayed in our mortal flesh" (v. 11); i.e., it
led to life for others. Harris 350: "Here his thought seems to be, 'I suffer "death" for

your sakes (cf. v. 15a); you enjoy more of the risen life of Christ as a consequence.' He apparently saw not only a causal but also a proportional relation between his 'death' and the 'life' of the Corinthian believers."

῞Ωστε is a conj. mng. "so then, in order that," but cf. Moule 144: "ὥστε is also, in certain contexts, simply an *inferential particle* as if ὥς τε, meaning *and so, accordingly*, etc.; e.g. . . . II Cor. iv.12, v. 16, 17." Ἐν, with dat. ἡμῖν, "in us." Ἐνεργεῖται, 3rd sg. pres. mid. indic. of ἐνεργέω, "work."

VERSE 13

ἔχοντες δὲ τὸ αὐτὸ πνεῦμα τῆς πίστεως κατὰ τὸ γεγραμμένον.
And since we have the same spirit of faith in keeping with what is written,

Δέ is prob. adversative; i.e., Paul is saying that despite death being at work in us we still operate in the same spirit of faith as the psalmist. Ἔχοντες, nom. pl. act. masc. of pres. act. ptc. of ἔχω, "have." Τὸ αὐτὸ πνεῦμα. When in the attrib. position αὐτό means "the same [spirit]." There has been debate whether "spirit of faith" refers to a human disposition, as indicated when the initial letter is rendered as lowercase ("spirit"—so Augustine, *ACCSC*, 234; Thrall 1:339) or to the Holy Spirit in which case the initial letter would be uppercase ("Spirit"—so Hafemann 187, Seifrid 209; Barnett 240 n. 7). The former is the better option as Paul is saying that like the psalmist, his faith in God persists despite the sufferings he encounters. He is not making a point about the Holy Spirit being the one who inspires faith. Τῆς πίστεως, descriptive gen. Κατά with acc. τὸ γεγραμμένον "according to what is written." Γεγραμμένον, acc. sg. neut. of pf. pass. ptc. of γράφω, "write."

Ἐπίστευσα, διὸ ἐλάλησα, καὶ ἡμεῖς πιστεύομεν, διὸ καὶ λαλοῦμεν.
I believed, therefore I spoke, we also believe, and therefore speak.

Paul quotes Ps. 116:10 (LXX Ps 115:1) to say that despite the difficulties of his ministry he operates with the same "spirit of faith" as the psalmist did in the midst of his distress, and in this faith Paul goes on speaking, either when (like the psalmist) he poured out his heart to the Lord or as he proclaimed God's word. Ἐπίστευσα, 1st sg. aor. act. indic. of πιστεύω, "believe." Διό, conj., "therefore." Ἐλάλησα, 1st sg. aor. act. indic. of λαλέω, "speak." Ἡμεῖς, emphatic. Πιστεύομεν, 1st pl. pres. act. indic. of πιστεύω, "believe." Λαλοῦμεν, 1st pl. pres. act. indic. of λαλέω, "speak."

VERSE 14

εἰδότες ὅτι ὁ ἐγείρας τὸν κύριον Ἰησοῦν καὶ ἡμᾶς σὺν Ἰησοῦ ἐγερεῖ καὶ παραστήσει σὺν ὑμῖν.
For we know that the one who raised the Lord Jesus will also raise us with Jesus and present us with you.

Paul's faith was strengthened by the knowledge that, should his sufferings intensify and culminate in death, the God who raised Jesus from the dead would also raise him along with Jesus. Εἰδότες, nom. pl. masc. of pf. act. ptc. of οἶδα, "know"; the ptc. is causal: "because we know . . ." Ἐγείρας, nom. sg. masc. of aor. act. ptc. of ἐγείρω, "raise." Σύν is a prep. with dat. Ἰησοῦ, "with Jesus," looking forward to future resurrection (cf. sim. use of σύν in relation to the resurrection in 1 Thess 4:14). Harris, *Prepositions*, 201: "It is clear that σύν cannot signify 'at the same time with' or 'in conjunction with,' for Jesus's resurrection lies in the past, not the future . . . Σύν Ἰησοῦ may be paraphrased 'by virtue of Jesus's resurrection' or 'in the wake of Jesus's resurrection,' reflecting Paul's belief that Christ or the resurrection of Christ was the firstfruits (ἀπαρχή) of believers' resurrection (1 Cor 15:20, 23)." Ἐγερεῖ, 3rd sg. fut. act. indic. of ἐγείρω, "raise." Παραστήσει [ἡμᾶς] σὺν ὑμῖν, the ἡμᾶς needs to be supplied. Παραστήσει, 3rd sg. fut. act. indic. of παρίστημι, "present." Σύν is a prep. with dat. ὑμῖν, "with you."

Resurrection is not an end in itself. It is the gateway to immortality in the presence of God. Paul looks forward to the day when being raised up he will be presented along with his converts to Christ in the presence of God (cf. 1:14; Phil 2:16; 1 Thess 2:19).

VERSE 15

We see in this verse both the penultimate purpose ("for your benefit") and the ultimate purpose ("to the glory of God") of Paul's ministry, through which God extends his grace to more and more people.

Harris 355–56 identifies four syntactical issues: (i) "is πλεονάσασα transitive ('having increased the thanksgiving'), or intransitive ('having increased')," and opts for the intransitive; (ii) "does διά govern τῶν πλειόνων or τὴν εὐχαριστίαν," and opts for τῶν πλειόνων; (iii) "is διὰ τῶν πλειόνων to be construed with πλεονάσασα or with τὴν εὐχαριστίαν," and opts for the former; (iv) "is περισσεύσῃ transitive ('cause (thanksgiving) to abound'), or intransitive ('abound')," and opts for the former. Harris 338 offers the translation: *"Yes, all this is for your benefit, so that when grace has widened its scope through more and more people, it may increase thanksgiving, to the glory of God."*

τὰ γὰρ πάντα δι᾽ ὑμᾶς, ἵνα ἡ χάρις πλεονάσασα διὰ τῶν πλειόνων
Indeed, everything is for your benefit so that, as grace extends through more and more people

Πάντα, nom. pl. neut. adj. πᾶς, πᾶσα, πᾶν, "all [things]"; a pres. tense verb needs to be supplied. Δι᾽ (contraction of διά) is a prep. with acc. ὑμᾶς, "for you, your benefit." Ἵνα with subjunc. περισσεύσῃ expresses purpose, "so that grace may increase." Χάρις, nom. sg. fem. χάρις, -ιτος, ἡ, "grace," BDAG 1080b: "divine beneficence in conversion." Πλεονάσασα, nom. sg. fem. of aor. act. ptc. of πλεονάζω, "increase, extend." Διά with gen. τῶν πλειόνων indicates, "through the many." Πλειόνων, gen. pl. masc. comp. adj. πολύς, πολλή, πολύ, "many."

τὴν εὐχαριστίαν περισσεύσῃ εἰς τὴν δόξαν τοῦ θεοῦ.
it may cause thanksgiving to increase to the glory of God.

Εὐχαριστίαν, acc. sg. fem. εὐχαριστία, -ας, ἡ, "thanksgiving." Περισσεύσῃ, 3rd sg. aor. act. subjunc. of περισσεύω following ἵνα, "so that grace may increase." Εἰς is a prep. with acc. τὴν δόξαν, "to the glory [of God]." Cf. Moule 108: "What is the force of II Cor. iv. 15 ἡ χάρις πλεονάσασα διὰ τῶν πλειόνων τὴν εὐχαριστίαν περισσεύσῃ εἰς τὴν δόξαν τοῦ θεοῦ? πλεονάσασα and περισσεύσῃ suggest that τῶν πλ. here means *the increasing numbers*." Harris 357: "Paul is envisaging that, with the expansion of God's grace by means of the conversion of an ever-growing multitude of people, the volume of thanksgiving to God for the receipt of illumination (cf. 4:6) would be greatly augmented and therefore God's greater glory would be achieved." Thrall 1:344: "The thought is that grace, having increased its influence through the response of more and more people, will cause an increase of thanksgiving, to the glory of God."

b. We Do Not Give Up (4:16–18)

In the light of the prospect of a future resurrection and the grace that is presently extending to more and more people though his ministry (vv. 14–15), Paul does not give up. And he is further enabled to do so because he knows that, while his "outer person is being destroyed," his "inner person is being renewed day by day" as he keeps his eyes fixed on that "eternal weight of glory" being prepared for him (vv. 16–18). These verses function as a transition from what precedes to what is to follow in 5:1–10; from apostolic suffering to future glory.

STRUCTURE

16   Διὸ οὐκ ἐγκακοῦμεν,
          ἀλλ᾽ εἰ καὶ ὁ ἔξω ἡμῶν ἄνθρωπος διαφθείρεται,
          ἀλλ᾽   ὁ ἔσω ἡμῶν ἀνακαινοῦται ἡμέρᾳ καὶ ἡμέρᾳ.
17   τὸ γὰρ παραυτίκα ἐλαφρὸν
                    τῆς θλίψεως ἡμῶν
                              καθ᾽ ὑπερβολὴν
                              εἰς ὑπερβολὴν
                         αἰώνιον βάρος δόξης
                    κατεργάζεται ἡμῖν,
18   μὴ σκοπούντων ἡμῶν τὰ βλεπόμενα
                              ἀλλὰ τὰ μὴ βλεπόμενα·
     τὰ γὰρ βλεπόμενα πρόσκαιρα,
     τὰ δὲ μὴ βλεπόμενα αἰώνια.

VERSE 16

Διὸ οὐκ ἐγκακοῦμεν,
Therefore we do not give up.

Refers back to vv. 14–15 as the ground for Paul not giving up. Cf. 4:1, where the same verb ἐγκακέω is also used. Διό is the conj. "therefore." Ἐγκακοῦμεν, 1st pl. pres. act. indic. of ἐγκακέω, "give up, be discouraged."

ἀλλ᾿ εἰ καὶ ὁ ἔξω ἡμῶν ἄνθρωπος διαφθείρεται,
Even though our outer person is being destroyed,

The prot. of a cond. sentence, formed with εἰ with the indic. διαφθείρεται, in which a situation is assumed to be correct for the sake of argument. Ἀλλ᾿ (contraction of ἀλλά) means "but." Εἰ καί, BDAG 278d: "even if, even though." Ὁ ἔξω ἡμῶν ἄνθρωπος, "our outer person," BDAG 354bc: "our outer being." R 766 describes this as an example of "the adjectival uses of the adverb." Ἔξω is the adv. "outer." Διαφθείρεται, 3rd sg. pres. pass. indic. of διαφθείρω, "destroy."

ἀλλ᾿ ὁ ἔσω ἡμῶν ἀνακαινοῦται ἡμέρᾳ καὶ ἡμέρᾳ.
our inner person is being renewed day by day.

The apod. of the cond. sentence. BDF (§448[5]): "Ἀλλά in an apodosis after εἰ . . . means 'yet, certainly, at least.'" Cf. ZG 542–43. Ὁ ἔσω ἡμῶν (contraction of ὁ ἔσω ἡμῶν ἄνθρωπος), "our inner person." R 681: "The attributive position of ἡμῶν . . . is not unusual." BDF (§184): "In ὁ ἔσω ἡμῶν . . . the gen. as in the preceding ὁ ἔξω ἡμῶν ἄνθ. is possessive." Ἔσω is the adv. "inner." Ἀνακαινοῦται, 3rd sg. pres. pass. indic. of ἀνακαινόω, "renew." The implied agent of this pass. verb is the Holy Spirit (cf. 3:18). Ἡμέρᾳ καὶ ἡμέρᾳ means "day by day." BDF (§200[1]): an instance of "the temporal dative to answer the question 'when?'" BDAG 438a: "day after day." Ἡμέρᾳ, dat. of time, cf. R 522.

The mng. of Paul's reference to his "outer person" and "inner person" has been the subject of debate. One view is that Paul adopted a dualistic view of the human constitution, one that regards the inner nature (soul) as good and destined for immortality, but regards the outer nature (body) as evil and destined to pass away. However, most recognize that this is at odds with Paul's personal eschatology, which involves a future existence, not as a disembodied soul, but as a whole person—with a resurrected body (cf. 1 Cor 15:35–38; 2 Cor 5:1–5).

Another view is that Paul was employing a general distinction between the physical body and the soul that would be readily understood by his predominantly Greco-Roman readers. However, more than the physical body is involved in the wasting away of "the outer man" as is indicated by his description of those afflictions that were causing it. These certainly included many that affected his physical body, but also those that affected his mind and spirit. For this reason it has been suggested that the "outer person" is the whole person from the standpoint of one's creaturely mortality, whereas the "inner person" is the whole person as a new creation (5:17), the renewed being of the believer (cf. Harris, 359–60; Seifrid 215–216; Thrall I 348–51).

VERSE 17

τὸ γὰρ παραυτίκα ἐλαφρὸν τῆς θλίψεως ἡμῶν
For our momentary light affliction

Paul's troubles were neither "light" nor "momentary" in themselves. They were the burdensome and virtually constant accompaniment of his ministry. Yet by comp. with the weighty and eternal character of the glory they were achieving for him, they were "light and momentary" (cf. Rom 8:17–23).

Τό . . . ἐλαφρὸν τῆς θλίψεως, lit. "the lightness of affliction,'" BDAG 314b: "insignificant affliction." Harris 361: "This construction has the effect of highlighting the idea of the adjective [ἐλαφρός, 'lightness'], probably in contrast with the following word βάρος ('weight')." Παραυτίκα is the adv. "momentary," an example of a compound adv. formed by the blending of two words (παρά and αὐτός); cf. R 297, 551. Ἐλαφρόν, nom. sg. neut. adj. ἐλαφρός, -ά, -όν, "light, having little weight," as subst. "lightness"; cf. BDF (§263[2]): "the use of a neuter sing. adjective like an abstract, mostly with a dependent gen." Τῆς θλίψεως, attrib. gen., descriptive of τό . . . ἐλαφρόν, lit. "(lightness) of affliction." Θλίψεως, gen. sg. fem. θλῖψις, -εως, ἡ, "affliction."

καθ' ὑπερβολὴν εἰς ὑπερβολὴν αἰώνιον βάρος δόξης κατεργάζεται ἡμῖν,
is producing for us an absolutely incomparable eternal weight of glory.

Καθ' (contraction of κατά) is a prep. with acc. mng. "according to." Καθ' ὑπερβολὴν εἰς ὑπερβολήν: The repetition of ὑπερβολή could simply denote intensification, or the two elements of the expression could be given due weight as in BDAG 1032d: "beyond all measure and proportion," or Thrall 1:347: "to an utterly extraordinary degree." Ὑπερβολήν, acc. sg. fem. ὑπερβολή, -ῆς, ἡ, "excess, extraordinary quality." Εἰς, prep. with acc. αἰώνιον, lit. "to the age," i.e., "eternal." Αἰώνιον βάρος δόξης κατεργάζεται, "produces an eternal weight of glory." Cf. Moule 186: "One ought also to mention [as a semitism] the collocation of βάρος δόξης in II Cor. iv.17, which may have been suggested by the fact that both *weight* and *glory* are expressed in Hebrew by the same consonants." Βάρος, acc. sg. neut. βάρος, -ους, τό, "weight." Κατεργάζεται, 3rd sg. pres. mid. indic. of κατεργάζομαι, "produce." Ἡμῖν, dat. 1st pl. "for us."

How are we to understand the causal connection between the experience of affliction and the glory to be revealed? Among Paul's Jewish contemporaries there was a belief that the messianic age would be ushered in by a def. and predetermined measure of afflictions to be experienced by the people of God. These afflictions were known as the birth pangs of the Messiah (cf. Mark 13:3–8, 17–20, 24–27 and parallels in Matthew 24 and Luke 21). It may be the belief that his afflictions were part of the birth pains of the new age that lies behind Paul's statement that the one "is producing" the other. On the other hand it may be better to see the connection simply in terms of God's gracious blessing of believers who suffer for the sake of his Son. Paul states this clearly in Romans 8:17–18: "Now if we are children, then we are heirs—heirs of God and co-heirs with Christ, if indeed we share in his sufferings in order that we may also share in his glory. I consider that our present sufferings are not worth comparing with the glory that will be revealed in us" (NIV; cf. Matt 10:32–33; 2 Tim 2:11–12). Calvin 64 rightly rejects the idea that "by afflictions we can merit the inheritance that comes to us only by the gracious adoption of God."

VERSE 18

μὴ σκοπούντων ἡμῶν τὰ βλεπόμενα ἀλλὰ τὰ μὴ βλεπόμενα·
So we do not focus on what is seen, but on what is unseen.

Σκοπούντων ἡμῶν is a gen. absolute cstr. used "to signify that a change of subject has occurred in relation to the subject of the main verb" (Forbes 91), in this case from the "momentary light affliction" that "is producing for us an absolutely incomparable eternal weight of glory" (v. 17) to the "we" of v. 18. Cf. BDF (§423[5]); R 1132. Harris 363 identifies four possible ways of construing the gen. absolute: "This genitive absolute may express a condition ('provided our eyes are fixed,' REB), a result ('So we fix our eyes, NIV), an attendant circumstance ('Meanwhile our eyes are fixed, NEB), or a reason ('because we look,' NRSV)." He opts for the causal sense. Σκοπούντων, gen. pl. masc. of pres. act. ptc. of σκοπέω, "pay attention to, watch closely," BDAG 931a–b: "to keep one's eyes on." Τὰ βλεπόμενα, ESV "the things that are seen," or NRSV "what can be seen." Βλεπόμενα, acc. pl. neut. of pres. pass. ptc. of βλέπω, "see." An example of a descriptive pres. ptc. (R 891). Τὰ μὴ βλεπόμενα, ESV "the things that are unseen."

τὰ γὰρ βλεπόμενα πρόσκαιρα, τὰ δὲ μὴ βλεπόμενα αἰώνια.
For what is seen is temporary, but what is unseen is eternal.

Πρόσκαιρα, nom. pl. neut. adj. πρόσκαιρος, -ον, "temporary, transitory." Αἰώνια, nom. pl. neut. adj. αἰώνιος, -ον, "eternal." When Paul contrasts "what is seen" with "what is unseen," he is not contrasting things that are visible with those that are inherently invisible. It is rather a contrast between what is now visible and what is not yet visible but about to be revealed, i.e., at the revelation of Christ and his kingdom at the second coming (cf. Rom 8:24–25; Col 3:1–4; Heb 11:1–3). Thrall 1:356: "The βλεπόμενα will include all that Paul means by the ἔξω ἄνθρωπος of v. 16, and all the outward material circumstances in which he is involved. . . . The μὴ βλεπόμενα will consist of all that is hoped for in the future, the total completion of the glory already in process of creation and the eternal heavenly dwelling Paul is confident of possessing."

FOR FURTHER STUDY

48. Catalogue of Afflictions (4:8–12)

Duff, P. "Apostolic Suffering and the Language of Processions in 2 Corinthians 4:7–10." *BTB* 21 (1991): 158–165.

Fitzpatrick, J. T. *Cracks in an Earthen Vessel: An Examination of the Catalogues of Hardships in the Corinthians Correspondence.* SBLDSS 99. Atlanta: Scholars Press, 1988. See pp. 166–180.

Kruse, C. G. *DPL* 18–20.

49. Death and Life (4:10)

Hafemann, S. J. *Suffering and Ministry in the Spirit: Paul's Defense of His Ministry in II Corinthians 2:14–3:3.* Grand Rapids: Eerdmans, 1990. See pp. 52–59.

Gräbe, P. J. "The All-Surpassing Power of God through the Holy Spirit in the Midst of Our Broken Earthly Existence: Perspectives on Paul's Use of *Dynamai* in 2 Corinthians." *Neot* 28 (1994): 147–56.

Kaithakottil, J. "'Death in Us, Life in You.' Ministry and Suffering: A Study of 2 Cor 4, 7-15." *Bible Bhashyam* 28 (2002): 433–60.

Best, E. "II Corinthians 4.7–15 Life Through Death." *IBS* 8 (1986): 2–7.

50. Believing and Speaking (4:13)

Campbell, D. A. "2 Corinthians 4:13: Evidence in Paul That Christ Believes." *JBL* 128 (2009): 337–56.

Stegman, T. D. "*Episteusa, Dio Elelēsa* (2 Corinthians 6.16c–18): Paul's Christological Reading of Psalm 115:1a LXX." *CBQ* 69 (2007): 725–45.

51. Future Hope/Resurrection (4:14)

Anderson, K. L. *DJG* 774–89.

Harris, M. J. "Resurrection and Immortality: Eight Theses." *Them* 1 (1976): 50–55.

Kreitzer, L. J. *DPL* 805–12.

Murphy-O'Connor, J. "Faith and Resurrection in 2 Cor 4:13–14." *RevBib* 95 (1988): 543–50.

Plevnik, J. "The Destination of the Apostle and the Faithful: Second Corinthians 4:13b–14 and First Thessalonians 4:14." *CBQ* 62 (2000): 83–95.

HOMILETICAL SUGGESTIONS

Treasure in Jars of Clay (4:7–15)

1. God releases the power of the gospel though the ministry of human beings (v. 7)
2. God sustains his messengers in the midst of their afflictions (vv. 8–9)
3. Sharing Jesus's "death" and experiencing his "life" (vv. 10–11)
4. "Death" in us means "life" for others (v. 12)
5. The ultimate (thanksgiving to God) and penultimate (grace extending to more people) results of gospel ministry (v.15)

Why We Do Not Lose Heart (4:16–18)

1. While our "outer" person is "destroyed," our "inner" person is "renewed" day by day (v. 16)

2. "Momentary and light affliction" produces for us an "incomparable weight of glory" (v. 17)
3. Our ultimate focus to be upon what is not yet seen but eternal (v.18)

c. The Heavenly Dwelling (5:1–10)

This passage is often studied in virtual isolation from the rest of 2 Corinthians because of its obvious importance for understanding Paul's views about life after death. However, in seeking a proper understanding of 5:1–10, it is essential to see it in its context, especially in relation to what immediately precedes, for in fact 4:16–5:10 constitutes one integrated section. It is in the light of the outer person "being destroyed" (4:16) and the fact that the "momentary light affliction is producing for us an absolutely incomparable eternal weight of glory" (4:17) that Paul proceeds to explain what he looks forward to "if our earthly tent we live in is destroyed" (5:1).

STRUCTURE

1 Οἴδαμεν γὰρ ὅτι
    ἐὰν ἡ ἐπίγειος ἡμῶν οἰκία τοῦ σκήνους καταλυθῇ,
      οἰκοδομὴν ἐκ θεοῦ ἔχομεν,
      οἰκίαν ἀχειροποίητον
      αἰώνιον ἐν τοῖς οὐρανοῖς.
2 καὶ γὰρ ἐν τούτῳ στενάζομεν
        τὸ οἰκητήριον ἡμῶν
        τὸ ἐξ οὐρανοῦ
        ἐπενδύσασθαι
      ἐπιποθοῦντες,
3 εἴ γε καὶ   ἐκδυσάμενοι
      οὐ γυμνοὶ εὑρεθησόμεθα.
4 καὶ γὰρ οἱ ὄντες ἐν τῷ σκήνει στενάζομεν
      βαρούμενοι,
   ἐφ' ᾧ οὐ θέλομεν ἐκδύσασθαι
    ἀλλ'   ἐπενδύσασθαι,
   ἵνα καταποθῇ τὸ θνητὸν ὑπὸ τῆς ζωῆς.
5 ὁ δὲ κατεργασάμενος ἡμᾶς εἰς αὐτὸ τοῦτο
θεός,
 ὁ   δοὺς ἡμῖν τὸν ἀρραβῶνα τοῦ πνεύματος.
6 Θαρροῦντες οὖν πάντοτε καὶ
   εἰδότες ὅτι   ἐνδημοῦντες ἐν τῷ σώματι
      ἐκδημοῦμεν ἀπὸ τοῦ κυρίου·
7 διὰ πίστεως γὰρ
περιπατοῦμεν,
   οὐ διὰ εἴδους·
8 θαρροῦμεν δὲ
καὶ εὐδοκοῦμεν μᾶλλον ἐκδημῆσαι ἐκ τοῦ σώματος
      καὶ ἐνδημῆσαι πρὸς τὸν κύριον.
9 διὸ καὶ φιλοτιμούμεθα,
     εἴτε ἐνδημοῦντες
     εἴτε ἐκδημοῦντες,

εὐάρεστοι αὐτῷ εἶναι.
10 τοὺς γὰρ πάντας ἡμᾶς φανερωθῆναι δεῖ
                      ἔμπροσθεν τοῦ βήματος τοῦ Χριστοῦ,
        ἵνα κομίσηται ἕκαστος τὰ διὰ τοῦ σώματος πρὸς ἃ ἔπραξεν,
                εἴτε ἀγαθὸν
                εἴτε φαῦλον.

VERSE 1

In many ways this verse is the interpretive crux for the whole of 5:1–10. How one interprets it determines to a large extent how one understands the rest of the passage. While most scholars agree that the destruction of the "earthly tent" refers to the death of the body, there is no agreement about the meaning of "a building from God . . . not made with hands." Suggestions include (i) a heavenly temple, understood either as the church in heaven, or heaven itself as the dwelling place of God in which Christians find their eternal habitation; (ii) a reference to Jesus's resurrection body understood corporately, so that those who believe in him share in it now; and (iii) the resurrection body.

The parallel passage in Rom 8:18–24 lends support to the third option. It also deals with the subject of suffering experienced by believers, comparing it with the glory to be revealed to them. What the believer looks forward to at the revelation of this glory is the redemption of the body (v. 23), clearly a reference to the resurrection of the body. Seeing that Rom 8:18–24 treats a sim. subject to that dealt with in 2 Cor 4:16–5:10, and seeing that Romans was written just a short time after 2 Corinthians, it is reasonable to interpret verse 1b in the light of Rom 8:23 and so conclude that the "building from God . . . not made with hands" refers to the resurrection body promised to the believer.

Οἴδαμεν γὰρ ὅτι ἐὰν ἡ ἐπίγειος ἡμῶν οἰκία τοῦ σκήνους καταλυθῇ,
For we know that if our earthly tent we live in is destroyed,

Γάρ is the coordinating. conj. "for," connecting what follows with what precedes in 4:16–18. Οἴδαμεν, 1st pl. pf. act. indic. of οἶδα, "know." Barnett 256 n. 6: "Gk. Οἴδαμεν . . . ὅτι suggests an introduction to a Christian teaching already known. The plural 'we know' must be applicable to believers in general . . . it is not a literary plural." Ἐὰν ἡ ἐπίγειος ἡμῶν οἰκία τοῦ σκήνους καταλυθῇ is the prot. of third-class cond. sentence (ἐάν with subjunc. in the prot.) postulating a future cond. "in the sense that a proposal is made regarding some form of action from which certain results will ensue if carried out. In other words, the use of the subjunctive makes a projection, not an assertion, about reality" (Forbes, 154). ZG, 534: "ἐάν w. aor. subj. an eventual condition." Harris 370: "Here the context indicates that ἐάν means 'if, as is probable.'" Seifrid 220, n. 417: "The genitive in the expression ἡ ἐπίγειος ἡμῶν οἰκία τοῦ σκήνους καταλυθῇ ('earthly house of a tent') is clearly epexegetic: 'our earthly house, which is a tent.'" Z §47: "Where two genitives depend upon the same noun, Paul commonly puts one of them before the other after that noun, e.g. 2 Cor 5,1 ἡ ἐπίγειος ἡμῶν οἰκία τοῦ σκήνους." Ἐπίγειος, nom. sg. fem. adj. ἐπίγειος, -ον, "earthly." Οἰκία τοῦ σκήνους, R 398–99: "Sometimes indeed the genitive is used where really the substantive is in apposition . . . So with ἡ οἰκία τοῦ σκήνους." Οἰκία, nom. sg. fem. οἰκία -ας, ἡ, "house."

Σκήνους, gen. sg. neut. σκῆνος, -ους, τό, "tent." Paul does not use here the usual word for tent (σκηνή), which is found extensively in the LXX and twenty times in the NT. Rather, he uses an unusual word, σκῆνος, which is found only twice in the NT (here and in v. 4), and only once in the LXX (Wis 9:15), where it is used figuratively to refer to the human body. It is also used in this manner in the papyri. This strongly suggests that σκῆνος should be understood in the same way here, and this is confirmed by the overall context of 4:16–5:10, where Paul is concerned with the effects of persecution and suffering. We may conclude that in the first part of the verse, then, he is referring to the final outcome of such a process, i.e., the destruction of the body in death. Καταλυθῇ, 3rd sg. aor. pass. subjunc. of καταλύω, "destroy."

οἰκοδομὴν ἐκ θεοῦ ἔχομεν, οἰκίαν ἀχειροποίητον αἰώνιον ἐν τοῖς οὐρανοῖς.
we have a building from God, an eternal dwelling in the heavens, not made with hands.

The apod. of the third-class cond. sentence ("if our earthly tent we live in is destroyed . . ."). Οἰκοδομήν, acc. sg. fem. οἰκοδομή, -ῆς, ἡ, "building." Seifrid 221: "The contrast between the present dwelling in a tent and the eternal 'building' from God recalls the replacement of the wilderness tabernacle by the temple." Ἐκ θεοῦ, gen. of source "from God." Ἔχομεν, 1st pl. pres. act. indic. of ἔχω, "have." Seifrid 225, commenting on the pres. tense of ἔχομεν, says this: "The dwelling is his, even if he possesses it presently *in spe non in re* ('in hope, not in substance')."

Harris 373: "οἰκίαν is in epexegetic apposition to οἰκοδομή." An important factor in determining the mng. of οἰκία here is the parallelism existing in this verse. What is earthly and threatened with destruction in v. 1a is to be replaced by something corresponding to it which is heavenly and eternal in v. 1b. If "the tent" that forms our earthly dwelling denotes the physical body of the believer, it is reasonable to regard the "building from God" as a reference to another body, the resurrection body of the believer. Cf. Rom 8:18–24. By referring to the resurrection body as a "building" Paul may be emphasizing its permanence, as compared with the impermanence of the present body he refers to as a "tent."

Ἀχειροποίητον, acc. sg. fem. adj. ἀχειροποίητος, -ον, "made without hands," qualifies οἰκίαν. Αἰώνιον, acc. sg. fem. adj. αἰώνιος, -ον, "eternal," further qualifying οἰκίαν. Ἐν is a prep. with dat. τοῖς οὐρανοῖς "in the heavens." Harris 373: "ἐν τοῖς οὐρανοῖς may be locative ('in heaven'), specifying the site of the inhabited οἰκία. But more prob. is it qualitative ('heavenly' = ἐπουράνιον)." See Harris 374–80 for detailed discussion of interpretations of what it means to "have" a building from God, in particular whether it denotes a "present possession of the spiritual body" or a "future acquisition of the spiritual body." He concludes that the preferred option is an "ideal possession of the spiritual body at death with real possession at the parousia." But cf. Thrall 1:368–70, 373, who adopts the view that "should a believer die before the Parousia, he will at that moment come into possession of a permanent (αἰώνιος), spiritual (ἀχειροποίητος), and heavenly (ἐν τοῖς οὐρανοῖς) form of existence. In view of the explicit contrast with the οἰκία τοῦ σκήνους, this must be seen as somatic existence and hence as the σῶμα πνευματικόν." Seifrid 221: "The contrast between the present dwelling in a tent and the eternal 'building' from God recalls the replacement of the wilderness tabernacle by the temple."

VERSE 2

καὶ γὰρ ἐν τούτῳ στενάζομεν
Indeed, we groan in this tent,

Harris 380: "καὶ γάρ introduces a confirmatory or additional reason ('for also,' 'moreover')." Ἐν is a prep. with dat. τούτῳ, "in this (tent understood)." Στενάζομεν, 1st pl. pres. act. indic. of στενάζω, "groan."

τὸ οἰκητήριον ἡμῶν τὸ ἐξ οὐρανοῦ ἐπενδύσασθαι ἐπιποθοῦντες,
desiring to put on our heavenly dwelling,

Οἰκητήριον, acc. sg. neut. οἰκητήριον, -ου, τό, "dwelling," dir. obj. of inf. ἐπενδύσασθαι. Τὸ ἐξ οὐρανοῦ, gen. prep. phrase indicates origin: "the one from heaven," qualifying οἰκητήριον. Ἐπενδύσασθαι, aor. mid. inf. of ἐπενδύομαι, "put on, be fully clothed." Thrall 1:371: "The verb ἐπενδύσασθαι is a double compound which means 'put on (in addition)'." Ἐπιποθοῦντες, nom. pl. masc. of pres. act. part. of ἐπιποθέω, "desire, long for." The parallel in Rom 8:18–24 is helpful and quite striking. Believers are depicted as groaning (the same verb, στενάζω, is used) as they wait for their adoption, interpreted as the redemption of their bodies (vv. 23–24). This supports the view that, when Paul talks about groaning and longing to put on the heavenly dwelling in the present context, he is speaking of the same thing. Seifrid 226 notes that Paul here moves from "the metaphor of a temple to that of clothing."

VERSE 3

εἴ γε καὶ ἐκδυσάμενοι οὐ γυμνοὶ εὑρεθησόμεθα.
since, when we have taken it off, we will not be found naked.

Cf. BDAG 278c: "Assuming, of course, that having put it off we shall not be found naked." Consistent with the line of interpretation adopted, the nakedness that Paul expects to avoid when he puts on the heavenly dwelling is the nakedness of a disembodied spirit. The promised heavenly body will save him from that. Εἴ γε, BDAG 278c: "if indeed." Harris 384: "In Pauline usage εἴ γε introduces a statement that makes explicit an assumption that lay behind some preceding assertion. . . . Thrall's detailed study of εἴ γε in Paul led her to conclude that these particles express assurance, not doubt: 'in the certain condition that.'" ZG 543: "γε particle strengthening the foregoing (or attached) word, εἴ γε καί *if, that is*." Ἐκδυσάμενοι, nom. pl. masc. of aor. mid. ptc. of ἐκδύω, "take off, strip." There is a var. rdg., ἐνδυσάμενοι ("put on") instead of ἐκδυσάμενοι ("taken off"). Metzger 511 concludes: "In view of its superior support the rdg. ἐνδυσάμενοι should be adopted, the rdg. ἐκδυσάμενοι being an early alteration to avoid apparent tautology."

Γυμνοί, nom. pl. masc. adj. γυμνός -ή, -όν, "naked." Harris 385–86: "Probably the most notorious crux of 5:1–10 is the mng. of γυμνοί. I will defend the view that in v. 3 Paul is expressing, not fear of temporary physical disembodiment or permanent spiritual disembodiment, but assurance of spiritual embodiment and rejection of any idealization of disembodiment that may have been advocated by certain gnosticizing Corinthians." So too Thrall 1:374–80. On the other hand, E. Earle Ellis, ("II Corinthians v.1–10 in Pauline Eschatology," *NTS* 6 [1960] 211–24), argues that being "found naked" here does not refer to existence as a disembodied spirit, but is to be understood ethically referring to the shame of exposure before the judgment seat of Christ. So too Hafemann 208–13, 217.

Εὑρεθησόμεθα, 1st pl. fut. pass. indic. of εὑρίσκω, "find." Harris 385: "If εὑρεθησόμεθα is a 'theological passive,' it refers to God's or Christ's 'discovery' of human beings at the Parousia (cf. 4:14; 5:10). But in NT Greek passives not infrequently have a refl. or intransitive sense, so that in v. 3 the passive of εὑρίσκειν may mean 'find oneself,' 'prove to be,' or 'be found to be' (French *se trouver*)."

VERSE 4

καὶ γὰρ οἱ ὄντες ἐν τῷ σκήνει στενάζομεν βαρούμενοι,
Indeed, we groan while we are in this tent, burdened as we are,

This verse repeats essentially what is found in vv. 2–3. Καὶ γάρ, Harris 386: "'for indeed,' 'for it is a fact that.'" Οἱ ὄντες ἐν τῷ σκήνει, subj. of στενάζομεν. Ὄντες, nom. pl. masc. of pres. act. ptc. of εἰμί, "be." Ἐν, prep. with locat. dat. τῷ σκήνει is an adv. phrase mng. "in the tent." Στενάζομεν, 1st pl. pres. act. indic. of στενάζω, "groan." Harris 388: "The nature of the sighing or groaning is nowhere specified in the passage. A comparison with a parallel use of this verb in Rom. 8:23 seems to indicate that this is Paul's term to describe the Christian's reaction to living 'between the times'—between the two advents of Christ. Βαρούμενοι, nom. pl. masc. of pres. pass. ptc. of βαρέω, BDAG 166d: "weigh down, burden."

ἐφ᾽ ᾧ οὐ θέλομεν ἐκδύσασθαι ἀλλ᾽ ἐπενδύσασθαι,
because we do not want to be unclothed but clothed,

Ἐφ᾽ ᾧ (= ἐπὶ τούτῳ ὅτι). ZG 543: "Ἐπί with dat. giving the grounds for an action." BDAG 365b: "*for this reason that, because.*" R 963: "ἐφ᾽ ᾧ is causal in 2 Cor. 5:4." Cf. Moule 132: "ἐφ᾽ ᾧ in II Cor.v.4 . . . almost certainly means *inasmuch as*"; so too Z §127. Θέλομεν, 1st pl. pres. act. indic. of θέλω, "will, want." Ἐκδύσασθαι, aor. mid. inf. of ἐκδύω, "remove clothing." Thrall 1:382 understands Paul's wish not to be "unclothed" as "unwillingness to experience the event of death," preferring "'over-clothing' with the heavenly body without prior death. He desires it so that mortality may be engulfed by life." Ἐπενδύσασθαι, aor. mid. inf. of ἐπενδύομαι, "clothe, put on."

ἵνα καταποθῇ τὸ θνητὸν ὑπὸ τῆς ζωῆς.
so that mortality may be swallowed up by life.

Ἵνα with subjunc. καταποθῇ expresses purpose. Καταποθῇ, 3rd sg. aor. pass. subjunc. of καταπίνω, "swallow." Ὑπό prep. with gen. τῆς ζωῆς expresses agency, "swallowed by life." Ζωῆς, gen. sg. fem. ζωή, -ῆς, ἡ, "life."

VERSE 5

ὁ δὲ κατεργασάμενος ἡμᾶς εἰς αὐτὸ τοῦτο θεός,
Now the one who prepared us for this very purpose is God,

Ὁ . . . κατεργασάμενος, subst. adj. ptc. phrase, "the one who prepared." Κατεργασάμενος, nom. sg. masc. of aor. mid. ptc. of κατεργάζομαι, "prepare." Ἡμᾶς, acc. dir. obj. of κατεργασάμενος. Εἰς, prep. with acc. αὐτὸ τοῦτο indicates purpose, BDAG 290d: "for this very reason." Prob. refers back to mortality being swallowed up by life. Αὐτό in the predicative position serves to emphasize: "this *very* (purpose)." The placement of θεός serves as emphasis. Harris 392 paraphrases: "Now he who has prepared us for this very destiny is none other than the God who is the creator and consummator of all things."

ὁ δοὺς ἡμῖν τὸν ἀρραβῶνα τοῦ πνεύματος.
who gave us the Spirit as a down payment.

A rel. clause qualifying θεός "the one who gave us. . . ." Δούς, nom. sg. masc. of aor. act. ptc. of δίδωμι, "give." Τὸν ἀρραβῶνα, dir. object of ptc. δούς. Ἀρραβῶνα, acc. sg. masc. ἀρραβών, -ῶνος, ὁ (as noted earlier in the commentary on 1:22) is a commercial term applied figuratively by Paul to the Spirit whom God gave him and to whose presence he appeals as a guarantee of bodily resurrection. Τοῦ πνεύματος, epex. gen., "pledge *of the Spirit*." R 498. ZG 543: "τοῦ πνεύματος of the Spirit, epexeg. = namely, the Spirit)." Barrett 266 n. 62: "The genitive τοῦ πνεύματος is appositional to τὸν ἀρραβῶνα and means 'the pledge consisting of the Spirit.'"

VERSE 6

Θαρροῦντες οὖν πάντοτε καὶ εἰδότες ὅτι ἐνδημοῦντες ἐν τῷ σώματι ἐκδημοῦμεν ἀπὸ τοῦ κυρίου·
So we are always confident and know that while we are at home in the body we are away from the Lord.

Θαρροῦντες, nom. pl. masc. of pres. act. ptc. of θαρρέω, "be confident," functions as an indic. and is equivalent to θαρροῦμεν. Οὖν, the conj. "therefore, so," introduces the reason for the confidence Paul experiences: the presence of the Spirit as God's pledge to him of bodily resurrection. Πάντοτε, temp. adv. "always." Εἰδότες, nom. pl. masc. of pf. act. ptc. of οἶδα, "know."

Ὅτι, the conj. "that," introduces the content of what the apostle knows. Ἐνδημοῦντες, nom. pl. masc. of pres. act. ptc. of ἐνδημέω, in the NT fig. "be at home." Ἐν is a prep. with locat. dat. τῷ σώματι, "in the body." Harris 395: "In the expression ἐνδημοῦντες ἐν τῷ σώματι . . . the article is anaphoric, referring back to the ἐπίγειος οἰκία of v. 1 and the σκῆνος of v. 4, so that ἐν τῷ σώματι means more than 'on earth.'" Ἐκδημοῦμεν, 1st pl. pres. act. indic. of ἐκδημέω, "be away, absent." Ἀπό, prep. with gen. τοῦ κυρίου "from the Lord."

What it means to be "at home in the body" and "away from the Lord" can be deduced from the parenthesis in v. 7, where Paul says, "For we walk by faith, not by sight." To be "at home in the body" means that God is not accessible to our sight (and in that sense we are away from the Lord); he is accessible to us only by faith (cf. John 20:29).

VERSE 7

διὰ πίστεως γὰρ περιπατοῦμεν, οὐ διὰ εἴδους·
For we walk by faith, not by sight.

A parenthetic statement following v. 6 before picking up the main stream of thought again in v. 8. Διὰ πίστεως . . . οὐ διὰ εἴδους, the prep. διά is used here to indicate manner of acting, or possibly circumstances, Z §114. Διά, prep. with gen. πίστεως could indicate instrumentality "by faith," but cf. Harris 397: "Because this περιπατεῖν διά combination is unique in Paul, διὰ πίστεως need not necessarily bear its customary sense of 'by means of faith,' especially since no object is expressed. It is preferable to conclude that both of the prepositional phrases in this verse describe accompanying circumstances ('we walk in the realm of faith, not of sight')." Γάρ, the conj. "for," introduces the reason why Paul could speak of being "away from the Lord." Περιπατοῦμεν, 1st pl. pres. act. indic. of περιπατέω, "walk." Διά, prep. with gen. εἴδους, "by sight." Εἴδους, gen. sg. neut. εἶδος, -ους, τό, "sight, the act of seeing." Barnett 270 n. 20: "The meaning is debated, depending on whether the phrase is taken as (1) active ('sight') or (2) passive ('what is seen'), either of which is possible. The context suggests the need for a symmetry with 'faith,' noting the matching διὰ πίστεως . . . διὰ εἴδους. Hence '. . . faith not sight,' i.e., option (1)."

VERSE 8

θαρροῦμεν δὲ καὶ εὐδοκοῦμεν μᾶλλον ἐκδημῆσαι ἐκ τοῦ σώματος καὶ ἐνδημῆσαι πρὸς τὸν κύριον.

In fact, we are confident, and we would prefer to be away from the body and at home with the Lord.

This verse picks up the thought of v. 6 following the parenthesis in v. 7. As the parenthesis threw light backward upon the mng. of v. 6, so too it throws light forward upon the statement in v. 8. To be "away from the body" means to be "at home with the Lord" in the sense that then the Lord will be accessible to sight, and no longer accessible only by faith. It would appear that Paul is saying he could prefer death (ἐκδημῆσαι ἐκ τοῦ σώματος) if that means being at home with the Lord (ἐνδημῆσαι πρὸς τὸν κύριον).

Θαρροῦμεν, 1st pl. pres. act. indic. of θαρρέω, "be confident, brave." BDAG 444b: "to have certainty in a matter." Εὐδοκοῦμεν, 1st pl. pres. act. indic. of εὐδοκέω, "prefer, or possibly be content." Barnett 270 n. 23 citing Plummer: "It is possible to long for one thing, and yet be content with, or even prefer another, because one knows the latter is well worth having, and perhaps better for one. . . . It was better to see the Lord than to be deprived of this bliss through being in the body." Μᾶλλον, an adv. mng. "rather." Ἐκδημῆσαι, aor. act. inf. of ἐκδημέω, "be absent, away." Ἐκ, prep. with gen. τοῦ σώματος, "away from the body." Ἐνδημῆσαι, aor. act. inf. of ἐνδημέω, "be present, at home." Πρός, prep. with acc. τὸν κύριον, "with the Lord," here locat. indicates position, so Moule 53. Cf. Barnett 271 n. 26: "face-to-face converse with the Lord (so John 1:1, 2)."

Paul recognizes that although he does not wish to experience a disembodied state, he may have to do so if he dies before the Parousia. But he is convinced that even if this should be his lot, it would be preferable to remaining "in the body" and so "away from the Lord" (v. 6). It may be helpful to think of this disembodied state being like the disembodied existence of Jesus Christ himself in the period between his death and resurrection. Harris 401–2: "But if ἐκδημῆσαι ἐκ τοῦ σώματος refers to death, and if Paul still believes that the resurrection body is acquired at the parousia (1 Cor 15:23, 42–44, 52), it is difficult not to conclude that he regarded the interval between the individual's death and the parousia as one of disembodiment."

VERSE 9

διὸ καὶ φιλοτιμούμεθα, εἴτε ἐνδημοῦντες εἴτε ἐκδημοῦντες, εὐάρεστοι αὐτῷ εἶναι.

Therefore, whether we are at home or away, we make it our aim to be pleasing to him

Διό, the conj. "therefore." Φιλοτιμούμεθα, 1st pl. pres. mid. indic. of φιλοτιμέομαι, "aspire, make it one's aim." Εἴτε . . . εἴτε, "whether . . . or." Εἴτε (= εἰ τέ), subord. cond. conj. "either/or." Ἐνδημοῦντες, nom. pl. masc. of pres. act. ptc. of ἐνδημέω, "be present, at home," i.e., in this earthly life. Ἐκδημοῦντες, nom. pl. masc. of pres. act.

ptc. of ἐκδημέω, "be absent, away," i.e., after this earthy life. Εὐάρεστοι, nom. pl. masc. verbal adj. εὐάρεστος, -ον, "pleasing, acceptable." Αὐτῷ, dat. 3rd sg. masc. αὐτός, -ή, -ό, "him." Εἶναι, pres. inf. of εἰμί, "be."

To overcome the problem of thinking that even after death, when believers are in the presence of Christ, they will still need to strive to please Christ, Thrall 1:393 says, "During his present life Paul aims so to act that both now and hereafter he will be pleasing to the Lord."

VERSE 10

τοὺς γὰρ πάντας ἡμᾶς φανερωθῆναι δεῖ ἔμπροσθεν τοῦ βήματος τοῦ Χριστοῦ,
For we must all appear before the judgment seat of Christ,

Τοὺς . . . πάντας ἡμᾶς, acc. subj. of inf. φανερωθῆναι. BDF (§275[7]): "τοὺς πάντας ἡμᾶς (not just he of whom Paul had previously spoken [cf. 1st pers. plur. in v. 9])." R 773: "we the whole number of us." Cf. 1 Cor 4:5; Rom 14:10. Φανερωθῆναι, aor. pass. inf. of φανερόω, "appear." Δεῖ, 3rd sg. pres. act. indic. of δέω, "be necessary." Ἔμπροσθεν, prep. with gen. τοῦ βήματος, "before the judgment seat." Βήματος, gen. sg. neut. βῆμα, -ατος, τό, "judgment seat." Τοῦ Χριστοῦ, gen. of possession, "of Christ, Christ's."

ἵνα κομίσηται ἕκαστος τὰ διὰ τοῦ σώματος πρὸς ἃ ἔπραξεν, εἴτε ἀγαθὸν εἴτε φαῦλον.
so that each may be repaid for what he has done in the body, whether good or evil.

Ἵνα with subjunc. κομίσηται expresses purpose: "so that (each) may be repaid." Κομίσηται, 3rd sg. aor. mid. subjunc. of κομίζω, "receive, be repaid." Ἕκαστος, nom. sg. masc. adj. ἕκαστος, -η, -ον, "each." BDAG 298c: "as subst. *each one, every one.*" Τὰ διὰ τοῦ σώματος, "the things (done) through the body." ZG 544: "διὰ τοῦ σώματος *in the body* (i.e. during his time on earth) though through (the instrumentality of) the body is also possible." Διά, prep. with gen. τοῦ σώματος, "through the body." Πρὸς ἃ ἔπραξεν, CSB: "for what he has done." Moule 53: "[πρός] in transferred senses . . . *in view of . . .* II Cor. v.10 πρὸς ἃ ἔπραξεν, in proportion to his deeds." BDF (§239[8]): "In accordance with. . . ." Ἔπραξεν, 3rd sg. aor. act. indic. of πράσσω, "do, accomplish." Εἴτε . . . εἴτε, "whether . . . or." Ἀγαθόν, acc. sg. neut. adj. ἀγαθός, -ή, -όν, "good." Φαῦλον, acc. sg. neut. adj. φαῦλος, -η, -ον, "evil."

Harris 408–9: "Since, then the tribunal of Christ is concerned with the assessment of works, not the determination of destiny, it will be apparent that the Pauline concepts of justification on the basis of faith and recompense in accordance with works may be complementary." Cf. Barnett 276: "Believers do not face condemnation at Christ's tribunal (see Rom 5:16, 18; 8:1) but rather *evaluation* with a view to the Master's commendation given or withheld (1 Cor 3:10–15; 4:5; cf. Luke 12:42–48)."

FOR FURTHER STUDY

52. Personal Eschatology (5:1–8)

Ellis, E. E. "II Corinthians v.1–10 in Pauline Eschatology." *NTS* 6 (1960): 211–24.
Gillman, J. "A Thematic Comparison: 1 Cor 15:50–57 and 2 Cor 5:1–5." *JBL* 107 (1988): 439–54.
Harris, M. J. "2 Corinthians 5:1–10: Watershed in Paul's Eschatology?" *TynBul* 22 (1971): 12–18.
———. *Raised Immortal: Resurrection and Immortality in the New Testament.* Grand Rapids: Eerdmans, 1991.
———. "Resurrection and Immortality: Eight Theses." *Them* 1 (1976): 50–55.
Kreitzer, L. J. *DPL* 253–69.
Osei-Bonsu, J. "Does 2 Cor. 5.1–10 Teach the Reception of the Resurrection Body at the Moment of Death?" *JSNT* 28 (1986): 81–101.
———. "Soul and Body in Life after Death: An Examination of the New Testament Evidence with Some Reference to Patristic Exegesis." Unpub. PhD thesis. University of Aberdeen, 1980.
Perriman, A. C. "Paul and the Parousia: 1 Corinthians 15:50–57 and 2 Corinthians 5:1–5." *NTS* 35 (1985): 512–21.
Sumney, J. L. "Post-Mortem Existence and Resurrection of the Body in Paul." *HBT* 31 (2009): 12–26.
Waters, L. J. "The Believer's Intermediate State after Death." *BibSac* 169 (2012): 283–303.
Yates, J. "Immediate or Intermediate? The State of the Believer upon Death." *Churchman* 101 (1987): 310–22.
Zorn, R. O. "II Corinthians 5:1–10: Individual Eschatology or Corporate Solidarity, Which?" *RTR* 47 (1988): 93–104.

53. General (5:1–10)

Cranford, L. "A New Look at 2 Corinthians 5:1–10." *SWJT* 19 (1976): 95–100.
Watson, N. M. "2 Cor. 5:1–10 in Recent Research." *ABR* 23 (1975): 33–36.

54. An Eternal Dwelling in the Heavens (5:1)

Danker, F. W. "Consolation in 2 Cor. 5:1–10," *CTM* (1968): 552–56.
Harris, *Prepositions*, 140–41, 192–93.
Sweet, J. P. M. "A House Not Made with Hands." Pages 368–90 in *Templum Amicitia: Essays on the Second Temple presented to Ernst Bammel.* Edited by W. Horbury. Sheffield: JSOT, 1991.

55. Pledge or Down Payment (Ἀρραβών) (5:5)

Erlemann, K. "*Der Geist als ἀρραβών (2 Kor 5, 5) im Kontext der paulinischen Eschatologie.*" *ZNW* 83 (1992): 202–23.
Kwon, Yon-Gyong "Arrabn as Pledge in Second Corinthians." *NTS* 54 (2008): 525–41.
Paige, T. *DPL* 404–13. See p. 411.

56. At Home in the Body, Away from the Lord (5:6–9)

Cassidy, R. "Paul's Attitude to Death in II Corinthians 6:1–10." *EvQ* 43 (1971): 210–17.

Craig, W. L. "Paul's Dilemma in 2 Corinthians 5:1–10: A Catch 22." *NTS* 34 (1987–88): 145–47.

Murphy-O'Connor, J. "Being at Home in the Body We Are in Exile from the Lord (2 Cor 5:6b)." *RB* 93/2 (1986): 214–21.

Thrall, M. E. "'Putting On' or 'Stripping Off' in 2 Corinthians 5:3." Pages 221–37 in *New Testament Textual Criticism. Its Significance for Exegesis: Essays in Honour of Bruce M. Metzger.* Edited by E. J. Epp and G. D. Fee. Oxford: Clarendon, 1981.

57. Appearing before the Judgment Seat of Christ (5:10)

Harris, *Prepositions*, 193–94.

Hiers, R. H. *ABD* 79–81. See pp. 80-81.

Morris, Leon, *The Biblical Doctrine of Judgment.* 1st ed. London: Tyndale Press, 1960.

Travis, S. H. *Christ and the Judgment of God: the Limits of Divine Retribution in New Testament Thought.* Milton Keynes, UK; Peabody, MA: Paternoster Press; Hendrickson, 2009.

———. *DPL* 516–17.

HOMILETICAL SUGGESTIONS

The Christian Hope (5:1–5)

1. An eternal dwelling in the heavens—the resurrection body replacing our earthly body (v. 1)
2. While we await our heavenly dwelling, we "groan" in our earthly body (v. 2)
3. Our hope is not for "nakedness," i.e., disembodiment, but for a resurrection body (vv. 3–4)
4. The presence of the Holy Spirit is God's pledge that our hope will be fulfilled (v. 5)

Living "Away from the Lord" (5:6–10)

1. Always confident even though we are "away from the Lord" (v. 6)
2. Walking by faith not by sight (v. 7)
3. Our aim is always to be pleasing to God (v. 9)
4. Evaluation of our works before the judgment seat of Christ (v. 10)

5. The Ministry of Reconciliation (5:11–21)

Having spoken of his aim to please the Lord whether he is at home in the body or away (5:9), and having reminded his readers that "all of us must appear before the judgment seat of Christ" (5:10 NRSV), Paul tells how he tries to persuade others to be reconciled to God (5:11). While doing so, he responds to criticisms of the way he conducts his ministry (5:11–15), and then spells out the theological basis upon which reconciliation with God rests (5:16–21).

a. Defense of His Ministry (5:11–15)

STRUCTURE

11   Εἰδότες οὖν τὸν φόβον τοῦ κυρίου
ἀνθρώπους πείθομεν,
     θεῷ δὲ
πεφανερώμεθα·
ἐλπίζω δὲ καὶ
     ἐν ταῖς συνειδήσεσιν ὑμῶν
          πεφανερῶσθαι.
12 οὐ πάλιν ἑαυτοὺς συνιστάνομεν ὑμῖν
     ἀλλ᾽ ἀφορμὴν διδόντες ὑμῖν καυχήματος ὑπὲρ ἡμῶν,
       ἵνα ἔχητε πρὸς τοὺς ἐν προσώπῳ καυχωμένους
              καὶ μὴ ἐν καρδίᾳ.
13 εἴτε γὰρ ἐξέστημεν, θεῷ·
     εἴτε σωφρονοῦμεν, ὑμῖν.
14 ἡ γὰρ ἀγάπη τοῦ Χριστοῦ συνέχει ἡμᾶς,
                         κρίναντας τοῦτο,
                            ὅτι εἷς ὑπὲρ πάντων ἀπέθανεν,
                               ἄρα οἱ πάντες ἀπέθανον·
15 καὶ ὑπὲρ πάντων ἀπέθανεν,
     ἵνα οἱ ζῶντες μηκέτι ἑαυτοῖς ζῶσιν
        ἀλλὰ   τῷ ὑπὲρ αὐτῶν ἀποθανόντι
                                 καὶ ἐγερθέντι.

VERSE 11

Εἰδότες οὖν τὸν φόβον τοῦ κυρίου ἀνθρώπους πείθομεν,
Therefore, since we know the fear of the Lord, we try to persuade people.

Εἰδότες, nom. pl. masc. of pf. act. ptc. of οἶδα, "know." Οὖν, the conj. "therefore," refers back to v. 10 as the basis of the fear that motivates Paul's efforts to persuade people to accept the gospel. He is not afraid of the Lord, but he does have a reverential awe of him and recognizes that his whole life and ministry will come under his scrutiny.

Τὸν φόβον τοῦ κυρίου, dir. obj. of εἰδότες. Τοῦ κυρίου, obj. gen. "the fear of the Lord." Ἀνθρώπους, acc. pl. masc. ἄνθρωπος, -ου, ὁ, "person," dir. obj. of πείθομεν. Πείθομεν, 1st pl. pres. act. indic. of πείθω, "persuade," can be construed in two ways: positively to persuade with a good motive, as in persuading people to embrace the gospel, or negatively to influence people with questionable motives. Paul could be conceding that he practices persuasion (which his opponents regarded as reprehensible) while asserting that his is not a persuasion that sacrifices the truth in order to please people. His persuasion is quite straightforward, carried out with a proper fear of the Lord. This interpretation finds support in the following statement.

But cf. Harris 413: "There is no need to find in the expression ἀνθρώπους πείθομεν an allusion to the rhetorical techniques of the orators of Paul's day or a slogan of Paul's opponents . . . which he cites and counters by claiming that *his* 'persuasion' arises from awareness of his responsibility before Christ . . . πείθομεν is probably a conative present ('we try to persuade'), referring not to action begun but either interrupted or unsuccessful, but to action that is incomplete, not yet fully accomplished."

θεῷ δὲ πεφανερώμεθα· ἐλπίζω δὲ καὶ ἐν ταῖς συνειδήσεσιν ὑμῶν πεφανερῶσθαι.
What we are is plain to God, and I hope it is also plain to your consciences.

Θεῷ, dat. indir. obj. of πεφανερώμεθα. Πεφανερώμεθα, 1st pl. pf. pass. indic. of φανερόω, "make known, make plain." Ἐλπίζω, 1st sg. pres. act. indic. of ἐλπίζω, "hope." Ἐν, prep. with locat. dat. ταῖς συνειδήσεσιν, "to your consciences." Συνειδήσεσιν, dat. pl. fem. συνείδησις, -εως, ἡ, "conscience." See note on 1:12 for an explanation of Paul's understanding of the nature and role of the conscience. Πεφανερῶσθαι, pf. pass. inf. of φανερόω, "make known, make plain." Obj. of inf. of ἐλπίζω, cf. R 909.

VERSE 12

οὐ πάλιν ἑαυτοὺς συνιστάνομεν ὑμῖν
We are not commending ourselves to you again,

Οὐ, the neg. particle "not." Πάλιν, the adv. "again." Ἑαυτούς, 3rd pl. masc. reflex. pron. ἑαυτοῦ, -ῆς, -οῦ, "oneself." Συνιστάνομεν, 1st pl. pres. act. indic. of συνίστημι, "commend." BDAG 972d: "*(re)commend someone to someone*. . . . Self-commendation . . . may be construed either as inappropriate . . . or as appropriate." Ὑμῖν, indir. obj. of συνιστάνομεν.

ἀλλ᾽ ἀφορμὴν διδόντες ὑμῖν καυχήματος ὑπὲρ ἡμῶν,
but giving you an opportunity to be proud of us,

Ἀφορμήν, acc. sg. fem. ἀφορμή, -ῆς, ἡ, "opportunity." Hafemann 237: "The word translated 'opportunity' (*aphorme*) in 5:12 is a military term used to designate a strategic base of operations as a launching pad for mounting an attack or defense (cf. its use in 11:12; Rom. 7:8; Gal. 5:13; 1 Tim. 5:14)." Διδόντες, nom. pl. masc. of pres. act.

ptc. of δίδωμι, "give." Moule 179 cites διδόντες here as an example of the use of a participle where normal Greek would have used a finite verb. Ἀφορμὴν διδόντες, BDAG 243b: *give an occasion* (for someth.)." Ὑμῖν, indir. obj. of διδόντες. Καυχήματος, gen. sg. neut. καύχημα, -ατος, τό, "boast, pride." Harris 415: "Here καύχημα denotes not the content or object of boasting, what one is proud of, but the act of boasting." Ὑπέρ, prep. with gen. ἡμῶν, "concerning us."

ἵνα ἔχητε πρὸς τοὺς ἐν προσώπῳ καυχωμένους καὶ μὴ ἐν καρδίᾳ.
so that you may have a reply for those who take pride in outward appearance rather than in the heart.

Ἵνα with subjunc. ἔχητε indicates purpose: "so that you may have." Ἔχητε, 2nd pl. aor. act. subjunc. of ἔχω, "have." Πρός, prep. with acc. τοὺς . . . καυχωμένους "with reference to those who boast." Cf. BDAG 875a. R 626: "Πρός does not of itself mean 'against,' though that may be the resultant idea . . . (2 Cor. 5:12)." Ἐν, prep. with dat. προσώπῳ, "in outward appearance." Μή, particle negating the prep. phrase. ἐν καρδίᾳ, in parallel with ἐν προσώπῳ modifying the subst. ptc. καυχωμένους.

VERSE 13

εἴτε γὰρ ἐξέστημεν, θεῷ· εἴτε σωφρονοῦμεν, ὑμῖν.
For if we are out of our mind, it is for God; if we are in our right mind, it is for you.

Εἴτε . . . εἴτε means "whether . . . or." Ἐξέστημεν, 1st pl. aor. act. indic. of ἐξίστημι, "be out of one's mind." There are two possible ways this could be taken. As an allusion to charges made by his opponents who said he was mad, to which Paul responds that what they regard as madness is in fact zeal for God. Alternatively, it is an allusion to charges that his ministry was unspiritual because it lacked evidence of ecstatic experience, to which Paul says his experience of ecstasy is something between himself and God, not something to be bragged about in support of the validity of his ministry. Θεῷ, dat. of advantage, "for God." Cf. BDF (§188[2]); R 539. Cf. 1 Cor 14:2, where Paul says of his tongue-speaking that it is "to God" (θεῷ).

Σωφρονοῦμεν, 1st pl. pres. act. indic. of σωφρονέω, "be in one's right mind." There are also two possible ways this could be taken. Alluding to those who said he was mad, Paul says to the Corinthians, "If I am in my right mind (as I am), that is for your sake (who benefit from the sober truth I speak)." Alluding to those who questioned the spiritual nature of his ministry, claiming it lacked ecstatic manifestations, he says to his readers, "If I experience ecstasy, that is something between me and God (not something to be spoken of as proof of the spiritual character of my ministry), but if I am in my right mind (and use reasonable, intelligible speech), that is for your benefit." Ὑμῖν, dat. of advantage, "for you." Cf. BDF (§188[2]); R 539; ZG 544.

Cf. Moule 195: "One is bound, however, to confess that it is difficult to detect a more than *rhetorical* antithesis in II Cor. v.13 . . . for what logic is there in saying that ecstasy is for God's sake, sanity for the sake of the Corinthians?" Cf. Hafemann, 238–39.

For a contrary view cf. Seifrid 242: "The language corresponds to that of the 'fool's speech' (11:16–12:10), in which Paul speaks out of character, 'in a state of boasting' (11:17). . . . Paul's statement is therefore not to be interpreted as a reference to an ecstatic experience, nor does it have reference to ecstatic experiences of his opponents. . . . It is highly unlikely that Paul is speaking here of the ecstasy of a vision; the verb *existēmi* does not normally bear this sense, nor does Paul give any indication of amazement or visible ecstasy on his part in his report of his vision, even if he was transported to heaven (12:1–10)."

VERSE 14

ἡ γὰρ ἀγάπη τοῦ Χριστοῦ συνέχει ἡμᾶς,
For the love of Christ compels us,

Γάρ, the conj. "since," introduces the reason why Paul, whether regarded as out of his mind or in his right mind, does things for the sake of the Corinthians. Ἀγάπη, nom. sg. fem. ἀγάπη, -ης, ἡ, "love." Τοῦ Χριστοῦ, either obj. gen. (Paul's love for Christ) or subj. gen. (Christ's love for Paul). The latter is preferable in the context where Christ's death for all is emphasized (though the sense of Christ's love for us generates our love for him; cf. 1 John 4:19: "We love because he first loved us"). Cf. R 499; Moule 41; Z §36. Συνέχει, 3rd pl. pres. act. indic. of συνέχω, "compel," a verb also found in Phil 1:23–24: "I am torn between the two. I long to depart and be with Christ—which is far better—but to remain in the flesh is more necessary for your sake." He felt the pressure of two alternatives so that he was motivated on the one hand to do one thing, but on the other hand to do the opposite. This illustrates the basic mng. of συνέχω, which is "to press together, constrain." It is the pressure applied not so much to control as to cause action. It is motivational rather than directional force. The pres. tense underlines the continuous nature of this pressure upon the apostle. Ἡμᾶς, acc. 1st pl. "us," dir. obj. of συνέχει.

κρίναντας τοῦτο, ὅτι εἷς ὑπὲρ πάντων ἀπέθανεν, ἄρα οἱ πάντες ἀπέθανον·
since we have reached this conclusion: If one died for all, then all died.

Κρίναντας τοῦτο, lit. "having judged this." NRSV: "because we are convinced." Κρίναντας, acc. pl. masc. of aor. act. ptc. of κρίνω, "judge." BDAG 568a: "make a judgment." Τοῦτο, acc. sg. neut. pron. "this," dir. obj. of κρίναντας. Κρίναντας is acc. because it is in appos. to ἡμᾶς.

Ὅτι, the conj. "that," introduces the content of the judgment made. Εἷς ὑπὲρ πάντων ἀπέθανεν: It was not the bare fact of Christ's historic death that moved Paul; it was his death understood in a particular way: "for all" (ὑπὲρ πάντων). Ὑπέρ may be understood to mean "instead of" (i.e., Christ dying "in place of" all) or "for the sake of" (i.e., "for the benefit of" all, understood to mean something less than "instead of" all). Against the former it has been argued that if Paul had meant to say Christ died "instead of" all, he would have used the Greek preposition ἀντί, which more clearly expresses that idea. It is true that ἀντί expresses the idea unambiguously, but while ὑπέρ need not denote "instead of," it may do so. The matter cannot be settled by consideration of this text in isolation. Other Pauline texts bearing upon the subject must guide us. E.g., in Gal 3:13 Paul says, "Christ redeemed us from the curse of the law by becoming a curse for [ὑπέρ] us, because it is written, **Cursed is everyone who is hung on a tree.**" There Christ clearly endured God's curse "instead of" us. There was absolutely no reason for him to endure God's curse otherwise. Guided by Gal 3:13, we may conclude that in the present context "one died for [ὑπέρ] all" means that Christ died "instead of all." This interpretation preserves the logical connection with what follows. Cf. Seifrid 244–45; R 631: "the notion of substitution must be understood because of Paul's use of ἄρα οἱ πάντες ἀπέθανον as the conclusion from εἷς ὑπὲρ πάντων ἀπέθανεν." Εἷς, nom. sg. masc. adj. εἷς, μία, ἕν, "one [person]." Ἀπέθανεν, 3rd sg. aor. act. indic. of ἀποθνήσκω, "die." The event denoted points back to the historic event of the cross. Ὑπέρ, prep with gen. πάντων "for all." Z §91: "Ὑπέρ generally means 'for' in the sense 'in favour of', but not rarely covers also 'for' in the sense 'in place of'."

Ἄρα, the conj. "then, therefore." Οἱ πάντες ἀπέθανον, "all died." If Christ did not die "instead of the all," then "the all" cannot be said to have died (the mng. of "the all" is discussed along with that of "the world" in the note on v. 19 below, where the latter is found). Only because Christ is the incarnate Son of God could the death of "the one" be for "the all." Only the death of this "one" could redeem us from the curse of the law; the death of a mere human being could never achieve this. Cf. Barnett 290: "'All' who are 'in Adam,' that is, all people regardless, do actually die as a result of Adam's sin (Rom 5:12, 18a, 19a). But the 'all' for whom Christ died, who also have 'died' in him, while potentially inclusive of 'all' who are 'in Adam,' is in actuality limited to those who are 'in Christ,' through faith-commitment to him." Cf. Harris 420–21: "The three uses of πάντες denote all people, οἱ ζῶντες [v. 15] describing those 'in Christ.'" Ἀπέθανον, 3rd pl. aor. act. indic. of ἀποθνήσκω, "die."

VERSE 15

In this verse Paul states the purpose of Christ's death insofar as the lives of those who benefit from it are concerned, stating it negatively in v. 15a, then positively in v. 15b.

καὶ ὑπὲρ πάντων ἀπέθανεν, ἵνα οἱ ζῶντες μηκέτι ἑαυτοῖς ζῶσιν
And he died for all so that those who live should no longer live for themselves,

Ὑπὲρ πάντων ἀπέθανεν, see note on v. 14 above. Cf. Moule 64. Harris, *Prepositions*, 213: "In 2Co 5:14–15 Paul is giving the reason why Christ's love governs him in everything. That ὑπέρ bears a substitutionary sense here . . . is shown by the conclusion (inferential ἄρα) Paul draws: 'therefore all died.' The death of Christ was the death of all human beings (πάντες), because he was dying the death they deserved. . . . He represented them by becoming their substitute." Cf. Harris 423: "There is universalism in the scope of redemption, since no person is excluded from God's offer of salvation; but there is a particularity in the application of redemption, since not everyone appropriates the benefits afforded by this universally offered salvation."

Ἵνα with subjunc. ζῶσιν expresses purpose. Ζῶσιν, 3rd pl. pres. act. subjunc. of ζάω, "live." Οἱ ζῶντες, ptc. phrase "those who live," subj of ζῶσιν. Ζῶντες nom. pl. masc. of pres. act ptc. of ζάω, "live." Μηκέτι, adv. mng. "no longer." Ἑαυτοῖς, dat. 3rd pl. masc. reflex. pron., "for themselves."

ἀλλὰ τῷ ὑπὲρ αὐτῶν ἀποθανόντι καὶ ἐγερθέντι.
but for the one who died for them and was raised.

Ἀλλά, advers. conj. "but." Τῷ . . . ἀποθανόντι καὶ ἐγερθέντι, dat. ptc. phrase "for the one who died and was raised." Ἀποθανόντι, dat. sg. masc. of aor. act. ptc. of ἀποθνῄσκω, "die." Καὶ ἐγερθέντι, (BDF §442[9]) "explicative καί . . . always used to particularize." Ἐγερθέντι, dat. sg. masc. of aor. pass. ptc. of ἐγείρω, "raise." Ὑπέρ, prep. with gen. αὐτῶν, "for them." Harris, *Prepositions*, 213: "in the case of ὑπὲρ αὐτῶν in v. 15b mere representation must be in mind if this phrase qualifies both τῷ . . . ἀποθανόντι and [τῷ] ἐγερθέντι . . . since Paul never portrays the resurrection of Jesus as being 'in the place of' believers."

b. God's Reconciling Act in Christ (5:16–21)

STRUCTURE

16　Ὥστε ἡμεῖς
　　　　ἀπὸ τοῦ νῦν
　　　　οὐδένα
　　　οἴδαμεν
　　　　κατὰ σάρκα·
　　εἰ καὶ ἐγνώκαμεν
　　　　κατὰ σάρκα
　　　　Χριστόν,
　ἀλλὰ　νῦν
　　　　οὐκέτι
　　　γινώσκομεν.
17　ὥστε εἴ τις ἐν Χριστῷ,
　καινὴ κτίσις·
　τὰ ἀρχαῖα παρῆλθεν,
　ἰδοὺ γέγονεν καινά·
18　τὰ δὲ πάντα ἐκ τοῦ θεοῦ

　　　　τοῦ καταλλάξαντος ἡμᾶς
　　　　ἑαυτῷ
　　　　διὰ Χριστοῦ

καὶ δόντος ἡμῖν τὴν διακονίαν τῆς καταλλαγῆς,
19   ὡς ὅτι θεὸς ἦν ἐν Χριστῷ
           κόσμον
           καταλλάσσων
           ἑαυτῷ,
       μὴ λογιζόμενος αὐτοῖς τὰ παραπτώματα αὐτῶν

       καὶ θέμενος ἐν ἡμῖν τὸν λόγον τῆς καταλλαγῆς.
20   ὑπὲρ Χριστοῦ
     οὖν πρεσβεύομεν
          ὡς τοῦ θεοῦ παρακαλοῦντος δι᾽ ἡμῶν·
           δεόμεθα ὑπὲρ Χριστοῦ,
               καταλλάγητε τῷ θεῷ.
21   τὸν μὴ γνόντα ἁμαρτίαν
               ὑπὲρ ἡμῶν
           ἁμαρτίαν
     ἐποίησεν,
        ἵνα ἡμεῖς γενώμεθα δικαιοσύνη θεοῦ ἐν αὐτῷ.

VERSE 16

Ὥστε ἡμεῖς ἀπὸ τοῦ νῦν οὐδένα οἴδαμεν κατὰ σάρκα·
From now on, then, we do not know anyone from a worldly perspective.

The reference to knowing Christ "from a worldly perspective" (lit. "according to [the] flesh"), led Bultmann to argue that Paul showed little interest in the historical Jesus (Christ after the flesh) but focused rather upon the Christ of faith. However, such a view can claim no support from this verse because Paul is talking about a *way* of knowing ("according to the flesh"), not about a particular *phase* of Christ's existence (Christ after the flesh = the historical Jesus). Cf. Harris, *Prepositions*, 149.
    Ὥστε, the conj. "therefore" introduces the first consequence of vv. 14–15. Moule 144: "ὥστε is also, in certain contexts, simply an *inferential particle* as if ὥς τε, meaning *and so, accordingly*, etc." Ἀπό, prep. with gen. art. τοῦ and subst. νῦν, "from now on" (BDAG 681c). Νῦν, adv. "now," as art. subst. τοῦ νῦν, "the present time." Οὐδένα, acc. sg. masc. subst. adj. οὐδείς, οὐδεμία, οὐδέν, "no one." Οἴδαμεν, 1st pl. pf. act. indic. of οἶδα, "know." ZG 544: "here used (like its Hebr. counterpart) in the sense of *consider, regard*." Κατά prep. with acc. σάρκα, lit. "according to the flesh," NRSV: "from a human point of view."

εἰ καὶ ἐγνώκαμεν κατὰ σάρκα Χριστόν, ἀλλὰ νῦν οὐκέτι γινώσκομεν.
Even if we have known Christ from a worldly perspective, yet now we no longer know him in this way.

Εἰ καί, "even if." Ἐγνώκαμεν, 1st pl. pf. act. indic. of γινώσκω, "know." Harris 427: "Clearly in this verse γινώσκομεν [κατὰ σάρκα] is synonymous with the earlier οἴδαμεν κατὰ σάρκα, both verbs meaning not 'know about,' but 'view,' 'regard,' 'appraise,' 'value' (cf. 1 Thess. 5:12)." Κατὰ σάρκα, see above. Χριστόν, obj. of ἐγνώκαμεν.

Ἀλλά, the advers. conj. "but." ZG 544–45: "in apodosis after εἰ has the force of *yet*." Νῦν, the adv. "now." Οὐκέτι, adv. mng. "no longer." Γινώσκομεν, 1st pl. pres. act. indic. of γινώσκω, "know."

Paul, before his conversion, like many of his fellow Jews, evaluated Christ "from a worldly perspective" and dismissed claims that he was the Messiah because he regarded it as unthinkable that God's Messiah could be crucified as a criminal.

VERSE 17

ὥστε εἴ τις ἐν Χριστῷ, καινὴ κτίσις· τὰ ἀρχαῖα παρῆλθεν, ἰδοὺ γέγονεν καινά·
Therefore, if anyone is in Christ, he is a new creation; the old has passed away, and see, the new has come!

Ὥστε, the conj. "therefore" introduces the second consequence of vv. 14–15. See note on v. 16 above. Rendered literally, εἴ τις ἐν Χριστῷ, καινὴ κτίσις reads "if anyone in Christ, a new creation." CSB renders καινὴ κτίσις as "he is a new creation"; however it lacks a copula and could also be rendered, "[there is] a new creation." Harris 432: "The rendering 'there is a new creation' . . . reproduces the ambiguity of the Greek, which could mean 'there is a newly-created being' . . . 'he or she is a newly-created person' or 'there is a new act of creation.' Εἴ, the conj. "if." Εν, prep. with dat. Χριστῷ, "in Christ." This has been variously interpreted: to belong to Christ; to live in the sphere of Christ's power; to be united to Christ; and to be a member of the Christian community through baptism. It is difficult to explain precisely what Paul intended by the expression here, and each of the options mentioned above is feasible. At a minimum to be "in Christ" means to belong to him through faith, but that can also mean living in the sphere of his power, being united with him through the Spirit, and to have become a part of the Christian community by baptism. Harris, *Prepositions*, 123: "Consequently, if anyone has been incorporated into Christ, there is a new creation." Καινή, nom. sg. fem. adj. subst. καινός, -ή, -όν, "new." Κτίσις, nom. sg. fem. κτίσις, -εως, ἡ, "creation, creature."

Ἀρχαῖα, nom. pl. neut. art. subst. adj. ἀρχαῖος, -αία, -αῖον, "the old." Cf. R 654. Παρῆλθεν, 3rd sg. aor. act. indic. of παρέρχομαι, "pass away." Ἰδού, dem. particle "behold, look, see." Γέγονεν, 3rd sg. pf. act. indic. of γίνομαι, "come to be." Καινά, nom. pl. neut. subst. adj. καινός, -ή, -όν, "(the) new."

When people are "in Christ," they become already part of the new creation. For the time being the old still persists and the new has not yet fully come (cf. Rom 8:18–25; Gal 5:15–26). Being "a new creation" now will culminate in transformation by resurrection to immortality in the new created order at the Parousia (cf. Isa 65:17–25; 66:22; Rom 8:19–23; Rev 21:1). Cf. Harris 434: "When a person becomes a Christian, he or she experiences a total restructuring of life that alters its whole fabric—thinking, feeling, willing, and acting. Anyone who is 'in Christ' is 'Under New Management.'"

VERSE 18

τὰ δὲ πάντα ἐκ τοῦ θεοῦ τοῦ καταλλάξαντος ἡμᾶς ἑαυτῷ διὰ Χριστοῦ
Everything is from God, who has reconciled us to himself through Christ

Πάντα, nom. pl. neut. subst. adj. πᾶς, πᾶσα, πᾶν, "all things." Ἐκ, prep. with gen. of source τοῦ θεοῦ, "from God." Cf. Harris, *Prepositions*, 105. Τοῦ καταλλάξαντος ἡμᾶς ἑαυτῷ, gen. attrib. ptc. clause describing God as the one "who has reconciled us." Καταλλάξαντος, gen. sg. masc. of aor. act. ptc. of καταλλάσσω, "reconcile." The language of reconciliation is peculiarly Pauline. The verbs "to reconcile" (καταλλάσσω, ἀποκαταλλάσσω) and the noun "reconciliation" (καταλλαγή) are found only in his letters in the NT (Rom 5:10, 11; 11:15; 1 Cor 7:11; 2 Cor 5:18, 19, 20; Eph 2:16; Col 1:20, 22). Seifrid 256–57: "In normal Greek usage, it is the (pers.) object of the active voice form of the verb *katallassō* ('reconcile') whose enmity is done away with. In other words, Paul is not speaking here of the overcoming of God's enmity against humanity, but that of the fallen humanity against God." Ἡμᾶς, acc. 1st pl. masc. pron. ἐγώ, "us," dir. obj. of καταλλάξαντος. Ἑαυτῷ, dat. 3rd sg. masc. reflex. pron. ἑαυτοῦ, -ῆς, -οῦ, "himself." Διά, prep. with gen. Χριστοῦ, "through Christ."

καὶ δόντος ἡμῖν τὴν διακονίαν τῆς καταλλαγῆς,
and has given us the ministry of reconciliation.

Δόντος, gen. sg. masc. of aor. act. attrib. ptc. of δίδωμι, "give," further describing God as the one who "has given (us the ministry of reconciliation)." Ἡμῖν, dat. 1st pl. masc. pron. ἐγώ, "us," indir. obj. of δόντος. Διακονίαν, acc. sg. fem. διακονία, -ας, ἡ, "ministry," dir. obj. of δόντος. Τῆς καταλλαγῆς, descriptive gen. qualifying διακονίαν. Καταλλαγῆς, gen. sg. fem. καταλλαγή, -ῆς, ἡ, "reconciliation."
In one sense reconciliation has been accomplished already. God through Christ has already "reconciled" us to himself (v. 18a). However, in another sense the process of reconciliation is still incomplete. Through the "ministry of reconciliation" (v. 18b), people are called to be reconciled to God, and unless they respond positively to that call, they do not actually experience reconciliation (cf. v. 20).

VERSE 19

ὡς ὅτι θεὸς ἦν ἐν Χριστῷ κόσμον καταλλάσσων ἑαυτῷ,
That is, in Christ, God was reconciling the world to himself,

Ὡς ὅτι, ZG 545: "that is." θεὸς ἦν ἐν Χριστῷ, Barnett 306: "There is a degree of ambiguity to the words [θεὸς ἦν ἐν Χριστῷ κόσμον καταλλάσσων ἑαυτῷ] . . . which in broad terms, have been taken either as 'God was in Christ reconciling the world to himself' (RV) or, preferably, as 'in Christ God was reconciling the world to himself' (RSV). The former would emphasize the incarnation, which, though mentioned in the letter (8:9), is not the burden of this passage. Rather, the death of Christ, which dominates the passage (vv.14–15 and v. 21) . . . provides the key to the interpretation." Cf. Harris, *Prepositions*, 126: "[this] does not refer to the incarnation (as if ἦν were equivalent to ἐσκήνωσεν, 'took up residence') but to the entire life of Christ on earth in which God was personally present and through which he revealed himself. Further, it seems that the finite verb (ἦν) and the participle (καταλλάσσων) are related as cause and effect; it was only because God in all his fullness had chosen to dwell in Christ (Col 1:19), only because there dwelt embodied in Christ the total plenitude of deity (Col 2:9), that reconciliation was accomplished. . . . A functional Christology presupposes and finds its ultimate basis in an ontological Christology."

ʾΗν . . . καταλλάσσων, impf. periph. ptc. "was reconciling." But cf. Moule 17–18: "In II Cor. v.19 it is debatable whether ἦν . . . καταλλάσσων is periphrastic or not." ʾΗν, 3rd sg. impf. act. indic. of εἰμί, "be." Καταλλάσσων, nom. sg. masc. of pres. act. ptc. of καταλλάσσω, "reconcile."

Ἐν, prep. with dat. Χριστῷ. God being "in Christ" may simply mean that it was through the agency of Christ that God reconciled the world to himself. However, prob. more is involved; see note on θεὸς ἦν ἐν Χριστῷ above.

Κόσμον, acc. sg. masc. κόσμος, -ου, ὁ, "world," dir. obj. of ἦν . . . καταλλάσσων. Here κόσμος refers to humanity, not the whole created order, as the context indicates when reconciliation is related to "not counting their trespasses against them" (elsewhere Paul does include the whole creation in the reconciliation; cf. Rom 8:19–22; Col 1:20). Ἑαυτῷ, dat. 3rd sg. masc. reflex. pron. ἑαυτοῦ, -ῆς, -οῦ, "himself," indir. obj. of ἦν . . . καταλλάσσων.

μὴ λογιζόμενος αὐτοῖς τὰ παραπτώματα αὐτῶν
not counting their trespasses against them,

Λογιζόμενος, nom. sg. masc. of pres. mid. ptc. of λογίζομαι, "take into account." Αὐτοῖς, dat. pl. masc. pron. αὐτός, -ή, -ό, "against them," dat. of personal disadvantage. R 683: "In 2 Cor. 5:19 αὐτοῖς refers to κόσμον." BDF (§282[3]) "The 3rd person pronoun αὐτοῦ etc. is often used without formal agreement, i.e. without a noun present in the same gender and number to which it would refer . . . (3) κόσμος . . . αὐτοῖς 2 C 5:19." Παραπτώματα, acc. pl. neut. παράπτωμα, -ατος, τό, "trespass," dir. obj. of λογιζόμενος. Αὐτῶν, poss. gen. 3rd pl. masc. pron. αὐτός, -ή, -ό, "them," qualifying παραπτώματα. Λογίζομαι is an accounting term used when crediting and debiting things to people's accounts. Cf. H. W. Heidland, *TDNT* 4.284–85. The non-counting of people's sins against them is expressed by Paul in Rom 4:8 citing Ps 32:2: "Blessed is the one whose sin the Lord will never count against them" (NIV). This blessing, Paul goes on to explain, is not restricted to Jews ("the circumcised") but is pronounced over all who believe, incl. Gentiles. Accordingly "the world" in v. 19a is best interpreted to apply to all who believe whether they be Jews or Gentiles, not extensively to every individual human being. Elsewhere Paul clearly implies that unless they repent, the sins of unbelievers are and shall be counted against them (cf. Rom 1:18–32; 2:5–11; Eph 5:3–6; Col 3:5–6). Nevertheless, it is vital to stress that the death of Christ is sufficient to atone for the sins of the whole world (cf. 1 John 2:2) and make reconciliation possible for everyone, but this becomes effective only in those who respond positively to the message of reconciliation.

καὶ θέμενος ἐν ἡμῖν τὸν λόγον τῆς καταλλαγῆς.
and he has committed the message of reconciliation to us.

Θέμενος, nom. sg. masc. of aor. mid. ptc. of τίθημι, "commit, entrust." Ἐν, prep. with dat. ἡμῖν, "to us," indir. obj. of θέμενος. Τὸν λόγον, dir. obj. of θέμενος. Τῆς καταλλαγῆς, gen. of content "(the message) of/about reconciliation." Καταλλαγῆς, gen. sg. fem. καταλλαγή, -ῆς, ἡ, "reconciliation."

The reconciling activity of God is manifested in two movements: the first is his own reconciliation of the world in Christ, and the second is his call to people to be reconciled on that basis through his messengers.

VERSE 20

ὑπὲρ Χριστοῦ οὖν πρεσβεύομεν ὡς τοῦ θεοῦ παρακαλοῦντος δι' ἡμῶν·
Therefore, we are ambassadors for Christ, since God is making his appeal through us.

Ὑπέρ, prep. with gen. Χριστοῦ, "for/on behalf of Christ." Οὖν, the conj. "therefore," introduces the result of Paul's being entrusted with the message of reconciliation. Πρεσβεύομεν, 1st pl. pres. act. indic. of πρεσβεύω, "be an ambassador." Lit. πρεσβεύω means "to be older or the eldest," but came to be used in connection with functions for which the wisdom of age was a necessary prerequisite. In the political sphere it was used of ambassadors who were commissioned and given authority to represent their nations. Harris, *Prepositions*, 213: "In saying ὑπὲρ Χριστοῦ οὖν πρεσβεύομεν, Paul is asserting more than the simple fact that he is 'Christ's ambassador' (which would be Χριστοῦ πρεσβεία/πρεσβευτής ἐσμεν). As Christ's envoy (πρεσβεύομεν v.20a) and also in issuing his impassioned entreaty (δεόμεθα v. 20b), he acts ὑπὲρ Χριστοῦ, both 'on behalf of Christ' and 'in the place of Christ' (cf. the ὑπέρ in 5:14). There is no need here to choose between the notions of representation and substitution for ὑπέρ; both concepts are present, in light of the implications of any ambassadorial role."

Ὡς, the comp. particle "since." R 1141: "In 2 Cor. 5:20 . . . Paul endorses the notion that he is an ambassador of God and ὡς is not to be interpreted as mere pretense," contra NIV: "as though." Τοῦ θεοῦ παρακαλοῦντος, gen. abs. depicting action taking place at the time of the main verb. Πρεσβεύομεν: "we are ambassadors . . . God is making his appeal through us." Παρακαλοῦντος, gen. sg. masc. of pres. act. ptc. of παρακαλέω, "make an appeal." Δι', prep. with gen. ἡμῶν, "through us."

δεόμεθα ὑπὲρ Χριστοῦ, καταλλάγητε τῷ θεῷ.
We plead on Christ's behalf: "Be reconciled to God."

Δεόμεθα, 1st pl. pres. mid. indic. of δέομαι, "plead, implore." Δεόμεθα has no direct object. This has led some exegetes to argue that Paul is not addressing his exhortation to his Corinthian readers. However, καταλλάγητε ("be reconciled") is a 2nd pl. impv. indicating that the exhortation is directed to them. Ὑπέρ, prep. with gen. Χριστοῦ, "on Christ's behalf." BDAG 1030c: "*as helpers of Christ we beg you.* Also prob. is *we beg you by* or *in the name of* Christ." Καταλλάγητε, 2nd pl. aor. pass. impv. of καταλλάσσω, "reconcile." Τῷ θεῷ, dat. "to God."

VERSE 21

τὸν μὴ γνόντα ἁμαρτίαν ὑπὲρ ἡμῶν ἁμαρτίαν ἐποίησεν,
He made the one who did not know sin to be sin for us,

Τὸν μὴ γνόντα ἁμαρτίαν, art. attrib. ptc. phrase "the one who did not know sin." To "know" sin in this context is not to know *about* sin but to know it by being personally *involved* in it. The consistent witness of the NT is that Jesus did not sin (cf. Matt 27:4, 24; Luke 23:47; John 8:46; Heb 4:15; 1 Pet 1:19; 2:22). It may be inferred from Paul's statement, Christ "did not know sin," that only a sinless one could, through his death, be the agent of reconciliation (cf. 1 Pet 1:19). Γνόντα, acc. sg. masc. of aor. act. ptc. of γινώσκω, "know." Ἁμαρτίαν, acc. sg. fem. ἁμαρτία, -ίας, ἡ, "sin." Ὑπέρ, prep. with gen. ἡμῶν, "for us." Ἁμαρτίαν ἐποίησεν, "he made . . . to be sin." ZG 545: "meaning that God treated him as if he had been sin's embodiment." See extended note below. Ἐποίησεν, 3rd sg. aor. act. indic. of ποιέω, "make."

There are various interpretations of τὸν μὴ γνόντα ἁμαρτίαν ὑπὲρ ἡμῶν ἁμαρτίαν ἐποίησεν: (a) God made Christ a sinner, (b) God made him a sin offering, (c) God made him bear the consequences of our sins. The first suggestion is rightly rejected out of hand. The second can be supported by appeal to Paul's use of sacrificial terminology elsewhere to bring out the significance of Christ's death (e.g., Rom 3:25; 1 Cor 5:7). It has also been noted that in Lev 4:24 and 5:12 (LXX) the same word, "sin" (ἁμαρτία), is used to mean "sin-offering." However, with only one possible exception (Rom 8:3), the word is never used in this way in the NT. The idea of Christ's death as a sacrifice for sin is certainly Pauline, but it is not the best way of understanding the present statement. The third suggestion then is to be preferred and is supported by the fact that in Gal 3:13 Paul interprets the work of Christ in terms of bearing the consequences of our sins: "Christ redeemed us from the curse of the law by becoming a curse for us, because it is written, **Cursed is everyone who is hung on a tree.**" This interpretation is further supported by the fact that "he made the one who did not know sin to be sin for us" (2 Cor 5:21a) is balanced in antithetical parallelism by the words, "so that in him we might become the righteousness of God" (v. 21b). If becoming "the righteous-ness of God" means God adjudicated in our favor and put us in right relationship with himself, then for Christ to be made sin, being its antithetical counterpart, will mean that God has adjudicated against Christ because he took upon himself the burden of our sins (cf. Isa 53:4–6, 12), with the result that the relationship of the human Jesus with God was (momentarily, but terribly beyond all human comprehension) severed.

Cf. Harris 454: "We conclude that in v. 21a Paul is not saying that at the crucifixion the sinless Christ became in some sense a sinner, yet he is affirming more that Christ became a sin-offering or even a sin bearer. In a sense beyond human comprehension, God treated Christ as 'sin,' aligning him so totally with sin and its dire consequences that from God's viewpoint he became indistinguishable from sin itself."

ἵνα ἡμεῖς γενώμεθα δικαιοσύνη θεοῦ ἐν αὐτῷ.
so that in him we might become the righteousness of God.

See note on v. 21a above. Ἵνα . . . with subjunc. γενώμεθα expresses purpose "that we might become." Ἡμεῖς emphatic. Γενώμεθα δικαιοσύνη θεοῦ, ZG 545: "a desperate attempt to put into words the inexpressible mystery whose inner principle transcends all human understanding." Γενώμεθα, 1st pl. aor. mid. subjunc. of γίνομαι, "become." Δικαιοσύνη, pred. nom. (following γενώμεθα) sg. fem. δικαιοσύνη, -ης, ἡ, "righteous-ness." Ἐν, prep. with dat. αὐτῷ, "in him."

FOR FURTHER STUDY

58. Self-Commendation (5:11–12)

> Hafemann, S. J. "'Self-Commendation' and Apostolic Legitimacy in 2 Corinthians: A Pauline Dialectic?" NTS (1990–91): 61–68.
> Kasch, W. TDNT 7.896–98.

59. Paul's Ecstasy or Madness? (5:13)

> Hubbard, M. "Was Paul Out of His Mind? Rereading 2 Corinthians 5:13." JSNT 70 (1998): 39–64.

60. Christ Died for All (5:14–15)

> Green, J. B. DPL 201–9.
> Riesenfeld, H. TDNT 8.509–10.

61. The Compelling Love of Christ (5:14)

> Hendry, G. S. "ἡ γὰρ ἀγάπη τοῦ Χριστοῦ συνέχει ἡμᾶς: 2 Cor 5:14." ExpTim 59 (1947–48): 82.

62. Paul's Knowledge of Christ (5:16)

> Frazer, J. W. "Paul's Knowledge of Jesus: 2 Corinthians 5.16 once more." NTS 17 (1971): 293–313.
> Wolff, C. "True Apostolic Knowledge of Christ: Exegetical Reflections on 2 Corinthians 5.14 ff." Pages 81–98 in Paul and Jesus. Collected Essays. JSNTSup 37. Edited by A. J. M. Wedderburn. Sheffield, 1981.

63. A New Creation (5:17)

Hubbard, M.V. *New Creation in Paul's Letters and Thought.* Cambridge: CUP, 2002.
Levison, J. R. *DPL* 189–90.

64. Reconciliation (5:18–19)

Beale, G. K. "The Old Testament Background of Reconciliation in 2 Cor 5–7 and Its
    Bearing on the Literary Problem of 2 Corinthians 6:14–7:1." *NTS* 35 (1989): 550–81.
Büchsel, F. *TDNT* 1.251–59.
Kim, S. "2 Cor. 5:11–21 and the Origin of Paul's Concept of 'Reconciliation.'" *NovT* 39
    (1997): 360–84.
Martin, R. P. *Reconciliation: A Study of Paul's Theology.* Atlanta: John Knox/London:
    Marshall, 1981.
Porter, S. E. "Reconciliation and 2 Corinthians 5,18–21." Pages 693–705 in *Studies on
    2 Corinthians.* Edited by R. Bieringer and J. Lambrecht. Leuven: Leuven University
    Press, 1996.

65. Paul as Ambassador (5:20)

Bornkamm, G. *TDNT* 6.681–83.

66. Made to Be Sin and Becoming the Righteousness of God (5:21)

Hooker, M. D. "Interchange in Christ." *JTS* n.s. 22 (1971): 349–61.
———. "On Becoming the Righteousness of God: Another Look at 2 Cor 5:21." *NovT* 50
    (2008): 358–75.

HOMILETICAL SUGGESTIONS

Setting the Record Straight (5:11–15)

1. Persuading others with integrity (v. 1)
2. Acting in a way that gives others a reason to take pride in us (v. 2)
3. Zeal for Christ can be misconstrued (v. 13)
4. Christ's love is what motivates us (v. 14)
5. Christ died for all so that all might live for him (v. 15)

Reconciliation and Its Implications (5:16–21)

1. The death of Christ for all changes our attitude to everyone (v. 16)
2. New creatures in Christ—the old has passed away, the new has come (v. 17)
3. God's reconciling act in Christ (vv. 18a, 19)
4. Pleading with people to be reconciled to God (vv. 18b–20)
5. Christ was made "to be sin" so that we might "become the righteousness of
   God" (v. 21)

6. Reconciliation Practiced (6:1–7:4)

Paul, having spoken in the previous chapter of the reconciling activity of God and his own role as an ambassador of Christ and a messenger of reconciliation, now in 6:1–7:4 enacts his role as a minister of reconciliation for the benefit of his readers. He was aware of the strains in the Corinthians' relationship with him because of the actions of the "offender" and the influence of intruders. In order that their relationship be fully restored, he exhorts them not to receive the grace of God in vain (vv. 1–2), makes another defense of his ministry (vv. 3–10), and appeals to them to open their hearts to him so as to be fully reconciled to their apostle (vv. 11–13; 7:2–4), interspersing a call to holy living (6:14–7:1).

a. An Appeal for Reconciliation (6:1–13)

STRUCTURE

1   Συνεργοῦντες δὲ καὶ
     παρακαλοῦμεν
          μὴ εἰς κενὸν τὴν χάριν τοῦ θεοῦ δέξασθαι ὑμᾶς·
2   λέγει γάρ,
          Καιρῷ δεκτῷ ἐπήκουσά σου
          καὶ ἐν ἡμέρᾳ σωτηρίας ἐβοήθησά σοι.
     ἰδοὺ νῦν καιρὸς εὐπρόσδεκτος,
     ἰδοὺ νῦν ἡμέρα σωτηρίας·
3   μηδεμίαν ἐν μηδενὶ διδόντες προσκοπήν
               ἵνα μὴ μωμηθῇ ἡ διακονία,
4   ἀλλ'   ἐν παντὶ
     συνιστάντες ἑαυτοὺς ὡς θεοῦ διάκονοι,
               ἐν ὑπομονῇ πολλῇ,
               ἐν θλίψεσιν,
               ἐν ἀνάγκαις,
               ἐν στενοχωρίαις,
5   ἐν πληγαῖς,
               ἐν φυλακαῖς,
               ἐν ἀκαταστασίαις,
               ἐν κόποις,
               ἐν ἀγρυπνίαις,
               ἐν νηστείαις,
6   ἐν ἁγνότητι,
               ἐν γνώσει,
               ἐν μακροθυμίᾳ,
               ἐν χρηστότητι,
               ἐν πνεύματι ἁγίῳ,
               ἐν ἀγάπῃ ἀνυποκρίτῳ,
7   ἐν λόγῳ ἀληθείας,

ἐν δυνάμει θεοῦ·
διὰ τῶν ὅπλων τῆς δικαιοσύνης
τῶν δεξιῶν
καὶ ἀριστερῶν,
8   διὰ δόξης καὶ ἀτιμίας,
διὰ δυσφημίας καὶ εὐφημίας·
ὡς πλάνοι καὶ ἀληθεῖς,
9   ὡς ἀγνοούμενοι καὶ ἐπιγινωσκόμενοι,
ὡς ἀποθνήσκοντες καὶ ἰδοὺ ζῶμεν,
ὡς παιδευόμενοι καὶ μὴ θανατούμενοι,
10   ὡς λυπούμενοι ἀεὶ δὲ χαίροντες,
ὡς πτωχοὶ πολλοὺς δὲ πλουτίζοντες,
ὡς μηδὲν ἔχοντες καὶ πάντα κατέχοντες.
11 Τὸ στόμα ἡμῶν ἀνέῳγεν πρὸς ὑμᾶς, Κορίνθιοι,
ἡ καρδία ἡμῶν πεπλάτυνται·
12 οὐ στενοχωρεῖσθε
ἐν ἡμῖν,
στενοχωρεῖσθε δὲ
ἐν τοῖς σπλάγχνοις ὑμῶν·
13   τὴν δὲ αὐτὴν ἀντιμισθίαν,
ὡς τέκνοις
λέγω,
πλατύνθητε καὶ ὑμεῖς.

VERSE 1

Συνεργοῦντες δὲ καὶ παρακαλοῦμεν μὴ εἰς κενὸν τὴν χάριν τοῦ θεοῦ δέξασθαι ὑμᾶς· Working together with him, we also appeal to you, "Don't receive the grace of God in vain."

Συνεργοῦντες, nom. pl. masc. of pres. act. ptc. of συνεργέω, "work together." The expression "working together with him" is the CSB translation of a single Greek word, συνεργοῦντες. Although the party with whom Paul works could conceivably be understood as one or more of his colleagues (so Seifrid 270), the context (cf. 5:20) supports the identification of Paul as a coworker of God. Καὶ παρακαλοῦμεν, Harris 456: "καί is not to be taken with δέ but with παρακαλοῦμεν, "we indeed appeal." Παρακαλοῦμεν, 1st pl. pres. act. indic. of παρακαλέω, "appeal, exhort," echoes 5:20: "since God is making his appeal through us."

Μή, neg. particle with inf. δέξασθαι. Εἰς, prep. with acc. sg. neut. adj. κενόν, "in vain." Harris 458–59: "without profit, without the intended effect being achieved." It is unlikely that Paul implies they were unbelievers (contra Seifrid 270) or their acceptance of the gospel was only superficial; rather, he knows they are easily influenced by those who criticize him (2:5; 7:12), resulting in reticence to receive his ministry and the grace of God mediated to them through it (cf. Barnett 316–17). Τὴν χάριν, dir. obj. of inf. δέξασθαι. Χάριν, acc. sing. fem. χάρις, -ιτος, ἡ, "grace." Harris 458: "within the wider context of the letter, 'the grace of God' will also refer to the present opportunity that the Corinthians have to become fully reconciled to Paul." Τοῦ θεοῦ, either gen. of source ("grace from God") or poss. gen. ("God's grace"). Δέξασθαι, aor. mid. inf. of δέχομαι, "receive." Harris 458: "as an aorist infinitive δέξασθαι expresses simply the act or acts of receiving without any reference to time . . . here it probably envisages multiple future acts of receiving, conceived as a unit." Ὑμᾶς, acc. 2nd pl. subj. of inf. δέξασθαι.

VERSE 2

To underline the gravity and urgency of his appeal in v. 1, Paul introduces a verbatim quotation from Isa 49:8 (LXX). In its original context these words are addressed to the Servant of the Lord and refer to the time of Israel's release from exile in Babylon.

λέγει γάρ, Καιρῷ δεκτῷ ἐπήκουσά σου καὶ ἐν ἡμέρᾳ σωτηρίας ἐβοήθησά σοι.
For he says: At an acceptable time I listened to you, and in the day of salvation I helped you.

Harris 461–62: "When Paul cites Isa. 49:8 he is thinking primarily of the Corinthians' experience, not his own. In their case, 'the time of God's favor' was the time of their conversion."

Λέγει γάρ introduces the basis for Paul's appeal not to "receive the grace of God in vain" (v.1). Καιρῷ δεκτῷ, dat. temp. phrase, "at an acceptable time." Καιρῷ, dat. sg. masc. καιρός, -οῦ, ὁ, "time, season," BDAG 497c: "a welcome time." Δεκτῷ, dat. sg. masc. adj. δεκτός, -ή, -όν, "acceptable," BDAG 217a: "pert. to being appropriate to circumstances, *favourable*, of time." Ἐπήκουσα, 1st sg. aor. act. indic. of ἐπακούω, "listen," BDAG 358a–b: "to pay close attention to what one is told w. implication of being responsive, *hear, listen to*." Σου, gen. 2nd sg. masc. σύ, "you," dir. obj. of ἐπήκουσα.

Ἐν ἡμέρᾳ σωτηρίας, dat. temp. phrase, "in the day of salvation." Ἡμέρᾳ, dat. sg. fem. ἡμέρα, -ας, ἡ, "day." Σωτηρίας, gen. sg. fem. σωτηρία, -ας, ἡ, "salvation," attrib. gen. qualifying ἡμέρᾳ; cf. R 497. Ἐβοήθησα, 1st sg. aor. act. indic. of βοηθέω, "help," BDAG 180b–c: "to render assistance to someone in need, *furnish aid*." Σοι, dat. 2nd sg. masc. σύ, "you," dir. obj. of ἐβοήθησα.

ἰδοὺ νῦν καιρὸς εὐπρόσδεκτος, ἰδοὺ νῦν ἡμέρα σωτηρίας·
See, now is the acceptable time; now is the day of salvation!

Ἰδού, "see, look!" BDAG 468b: "demonstrative or presentative particle that draws attention to what follows. . . . It is actually the aor. mid. impv. of εἶδον, ἰδοῦ, except that it is accented w. the acute when used as a particle." Νῦν, temp. adv. "now." Καιρός, -οῦ, ὁ, "time, season." Εὐπρόσδεκτος, nom. sg. masc. adj. εὐπρόσδεκτος, -ον, "acceptable." Ἡμέρα, nom. sg. fem. "day." Σωτηρίας, attrib. gen. sg. fem. "salvation."

VERSE 3

μηδεμίαν ἐν μηδενὶ διδόντες προσκοπήν, ἵνα μὴ μωμηθῇ ἡ διακονία,
We are not giving anyone an occasion for offense, so that the ministry will not be blamed.

Μηδεμίαν, acc. sg. fem. adj. μηδείς, μηδεμία, μηδέν, "no, none," qualifying προσκοπήν "no (occasion/opportunity)." Ἐν, prep. with dat. subst. adj. μηδενί, "in nothing." BDAG 647c: "*in no way* or *respect.*" Μηδενί, dat. sg. neut. subst. adj. μηδείς, μηδεμία, μηδέν, "nothing." Διδόντες, nom. pl. masc. of pres. act. ptc. of δίδωμι, "give." Harris 468: "given the frequency with which participles stand for finite verbs in 2 Corinthians, it is better (as in 5:12) to construe διδόντες as equivalent to δίδομεν." Προσκοπήν, acc. sg. fem. προσκοπή, -ῆς, ἡ, "occasion." BDAG 882a–b: "*an occasion for taking offense.*" Ἵνα with subjunc. μωμηθῇ expresses purpose: "so that (the ministry) will not be blamed." Μωμηθῇ, 3rd sg. aor. pass. subjunc. of μωμάομαι, "blame." Διακονία, nom. sg. fem. διακονία, -ας, ἡ, "ministry," subj. of pass. verb μωμηθῇ.

VERSES 4–5

Having insisted in v. 3 that he seeks to give no offense so that the ministry of the gospel will not be blamed, in vv. 4–5 Paul lists ways he seeks to commend his ministry. He begins with a general statement in v. 4a:

ἀλλ᾽ ἐν παντὶ συνιστάντες ἑαυτοὺς ὡς θεοῦ διάκονοι,
Instead, as God's ministers, we commend ourselves in everything:

Barnett 325: "In v. 4a Paul turns from defense to positive affirmation. Here his 'in nothing' of v. 3 is reversed by 'in everything' and his denial of 'giving offense' is reversed by his 'commendation' of himself."
Ἀλλ᾽ (contraction of ἀλλά), "but, instead." Ἐν, prep. with dat. παντί, "in everything." Moule 78 asks whether the adverbial ἐν παντί means "in every respect" or if it is temporal "on every occasion." Συνιστάντες, nom. pl. masc. of pres. act. ptc. of συνίστημι, "commend." Ἑαυτούς, acc. 3rd pl. masc. pron. ἑαυτοῦ, -ῆς, -οῦ, "ourselves." Ὡς is the particle "as." BDAG 1104d: "introducing the perspective from which a pers. . . . is viewed or understood as to . . . role." Here "as God's ministers." Θεοῦ, poss. gen. sg. masc. θεός, -οῦ, ὁ, "of God, God's," qualifying διάκονοι. Διάκονοι, nom. pl. masc. διάκονος, -ου, ὁ, "servant/ minister."
In vv. 4b–5 Paul illustrates his general statement (v. 4a) with three sets of factors that commend his ministry, all of which are in the form of the prep. ἐν with the various factors in the dat. case:
The first set is expressed in more general terms:
Ἐν ὑπομονῇ (ὑπομονή, -ῆς, ἡ) πολλῇ, "in/by great endurance." Harris, *Prepositions*, 116: "This phrase, an instrumental dative, stands as a general heading for the following 17 instances of ἐν that describe first his outward circumstances (vv. 4b–5), then his

qualities of character (v. 6) and spiritual equipment (v. 7). Nine instances of a locat. dat., grouped in three triads (vv. 4b–5), are followed by eight cases of the instrumental dative in a pair of triads (vv. 6–7a)."

The first set relates to outward circumstances:

Ἐν θλίψεσιν (θλῖψις, -εως, ἡ), "in/by afflictions."

Ἐν ἀνάγκαις (ἀνάγκη, -ης, ἡ), "in/by hardships."

Ἐν στενοχωρίαις (στενοχωρία, -ας, ἡ), "in/by difficulties."

The second set represents particular examples:

Ἐν πληγαῖς (πληγή, -ῆς, ἡ), "in/by beatings."

Ἐν φυλακαῖς (φυλακή, -ῆς, ἡ), "in/by imprisonments."

Ἐν ἀκαταστασίαις (ἀκαταστασία, -ας, ἡ), "in/by riots."

The third set lists hardships voluntarily undertaken:

Ἐν κόποις (κόπος,- ου, ὁ), "in/by labors."

Ἐν ἀγρυπνίαις (ἀγρυπνία, -ας, ἡ), "in/by sleepless nights."

Ἐν νηστείαις (νηστεία, -ας, ἡ), "in/by times of hunger."

VERSES 6–7

In vv. 6–7, to further commend his ministry, Paul speaks first of moral integrity, again employing the prep. ἐν with the various elements in the dat. case (v. 6):

Ἐν ἁγνότητι (ἁγνότης, -ητος, ἡ), "in/by purity."

Ἐν γνώσει (γνῶσις, -εως, ἡ), "in/by knowledge."

Ἐν μακροθυμίᾳ (μακροθυμία, -ας, ἡ), "in/by patience."

Ἐν χρηστότητι (χρηστότης, -ητος, ἡ), "in/by kindness."

Ἐν πνεύματι ἁγίῳ, "in/by the Holy Spirit."

Ἐν ἀγάπῃ ἀνυποκρίτῳ (ἀνυπόκριτος, -ον), "in/by sincere love."

He then describes the "weapons" he employs (v. 7), listed again with the prep. ἐν and the various weapons in the dat. case, except the last, in which he uses the prep. διά with the gen. case:

Ἐν λόγῳ ἀληθείας (ἀλήθεια, -ας, ἡ), "by the word of truth."

Ἐν δυνάμει (δύναμις, -εως, ἡ), θεοῦ, "by the power of God."

Διὰ τῶν ὅπλων (ὅπλον, -ου, τό), τῆς δικαιοσύνης, "through/by the weapons of righteousness." R 582: "The agent may also be expressed by διά." Moule 58: "διὰ τῶν ὅπλων might be instrumental."

Τῶν δεξιῶν (gen. pl. fem adj. δεξιός, -ά, -όν) καὶ ἀριστερῶν (gen. pl. fem adj. ἀριστερός, -α, -όν), "for the right hand and the left," a military metaphor for being equipped for both offense and defense.

VERSES 8–10

In vv. 8–10 Paul further commends his ministry by setting forth nine antitheses. In each case one part of the antithesis represents an evaluation of his ministry "from a human point of view," and the other part, the view of one "in Christ."

The first two antitheses in v. 8a are expressed with the prep. διά with the elements of the antitheses in gen. case:

Διὰ δόξης (δόξα, -ης, ἡ) καὶ ἀτιμίας (ἀτιμία, -ας, ἡ), "through glory and dishonor." Διὰ δυσφημίας (δυσφημία, -ας, ἡ) καὶ εὐφημίας (εὐφημία, -ας, ἡ), "through slander and good report." NB the play on words: δυσ-φημία and εὐ-φημία.

The next seven antitheses in vv. 8b–10 are introduced with the particle ὡς (BDAG 1104d: "marker introducing the perspective from which a pers., thing, or activity is viewed or understood as to character, function, or role, *as*)."

Ὡς πλάνοι (nom. pl. masc. subst. adj. πλάνος, -ον) καὶ ἀληθεῖς (nom. pl. masc. adj. ἀληθής, -ές), "as deceivers, yet true."

Ὡς ἀγνοούμενοι (nom. pl. masc. of pres. pass. ptc. of ἀγνοέω) καὶ ἐπιγινωσκόμενοι (nom. pl. masc. of pres. pass. ptc. of ἐπιγινώσκω), "as unknown, yet recognized."

Ὡς ἀποθνῄσκοντες (nom. pl. masc. of pres. act. ptc. of ἀποθνῄσκω) καὶ ἰδοὺ ζῶμεν (1st pl. pres. act. indic. of ζάω), "as dying, yet see—we live."

Ὡς παιδευόμενοι (nom. pl. masc. of pres. pass. ptc. of παιδεύω) καὶ μὴ θανατούμενοι (nom. pl. masc. of pres. pass. ptc. of θανατόω), "as being disciplined, yet not killed."

Ὡς λυπούμενοι (nom. pl. masc. of pres. mid. ptc. of λυπέω) ἀεὶ (ἀεί adv., "always") δὲ χαίροντες (nom. pl. masc. of pres. act. ptc. of χαίρω), "as grieving, yet always rejoicing."

Ὡς πτωχοὶ (nom. pl. masc. adj. πτωχός, -ή, -όν) πολλοὺς (acc. pl. masc. adj., "many") δὲ πλουτίζοντες (nom. pl. masc. of pres. act. ptc. of πλουτίζω), "as poor, yet enriching many."

Ὡς μηδὲν ἔχοντες (nom. pl. masc. of pres. act. ptc. of ἔχω) καὶ πάντα κατέχοντες (nom. pl. masc. of pres. act. ptc. of κατέχω), "as having nothing, yet possessing everything."

The purpose of Paul's long commendation in vv. 3–10 is to show that no fault was to be found in his ministry, and thereby to clear the ground for the appeal he makes to the Corinthians in vv. 11–13 for a full reconciliation with their apostle.

Moule 196: "II Cor. vi.4–10 is an impassioned and almost lyrical passage, where precision in the interpretation of the prepositions is probably impossible because the 'catalogue' has lured the writer into repeating a preposition in some instances where in sober prose it might have been unnatural."

VERSE 11

Τὸ στόμα ἡμῶν ἀνέῳγεν πρὸς ὑμᾶς, Κορίνθιοι, ἡ καρδία ἡμῶν πεπλάτυνται·
We have spoken openly to you, Corinthians; our heart has been opened wide.

When literally translated, τὸ στόμα ἡμῶν ἀνέῳγεν would be "we have opened our mouth." Sim. expressions are used of Jesus speaking (cf. Matt 5:2; 13:35) and reflect a common Hebraic idiom mng. simply "to speak." However, τὸ στόμα ἡμῶν ἀνέῳγεν is also a Greek idiom denoting candor, or straightforward speech. Στόμα, nom. sg. neut. στόμα, -ατος, τό, "mouth," subj. of ἀνέῳγεν. Ἀνέῳγεν, 3rd sg. pf. act. indic. of ἀνοίγω, "open." Πρός, prep. with acc. ὑμᾶς "to you." Κορίνθιοι, voc. pl. masc. Κορίνθιος, -ου, ὁ, "Corinthian." Ἡ καρδία ἡμῶν πεπλάτυνται, "our heart has been opened wide," implies there is plenty of room for the Corinthians in Paul's affections. Καρδία, nom. sg. fem. καρδία, -ας, ἡ, "heart." Ἡμῶν, poss. gen. 1st pl. masc. ἐγώ, "our," qualifying καρδία. πεπλάτυνται, 3rd sg. pf. pass. indic. of πλατύνω, "enlarge, open wide."

VERSE 12

οὐ στενοχωρεῖσθε ἐν ἡμῖν, στενοχωρεῖσθε δὲ ἐν τοῖς σπλάγχνοις ὑμῶν·
We are not withholding our affection from you, but you are withholding yours from us.

Στενοχωρεῖσθε, 2nd pl. pres. mid. indic. of στενοχωρέω, "withhold, restrict." BDAG 942d: "to confine or restrict to a narrow space, *crowd, cramp, confine, restrict.*" In this context it indicates that the Corinthians are not restricted to a narrow place in Paul's affections, but that they are restricting Paul to a narrow place in their hearts. Cf. Harris 490: "In using the second person (στενοχωρεῖσθε) in v. 12b as well as in v. 12a, Paul skillfully focuses attention on the Corinthians' attitude; to have written στεοχωρούμεθα δὲ ἡμεῖς κτλ. would have emphasized Paul's deprivation, not their shortcomings." Ἐν, prep. with dat. pl. ἡμῖν, "in us." Ἐν, prep. with dat. τοῖς σπλάγχνοις ὑμῶν, "in your affections." Σπλάγχνοις, dat. pl. neut. σπλάγχνον, -ου, τό, "affection, entrails, heart." Harris 490: "Metaphorically, σπλάγχνα refers to the seat of the emotions, thus 'feelings' or 'affections,' especially those of pity and love."

VERSE 13

τὴν δὲ αὐτὴν ἀντιμισθίαν, ὡς τέκνοις λέγω, πλατύνθητε καὶ ὑμεῖς.
I speak as to my children; as a proper response, open your heart to us.

Τὴν . . . αὐτὴν ἀντιμισθίαν, lit. "the same response." In the attrib. position αὐτήν with same gender, case, and number = "the same." Moule 34: "this is possibly adverbial—*with the same recompense*, i.e. *by way of recompense in kind.*" Moule 36: "τὴν δὲ αὐτὴν ἀντιμισθίαν may be an instance of an adverbial phrase made up upon a basis other than that of a neuter noun: it looks like a subtle blend of τὸ δε αὐτό, *in the same way*, and κατ' ἀντιμισθίαν, *by way of recompense*, and on this showing, might be rendered *and accordingly, by way of response on your part.*" Ἀντιμισθίαν, acc. sg. fem. ἀντιμισθία, -ας, ἡ, "response." BDAG 90a: "requital based upon what one deserves, *recompense, exchange.*" Ὡς τέκνοις λέγω, "I speak as to children." Τέκνοις, dat. pl. neut. τέκνον, -ου, τό, "child." Πλατύνθητε καὶ ὑμεῖς, BDAG 823d: "*you must open your hearts (wide), too.*" Πλατύνθητε, 2nd pl. aor. pass. impv. of πλατύνω, "enlarge."

FOR FURTHER STUDY

67. Now Is the Day of Salvation (6:2–3)

Gignilliat, M. "2 Corinthians 6:2: Paul's Eschatological 'Now' and Hermeneutical Invitation," *WJT* 67 (2005): 147–61.

Lambrecht, J. "The Favorable Time: A Study of 2 Cor 6,2a in Its Context." Pages 377–92 in *Vom Urchristentum zu Jesus. Für Joachim Gnilka*. Edited by H. Frankemölle and K. Kertelge. Freiburg, Basel, and Vienna: Herder, 1989.

68. Self-Commendation (6:4)

Forbes, C. "Comparison, Self-Praise and Irony: Paul's Boasting and the Conventions of Hellenistic Rhetoric." *NTS* 32 (1986): 1–30.

Hafemann, S. J. "'Self-Commendation' and Apostolic Legitimacy in 2 Corinthians: A Pauline Dialectic." *NTS* 36 (1990): 66–88.

Kasch, W. *TDNT* 7. 896–98.

69. Paul's Hardship Lists (6:4–5)

Manus, C. U. "Apostolic Suffering (2 Cor 6:4–10): The Sign of Christian Existence and Identity." *Asia Journal of Theology* 1 (1987): 41–54.

Seifrid, M. A. "Excursus: Paul's List of Hardships—and the Works of God." In *The Second Letter to the Corinthians*, 274–76. Grand Rapids: Eerdmans, 2014.

HOMILETICAL SUGGESTIONS

Paul's Appeal (6:1–2)

1. The danger of receiving the grace of God in vain when relationships are broken (v. 1)
2. The present time is the time for restoration of relationships (v. 2)

Giving No Offense (6:3–10)

1. The importance of avoiding unnecessary offense in our ministry (v. 3)
2. Commending our ministry by the way hardships are endured (vv. 4–5)
3. Commending our ministry by godly character and the power of God (vv. 6–7)
4. Commending ourselves in the ups and downs of ministry (vv. 8–10)

Frank and Openhearted Communication (6:11–13)

1. The importance of plain speaking with an open heart (v. 11)
2. Genuine affection between people and their pastors to be highly valued (vv. 12–13)

b. A Call for Holy Living (6:14–7:1)

This passage poses many problems because its connection with what precedes and follows is not obvious, and therefore some regard it as a later interpolation. Hafemann 278 n.1, while not regarding it as an interpolation, notes that "six of the fifty New Testament *hapax legomenon* found in 2 Corinthians occur in this passage." But the interpolation theory raises more problems than it solves, as it is difficult then to explain why anyone would introduce such a passage at this point.

If it is not a later interpolation, we have two tasks before us: to understand the message of 6:14–7:1 itself, and to relate it somehow to the rest of the letter, especially its immediate context. Various suggestions have been made, all of which have some merit, incl.: (a) Paul is picking up his exhortation that his readers "not receive God's grace in vain" (6:1), something they would be doing should they become involved again in idolatry; (b) being deeply concerned to reestablish fellowship with the Corinthians (cf. 6:11–13; 7:2–4), Paul reminds them that full restoration of fellowship can be achieved only if they cease all involvement with idol worship; (c) Paul is warning his readers that if they were to join the opposition to him and his gospel, such action would be tantamount to siding with Satan, Belial. He calls on them to avoid any such liaison and to be reconciled with their true apostle instead.

STRUCTURE

The passage consists of (1) an introductory exhortation not to be partners with unbelievers (6:14a), (2) five rhetorical questions supporting the exhortation (6:14b–16a), (3) an affirmation of believers' unique relationship with God (6:16b), (4) a number of quotations from the OT that highlight the privilege involved in this relationship and reiterate the content of the exhortation (6:16c–18), and (5) a concluding call to be cleansed "from every impurity of the flesh and spirit, bringing holiness to completion in the fear of God" (7:1).

14 Μὴ γίνεσθε ἑτεροζυγοῦντες ἀπίστοις·
        τίς γὰρ μετοχὴ   δικαιοσύνῃ καὶ ἀνομίᾳ,
        ἢ τίς   κοινωνία   φωτὶ πρὸς σκότος;
15   τίς δὲ   συμφώνησις Χριστοῦ πρὸς Βελιάρ,
        ἢ τίς   μερὶς   πιστῷ μετὰ ἀπίστου;
16   τίς δὲ συγκατάθεσις ναῷ θεοῦ μετὰ εἰδώλων;
        ἡμεῖς γὰρ ναὸς θεοῦ ἐσμεν ζῶντος,
        καθὼς εἶπεν ὁ θεὸς ὅτι
                        Ἐνοικήσω ἐν αὐτοῖς καὶ ἐμπεριπατήσω
                        καὶ ἔσομαι αὐτῶν θεὸς
                        καὶ αὐτοὶ ἔσονταί μου λαός.
17   διὸ ἐξέλθατε ἐκ μέσου αὐτῶν καὶ ἀφορίσθητε,
                            λέγει κύριος,
                        καὶ ἀκαθάρτου μὴ ἅπτεσθε·
                        κἀγὼ εἰσδέξομαι ὑμᾶς

18   καὶ ἔσομαι ὑμῖν εἰς πατέρα
                                        καὶ ὑμεῖς ἔσεσθέ μοι εἰς υἱοὺς καὶ θυγατέρας,
                                            λέγει κύριος παντοκράτωρ.
7:1   ταύτας οὖν ἔχοντες τὰς ἐπαγγελίας, ἀγαπητοί,
        καθαρίσωμεν ἑαυτοὺς
            ἀπὸ παντὸς μολυσμοῦ
                        σαρκὸς καὶ πνεύματος,
            ἐπιτελοῦντες ἁγιωσύνην
                ἐν φόβῳ θεοῦ.

VERSE 14

Μὴ γίνεσθε ἑτεροζυγοῦντες ἀπίστοις·
Don't become partners with those who do not believe.

Μή, neg. particle with impv. γίνεσθε. Γίνεσθε ἑτεροζυγοῦντες, periph. pres.; cf. R 330, 375. Γίνεσθε, 2nd pl. pres. mid. impv. of γίνομαι, "become." Ἑτεροζυγοῦντες, nom. pl. masc. of pres. act. ptc. of ἑτεροζυγέω, "become a partner." BDF (§354): "a present or perfect participle is sometimes also used . . . to denote the beginning or a state or condition: 2 C 6:14." BDAG 399a: "be unevenly yoked, be mismated." This verb is found only here in the NT, but is used in the LXX in Lev 19:19 as part of a prohibition on yoking different types of animals together. Ἀπίστοις, dat. pl. masc. subst. adj. ἄπιστος, -ον, "unbeliever" (cf. BDF §189[1]), indir. obj. of γίνεσθε.

This opening exhortation is backed up by five rhetorical questions that underline its importance:

τίς γὰρ μετοχὴ δικαιοσύνῃ καὶ ἀνομίᾳ,
For what partnership is there between righteousness and lawlessness?

ZG 547: "lit. 'What partnership is there to δ. and to ἀν?' i.e. *what has r. to do with i.?*" Τίς, nom. sg. fem. interr. pron. τίς, τί, "what?" Μετοχή, nom. sg. fem. μετοχή, -ῆς, ἡ, "partnership, participation." Δικαιοσύνῃ, dat. sg. fem. δικαιοσύνη, -ης, ἡ, "righteousness." Ἀνομίᾳ, dat. sg. fem. ἀνομία, -ας, ἡ, "lawlessness."

ἢ τίς κοινωνία φωτὶ πρὸς σκότος;
Or what fellowship does light have with darkness?

ZG 547: "*what have light and darkness in common?*" Ἤ is the particle "or." Τίς, see above. Κοινωνία, nom. sg. fem. κοινωνία, -ας, ἡ, "fellowship." Πρός, prep. with acc. σκότος "with darkness"; cf. R 625, indicating a relationship (to be avoided). Σκότος, acc. sg. neut. σκότος, -ους, τό, "darkness."

VERSE 15

τίς δὲ συμφώνησις Χριστοῦ πρὸς Βελιάρ,
What agreement does Christ have with Belial?

Τίς, see above. Συμφώνησις, nom. sg. fem. συμφώνησις, -εως, ἡ, "agreement." Πρός, prep. with acc. Βελιάρ "with Belial." Βελιάρ, acc. sg. masc. Βελιάρ, ὁ (indecl.), "Belial." BDAG 173d: "name for the devil. . . . The Antichrist, too, is given this name. . . . Both mngs. are prob."

ἢ τίς μερὶς πιστῷ μετὰ ἀπίστου;
Or what does a believer have in common with an unbeliever?

ZG 547: "*what part or lot* has a believer with . . . ?" Ἤ is the particle "or." Τίς, see above. Μερίς, nom. sg. fem. μερίς, -ίδος, ἡ, "part, share, portion." Μετά, prep. with gen. ἀπίστου, "with an unbeliever." Ἀπίστου, gen. sg. masc. subst. adj. ἄπιστος, -ον, "unbeliever."

VERSE 16

τίς δὲ συγκατάθεσις ναῷ θεοῦ μετὰ εἰδώλων;
And what agreement does the temple of God have with idols?

Τίς, see above. Συγκατάθεσις, nom. sg. fem. συγκατάθεσις, -εως, ἡ, "agreement." Ναῷ, dat. sg. masc. ναός, -οῦ, ὁ, "temple." Θεοῦ, poss. gen. sg. masc. θεός, -οῦ, ὁ, "of God, God's." Μετά, prep. with gen. εἰδώλων "with idols." Εἰδώλων, gen. pl. neut. εἴδωλον, -ου, τό, "idol." This final question with its temple imagery supports the view that the earlier questions also constitute a call to have no involvement in worship in idol temples.

ἡμεῖς γὰρ ναὸς θεοῦ ἐσμεν ζῶντος,
For we are the temple of the living God,

Ἡμεῖς, emphatic. Ναός, nom. sg. masc. ναός, -οῦ, ὁ, "temple." Θεοῦ, poss. gen. sg. masc. θεός, -οῦ, "of God, God's." Ἐσμεν, 1st pl. pres. act. indic. of εἰμί, "we are." Ζῶντος, descriptive gen. sg. masc. of pres. act. ptc. of ζάω, "live," qualifying θεοῦ. In 1 Corinthians Paul speaks of both the individual Christian's body (1 Cor 6:16–20) and the Christian community as a whole (1 Cor 3:16–17) as God's temple. It is the latter sense that he employs here.

καθὼς εἶπεν ὁ θεὸς ὅτι Ἐνοικήσω ἐν αὐτοῖς καὶ ἐμπεριπατήσω
as God said: **I will dwell and walk among them,**

In this OT quotation and those that follow, God is in fact the speaker in each case, and the people of Israel are those addressed. Paul here applies them to the Christian community in Corinth. Seifrid 296 comments: "The twofold imagery of 'dwelling in [or among] them and walking among [them],' which appears in Lev 26:11–12, reflects the period of the tabernacle, even if the context anticipates the temple."

Καθώς is the conj. "as." Εἶπεν, 3rd sg. aor. act. indic. of λέγω, "say." Ὅτι, a conj., introduces dir. speech. Ἐνοικήσω, 1st sg. fut. act. indic. of ἐνοικέω, "dwell among." Ἐν, prep. with dat. αὐτοῖς, "among them." Ἐμπεριπατήσω, 1st sg. fut. act. indic. of ἐμπεριπατέω, "walk among."

καὶ ἔσομαι αὐτῶν θεὸς καὶ αὐτοὶ ἔσονταί μου λαός.
and I will be their God, and they will be my people.

Ἔσομαι, 1st sg. fut. indic. of εἰμί. Αὐτῶν, poss. gen. 3rd pl. masc. pron. αὐτός, -ή, -ό, "their," qualifying θεὸς (pred. nom. following εἰμί). Αὐτοί, nom. 3rd pl. masc. pron. αὐτός, -ή, -ό, "they," subj. of ἔσονταί (3rd pl. fut. indic. of εἰμί). Μου, poss. gen. 1st sg. pron. ἐγώ, "my," qualifying λαός (nom. sg. masc. λαός, -οῦ, ὁ, "people," pred. nom. following εἰμί).

VERSE 17

διὸ ἐξέλθατε ἐκ μέσου αὐτῶν καὶ ἀφορίσθητε, λέγει κύριος,
Therefore, **come out from among them** and **be separate, says the Lord;**

In substance this quotation is taken from Isa 52:11, where the Jewish exiles are urged to leave Babylon and return to Judea and Jerusalem. Paul applies the text to the Corinthians, calling them to separate themselves from idolatry in Corinth. Διό is a conj. mng. "therefore." Ἐξέλθατε, 2nd pl. aor. act. impv. of ἐξέρχομαι, "come out." Ἐκ is a prep. with gen. μέσου, mng. "from the midst (αὐτῶν, of them)." Μέσου, gen. sg. neut. subst. adj. μέσος, -η, -ον, "the midst." Ἀφορίσθητε, 2nd pl. aor. pass. impv. of ἀφορίζω, "separate."

καὶ ἀκαθάρτου μὴ ἅπτεσθε· κἀγὼ εἰσδέξομαι ὑμᾶς
do not touch any unclean thing, and I will welcome you.

Ἀκαθάρτου, gen. sg. neut. subst. adj. ἀκάθαρτος, -ον, "unclean thing," gen. dir. obj. of ἅπτεσθε. Ἅπτεσθε, 2nd pl. pres. mid. impv. of ἅπτω, "touch." Negated by μή, the pres. impv. has traditionally been regarded as a command not to continue to do something. Cf. Harris 508: "μὴ ἅπτεσθε could be enjoining and end to an action ('Stop touching . . .') or the perpetual avoidance of an action ('Do not touch . . .')." Κἀγώ, contraction of καί and ἐγώ. Εἰσδέξομαι, 1st sg. fut. mid. indic. of εἰσδέχομαι, "receive." Ὑμᾶς, acc. 2nd pl. σύ, "you," dir. obj. of εἰσδέχομαι.

VERSE 18

καὶ ἔσομαι ὑμῖν εἰς πατέρα καὶ ὑμεῖς ἔσεσθέ μοι εἰς υἱοὺς καὶ θυγατέρας, λέγει κύριος παντοκράτωρ.

And **I will be a Father** to you, **and** you will be **sons** and daughters **to me, says the Lord Almighty.**

Paul exchanges the temple imagery of vv. 16–17 for that of the family when quoting 2 Sam 7:8, 14 (LXX) here. Ἔσομαι, 1st sg. fut. indic. of εἰμί. Ὑμῖν, poss. dat. 2nd pl. σύ, "to you." Εἰς, prep. with acc. πατέρα, BDAG 291b: "The predicate nom. and the predicate acc. are somet. replaced by εἰς w. acc. under Semitic influence, which has strengthened Gk. tendencies in the same direction." Cf. ZG 547. Πατέρα, acc. sg. masc. πατήρ, πατρός, ὁ, "father." Ἔσεσθέ, 2nd pl. fut. indic. of εἰμί. Μοι, poss. dat. 1st sg. ἐγώ, "to me." Εἰς, prep. with acc. υἱοὺς καὶ θυγατέρας, "sons and daughters"; see note on εἰς πατέρα above. Cf. R 595. Harris 509: "The construction with the accusative, found twice in this verse [ἔσομαι . . . εἰς πατέρα and ἔσεσθέ . . . εἰς υἱοὺς καὶ θυγατέρας], is used in place of a predicate nominative." Παντοκράτωρ, nom. sg. masc. παντοκράτωρ, -ορος, ὁ. BDAG 755b: "the *Almighty All-Powerful, Omnipotent (One)* only of God (as transl. of צָבָאֹות . . . and שַׁדַּי)," in appos. with κύριος.

VERSE 7:1

ταύτας οὖν ἔχοντες τὰς ἐπαγγελίας, ἀγαπητοί,
So then, dear friends, since we have these promises,

Οὖν, conj. mng. "therefore." Ταύτας . . . τὰς ἐπαγγελίας, "these promises"; the dem. pron. ταύτας occupies the pred. position. Ἐπαγγελίας, acc. pl. fem. ἐπαγγελία, -ας, ἡ, "promise," dir. obj. of ptc. ἔχοντες. Ἔχοντες, nom. pl. masc. of pres. act. ptc. of ἔχω, "have." Ἀγαπητοί, voc. pl. masc. subst. adj. "beloved."

καθαρίσωμεν ἑαυτοὺς ἀπὸ παντὸς μολυσμοῦ σαρκὸς καὶ πνεύματος,
let us cleanse ourselves from every impurity of the flesh and spirit,

Καθαρίσωμεν, 1st pl. aor. act. hort. subjunc. of καθαρίζω, "cleanse." Ἑαυτούς, the reflexive pronoun ("ourselves"), shows that Paul includes himself with his readers as those who must fulfill the exhortation. Ἀπό, prep. with gen. παντὸς μολυσμοῦ, "from every impurity." Μολυσμοῦ, gen. sg. masc. μολυσμός, -οῦ, ὁ, "impurity, defilement." The word found only here in the NT and only three times in the LXX (Jer 23:15; 1 Esdr 8:80; 2 Macc 5:27). In all cases it denotes religious defilement. Σαρκὸς καὶ πνεύματος, descriptive gen. "of flesh and spirit," qualifying μολυσμοῦ.

ἐπιτελοῦντες ἁγιωσύνην ἐν φόβῳ θεοῦ.
bringing holiness to completion in the fear of God.

Harris 513: "(And let us) complete our consecration by our reverence for God." Ἐπιτελοῦντες, nom. pl. masc. of pres. act. ptc. of ἐπιτελέω, "bring to completion." Ἁγιωσύνην, acc. sg. fem. ἁγιωσύνη, -ης, ἡ, "holiness," dir. obj. of ptc. ἐπιτελοῦντες. Paul uses ἁγιωσύνη in Rom 1:4, where he speaks of "the Spirit of holiness" (πνεῦμα ἁγιωσύνης) by whom Christ was designated Son of God with power, and also in 1 Thess 3:13, where he says, "May he make your hearts blameless in holiness [ἐν ἁγιωσύνῃ] before our God and Father at the coming of our Lord Jesus with all his saints. Amen." This indicates complete perfection in holiness is experienced only at the Parousia. Ἐν, prep. with dat. φόβῳ, "in fear." Φόβῳ, dat. sg. masc. φόβος, -ου, ὁ, "fear." Θεοῦ, obj. gen. sg. masc. θεός, -οῦ, ὁ, "(fear of) God."

c. A Further Appeal for Reconciliation (7:2–4)

Following the section calling for no compromise with paganism (6:14–7:1), here in 7:2–4 Paul renews his appeal for reconciliation with the Corinthians begun in 6:1–13. Barnett 359 n.1: "7:2–4 is one of a number of transitional or bridge passages within 2 Corinthians that repeat words or ideas from earlier passages (καρδία–6:11; 7:3) and that introduce words or ideas that will carry forward (παράκλησις–7:4, 7, 13; 8:4, 17) into passages following."

STRUCTURE

2   Χωρήσατε ἡμᾶς·
        οὐδένα ἠδικήσαμεν,
        οὐδένα ἐφθείραμεν,
        οὐδένα ἐπλεονεκτήσαμεν.
3   πρὸς κατάκρισιν
     οὐ λέγω·
     προείρηκα γὰρ
        ὅτι ἐν ταῖς καρδίαις ἡμῶν ἐστε
            εἰς τὸ συναποθανεῖν
            καὶ συζῆν.
4   πολλή μοι παρρησία
        πρὸς ὑμᾶς,
     πολλή μοι καύχησις
        ὑπὲρ ὑμῶν·
     πεπλήρωμαι
        τῇ παρακλήσει,
     ὑπερπερισσεύομαι
        τῇ χαρᾷ
        ἐπὶ πάσῃ τῇ θλίψει ἡμῶν.

VERSE 2

Χωρήσατε ἡμᾶς· οὐδένα ἠδικήσαμεν, οὐδένα ἐφθείραμεν, οὐδένα ἐπλεονεκτήσαμεν.
Make room for us in your hearts. We have wronged no one, corrupted no one, taken
advantage of no one.

To support this renewed appeal, Paul defends his integrity on three levels, claiming
he has wronged no one, corrupted no one, and taken advantage of no one. Χωρήσατε,
2nd pl. aor. act. impv. of χωρέω, "receive, make room." Ἡμᾶς, acc. 1st pl. ἐγώ, dir. obj.
of χωρήσατε.

Οὐδένα, acc. sg. masc. subst. adj. οὐδείς, οὐδεμία, οὐδέν, "no one." Ἠδικήσαμεν, 1st
pl. aor. act. indic. of ἀδικέω, "wrong, do wrong to."

Ἐφθείραμεν, 1st pl. aor. act. indic. of φθείρω, "corrupt, defraud." Φθείρω is used
three times in the Corinthian correspondence. In 1 Cor 3:17, after speaking of building
the church on the foundation of Christ by various ministers, all of whose work is to be
tested, Paul says anyone who "destroys" (φθείρει) God's temple, God will "destroy"
(φθείρει). In 1 Cor 15:33 he says bad company "corrupts" (φθείρουσιν) good character
(NIV). A parallel use is found in Eph 4:22, where the "old self" is said to be "corrupted" (φθειρόμενον) by deceitful desires. In all probability, therefore, Paul's mng. in
the present context is that he has caused the church no harm; his teaching and example
have not corrupted it or encouraged immoral behavior.

Ἐπλεονεκτήσαμεν, 1st pl. aor. act. indic. of πλεονεκτέω, "take advantage of." BDAG
824b: *exploit, outwit, defraud. cheat.*" In 12:16–18 Paul had to deny explicitly that
he was guilty of taking advantage of the Corinthians financially by means of the collection for the poor.

VERSE 3

πρὸς κατάκρισιν οὐ λέγω·
I don't say this to condemn you,

Paul may have said this because he felt the strong defense of his own integrity
in v. 2 could be taken as a criticism of the Corinthians' integrity. Πρός, prep. with
acc. κατάκρισιν, "for condemnation." Κατάκρισιν, acc. sg. fem. κατάκρισις, εως, ἡ,
"condemnation."

προείρηκα γὰρ ὅτι ἐν ταῖς καρδίαις ἡμῶν ἐστε εἰς τὸ συναποθανεῖν καὶ συζῆν.
since I have already said that you are in our hearts, to die together and to live together.

Προείρηκα, 1st sg. pf. act. indic. of προλέγω, "say beforehand." Γάρ, the conj.
"since" signals that what follows provides the reason why Paul will not condemn the
Corinthians. Ἐν, prep. with dat. ταῖς καρδίαις ἡμῶν, "in our hearts." Καρδίαις, dat. pl.
fem. καρδία, -ας, ἡ, "heart." Ἐστε, 2nd pl. pres. indic. of εἰμί. Εἰς, prep. with art. inf. τὸ
συναποθανεῖν καὶ συζῆν, "to die together and live together." Here εἰς with inf. expresses

the result of Paul having his converts in his heart. The NIV reverses the order of Paul's affirmation, making it sim. to what is found in the papyri, "live or die with you." Συναποθανεῖν, aor. act. inf. of συναποθνῄσκω, "die together." Συζῆν, pres. act. inf. of συζάω, "live together."

VERSE 4

πολλή μοι παρρησία πρὸς ὑμᾶς, πολλή μοι καύχησις ὑπὲρ ὑμῶν·
I am very frank with you; I have great pride in you.

Πολλή μοι παρρησία, lit. "(there is) great frankness with me," CSB: "I am very frank." Πολλή, nom. sg. fem. adj. πολύς, πολλή, πολύ, "great." Παρρησία, nom. sg. fem. παρρησία, -ας, ἡ, "frankness, openness." Πρός, prep. with acc. ὑμᾶς, "in relation to you."

Πολλή μοι καύχησις, lit. "(there is) great pride with me," CSB: "I have great pride." Καύχησις, nom. sg. fem. καύχησις, -εως, ἡ, "boasting, pride." Ὑπέρ, prep. with gen. ὑμῶν, "in, for."

πεπλήρωμαι τῇ παρακλήσει, ὑπερπερισσεύομαι τῇ χαρᾷ ἐπὶ πάσῃ τῇ θλίψει ἡμῶν.
I am filled with encouragement; I am overflowing with joy in all our afflictions.

Πεπλήρωμαι 1st sg. pf. pass. indic. of πληρόω, "fill." Τῇ παρακλήσει, dat. of content "(filled) with encouragement." Παρακλήσει, dat. sg. fem. παράκλησις, -εως, ἡ, "encouragement." Ὑπερπερισσεύομαι, 1st sg. pres. mid. indic. of ὑπερπερισσεύω, "overflow." Τῇ χαρᾷ, dat. of manner "(overflowing) with joy." Ἐπί, prep. with dat. πάσῃ τῇ θλίψει ἡμῶν, "in all our afflictions," dat. prep. phrase describing circumstances in which Paul experienced overflowing joy. Πάσῃ, dat. sg. fem. "all," qualifying τῇ θλίψει ἡμῶν. Θλίψει, dat. sg. fem. θλῖψις, -εως, ἡ, "affliction."

FOR FURTHER STUDY

70. Understanding 2 Cor 6:14–7:1

Adewuya, A. J. Holiness and Community in 2 Cor. 6:14–7:1: Paul's View of Communal Holiness in the Corinthian Correspondence. New York: Lang, 2001.

Beale, G. K. "The Old Testament Background of Reconciliation in 2 Corinthians 5–7 and Its Bearing on the Literary Problem of 2 Corinthians 6.14–7.1." NTS 35 (1989–90): 550–81.

Betz, H. D. "2 Cor 6:14–7:1: An Anti-Pauline Fragment?" JBL 92 (1973): 88–108.

Dahl, N. A. "A Fragment and Its Context: 2 Cor 6:14–7:1." Studies in Paul: Theology for the Early Christian Mission, 62–69. Minneapolis: Augsburg, 1977.

Fee, G. D. "II Corinthians vi.14–vii.1 and Food Offered to Idols." NTS 23 (1977): 140–61.

Lambrecht, J. "The Fragment 2 Cor vi 14–vii 1: A Plea for Its Authenticity." In Miscellanea Neotestamentica 2:143–61. Edited by T. Baarda, A. F. J. Klijn, and W. C. van Unnik. NovTSup 47. Leiden: Brill, 1978.

Thrall, M. E. "The Problem of II Cor. vi.14–vii.1 in some Recent Discussion." *NTS* 24 (1977–78): 132–48.

71. Unequally Yoked Together (6:14)

McDougall, D. G. "Unequally Yoked—A Re-Examination of 2 Corinthians 6:11–7:4." *TMSJ* 10 (1999): 113–37.
Webb, W. J. "Unequally Yoked Together with Unbelievers: Who Are the Unbelievers (*apistoi*) in 2 Corinthians 6:14? Part 1 (of 2 parts)." *BSac* 149 (1992): 27–44.
———. "Unequally Yoked Together with Unbelievers. Part 2 (of 2 parts): What Is the Unequal Yoke (*heterozygountes*) in 2 Corinthians 6:14?" *BSac* 149 (1992): 162–79.

72. Belial (6:15)

Elgvin, T. *DNTB* 153–157.
Huppenbauer, H. W. "Belial in den Qumrantexten." *TZ* 15 (1959): 81–89.

73. Paul's Use of Scripture (6:16–18)

Ellis, E. E. *Paul's Use of the Old Testament*. Edinburgh: Oliver & Boyd, 1957.
Moyise, S. *Paul and Scripture: Studying the New Testament Use of the Old Testament*. Grand Rapids: Baker, 2010.
Scott, J. M. "The Use of Scripture in 2 Corinthians 6.16c–18 and Paul's Restoration Theology." *JSNT* 56 (1994): 73–99.

74. Dying and Living (7:3)

Lambrecht, J. "To Die together and to Live Together: A Study of 2 Corinthians 7,3." In R. Bieringer and J. Lambrecht. *Studies in 2 Corinthians*, 571–87. Leuven: Leuven University, 1994.
Tannehill, R. C. *Dying and Rising with Christ: A Study in Pauline Theology*. Berlin: Topelmann, 1967.

HOMILETICAL SUGGESTIONS

Paul's Exhortation (6:14–15a)

1. The need to avoid involvement with wrongdoers (v. 14a)
2. The incompatibility of Christian belief and pagan/occult practices (vv. 14b–16a)
3. Believers are blessed to be the temple of the living God (v. 16a)

The Promises of God (6:16–18)

1. God's promise to dwell with believers and walk with them (v. 16b)
2. The great promise of God: "I will be their God, and they will be my people" (v. 16b)
3. Believers must reject religious defilement to enjoy being children of God (vv. 17–18)

Paul's Appeal (7:1–4)
1. The call for purity and holiness (v. 1)
2. Make the effort to maintain affectionate relationships between pastor and people (vv. 2–3)
3. The importance of affirmation (v. 4)

7. Paul's Joy after a Crisis Resolved (7:5–16)

In this section Paul returns to the account of his travels broken off at 2:13 to include the long treatment of the nature, integrity, and divine enabling of his ministry (2:14–7:4). He recounts the relief he experienced when he finally met up with Titus in Macedonia and received a good report of affairs in Corinth (vv. 5–7). He tells how, in light of the events reported by Titus, he no longer regretted writing the "severe letter," though shortly after sending it he had done so. This change had been brought about by learning of the positive benefits resulting from that letter (vv. 8–13a). Finally, Paul tells how he was also relieved because the confidence he expressed to Titus about the Corinthians proved to be justified (vv. 13b–16).

a. Paul's Relief When Titus Arrived (7:5–7)

STRUCTURE

5   Καὶ γὰρ ἐλθόντων ἡμῶν εἰς Μακεδονίαν
οὐδεμίαν ἔσχηκεν ἄνεσιν ἡ σὰρξ ἡμῶν
   ἀλλ᾽ ἐν παντὶ θλιβόμενοι·
    ἔξωθεν μάχαι,
    ἔσωθεν φόβοι.
6 ἀλλ᾽ ὁ <u>παρακαλῶν</u> τοὺς ταπεινοὺς <u>παρεκάλεσεν</u> ἡμᾶς
  ὁ θεὸς
           ἐν τῇ παρουσίᾳ Τίτου,

7   οὐ μόνον δὲ ἐν τῇ παρουσίᾳ αὐτοῦ
       ἀλλὰ καὶ ἐν τῇ <u>παρακλήσει</u>
         ἧ <u>παρεκλήθη</u> ἐφ᾽ ὑμῖν,

  ἀναγγέλλων ἡμῖν τὴν ὑμῶν ἐπιπόθησιν,
   τὸν ὑμῶν ὀδυρμόν,
   τὸν ὑμῶν ζῆλον ὑπὲρ ἐμοῦ
    ὥστε με μᾶλλον χαρῆναι.

VERSE 5

Καὶ γὰρ ἐλθόντων ἡμῶν εἰς Μακεδονίαν
In fact, when we came into Macedonia,

Καὶ γάρ, "for even . . . "; CSB, "In fact." Ἐλθόντων ἡμῶν, gen. abs. "when we came," depicts action occurring at the time of the main verb, i.e., "we had no rest." Ἐλθόντων, gen. pl. masc. of aor. act. ptc. of ἔρχομαι, "come." Εἰς, prep. with acc. Μακεδονίαν, "into Macedonia."

οὐδεμίαν ἔσχηκεν ἄνεσιν ἡ σὰρξ ἡμῶν
we had no rest [lit., "our flesh had no rest"].

Οὐδεμίαν, acc. sg. fem. adj. οὐδείς, οὐδεμία, οὐδέν, "no, none." Ἔσχηκεν, 3rd sg.
pf. act. indic. ἔχω, "have." Moule 14: notes the pf. here is used as an aor.; so too
Harris 525. R 897 cites it as an example of a "vivid perfect." Ἄνεσιν, acc. sg. fem.
ἄνεσις, -εως, ἡ, "rest, relief," dir. obj. of ἔσχηκεν. Ἡ σὰρξ ἡμῶν, lit. "our flesh," subj.
of ἔσχηκεν, stands for Paul's whole person here, not just his body. Thrall 1:487: "σάρξ
whilst including the physical element, has a wider scope, i.e., that it refers to the whole
person and is the equivalent of ἡμεῖς."

ἀλλ' ἐν παντὶ θλιβόμενοι· ἔξωθεν μάχαι, ἔσωθεν φόβοι.
Instead, we were troubled in every way: conflicts on the outside, fears within.

BDF (§468[1]): "Paul is fond of continuing construction begun with a finite verb
by means of co-ordinated participles, sometimes in a long series. E.g. 2 C 7:5 οὐδεμίαν
. . . φόβοι (short exclamations: 'always plagued!' etc . . .)." Cf. Z §374. Ἐν, prep. with
dat. sg. neut. παντί, "in everything, every way." Θλιβόμενοι, nom. pl. masc. of pres.
pass. ptc. of θλίβω, "trouble, oppress." Moule 179 notes that the ptc. θλιβόμενοι is used
here "where normal Greek would have used a finite verb." Thrall 1:487: "This verse
has a logical connection (καὶ γάρ) with v.4, in that θλιβόμενοι offers an explanatory
example of the preceding ἐπὶ πάσῃ τῇ θλίψει ἡμῶν. Substantially, however, it takes
the reader back to 2.13 and resumes the account of Paul's journey in search of Titus."
Ἔξωθεν, adv. of place, "outside." Μάχαι, nom. pl. fem. μάχη, -ης, ἡ, "conflict."
"Conflicts on the outside" may refer to Paul's sharing the persecution in which the
Macedonian churches were immersed (cf. 8:1–2). However, where found elsewhere
in the NT, μάχαι refers only to quarrels and disputes (cf. 2 Tim 2:23; Titus 3:9; Jas
4:1), so here they may refer to heated disputations with unbelievers (cf. Acts 17:5–14)
or Christian opponents (cf. Phil 3:2) in Macedonia. Ἔσωθεν, adv. of place, "inside,
within." Φόβοι nom. pl. masc. φόβος, -ου, ὁ, "fear." "Fears within" could refer either to
fear of persecution (during his first visit to Corinth, Paul had been in danger of being
reduced to silence through fear; cf. Acts 18:9) or fear about the spiritual losses that
would be incurred if the Corinthians did not react positively to his "severe letter" (cf.
11:3). The latter is more likely seeing that the arrival of Titus with good news about the
situation in Corinth brought relief.

VERSE 6

ἀλλ' ὁ παρακαλῶν τοὺς ταπεινοὺς παρεκάλεσεν ἡμᾶς ὁ θεὸς ἐν τῇ παρουσίᾳ Τίτου,
But God, who comforts the downcast, comforted us by the arrival of Titus,

Ὁ παρακαλῶν τοὺς ταπεινούς stands in appos. with ὁ θεός. Barnett 369: "The vocabulary calls to mind God's comfort to his people through the prophet Isaiah (LXX Isa
40:1; 49:13; 51:3, 12, 19; 52:9; 61:2; 66:13); the 'consolation [i.e., comforting] of

Israel' (Luke 2:25) described the long-awaited messianic age." Ὁ παρακαλῶν, adj.
ptc. phrase "he (God) who comforts." Παρακαλῶν, nom. sg. masc. of pres. act. ptc. of
παρακαλέω. Τοὺς ταπεινούς, acc. pl. masc. subst. adj. ταπεινός, -ή, -όν, "the downcast/
humble." Παρεκάλεσεν, 3rd sg. aor. indic. act. of παρακαλέω, "comfort." Ἡμᾶς, acc.
1st pl. ἐγώ, "us," dir. obj. of παρεκάλεσεν. Ὁ θεός, subj. of παρεκάλεσεν. Ἐν, prep. with
dat. τῇ παρουσίᾳ, "by the arrival/coming (of Titus)." Seifrid 307: "God uses earthly
means to provide comfort: he comforted Paul with the arrival of Titus."

VERSE 7

οὐ μόνον δὲ ἐν τῇ παρουσίᾳ αὐτοῦ ἀλλὰ καὶ ἐν τῇ παρακλήσει ᾗ παρεκλήθη ἐφ' ὑμῖν,
and not only by his arrival but also by the comfort he received from you.

Ἐν, prep. with instr. dat. τῇ παρουσίᾳ, "by the arrival." Ἐν, prep. with instr. dat.
τῇ παρακλήσει, "by the comfort." Παρουσίᾳ, dat. sg. fem. παρουσία, -ας, ἡ, "arrival."
Παρακλήσει, dat. sg. fem. παράκλησις, -εως, ἡ, "comfort." Ἧ παρεκλήθη ἐφ' ὑμῖν, adj.
phrase qualifying παρακλήσει. Παρεκλήθη, 3rd sg. aor. pass. indic. of παρακαλέω,
"comfort." Ἐφ' is a prep. (contraction of ἐπί) with dat. ὑμῖν, "from, by you."

ἀναγγέλλων ἡμῖν τὴν ὑμῶν ἐπιπόθησιν, τὸν ὑμῶν ὀδυρμόν, τὸν ὑμῶν ζῆλον ὑπὲρ ἐμοῦ
He told us about your deep longing, your sorrow, and your zeal for me,

Ἀναγγέλλων, nom. sg. masc. of pres. act. ptc. of ἀναγγέλλω, "report, tell." Harris
530: "In the place of the form ἀναγγέλλων, which is anacoluthic, we might have
expected either a genitive absolute construction, ἀναγγέλλοντος αὐτοῦ, or a participle,
ἀναγγέλλοντος, that agreed with the preceding αὐτοῦ. This may be a case of 'construction according to sense' with the participle ἀναγγέλλων adverting to the subject of
παρεκλήθη (i.e., Titus), or better, an instance of the nominative absolute . . . here used
in a causal sense (= ἀνηγγειλεν γάρ), 'for he reported.'" Ἡμῖν, dat. 1st pl. ἐγώ, "us,"
indir. obj. of ἀναγγέλλων. Τὴν ὑμῶν ἐπιπόθησιν, τὸν ὑμῶν ὀδυρμόν, τὸν ὑμῶν ζῆλον ὑπὲρ
ἐμοῦ functions as dir. obj. of ἀναγγέλλων. Ἐπιπόθησιν, acc. sg. fem. ἐπιπόθησις, -εως,
ἡ. BDAG 377d: "yearning desire for, longing," perhaps for a restored relationship with
Paul. Ὀδυρμόν, acc. sg. masc. ὀδυρμός, -οῦ, ὁ, "sorrow, mourning," perhaps over the
Corinthians' past failure to defend Paul against attack, or as Thrall 1:489 suggests, "on
account of Paul's decision that it would be better to keep away from Corinth." Ζῆλον,
acc. sg. masc. ζῆλος, -ου, ὁ, "zeal, ardor," prob. in disciplining the offender. Ὑπέρ, prep.
with gen. ἐμοῦ, "for me."

ὥστε με μᾶλλον χαρῆναι.
so that I rejoiced even more.

Ὥστε, conj. with inf. χαρῆναι expresses result: "so that I rejoiced." Cf. R 1091. Με,
acc. 1st sg. ἐγώ, "me," acc. subj. of inf. χαρῆναι. Μᾶλλον, comp. adv., "even more." Cf.
R 665. Χαρῆναι, aor. pass. inf. of χαίρω, "rejoice."

b. The "Severe Letter" and Its Effects (7:8–13a)

STRUCTURE

8   ὅτι εἰ καὶ ἐλύπησα ὑμᾶς
                 ἐν τῇ ἐπιστολῇ,
    οὐ μεταμέλομαι·
       εἰ καὶ μετεμελόμην,
    βλέπω [γὰρ]
       ὅτι ἡ ἐπιστολὴ ἐκείνη
                            εἰ καὶ πρὸς ὥραν
                            ἐλύπησεν ὑμᾶς,
9   νῦν χαίρω,
       οὐχ ὅτι ἐλυπήθητε
       ἀλλ᾽ ὅτι ἐλυπήθητε εἰς μετάνοιαν·
    ἐλυπήθητε γὰρ κατὰ θεόν,
       ἵνα ἐν μηδενὶ ζημιωθῆτε ἐξ ἡμῶν.
10 ἡ γὰρ κατὰ θεὸν λύπη μετάνοιαν
                 εἰς σωτηρίαν
                 ἀμεταμέλητον ἐργάζεται·
    ἡ δὲ τοῦ κόσμου λύπη θάνατον κατεργάζεται.
11 ἰδοὺ γὰρ αὐτὸ τοῦτο τὸ
                            κατὰ θεὸν
               λυπηθῆναι
               πόσην κατειργάσατο ὑμῖν σπουδήν,
               ἀλλ᾽ ἀπολογίαν,
               ἀλλ᾽ ἀγανάκτησιν,
               ἀλλὰ φόβον,
               ἀλλ᾽ ἐπιπόθησιν,
               ἀλλὰ ζῆλον,
               ἀλλ᾽ ἐκδίκησιν.
    ἐν παντὶ
    συνεστήσατε ἑαυτοὺς ἁγνοὺς εἶναι τῷ πράγματι.
12   ἄρα εἰ καὶ ἔγραψα ὑμῖν,
    οὐχ ἕνεκεν τοῦ ἀδικήσαντος
    οὐδὲ ἕνεκεν τοῦ ἀδικηθέντος
    ἀλλ᾽ ἕνεκεν τοῦ φανερωθῆναι τὴν σπουδὴν ὑμῶν
                            τὴν ὑπὲρ ἡμῶν πρὸς ὑμᾶς ἐνώπιον τοῦ θεοῦ.
13 διὰ τοῦτο παρακεκλήμεθα.

VERSE 8

ὅτι εἰ καὶ ἐλύπησα ὑμᾶς ἐν τῇ ἐπιστολῇ,
For even if I grieved you with my letter,

The prot. of a first-class cond. sentence formed with εἰ + indic., which postulates a certain situation, the result of which is stated in the apod. Εἰ καὶ, "even if." Moule 167: "εἰ καί is concessive (*even if, etsi*), II Cor. vii.8 (thrice)." Ἐλύπησα, 1st sg. aor. act. indic. of λυπέω, "cause grief." Ὑμᾶς, acc. 2nd pl. σύ, "you," dir. obj. of ἐλύπησα. Ἐν, prep. with dat. τῇ ἐπιστολῇ, "with the letter." Ἐπιστολῇ, dat. sg. fem. ἐπιστολή, -ῆς, ἡ, "letter."

οὐ μεταμέλομαι· εἰ καὶ μετεμελόμην,
I don't regret it. And if I regretted it—

The apod. of the first-class cond. sentence. However, if εἰ καὶ μετεμελόμην begins a second cond. sentence, then νῦν χαίρω . . . (v. 9) forms the apod. Cf. Harris 534. Μεταμέλομαι, 1st sg. pres. mid. indic. of μεταμέλομαι, "regret." ZG 548: "lit. 'change what one has at heart (μέλει)', *change one's mind*; hence, *regret, be sorry.*" R 1008 notes that "there is perfect liberty to mix tenses" between the prot. and apod. "So past and present (. . . 2 Cor. 7:8)."

Εἰ καί, "even if." Μετεμελόμην, 1st sg. impf. mid. indic. of μεταμέλομαι, "regret," pointing to a past progressive action (cf. Porter *Idioms* 34; Harris 535). There is an important difference between the "regret" (μεταμέλομαι) Paul felt and the "repen-tance" (μετάνοια) to which the Corinthians were led. Paul felt regret when he became concerned about the effect his "severe letter" might have upon the Corinthians. The Corinthians' repentance produced grief as they realized what they had done and not done, and this resulted in a marked change in their behavior. Harris 536–37: "Etymologically, μετανοέω denotes an altered (μετα-) view or attitude (νοῦς), and μεταμέλομαι an altered (μετα-) mood or interest (μελεῖ, 'it is an object of concern'). The distinction between these verbs and between the corresponding nouns, μετάνοια ('a change of mind') and μεταμέλεια ('remorse') (a word not found in the NT), is preserved in Classical Greek, but Hellenistic usage often blurs the distinction. In the present context there is a clear difference between the two concepts."

βλέπω [γὰρ] ὅτι ἡ ἐπιστολὴ ἐκείνη εἰ καὶ πρὸς ὥραν ἐλύπησεν ὑμᾶς,
since I saw that the letter grieved you, yet only for a while—

Βλέπω, 1st sg. pres. act. indic. of βλέπω, "see." Ὅτι, conj., "that." BDAG 731c–d: "marker of narrative or discourse content, direct or indirect, that. Used after verbs that denote mental or sense perception, or the transmission of such perception, or an act of the mind, to indicate the content of what is said, etc." Ἡ ἐπιστολὴ ἐκείνη, "that letter." Εἰ καί, "even if." CSB: "yet." Πρός, prep. with acc. ὥραν, "for an hour." ZG 548 "*only for a time.*" Ὥραν, acc. sg. fem. ὥρα, -ας, ἡ, "hour." BDAG 1102d: "a short period of time." Ἐλύπησεν, 3rd sg. aor. act. indic. of λυπέω, "cause grief." Ὑμᾶς, acc. 2nd pl. σύ, "you," dir. obj. of ἐλύπησεν.

VERSE 9

νῦν χαίρω, οὐχ ὅτι ἐλυπήθητε ἀλλ᾽ ὅτι ἐλυπήθητε εἰς μετάνοιαν·
I now rejoice, not because you were grieved, but because your grief led to repentance.

Χαίρω, 1st sg. pres. act. indic. "rejoice." Οὐχ ὅτι . . . ἀλλ᾽ expresses "sharp antithesis" (R 1166). Ὅτι, conj. "that." See note above. Ἐλυπήθητε, 2nd pl. aor. pass. indic.
of λυπέω, "cause grief." R 834 cites this as an ingressive aorist. Εἰς, prep. with acc.
μετάνοιαν, "(leading) to repentance." Harris 536: "εἰς is resultative." Μετάνοιαν, acc.
sg. fem. μετάνοια, -ας, ἡ, "repentance."

ἐλυπήθητε γὰρ κατὰ θεόν, ἵνα ἐν μηδενὶ ζημιωθῆτε ἐξ ἡμῶν.
For you were grieved as God willed, so that you didn't experience any loss from us.

Ἐλυπήθητε, see above. Γάρ, explanatory conj., "for, because." Κατά, prep. with
acc. θεόν, lit. "according to God." BDAG 407c: "to introduce the norm which governs someth.," here God. Moule 59: "in a godly way." Cf. Harris, *Prepositions*, 153:
"Since this sorrow is contrasted with ἡ δὲ τοῦ κόσμου λύπη (v. 10b), 'worldly sorrow,'
it is tempting to render κατὰ θεόν by a matching 'godly' (as Moule 59). But the context suggests a more expressive rendering, such as '[sorrow] borne in God's way' or
'[sorrow] experienced as God intends.' God's intent was that the λύπη should lead to
repentance . . . 'a repentance that results in salvation and so is not regretted.'" So too
ZG 548; Hafemann 312. Thrall 1:491: "in accordance with God's will."
Ἵνα with subjunc. ζημιωθῆτε expresses result: "so that you didn't experience any
loss (from us)." Thrall 1:491: "He does not explain what kind of damage he has in
mind. Perhaps the point is that they would eventually have suffered spiritual harm,
had he refrained from rebuking their behavior, and urging amendment. Conversely,
he might mean that he would have been compelled to discipline them, with some
severity, had they not responded positively." Ζημιωθῆτε, 2nd pl. aor. pass. subjunc. of
ζημιόω, "suffer loss." Paul uses ζημιόω also in 1 Cor 3:15 of those who will suffer loss
of reward if their works do not pass God's test on the last day. Paul may have felt that
the Corinthians' positive response to his "severe letter" had saved them from such a
loss. Ἐξ, prep. with gen. of source ἡμῶν, "from us." R 598–99 cites this as an example
"of cause or occasion which may also be conveyed by ἐκ."

VERSE 10

ἡ γὰρ κατὰ θεὸν λύπη μετάνοιαν εἰς σωτηρίαν ἀμεταμέλητον ἐργάζεται·
For godly grief produces a repentance that leads to salvation without regret,

Γάρ, explanatory conj. "for, because." Κατὰ θεὸν λύπη, attrib. prep. phrase qualifying μετάνοιαν, "godly grief." Κατὰ θεόν, Moule 59: "in a godly way." Λύπη, nom. sg.
fem. λύπη, -ης, ἡ, "grief, sorrow."

Μετάνοιαν εἰς σωτηρίαν: Commenting on this phrase, Harris 538–39 says that Paul "is relating repentance to salvation not as cause and effect but as antecedent and result, 'a repentance that leads to (εἰς) salvation,' a repentance 'whose fruit is salvation.'" Μετάνοιαν, acc. sg. fem. μετάνοια, -ας, ἡ, "repentance." Εἰς, prep. with acc. σωτηρίαν, "(leading) to salvation." Σωτηρίαν, acc. sg. fem. σωτηρία, -ας, ἡ, "salvation," dir. obj. of ἐργάζεται.

Ἀμεταμέλητον, verbal adj. ἀμεταμέλητος, -ον, "without regret." Barnett 376–77: "Critical to this verse is the word *ametamelēton*, meaning 'without regret' ('unregretted'), which deliberately reverses the twice-repeated verb 'regret' (*metamelomai*) of v. 8, which contrasted how Paul felt when he first dispatched the letter with his present positive feelings in the light of their reported 'repentance.'" Harris 539: "In spite of the difficulty of the word order—which is merely apparent—it is preferable to take ἀμεταμέλητον with μετάνοιαν, which creates an oxymoron by means of *paronomasia* (μετά), 'repentance not to be repented of.'" Ἐργάζεται, 3rd sg. pres. mid. indic. of ἐργάζομαι, "produce."

ἡ δὲ τοῦ κόσμου λύπη θάνατον κατεργάζεται.
but worldly grief produces death.

Δέ, adversative conj., "but." Τοῦ κόσμου, gen. attrib. phrase qualifying λύπη: "worldly grief." Λύπη, nom. sg. fem. λύπη, -ης, ἡ, "grief, sorrow." Θάνατον, acc. sg. masc. θάνατος, -ου, ὁ, "death," dir. obj. of κατεργάζεται. Κατεργάζεται, 3rd sg. pres. mid. indic. of κατεργάζομαι, "produce."

"Godly grief," which issues in repentance when coupled with faith in God, leads to salvation. Repentance itself is not the cause of salvation; rather, God saves us and freely forgives our sins only when our repentance shows that we have renounced them. Harris 538 says Paul "is relating repentance to salvation not as cause and effect but as antecedent and result."

On the other hand, "worldly grief" does not progress beyond remorse. There are regrets over what has happened, but no accompanying change of mind and heart, nor any willingness to change behavior, nor any faith in God. The result is not salvation, but death (cf. Rom 6:15–23). Biblical examples of godly grief can be seen in the cases of David (2 Sam 12:13; Ps 51:1–11), Peter (Mark 14:72), and Paul himself (Acts 9:1–22), while examples of worldly grief are to be found in the cases of Esau (Gen 27:1–40; Heb 12:15–17) and Judas (Matt 27:3–5).

VERSE 11

ἰδοὺ γὰρ αὐτὸ τοῦτο τὸ κατὰ θεὸν λυπηθῆναι πόσην κατειργάσατο ὑμῖν σπουδήν,
For consider how much diligence this very thing—this grieving as God wills—has produced in you:

Αὐτὸ τοῦτο τὸ κατὰ θεὸν λυπηθῆναι ZG 548: "*This very experience of godly sorrow*, τοῦτο connoting 'well known to you.'" Αὐτὸ τοῦτο is translated by the CSB as "this very thing" because αὐτό, being in the pred. position and in the same case and number as τοῦτο, functions as an emphasizing pron. Αὐτὸ τοῦτο is anaphoric, referring to something previously mentioned, i.e., "godly grief" (v. 10); cf. BDF (§399[1]). Harris 541: "αὐτὸ τοῦτο (literally, 'this very thing') is nominative after ἰδού but may be translated as though it were a direct object." Τὸ . . . λυπηθῆναι, art. inf. functioning as a verbal noun, "the grieving," stands in appos. with αὐτὸ τοῦτο (cf. R 1078). Κατὰ θεόν, lit. "according to God," = "godly," or as in CSB, "as God wills." Moule 59: "in a godly way." Λυπηθῆναι, aor. pass. inf. of λυπέω, "grieve." R 1059: "In 2 Cor. 7:11 the substantival aspect of the inf, is shown by the use of the pronoun in the nominative with αὐτὸ τοῦτο τὸ λυπηθῆναι." Πόσην, acc. sg. fem. pron. πόσος, -η, -ον expresses degree or magnitude (BDAG 855d) "how much," qualifying σπουδήν. R 741 cites this as an example of the exclamatory use of the pron. Harris 541: "Instead of repeating the exclamatory πόσος . . . with each of the seven nouns in his list, Paul follows up the initial πόσην . . . σπουδήν with six instances of ἀλλά. This conjunction is here not adversative but copulative, forming a series of emphatic additions, 'not only this, but also.'" Σπουδήν, acc. sg. fem. σπουδή, -ῆς, ἡ, "diligence, earnestness," obj. of κατειργάσατο, i.e., diligence in dealing with the offender. Κατειργάσατο, 3rd sg. aor. mid. indic. of κατεργάζομαι, "produce, bring about." Ὑμῖν, locat. dat. following κατειργάσατο (cf. R 523), "has produced *in you*."

ἀλλ᾽ ἀπολογίαν, ἀλλ᾽ ἀγανάκτησιν, ἀλλὰ φόβον, ἀλλ᾽ ἐπιπόθησιν, ἀλλὰ ζῆλον, ἀλλ᾽ ἐκδίκησιν.
what a desire to clear yourselves, what indignation, what fear, what deep longing, what zeal, what justice!

Ἀλλ᾽ (contraction of ἀλλά), conj. "what!" BDAG 45c: "rhetorically ascensive . . . yes indeed." introduces a series of responses to Paul's letter: Ἀπολογίαν, acc. sg. fem. ἀπολογία, -ας, ἡ, "defense"; CSB, "desire to clear (yourselves)." Ἀγανάκτησιν, acc. sg. fem. ἀγανάκτησις, -εως, ἡ, "indignation." The indignation was prob. directed toward the "offender" who was at the cause of the trouble (cf. 2:5; 7:12). Φόβον, acc. sg. masc. φόβος, -ου, ὁ, "fear." This may have been fear of God when they realized they had not accorded his apostle proper respect. Ἐπιπόθησιν, acc. sg. fem. ἐπιπόθησις, -εως, ἡ, "longing, desire," prob. their desire for a restoration of their relationship with Paul. Ζῆλον, acc. sg. masc. ζῆλος, -ου, ὁ, "zeal," either in disciplining the offender or in their desire for a restored relationship with Paul. Ἐκδίκησιν, acc. sg. fem. ἐκδίκησις, -εως, ἡ, "punishment, justice," would relate to the Corinthians' disciplining of the offender as Paul had demanded (cf. 2:6).

ἐν παντὶ συνεστήσατε ἑαυτοὺς ἁγνοὺς εἶναι τῷ πράγματι.
In every way you showed yourselves to be pure in this matter.

Ἐν παντί, lit., "in everything"; CSB, "in every way"; NIV, NRSV, "at every point." Συνεστήσατε, 2nd pl. aor. act. indic. of συνίστημι, "show, demonstrate." BDAG 973a: "to provide evidence of a personal characteristic or claim through action." Ἑαυτούς, acc. 3rd pl. masc. reflex. pron. ἑαυτοῦ, -ῆς, -οῦ, "yourselves." Ἁγνούς, acc. pl. masc. adj. ἁγνός, -ή, -όν, "pure, innocent." Εἶναι, pres inf. of εἰμί, "be." Τῷ πράγματι, dat. phrase "in the matter." BDF (§197): "dative of respect . . . perhaps εἶναι is corrupted from ἐν (εἶναι ἐν . . .)." Cf. Z §53. Πράγματι, dat. sg. neut. πρᾶγμα,-ατος, τό, "matter, thing." BDAG 858d: *the matter* under discussion." Hafemann 313: "The word . . . can be used in a technical sense to refer to a legal case (cf. 1 Cor 6:1) and most likely carries such a 'quasi-legal connotation in our present passage.'"

It seems that while the congregation as a whole may not have sprung to the apostle's defense when he was maligned in their presence by the "offender," and while they had been lax in responding to earlier calls to discipline him, nevertheless they were not involved in maligning him. In that matter at least they proved to be guiltless when they finally acted to discipline the offender.

Harris 543: "This crowning affirmation has been understood in two ways. According to Barrett, the aorist συνεστήσατε refers to the time of Titus's visit to Corinth with the 'severe letter' when to his satisfaction—and now Paul's—the Corinthians had proved that they were and always had been completely innocent (ἁγνοί) of any complicity in the wrong doing of ὁ ἀδικήσας. . . . On the other view . . . Paul is saying that by their repentance (7:9) and subsequent conduct (7:11a) as reported by Titus, the Corinthians have demonstrated that they are *now* completely in the right."

VERSES 12–13a

ἄρα εἰ καὶ ἔγραψα ὑμῖν, οὐχ ἕνεκεν τοῦ ἀδικήσαντος οὐδὲ ἕνεκεν τοῦ ἀδικηθέντος
So even though I wrote to you, it was not because of the one who did wrong, or because of the one who was wronged,

Ἄρα, inferential conj., "so, therefore." Εἰ καί, "even if, even though." Ἔγραψα, 1st sg. aor. act. indic. of γράφω, "write." Harris 544: "It is interesting to note that whenever ἔγραψα is used, it is followed by a statement of purpose (ἵνα, 2:3, 4, 9; ἕνεκεν, 7:12 [third instance])." Ὑμῖν, dat. 2nd pl. σύ, "you," indir. obj. of ἔγραψα.

Ἕνεκεν, prep. (with gen.), "on account of, because of." BDF (§216[1]): "The meaning of ἕνεκεν is almost always *propter* (hardly distinguished from διά with acc.)." BDF (§403): "In 2 C 7:12 ἕνεκεν τοῦ is formed on the model of the preceding ἕνεκεν τοῦ ἀδικήσαντος etc.; otherwise ἕν. would be superfluous." R 1073: "(ἕνεκεν) is clearly causal as with the two preceding participles, (a good passage to note the distinction between the inf. and the part.)." Τοῦ ἀδικήσαντος, gen. ptc. phrase, "the one who did the wrong," i.e., the "offender." Ἀδικήσαντος, gen. sg. masc. of aor. act. ptc. of ἀδικέω, "do wrong, harm." Paul himself was the one who "was wronged."

ἀλλ᾽ ἕνεκεν τοῦ φανερωθῆναι τὴν σπουδὴν ὑμῶν τὴν ὑπὲρ ἡμῶν πρὸς ὑμᾶς ἐνώπιον τοῦ θεοῦ.
but in order that your devotion to us might be made plain to you in the sight of God.

The third use of ἕνεκεν in this verse expresses Paul's positive purpose in writing ("in order that your devotion to us might be made plain to you"), unlike the earlier two, used here to express Paul's neg. reasons for writing (cf. Harris 544). Ἀλλ', R 429: "the use of ἀλλά in the apodosis accents the logical connection of thought." Moule 83: "in II Cor. vii.12 ἕνεκεν τοῦ φανερωθῆναι . . . is practically a final [= purpose] clause. It is not used in the N.T. as an adverb." Τοῦ φανερωθῆνα, gen. art. pass. inf., expresses purpose: "to be made plain." Φανερωθῆνα, aor. pass. inf. of φανερόω, "make plain, make known." Σπουδήν, acc. sg. fem. σπουδή, -ῆς, ἡ, "devotion, zeal." BDAG 939d: "earnest commitment in discharge of an obligation or experience of a relationship." Τὴν ὑπὲρ ἡμῶν, prep. phrase "(your devotion) to/for us." Πρός, prep. with acc. ὑμᾶς, "to you." Ἐνώπιον, prep. with gen. τοῦ θεοῦ, "before, in the sight of God." Harris 546: "ἐνώπιον τοῦ θεοῦ is emphatic by position and belongs with φανερωθῆναι . . . rather than the remote ἔγραψα." Barnett 381–82: "This is one of a number of phrases used in 2 Corinthians that calls for appropriate actions in the present in the light of the great eschatological moment when all things will be revealed, including the true relationship between the apostle and his people."

διὰ τοῦτο παρακεκλήμεθα.
For this reason we have been comforted.

Διά, prep. with acc. τοῦτο, "because of this, for this reason." Παρακεκλήμεθα, 1st pl. pf. pass. indic. of παρακαλέω, "comfort." Although pl. in form, παρακεκλήμεθα refers to Paul alone, as the context indicates.

c. Titus's Happiness and Affection for the Corinthians (7:13b–16)

STRUCTURE

13   Ἐπὶ δὲ τῇ παρακλήσει ἡμῶν
<u>περισσοτέρως μᾶλλον ἐχάρημεν</u>
                 ἐπὶ τῇ χαρᾷ Τίτου,
         ὅτι ἀναπέπαυται τὸ πνεῦμα αὐτοῦ
            ἀπὸ πάντων ὑμῶν·
14   ὅτι εἴ τι αὐτῷ ὑπὲρ ὑμῶν <u>κεκαύχημαι</u>,
οὐ κατῃσχύνθην,
         ἀλλ' ὡς πάντα ἐν ἀληθείᾳ ἐλαλήσαμεν ὑμῖν,
            οὕτως καὶ ἡ <u>καύχησις</u> ἡμῶν
               ἡ ἐπὶ Τίτου ἀλήθεια ἐγενήθη.
15 καὶ τὰ σπλάγχνα αὐτοῦ <u>περισσοτέρως</u> εἰς ὑμᾶς ἐστιν
      ἀναμιμνῃσκομένου τὴν πάντων ὑμῶν ὑπακοήν,
      ὡς μετὰ φόβου καὶ τρόμου ἐδέξασθε αὐτόν.
16 <u>χαίρω</u> ὅτι ἐν παντὶ θαρρῶ ἐν ὑμῖν.

VERSE 13b

Ἐπὶ δὲ τῇ παρακλήσει ἡμῶν περισσοτέρως μᾶλλον ἐχάρημεν ἐπὶ τῇ χαρᾷ Τίτου,
In addition to our own comfort, we rejoiced even more over the joy Titus had,

Ἐπὶ δὲ τῇ παρακλήσει ἡμῶν . . . ἐχάρημεν, "we rejoiced over the comfort." Ἐπί, prep.
with dat. τῇ παρακλήσει, "over the comfort." Περισσοτέρως, comp. adv. "even more
so." ZG 549: "more than ever." Μᾶλλον, comp. adv., "more, rather." R 663: "Double
comparison. Sometimes indeed μᾶλλον occurs with the comparative form itself . . .
περισσοτέρως μᾶλλον (2 Cor. 7:13)." R 1205 cites this also as a *pleonasm* and adds,
"This redundancy is usually due to the custom of the language with no thought of the
repetition, as in . . . περισσοτέρως μᾶλλον (2 Cor. 7:13)." Ἐχάρημεν, 1st pl. aor. pass.
indic. of χαίρω, "rejoice." Ἐπί, prep. with dat. τῇ χαρᾷ, "over the joy." Χαρᾷ, dat. sg.
fem. χαρά, -ᾶς, ἡ, "joy."

Hafemann 315: "At first such an emphasis on Titus is puzzling. The reason becomes
clear, however, in 7:14, where we learn that Paul had put himself on the line for the
sake of the Corinthians. He had risked embarrassment by declaring in advance that
they would respond positively to his 'tearful letter' and to Titus's ministry, even though
Titus himself had reservations about taking the letter to Corinth."

ὅτι ἀναπέπαυται τὸ πνεῦμα αὐτοῦ ἀπὸ πάντων ὑμῶν·
because his spirit was refreshed by all of you.

Ὅτι, conj., "because." Ἀναπέπαυται, 3rd sg. pf. pass. indic. of ἀναπαύω, "refresh,
set at rest." Τὸ πνεῦμα αὐτοῦ, "his spirit," subj. of pass. verb. ἀναπέπαυται. Ἀπό, prep.
with gen. πάντων ὑμῶν, "by all of you." Harris 548: "Although the ὅτι clause could
define the content of Paul's joy (ἐχάρημεν), 'we rejoiced . . . that . . . ,' more probably
it denotes the reason (causal ὅτι) for Titus's joy."

VERSE 14

ὅτι εἴ τι αὐτῷ ὑπὲρ ὑμῶν κεκαύχημαι, οὐ κατῃσχύνθην,
For if I have made any boast to him about you, I have not been disappointed;

Ὅτι, the conj. "because" introduces the reason Paul's spirit was refreshed (v. 13b).
Εἴ τι . . . κεκαύχημαι, "if I say something boastingly" (cf. BDAG 536d). Αὐτῷ, 3rd sg.
dat. masc. αὐτός, -ή, -ό, "to him." Ὑπέρ, prep. with gen. ὑμῶν, "about you." Κεκαύχημαι,
1st sg. pf. mid. indic. of καυχάομαι, "boast." Κατῃσχύνθην, 1st sg. aor. pass. indic. of
καταισχύνω, "put to shame, disappoint." This reflects something less than complete
confidence about the Corinthians' attitude, and it explains why Paul was so relieved
when he heard the good news about their reception of Titus.

ἀλλ᾽ ὡς πάντα ἐν ἀληθείᾳ ἐλαλήσαμεν ὑμῖν,
but as I have spoken everything to you in truth,

Ὡς, conj., "as." R 968: "Usually ὡς has a correlative. Thus . . . ὡς–οὕτως καί (2 Cor. 7:14)." Πάντα, acc. pl. neut. adj. πᾶς, πᾶσα, πᾶν, "all things, everything," dir. obj. of ἐλαλήσαμεν. Ἐν, prep. with dat. ἀληθείᾳ, "in truth." Ἐλαλήσαμεν, 1st pl. aor. act. indic. of λαλέω, "speak." Ὑμῖν, indir. obj. of ἐλαλήσαμεν.

οὕτως καὶ ἡ καύχησις ἡμῶν ἡ ἐπὶ Τίτου ἀλήθεια ἐγενήθη.
so our boasting to Titus has also turned out to be the truth.

Οὕτως, dem. adv., "so." Καί, adv., "also." Καύχησις, nom. sg. fem. καύχησις, -εως, ἡ, "boasting," subj. of ἐγενήθη. Ἡ ἐπὶ Τίτου, explanatory phrase qualifying καύχησις. Ἐπί, prep. with gen. Τίτου, "to Titus." R 603: "With persons ἐπί and the genitive may yield the resultant meaning of 'before' or 'in the presence of.' Thus . . . ἐπὶ Τίτου in 2 Cor. 7:14." Ἀλήθεια, nom. sg. fem. ἀλήθεια, -ας, ἡ, "truth," pred. nom. of ἐγενήθη.

Despite the Corinthians' earlier failure to defend their apostle when he was maligned, it would appear Paul still believed there would be a basic readiness to respond positively to his "severe letter," and he had assured Titus along these lines when he sent him to Corinth. The Corinthians' response to Titus when he visited them proved that Paul's boasting about them was true.

VERSE 15

καὶ τὰ σπλάγχνα αὐτοῦ περισσοτέρως εἰς ὑμᾶς ἐστιν ἀναμιμνησκομένου τὴν πάντων ὑμῶν ὑπακοήν,
And his affection toward you is even greater as he remembers the obedience of all of you,

Σπλάγχνα, nom. pl. neut. σπλάγχνον,-ου, τό, "affection, heart," subj. of ἐστίν. Περισσοτέρως, adv. "even greater, even more so." Εἰς, prep. with acc. ὑμᾶς, "toward you." Ἀναμιμνησκομένου, gen. sg. masc. of pres. mid. ptc. of ἀναμιμνήσκω, "remember," gen. abs. depicting action occurring at the time of the main verb; i.e., Titus's affection became greater as he remembered the Corinthians' obedience to the demands in Paul's severe letter that he had delivered. Τὴν πάντων ὑμῶν ὑπακοήν, dir. obj. of ptc. ἀναμιμνησκομένου, "the obedience of you all." Ὑπακοήν, acc. sg. fem. ὑπακοή, -ῆς, ἡ, "obedience."

ὡς μετὰ φόβου καὶ τρόμου ἐδέξασθε αὐτόν.
and how you received him with fear and trembling.

Ὡς, conj., "how." Μετά, prep. with. gen. φόβου καὶ τρόμου, "with fear and trembling." R 611–12: "The metaphorical use (of μετά) for the idea of accompaniment occurs like . . . μετὰ φόβου καὶ τρόμου (2 Cor. 7:15)." Z §64 notes that sometimes, as here, μετά with gen. is used instead of ἐν with dat. Hafemann 315: "Paul is the only New Testament author to use the expression 'with fear and trembling' to describe the believer's reaction to being part of God's great salvation. He uses this expression in

Philippians 2:12 and Ephesians 6:5 in connection with the believer's obedience, and in I Corinthians 2:3 to describe his own attitude in preaching the gospel. If obedience is the action that grows from the gospel having taken root, then 'fear and trembling' is its corresponding attitude. Those who recognize that obedience is the fruit of genuine faith do not take sin lightly." Harris 552: "The Corinthians were aware of what was at stake in the way they treated Titus, who was Paul's envoy and so God's representative as well. They knew they would have to give account to God for their conduct—hence their warm receptiveness." Φόβου, gen. sg. masc. φόβος, -ου, ὁ, "fear." Ἐδέξασθε, 2nd pl. aor. mid. indic. of δέχομαι, "receive." Αὐτόν, dir. obj. of ἐδέξασθε.

VERSE 16

χαίρω ὅτι ἐν παντὶ θαρρῶ ἐν ὑμῖν.
I rejoice that I have complete confidence in you.

Χαίρω, 1st sg. pres. act. indic., "rejoice." Ἐν, prep. with dat. παντί, "in everything, complete." Θαρρῶ, 1st sg. pres. act. indic. θαρρέω, "have confidence, depend on." Ἐν, prep. with dat. ὑμῖν, "in you." Seifrid 313: "His affirmation is intended to have a definite rhetorical effect. Paul seeks to build up the success achieved in Titus's mission." Thrall 1:501: "This verse sums up the renewed confidence in the Corinthians which Paul has expressed in various ways in the preceding verses, and forms a fitting transition to chap. 8, where he begs them to resume their activity in the matter of the collection."

FOR FURTHER STUDY

75. Comfort (7:6–7)

Braumann, G. NIDNTT, 1.567–71. See p. 571.
Clarke, A. D. "'Refresh the Hearts of the Saints': A Unique Pauline Context?" TynBul 47 (1996): 277–300.
Schmitz, O. G. TDNT 5.773–99.

76. Titus (7:6)

Barrett, C. K. "Titus." In Essays on Paul, 118–131. Philadelphia: Westminster/London: SPCK, 1982.
Ellis, E. E. "Paul and His Co-Workers." NTS 17 (1970–71): 437–52.
Kantzer, R. F. "Titus and Corinth." TJ 2 (1972): 84–97.
Mitchell, M. M. "NT Envoys in the Context of Greco-Roman Diplomatic and Epistolary Conventions: The Example of Timothy and Titus." JBL 111 (1991): 641–62.

77. Repentance (7:9–10)

Moncure, J. "II Corinthians 7:8–10." RevExp 16 (1919): 476–77.
Thomson, E. G. "Μετανοέω and μεταμέλει in Greek Literature until 100 A.D." In Historical and Linguistic Studies in Literature Related to the New Testament. Second series, 1:358–64. Chicago: University of Chicago, 1909.

78. Discipline (7:11)

Lampe, G. W. H. "Church Discipline and the Interpretation of the Epistles to the Corinthians." In *Christian History and Interpretation*, edited by W. R. Farmer, 337–61. Cambridge: Cambridge University Press, 1967.
Schmidt, T.E. *DPL* 214–18.

79. The Offender (7:12)

Barrett, C. K. "Ο ΑΔΙΚΗΣΑΣ (2 Cor. 7,12)." In *Essays on Paul*, 108–17. Philadelphia: Westminster/London: SPCK 1982.
Kruse, C. G. "The Offender and the Offence in 2 Corinthians 2:5 and 7:12." *EvQ* 60 (1988): 129–39.

HOMILETICAL SUGGESTIONS

Paul's Anxiety and Comfort (7:5–7)

1. The importance of honestly acknowledging anxiety in the face of conflicts (v. 5)
2. God comforts those who are anxious through reunions with fellow workers (v. 6)
3. God comforts the downcast through good news (v. 7; cf. Prov 12:25; 15:30)

Regrets Giving Way to Joy (7:8–11)

1. Tough decisions may give rise to initial regret (v. 8)
2. Seeing the positive results of a necessary tough decision leads to joy (v. 9)
3. Godly grief produces repentance, leads to salvation, and is reflected in godly action (vv.10–11)
4. Worldly grief without repentance ends in remorse and produces death (v. 10b)

Godly Motivation (7:12)

1. Does not seek to blame others or just to defend oneself (v. 12a)
2. Helps others to value Christian relationships (v. 12b)

Risk-Taking for the Greater Good (7:14)

1. Going out on a limb in difficult circumstances to speak well of others (v. 14a)
2. Risk-taking rewarded as people rise to the occasion by God's grace (vv. 14b–15)

The Importance of Affirmation (7:16)

1. Past problems not allowed to prevent Paul's expression of confidence in his converts (v. 16)

C. THE MATTER OF THE COLLECTION (8:1–9:15)

Having spoken of his joy and relief when hearing the news Titus brought of the Corinthians' response to his "severe letter," Paul proceeds to raise with them the matter of the collection being taken up among the Gentile churches to assist the poor Jewish believers in Judea. They had been hit hard by famine during the reign of the emperor Claudius (AD 41–54), and the largely Gentile church at Antioch (Syria) had responded quickly by sending relief by the hand of Barnabas and Saul (Paul) (Acts 11:27–30). In Gal 2:10 Paul tells how the leaders of the Jerusalem church, having recognized his apostolate to the Gentiles, urged him to continue remembering the poor, which, he said, he was eager to do. By the time he wrote 1 Corinthians (c. AD 55) he had already begun soliciting aid from the churches of Galatia, and the Corinthians had heard about it and asked to be allowed to share in this ministry (1 Cor 16:1–4). And by the time 2 Corinthians was written (c. AD 56), Paul had contacted the Macedonian churches who had begged him "for the privilege of sharing in this ministry to the saints" (8:4). He was now using the example of their generosity to stimulate the Corinthians to carry out what they had earlier shown themselves ready to do (8:1–7; cf. 1 Cor 16:1–4), just as he had previously used the example of the Corinthians' readiness to motivate the Macedonians (9:1–15).

1. The Example of the Macedonians (8:1–6)

In these verses Paul uses the example of the Macedonian believers' remarkably generous response to the collection appeal to motivate the Corinthian believers to carry out what they had previously shown themselves ready to do: to provide relief for the believers in Jerusalem.

STRUCTURE

```
1   Γνωρίζομεν δὲ ὑμῖν, ἀδελφοί,
          τὴν χάριν τοῦ θεοῦ
          τὴν δεδομένην ἐν ταῖς ἐκκλησίαις τῆς Μακεδονίας,
2         ὅτι ἐν πολλῇ δοκιμῇ θλίψεως
    ἡ περισσεία τῆς χαρᾶς αὐτῶν
    καὶ ἡ κατὰ βάθους πτωχεία αὐτῶν ἐπερίσσευσεν
                              εἰς τὸ πλοῦτος τῆς ἁπλότητος αὐτῶν·
3         ὅτι κατὰ δύναμιν,
    μαρτυρῶ,
          καὶ παρὰ δύναμιν,
          αὐθαίρετοι
4             μετὰ πολλῆς παρακλήσεως
          δεόμενοι ἡμῶν τὴν χάριν
                 καὶ τὴν κοινωνίαν τῆς διακονίας
                        τῆς εἰς τοὺς ἁγίους,
5   καὶ οὐ καθὼς ἠλπίσαμεν
```

ἀλλ᾽ ἑαυτοὺς ἔδωκαν πρῶτον τῷ κυρίῳ
        καὶ ἡμῖν διὰ θελήματος θεοῦ
6   εἰς τὸ <u>παρακαλέσαι</u> ἡμᾶς Τίτον,
        ἵνα καθὼς προενήρξατο
        οὕτως καὶ ἐπιτελέσῃ εἰς ὑμᾶς καὶ τὴν <u>χάριν</u> ταύτην.

VERSE 1

Γνωρίζομεν δὲ ὑμῖν, ἀδελφοί, τὴν χάριν τοῦ θεοῦ
We want you to know, brothers and sisters, about the grace of God

Γνωρίζομεν . . . ὑμῖν, lit. "we make known to you." Γνωρίζομεν, 1st pl. pres. act. indic. of γνωρίζω, "make known, reveal." Ὑμῖν, indir. obj. of γνωρίζομεν. Ἀδελφοί, nom. pl. masc. ἀδελφός, -οῦ, ὁ, "brother." Χάριν, dir. obj. of γνωρίζομεν. Χάριν, acc. sg. fem. χάρις, -ιτος, ἡ, "grace." Τοῦ θεοῦ, either gen. of source ("grace from God") or poss. gen. ("God's grace").

τὴν δεδομένην ἐν ταῖς ἐκκλησίαις τῆς Μακεδονίας,
that was given to the churches of Macedonia:

Attrib. clause qualifying τὴν χάριν τοῦ θεοῦ. Δεδομένην, acc. sg. fem. of pf. pass. ptc. of δίδωμι, "give," a divine pass. "given by God." Ἐν, prep. with dat. ταῖς ἐκκλησίαις, "to the churches." Here ἐν is a substitute for εἰς; cf. BDF (§218); Moule 75–76. Z §120: "The great extension of the use of ἐν in the evolution of Hellenistic Greek goes so far as its addition, without any special significance, to the simple dative." Τῆς Μακεδονίας, attrib. gen. qualifying ταῖς ἐκκλησίαις, "(the churches) of Macedonia."

VERSE 2

ὅτι ἐν πολλῇ δοκιμῇ θλίψεως
During a severe trial brought about by affliction,

Ὅτι, Barnett 392: "The initial 'that' (untranslated) is a bridge from the previous verse introducing an explanation of 'the grace of God given the Macedonian churches.' God's grace to them is now revealed in their grace to others, shown in the midst of great affliction." Ἐν πολλῇ δοκιμῇ θλίψεως, dat. prep. phrase, "in a great trial of affliction," explaining the situation in which the Macedonians' joy overflowed in generosity. Δοκιμῇ, dat. sg. fem. δοκιμή, -ῆς, ἡ, "trial, ordeal." BDAG 256a: "*in a great ordeal of affliction.*" Θλίψεως, gen. sg. fem. θλῖψις, -εως, ἡ, "affliction," epex. gen.; explains the nature of the trial.

ἡ περισσεία τῆς χαρᾶς αὐτῶν καὶ ἡ κατὰ βάθους πτωχεία αὐτῶν ἐπερίσσευσεν
their abundant joy and their extreme poverty overflowed

Περισσεία, nom. sg. fem. περισσεία, -ας, ἡ, "abundance." Τῆς χαρᾶς αὐτῶν, gen. attrib. phrase qualifying ἡ περισσεία, "(the abundance) of their joy." Ἡ κατὰ βάθους πτωχεία αὐτῶν, lit. "according to the depth of their poverty." Moule 60, noting the general sense of κατά with the gen. ("down"), offers this translation: "their profound (perhaps = down to the depths) poverty." Κατά, prep. with gen. βάθους πτωχεία, BDAG 511a: "of position relatively deep, *into someth . . . extreme* (lit. 'reaching down into the depths' . . .) or *abysmal poverty.*" Cf. R 607. Βάθους, gen. sg. neut. βάθος, -ους, τό, "depth." Πτωχεία, nom. sg. fem. πτωχεία, -ας, ἡ, "poverty." Ἐπερίσσευσεν, 3rd sg. aor. act. indic. of περισσεύω, "abound, overflow."

εἰς τὸ πλοῦτος τῆς ἁπλότητος αὐτῶν·
in a wealth of generosity on their part.

Εἰς, prep. with acc. τὸ πλοῦτος, "in the wealth." Πλοῦτος, acc. sg. neut. πλοῦτος, -ου, τό, "wealth, riches, abundance." Τῆς ἁπλότητος αὐτῶν, gen. attrib. phrase qualifying πλοῦτος, "(wealth) of their generosity." Ἁπλότητος, gen. sg. fem. ἁπλότης, -ητος, ἡ, "generosity, liberality." Seifrid 321: "The term *haplotēs*, which is rendered 'generosity' in the major English translations (ESV, NIV, NRSV), should be interpreted instead in its usual sense as 'simplicity,' not only here, but also in 9:11, 13. There is no good reason to introduce an otherwise unattested meaning of the term in these contexts. God's grace effects a 'simplicity' in human beings that opens them to a receiving-and-giving in which hidden self-seeking motives are overcome." Thrall 2:523–24: "When the term is applied to persons, the usual meaning is 'simplicity,' 'frankness,' or 'sincerity.' Certainly the lexicons do also give 'liberality' but it is the Pauline occurrences in 2 Corinthians and Rom 12.8 that provide the basic evidence. . . . To give unconditionally is to give generously, with sincere and inward integrity.

Seifrid 320 notes two paradoxes in this verse: (1) "in the midst of 'much affliction' the Macedonians had and abundance of joy"; (2) their "deep poverty" abounded in "a wealth of generosity." Likewise Harris 564.

VERSE 3

ὅτι κατὰ δύναμιν, μαρτυρῶ, καὶ παρὰ δύναμιν, αὐθαίρετοι
I can testify that, according to their ability and even beyond their ability, of their own accord,

Describes the manner in which they begged to be able to contribute to the collection (cf. v. 4). Κατά, prep. with acc. δύναμιν, "according to (their) ability." Cf. Harris, *Prepositions*, 152. Κατὰ δύναμιν is very common in the papyri, especially in marriage contracts where a husband promises to provide food and clothing for his wife as much as he is able. Μαρτυρῶ, 1st sg. pres. act. indic. of μαρτυρέω, "bear witness, testify," i.e., to the Macedonians' willing desire, even beyond their ability, to contribute to the collection. BDF (§465[2]): "A short finite verb [μαρτυρῶ] is occasionally thrown into a construction . . . forming a slight parenthesis . . . e.g. 2 C 8:3." Cf. R 434. Παρά, prep. with acc. δύναμιν, "beyond (their) ability." Moule 51: "παρὰ δύναμιν, beyond their power, contrasted with κατὰ δύναμιν (there is a significant variant ὑπέρ for παρά here)." Cf. BDF §236[2]; Harris, *Prepositions*, 171. Παρὰ δύναμιν is found in the context of a man's complaint against his wife for whom he has provided beyond what his means really allowed. Αὐθαίρετοι, nom. pl. masc. adj. αὐθαίρετος, -ον, "of one's own accord."

VERSE 4

μετὰ πολλῆς παρακλήσεως δεόμενοι ἡμῶν τὴν χάριν
they begged us earnestly for the privilege

Μετά, prep. with gen. πολλῆς παρακλήσεως, "with much encouragement," adv. phrase modifying δεόμενοι. BDAG 766a–b: *"request earnestly."* Παρακλήσεως, gen. sg. fem. παράκλησις, -εως, ἡ, "encouragement." Δεόμενοι, nom. pl. masc. of pres. mid. ptc. of δέομαι, "beg, ask." Moule 179 cites this as an example of the use of a ptc. "where normal Greek would have used a finite verb or imperative." δέομαι, takes gen. of person besought (ἡμῶν) and acc. of the thing requested (τὴν χάριν καὶ τὴν κοινωνίαν). BDAG 218b: "begging us for the favour." Χάριν, acc. sg. fem. χάρις, -ιτος, ἡ, "favor, privilege."

καὶ τὴν κοινωνίαν τῆς διακονίας τῆς εἰς τοὺς ἁγίους,
of sharing in the ministry to the saints,

Τὴν χάριν καὶ τὴν κοινωνίαν, ZG 549: "a hendiadys: favour of sharing in sth." Κοινωνίαν, acc. sg. fem. κοινωνία, -ας, ἡ, "share, part." Τῆς διακονίας τῆς εἰς τοὺς ἁγίους indicates what they wanted a share in, "the ministry to the saints." Εἰς, prep. with acc. τοὺς ἁγίους, "to/for the saints." ZG 549: "εἰς for dat. of advantage." Ἁγίους, acc. pl. masc. subst. adj. ἅγιος, -ία, -ον, "saints," referring here to the Jewish believers.

In v. 4 three key words are used in relation to the collection: (1) "Privilege" (χάρις) is used to show that the Macedonians regarded the opportunity to contribute as a favor, not a burden. (2) "Sharing" (κοινωνία) indicates that their involvement was seen as participation in a larger entity, i.e., an "ecumenical" act of compassion. (3) "Service" (διακονία) reflects the fact that contributing to the collection was viewed as Christian "service." Harris 566: "In Paul's letters κοινωνία always implies an active involvement rather than a passive partnership."

VERSE 5

καὶ οὐ καθὼς ἠλπίσαμεν
and not just as we had hoped.

Καθώς, conj., "as, just as." Ἠλπίσαμεν, 1st pl. aor. act. indic. of ἐλπίζω, "hope."

ἀλλ᾽ ἑαυτοὺς ἔδωκαν πρῶτον τῷ κυρίῳ καὶ ἡμῖν διὰ θελήματος θεοῦ
Instead, they gave themselves first to the Lord and then to us by God's will.

Ἑαυτούς, acc. 3rd pl. masc. reflex. pron. ἑαυτοῦ, -ῆς, -οῦ, "themselves," dir. obj. of ἔδωκαν. Κυρίῳ, Harris 568: "ἑαυτοὺς ἔδωκαν . . . τῷ κυρίῳ cannot refer to their conversion experience because of the καὶ ἡμῖν that follows. It must have been a rededication of their lives . . . for a specific task that involved Paul, namely the facilitating of the collection." Ἔδωκαν, 3rd pl. aor. act. indic. of δίδωμι, "give." Πρῶτον, adv. "first." BDAG 894a: "in the first place . . . first of all." Cf. Hafemann 334: "That the Macedonians gave themselves 'first' to the Lord is not a reference to a temporal sequence but to the priority of allegiance to God (contra the NIV [and the CSB], the word 'then' is not necessarily implicit in the text)." Τῷ, prep. with dat. κυρίῳ καὶ ἡμῖν, "to the Lord and to us," indir. obj. of ἔδωκαν.

Διὰ θελήματος θεοῦ, gen. prep. phrase, "by the will of God" (BDAG 224d: "of efficient cause"), indicates what caused the Macedonians to give themselves to Paul (cf. Phil 2:13: "For it is God who is working in you both to will and to work according to his good purpose"). Θελήματος, gen. sg. neut. θέλημα, -ατος, τό, "will (of God)." Θεοῦ, subj. gen. "(what) God wills." "By the will of God" is a peculiarly Pauline expression, found seven times in his letters and nowhere else in the NT. Five times it relates to Paul's call to be an apostle (1 Cor 1:1; 2 Cor 1:1; Eph 1:1; Col 1:1; 2 Tim 1:1). Once it relates to his plans to visit the believers in Rome (Rom 15:32), and here in 8:5 it relates to the Corinthians' dedication of themselves to the Lord and his apostle.

VERSE 6

εἰς τὸ παρακαλέσαι ἡμᾶς Τίτον, ἵνα καθὼς προενήρξατο
So we urged Titus that just as he had begun,

Εἰς, prep. with art. inf. τὸ παρακαλέσαι expresses result, "so we urged Titus." Cf. Moule 141; R1003; Harris, Prepositions, 90. BDF (§402[2]): "εἰς τό is used to denote purpose or result, apparently not differing from τοῦ and the infinitive." Παρακαλέσαι, aor. act. inf. of παρακαλέω, "urge, exhort." Ἡμᾶς, acc. subj. of inf. παρακαλέσαι. Ἵνα, conj. with subjunc. ἐπιτελέσῃ. ZG 549: "standing for obj. inf." Harris 570: "ἵνα is epexegetic rather than telic [indicating purpose]." Καθώς, conj. "just as," when followed by οὕτως: "just as . . . so" (cf. BDAG 493c). Προενήρξατο, 3rd sg. aor. mid. indic. of προενάρχομαι, "begin beforehand," prob. referring to the visit mentioned in 8:6, 10; 9:2, 12:17–18, as Hafemann 334 suggests.

οὕτως καὶ ἐπιτελέσῃ εἰς ὑμᾶς καὶ τὴν χάριν ταύτην.
so he should also complete among you this act of grace.

Οὕτως, conj., "so," when preceded by καθώς: "just as . . . so" (cf. BDAG 493a).
Ἐπιτελέσῃ, 3rd sg. aor. act. subjunc. of ἐπιτελέω, "complete, bring to an end," preceded by ἵνα, expresses purpose. Εἰς, prep. with acc. ὑμᾶς, "for or among you." Τὴν
χάριν ταύτην, "this act of grace," dir. obj. of ἐπιτελέσῃ (ταύτην in the pred. position).
Χάριν, acc. sg. fem. χάρις, -ιτος, ἡ, "(act of) grace."

2. Paul Exhorts the Corinthians to Finish What They Began (8:7–15)

STRUCTURE

7 ἀλλ' ὥσπερ ἐν παντὶ <u>περισσεύετε</u>,
         πίστει
      καὶ λόγῳ
      καὶ γνώσει
      καὶ πάσῃ σπουδῇ
      καὶ τῇ ἐξ ἡμῶν ἐν ὑμῖν ἀγάπῃ,
      ἵνα καὶ ἐν ταύτῃ τῇ χάριτι <u>περισσεύητε</u>.
8   Οὐ κατ' ἐπιταγὴν
λέγω
    ἀλλὰ   διὰ τῆς ἑτέρων σπουδῆς
              καὶ τὸ τῆς ὑμετέρας ἀγάπης γνήσιον
    δοκιμάζων·
9 γινώσκετε γὰρ τὴν χάριν τοῦ κυρίου ἡμῶν Ἰησοῦ Χριστοῦ,
      ὅτι   δι' ὑμᾶς
         ἐπτώχευσεν
         πλούσιος ὤν,
         ἵνα ὑμεῖς
                        τῇ ἐκείνου πτωχείᾳ
                        πλουτήσητε.
10 καὶ γνώμην ἐν τούτῳ δίδωμι·
τοῦτο γὰρ ὑμῖν συμφέρει,
         οἵτινες οὐ μόνον τὸ ποιῆσαι
            ἀλλὰ καὶ τὸ θέλειν προενήρξασθε
                              ἀπὸ πέρυσι·
11 νυνὶ δὲ καὶ τὸ ποιῆσαι ἐπιτελέσατε,
      ὅπως καθάπερ ἡ προθυμία τοῦ θέλειν,
      οὕτως καὶ τὸ ἐπιτελέσαι ἐκ τοῦ ἔχειν.
12   εἰ γὰρ ἡ προθυμία πρόκειται,
      καθὸ ἐὰν ἔχῃ εὐπρόσδεκτος,
      οὐ καθὸ οὐκ ἔχει.
13 οὐ γὰρ ἵνα ἄλλοις ἄνεσις,
            ὑμῖν θλῖψις,
      ἀλλ' ἐξ ἰσότητος·
14   ἐν τῷ νῦν καιρῷ

τὸ ὑμῶν <u>περίσσευμα</u>   εἰς τὸ ἐκείνων ὑστέρημα,
  ἵνα καὶ τὸ ἐκείνων <u>περίσσευμα</u> γένηται
               εἰς τὸ ὑμῶν ὑστέρημα,
  ὅπως γένηται ἰσότης,
15 καθὼς γέγραπται,
    Ὁ τὸ πολὺ οὐκ ἐπλεόνασεν,
  καὶ ὁ τὸ ὀλίγον οὐκ ἠλαττόνησεν.

VERSE 7

ἀλλ᾽ ὥσπερ ἐν παντὶ περισσεύετε,
Now as you excel in everything—

Ὥσπερ, conj. followed by καί, "just as . . . so." BDAG 1106d: "ὥσπερ . . . , ἵνα καί w. subjunctive [περισσεύητε v. 7b] (as a substitute for the impv.) 2 Cor 8:7." Ἐν, prep. with dat. παντί, "in everything." Περισσεύετε, 2nd pl. pres. act. indic. of περισσεύω, "excel, abound."

πίστει καὶ λόγῳ καὶ γνώσει καὶ πάσῃ σπουδῇ καὶ τῇ ἐξ ἡμῶν ἐν ὑμῖν ἀγάπῃ,
in faith, speech, knowledge, and in all diligence, and in your love for us—

Πίστει, dat. sg. fem. πίστις, -εως, ἡ, "faith." Λόγῳ, dat. sg. masc. λόγος, -ου, ὁ, "speech, word." Cf. 1 Cor 1:5. Γνώσει, dat. sg. fem. γνῶσις, -εως, ἡ, "knowledge." Cf. 1 Cor 1:5. Πάσῃ σπουδῇ, "all diligence." Σπουδῇ, dat. sg. fem. σπουδή, -ῆς, ἡ, "diligence, eagerness, earnestness, zeal." Τῇ ἐξ ἡμῶν ἐν ὑμῖν ἀγάπῃ, lit. "in the love from us in you." NRSV, ESV: "in our love for you." Cf. CSB: "in your love for us," NIV: "in the love we have kindled in you." For a discussion of the var. τῇ ἐξ ὑμῶν ἐν ἡμῖν ἀγάπῃ, see Metzger 512; Thrall 2:529–30; Harris 573 n. a. Ἐξ, prep. with gen. of agency ἡμῶν. Harris, *Prepositions*, 104: "the love we inspired in you." Ἐν, prep. with locat. dat. ὑμῖν, "in you." Ἀγάπῃ, dat. sg. fem. ἀγάπη, -ης, ἡ, "love."

ἵνα καὶ ἐν ταύτῃ τῇ χάριτι περισσεύητε.
excel also in this act of grace

Ἵνα with subjunc. περισσεύητε, "excel (also in this . . .)," an instance of ἵνα plus the subjunc. becoming imperative in sense. Cf. Moule 144; BDF §387[3]; R 933; Harris 575. Z §415 cites this as an example of an "independent wish or exhortation." ZG 550: "ἵνα abs. introducing a wish, may you. . . ." Cf. Thrall 2:529. Περισσεύητε, 2nd pl. pres. act. subjunc. of περισσεύω, "excel, abound." Ἐν, prep with dat. ταύτῃ τῇ χάριτι, "in this (act of) grace." Ταύτῃ, dat. sg. fem. dem. pron. οὗτος, αὕτη, τοῦτο, in the pred. position "this." Χάριτι, dat. sg. fem. χάρις, -ιτος, ἡ, "(act of) grace."

VERSE 8

Οὐ κατ᾽ ἐπιταγὴν λέγω ἀλλὰ διὰ τῆς ἑτέρων σπουδῆς
I am not saying this as a command. Rather, by means of the diligence of others,

Οὐ κατ᾽, prep. with acc. ἐπιταγήν, "not as a command, voluntary." Cf. Harris, *Prepositions*, 156. Ἐπιταγήν, acc. sg. fem. ἐπιταγή, -ῆς, ἡ, "command, order." Διά, prep. with gen. τῆς ἑτέρων σπουδῆς, "by the diligence of others." Ἑτέρων, gen. pl. masc. adj. ἕτερος, -α, -ον, "others," i.e., the Macedonians who provided an example of diligence (ἑτέρων is better not regarded as an obj. gen. [i.e., "for others"] referring to the recipients of the collection; cf. Thrall 2:532). Σπουδῆς, gen. sg. fem. σπουδή, -ῆς, ἡ, "diligence, eagerness."

In 1 Cor 7:6, when giving advice to the married about temporary sexual abstinence to devote themselves to prayer, Paul uses the same expression, οὐ κατ᾽ ἐπιταγήν. When here in 8:8 he urges the Corinthians to excel in "this act of grace," it was not a command to be obeyed, but an exhortation to take the opportunity to demonstrate the genuineness of their own love and diligence.

καὶ τὸ τῆς ὑμετέρας ἀγάπης γνήσιον δοκιμάζων·
I am testing the genuineness of your love.

BDF (§263[2]): "Peculiar to Paul (Heb) is the use of a neuter sing. adjective like an abstract mostly with a dependent gen. . . . 2 C 8:8 τὸ τῆς ὑμετέρας ἀγάπης γνήσιον ('what is genuine with respect to your love')." Moule 96 cites this as an instance of an adj. functioning as a noun, something that "is easy enough to understand whenever a noun can be mentally supplied. . . . But on occasion there seems to be no implied noun, or at least it is hard to conceive of one: II Cor. viii.8 τὸ γνήσιον." Τῆς ὑμετέρας ἀγάπης, "your love." Ὑμετέρας, gen. sg. fem. poss. adj. ὑμέτερος, -α, -ον, "your." Γνήσιον, acc. sg. neut. subst. adj. γνήσιος, -α, -ον, "genuineness." Δοκιμάζων, nom. sg. masc. of pres. act. ptc. of δοκιμάζω, "test, prove." Harris 576: "It [the ptc.] may bear a telic sense ('in order to prove' . . .)."

VERSE 9

γινώσκετε γὰρ τὴν χάριν τοῦ κυρίου ἡμῶν Ἰησοῦ Χριστοῦ,
For you know the grace of our Lord Jesus Christ:

Γινώσκετε, 2nd pl. pres. act. indic. of γινώσκω, "know." Τὴν χάριν, dir. obj. of γινώσκετε. Τοῦ κυρίου ἡμῶν, either gen. of source ("[grace] from our Lord") or poss. gen. ("our Lord's [grace]"). Ἰησοῦ Χριστοῦ, gen. sg. in appos. with τοῦ κυρίου ἡμῶν.

ὅτι δι᾽ ὑμᾶς ἐπτώχευσεν πλούσιος ὤν,
Though he was rich, for your sake he became poor,

Ὅτι, conj., "that." BDAG 731d: "marker of discourse content . . . after verbs that denote mental perception . . . γινώσκω." Δι᾽, prep. with acc. ὑμᾶς, "for your sake." Ἐπτώχευσεν, 3rd sg. aor. act. indic. of πτωχεύω, "become poor." An ingressive aor.; cf. Moule 11. Πλούσιος, nom. sing. masc. adj. πλούσιος, -ία, -ιον, "rich." Ὤν, nom. sg. masc. of pres. ptc. of εἰμί, "be." Seifrid 329–30: "The participial construction should not be interpreted as concessive but as modal: 'for your sake he became poor, being rich.' Christ's wealth is present within his poverty . . . the riches of Christ, hidden in his poverty, are the riches that make the Corinthians rich."

For a detailed discussion of Jesus's "poverty" and "wealth," see Thrall 2:532–34, who adopts the traditional view: "The phrase πλούσιος ὤν refers to Christ's pre-existent state, and the ἐπτώχευσεν to his incarnation. The assertion is seen to be parallel in general sense to Phil 2.6–8 as traditionally interpreted." So too Harris 579; Barnett 408.

ἵνα ὑμεῖς τῇ ἐκείνου πτωχείᾳ πλουτήσητε.
so that by his poverty you might become rich.

Ἵνα, with subjunc. πλουτήσητε, "so that you might become rich." Ὑμεῖς, nom. 2nd pl. subj. of πλουτήσητε. Πλουτήσητε, 2nd pl. aor. act. subjunc. of πλουτέω, "become rich," an ingressive aor. Τῇ ἐκείνου πτωχείᾳ, dat. phrase "by his poverty." Ἐκείνου, gen. sg. masc. dem. pron. ἐκεῖνος, -η, -ο, "that one, his." Πτωχείᾳ, dat. sg. fem. πτωχεία, -ας, ἡ, "poverty." Hafemann 337: "Decoded, this means that Jesus underwent his incarnation (i.e., his becoming 'poor'), in spite of his position in heaven (i.e., the fact that he was 'rich'), in order that we might be saved (our justification through Jesus' death means our becoming 'rich' through his 'poverty;' cf. Rom. 10:12; 11:12; 2 Cor. 5:21; 6:10)."

VERSE 10

καὶ γνώμην ἐν τούτῳ δίδωμι· τοῦτο γὰρ ὑμῖν συμφέρει,
And in this matter I am giving advice because it is profitable for you,

Γνώμην, acc. sg. fem. γνώμη, -ης, ἡ, "advice, opinion, judgment." The apostle was not averse to making demands that he regarded as commands of the Lord (cf. 1 Cor 14:37–38), but he distinguished his own advice or opinions as an apostle from such authoritative commands (cf. 1 Cor 7:25, 40), as he does here when prefacing it with "I am giving advice." Ἐν, prep. with dat. τούτῳ, "in this (matter)." Δίδωμι, 1st sg. pres. act. indic. of δίδωμι, "give."

Τοῦτο, "this (advice)." Ὑμῖν, dat. 2nd pl. indir. obj. of συμφέρει. Συμφέρει, 3rd sg. pres. act. indic. of συμφέρω, "be better, benefit, useful." BDAG 960a: "impers. συμφέρει τι someth. is good (for someone or someth)." Harris 581: "The expediency implied by συμφέρει ('it is expedient/advantageous/fitting') did not involve some benefit that would accrue to the Corinthians if they completed their collection, but rather was appropriate or advantageous action that Paul himself was taking in the case of the Corinthians (ὑμῖν, 'in your case')."

οἵτινες οὐ μόνον τὸ ποιῆσαι ἀλλὰ καὶ τὸ θέλειν προενήρξασθε ἀπὸ πέρυσι·
who began last year not only to do something but also to want to do it.

Οἵτινες, nom. pl. masc. pron. ὅστις, ἥτις, ὅ τι, "who." BDAG 730a: "Quite oft. ὅστις takes the place of the simple rel. ὅς, ἥ, ὅ; this occurs occasionally in ancient Gk. usage." Οὐ μόνον, "not only." Τὸ ποιῆσαι, aor. act. art. inf., lit. "the doing." Τὸ θέλειν, pres. act. art. inf., lit. "the willing." Προενήρξασθε, 2nd pl. aor. mid. indic. of προενάρχομαι, "begin beforehand." Ἀπὸ πέρυσι, BDAG 105c: "*since last year.*" Thrall 2:536–37: "Paul is thinking of the initial interest in the collection to which he refers in 1 Cor 16:1–4, and which he heard of in the letter the Corinthians had written to him." Πέρυσι, adv., "last year, a year ago."

VERSE 11

νυνὶ δὲ καὶ τὸ ποιῆσαι ἐπιτελέσατε, ὅπως καθάπερ ἡ προθυμία τοῦ θέλειν,
Now also finish the task, so that just as there was an eager desire,

Νυνὶ δὲ harks back to ἀπὸ πέρυσι in v. 10. Τὸ ποιῆσαι, aor. act. art. inf. of ποιέω, "do," lit. "the doing." Ἐπιτελέσατε, 2nd pl. aor. act. impv. of ἐπιτελέω, "complete, finish, bring to an end," prob. refers to the practice of setting "something aside" for the collection on the first day of the week (1 Cor 16:2). Ὅπως, conj., "so that." Καθάπερ, conj., "just as" followed by οὕτως, "just as . . . so." Προθυμία, nom. sg. fem. προθυμία, -ας, ἡ, "eagerness, readiness, willingness." Τοῦ θέλειν, pres. act. art. inf. of θέλω, expresses purpose "to desire." Ἡ προθυμία τοῦ θέλειν, ESV, "your readiness in desiring it."

οὕτως καὶ τὸ ἐπιτελέσαι ἐκ τοῦ ἔχειν.
there may also be a completion, according to what you have.

Οὕτως, adv., "so, thus," preceded by καθάπερ, "just as . . . so." Τὸ ἐπιτελέσαι, aor. act. explanatory. art. inf., "(an eager desire) to complete." Ἐκ, prep. with gen. denotes derivation "from"; cf. BDAG 296d. Harris, *Prepositions*, 104: denotes basis of action. Ἐκ, prep. with pres. act. subst. inf. τοῦ ἔχειν, "from what you have," Harris, *Prepositions*, 157: "as resources permit."

VERSE 12

εἰ γὰρ ἡ προθυμία πρόκειται,
For if the eagerness is there,

Προθυμία, nom. sg. fem. προθυμία, -ας, ἡ, "eagerness, readiness." Πρόκειται, 3rd sg. pres. mid. indic. of πρόκειμαι, "be present, there, lie before."

καθὸ ἐὰν ἔχῃ εὐπρόσδεκτος, οὐ καθὸ οὐκ ἔχει.
the gift is acceptable according to what a person has, not according to what he does not have.

Καθὸ ἐὰν ἔχῃ, "according to what a person has." Moule 59, "in proportion to what one has." Καθό, adv. BDAG 493a: "marker of degree, *in so far as, to the degree that.*" Ἔχῃ, 3rd sg. pres. act. subjunc. of ἔχω, "have." ZG 550: "supply τις as subject." Εὐπρόσδεκτος, nom. sg. masc. adj. εὐπρόσδεκτος, -ον, "acceptable." Εὐπρόσδεκτος is found in three other contexts in Paul's letters: In Rom 15:16 Paul speaks of the Gentiles being an "acceptable" sacrifice to God; in Rom 15:31 he expresses his hope that the collection will be "acceptable" to the Judean Christians; and in 2 Cor 6:2 it is used of the "acceptable time," i.e., "the day of salvation." Thus Paul uses εὐπρόσδεκτος of acceptability both to God and to human beings. In our present context, where the word is used in an absolute sense, and where no human acceptance is in view, acceptability before God of the Corinthians' gift is intended.

Οὐ καθὸ οὐκ ἔχει, "not according to what he does not have." Thrall 2:538–39: "The point must be that the demands of piety do not go beyond what is proportionate to one's resources, not that it would be displeasing to God to exceed them."

VERSE 13

οὐ γὰρ ἵνα ἄλλοις ἄνεσις, ὑμῖν θλῖψις, ἀλλ' ἐξ ἰσότητος·
It is not that there should be relief for others and hardship for you, but it is a question of equality.

Ἵνα ἄλλοις ἄνεσις, a subjunc. form of εἰμί is implied, "that there should be relief for others." Ἄλλοις, dat. pl. masc. adj. ἄλλος, -η, -ο, "others," dat. of respect. Ἄνεσις, nom. sg. fem. ἄνεσις, -εως, ἡ, "relief." Ὑμῖν, dat. 2nd pl. σύ, "you," dat. of respect. Θλῖψις, nom. sg. fem. θλῖψις, -εως, ἡ, "hardship, trouble." Ἀλλ' (contraction of ἀλλά), adversative particle "but," introduces Paul's real reason for advocating participation in the collection. Ἐξ, prep. with gen. ἰσότητος. ZG 550: "by equality," BDAG 481a: "*as a matter of equality.*" Ἰσότητος, gen. sg. fem. ἰσότης, -ητος, ἡ, "equality." Thrall 2:540: "He is not concerned to promote a state of general financial equality between all Christian churches, since in that case he would surely have been asking for assistance for the Macedonians, rather than accepting a donation from them."

VERSE 14

ἐν τῷ νῦν καιρῷ τὸ ὑμῶν περίσσευμα εἰς τὸ ἐκείνων ὑστέρημα,
At the present time your surplus is available for their need,

Ἐν, prep. with dat. τῷ νῦν καιρῷ, "at the present time." Περίσσευμα, nom. sg. neut. περίσσευμα, -ατος, τό, "surplus, abundance." Harris 590–91: "It was this 'surplus,' accumulated in weekly instalments (1 Cor. 16:2), that would meet the 'deficiency' or 'shortage' or 'shortfall' . . . of those in Jerusalem." Εἰς τὸ ἐκείνων ὑστέρημα with a form of εἰμί implied "(is) for their need." Ὑστέρημα, acc. sg. neut. ὑστέρημα, -ατος, τό, "need, lack of what is needed, deficiency."

ἵνα καὶ τὸ ἐκείνων περίσσευμα γένηται εἰς τὸ ὑμῶν ὑστέρημα, ὅπως γένηται ἰσότης,
so that their abundance may in turn meet your need, in order that there may be equality.

Ἵνα with subjunc. γένηται expresses purpose. Γένηται, 3rd sg. aor. mid. subjunc. of γίνομαι, "be." Περίσσευμα, nom. sg. neut. περίσσευμα, -ατος, τό, "surplus, abundance." Εἰς, prep. with acc. τὸ ὑμῶν ὑστέρημα, "for your need." Ὑστέρημα, acc. sg. neut. ὑστέρημα, -ατος, τό, "need, lack of what is needed." Ὅπως, conj., "in order that." BDF (§369[4]): "ὅπως is evidently used for the sake of variety since ἵνα has just preceded." Γένηται, see above. Ἰσότης, nom. sg. fem. ἰσότης, -ητος, ἡ, "equality." NRSV, "a fair balance"; ESV, "fairness."

VERSE 15

καθὼς γέγραπται, Ὁ τὸ πολὺ οὐκ ἐπλεόνασεν, καὶ ὁ τὸ ὀλίγον οὐκ ἠλαττόνησεν.
As it is written: **The person who had much did not have too much, and the person who had little did not have too little.**

Καθώς, conj., "as." Γέγραπται, 3rd sg. pf. pass. indic. of γράφω, "write." Ὁ τὸ πολύ, "the one who (gathered) much." Πολύ, acc. sg. neut. subst. adj. πολύς, πολλή, πολύ, "much." Ἐπλεόνασεν, 3rd sg. aor. act. indic. of πλεονάζω, "have much." BDAG 824b: *"have more than is necessary, have too much."* Ὁ τὸ ὀλίγον, "the one who (gathered) little." Ὀλίγον, acc. sg. neut. subst. adj. ὀλίγος, -η, -ον, "little." Ἠλαττόνησεν, 3rd sg. aor. act. indic. of ἐλαττονέω, "lack, have less, too little." BDAG 313d: "to be in possession of relatively less, have less, have too little." Harris 594: "Both ἐπλεόνασεν and ἠλαττόνησεν are constative aorists that view repeated states in a summary fashion."

3. Commendation of Those Who Will Receive the Collection (8:16–24)

Here Paul commends the three brothers who are to travel to Corinth to administer the collection. Titus is commended first (vv. 16–17), then the brother "who is praised among all the churches for his gospel ministry" (vv. 18–19), and thirdly "our brother" who has been "often tested" and found "to be diligent" (v. 22). The passage concludes with a summary commendation of all three (v. 23) and an exhortation that the Corinthians give proof of their love (for Paul) and the truth of his boasting about them (to the Macedonians) when the three brothers arrive (v. 24). Between the commendations of those whom he is sending, Paul digresses briefly to say he is trying to avoid any criticism of the way he is administering this "large sum" (vv. 20–21). It is this concern that prob. accounts for the rather full commendations Paul makes.

STRUCTURE

16   Χάρις δὲ τῷ θεῷ
              τῷ δόντι τὴν αὐτὴν σπουδὴν
                     ὑπὲρ ὑμῶν
                     ἐν τῇ καρδίᾳ Τίτου,
17   ὅτι τὴν μὲν παράκλησιν ἐδέξατο,
                             σπουδαιότερος δὲ ὑπάρχων
                             αὐθαίρετος ἐξῆλθεν πρὸς ὑμᾶς.

18   συνεπέμψαμεν δὲ
                     μετ᾽ αὐτοῦ
                     τὸν ἀδελφὸν
                     οὗ ὁ ἔπαινος
                            ἐν τῷ εὐαγγελίῳ
                            διὰ πασῶν τῶν ἐκκλησιῶν,
19   οὐ μόνον δέ,
          ἀλλὰ καὶ χειροτονηθεὶς
                     ὑπὸ τῶν ἐκκλησιῶν
                     συνέκδημος ἡμῶν
                     σὺν τῇ χάριτι ταύτῃ
                            τῇ διακονουμένῃ ὑφ᾽ ἡμῶν
                            πρὸς τὴν [αὐτοῦ] τοῦ κυρίου <u>δόξαν</u>
                            καὶ προθυμίαν ἡμῶν,
20   στελλόμενοι τοῦτο,
                 μή τις ἡμᾶς μωμήσηται
                            ἐν τῇ ἁδρότητι ταύτῃ
                                 τῇ διακονουμένῃ ὑφ᾽ ἡμῶν·
21   προνοοῦμεν γὰρ καλὰ
          οὐ μόνον ἐνώπιον κυρίου
          ἀλλὰ καὶ ἐνώπιον ἀνθρώπων.
22   συνεπέμψαμεν δὲ
          αὐτοῖς   τὸν ἀδελφὸν ἡμῶν
                            ὃν ἐδοκιμάσαμεν
                                 ἐν πολλοῖς πολλάκις
                                 σπουδαῖον ὄντα,
                            νυνὶ δὲ πολὺ σπουδαιότερον
                                 πεποιθήσει πολλῇ
                                 τῇ εἰς ὑμᾶς.
23   εἴτε ὑπὲρ Τίτου,
              κοινωνὸς ἐμὸς
              καὶ εἰς ὑμᾶς συνεργός·
      εἴτε   ἀδελφοὶ ἡμῶν,
                 ἀπόστολοι ἐκκλησιῶν,
                 <u>δόξα</u> Χριστοῦ.

24   τὴν οὖν ἔνδειξιν
τῆς ἀγάπης ὑμῶν
καὶ ἡμῶν καυχήσεως ὑπὲρ ὑμῶν
εἰς αὐτοὺς
ἐνδεικνύμενοι
εἰς πρόσωπον τῶν ἐκκλησιῶν.

VERSE 16

Χάρις δὲ τῷ θεῷ τῷ δόντι τὴν αὐτὴν σπουδὴν ὑπὲρ ὑμῶν ἐν τῇ καρδίᾳ Τίτου,
Thanks be to God, who put the same concern for you into the heart of Titus.

Χάρις, nom. sg. fem. χάρις, -ιτος, ἡ, "grace," here "thanks," BDAG 1080c: "response to generosity or beneficence, *thanks, gratitude*." Τῷ θεῷ, dat. phrase indir. obj. of implied form of εἰμί, "(thanks) be to God." Τῷ δόντι, "the one who gave/put," attrib. phrase describing τῷ θεῷ. Δόντι, dat. sg. masc. of aor. act. ptc. of δίδωμι, "give." Τὴν αὐτὴν σπουδήν, with αὐτήν in the attrib. position: "the same concern." Titus's "same concern" for the Corinthians as Paul had in this matter arose perhaps because he realized it was a test of the sincerity of their love (v. 8) and he was anxious that they not be found to have failed the test. Σπουδήν, acc. sg. fem. σπουδή, -ῆς, ἡ, "diligence, eagerness, zeal." Ὑπέρ, prep. with gen. ὑμῶν, "for you." Ἐν, prep. with locat. dat. τῇ καρδίᾳ (Τίτου), "in the heart (of Titus)." Here ἐν appears to have been substituted for εἰς; cf. BDF §218; Moule 76; Harris, *Prepositions*, 117.

VERSE 17

ὅτι τὴν μὲν παράκλησιν ἐδέξατο, σπουδαιότερος δὲ ὑπάρχων αὐθαίρετος ἐξῆλθεν πρὸς ὑμᾶς.
For he welcomed our appeal and, being very diligent, went out to you by his own choice.

Παράκλησιν, acc. sg. fem. παράκλησις, -εως, ἡ, "exhortation, appeal." Ἐδέξατο, 3rd sg. aor. mid. indic. of δέχομαι, "accept, welcome." Σπουδαιότερος, nom. sg. masc. (comp. of σπουδαῖος) adj., "very/more diligent, earnest, eager." Thrall 2:546: "The sense might be: 'more enthusiastic than the mere acceptance of a request implies.'" Ὑπάρχων, nom. sg. masc. of pres. act. ptc. of ὑπάρχω, "be." BDAG 1029d: "a widely used substitute . . . for εἶναι." Αὐθαίρετος, nom. sg. masc. adj. "of one's own accord." Titus undertook his mission "by his own choice" (αὐθαίρετος), just as the Macedonians had participated in the collection "of their own accord" (8:3: αὐθαίρετοι). Ἐξῆλθεν, 3rd sg. aor. act. indic. of ἐξέρχομαι, "go out." Πρός, prep with acc. ὑμᾶς, "to you."

VERSE 18

συνεπέμψαμεν δὲ μετ᾽ αὐτοῦ τὸν ἀδελφὸν οὗ ὁ ἔπαινος ἐν τῷ εὐαγγελίῳ διὰ πασῶν τῶν ἐκκλησιῶν,
We have sent with him the brother who is praised among all the churches for his gospel ministry.

Συνεπέμψαμεν, 1st pl. aor. act. indic. of συμπέμπω. BDAG 959a: "send someone together with someone else, *send with or at the same time*." Μετ᾽, prep. with gen. αὐτοῦ, "with him." Τὸν ἀδελφόν, "the brother," dir. obj. of συνεπέμψαμεν. Οὗ ὁ ἔπαινος, "whose praise." Οὗ, gen. sg. masc. pron. ὅς, ἥ, ὅ, "whose, of whom." Ἔπαινος, nom. sg. masc. ἔπαινος, -ου, ὁ, "praise, approval, recognition." Ἐν, prep. with dat. τῷ εὐαγγελίῳ, dat. of respect "in (respect of) the gospel." Διά, prep. with gen. πασῶν τῶν ἐκκλησιῶν, "among all the churches." BDAG 224a: "[διά] w. other verbs that include motion: οὗ ὁ ἔπαινος διὰ πασῶν τ. ἐκκλησιῶν (sc. ἀγγέλλεται) *throughout all the congregations* 2 Cor 8:18."

VERSE 19

οὐ μόνον δέ, ἀλλὰ καὶ χειροτονηθεὶς ὑπὸ τῶν ἐκκλησιῶν συνέκδημος ἡμῶν
And not only that, but he was also appointed by the churches to accompany us

Οὐ μόνον δέ, ἀλλὰ καί, "and not only but also." Cf. BDAG 658d. Χειροτονηθείς, nom. sg. masc. of aor. pass. ptc. of χειροτονέω, "appoint, choose." ZG 551: "ptc. instead of finite vb." Cf. Z §374. Harris 602: "χειροτονηθείς must be regarded as an absolute participle that is coordinate with a finite verb (συνεπέμψαμεν, v. 18) and stands for a finite verb, in this case in the indicative (ἐχειροτονήθη)." Ὑπό, prep. with gen. τῶν ἐκκλησιῶν, "by the churches," as their representative in the group conveying the money collected to Jerusalem. Συνέκδημος, nom. sg. masc. subst. adj., "traveling companion," in appos. to subj. of χειροτονηθείς.

σὺν τῇ χάριτι ταύτῃ τῇ διακονουμένῃ ὑφ᾽ ἡμῶν
with this gracious gift that we are administering

Σύν, prep. with dat. τῇ χάριτι ταύτῃ, "with this gracious gift," the dem. ταύτῃ is in the pred. position. Τῇ διακονουμένῃ ὑφ᾽ ἡμῶν, dat. attrib. ptc. phrase "administered by us," qualifies τῇ χάριτι ταύτῃ. Διακονουμένη, dat. sg. fem. of pres. pass. ptc. of διακονέω, "administer, serve." BDAG 229d: "Of delivery of an object: χάρις διακονουμένη ὑφ᾽ ἡμῶν *gift that we are transmitting* (a ref. to the collection for whose delivery they have accepted responsibility) 2 Cor 8:19." Ὑφ᾽, prep. with gen. ἡμῶν, expresses agency "by us."

πρὸς τὴν [αὐτοῦ] τοῦ κυρίου δόξαν καὶ προθυμίαν ἡμῶν,
for the glory of the Lord himself and to show our eagerness to help.

Πρός, prep. with acc. τὴν . . . δόξαν expresses result or purpose: "for the glory (of the Lord [himself])." [Αὐτοῦ] τοῦ κυρίου. In the pred. position αὐτοῦ is an emphasizing pron. "the Lord [himself]." Πρός, prep. with acc. . . . προθυμίαν ἡμῶν "for/to show our eagerness." Thrall 2:550: "The result of the appointment has been an increase in Paul's own eagerness for the project. Perhaps he has been freed from anxiety lest his motives might be mistrusted, or the prospects for the success of the enterprise have been increased on account of this extra assistance." Προθυμίαν, acc. sg. fem. προθυμία, -ας, ἡ, "eagerness, willingness." BDAG 870a: "exceptional interest in being of service, *willingness, readiness, goodwill* 2 Cor 8:19."

VERSE 20

στελλόμενοι τοῦτο, μή τις ἡμᾶς μωμήσηται ἐν τῇ ἁδρότητι ταύτῃ τῇ διακονουμένῃ ὑφ᾿ ἡμῶν·
We are taking this precaution so that no one will criticize us about this large sum that we are administering.

Στελλόμενοι τοῦτο, μή τις, BDAG 942c: "*trying to avoid this, lest someone* 2 Cor 8:20." Harris 605: "στελλόμενοι is best regarded as an absolute participle, standing for a finite verb (στελλόμεθα) in a construction that is anacoluthic since this participle does not accord with χειροτονηθεὶς . . . συνέκδημος." Στελλόμενοι, nom. pl. masc. of pres. mid. ptc. of στέλλω, "avoid, take precaution." Ἡμᾶς, dir. obj. of μωμήσηται. Μωμήσηται, 3rd sg. aor. mid. subjunc. of μωμάομαι, "criticize, find fault." Ἐν, prep. with dat. of respect τῇ ἁδρότητι ταύτῃ, "in respect of this large sum." Ἁδρότητι, dat. sg. fem. ἁδρότης, -ητος, ἡ, lit. "abundance." CSB, "large sum"; BDAG 21d: "*lavish gift.*" Τῇ διακονουμένῃ ὑφ᾿ ἡμῶν, dat. attrib. ptc. phrase "administered by us," qualifying τῇ ἁδρότητι ταύτῃ. Διακονουμένῃ, dat. sg. fem. of pres. pass. ptc. of διακονέω, "administer."

VERSE 21

προνοοῦμεν γὰρ καλὰ οὐ μόνον ἐνώπιον κυρίου ἀλλὰ καὶ ἐνώπιον ἀνθρώπων.
Indeed, we are giving careful thought to do what is right, not only before the Lord but also before people.

Προνοοῦμεν, 1st pl. pres. act. indic. of προνοέω, "care for." Οὐ μόνον ἐνώπιον κυρίου ἀλλὰ καὶ ἐνώπιον ἀνθρώπων appears to be an adaptation of Prov 3:4 (LXX). Καλά, acc. pl. neut. subst. adj. καλός, -ή, -όν, "what is good, honorable." BDAG 504d: "of moral quality . . . *good, noble.*" Οὐ μόνον . . . ἀλλὰ καί, "not only . . . but also." Cf. BDAG 659b. Ἐνώπιον, prep. with gen. κυρίου, "before (the) Lord." Ἐνώπιον, prep. with gen. ἀνθρώπων, "before men/people."

VERSE 22

συνεπέμψαμεν δὲ αὐτοῖς τὸν ἀδελφὸν ἡμῶν
We have also sent with them our brother.

Συνεπέμψαμεν, 1st pl. aor. act. indic. of συμπέμπω, "send someone with someone else or at the same time." Αὐτοῖς, 3rd pl. masc. dat. pron. αὐτός, -ή, -ό, "with them." Ἀδελφόν, acc. sg. masc. ἀδελφός, -οῦ, ὁ, "brother," dir. obj. of συνεπέμψαμεν." Ἡμῶν, 1st pl. poss. gen., "our."

ὃν ἐδοκιμάσαμεν ἐν πολλοῖς πολλάκις σπουδαῖον ὄντα,
We have often tested him in many circumstances and found him to be diligent—

Ὅν, acc. sg. masc. rel. pron. ὅς, ἥ, ὅ, "whom." Ἐδοκιμάσαμεν, 1st pl. aor. act. indic. of δοκιμάζω, "test, approve." Harris 609: "ἐδοκιμάσαμεν is a summary or constative aorist, comprehending all the occasions and ways in a single glance." Ἐν, prep. with dat. πολλοῖς "in many matters/circumstances." Πολλάκις, adv., "often." Σπουδαῖον, acc. sg. masc. adj. σπουδαῖος, -α, -ον, "diligent," BDAG 939c: "pert. to being conscientious in discharging a duty or obligation." Ὄντα, acc. sg. masc. of pres. ptc. of εἰμί, "be."

νυνὶ δὲ πολὺ σπουδαιότερον πεποιθήσει πολλῇ τῇ εἰς ὑμᾶς.
and now even more diligent because of his great confidence in you.

Πολύ, adv., "much more," used to strengthen the comp. σπουδαιότερον; cf. R 664. Σπουδαιότερον, acc. sg. masc. comp. adj. σπουδαῖος, -α, -ον, "more diligent/earnest." Πεποιθήσει, dat. sg. fem. πεποίθησις, -εως, ἡ, "confidence." Πολλῇ τῇ εἰς ὑμᾶς, dat. phrase qualifying πεποίθησις, "great (confidence) in you." Εἰς, prep. with acc. ὑμᾶς, "in you."

VERSE 23

εἴτε ὑπὲρ Τίτου, κοινωνὸς ἐμὸς καὶ εἰς ὑμᾶς συνεργός·
As for Titus, he is my partner and coworker for you;

Εἴτε . . . εἴτε "as for . . . as for." BDF (§454[3]): "The correlatives εἴτε . . . εἴτε . . . appear only in Paul and 1 P[et], either with a finite verb or more frequently in abbreviated expressions without a verb." Harris 610: "When the correlatives εἴτε . . . εἴτε . . . are not followed by a finite verb, there is an ellipsis . . . here, 'if [someone asks]' or 'if [there is any question].'" Εἴτε (= εἰ τέ), subord. cond. conj., "either/or." Ὑπέρ, prep. with gen. Τίτου, "as for Titus"; cf. Moule 65. R 632: "Here ὑπέρ encroaches on the province of περί." Cf. Z §96. Harris, *Prepositions*, 180: "Since both περί and ὑπέρ can mean 'about/concerning,' and since both can depict the person or thing on whose behalf or in whose interest something takes place, it is not surprising that each preposition often appears as a variant reading for the other." Betz 79 notes that the word ὑπέρ was used when making "a legal statement on someone's behalf" reinforcing the view that Paul was introducing Titus as his official representative.

Κοινωνός, nom. sg. masc. κοινωνός, -οῦ, ὁ, "partner." This is the only place Paul uses the word "partner" (κοινωνός) of a colleague, but he uses "coworker" (συνεργός) several times to denote both male and female colleagues (Rom 16:3, 9, 21; Phil 2:25; 4:3; Col 4:11; 1 Thess 3:2; Phlm 1, 24). Ἐμός, nom. sg. masc. poss. pron. ἐμός, -ή, -όν, "my." Εἰς, prep. with acc. ὑμᾶς, "for you." Συνεργός, nom. sg. masc. subst. adj. συνεργός, -όν, "coworker."

εἴτε ἀδελφοὶ ἡμῶν, ἀπόστολοι ἐκκλησιῶν, δόξα Χριστοῦ.
as for our brothers, they are the messengers of the churches, the glory of Christ.

Εἴτε, see above. Ἀδελφοί, nom. pl. masc. ἀδελφός, -οῦ, ὁ, "brother." Ἀπόστολοι ἐκκλησιῶν, "apostles/messengers of the churches (cf. Phil 2:25)," in appos. to ἀδελφοί. Harris 611: "By using the term ἀπόστολος of these two Christian brothers, Paul is not suggesting that they shared his status as ἀπόστολος Χριστοῦ (1:1)." Δόξα Χριστοῦ, "the glory of Christ," in appos. with ἀπόστολοι ἐκκλησιῶν. "The glory of Christ" could refer to "the messengers of the churches" (implied in the NIV), in which case it may imply that these men worked for the "glory of Christ" in that they participated in the administration of a collection that was "to honor the Lord himself" (v. 19 NIV); sim. Thrall 2:555: "It is more likely that the sense of the phrase δόξα Χριστοῦ is 'promoting the glory of Christ.'" Betz 82 argues that the very vagueness of the expression reflects "the language of diplomacy," in this case to enhance the status of these brothers.

Cf. Hafemann 362: "Since Christ is the one who creates in them their eager desire to serve the Corinthians, these 'apostles,' like the apostle Paul (cf. 1:1), are manifestations of Christ's life-changing glory. This means to reject their work among the Corinthians is to reject the reality of Christ in his church and within her apostles." Cf. Seifrid 346.

Alternatively, "the glory of Christ" could refer to the churches (as implied by the punctuation in the CSB ("they are the messengers of the churches, the glory of Christ"). Barnett 427 suggests that the churches were "the glory of Christ" because, against the dark background in which they were situated, they shone brightly and so glorified Christ.

Harris 612: "The delegates are said to be 'the glory of Christ' in that they were 'an honor to Christ' (TCNT) or 'a credit to Christ' (Goodspeed) either by their exemplary lives and service or because they were trophies of Christ's saving grace; or in that they were an embodiment or worthy reflection of Christ's glory; or in that they were 'men in whom Christ is glorified' (Weymouth); or in that they promoted Christ's glory."

VERSE 24

τὴν οὖν ἔνδειξιν . . . εἰς αὐτοὺς ἐνδεικνύμενοι
Therefore, show them proof

Harris 612: "τὴν . . . ἔνδειξιν . . . ἐνδεικνύμενοι is clearly a play on words. . . . 'The noun describes a demonstration properly speaking, a means of proving something hidden; the verb refers to a manifestation of the proof by its being brought to the attention of others.' Thus, 'give public proof. . . .'" Ἔνδειξιν, acc. sg. fem. ἔνδειξις, -εως, ἡ, "proof, evidence," dir. obj. of ἐνδεικνύμενοι. Εἰς, prep. with acc. αὐτούς, "to them," indir. obj. of ἐνδεικνύμενοι. Ἐνδεικνύμενοι, nom. pl. masc. of pres. mid. ptc. of ἐνδείκνυμι, "give proof, show, demonstrate." The ptc. functions here as an imperative.

εἰς πρόσωπον τῶν ἐκκλησιῶν.
before the churches

Εἰς, prep. with acc. πρόσωπον, lit. "before the face." Ἐκκλησιῶν, gen. pl. fem. ἐκκλησία, -ας, ἡ, "church." Harris 614: "presumably the Macedonian churches from which the delegates probably came, but it is not impossible that ἐκκλησίαι here includes all Christian congregations of the time, but notably the mother-church in Jerusalem."

τῆς ἀγάπης ὑμῶν καὶ ἡμῶν καυχήσεως ὑπὲρ ὑμῶν
of your love and of our boasting about you.

A gen. explanatory phrase qualifying ἔνδειξιν. Ἀγάπης, gen. sg. fem ἀγάπη, -ης, ἡ, "love." Καυχήσεως, gen. sg. fem. καύχησις, -εως, ἡ, "boasting, pride." Ὑπέρ, prep. with gen. ὑμῶν, "about you."

FOR FURTHER STUDY

80. The Collection (8:1–24)

Ascough, R. S. "The Completion of a Religious Duty: The Background of 2 Cor 8.1–15." *NTS* 42 (1995–96): 584–99.

Berger, K. "Almosen für Israel. Zum Historischen Kontext der Paulinischen Kollekte." *NTS* 23 (1976–77): 180–204.

Betz, H. D. *2 Corinthians 8 and 9*. Hermeneia. Philadelphia: Fortress, 1985. See pages 37–86.

Buck, C. H. Jr. "The Collection for the Saints." *HTR* 43 (1950): 1–29.

Dockx, S. "Chronologie Paulinienne de L'année de la grande collecte." *RB* 81 (1974): 183–95.

Joubert, S. J. *Paul as Benefactor: Reciprocity, Strategy and Theological Reflection in Paul's Collection*. WUNT 1/124. Tübingen: Mohr, 2000.

Keck, L. E. "The Poor among the Saints in Jewish Christianity and Qumran." *ZNW* 57 (1966): 54–78.

Lodge, J. G. "The Apostle's Appeal and Readers' Response: 2 Corinthians 8 and 9." *ChicStud* 30 (1991): 59–75.

Nickle, K. F. *The Collection: A Study in Paul's Theology*. London: SCM, 1966.

81. Κοινωνία (8:4)

Bruce, F. F. "Paul and Jerusalem." *TynBul* 19 (1968): 3–25.

McDermott, J. M. "The Biblical Doctrine of ΚΟΙΝΩΝΙΑ." *BZ* n.f. 19 (1975): 64–77, 219–13.
Panikulam G. *Koinonia in the New Testament: A Dynamic Expression of Christian Life.* Rome: Pontifical Biblical Institute, 1979.

82. Paul and Persuasion (8:7–15)

Joubert, S. J. "Behind the Mask of Rhetoric: 2 Corinthians 8 and the Intra-Textual Relation between Paul and the Corinthians." *Neot* 26 (1992): 101–12.
O'Mahoney, K. J. *Pauline Persuasion: A Sounding in 2 Corinthians 8-9.* JSNTSup 199. Sheffield: Sheffield Academic, 2000.
———. "The Rhetoric of Benefaction." *PIBA* 22 (1999): 9–40.
Verbrugge, V. D. *Paul's Style of Church Leadership Illustrated by His Instructions to the Corinthians on the Collection.* San Francisco: Mellen Research University, 1992.

83. Financial Integrity (8:18–23)

Stowers, S. K. "Περὶ μὲν γάρ and the Integrity of 2 Corinthians 8 and 9." *NovT* 32 (1980): 340–48.
Talbert, C. H. "Money Management in Early Mediterranean Christianity: 2 Corinthians 8–9." *RevExp* 86 (1989): 359–70.

84. The Glory of Christ (8:23)

Harrison, J. R. "The Brothers as the 'Glory of Christ' (2 Cor 8:23): Paul's *Doxa* Terminology in Its Ancient Benefaction Context." *NovT* 52 (2010): 156–88.

85. Boasting and Joy (8:24)

Lambrecht, J. "Paul's Boasting about the Corinthians: A Study of 2 Cor. 8:24–9:5." *NovT* 40 (1998): 352–68.
Morrice, W. G. *Joy in the New Testament.* Grand Rapids: Eerdmans, 1985.

HOMILETICAL SUGGESTIONS

The Power of a Godly Example (8:1–6)

1. The experience of the grace of God expressed through generosity (vv. 1–3)
2. Giving oneself to God precedes and is expressed in giving aid to others (v.5)
3. The importance of carrying good intentions through to completion in action (v. 6)

Motivation for and Practical Advice Regarding Christian Giving (8:7–15)

1. Excellence in matters of faith, speech, and knowledge to be complemented by excellence in the grace of giving (v. 7)
2. The example of Christ becoming poor in order to enrich others (v. 9)
3. The practice of generosity in accordance with one's means (vv. 11–12)
4. Using one's "abundance" to meet the needs of others (vv. 12–15)

Ensuring the Administration of Aid Is above Reproach (8:16–24)

1. Titus's desire to participate was God-given, and by his own choice (vv. 16–17)
2. Things need to be seen to be right not only in the sight of God but also in the sight of people (vv. 18–21)
3. The key importance of diligence in Christian service (v. 21)

4. Be Prepared and Avoid Humiliation (9:1–5)

STRUCTURE

1   Περὶ μὲν γὰρ τῆς διακονίας
                                              τῆς εἰς τοὺς ἁγίους
περισσόν μοί ἐστιν τὸ γράφειν ὑμῖν·
2   οἶδα γὰρ τὴν προθυμίαν ὑμῶν
                        ἣν ὑπὲρ ὑμῶν καυχῶμαι Μακεδόσιν,
                        ὅτι Ἀχαΐα παρεσκεύασται ἀπὸ πέρυσι,
     καὶ τὸ ὑμῶν ζῆλος ἠρέθισεν τοὺς πλείονας.
3   ἔπεμψα δὲ τοὺς ἀδελφούς,
        ἵνα μὴ τὸ καύχημα ἡμῶν τὸ ὑπὲρ ὑμῶν κενωθῇ
                                              ἐν τῷ μέρει τούτῳ,
        ἵνα   καθὼς ἔλεγον
              παρεσκευασμένοι ἦτε,
4   μή πως ἐὰν ἔλθωσιν σὺν ἐμοὶ Μακεδόνες
               καὶ εὕρωσιν ὑμᾶς ἀπαρασκευάστους
     καταισχυνθῶμεν ἡμεῖς,
        ἵνα μὴ λέγω ὑμεῖς,
              ἐν τῇ ὑποστάσει ταύτῃ.
5   ἀναγκαῖον οὖν ἡγησάμην παρακαλέσαι τοὺς ἀδελφούς,
        ἵνα προέλθωσιν εἰς ὑμᾶς
     καὶ προκαταρτίσωσιν τὴν προεπηγγελμένην εὐλογίαν ὑμῶν,
                        ταύτην ἑτοίμην εἶναι
                                    οὕτως ὡς εὐλογίαν
                                    καὶ μὴ ὡς πλεονεξίαν.

VERSE 1

Περὶ μὲν γὰρ τῆς διακονίας τῆς εἰς τοὺς ἁγίους
Now concerning the ministry to the saints,

Περί, prep. with gen. τῆς διακονίας, "concerning the ministry." Διακονίας, gen. sg. fem. διακονία, -ας, ἡ, "ministry." Τῆς εἰς τοὺς ἁγίους, attrib. phrase describing διακονίας. Εἰς, prep. with acc. τοὺς ἁγίους, "to the saints." Ἁγίους, acc. pl. masc. subst. adj. ἅγιος, -ία, -ον, "saints."

περισσόν μοί ἐστιν τὸ γράφειν ὑμῖν·
it is unnecessary for me to write to you.

Περισσόν, nom. sg. neut. adj. περισσός, -ή, -όν, "unnecessary, superfluous." Betz 90–91: "Paul figured that his readers were so familiar with the subject of the collection that they had grown tired of hearing of it. . . . To relieve the tiresomeness of the subject, Paul employed a contemporary epistolary tag, a variation on the basic notion that 'though I have nothing to say to you, I am writing to you all the same.' A denial of this kind was, and remains, one of the simplest devices for beginning a letter that introduces a subject which has grown tiresome to its readers." Μοί, dat. 1st sg. pron., "for me." Τὸ γράφειν, nom. art. inf., subj. of ἐστίν. Ὑμῖν, dat. 2nd pl. σύ, "you," indir. obj. of γράφειν.

Harris 618: "When Paul comments 'It is superfluous for me to write . . . ,' yet proceeds to speak further (in 9:2–15) about this charitable project, he is employing a rhetorical device known as *paraleipsis*. In this 'figure of thought' (σχῆμα διανοίας) a speaker or writer professes to pass over a certain matter only to mention or expound it. Heb. 11:32–38 is the most celebrated NT example."

Thrall 2:563–64: "Despite his opening words ['Now concerning the ministry to the saints, it is unnecessary for me to write to you'], Paul is more than a little apprehensive about the adequacy of the Corinthians' activity in respect of the collection. There is a further reason, it seems, for the dispatch of the envoys: They are to make sure that the Corinthian contribution is ready before Paul arrives in person."

VERSE 2

οἶδα γὰρ τὴν προθυμίαν ὑμῶν ἣν ὑπὲρ ὑμῶν καυχῶμαι Μακεδόσιν,
For I know your eagerness, and I boast about you to the Macedonians:

Οἶδα, 1st sg. pf. act. indic. οἶδα, "know." Γάρ, conj., "for," introduces the reason Paul found it unnecessary to write to the Corinthians. Προθυμίαν, acc. sg. fem. προθυμία, -ας, ἡ, "eagerness." BDAG 870a: "exceptional interest in being of service." Ἥν, acc. sg. fem. rel. pron. "which," referring to προθυμίαν. Ὑπέρ, prep. with gen. ὑμῶν, "about you." Cf. Z §96: ὑπέρ = περί, Καυχῶμαι, 1st sg. pres. mid. indic. of καυχάομαι, "boast." Μακεδόσιν, dat. pl. masc. Μακεδών, -όνος, ὁ, "Macedonian," indir. obj. of καυχῶμαι.

ὅτι Ἀχαΐα παρεσκεύασται ἀπὸ πέρυσι,
"Achaia has been ready since last year,"

Ἀχαΐα, nom. sg. fem. Ἀχαΐα, -ας, ἡ, "Achaia." Hafemann 363: "Paul employs the geographical designation of 'Achaia' here to match his corresponding reference to the 'Macedonians,' especially since Corinth was the senatorial and provincial capital of Achaia." Ὅτι, conj. introduces the content of Paul's boast. Παρεσκεύασται, 3rd sg. pf. mid. indic. παρασκευάζω, "be ready." BDAG 771a–b: "Mid., to make oneself ready for some purpose *prepare (oneself)*." Ἀπό, prep. with πέρυσι adv. of time "since last year." Harris 620: "It is the sequence τὴν προθυμίαν ὑμῶν ἣν . . . καυχῶμαι . . . ὅτι . . . παρεσκεύασται that suggests that the 'readiness' actually was the 'eager willingness' to contribute the charitable offering. . . . On this interpretation of παρεσκεύασται, Paul was being completely truthful, neither going 'somewhat' beyond the facts (as Plummer [254] suggests) nor 'perhaps' being overly optimistic (as Barrett [234] submits)."

καὶ τὸ ὑμῶν ζῆλος ἠρέθισεν τοὺς πλείονας.
and your zeal has stirred up most of them.

Τὸ ὑμῶν ζῆλος, "your zeal." Ὑμῶν, subj. gen. Cf. BDF §212, contra BDF §284[2] poss. gen. Ζῆλος, nom. sg. neut. ζῆλος, -ους, τό, "zeal, enthusiasm." Ἠρέθισεν, 3rd sg. aor. act. indic. of ἐρεθίζω, "stir to action," BDAG 391c: "to cause someone to react in a way that suggests acceptance of a challenge . . . mostly in bad sense *irritate, embitter*. . . . In a good sense of an encouraging example." Harris 621: "Those who were spurred on by Paul's account of the enthusiasm of the Corinthians were roused not to compete with them (as Betz 93) and not so much to emulate them (Barrett 234) as simply to follow the example of their keenness, which led these Macedonians to give sacrificially and generously (8:2)." Τοὺς πλείονας, "most of them." Moule 108: "In II Cor. ix.2 τοὺς πλείονας perhaps means the majority (though not all). Cf. ii.6." Πλείονας, acc. pl. masc. comp. adj. "most," BDAG 847c–d: "πολύς, πολλή, πολύ . . . Comparative πλείων, πλεῖον."

VERSE 3

ἔπεμψα δὲ τοὺς ἀδελφούς, ἵνα μὴ τὸ καύχημα ἡμῶν τὸ ὑπὲρ ὑμῶν κενωθῇ ἐν τῷ μέρει τούτῳ,
But I am sending the brothers so that our boasting about you in this matter would not prove empty,

Ἔπεμψα, 1st sg. aor. act indic. of πέμπω, "send." An instance of the epistolary aor. Cf. Moule 12: "*The Epistolary Aorist* is an understandable idiom—and a rather gracious one, though it causes more ambiguity than the English—whereby the writer courteously projects himself in imagination into the position of the reader for whom actions contemporaneous with the time of writing will be past." Τοὺς ἀδελφούς, acc. pl. masc. ἀδελφός, -οῦ, ὁ, "brothers," dir. obj. of ἔπεμψα.
Ἵνα, conj. with subjunc. κενωθῇ, expresses purpose "so that (our boasting . . .) would not prove empty." Κενωθῇ, 3rd sg. aor. pass. subjunc. of κενόω, "make empty." Καύχημα, nom. sg. neut. καύχημα, -ατος, τό, "object of boasting." Cf. BDAG 537a: "*so that what we say in praise of you may not prove to be empty words.*" Τὸ ὑπὲρ ὑμῶν, attrib. phrase qualifying καύχημα ἡμῶν. Ὑπέρ, prep. with gen. ὑμῶν, "about you." Ἐν τῷ μέρει τούτῳ, dat. attrib. phrase "in this matter," qualifying καύχημα ἡμῶν. Ἐν τῷ μέρει, BDAG 633d: "*in the matter of, with regard to.*" Μέρει, dat. sg. neut. μέρος, -ους, τό, "matter."

ἵνα καθὼς ἔλεγον παρεσκευασμένοι ἦτε,
and so that you would be ready just as I said.

Ἵνα with subjunc. ἦτε expresses purpose "so that you would be (ready)." Καθώς, conj. "as, just as." Ἔλεγον, 1st sg. impf. act. indic. of λέγω, "say." The impf. is prob. either progressive ("was saying") or iterative ("kept on saying"). Παρεσκευασμένοι with ἦτε

(2nd pl. pres. subjunc. of εἰμί), pf. periph. ptc. "you would be ready." Παρεσκευασμένοι, nom. pl. masc. of pf. mid. ptc. of παρασκευάζω, "be ready, prepared."

VERSE 4

μή πως ἐὰν ἔλθωσιν σὺν ἐμοὶ Μακεδόνες καὶ εὕρωσιν ὑμᾶς ἀπαρασκευάστους
Otherwise, if any Macedonians come with me and find you unprepared,

Μή πως, BDAG 901d: "in clauses that in effect qualify as purpose clauses . . . *lest somehow* w. aor. subj." [in this case καταισχυνθῶμεν: "otherwise/lest we . . . would be put to shame"]. Harris 625: "The word order μή πως ἐάν (not μή ἐάν πως) indicates that the uncertainty expressed by the enclitic particle πώς . . . relates to καταισχυνθῶμεν and not ἔλθωσιν, or εὕρωσιν: 'lest if . . . , we perhaps be put to shame.'" Ἔλθωσιν, 3rd pl. aor. act. subjunc. of ἔρχομαι, "come." Σύν, prep. with dat. ἐμοί, "with me." Μακεδόνες, nom. pl. masc. Μακεδών, -όνος, ὁ, "Macedonian," subj. of ἔλθωσιν. Εὕρωσιν, 3rd pl. aor. act. subjunc. of εὑρίσκω, "find." Ὑμᾶς, acc. 2nd pl. σύ, "you," dir. obj. of εὕρωσιν. Ἀπαρασκευάστους, acc. pl. masc. adj. ἀπαρασκεύαστος, -ον, "unprepared."

καταισχυνθῶμεν ἡμεῖς, ἵνα μὴ λέγω ὑμεῖς, ἐν τῇ ὑποστάσει ταύτῃ.
we, not to mention you, would be put to shame in that situation.

Καταισχυνθῶμεν, 1st pl. aor. pass. subjunc. of καταισχύνω, "put to shame," following μή πως. Ἡμεῖς, 1st pl. nom. "we," subj. of καταισχυνθῶμεν. Ἵνα with subjunc. (μὴ) λέγω expresses (neg.) result, "not to mention (you)." Ὑμεῖς, 2nd pl. nom. "you," subj. of καταισχυνθῶμεν. Ἐν, prep. with dat. τῇ ὑποστάσει ταύτῃ, "in that situation." Ὑποστάσει, dat. sg. fem. ὑπόστασις, -εως, ἡ, a word with varied mngs.; cf. CSB: "situation." BDAG 1040d: "*undertaking* i.e. the collection for Jerusaalem." ZG 552: "that which underlies, e.g. *foundation*, so *ground of hope*, then *hope, confidence* itself." Thrall 2:569–70 adopts the view that ὑποστάσει is best translated in this verse as "project," so too Betz 95.

Harris 623: "Paul gives three reasons—two negative and one positive—for his sending of the three brothers to Corinth: (a) to prevent his boasting . . . from turning out to be unjustified (v. 3a); (b) to make sure the Corinthians were in a state of full readiness with regard to the collection when he arrived (v. 3b); (c) to avoid humiliation in the event that some Macedonians should come with him and find the Corinthians unprepared (v. 4)."

VERSE 5

ἀναγκαῖον οὖν ἡγησάμην παρακαλέσαι τοὺς ἀδελφούς,
Therefore I considered it necessary to urge the brothers

Ἀναγκαῖον, nom. sg. neut. adj. ἀναγκαῖος, -α, -ον, "necessary." Ἡγησάμην, 1st sg. aor. mid. indic. of ἡγέομαι, "think, consider." Παρακαλέσαι, aor. act. inf. of παρακαλέω, "urge, exhort." BDAG 765b: "to make a strong request for someth., *request, implore, entreat.*" Ἀδελφούς, acc. pl. masc. ἀδελφός, -οῦ, ὁ, "brother," dir. obj. of παρακαλέσαι.

ἵνα προέλθωσιν εἰς ὑμᾶς καὶ προκαταρτίσωσιν τὴν προεπηγγελμένην εὐλογίαν ὑμῶν,
to go on ahead to you and arrange in advance the generous gift you promised,

 Ἵνα with subjunc. προέλθωσιν expresses purpose, "to visit (you) in advance." But cf. Harris 627: "ἵνα προέλθωσιν . . . καὶ προκαταρτίσωσιν defines not the purpose but the content of the παράκλησις, and is equivalent to an infinitive expressing the object after a verb of asking such as παρακαλέω, as if Paul had written . . . παρακαλέσαιτοὺς ἀδελφοὺς προελθεῖν . . . καὶ προκαταρτίσαι." Προέλθωσιν, 3rd pl. aor. act. subjunc. of προέρχομαι, "go before, ahead." Εἰς, prep. with acc. ὑμᾶς, "to you." Προκαταρτίσωσιν, 3rd pl. aor. act. subjunc. προκαταρτίζω, "make arrangements in advance, prepare ahead of time." Προεπηγγελμένην, acc. sg. fem. of pf. pass. ptc. of προεπαγγέλλω, "promise," qualifying εὐλογίαν. Εὐλογίαν, acc. sg. fem. εὐλογία, -ας, ἡ, "gift, blessing, benefit," Paul's use of which may foreshadow the spiritual as well as the material effects of the gift (cf. vv. 12–14). Harris 628: "in the LXX εὐλογία sometimes denotes a gift that is bestowed by one person on another as a 'blessing.' It is this latter usage that supports the view that in 9:5 εὐλογία means 'gift of blessing,' referring to the collection as the love-gift of the Corinthians that would be a blessing to the destitute believers in Jerusalem (9:12), that would prompt the Jerusalemites to bless God (9:11–13), and that would lead to God's gracious blessing on their own lives (9:8–10)."

ταύτην ἑτοίμην εἶναι οὕτως ὡς εὐλογίαν καὶ μὴ ὡς πλεονεξίαν.
so that it will be ready as a gift and not as an extortion.

 R 1086: "A good instance of the epexegetical inf. is seen in 2 Cor. 9:5, where ταύτην ἑτοίμην εἶναι οὕτως ὡς εὐλογίαν is subsidiary to the ἵνα clause preceding, as is often the case." Ταύτην ἑτοίμην εἶναι. Moule 141: "the simple Acc. and Infin. without ὥστε might be consecutive [result] in meaning. . . . But it might equally well be final [purpose]." Ταύτην, acc. sg. fem. dem. pron. οὗτος, αὕτη, τοῦτο, "this," refers back to εὐλογία and is the acc. subj. of inf. εἶναι. Ἑτοίμην, acc. sg. fem. adj. ἕτοιμος, -η, -ον, "ready," qualifying ταύτην. Οὕτως ὡς, "thus as, in this way." Ὡς εὐλογίαν καὶ μὴ ὡς πλεονεξίαν. Betz 97: "Paul drew attention to two attitudes towards wealth. A gift of blessing is given in response to blessings received, while greed represents a failure to respond in kind, owing to one's failure to receive anything as a gift." Εὐλογίαν, acc. sg. fem. εὐλογία, -ας, ἡ, "(generous) gift." Μὴ ὡς πλεονεξίαν, "not as one grudgingly given, not as an exaction."
 Πλεονεξίαν, acc. sg. fem. πλεονεξία, -ας, ἡ, "exaction, something grudgingly given." BDAG 824d: "In 2 Cor 9:5 the context calls for the pregnant mng. *a gift that is grudgingly granted by avarice.*" Cf. Thrall 2:573: "The Corinthian contribution to the collection is not to be an expression of any such 'desire to have more' [avarice] than their fellow Christians of the mother church. In other words, it is not to be a sparing contribution. It is to be ὡς εὐλογίαν, i.e., 'as a bountiful gift.'" Cf. Hafemann 365: "In 9:5,

Paul is consequently pointing to two opposite ways of giving: the kind of generosity that flows from experiencing God's blessing and from trusting in the sufficiency of God's grace, versus the kind of begrudging greediness and self-reliance that selfishly seeks to keep as much as possible for oneself."

Barnett 435 comments on vv. 1–5: "So far from opportunistically playing off one church against another, as is often concluded from this passage, Paul is, rather, seeking to preserve the reputation of the Corinthians in a situation of potential misunderstanding in which they would have lost face."

5. An Exhortation to Be Generous (9:6–15)

STRUCTURE

6   Τοῦτο δέ,
    ὁ σπείρων φειδομένως φειδομένως καὶ θερίσει,
  καὶ ὁ σπείρων ἐπ' εὐλογίαις ἐπ' εὐλογίαις καὶ θερίσει.
7   ἕκαστος
    καθὼς προῄρηται τῇ καρδίᾳ,
    μὴ ἐκ λύπης ἢ ἐξ ἀνάγκης·
  ἱλαρὸν γὰρ δότην ἀγαπᾷ ὁ θεός.
8   δυνατεῖ δὲ ὁ θεὸς πᾶσαν χάριν περισσεῦσαι εἰς ὑμᾶς,
    ἵνα
            ἐν παντὶ
            πάντοτε
            πᾶσαν αὐτάρκειαν
        ἔχοντες
      περισσεύητε
            εἰς πᾶν ἔργον ἀγαθόν,
9   καθὼς γέγραπται,
            Ἐσκόρπισεν, ἔδωκεν τοῖς πένησιν,
            ἡ δικαιοσύνη αὐτοῦ μένει εἰς τὸν αἰῶνα.
10 ὁ δὲ ἐπιχορηγῶν σπόρον
          τῷ σπείροντι
      καὶ ἄρτον
         εἰς βρῶσιν
            χορηγήσει
           καὶ πληθυνεῖ τὸν σπόρον ὑμῶν
           καὶ αὐξήσει τὰ γενήματα
                 τῆς δικαιοσύνης ὑμῶν·
11   ἐν παντὶ πλουτιζόμενοι
            εἰς πᾶσαν ἁπλότητα,
               ἥτις κατεργάζεται
                  δι' ἡμῶν
                     εὐχαριστίαν

τῷ θεῷ·

12   ὅτι ἡ διακονία τῆς λειτουργίας ταύτης
            οὐ μόνον ἐστὶν προσαναπληροῦσα τὰ ὑστερήματα τῶν ἁγίων,
            ἀλλὰ καὶ περισσεύουσα διὰ πολλῶν εὐχαριστιῶν τῷ θεῷ.
13   διὰ τῆς δοκιμῆς τῆς διακονίας ταύτης
        δοξάζοντες τὸν θεὸν
            ἐπὶ τῇ ὑποταγῇ τῆς ὁμολογίας ὑμῶν
                εἰς τὸ εὐαγγέλιον τοῦ Χριστοῦ
            καὶ ἁπλότητι τῆς κοινωνίας
                εἰς αὐτοὺς καὶ εἰς πάντας,
14   καὶ αὐτῶν δεήσει ὑπὲρ ὑμῶν ἐπιποθούντων ὑμᾶς
            διὰ τὴν ὑπερβάλλουσαν χάριν τοῦ θεοῦ ἐφ' ὑμῖν.
15 χάρις τῷ θεῷ
            ἐπὶ τῇ ἀνεκδιηγήτῳ αὐτοῦ δωρεᾷ.

VERSE 6

Τοῦτο δέ, ὁ σπείρων φειδομένως φειδομένως καὶ θερίσει,
The point is this: The person who sows sparingly will also reap sparingly,

A possible allusion to Prov 22:8 LXX. Τοῦτο δέ, lit. "And this . . . ," an example of ellipsis. BDF (§481) says we need to supply φημί [cf. 1 Cor 7:29; 15:15], and that in ellipses "the writer can count on the knowledge which the recipient shares with himself and where he imitates ordinary speech." Ὁ σπείρων, ptc. phrase "the one who sows." Σπείρων, nom. sing. masc. of pres. act. ptc. of σπείρω, "sow seed." Φειδομένως, adv. "sparingly." Θερίσει, 3rd sg. gnomic fut. act. indic. θερίζω, "reap."

καὶ ὁ σπείρων ἐπ' εὐλογίαις ἐπ' εὐλογίαις καὶ θερίσει.
and the person who sows generously will also reap generously.

Ὁ σπείρων, see above. Ἐπ', prep. with dat. εὐλογίαις "with generosity, bountifully." Εὐλογίαις, dat. pl. fem. εὐλογία, -ας, ἡ, lit. "blessing." But cf. BDAG 409a: "Since the concept of blessing connotes the idea of bounty, εὐ. also bears the mng. *generous gift* . . . ἐπ' εὐλογίαις (opp. φειδομένως) *bountifully*." Cf. Seifrid 355: "Paul's use of the term 'blessing' (*eu-logia*) suggests that he understands bountiful giving as a 'speech act,' a response to the address of the good Creator, a 'speaking forth' of the spoken blessing that has been received. This reading correlates with Paul's following description of the Corinthian gift as a confession of the Gospel (v. 13)." Θερίσει, see above.

VERSE 7

ἕκαστος καθὼς προῄρηται τῇ καρδίᾳ,
Each person should do as he has decided in his heart—

Ἕκαστος, nom. sg. masc. subst. adj. ἕκαστος, -η, -ον, "each one, everyone," an example of ellipsis. ZG 552: "understand 'let each one give,'"; cf. BDF §481. Harris 635: "With ἕκαστος we may supply the aorist optative δώη . . . 'May each give,' or some imperative such as δότω . . . 'Let each give,' or ποιείτω . . . 'Let each act,' 'Let each do this [sow generously, v. 6].'" Καθώς, conj., "as, just as." Προήρηται, 3rd sg. pf. mid. indic. of προαιρέω, "decide, make up one's mind." BDAG 865a–b: "mid. to reach a decision beforehand, *choose (for oneself), commit oneself to, prefer* . . . καθὼς προήρηται τῇ καρδίᾳ *as he has made up his mind.*" Τῇ καρδίᾳ, dat. sg. fem., lit. "in the heart."

μὴ ἐκ λύπης ἢ ἐξ ἀνάγκης· ἱλαρὸν γὰρ δότην ἀγαπᾷ ὁ θεός.
not reluctantly or out of compulsion, since God loves a cheerful giver.

Ἐκ, adv. prep. with gen. λύπης, lit. "out of/from pain," i.e., "reluctantly." Λύπης, gen. sg. fem. λύπη, -ης, ἡ, "pain, grief." Ἐξ, prep. with gen. ἀνάγκης, "out of compulsion." Ἀνάγκης, gen. sg. fem. ἀνάγκη, -ης, ἡ, "compulsion, necessity." Ἱλαρὸν γὰρ δότην ἀγαπᾷ ὁ θεός. Moule 8 cites this as an example of the gnomic present, "i.e. that used in a γνώμη, a maxim or generalization." Paul draws upon Prov 22:8a (LXX). Ἱλαρόν, acc. sg. masc. adj. ἱλαρός, -ά, -όν, "cheerful." Δότην, acc. sg. masc. δότης, -ου, ὁ, "giver." Ἀγαπᾷ, 3rd sg. pres. act. indic. of ἀγαπάω, "love." See Deut 15:10 for an example of reluctant giving and Acts 11:29 for an example of cheerful giving.

VERSE 8

δυνατεῖ δὲ ὁ θεὸς πᾶσαν χάριν περισσεῦσαι εἰς ὑμᾶς,
And God is able to make every grace overflow to you,

Δυνατεῖ . . . περισσεῦσαι, complementary inf. cstr.: '(God) is able to cause (all grace) to abound." Δυνατεῖ, 3rd sg. pres. act. indic. of δυνατέω, "be able, powerful." Πᾶσαν χάριν, "every grace." Thrall 2:578: "If we take πᾶσαν χάριν in a comprehensive sense, we can see Paul as amplifying or elucidating his scriptural quotation: God is able most abundantly to bestow both the spiritual quality of cheerful generosity and the practical resources for its implementation, so that the individual Corinthian may truly fulfil the role of the ἱλαρὸς δότης." Πᾶσαν, acc. sg. fem. adj. πᾶς, πᾶσα, πᾶν, "all," qualifying χάριν. Χάριν, acc. sg. fem. χάρις, -ιτος, ἡ, "grace," dir. obj. of inf. περισσεῦσαι. Περισσεῦσαι, aor. act. inf. of περισσεύω, "abound." Εἰς, prep. with acc. ὑμᾶς "to you."

ἵνα ἐν παντὶ πάντοτε πᾶσαν αὐτάρκειαν ἔχοντες
so that in every way, always having everything you need,

Barnett 439: "This great power of God is expressed in a string of universals: 'God is able to make *all* grace overflow toward you so that, having sufficient [*sic*] in *all* things at *all* times, you might overflow for *every* good work.'" Ἵνα with subjunc. περισσεύητε may express purpose, "so that you may have," or result, "thus you will have"; cf.

Harris 637. NB the use of the rhetorical alliteration device (*paronomasia*) for emphasis: παντὶ πάντοτε πᾶσαν, (cf. BDF §488[1a]). Ἐν, prep. with dat. παντί, "in every way," NIV "in all things." Πάντοτε, adv. "always." Πᾶσαν αὐτάρκειαν, "everything you need," dir. obj. of ptc. ἔχοντες. Πᾶσαν, acc. sg. fem. adj. πᾶς, πᾶσα, πᾶν, "every, all," qualifies αὐτάρκειαν. Αὐτάρκειαν, acc. sg. fem. αὐτάρκεια, -ας, ἡ, "what is needed, sufficiency," BDAG 152a: "*have enough of everything.*" ZG 552: "*self-sufficiency.*" In Cynic and stoic philosophy, it was used of the person who was self-sufficient. Seneca understood it as that proud independence of outward circumstances and other people that constituted true happiness. For Paul it meant the sufficiency provided by God's grace, and as such made possible, not independence of others, but the ability to abound in good works toward them. Ἔχοντες, nom. pl. masc. of pres. act. ptc. of ἔχω, "have."

περισσεύητε εἰς πᾶν ἔργον ἀγαθόν,
you may excel in every good work.

Περισσεύητε, 2nd pl. pres. act. subjunc. of περισσεύω, "excel, abound." The readers are able to excel (περισσεύητε) in every good work because God is able to make every grace overflow (περισσεῦσαι) to them. Εἰς, prep. with acc. πᾶν ἔργον ἀγαθόν, "in every good work." Πᾶν, acc. sg. neut. adj. πᾶς, πᾶσα, πᾶν, "every, all," qualifies ἔργον. Ἔργον, acc. sg. neut. ἔργον, -ου, τό, "work." Ἀγαθόν, acc. sg. neut. adj. ἀγαθός, -ή, -όν, "good," qualifies ἔργον.

VERSE 9

καθὼς γέγραπται, Ἐσκόρπισεν, ἔδωκεν τοῖς πένησιν, ἡ δικαιοσύνη αὐτοῦ μένει εἰς τὸν αἰῶνα.
As it is written: **He distributed freely; he gave to the poor; his righteousness endures forever.**

Paul here quotes verbatim from Ps 112:9 (LXX 111:9). Καθώς, conj., "as, just as." Γέγραπται, 3rd sg. pf. pass. indic. of γράφω, "write." Ἐσκόρπισεν, 3rd sg. gnomic aor. act. indic. of σκορπίζω, "distribute, scatter." Ἔδωκεν, 3rd sg. gnomic aor. act. indic. of δίδωμι, "give." Thrall 2:583: "the representative Corinthian contributor is the implicit subject of ἐσκόρπισεν and ἔδωκεν, and the point of reference of αὐτοῦ." Τοῖς πένησιν, dat. phrase "to the poor." Πένησιν, dat. pl. masc. subst. adj. πένης, -ητος, "(the) poor." ZG 552: "*poor man* (obliged to labour (πένεσθαι) but not destitute like πτωχός)."

Δικαιοσύνη, nom. sg. fem. δικαιοσύνη, -ης, ἡ, "righteousness." Thrall 2:582–83 suggests righteousness here means benevolence, something enabled by God who provides the means (cf. v. 10) so that it continues for ever (i.e., throughout life). Cf. Hafemann 368: "The 'righteousness' of the one who gives to the poor 'endures forever' (Ps. 112.9) *only because* it is created and sustained by the Lord's 'righteousness,' which also 'endures forever' (111:3);" Seifrid 359: "Their 'righteousness' is an abundance that comes ever again in blessing from the Lord. It thus abides forever. The psalm makes the point that the abundance of the righteous is not the result of their work or their hoarding of possessions. Just the opposite. It is blessing that is ever given and ever received afresh, in the relationship of trust and fear of the Lord, an abundance found in the relationship of receiving and giving."

But cf. Barnett 440: "This 'righteousness' of God is here taken to mean his covenantal loyalty, his faithfulness to his people ('God is faithful'—1:18), as evidenced in his watchful care over them and active generosity toward them."

Αὐτοῦ, gen. sg. masc. poss. pron. αὐτός, -ή, -ό, "his." Μένει, 3rd sg. pres. act. indic. of μένω, "endure, remain." Εἰς, prep. with acc. τὸν αἰῶνα adv. phrase, "forever." Αἰῶνα, acc. sg. masc. αἰών, -ῶνος, ὁ, "age, eternity." BDAG 32b: "of time to come which, if it has no end, is also known as *eternity*."

VERSE 10

ὁ δὲ ἐπιχορηγῶν σπόρον τῷ σπείροντι καὶ ἄρτον εἰς βρῶσιν
Now the one who provides seed for the sower and bread for food

Paul alludes here to Isa 55:10. Ἐπιχορηγῶν, nom. sg. masc. of pres. act. ptc. of ἐπιχορηγέω, "provide, supply." Σπόρον, acc. sg. masc. σπόρος, -ου, ὁ, "seed," dir. obj. of ἐπιχορηγῶν. Τῷ σπείροντι, subst. adj. ptc. "the sower/ the one who sows," indir. obj. of ἐπιχορηγῶν. Σπείροντι, dat. sg. masc. of pres. act. ptc. of σπείρω, "sow." Ἄρτον, acc. sg. masc. ἄρτος, -ου, ὁ, "bread," dir. obj. of χορηγήσει. Εἰς, prep. with acc. βρῶσιν, "for food." Βρῶσιν, acc. sg. fem. βρῶσις, -εως, ἡ, "food."

χορηγήσει καὶ πληθυνεῖ τὸν σπόρον ὑμῶν καὶ αὐξήσει τὰ γενήματα τῆς δικαιοσύνης ὑμῶν·
will also provide and multiply your seed and increase the harvest of your righteousness.

Paul alludes here to Hos 10:12. Χορηγήσει, 3rd sg. fut. act. indic. of χορηγέω, "provide, supply." Πληθυνεῖ, 3rd sg. fut. act. indic. of πληθύνω, "multiply, increase." Σπόρον, acc. sg. masc. σπόρος, -ου, ὁ, "seed," dir. obj. of χορηγήσει and πληθυνεῖ. Αὐξήσει, 3rd sg. fut. act. indic. of αὐξάνω, "cause to grow, increase." Γενήματα, acc. pl. neut. γένημα, -ατος, τό, "harvest," dir. obj. of αὐξήσει. Τῆς δικαιοσύνης, descriptive. gen. "(harvest) of righteousness." Δικαιοσύνης, gen. sg. fem. δικαιοσύνη, -ης, ἡ, "righteousness." Barnett 442: "We take it that 'the harvest of your righteousness' is the fruit of God's justification of his people in Christ (5:21), expressed in their generosity toward needy saints."

VERSE 11

ἐν παντὶ πλουτιζόμενοι εἰς πᾶσαν ἁπλότητα,
You will be enriched in every way for all generosity,

Ἐν, prep. with dat. παντί, "in every way." Πλουτιζόμενοι, nom. pl. masc. of pres. pass. ptc. of πλουτίζω, "enrich." Moule 31: "II Cor. ix. 11, 13 ἐν παντὶ πλουτιζόμενοι . . . δοξάζοντες τὸν θεὸν . . . the participles may stand—perhaps by Semitic idiom . . . for imperatives or indicatives." Cf. Harris: "To take πλουτιζόμενοι as standing for a future indicative seems preferable, given the three preceding futures." Εἰς, prep. with acc. ἁπλότητα, "for generosity." Ἁπλότητα, acc. sg. fem. ἁπλότης, -ητος, ἡ, "generosity."

ἥτις κατεργάζεται δι᾽ ἡμῶν εὐχαριστίαν τῷ θεῷ·
which produces thanksgiving to God through us.

Ἥτις, nom. sg. fem. rel. pron. ὅστις, ἥτις, ὅ τι, "which." Κατεργάζεται, 3rd sg. pres. mid. indic. of κατεργάζομαι, "produce, bring about." Δι᾽, prep. with gen. ἡμῶν, "through us." Εὐχαριστίαν, acc. sg. fem. εὐχαριστία, -ας, ἡ, "thanksgiving," dir. obj. of κατεργάζεται. Τῷ θεῷ, dat. indir. obj. of κατεργάζεται, "to God." R 439: "In 2 Cor. 9:11,13, the participles πλουτιζόμενοι and δοξάζοντες have no formal connection with a principal verb and are separated by a long parenthesis in verse 12. But these participles may be after all tantamount to the indicative and not mere anacoluthon."

VERSE 12

ὅτι ἡ διακονία τῆς λειτουργίας ταύτης οὐ μόνον ἐστὶν προσαναπληροῦσα τὰ ὑστερήματα τῶν ἁγίων,
For the ministry of this service is not only supplying the needs of the saints

Ὅτι, conj., "because." Διακονία, nom. sg. fem. διακονία, -ας, ἡ, "ministry, service." Τῆς λειτουργίας ταύτης, epex. gen. phrase "of this service," qualifying διακονία. Λειτουργίας, gen. sg. fem. λειτουργία, -ας, ἡ, "service." ZG 553: "any *public service*, religious or secular, in NT always w. religious connotation." Μόνον, adv., "only." Harris 650: "οὐ μόνον . . . ἀλλὰ καὶ here is ascensive, with the first, historic purpose subsidiary to the second, theological aim." Ἐστὶν προσαναπληροῦσα, periph. pres. cf. R 881. Προσαναπληροῦσα, nom. sg. fem. of pres. act. ptc. of προσαναπληρόω, "supply, fill up." BDAG 876b: "*supply [someone's] wants*." Ὑστερήματα, acc. pl. neut. ὑστέρημα, -ατος, τό, "needs, what is lacking. Τῶν ἁγίων epex. gen. "of the saints," qualifying τὰ ὑστερήματα.

ἀλλὰ καὶ περισσεύουσα διὰ πολλῶν εὐχαριστιῶν τῷ θεῷ.
but is also overflowing in many expressions of thanks to God.

Περισσεύουσα, nom. sg. fem. of pres. act. ptc. of περισσεύω, "overflow, abound," (with preceding ἐστὶν periph. ptc.). Διά, prep. with gen. πολλῶν εὐχαριστιῶν, "in/with many thanksgivings." Εὐχαριστιῶν, gen. pl. fem. εὐχαριστία, -ας, ἡ, "thanksgiving." Τῷ θεῷ, dat. indir. obj. of περισσεύουσα, "to God." Verse 12 constitutes a long parenthesis; cf. R 435.

VERSE 13

διὰ τῆς δοκιμῆς τῆς διακονίας ταύτης
Because of the proof provided by this ministry,

Διά, prep. with gen. τῆς δοκιμῆς, "because of the proof. . . ." Unusually, here διά with gen. denotes cause; cf. Harris, *Prepositions*, 73. Δοκιμῆς, gen. sg. fem. δοκιμή, -ῆς, ἡ, "proof." Barnett 445: "He spells out this 'proof' as occurring (1) 'at' the obedience of their confession of the gospel of Christ, and (2) 'at' the generosity of their sharing in this ministry." Διακονίας, epex. gen. sg. fem. διακονία, -ας, ἡ, "ministry," qualifying τῆς δοκιμῆς. Ταύτης, gen. sg. fem. dem. pron. οὗτος, αὕτη, τοῦτο, "this," takes pred. position.

δοξάζοντες τὸν θεὸν ἐπὶ τῇ ὑποταγῇ τῆς ὁμολογίας ὑμῶν εἰς τὸ εὐαγγέλιον τοῦ Χριστοῦ
they will glorify God for your obedient confession of the gospel of Christ,

Δοξάζοντες, nom. pl. masc. of pres. act. ptc. of δοξάζω, "glorify," functioning here as a pres. indic. Ἐπί, prep. with dat. τῇ ὑποταγῇ denoting cause, "the obedience . . ."; cf. Harris, *Prepositions*, 138; Moule 179. Ὑποταγῇ, dat. sg. fem. ὑποταγή, -ῆς, ἡ, "obedience." Τῆς ὁμολογίας ὑμῶν, epex. gen. qualifies τῇ ὑποταγῇ, "(the obedience) of your confession." Ὁμολογίας, gen. sg. fem. ὁμολογία, -ας, ἡ, "confession." Harris 654: "a subjective genitive: a confessional adherence to the gospel produces obedience." Εἰς, prep. with acc. τὸ εὐαγγέλιον, "to the gospel." Εὐαγγέλιον, acc. sg. neut. εὐαγγέλιον, -ου, τό, "gospel." Τοῦ Χριστοῦ, either epex. gen., "the gospel about Christ," or poss. gen., "Christ's gospel."

καὶ ἁπλότητι τῆς κοινωνίας εἰς αὐτοὺς καὶ εἰς πάντας,
and for your generosity in sharing with them and with everyone.

Ἁπλότητι, dat. sg. fem. (following prior prep. ἐπί) ἁπλότης, -ητος, ἡ, "generosity." Τῆς κοινωνίας, epex. gen. "(generosity) of sharing." Εἰς, prep. with acc. αὐτούς, "with them." Εἰς, prep. with acc. πάντα, "with everyone." Thrall 2:591: "The Corinthians' state or sense of fellowship with the Jerusalem church, attested by the collection, could readily be supposed to extend to all other Christian communities."

In v. 13 Paul identifies two things for which he thinks the Jerusalem believers will thank God: (1) the Corinthians' obedient response to the gospel expressed in (2) their generosity in the matter of the collection.

VERSE 14

καὶ αὐτῶν δεήσει ὑπὲρ ὑμῶν ἐπιποθούντων ὑμᾶς
And as they pray on your behalf, they will have deep affection for you

Αὐτῶν . . . ἐπιποθούντων, gen. abs. "they have deep affection as they pray." Cf. Harris 657; Thrall 2:592. Δεήσει ὑπὲρ ὑμῶν, dat. phrase, "as they pray for you," lit. "in prayer for you." Δεήσει, dat. sg. fem. δέησις, -εως, ἡ, "prayer." Ἐπιποθούντων, gen. pl. masc. of pres. act. ptc. of ἐπιποθέω, "have deep affection, long for." Ὑμᾶς, acc. 2nd pl. pron. "you," dir. obj. of ἐπιποθούντων.

διὰ τὴν ὑπερβάλλουσαν χάριν τοῦ θεοῦ ἐφ᾽ ὑμῖν.
because of the surpassing grace of God in you.

Διά, prep. with acc. τὴν . . . χάριν, "because of the grace. . . ." Ὑπερβάλλουσαν, acc. sg. fem. of pres. act. ptc. of ὑπερβάλλω, "surpass," qualifies χάριν. Τοῦ θεοῦ, poss. gen. "God's grace." Ἐφ᾽, prep. with dat. ὑμῖν, "in you."

VERSE 15

χάρις τῷ θεῷ ἐπὶ τῇ ἀνεκδιηγήτῳ αὐτοῦ δωρεᾷ.
Thanks be to God for his indescribable gift!

Χάρις τῷ θεῷ (a form of εἰμί understood), "thanks (be) to God." Ἐπί, prep. with dat. τῇ . . . δωρεᾷ, "for the . . . gift." Ἀνεκδιηγήτῳ, dat. sg. fem. adj. ἀνεκδιήγητος, -ον, "unspeakable." This word is found neither in classical Greek nor in the papyri. It appears first in the NT and only in this verse. It appears to be a word the apostle himself coined to describe the ineffable character of God's gift. Once coined by Paul, it was used by Clement of Rome in his letter to the Corinthians (written c. AD 95) when writing of God's "indescribable" judgments, love, and power (1 Clem 20:5; 49:4; 61:1). God's "indescribable gift" is here is most likely the gift of his Son. Cf. Seifrid 367: "The term that he uses, *anekdiēgetos*, signifies that his gift cannot be recounted, narrated, or told. It implies a story that is beyond all telling, a story that again and again calls forth amazement, wonder, and praise." Δωρεᾷ, dat. sg. fem. δωρεά, -ᾶς, ἡ, "gift."

FOR FURTHER STUDY

86. The Collection (9:1–13)

Berger, K. "Almosen für Israel. Zum Historischen Kontext der Paulinischen Kollekte." *NTS* 23 (1976–77): 180–204.

Betz, H. D. *2 Corinthians 8 and 9*. Hermeneia. Philadelphia: Fortress, 1985. See pages 90–129.

Bruce, F. F. "Paul and Jerusalem." *TynBul* 19 (1968): 3–25.

Buck, C. H. Jr. "The Collection for the Saints." *HTR* 43 (1950): 1–29.

Dockx, S. "Chronologie Paulinienne de L'année de la Grande Collecte." *RB* 81(1974): 183–95.

Georgi, D. *Remembering the Poor: The History of Paul's Collection for Jerusalem*. Nashville: Abingdon, 1992.

194   I. PAUL'S RESPONSE TO A CRISIS RESOLVED (1:1–9:15)

Joubert, S. J. *Paul as Benefactor: Reciprocity, Strategy and Theological Reflection in Paul's Collection.* WUNT 1/124. Tübingen: Mohr, 2000.
Keck, L. E. "The Poor among the Saints in Jewish Christianity and Qumran." *ZNW* 57 (1966): 54–78.
Murphy-O'Connor, J. "Paul and Macedonia." *JSNT* 25 (1985): 99–103.
Nickle, K. F. *The Collection: A Study in Paul's Theology.* London: SCM, 1966.

87. Paul and Persuasion (9:1–14)

Bruehler, B. B. "Proverbs, Persuasion and People: A Three-Dimensional Investigation of 2 Cor 9.6–15." *NTS* 48 (2002): 209–24.
Lodge, J. G. "The Apostle's Appeal and Readers' Response: 2 Corinthians 8 and 9." *ChicStud* 30 (1991): 59–75.
Mitchell, M. M. "New Testament Envoys in the Context of Greco-Roman Diplomatic Epistolary Conventions: The Example of Timothy and Titus." *JBL* 111 (1992): 641–62.
O'Mahony, K. J. *Pauline Persuasion: A Sounding in 2 Corinthians 8–9.* JSNTSup 199. Sheffield: Sheffield Academic, 2000.
———. "The Rhetoric of Benefaction." *PIBA* 22 (1999): 9–40.
Verbrugge, V. D. *Paul's Style of Church Leadership Illustrated by His Instructions to the Corinthians on the Collection.* San Francisco: Mellen Research University, 1992.

88. Boasting and Joy (9:3–4)

Lambrecht, J. "Paul's Boasting about the Corinthians: A Study of 2 Cor. 8:24–9:5," *NovT* 40 (1998): 352–68.
Morrice, W. G. *Joy in the New Testament.* Grand Rapids: Eerdmans. 1985.

89. Financial Integrity (9:5)

Stowers, S. K. "Περὶ μὲν γάρ and the Integrity of 2 Corinthians 8 and 9." *NovT* 32 (1980): 340–48.
Talbert, C. H. "Money Management in Early Mediterranean Christianity: 2 Corinthians 8–9." *RevExp* 86 (1989): 359–70.

90. Word Studies

Balz, H. "λειτουργία, κτλ," *EDNT* 2.347–49.
Kittel, G. "αὐτάρκεια," *TDNT* 1.466–67.
Klaar, .E. "Πλεονεξία, -έκτης -εκτεῖν," *TZ* 10 (1954): 395–97.
Köster, H. "ὑπόστασις," *TDNT* 8.572–89.
Strathmann, H. "λειτουργία," *TDNT* 4.226–31.

HOMILETICAL SUGGESTIONS

Practical Incentives (9:1–5)

1. Remember the eagerness to participate you once had (v. 2a)
2. Don't let my boasting about you prove to be baseless (vv. 2b–3)
3. Avoid the shame of being found unprepared (vv. 4–5a)
4. Care for the poor should constitute a gift, not result from extortion (v. 5)

Theological Incentives (9:6–11)
    1. What you "sow" determines what you "reap" (v. 6)
    2. Give as you decide in your heart: God loves a "cheerful giver" (v. 7)
    3. God enriches people for generosity (vv. 8–11)

Practical Outcomes (9:12–14)
    1. Contributing to the collection not only meets the needs of the poor; it over-flows in thanksgiving to God (vv. 16–17)
    2. Generosity is evidence of commitment to Christ (v. 13)
    3. Generosity promotes genuine affection in the hearts of the recipients for their donors (v. 14)

God's Indescribable Gift (9:15)
    1. Giving to God's people in need reflects our appreciation of what God has done for us in giving up his own Son for our salvation (v. 15)

II. Paul Responds to a New Crisis (10:1–13:14)

In chapters 10–13 Paul faces determined opposition. His opponents were Jewish Christians who put themselves forward as apostles of Christ. They highly prized eloquent speech, displays of authority, visions and revelations, and the performance of mighty works as the signs of a true apostle. They had earlier infiltrated the Corinthian church, and their criticisms of Paul prob. provided some of the "ammunition" used by the offender (i.e., the one who caused pain, 2:5; who did the wrong, 7:12) in his attack against Paul. By writing the "severe letter," Paul succeeded in moving the church to discipline the offender, and then in his next letter, he urged them to express their love to the now presumably repentant offender and to reinstate him lest Satan gain the advantage (2:5–11). In the same letter he called upon the Corinthians to open their hearts fully to him as his own heart was open toward them (7:2–4). Seeing Paul being thus reinstated in the affections of the Corinthians, and his authority reestablished among them, the infiltrators mounted their own frontal attack against the validity and integrity of his apostolate (10:9–11). They succeeded in winning over the Corinthians to their point of view and getting them to submit to their authority (11:1–6). Paul, finding his authority usurped and his apostleship called into question, was forced, against his better judgment, to provide a strong pers. defense and to mount a vigorous counterattack against his opponents (11:16–12:13). The crisis Paul faced in this situation was the most crucial in all his relationships with the Corinthians, and this fact colors both the tone and content of chapters 10–13.

A. PAUL'S EXERCISE OF APOSTOLIC AUTHORITY (10:1–18)

Paul opens his response to this crisis by responding to criticisms that he lacks courage when present and that he conducts his ministry according to mere human standards. He insists that the "weapons" he fights with have "divine power." He says he is ready to "punish" disobedience, even though his ministry is essentially for building up, not tearing down (vv. 1–11). He refuses to engage in pointless comparisons of his ministry with that of his opponents, and he insists that he operates only in the sphere assigned to him by God. He does not boast of work done in another's territory, as his opponents were doing, as his aim is to preach in "regions beyond" (vv. 12–18).

1. Paul Responds to Criticisms (10:1–11)

Paul appeals to the Corinthians to so act that when he comes on his third visit he will not need to take action against them as he is resolved to do against those who question the validity of his apostleship (vv. 1–2). He denies charges that he acts in a worldly fashion, assuring his readers that he conducts his ministry with "weapons" that have divine power (vv. 3–5). He informs them that he is ready to punish his opponents in Corinth, as soon as the Corinthians' own obedience is complete (v. 6). He responds to the criticisms leveled against him by his opponents: first, that he was no true servant of Christ, while they were (vv. 7–8); and second, that while his letters were "weighty and powerful," "his physical presence is weak," and "his public speaking amounts to nothing" (vv. 9–11).

STRUCTURE

1 Αὐτὸς δὲ ἐγὼ Παῦλος παρακαλῶ ὑμᾶς
        διὰ τῆς πραΰτητος καὶ ἐπιεικείας τοῦ Χριστοῦ,
    ὃς κατὰ πρόσωπον μὲν ταπεινὸς ἐν ὑμῖν,
    ἀπὼν δὲ θαρρῶ εἰς ὑμᾶς·
2 δέομαι δὲ τὸ μὴ παρὼν θαρρῆσαι τῇ πεποιθήσει ᾗ λογίζομαι τολμῆσαι
    ἐπί τινας τοὺς λογιζομένους ἡμᾶς ὡς κατὰ σάρκα περιπατοῦντας.
3   ἐν σαρκὶ γὰρ
   περιπατοῦντες
     οὐ κατὰ σάρκα
 στρατευόμεθα,
4 τὰ γὰρ ὅπλα τῆς στρατείας ἡμῶν οὐ σαρκικὰ
      ἀλλὰ δυνατὰ τῷ θεῷ
        πρὸς καθαίρεσιν ὀχυρωμάτων,
        λογισμοὺς καθαιροῦντες
5   καὶ πᾶν ὕψωμα ἐπαιρόμενον
        κατὰ τῆς γνώσεως τοῦ θεοῦ,
        καὶ αἰχμαλωτίζοντες πᾶν νόημα
        εἰς τὴν ὑπακοὴν τοῦ Χριστοῦ,
6   καὶ ἐν ἑτοίμῳ ἔχοντες ἐκδικῆσαι πᾶσαν
        παρακοήν,
        ὅταν πληρωθῇ ὑμῶν ἡ ὑπακοή.
7 Τὰ κατὰ πρόσωπον βλέπετε.
    εἴ τις πέποιθεν ἑαυτῷ Χριστοῦ εἶναι,
   τοῦτο λογιζέσθω πάλιν ἐφ᾽ ἑαυτοῦ,
    ὅτι καθὼς αὐτὸς Χριστοῦ,
     οὕτως καὶ ἡμεῖς.
8   ἐάν [τε] γὰρ περισσότερόν τι καυχήσωμαι
        περὶ τῆς ἐξουσίας ἡμῶν
         ἧς ἔδωκεν ὁ κύριος
         εἰς οἰκοδομὴν

καὶ οὐκ εἰς καθαίρεσιν ὑμῶν,
οὐκ αἰσχυνθήσομαι.
9   ἵνα μὴ δόξω ὡς ἂν ἐκφοβεῖν ὑμᾶς
                διὰ τῶν ἐπιστολῶν·
10   ὅτι,
        Αἱ ἐπιστολαὶ μέν, φησίν, βαρεῖαι καὶ ἰσχυραί,
        ἡ δὲ παρουσία τοῦ σώματος ἀσθενὴς
        καὶ ὁ λόγος ἐξουθενημένος.
11   τοῦτο λογιζέσθω ὁ τοιοῦτος,
        ὅτι οἷοί ἐσμεν τῷ λόγῳ δι’ ἐπιστολῶν ἀπόντες,
        τοιοῦτοι καὶ παρόντες τῷ ἔργῳ.

VERSE 1

Αὐτὸς δὲ ἐγὼ Παῦλος παρακαλῶ ὑμᾶς διὰ τῆς πραΰτητος καὶ ἐπιεικείας τοῦ Χριστοῦ,
Now I Paul, myself, appeal to you by the meekness and gentleness of Christ—

Harris 666: "Αὐτὸς ἐγὼ Παῦλος, a *hapax legomenon* . . . stresses the intensely personal nature of his appeal, reflects his recognition of the great significance of the issue
to be discussed, and alludes to his apostolic authority." Αὐτός is in the pred. position,
emphasizing the pron. "myself." Ἐγώ, emphatic. Παρακαλῶ, 1st sg. pres. act. indic. of
παρακαλέω, "appeal, exhort." Ὑμᾶς, dir. obj. of παρακαλῶ.
        Διά, prep. with gen. τῆς πραΰτητος καὶ ἐπιεικείας . . . "by the meekness and gentle-
ness . . . ," an oath formula (Hafemann, 392). Harris, *Prepositions*, 127: "διά bears the
sense 'by means of [the example of]' = 'on the basis of')." Πραΰτητος, gen. sg. fem.
πραΰτης, -ητος, ἡ, "meekness." Among the Greeks from classical times on, πραΰτης
denoted a "mild and gentle friendliness," a highly prized social virtue and the opposite
of brusqueness or sudden anger. It was regarded as virtuous to show mildness to one's
own people and harshness to one's enemies. Mildness on the part of the judge meant
sentencing offenders with more leniency than the law prescribed. Ἐπιεικείας, gen. sg.
fem. ἐπιείκεια, -ας, ἡ, "gentleness." The essential mng. of ἐπιείκεια is "suitable" or
"fitting," and when used in a moral sense, "reasonable" or "fair." Applied to rulers, it
denoted kindness, equity, and leniency (cf. Acts 24:4). In the present context it is part
of a hendiadys (the use of two words joined by "and" to express one idea); therefore its
mng. is defined by that of πραΰτης, and so is rendered "gentleness" in the CSB. In the
case of Christ, "meekness and gentleness" did not mean weakness, and this was also
true of Paul. Hafemann 393 comments, "Far from timidity, his [Christ's] 'meekness' is
his slowness to anger, far from lacking conviction, his 'gentleness' is his forbearance,
in contrast to being vindictive." Τοῦ Χριστοῦ, poss. gen. ("belonging to Christ)" or a
subj. gen. ("shown by Christ"); cf. Harris 668. Barnett 457: "These striking terms,
'meekness and gentleness,' are clearly related to the loaded phrases '"timid" when
face to face . . . "bold" when away,' each of which stands in symmetrical counter-
balance to the other."

Ὅς κατὰ πρόσωπον μὲν ταπεινὸς ἐν ὑμῖν, ἀπὼν δὲ θαρρῶ εἰς ὑμᾶς·
I who am humble among you in person but bold toward you when absent.

An allusion to criticisms Paul's opponents made of him (cf. v.10). Ὅς, nom. masc. sg. rel. pron. ὅς, ἥ, ὅ, "who," antecedent: Αὐτὸς . . . ἐγὼ Παῦλος. Κατά, prep. with acc. πρόσωπον, lit. "according to face" = "in person." Ταπεινός, nom. sg. masc. adj. ταπεινός, -ή, -όν, "humble." BDAG 989c: "pert. to being servile in manner, *pliant, subservient, abject* a neg. quality that would make one lose face in the Gr-Rom. world, opp. of a free person's demeanour . . . in a judgment pronounced by Paul's opponents upon him 2 Cor 10:1." A reference to Paul's demeanor during his "painful visit." Harris 670: "ταπεινός does not bear its positive NT sense of 'humble,' but carries a pejorative meaning, 'timid' . . . 'feeble' . . . 'obsequious,' or 'servile.'" Ἐν, prep. with dat. ὑμῖν, "among you." Ἀπών, nom. sg. masc. of pres. act. ptc. of ἄπειμι, "be absent." Θαρρῶ, 1st sg. pres. act. indic. of θαρρέω, "be bold." Being bold "when absent" is prob. a reference to the opponents' criticism of Paul when he sent the "severe letter" rather than making another visit. Εἰς, prep. with acc. ὑμᾶς, "toward you."

VERSE 2

δέομαι δὲ τὸ μὴ παρὼν θαρρῆσαι τῇ πεποιθήσει
I beg you that when I am present I will not need to be bold with the confidence

Barnett 460: "This verse carries forward the 'bold when absent' accusation implicit in the previous verse. Now however, he turns it back on the Corinthians. He 'begs' them not to have to be 'bold *when present*.'" Δέομαι, 1st sg. pres. mid. indic. of δέομαι, "beg, ask, request." Δέομαι τὸ μὴ παρὼν θαρρῆσαι expresses the content of the request: "when I am present (I will) not need to be bold." BDF (§399[3]): "Here τὸ μή (like τοῦ μή §400) is the equivalent of a ἵνα μή-clause." BDF (§405[1]): "In the majority of cases in the NT too, a subject already given in or with the main verb is not repeated with the infinitive." Παρών, nom. sg. masc. of pres. ptc. of πάρειμι, "be present." Harris 672: "The adverbial participle ('when present') is nominative, as opposed to the accusative that one expects for the 'subject' of an infinitive, because it agrees with the subject of δέομαι." Θαρρῆσαι, aor. act. inf. of θαρρέω, "be bold." Πεποιθήσει, dat. sg. fem. πεποίθησις, -εως, ἡ, "confidence."

ἧ λογίζομαι τολμῆσαι ἐπί τινας τοὺς λογιζομένους ἡμᾶς ὡς κατὰ σάρκα περιπατοῦντας.
by which I plan to challenge certain people who think we are behaving according to the flesh.

Ἧ, dat. sg. fem. rel. pron. ὅς, ἥ, ὅ, "which," antecedent πεποιθήσει. Λογίζομαι, 1st sg. pres. mid. indic. of λογίζομαι, "plan." BDAG 598a: "to give careful thought to a matter, *think (about), consider, ponder.*" Τολμῆσαι, aor. act. inf. of τολμάω, "challenge." BDAG 1010c: "τολμῆσαι ἐπί τινα *show courage* or *boldness toward* or *against someone.*" Ἐπί, prep. with acc. τινας, "to certain people," a reference to Paul's opponents in

Corinth. Τοὺς λογιζομένους ἡμᾶς ὡς κατὰ σάρκα περιπατοῦντας, epex. qualifying τινας, and introducing the opponents' critique of Paul. Λογιζομένους, acc. pl. masc. of pres. mid. ptc. of λογίζομαι, "think." BDAG 597d: "*consider, look upon someone as.*" Ἡμᾶς, dir. obj. of λογιζομένους. Ὡς, particle "as." Κατά, prep. with acc. σάρκα, "according to (the) flesh." Περιπατοῦντας, acc. pl. masc. of pres. act. ptc. of περιπατέω, lit. "walk," metaphorical "behave."

Harris 675: "The gist of vv. 1b–2 may be stated as follows. 'Some say I am timid and servile when present with you but full of courage and boldness in my letters when at a safe distance. Let me state my intent . . . I shall be bold and confident, when I see you shortly, against certain persons of your number—those who persist in thinking and claiming that my outlook and behavior lack the signs of the Spirit's presence."

VERSE 3

ἐν σαρκὶ γὰρ περιπατοῦντες οὐ κατὰ σάρκα στρατευόμεθα,
For although we live in the flesh, we do not wage war according to the flesh,

In vv. 3–6 Paul employs military metaphors to make his point. He refers to waging war (v. 3); weapons and strongholds (v. 4); things raised up, e.g., towers/ramparts, and taking captives (v. 5); and punishing disobedience, e.g., by court-martial (v. 6). Harris 677 notes: "The imagery of Greco-Roman siegecraft was in common use by the first century A.D., especially among Stoics."

Having said in v. 2 that he intends to challenge those who think he behaves "according to the flesh" (κατὰ σάρκα), here in v. 3 Paul insists that while he lives "in the flesh" (ἐν σαρκί), he does not wage war "according to the flesh" (κατὰ σάρκα). Ἐν σαρκὶ . . . περιπατοῦντες, concessive use of the ptc., "although we live in the flesh," (cf. Moule 102; ZG 553–554). Κατὰ σάρκα. Moule 59: "*in accordance with material standards* (to be distinguished in meaning from κατὰ σάρκα, Rom. i.3, and τὸ κατὰ σάρκα, Rom. ix.5." Περιπατοῦντες, nom. pl. masc. of pres. act. ptc. of περιπατέω, lit. "walk," metaphorical "live." Στρατευόμεθα, 1st pl. pres. mid. indic. of στρατεύω, "wage war." Barnett 463: "The general martial allusion 'wages war' will lead into the imagery of the ministry as siege warfare that he expresses elaborately in vv. 4–6."

Commenting on vv. 2b–3, Harris, *Prepositions*, 150, says this: "two opposing uses of σάρξ are juxtaposed. In the phrase ἐν σαρκί it refers to life on earth in its totality, the universal human condition shared by believer and unbeliever alike . . . Κατὰ σάρκα, by contrast, here means 'by human methods' (NJB) or 'with human resources,' and points forward to the next verses that describe divine resources and methods of warfare." Cf. Seifrid 379: "Paul . . . concedes that he 'walks in the flesh.' In other words, he is subject to weakness, distress, and suffering. This has been his theme in this letter, and also in his self-description in First Corinthians."

VERSE 4

τὰ γὰρ ὅπλα τῆς στρατείας ἡμῶν οὐ σαρκικὰ ἀλλὰ δυνατὰ τῷ θεῷ
since the weapons of our warfare are not of the flesh, but are powerful through God

῞Οπλα, nom. pl. neut. ὅπλον,-ου, τό, "weapon." Στρατείας, gen. sg. fem. στρατεία, -ας, ἡ, "warfare." Σαρκικά, nom. pl. neut. adj. σαρκικός, -ή, -όν, "of the flesh." BDAG 914b: "sinful *earthly, mediocre, merely human, worldly.*" Δυνατά, nom. pl. neut. adj. δυνατός, -ή, -όν, "powerful." Τῷ θεῷ, dat. sg. masc. "through God." Possibly a Semitism; an intensive use of God's name to underline the great power of the weapons of Paul's warfare (cf. Moule 46, 184; Z §56). ZG 554: "either *because of God*, (NEB) *divinely potent*, or dat. of advantage, *for God.*" Thrall 2:610: "in God's service," sim. Harris 679–80.

Paul does not, in this passage, identify these powerful weapons, but statements elsewhere in the Corinthian correspondence suggest they consist in the proclamation of the gospel, through which divine power is released (4:1–6; 1 Cor 1:17–25; 2:1–5; cf. Rom 1:16; Eph 6:11–17).

πρὸς καθαίρεσιν ὀχυρωμάτων, λογισμοὺς καθαιροῦντες
for the demolition of strongholds. We demolish arguments

Πρός, prep. with acc. καθαίρεσιν "for demolition." Καθαίρεσιν, acc. sg. fem. καθαίρεσις, -εως, ἡ, "demolition." BDAG 487c: "*tearing down, destruction.*" Ὀχυρωμάτων, obj. gen. pl. neut. ὀχύρωμα, -ατος, τό, "stronghold, fortress." The word ὀχύρωμα is found only here in the NT. It is used in a literal sense in Prov 21:22 (LXX), while Philo uses it figuratively of a stronghold prepared by persuasive words against the honor of God (*Confusion of Tongues*, 129). The military practice of building strongholds (there was a large one on Acrocorinth) provided the imagery used by Cynic and Stoic philosophers, and in particular by Seneca, a contemporary of Paul, to describe the fortification of the soul by reasonable arguments to render it impregnable under the attack of adverse fortune. In the next verse Paul speaks of destroying arguments that stand against the knowledge of God, suggesting that the "strongholds" he had in mind were the intellectual arguments of unbelievers that have to be demolished so that the truth of the gospel might gain entry. Cf. Hafemann 396: "The arguments in view here are the objections being raised against his apostolic authority and message."

Λογισμούς, acc. pl. masc. λογισμός, -οῦ, ὁ, "arguments, reasoning," dir. obj. of καθαιροῦντες. Καθαιροῦντες, nom. pl. masc. of pres. act. ptc. of καθαιρέω, "demolish, tear down." Λογισμοὺς καθαιροῦντες. BDAG 598d: "*we demolish sophistries.*"

VERSE 5

καὶ πᾶν ὕψωμα ἐπαιρόμενον κατὰ τῆς γνώσεως τοῦ θεοῦ,
and every proud thing that is raised up against the knowledge of God,

Πᾶν, acc. sg. neut. adj. πᾶς, πᾶσα, πᾶν, "every." Ὕψωμα, acc. sg. neut. ὕψωμα, -ατος, τό, "high thing." The expression πᾶν ὕψωμα ἐπαιρόμενον relates to the world of ancient warfare and denotes a tower or raised rampart built to withstand the enemy. Both the ὀχύρωμα of v. 4 and the ὕψωμα of this verse stand for intellectual arguments employed by people in their rejection of the gospel. ZG 554: "*a height* (lit. of enemy defences) meaning their *arrogance*." So too Thrall 2:613. Ἐπαιρόμενον, acc. sg. neut. of pres. pass. ptc. of ἐπαίρω, "raise up." Κατά, prep. with. gen. τῆς γνώσεως, "against the knowledge." Γνώσεως, gen. sg. fem. γνῶσις, -εως, ἡ, "knowledge." Τοῦ θεοῦ, descriptive gen. "(knowledge) about God."

καὶ αἰχμαλωτίζοντες πᾶν νόημα εἰς τὴν ὑπακοὴν τοῦ Χριστοῦ,
and we take every thought captive to obey Christ.

Thrall 2:613: "Paul's military metaphor has been that of a siege. First, the fortifications of the city have been destroyed and now its inhabitants are taken prisoner, captured 'for obedience to Christ.'"
Αἰχμαλωτίζοντες, nom. pl. masc. of pres. act. ptc. of αἰχμαλωτίζω, "take captive." Νόημα, acc. sg. neut. νόημα, -ατος, τό, "thought." Εἰς, prep. with acc. τὴν ὑπακοήν, "for obedience." Cf. R 593–94. Ὑπακοήν, acc. sg. fem. ὑπακοή, -ῆς, ἡ, "obedience." Τοῦ Χριστοῦ, obj. gen. (obedience) to Christ." Cf. R 500.

VERSE 6

καὶ ἐν ἑτοίμῳ ἔχοντες ἐκδικῆσαι πᾶσαν παρακοήν, ὅταν πληρωθῇ ὑμῶν ἡ ὑπακοή.
And we are ready to punish any disobedience, once your obedience is complete.

Ἐν ἑτοίμῳ ἔχοντες, idiomatic phrase: "be ready," an expression used of military preparedness. Ἐν, prep. with dat. ἑτοίμῳ, "in readiness." Ἑτοίμῳ, dat. sg. neut. adj. ἕτοιμος, -η, -ον, "ready," as subst. "readiness," dir. obj. of ἔχοντες. Ἔχοντες, nom. pl. masc. of pres. act. ptc. of ἔχω, "have." Ἐκδικῆσαι, aor. act. inf. ἐκδικέω, "punish." The punishment intended is prob. the exclusion of Paul's opponents from the congregation, something he could only effect when the Corinthians' "obedience is complete," and when they are ready to support such action. Πᾶσαν, acc. sg. fem. adj. πᾶς, πᾶσα, πᾶν, "every." Παρακοήν, acc. sg. fem. παρακοή, -ῆς, ἡ, "disobedience."
Ὅταν, conj., "when." Πληρωθῇ, 3rd sg. aor. pass. subjunc. of πληρόω, "complete, finish." Ὑπακοή, nom. sg. fem. ὑπακοή, -ῆς, ἡ, "obedience." Thrall 2:615: "Obedience to Christ must be meant, in view of v. 5, and what is required will be their detachment from the influence of the rival missionaries whom Paul later castigates as intermediaries of Satan (11.14–15), the opponents of Christ and the gospel."
Harris 681: "So with regard to the structure of vv. 3–6 which form one sentence in Greek, we conclude: that v. 4 is not parenthetical; that it affords the evidence that Paul was not conducting his campaign using worldly resources (v. 3b)."

VERSE 7

Τὰ κατὰ πρόσωπον βλέπετε.
Look at what is obvious.

Τὰ κατὰ πρόσωπον, BDAG 888b: *"what is before your eyes."* Moule 58: *"what is in front of you,"* presumably the evidence that Paul is a true servant who "belongs to Christ." Harris 686: "Look at what is staring you in the face." Τά, neut. pl. acc. article "the (things)," dir. obj. of βλέπετε. Κατά, prep. with acc. πρόσωπον, idiomatic: "evident"; cf. BDAG 511d: *"is obvious."* Βλέπετε, 2nd pl. pres. act. either impv. (CSB; Thrall 2:618; Hafemann 397; Harris 687) or indic. (NIV; Seifrid 385), βλέπω, "look."

εἴ τις πέποιθεν ἑαυτῷ Χριστοῦ εἶναι, τοῦτο λογιζέσθω πάλιν ἐφ᾽ ἑαυτοῦ,
If anyone is confident that he belongs to Christ, let him remind himself of this:

A first-class cond. sentence (with εἴ plus the indic. in the prot.) consisting of a prot., which postulates a certain situation, and an apod., stating the consequence of that situation. Πέποιθεν, 3rd sg. pf. act. indic. of πειθώ, "be confident, persuade." Ἑαυτῷ, dat. 3rd sg. masc. refl. pron. ἑαυτοῦ, -ῆς, -οῦ, "himself."
There has been much debate about the mng. of Χριστοῦ εἶναι, lit. "to be of Christ." It has been variously understood to mean: (a) to be a Christian, (b) to have been a disciple of the earthly Jesus, (c) to be a servant or apostle of Christ, and (d) to be part of Christ (understood along Gnostic lines). The view that it means to be a servant of Christ or an apostle commends itself most in the light of both 11:23 ("are they servants of Christ? . . . I'm a better one") and the fact that throughout chaps. 10–13 Paul is defending his apostolate. Cf. Harris 689. Barnett 470: "In our view, this means that they [Paul's opponents] doubted that he was a Spirit-empowered minister." Εἶναι, pres. inf. of εἰμί, "be." Τοῦτο, acc. sg. neut. dem. pron. "this." Λογιζέσθω, 3rd sg. pres. mid. impv. of λογίζομαι, "remind, think, count." Πάλιν, adv. "again." Ἐφ᾽, prep. (contraction of ἐπί) with gen. ἑαυτοῦ, ZG 554: "for himself."

ὅτι καθὼς αὐτὸς Χριστοῦ, οὕτως καὶ ἡμεῖς.
Just as he belongs to Christ, so do we.

Ὅτι, conj., "that." Καθώς, conj., "just as." Αὐτός, nom. 3rd sg. masc. pron. αὐτός, -ή, -ό, "he." Χριστοῦ, poss. gen., "belongs to Christ." Καθώς . . . οὕτως, "just as . . . so." Καὶ ἡμεῖς, "and (do) we."

VERSE 8

ἐάν [τε] γὰρ περισσότερόν τι καυχήσωμαι περὶ τῆς ἐξουσίας ἡμῶν
For if I boast a little too much about our authority,

This clause introduces a third-class cond. sentence (ἐάν plus subjunc. in the prot.) described by Forbes, 154, "as the future cond., in the sense that a proposal is made regarding some form of action from which certain results will ensue if carried out. In other words, the use of the subjunctive makes a projection, not an assertion, about reality." Τε, conj., "even." BDAG 993d: "marker w. ascensive stress and serving without copulative force, *even.* Ἐάν τε γὰρ περισσότερόν τι καυχήσωμαι *for suppose I (even) do boast a little too much.*" BDF (§443[3]): "In the connection of clauses, τε indicates rather close connection and relationship." Περισσότερον, BDAG 806a: "περισσότερος, τέρα, ον comp. of περισσός . . . pert. to being beyond a standard of abundance, *greater, more, even more.*" Τι, acc. sg. neut. indef. pron. τις, τι, "a little." Καυχήσωμαι, 1st sg. aor. mid. subjunc. of καυχάομαι, "boast." περί, prep. with gen. τῆς ἐξουσίας, "concerning the authority." Ἐξουσίας, gen. sg. fem. ἐξουσία, -ας, ἡ, "authority." Ἡμῶν, gen. 1st pl. poss. pron. ἐγώ, "our."

ἧς ἔδωκεν ὁ κύριος εἰς οἰκοδομὴν καὶ οὐκ εἰς καθαίρεσιν ὑμῶν, οὐκ αἰσχυνθήσομαι.
which the Lord gave for building you up and not for tearing you down, I will not be put to shame.

Ἧς, gen. sg. fem. rel. pron. ὅς, ἥ, ὅ, "which," antecedent ἐξουσίας. Ἔδωκεν, 3rd sg. aor. act. indic. of δίδωμι, "give." Harris 693: "In the present context the aorist ἔδωκεν points to a single event—Christ's appointment of Paul as an authoritative apostle at the time of his conversion." Εἰς, prep. with acc. οἰκοδομήν, "for building up." Οἰκοδομήν, acc. sg. fem. οἰκοδομή, -ῆς, ἡ, "building up, edification." Εἰς, prep. with acc. καθαίρεσιν, "for tearing down." Καθαίρεσιν, acc. sg. fem. καθαίρεσις, -εως, ἡ, "tearing down, destruction." Οὐκ αἰσχυνθήσομαι, apod. of cond. sentence following ἐάν [τε] γὰρ περισσότερόν τι καυχήσωμαι, "I will not be put to shame." Αἰσχυνθήσομαι, 1st sg. fut. pass. indic. of αἰσχύνω, "be put to shame."

VERSE 9

ἵνα μὴ δόξω ὡς ἂν ἐκφοβεῖν ὑμᾶς διὰ τῶν ἐπιστολῶν·
I don't want to seem as though I am trying to terrify you with my letters.

Ἵνα, conj. with subjunc. δόξω, "so that I (don't) seem." Δόξω, 1st sg. aor. act. subjunc. of δοκέω, "seem, appear." Ὡς ἄν, BDAG 1106b: "marker indicating perspective or point of view, with component of cautious statement, *as if, as it were, so to speak.*" R 959: "There is one instance of ἄν with the infinitive in the N.T. (2 Cor. 10:9) . . . but ἄν is here probably the same as ἐάν and ὡς ἄν = 'as if.'" Ἐκφοβεῖν, pres. act. inf. ἐκφοβέω, "terrify, frighten." R 969: "In 2 Cor. 10:9 we have ὡς ἂν ἐκφοβεῖν (here alone in the N.T. with the infinitive) = 'as if to frighten.'" Ὑμᾶς, dir. obj. of ἐκφοβεῖν. Διά, prep. with gen. τῶν ἐπιστολῶν, "with/through letters." BDF (§223[3]): "to denote . . . the medium."

The grammatical connection with what precedes is not apparent. Thrall 2:626–27 suggests there must be "some intermediate thought" that would connect it to v. 8.

She says, "The connecting link would then be: 'I say this.' And the meaning of the verse would be: 'so that I may not seem to be operating, so to speak, an epistolary "terror-campaign."'" Cf. Harris 697.

VERSE 10

ὅτι, Αἱ ἐπιστολαὶ μέν, φησίν, βαρεῖαι καὶ ἰσχυραί,
For it is said, "His letters are weighty and powerful,

Here Paul provides the background to his reference to terrifying the Corinthians with letters in v. 9, explaining that people are criticizing him for sending "weighty and powerful" letters, while in person he "is weak and his public speaking amounts to nothing." Ἐπιστολαί, nom. pl. fem. ἐπιστολή, -ῆς, ἡ, "letter." Φησίν, 3rd sg. pres. act. indic. of φημί, "say." Moule 29: "suggests that φησίν . . . is the idiom of the 'diatribe,' and refers to a supposed objector; *someone will say.*" Βαρεῖαι, nom. pl. fem. adj. βαρύς, -εῖα, -ύ, "weighty." BDAG 167d, *"severe."* Thrall 2:630: "In the present context βαρύς more probably means 'weighty' in the sense of 'impressive.' It is contrasted with ἐξουθενημένος, 'contemptible.' It may have some connotation of rhetorical impressiveness. The other adjective ἰσχυρός means 'effective,' in a strong sense, again perhaps, as inclusive of an oratorical quality." Ἰσχυραί, nom. pl. fem. adj. ἰσχυρός, -ά, -όν, "powerful, strong."

ἡ δὲ παρουσία τοῦ σώματος ἀσθενὴς καὶ ὁ λόγος ἐξουθενημένος.
but his physical presence is weak and his public speaking amounts to nothing."

Παρουσία, nom. sg. fem. παρουσία, -ας, ἡ, "presence." Τοῦ σώματος, attrib. gen. qualifying παρουσία, "bodily/physical (presence)." Σώματος, gen. sg. neut. σῶμα, -ατος, τό, "body." Ἀσθενής, nom. sg. fem. adj. ἀσθενής, -ές, "weak." Λόγος, nom. sg. masc. λόγος, -ου, ὁ, "speech." Ἐξουθενημένος, nom. sg. masc. of pf. mid. ptc. of ἐξουθενέω, "despise." With a form of εἰμί understood, it functions as a periph. ptc., "is despicable," or as CSB: "amounts to nothing."

Barnett 476–77: "While their negative views of his 'person' and 'speech,' broadly speaking, probably have overtones of disappointment in his lack of expertise in rhetorical skills and lack of physical 'presence,' the context of vv. 1–11 makes it probable that their primary criticisms were directed at his unimpressive attempts to discipline the morally wayward during the recent visit (cf. 13:2; 12:21; 10:1–2), and the dispatch, instead, of a letter when they were expecting a return visit (1:15–2:3)."

VERSE 11

τοῦτο λογιζέσθω ὁ τοιοῦτος,
Let such a person consider this:

Seifrid 389: "The plurality of opponents again shifts to the singular: Paul again focuses upon the likelihood of an individual confrontation in Corinth, as he does in v. 7." Τοῦτο, acc. sg. neut. pron. οὗτος, αὕτη, τοῦτο, "this," dir. obj. of λογιζέσθω. Λογιζέσθω, 3rd sg. pres. mid. impv. λογίζομαι, "consider." Ὁ τοιοῦτος, ZG 555: *this individual.* Τοιοῦτος, nom. sg. masc. pron. τοιοῦτος, -αύτη, -οῦτον, "such a person."

ὅτι οἷοί ἐσμεν τῷ λόγῳ δι᾽ ἐπιστολῶν ἀπόντες,
What we are in our letters, when we are absent,

Ὅτι, a conj., introduces what the apostle wants the Corinthians to consider. Οἷοι, nom. pl. masc. pron. οἷος, -α, -ον, "what, what sort of person." Ἐσμέν, 1st pl. pres. indic. of εἰμί, "be, are." Τῷ λόγῳ dat. phrase, lit. "in word." Δι᾽, prep. with gen. ἐπιστολῶν, "in letters." Z §114: "διά with the genitive is used of the manner of acting. The means whereby a thing is done is already in a certain sense a manner in which it is done, e.g. διὰ λόγου «orally» Acts 15,27 as opposed to διὰ τῆς ἐπιστολῆς 2 Cor 10,11." Ἀπόντες, nom. pl. masc. of pres. ptc. of ἄπειμι, "be absent."

τοιοῦτοι καὶ παρόντες τῷ ἔργῳ.
we will also be in our actions when we are present.

Τοιοῦτοι, nom. pl. masc. pron. τοιοῦτος, -αύτη, -οῦτον, "such a kind of person." Παρόντες, nom. pl. masc. of pres. ptc. of πάρειμι, "be absent." Τῷ ἔργῳ, dat. phrase "in action." Ἔργῳ, dat. sing. neut. ἔργον, -ου, τό, "work, action." BDAG 390b: "that which displays itself in activity of any kind, *deed, action.*"

2. Boasting within Proper Limits (10:12–18)

In the previous section Paul defended himself against those who claimed that while he could write boldly from a distance, his lack of authority was plain for all to see when he was present in person. In 10:12–18 Paul takes the offensive. He satirizes his opponents who commend themselves (by comparing themselves with one another!). By contrast his own boasting, he says, is carefully measured and based upon actual work done in the sphere of operations assigned to him by the Lord. He concludes, clearly having his opponents in mind: "For it is not the one commending himself who is approved, but the one the Lord commends."

STRUCTURE

12 Οὐ γὰρ τολμῶμεν ἐγκρῖναι
       ἢ συγκρῖναι ἑαυτούς
       τισιν τῶν ἑαυτοὺς συνιστανόντων,
  ἀλλ᾽ αὐτοὶ   ἐν ἑαυτοῖς ἑαυτοὺς
       μετροῦντες
       καὶ συγκρίνοντες ἑαυτοὺς ἑαυτοῖς
       οὐ συνιᾶσιν.
13 ἡμεῖς δὲ οὐκ εἰς τὰ ἄμετρα καυχησόμεθα
   ἀλλὰ κατὰ τὸ μέτρον τοῦ κανόνος
       οὗ ἐμέρισεν ἡμῖν ὁ θεὸς μέτρου,
       ἐφικέσθαι ἄχρι καὶ ὑμῶν.
14 οὐ γὰρ   ὡς μὴ ἐφικνούμενοι εἰς ὑμᾶς
       ὑπερεκτείνομεν ἑαυτούς,
   ἄχρι γὰρ καὶ ὑμῶν ἐφθάσαμεν
       ἐν τῷ εὐαγγελίῳ τοῦ Χριστοῦ,
15 οὐκ εἰς τὰ ἄμετρα καυχώμενοι
   ἐν ἀλλοτρίοις κόποις,
   ἐλπίδα δὲ ἔχοντες
       αὐξανομένης τῆς πίστεως ὑμῶν
   ἐν ὑμῖν μεγαλυνθῆναι
       κατὰ τὸν κανόνα ἡμῶν
       εἰς περισσείαν
16 εἰς τὰ ὑπερέκεινα ὑμῶν εὐαγγελίσασθαι,
           οὐκ ἐν ἀλλοτρίῳ κανόνι
           εἰς τὰ ἕτοιμα καυχήσασθαι.
17 Ὁ δὲ καυχώμενος ἐν κυρίῳ καυχάσθω·
18 οὐ γὰρ ὁ ἑαυτὸν συνιστάνων,
       ἐκεῖνός ἐστιν δόκιμος,
   ἀλλ᾽ ὃν ὁ κύριος συνίστησιν.

VERSE 12

Οὐ γὰρ τολμῶμεν ἐγκρῖναι ἢ συγκρῖναι ἑαυτούς τισιν τῶν ἑαυτοὺς συνιστανόντων,
For we don't dare classify or compare ourselves with some who commend themselves.

Τολμῶμεν, 1st pl. pres. act. indic. of τολμάω, "dare, presume." Ἐγκρῖναι, aor. act. inf. of ἐγκρίνω, "classify." Συγκρῖναι, aor. act. inf. of συγκρίνω, "compare." Barnett 482 n. 11: "Gk. ἐγκρῖναι ἢ συγκρῖναι. There is a play on words . . . something in which Paul evidently takes some pleasure. The one—ἐγκρῖναι—means to judge within a class (as, e.g., among a group of enlisted soldiers or athletes in a contest . . .); the other—συγκρῖναι—means to contrast or compete with something outside its class." Ἑαυτούς, acc. 3rd pl. masc. pron. ἑαυτοῦ, -ῆς, -οῦ, "ourselves," dir. obj. of ἐγκρῖναι and συγκρῖναι. Τισιν, dat. pl. masc. τις, τι, "certain one(s)." Τῶν . . . συνιστανόντων, art. subst. ptc., "those who commend (themselves)." Ἑαυτούς, dir. obj. of συνιστανόντων. Συνιστανόντων, gen. pl. masc. of pres. act. ptc. of συνίστημι, "commend."

ἀλλ᾽ αὐτοὶ ἐν ἑαυτοῖς ἑαυτοὺς μετροῦντες καὶ συγκρίνοντες ἑαυτοὺς ἑαυτοῖς οὐ συνιᾶσιν. But in measuring themselves by themselves and comparing themselves to themselves, they lack understanding.

ZG 555: "measuring themselves by their own standards and comparing themselves with each other they are not showing themselves very intelligent." Ἀλλ᾽ (contraction of ἀλλά) introduces the contrast between Paul's attitude and the behavior of his opponents. Αὐτοί, nom. 3rd pl. masc. pron. αὐτός, -ή, -ό, emphasizes the subject of μετροῦντες and συγκρίνοντες. BDF (§283[4]): "The strengthening of the reflexive with αὐτός, frequent in Attic, appears only in scattered instances (literary language): 2 C 10:12 αὐτοὶ ἐν ἑαυτοῖς ἑαυτοὺς μετροῦντες." Cf. R 687. Ἐν, prep. with dat. ἑαυτοῖς, "by themselves." Ἑαυτούς, dir. obj. of μετροῦντες. Μετροῦντες, nom. pl. masc. of pres. act. ptc. of μετρέω, "measure, evaluate." Συγκρίνοντες, nom. pl. masc. of pres. act. ptc. of συγκρίνω, "compare." Ἑαυτούς, dir. obj. of συγκρίνοντες. Ἑαυτοῖς, dat. 3rd pl. masc. pron. ἑαυτοῦ, -ῆς, οῦ, "to themselves," instrumental dat. cf. R 529.

We cannot be certain about the criteria Paul's opponents employed in this measurement. However, it is likely that they employed the same criteria when comparing themselves with Paul, and hints in 2 Corinthians suggest these were: an authoritative presence and impressive speech (10:1, 10; 11:20–21), the levying of a fee for the message proclaimed (11:7–11), an impeccable Jewish ancestry (11:21b–22), impressive spiritual experiences (12:1-6), the performance of apostolic signs (12:12), and some show of power and authority (11:19–20) to prove that Christ spoke through them (13:3). The triumphalist nature of these criteria should be noted. There is no room for weakness, suffering, persecution and imprisonment, which were often Paul's lot, and which Jesus said would be the experience of those who followed him. If the understanding of the criteria adopted by Paul's opponents suggested here is valid, it is no wonder Paul says of these people, "They lack understanding." For a discussion of other possible criteria, see Thrall 2:641–43.

Συνιᾶσιν, 3rd pl. pres. act. indic. of συνίημι, "understand." Seifrid 391: "The term Paul uses to describe the failure of his opponents is deliciously ironic. This verb for understanding is a compound form (syn-iēmi) that appears at the end of a list of similar compounds with the prefix syn- ('together'). Paul will not compare himself (syn-krinō) with those who commend themselves (syn-istanō); when they compare themselves (syn-krinō) they do not understand (syn-iēmi). The opponents make comparisons in which they put things together, but they cannot put it together." For a discussion of the absence of οὐ συνιᾶσιν. ἡμεῖς δὲ in some manuscripts, see Metzger 514; Thrall 2:636–39.

VERSE 13

ἡμεῖς δὲ οὐκ εἰς τὰ ἄμετρα καυχησόμεθα
We, however, will not boast beyond measure

Ἡμεῖς, 1st pl. nom. pron. used to emphasise the subject of the verb (οὐκ) καυχησόμεθα. Εἰς, prep. with acc. τὰ ἄμετρα, adv. phrase "beyond measure." Moule 71: "does this mean *by reference to a standard which we have no right to use?* Or does it simply mean *with reference to what lies outside our scope?*" Ἄμετρα, acc. pl. neut. adj. ἄμετρος, -ον, "boundless, excessive." BDAG 53c: "εἰς τὰ ἄ. καυχᾶσθαι *boast beyond limits.*" Seifrid 392: "immeasurable things. . . . Paul's thought here corresponds to his admonition to the Roman Christians 'not to think more highly of oneself than one ought to think, but to think with sound judgment, because God has measured to each a measure of faith' (Rom. 12:3)." Καυχησόμεθα, 1st pl. fut. mid. indic. of καυχάομαι, "boast."

ἀλλὰ κατὰ τὸ μέτρον τοῦ κανόνος οὗ ἐμέρισεν ἡμῖν ὁ θεὸς μέτρου, ἐφικέσθαι ἄχρι καὶ ὑμῶν.
but according to the measure of the area of ministry that God has assigned to us, which reaches even to you.

Κατά, prep. with acc. τὸ μέτρον, "according to the measure." Μέτρον, acc. sg. neut. μέτρον, -ου, τό, "measure." Τοῦ κανόνος, gen. sg. masc. κανών, -όνος, ὁ. The basic mng. of κανών is "a rule" or "a standard of measurement." In recently published papyri (*New Docs* I, 36–45), there is evidence for the use of the word to denote services rendered within "a specified geographical area," and the same sense of the word is required here. The area (κανών) of ministry that God assigned to Paul was the preaching of the gospel in Gentile lands (cf. Rom 1:5, 13–14; 15:18–19; Gal 2:7–8) and, as the success of his ministry in Corinth showed, the people of that city were included in his God-ordained area of ministry: "which reaches even to you." Cf. Harris 714. Οὗ ἐμέρισεν ἡμῖν ὁ θεὸς μέτρου, "which measure God has assigned to us." Οὗ, ZG 555: "seemingly attracted into the case of κανόνος (which is not its antecedent) and μέτρου then added to make this clearer." Ἐμέρισεν, 3rd sg. aor. act. indic. of μερίζω, "assign." BDF (§294[5]): "κατὰ τὸ μέτρον τοῦ κανόνος οὗ ἐμέρισεν ἡμῖν ὁ θεὸς μέτρου is difficult; οὗ is probably attracted from ὅ (referring to μέτρον) to κανόνος and then μέτρου repeated, lest οὗ be referred to κανόνος." Cf. R 719. Ἐφικέσθαι, aor. mid. inf. of ἐφικνέομαι, "reach." R 1078 cites this as an example of the appos. inf. Ἄχρι, prep. with gen. (of place) ὑμῶν, "as far as you." BDAG 161a: "ἄχρι . . . marker of extension up to a certain point, *as far as.*"

VERSE 14

οὐ γὰρ ὡς μὴ ἐφικνούμενοι εἰς ὑμᾶς ὑπερεκτείνομεν ἑαυτούς,
For we are not overextending ourselves, as if we had not reached you,

BDF (§433[3]): "ὡς is treated as a preposition in 2 C 10:14 . . . 'as not (actually) reaching you.'" Ἐφικνούμενοι, nom. pl. masc. of pres. mid. ptc. of ἐφικνέομαι, "reach." Εἰς, prep. with acc. ὑμᾶς, "to you." Ὑπερεκτείνομεν, 1st pl. pres. act. indic. of ὑπερεκτείνω, "overextend." Ἑαυτούς, acc. 3rd pl. masc. reflex. pron. ἑαυτοῦ, -ῆς, -οῦ, here "ourselves."

Barnett 488: "But what is Paul implying about the movements of the intruders? In reaching Corinth they have 'overextended' themselves. The 'field' of mission God has assigned to them is either in Judaea or with the Jews of the Diaspora living among the Gentiles."

ἄχρι γὰρ καὶ ὑμῶν ἐφθάσαμεν ἐν τῷ εὐαγγελίῳ τοῦ Χριστοῦ,
since we have come to you with the gospel of Christ.

Ἄχρι, prep. with gen. ὑμῶν, "to/as far as you." Ἐφθάσαμεν, 1st pl. aor. act. indic. of φθάνω, "come, reach." ZG 555: "perh. w. class. connotation, *we were the first to come*"; sim. Thrall 2:648. Ἐν, prep. with dat. τῷ εὐαγγελίῳ, "with the gospel." Τοῦ Χριστοῦ, either poss. gen. ("Christ's gospel") or descriptive gen. ("the gospel about Christ").

VERSE 15

οὐκ εἰς τὰ ἄμετρα καυχώμενοι ἐν ἀλλοτρίοις κόποις,
We are not boasting beyond measure about other people's labors.

Paul is prob. implying that this is what his opponents do. Εἰς, prep. with acc. τὰ ἄμετρα, "beyond measure." See notes on v. 13. Ἄμετρα, acc. pl. neut. adj. ἄμετρος, -ον, "excessive, immeasurable, limitless." Καυχώμενοι, nom. pl. masc. of pres. mid. ptc. of καυχάομαι, "boast." ZG 555: "καυχώμενοι . . . ἔχοντες ptcs. taking the place of finite vbs." Ἐν, prep. with dat. ἀλλοτρίοις κόποις, "in other people's labors." Ἀλλοτρίοις, dat. pl. masc. adj. ἀλλότριος, -ία, -ον, "belonging to another." Κόποις, dat. pl. masc. κόπος, -ου, ὁ, "labor."

ἐλπίδα δὲ ἔχοντες αὐξανομένης τῆς πίστεως ὑμῶν
On the contrary, we have the hope that as your faith increases,

Ἐλπίδα, acc. sg. fem. ἐλπίς, -ίδος, ἡ, "hope," obj. of ἔχοντες. Ἔχοντες, nom. pl. masc. of pres. act. ptc. of ἔχω, "have." Αὐξανομένης τῆς πίστεως ὑμῶν, gen. abs. "as your faith increases," depicts action occurring at the time of the main verb, i.e., "we have (hope)." Αὐξανομένης, gen. sg. fem. of pres. mid. ptc. of αὐξάνω, "increase, cause to grow."

ἐν ὑμῖν μεγαλυνθῆναι κατὰ τὸν κανόνα ἡμῶν εἰς περισσείαν
our area of ministry [among you] will be greatly enlarged,

Ἐν, prep. with dat. ὑμῖν, "among you." Μεγαλυνθῆναι, aor. pass. inf. of μεγαλύνω, "enlarge, increase." Κατά, prep. with acc. τὸν κανόνα, "according to our area of ministry." Κανόνα, acc. sg. masc. κανών, -όνος, ὁ, "area of ministry." Εἰς, prep. with acc. περισσείαν, lit., "for abundance." Περισσείαν, acc. sg. fem. περισσεία, -ας, ἡ, "abundance."

Calvin 137 comments: "As if he had said, 'If you had progressed as far as you ought, I should by now be occupied in gaining new churches and I should have your assistance in doing so. But, as things are, you are delaying me by your weakness.'"

VERSE 16

εἰς τὰ ὑπερέκεινα ὑμῶν εὐαγγελίσασθαι,
so that we may preach the gospel to the regions beyond you

Εἰς, with inf. εὐαγγελίσασθαι, expresses purpose, "to preach the gospel." Τὰ ὑπερέκεινα ὑμῶν, indir obj. of εὐαγγελίσασθαι, "the regions beyond you," a prob. reference to Paul's ambition to take the gospel to Spain. Ὑπερέκεινα, adv. "beyond," takes gen. ὑμῶν, "beyond you." Moule 86: "ὑπερέκεινα only occurs once in the N.T. (II Cor. x.16) and then as a preposition with the Genitive = beyond." Cf. Harris, Prepositions, 250. Εὐαγγελίσασθαι, aor. mid. inf. of εὐαγγελίζω, "preach the gospel."

οὐκ ἐν ἀλλοτρίῳ κανόνι εἰς τὰ ἕτοιμα καυχήσασθαι.
without boasting about what has already been done in someone else's area of ministry.

Ἐν, prep. with dat. ἀλλοτρίῳ κανόνι, "in someone else's area of ministry." Ἀλλοτρίῳ, dat. sg. masc. adj. ἀλλότριος, -ία, -ον, "belonging to another." Κανόνι, dat. sg. masc. κανών, -όνος, ὁ, "area of ministry." Εἰς with inf. καυχήσασθαι expresses purpose, "to boast about (things already done)." Τὰ ἕτοιμα, acc. pl. neut. subst. adj. ἕτοιμος, -η, -ον, "the things already done." Καυχήσασθαι, aor. mid. inf. of καυχάομαι, "boast."

ZG 556: "Vv. 15,16 may be fairly lit. transl. *We do not boast outside our limits about work done by others but we have the hope that as your faith increases we may be enlarged among you—(always) within our proper field—to a vast extent, even to (the point of) spreading the gospel to places beyond you, (though) not so as to boast about another's sphere of places already evangelized.*"

VERSE 17

Ὁ δὲ καυχώμενος ἐν κυρίῳ καυχάσθω
So **let the one who boasts, boast in the Lord.**

Ὁ καυχώμενος, subst. ptc., "the one who boasts." Καυχώμενος, nom. sg. masc. of pres. mid. ptc. of καυχάομαι, "boast." Ἐν, prep. with dat. κυρίῳ, "in the Lord." Καυχάσθω, 3rd sg. pres. mid. impv. καυχάομαι, "let him boast." Here (and in 1 Cor 1:31) Paul draws on Jer 9:23–24, where the wise, the mighty, and the rich are counseled against glorying in their advantages. They are urged to glory in the fact that they know the Lord. Jesus taught the Seventy the same lesson when they came back from their mission rejoicing that they had seen even the demons subject to them (Luke 10:17–20). Harris, *Prepositions*, 133: "κύριος refers to Christ: the prepositional phrase ἐν κυρίῳ regularly refers to Christ in Paul's letters. . . . Paul is not averse to applying to Christ OT passages that refer to Yahweh (e.g., Isa 28:16 in Rom. 9:33; 10:11)."

VERSE 18

οὐ γὰρ ὁ ἑαυτὸν συνιστάνων, ἐκεῖνός ἐστιν δόκιμος, ἀλλ᾿ ὃν ὁ κύριος συνίστησιν.
For it is not the one commending himself who is approved, but the one the Lord commends.

Ὁ συνιστάνων, subst. ptc. "the one who commends (himself)." Συνιστάνων, nom. sg. masc. of pres. act. ptc. of συνίστημι, "commend." Ἑαυτόν, acc. 3rd sg. masc. pron. ἑαυτοῦ, -ῆς, -οῦ "himself." Harris 728: "The phrase ἐκεῖνός ἐστιν δόκιμος is the pivot on which the verse turns. ἐκεῖνός is emphatic, 'he and he alone' (NEB)." Ἐκεῖνός, nom. sg. masc. pron. ἐκεῖνος, -η, -ο, "that one." Δόκιμος, nom. sg. masc. adj. δόκιμος, -ον, "approved." BDAG 256b: "pert. to being genuine on the basis of testing, *approved (by test), tried and true, genuine.*" Paul uses δόκιμος to describe a tried and tested servant of Christ, one whose worth has been proved (Rom 16:10; cf. 2 Tim 2:15). He uses the cognate verb, δοκιμάζω, in reference to the testing of Christian workers (2 Cor 8:22) and the works of believers (1 Cor 3:13; Gal 6:4). Ὅν, acc. sg. masc. pron. ὅς, ἥ, ὅ, "the one whom (the Lord commends)." Συνίστησιν, 3rd sg. pres. act. indic. of συνίστημι, "commend."

FOR FURTHER STUDY

91. Appeal by the Meekness and Gentleness of Christ (10:1)

Carson, D.A. "Disobedience Versus Discipline: An Appeal for Obedient Faith (10:1–6)." In *From Triumphalism to Maturity: An Exposition of 2 Corinthians 10–13*, 31–55. Grand Rapids: Baker, 1984.

Lambrecht, J. "Paul's Appeal and the Obedience to Christ: The Line of Thought in 2 Corinthians 10:1–6." *Bib* 77 (1996): 398–416.

Leivestad, R. "'The Meekness and Gentleness of Christ' II Cor. X.1," *NTS* 12 (1965–66): 156–64.

Weber. V. "Erklärung von 2 Kor. 10,1–6." *BZ* 1 (1903): 64–78.

92. Military Metaphors (10:3–6)

Gale, H. M. *The Use of Analogy in the Letters of Paul.* Philadelphia: Westminster, 1964.

Malherbe, A. J. "Antisthenes and Odysseus and Paul at War." *HTR* 76 (1983): 143–73.

Murphy-O'Connor, J. "Paul Takes the Offensive (10:1–18)." In *The Theology of the Second Letter to the Corinthians*, 99–106. Cambridge: Cambridge University Press, 1991.

Roetzel, C. J. "The Language of War (2 Cor. 10:1–6) and the Language of Weakness (2 Cor. 11:21b–13:10)." *BibInt* 17 (2007): 77–99.

93. Ministry Rights and χανών *(10:13–15)*

Catchpole, D. R. "Paul, James and the Apostolic Decree." *NTS* 23 (1977): 436–39.

Goulder, M. D. *Early Christian Conflict in Corinth: Paul and the Followers of Peter.* Peabody, MA: Hendrickson, 2001.

Judge, E. A. "The Regional χανών for Requisitioned Transport." In G. H. R. Horsley, *New Documents Illustrating Early Christianity: A Review of the Greek Inscriptions and Papyri Published in 1976,* 1:36–45. North Ryde, UK: Macquarie University, 1981.

Strange, J. F. "2 Corinthians 10:13–16 Illuminated by a Recently Published Inscription." *BA* 46 (1983): 167–68.

Wong, K. H. *Boasting and Foolishness: A Study of 2 Cor 10, 12–18 and 11, 1a.* Hong Kong: Alliance Bible Seminary, 1998.

94. Boasting and Self-Commendation *(10:12–18)*

Carson, D. A. "The Ugliness of Spiritual One-Upmanship: How Not to Boast in the Lord (10:7–18)." In *From Triumphalism to Maturity: An Exposition of 2 Corinthians 10–13,* 57–80. Grand Rapids: Baker, 1984.

Dewey, A. J. "A Matter of Honor: A Social-Historical Analysis of 2 Corinthians 10." *HTR* 78 (1985): 209–17.

Fahy, T. "St. Paul's 'Boasting' and 'Weakness.'" *ITQ* 31 (1964): 214–27.

Forbes, C. B. "Comparison, Self-Praise and Irony: Paul's Boasting and the Conventions of Hellenistic Rhetoric." *NTS* 32 (1986): 1–30.

Hafemann, S. J. "'Self-Commendation' and Apostolic Legitimacy in 2 Corinthians: A Pauline Dialectic." *NTS* 36 (1990): 66–88.

Henning J. "The Measure of Man: A Study of 2 Cor. 10:12." *CBQ* 8 (1946): 332–43.

Judge, E. A. "Paul's Boasting in Relation to Contemporary Professional Practice." *ABR* 16 (1968): 37–50.

Lambrecht, J. "Dangerous Boasting: Paul's Self-Commendation in 2 Corinthians 10–13." In *The Corinthian Correspondence,* edited by R. Bieringer, 325–46. Leuven: Leuven University, 1996.

Travis, S. "Paul's Boasting in 2 Corinthians 10–12." *SE* 6 (1973): 527–32.

95. Paul's Use of the OT *(10:17–18)*

Capes, D. *Old Testament Yahweh Texts in Paul's Christology.* WUNT 2/47. Tübingen: Mohr, 1992.

Wong, E. "'Lord' in 2 Corinthians 10.17." *LouvStud* 17 (1992): 243–53.

HOMILETICAL SUGGESTIONS

Christian "Warfare" *(10:2–6)*

1. Living in the world but not waging war by the standards of the world (v. 3)
2. "Weapons" for destroying "strongholds," i.e., arguments against the knowledge of God (vv. 4–5a)

3. Taking every thought captive to Christ and dealing with disobedience (vv. 5b–6)

The Purpose of Ministry: To Build People Up, Not Tear Them Down (10:8–11)

1. Ministerial authority is given for building up, not tearing down (v. 8)
2. There is a time for confronting unfair criticism (vv. 9–11)
3. The need for consistency in written and face-to-face communication (v. 11)

Boasting within Appropriate Limits (10:12–18)

1. Avoid involvement in inappropriate comparisons with other people (v. 12)
2. Restrict boasting to work done in the field to which God has assigned us (vv. 13–14)
3. Don't take credit for work done by others (vv. 15–16)
4. Boasting is best to be about the Lord, from whom true commendation comes (vv. 17–18)

B. A PLEA FOR TOLERANCE AND CONDEMNATION OF THE OPPONENTS (11:1–15)

In this passage Paul foreshadows the "fool's speech," which follows in 11:16–12:13. He explains that his great concern about his readers' gullibility forces him to make this speech. He is concerned lest their minds be led astray from devotion to Christ (vv. 2–3) by those who question his credentials and proclaim a different gospel (v. 4). He insists that he is in no way inferior to these "super-apostles" (vv. 5–6). He responds to criticisms of his practice of not asking for or accepting financial support from the Corinthians (vv. 7–8). He appears to have come under criticism on two counts. First, the Corinthians felt affronted because he refused to accept their assistance, especially when by so doing he was forced to undertake menial work to support himself, work they regarded as degrading for an apostle, while accepting support from other churches (vv. 7–9). Second, this refusal was misconstrued as evidence that Paul did not really love the Corinthians. If he would not accept their money, surely that meant he had no real affection for them (v. 11). Despite these criticisms Paul informs his readers that he has no intention of changing his practice, because he wishes to undercut claims made by his opponents to work on the same basis as he does (v. 12). There follows a strong verbal attack in which Paul dispenses with irony and reveals clearly his opinion of his opponents (vv. 13–15).

1. The Corinthians' Gullibility (11:1–6)

STRUCTURE

1 Ὄφελον ἀνείχεσθέ μου μικρόν τι ἀφροσύνης·
  ἀλλὰ καὶ ἀνέχεσθέ μου.
2 ζηλῶ γὰρ ὑμᾶς θεοῦ ζήλῳ,
  ἡρμοσάμην γὰρ ὑμᾶς
    ἑνὶ ἀνδρὶ παρθένον ἁγνὴν
    παραστῆσαι τῷ Χριστῷ·
3 φοβοῦμαι δὲ μή πως,
  ὡς ὁ ὄφις ἐξηπάτησεν Εὕαν
      ἐν τῇ πανουργίᾳ αὐτοῦ,
  φθαρῇ τὰ νοήματα ὑμῶν
    ἀπὸ τῆς ἁπλότητος [καὶ τῆς ἁγνότητος]
    τῆς εἰς τὸν Χριστόν.
4   εἰ μὲν γὰρ   ὁ ἐρχόμενος
              ἄλλον Ἰησοῦν κηρύσσει
              ὃν οὐκ ἐκηρύξαμεν,
            ἢ πνεῦμα ἕτερον λαμβάνετε
              ὃ οὐκ ἐλάβετε,
            ἢ εὐαγγέλιον ἕτερον
              ὃ οὐκ ἐδέξασθε,
  καλῶς ἀνέχεσθε.

5   λογίζομαι γὰρ μηδὲν ὑστερηκέναι
                    τῶν ὑπερλίαν ἀποστόλων.
6   εἰ δὲ καὶ ἰδιώτης τῷ λόγῳ,
    ἀλλ᾿ οὐ   τῇ γνώσει,
    ἀλλ᾿ ἐν παντὶ φανερώσαντες
    ἐν πᾶσιν εἰς ὑμᾶς.

VERSE 1

Ὄφελον ἀνείχεσθέ μου μικρόν τι ἀφροσύνης· ἀλλὰ καὶ ἀνέχεσθέ μου.
I wish you would put up with a little foolishness from me. Yes, do put up with me!

Paul regarded the parading of his credentials in the "fool's speech," which is to follow (11:16–12:13), as an act of folly. Yet the situation in Corinth forced him to do so,
and that, not as he would have chosen, but in accordance with the criteria favored by
his opponents and apparently accepted by his converts.

BDF (§448[6]): "᾿Ὄφελον . . .· ἀλλὰ καὶ ἀνέχεσθε ('I will not only express the
wish, but I forthwith entreat you [ἀνέχεσθε taken as impera.], or 'but you have already
done it' [ἀνέχ. taken as indic.])." Ὄφελον, particle, "I wish." ZG 556: *would that / if
only!* w. past tense of indic. introducing an unrealized (or improbable) wish, w. impf.
ref. pres. time, 'if only you would put up with. . . .'" BDAG 743d: "an expression of
a wish that someth. had taken place or would take place, *or that, would that* w. the
impf. to express present time." Moule 137: "although in II Cor xi.1 the wish is, after
all, realized, the ὄφελον clause itself regards it as unattainable." Seifrid 401: "Paul's
expression of unattainable wish . . . may be taken in two senses . . . [1] it constitutes
a request of the Corinthians to allow him to speak foolishly . . . [2] The foolishness
that Paul requests the Corinthians to endure may be understood as that which *they*
regard as foolish." Cf. R 923. Ἀνείχεσθε, 2nd pl. impf. mid. indic. of ἀνέχω. BDAG
78b: "to regard w. tolerance, *endure, bear with, put up with,*" takes gen. of person
tolerated: μου. Μου, 1st sg. gen. ἐγώ, dir. obj. of ἀνέχεσθε. Μικρόν τι, ZG 556: "*a little,*
w. partitive gen. *a little (bit of).*" Μικρόν, acc. sg. neut. adj. μικρός, -ά, -όν, "little." R
486: an adv. acc. Ἀφροσύνης, gen. sg. fem. ἀφροσύνη, -ης, ἡ, "foolishness." Harris 732:
"ἀφροσύνης, which may be classed as a partitive genitive . . . could refer to the foolish
talk or more specifically, to the foolish boasting that was forced on Paul by circumstances at Corinth (cf. 12:11)."

Ἀλλὰ καί, ZG 556: "with indic. *but in fact you do,* or impv. 2nd pl. *nay, you must. . . .*"
Ἀνέχεσθε, 2nd pl. pres. mid. indic. of ἀνέχω, "put up with." When Paul entreats his
readers to put up with him, it is prob. a sign of his own embarrassment about the whole
exercise rather than any concern that they might see it as inappropriate. R 1186: "In
2 Cor. 11:1, ἀλλὰ καὶ ἀνέχεσθε, the tone of irony makes it doubtful whether to take
ἀλλά as copulative or adversative." Μου, gen. 1 sg. ἐγώ, dir. obj. of ἀνείχεσθε.

Thrall 2:659: "There is some ambiguity in the second part of the verse, since the
verb ἀνέχεσθέ may be either indicative or imperative . . . the indicative, affirming that

his readers do bear with him. . . . It is preferable to understand the ἀνέχεσθε of v. 1 as also an imperative. . . . From the point of view of rhetorical technique, Paul is employing . . . the method of 'prodiorthosis': he asks in advance for his readers' toleration of anything he may say that they might find uncongenial." Barnett 498 prefers the indic.

Carson 83: "If the Corinthians can put up with his foolishness as *they* measure foolishness, surely they will put up with a little of his foolishness as *he* measures foolishness! Alternatively, it is just possible he means something a little different, but no less ironical: the Corinthians have already shown they are prepared to put up with the species of conduct Paul calls foolishness, for it is just such conduct that characterizes the intruders."

VERSE 2

ζηλῶ γὰρ ὑμᾶς θεοῦ ζήλῳ,
For I am jealous for you with a godly jealousy,

Ζηλῶ, 1st sg. pres. act. indic. of ζηλόω, "be jealous." Ὑμᾶς, 2nd pl. pers. pron., σύ "you." Θεοῦ ζήλῳ, lit. "with a jealousy of God." CSB: "a godly jealousy." Moule 184: "Is II Cor. xi.2 θεοῦ ζήλῳ to be interpreted as a *divine* (i.e. *supernaturally great*) *eagerness*, or is it nearer to the meaning *an eagerness which is God's own eagerness* (or *which springs from God Himself*)?" Carson 84: "Divine jealousy . . . is a form of holy outrage mingled with love." Θεοῦ, gen. sg. masc. descriptive gen. Ζήλῳ, dat. sg. masc. ζῆλος, -ου, ὁ, "jealousy."

ἡρμοσάμην γὰρ ὑμᾶς ἑνὶ ἀνδρί
because I have promised you in marriage to one husband—

Paul saw himself as the agent of God through whom his converts were betrothed to Christ (the "father" of the bride, as it were), and felt under obligation to ensure that they would be presented as a pure virgin to her one husband at the nuptial ceremony, when the marriage is consummated at the parousia of Christ (cf. Eph 5:27; Col 1:22). Ἡρμοσάμην, 1st sg. aor. mid. indic. of ἁρμόζω, "betroth." BDF (§316[1]): "The middle is occasionally used . . . where an active is expected. . . . ἡρμοσάμην ὑμᾶς ἀνδρί 2 C 11:2 'betrothed' for ἥρμοσα." Ὑμᾶς, 2nd pl. pers. pron. "you," dir. obj. of ἡρμοσάμην. Ἑνὶ ἀνδρί, "to one husband," indir. obj. of ἡρμοσάμην. Ἑνί, dat. sg. masc. adj., "one." Ἀνδρί, dat. sg. masc. ἀνήρ, ἀνδρός, ὁ, "husband."

παρθένον ἁγνὴν παραστῆσαι τῷ Χριστῷ·
to present a pure virgin to Christ.

Παρθένον, acc. sg. fem. παρθένος, -ου, ἡ, "virgin," dir. obj. of παραστῆσαι, stands in appos. with ὑμᾶς. Ἁγνήν, acc. sg. fem. adj. ἁγνός, -ή, -όν, "pure," qualifies παρθένον. Παραστῆσαι, aor. act. inf. of παρίστημι, "present." Τῷ Χριστῷ, dat. sg. masc. indir. obj. of παραστῆσαι "to Christ."

VERSE 3

φοβοῦμαι δὲ μή πως, ὡς ὁ ὄφις ἐξηπάτησεν Εὕαν ἐν τῇ πανουργίᾳ αὐτοῦ,
But I fear that, as the serpent deceived Eve by his cunning,

Φοβοῦμαι, 1st sg. pres. mid. indic. of φοβέω, "fear, be afraid." Μή πως. BDAG 901d: "as conj . . . marker of a neg. perspective expressing misgiving, frequently rendered *lest*." Ὡς, conj., "as." Ὄφις, nom. sg. masc. ὄφις, -εως, ὁ, "serpent." Ἐξηπάτησεν, 3rd sg. aor. act. indic. of ἐξαπατάω, "deceive." Εὕαν, acc. sg. fem. proper noun Εὕα,-ας, ἡ, "Eve." Ἐν, prep. with dat. τῇ πανουργίᾳ αὐτοῦ, "by his cunning." Πανουργίᾳ, dat. sg. fem. πανουργία,-ας, ἡ, "cunning, craftiness."

φθαρῇ τὰ νοήματα ὑμῶν ἀπὸ τῆς ἁπλότητος [καὶ τῆς ἁγνότητος] τῆς εἰς τὸν Χριστόν.
your minds may be seduced from a sincere and pure devotion to Christ.

Φθαρῇ, 3rd sg. aor. pass. subjunc. of φθείρω, "seduce." Νοήματα, acc. pl. neut. νόημα, -ατος, τό, "mind." Harris 739: "νοήματα here refers to 'thinking processes' and 'attitudes,' as in 3:14; 4:4, not to 'stratagems' (as in 2:11) or (in the singular) to 'design' (10:5)." Ἀπό, prep. with gen. τῆς ἁπλότητος, "from the sincerity," ἀπό, with gen. designating separation (cf. BDF §211). Ἁπλότητος, gen. sg. fem. ἁπλότης,-ητος, ἡ, "sincerity." Ἁγνότητος, gen. sg. fem. ἁγνότης, -ητος, ἡ, "purity." Τῆς εἰς τὸν Χριστόν, descriptive phrase qualifying τῆς ἁπλότητος [καὶ τῆς ἁγνότητος], "that is to Christ."

Harris, *Prepositions*, 61: "The main danger confronting the Corinthian church was intellectual deception—their adulterous flirting with a false gospel (2Co 11:4c) and their countenancing of a different Jesus and an alien Spirit (2Co 11:4a–b). If such deception took place, the casualty would be their singleness of outlook and purpose and their original virginity as a church betrothed to Christ, her heavenly bridegroom and one husband (2Co 12:2)."

VERSE 4

εἰ μὲν γὰρ ὁ ἐρχόμενος ἄλλον Ἰησοῦν κηρύσσει ὃν οὐκ ἐκηρύξαμεν,
For if a person comes and preaches another Jesus, whom we did not preach,

Εἰ μὲν γὰρ ὁ ἐρχόμενος . . . , the prot. of a first-class cond. sentence (formed with εἰ plus the indic.) that assumes that a situation is correct for the sake of the argument. Ὁ ἐρχόμενος, "he who comes . . ."; CSB, "a person comes." Ἐρχόμενος, nom. sg. masc. of pres. mid. ptc. of ἔρχομαι, "come." Ἄλλον Ἰησοῦν, "another Jesus," dir. obj. of κηρύσσει. Paul's opponents were apparently triumphalist in character and left no room for the experience of weakness or suffering. It may be that in their preaching Paul's opponents stressed the power and glory of Christ to the virtual exclusion of the fact that he had also known weakness, humiliation, persecution, suffering, and death. Paul preached Christ crucified as Lord, so a proclamation like that outlined above would seem to him to be the preaching of "another Jesus." Ἄλλον, acc. sg. masc. adj. ἄλλος,

-η, -ο, "another." BDAG 47a: *"different in kind . . .* interchanging w. ἕτερος. . . ." R 1186–87: "Just as ἄλλος (cf. 2 Cor. 11:4) can be used in the sense of ἕτερος (when it means 'different,' not merely 'second'), so ἀλλά can mean 'another' in contrast to the preceding." Κηρύσσει, 3rd sg. pres. act. indic. of κηρύσσω, "preach, proclaim." Ὅν, acc. sg. masc. rel. pron. ὅς, ἥ, ὅ, "who(m)," dir. obj. of (οὐκ) ἐκηρύξαμεν. Ἐκηρύξαμεν, 1st pl. aor. act. indic. of κηρύσσω, "preach, proclaim."

ἢ πνεῦμα ἕτερον λαμβάνετε ὃ οὐκ ἐλάβετε,
or you receive a different spirit, which you had not received,

Ἤ, particle, "or." Πνεῦμα ἕτερον, "another spirit," dir. obj. of λαμβάνετε. Ἕτερον, acc. sg. neut. adj. ἕτερος, -α, -ον, "different," qualifies πνεῦμα. Λαμβάνετε, 2nd pl. pres. act. indic. of λαμβάνω, "receive." Ὁ οὐκ ἐλάβετε, "which you had not received." Ὁ, acc. sg. neut. rel. pron. ὅς, ἥ, ὅ, "which." Ἐλάβετε, 2nd pl. aor. act. indic. of λαμβάνω, "receive."

Hafemann 428–29: "A *mistaken* emphasis on the miraculous by these so-called super-apostles (11:5) resulted in a construal of the Spirit as a wonder-worker rather than a guarantor of the kerygma." L. L. Belleville, "Paul's Polemic and the Theology of the Spirit in Second Corinthians," *CBQ* 58 (1966): 281–304.

ἢ εὐαγγέλιον ἕτερον ὃ οὐκ ἐδέξασθε, καλῶς ἀνέχεσθε.
or a different gospel, which you had not accepted, you put up with it splendidly!

Ἤ, particle, "or." Εὐαγγέλιον ἕτερον, "another gospel," dir. obj. of (οὐκ) ἐδέξασθε. Εὐαγγέλιον, acc. sg. neut. εὐαγγέλιον, -ου, τό, "gospel." Ἕτερον, acc. sg. neut. adj. ἕτερος, -α, -ον, "different," qualifies εὐαγγέλιον. BDF (§306[4]): "Ἄλλος and ἕτερος are sometimes combined, it seems, only for the sake of variety: 2 C 11:4 ἄλλον Ἰησοῦν . . . πνεῦμα ἕτερον . . . εὐαγγέλιον ἕτερον." Cf. R 747, 748. Ὁ οὐκ ἐδέξασθε, "which you had not accepted." Ἐδέξασθε, 2nd pl. aor. mid. indic. of δέχομαι, "accept."

Καλῶς ἀνέχεσθε, apod. of first-class cond. sentence, "you accept it well (enough)." BDAG 506a: *"you put up with it all right."* Καλῶς, adv., "well." ZG 556: "here ironic, *with ease."* Ἀνέχεσθε, 2nd pl. pres. mid. indic. of ἀνέχω, "put up with, bear," Paul uses the same word in v. 1.

Barnett 506: "By saying they 'preached another Jesus' and that 'you receive a different spirit . . . a different gospel,' he may be pointing up the very absurdity of the idea (cf. Gal 1:6–7)." Cf. Thrall 2: Excursus IX 667–71.

VERSE 5

λογίζομαι γὰρ μηδὲν ὑστερηκέναι τῶν ὑπερλίαν ἀποστόλων.
Now I consider myself in no way inferior to those "super-apostles."

Λογίζομαι, 1st sg. pres. mid. indic. of λογίζομαι, "consider." Γάρ, ZG 556: *"for* would imply an ellipsis, e.g. 'you accept them, why not me?'" Μηδέν as subst., "nothing."

CSB: "in no way." BDAG 647c: "can be rendered *not . . . at all, in no way.*" ZG 556: "acc. of respect." Ὑστερηκέναι, pf. act. inf. of ὑστερέω, "lack, be inferior," takes gen. of comp. Harris 746: "ὑστερηκέναι is a complementary infinitive after λογίζομαι, with the subject of the infinitive identical with that of the governing verb." Τῶν ὑπερλίαν ἀποστόλων, gen. of comp. "to those super-apostles." Ὑπερλίαν adv. "beyond measure, super-." Ἀποστόλων, gen. pl. masc. ἀπόστολος, -ου, ὁ, "apostle."

VERSE 6

εἰ δὲ καὶ ἰδιώτης τῷ λόγῳ, ἀλλ᾽ οὐ τῇ γνώσει,
Even if I am untrained in public speaking, I am certainly not untrained in knowledge.

This statement could be understood in two ways: (1) as a straightforward conces-sion that in respect of rhetorical skills in public speaking, Paul is inferior to his oppo-nents; and (2) as a rhetorical device by which he places himself in an inferior position vis-à-vis his opponents even though he knows (and expects his readers to know) that he is in fact superior to them. The former alternative fits the context better. Paul's pur-pose seems to be, while conceding inferiority in the less important area of rhetorical skills, to claim superiority in the far more important area of knowledge. Cf. Barnett 509–10: "That he was inferior to them (and Apollos?) does not logically require that he was without gifts in that respect. Paul's dialectic in this verse should not lead us to draw wrong conclusions."
Ἰδιώτης, nom. sg. masc. ἰδιώτης, -ου, ὁ, "untrained person." ZG 557: "an *amateur* (in Eng. sense), *not a specialist, not proficient,*" εἰμί omitted (cf. BDF §128[2]). Τῷ λόγῳ, dat. of respect "in speaking." Λόγῳ, dat. sg. masc. λόγος, -ου, ὁ, "word, speech." Τῇ γνώσει, dat. of respect "in knowledge." Γνώσει, dat. sg. fem. γνῶσις, -εως, ἡ, "knowl-edge." Thrall 2:678: "Allowing, though only conditionally, that in this respect he can-not match their professionalism, Paul nevertheless insists that in respect of knowledge he is their equal, or indeed their superior."

ἀλλ᾽ ἐν παντὶ φανερώσαντες ἐν πᾶσιν εἰς ὑμᾶς.
Indeed, we have in every way made that clear to you in everything.

Ἐν, prep. with dat. παντί "in every way." Παντί, dat. sg. neut. adj. πᾶς, πᾶσα, πᾶν, "all, every." Φανερώσαντες, nom. pl. masc. of aor. act. ptc. of φανερόω, "make known." Moule 119: "in II Cor. xi.6 there appears to be an obviously 'epistolary' plural par-ticiple." Z §8: "another use of the plural for a single person is the epistolary plural, whereby the writer as it were associates himself with the reader. This plural seems to be rare in the Pauline letters, but is found . . . especially [in] the alternation of singular and plural in 2 Cor 10, 1–11, 6, where Paul is certainly speaking of himself alone. For this reason it is rash to regard Paul's «we» as always referring to the apostle along with his associates." Ἐν, prep. with dat. πᾶσιν, "in all things." Πᾶσιν, dat. pl. neut. adj. πᾶς, πᾶσα, πᾶν, "all, every." Εἰς, prep. with acc. ὑμᾶς, "to you."

2. The Matter of Financial Remuneration (11:7–15)

STRUCTURE

7 Ἡ ἁμαρτίαν ἐποίησα ἐμαυτὸν ταπεινῶν
  ἵνα ὑμεῖς ὑψωθῆτε,
  ὅτι δωρεὰν τὸ τοῦ θεοῦ εὐαγγέλιον εὐηγγελισάμην ὑμῖν;
8 ἄλλας ἐκκλησίας ἐσύλησα
  λαβὼν ὀψώνιον
  πρὸς τὴν ὑμῶν διακονίαν,
9   καὶ παρὼν πρὸς ὑμᾶς καὶ ὑστερηθεὶς
  οὐ κατενάρκησα οὐθενός·
  τὸ γὰρ ὑστέρημά μου προσανεπλήρωσαν οἱ ἀδελφοὶ ἐλθόντες ἀπὸ Μακεδονίας,
  καὶ ἐν παντὶ ἀβαρῆ ἐμαυτὸν ὑμῖν ἐτήρησα
          καὶ τηρήσω.
10 ἔστιν ἀλήθεια Χριστοῦ ἐν ἐμοὶ
  ὅτι ἡ καύχησις αὕτη οὐ φραγήσεται εἰς ἐμὲ
          ἐν τοῖς κλίμασιν τῆς Ἀχαΐας.
11 διὰ τί;
  ὅτι οὐκ ἀγαπῶ ὑμᾶς;
  ὁ θεὸς οἶδεν.
12 Ὁ δὲ ποιῶ,
  καὶ ποιήσω,
  ἵνα ἐκκόψω τὴν ἀφορμὴν τῶν θελόντων ἀφορμήν,
  ἵνα ἐν ᾧ καυχῶνται εὑρεθῶσιν καθὼς καὶ ἡμεῖς.
13 οἱ γὰρ τοιοῦτοι ψευδαπόστολοι,
          ἐργάται δόλιοι,
          μετασχηματιζόμενοι εἰς ἀποστόλους Χριστοῦ.
14 καὶ οὐ θαῦμα·
  αὐτὸς γὰρ ὁ Σατανᾶς μετασχηματίζεται
          εἰς ἄγγελον φωτός.
15 οὐ μέγα οὖν
  εἰ καὶ οἱ διάκονοι αὐτοῦ μετασχηματίζονται
          ὡς διάκονοι δικαιοσύνης·
          ὧν τὸ τέλος ἔσται κατὰ τὰ ἔργα αὐτῶν.

VERSE 7

Ἡ ἁμαρτίαν ἐποίησα ἐμαυτὸν ταπεινῶν ἵνα ὑμεῖς ὑψωθῆτε,
Or did I commit a sin by humbling myself so that you might be exalted,

According to Acts 18:1–4, Paul worked as a tentmaker to provide for his needs during his first stay in Corinth. By so doing he "humbled" himself, for among the Greeks it was regarded as degrading for philosophers or itinerant teachers to engage in manual work to supply their needs. No doubt aware of this, Paul asks with ironic exaggeration whether he committed a "sin" by so humbling himself when he preached God's gospel free of charge. Alternatively, it has been suggested that Paul's practice was a "sin" because it contravened the dominical teaching that those who preach the gospel should receive their living from the gospel (cf. 1 Cor 9:14). Another view is that Paul's preaching free of charge was a "sin" because it involved a refusal of the Corinthians' offer of financial support. To refuse benefaction in the ancient world was a rejection of friendship and constituted an insult to those who offered it. While each of these suggestions has merit, the first seems to fit best in the context where Paul's question includes the notion of humbling himself while preaching free of charge. The expected answer to Paul's question is, of course, a resounding "No."

Ἦ, interr. particle. ZG 557: "introducing a [rhetorical] question." Cf. BDF §440[1]. Ἁμαρτίαν, acc. sg. fem. ἁμαρτία, -ίας, ἡ, "sin," dir. obj. of ἐποίησα. Ἐποίησα, 1st sg. aor. act. indic. of ποιέω, "commit." BDAG 840d: "do, commit, be guilty of sins and vices." Barnett 513: "Paul's 'sin' was that he did not accept financial support from the Corinthians while preaching the gospel of God to them. To be sure, from their viewpoint Paul had painfully breached social conventions in rejecting their patronage of money, gifts, and hospitality, which were at that time conventionally given to those who taught and lectured." Ἐμαυτόν, acc. 1st sg. masc. reflex. pron. ἐμαυτοῦ, -ῆς, "myself," dir. obj. of ταπεινῶν. Ταπεινῶν, nom. sg. masc. of pres. act. ptc. of ταπεινόω, "humble." Ἵνα, with subjunc. ὑψωθῆτε expresses purpose, "so that you may be exalted." Ὑψωθῆτε, 2nd pl. aor. pass. subjunc. ὑψόω "exalt." Ὑμεῖς, nom. 2nd pl. pron. "you," subj. of ὑψωθῆτε.

ὅτι δωρεὰν τὸ τοῦ θεοῦ εὐαγγέλιον εὐηγγελισάμην ὑμῖν;
because I preached the gospel of God to you free of charge?

Ὅτι, a conj., introduces the reason why Paul "humbled" himself. δωρεάν, adv., "freely, free of charge," qualifies εὐηγγελισάμην. ZG 557: "gratis, freely, without payment." Τὸ τοῦ θεοῦ εὐαγγέλιον, "the gospel of God." Τοῦ θεοῦ, poss. gen. "God's (gospel)." Εὐαγγέλιον, acc. sg. neut. εὐαγγέλιον, -ου, τό, "gospel." Εὐηγγελισάμην, 1st sg. aor. mid. indic. of εὐαγγελίζω, "preach the gospel/good news." Ὑμῖν, dat. 2nd pl. σύ, "you," indir. obj. of εὐηγγελισάμην.

VERSE 8

ἄλλας ἐκκλησίας ἐσύλησα λαβὼν ὀψώνιον πρὸς τὴν ὑμῶν διακονίαν,
I robbed other churches by taking pay from them to minister to you.

BDAG 955c: "I sacked (or looted/raided) other churches and thus obtained the money that enabled me to serve you free of charge." Ἄλλας, acc. pl. fem. adj. ἄλλος, -η, -ο, "other." Ἐκκλησίας, acc. pl. fem. ἐκκλησία, -ας, ἡ, "church." Ἐσύλησα, 1st sg. aor. act. indic. of συλάω, "rob." This verb is used in the papyri with the mng. "to pillage," and in classical Greek it was used predominantly in a military context mng. "to strip" (a dead soldier of his armor). Why Paul chose such a strong word is difficult to determine. Perhaps he wanted to bring home to the Corinthians the lengths to which he had gone to make the gospel available to them free of charge, i.e., even to the extent of "robbing" other churches by accepting support from them while working in Corinth, work from which the donors would receive no benefits. Thrall 2:684: "Paul's manner of expression here may be designed to dispel the suspicion that, having rejected would-be benefactors in Corinth, he had willingly become the client of other Christian patrons. The verb ἐσύλησα means, 'I plundered,' and this is the opposite of receiving something as a benefaction."

Λαβὼν ὀψώνιον πρὸς τὴν ὑμῶν διακονίαν explains the nature of Paul's "robbery" of other churches. Λαβών, nom. sg. masc. of aor. act. ptc. of λαμβάνω, "take, accept payment" Ὀψώνιον, acc. sg. neut. ὀψώνιον, -ου, τό, "pay, wages." Πρός, prep. with acc. τὴν . . . διακονίαν, "for the ministry." Ὑμῶν, obj. gen. "to you."

VERSE 9

καὶ παρὼν πρὸς ὑμᾶς καὶ ὑστερηθεὶς οὐ κατενάρκησα οὐθενός·
When I was present with you and in need, I did not burden anyone,

παρών, nom. sg. masc. of pres. ptc. of πάρειμι, "be present." Πρός, prep. with acc. ὑμᾶς, "with you." Ὑστερηθείς, nom. sg. masc. of aor. pass. ptc. of ὑστερέω, "suffer lack." ZG 557: "aor. inceptive, *run short*." Κατενάρκησα, 1st sg. aor. act. indic. of καταναρκάω, with gen. "be a burden (to someone)." Οὐθενός, gen. sg. masc. indef. adj. οὐθείς, "no one."

τὸ γὰρ ὑστέρημά μου προσανεπλήρωσαν οἱ ἀδελφοὶ ἐλθόντες ἀπὸ Μακεδονίας,
since the brothers who came from Macedonia supplied my needs.

Ὑστέρημα, acc. sg. neut. ὑστέρημα, -ατος, τό, "What is lacking, needs," dir. obj. προσανεπλήρωσαν. Προσανεπλήρωσαν, 3rd pl. aor. act. indic. of προσαναπληρόω, "supply, fill up." Ἀδελφοί, nom. pl. masc. ἀδελφός, οῦ, ὁ, "brother," subj. of προσανεπλήρωσαν. Ἐλθόντες, nom. pl. masc. of aor. act. ptc. of ἔρχομαι, "come." Ἀπό, prep. with gen. Μακεδονίας, "from Macedonia." Μακεδονίας, gen. sg. fem. Μακεδονία, -ας, ἡ, "Macedonia."

Harris 760: "while resident in Corinth, Paul 'ran short' of funds to supply the necessities of life, but even during the resulting period of need, he never squeezed charity from anyone."

καὶ ἐν παντὶ ἀβαρῆ ἐμαυτὸν ὑμῖν ἐτήρησα καὶ τηρήσω.
I have kept myself, and will keep myself, from burdening you in any way.

Ἐν, prep. with dat. παντί, "in everything." Ἀβαρῆ, acc. sg. masc. adj. ἀβαρής, -ές, "not burdensome." Ἐμαυτόν, acc. 1st sg. masc. reflex. pron. ἐμαυτοῦ, -ῆς, "myself," dir. obj. of ἐτήρησα. Ὑμῖν, dat. 2nd pl. σύ, "to you," indir. obj. of ἐτήρησα. Ἐτήρησα, 1st sg. aor. act. indic. of τηρέω, "keep." Τηρήσω, 1st sg. fut. act. indic. of τηρέω, "keep."

VERSE 10

ἔστιν ἀλήθεια Χριστοῦ ἐν ἐμοὶ ὅτι
As the truth of Christ is in me,

An oath formula, introduces an important affirmation by the apostle. ZG 557: "ἔστιν . . . ὅτι form of asserration, by the truth of Christ in me *(I assure you) that.* BDF (§397[3]): "Verbs of saying etc. take ὅτι to a very large extent . . . ἔστιν ἀλήθεια Χριστοῦ ἐν ἐμοί, ὅτι 2 C 11:10." Moule 112: "II Cor xi.10 ἔστιν ἀλήθεια Χριστοῦ ἐν ἐμοὶ ὅτι . . . presumably means *I am speaking Christian truth when I say that* . . . : if so, it is a much smaller and more particularized sense of ἀλήθεια as associated with Christ." Cf. R 1034. Ἀλήθεια, nom. sg. fem. ἀλήθεια, -ας, ἡ, "truth." Χριστοῦ, either poss. gen. ("Christ's truth"), gen. of source ("truth from Christ"), descriptive gen. ("truth of/ about Christ"), or subj. gen. ("truth given by Christ"). Harris 763: "Paul's appeal is not to 'truth about Christ' (objective genitive) that is communicated in his preaching but to divine 'truth given by Christ' (subjective genitive) that he has personally appropriated and is therefore in him (cf. 13:3) in the same way that the mind of Christ (1 Cor. 2:16) and the Spirit of Christ (Rom. 8:9) dwell in him." Ἐν, prep. with dat. ἐμοί, "in me."

ἡ καύχησις αὕτη οὐ φραγήσεται εἰς ἐμὲ ἐν τοῖς κλίμασιν τῆς Ἀχαΐας.
this boasting of mine will not be stopped in the regions of Achaia.

Καύχησις, nom. sg. fem. καύχησις, -εως, ἡ, "boasting." Αὕτη, nom. sg. fem. dem. pron. οὗτος, αὕτη, τοῦτο, "this." Φραγήσεται, 3rd sg. fut. pass. indic. of φράσσω, "silence." BDAG 1065a: "fig. ext. of 1a: *close* or *stop* the mouth, so that the pers. must remain silent." Εἰς, prep. with acc. ἐμέ, ZG 557: "*against me*; not directly translatable into Eng . . . ; *I will not be stopped from boasting, this boasting will never be stifled in me*." Ἐν, prep. with locat. dat. τοῖς κλίμασιν, "in the regions." Κλίμασιν, dat. pl. neut. κλίμα, -ατος, τό, "region." ZG 557: "*district, territory* (smaller than a χώρα)." Τῆς Ἀχαΐας, descriptive gen. "(regions) of Achaia," denotes the Roman province of Achaia, of which Corinth was the major city and administrative center. Ἀχαΐας, gen. sg. fem. Ἀχαΐα, -ας, ἡ, "Achaia."

VERSE 11

διὰ τί; ὅτι οὐκ ἀγαπῶ ὑμᾶς; ὁ θεὸς οἶδεν.
Why? Because I don't love you? God knows I do!

Διὰ τί, "why?" Ἀγαπῶ, 1st sg. pres. act. indic. of ἀγαπάω, "love." Ὑμᾶς, acc. 2nd pl. pron. σύ, "you," dir. obj. of ἀγαπῶ. Οἶδεν, 3rd sg. pf. act. indic. of οἶδα, "know." Because Paul's opponents could not silence his boasting, they tried to undermine his relationship with the Corinthians by suggesting his refusal to accept their assistance was proof that he did not really love them. Paul does not dignify their accusations with a reasoned reply. Instead, calling upon God as his witness, he simply affirms his love for his readers: "God knows I do!" (another oath formula?).

VERSE 12

Ὃ δὲ ποιῶ, καὶ ποιήσω,
But I will continue to do what I am doing,

Ὃ, acc. sg. neut. rel. pron. ὅς, ἥ, ὅ, "what." Ποιῶ, 1st sg. pres. act. indic. of ποιέω, "do." Ποιήσω, 1st sg. fut. act. indic. of ποιέω, "do."

ἵνα ἐκκόψω τὴν ἀφορμὴν τῶν θελόντων ἀφορμήν,
in order to deny an opportunity to those who want an opportunity (NRSV)

Ἵνα, with subjunc. ἐκκόψω expresses purpose, lit. "to cut off." Ἐκκόψω, 1st sg. aor. act. subjunc. of ἐκκόπτω, "cut off." BDAG 305b: "remove the occasion (= stop them from)." Ἀφορμήν, acc. sg. fem. ἀφορμή, -ῆς, ἡ, "opportunity, occasion." ZG 557: "*pretext, opportunity.*" Ἐκκόψω τὴν ἀφορμήν, ZG 557: "Eng. *I will cut the ground from under the feet.*" Θελόντων, gen. pl. masc. of pres. act. ptc. of θέλω, "want, desire."

ἵνα ἐν ᾧ καυχῶνται εὑρεθῶσιν καθὼς καὶ ἡμεῖς.
to be recognized as our equals in what they boast about (NRSV).

Ἵνα with subjunc. εὑρεθῶσιν expresses purpose "to be found, recognized." Εὑρεθῶσιν, 3rd pl. aor. pass. subjunc. εὑρίσκω, "find." Ἐν, prep. with dat. ᾧ, "in what (they boast about)." Harris, *Prepositions*, 132: "in the matter about which [ἐν ᾧ] they boast." Καυχῶνται, 3rd pl. pres. mid. indic. of καυχάομαι, "boast." Καθὼς καὶ ἡμεῖς, "even as we (are)." CSB: "as our equals." Καθώς conj. "as, just as."

Carson 99: "Paul's argument is psychologically effective; for it exposes the intruders as moneygrubbers, not humble and self-sacrificing leaders intent on the Corinthians' well-being."

Harris 770: "Paul, however, resolved not to surrender his advantage over his rivals, namely that no one could ever charge him with preaching for a fee or for profit or with burdening his converts. Rather he planned to continue his present policy in order to undercut his rivals' desire to be on a par with him with regard to financial support."

VERSE 13

οἱ γὰρ τοιοῦτοι ψευδαπόστολοι, ἐργάται δόλιοι,
For such people are false apostles, deceitful workers,

Paul now dispenses with irony, pers. defense, and explanations of his policy in money matters, and with striking virulence exposes the true character of his opponents. Τοιοῦτοι, nom. pl. masc. dem. pron. τοιοῦτος, -αύτη, -οῦτον, "such people." Ψευδαπόστολοι, nom. pl. masc. ψευδαπόστολος, -ου, ὁ, "false apostle." Ἐργάται, nom. pl. masc. ἐργάτης, -ου, ὁ, "worker." Δόλιοι, nom. pl. masc. adj. δόλιος, -ία, -ον, "deceitful."

μετασχηματιζόμενοι εἰς ἀποστόλους Χριστοῦ.
disguising themselves as apostles of Christ.

Μετασχηματιζόμενοι, nom. pl. masc. of pres. mid. ptc. of μετασχηματίζω, "disguise." BDAG 641d: "to feign to be what one is not, *change/disguise oneself.*" Εἰς, prep. with acc. ἀποστόλους, "as apostles." Χριστοῦ, either poss. gen. ("belonging to Christ") or subj. gen. ("sent by Christ").

Carson 100: "In light of the appalling directions the church is taking because of these false apostles, it is not surprising that the apostle's language is so strong. Two and a half centuries ago Bengel remarked that 'the Indifferentism, which is so pleasant to many in the present day, was not cultivated by Paul. He was no pleasant teacher of toleration.'"

VERSE 14

καὶ οὐ θαῦμα· αὐτὸς γὰρ ὁ Σατανᾶς μετασχηματίζεται εἰς ἄγγελον φωτός.
And no wonder! For Satan disguises himself as an angel of light.

Paul may be thinking here of Gen 3 and the deceitfulness of the serpent who "enlightened" Eve. Alternatively, there are stories in Jewish pseudepigraphical works in which Satan appears as an angel to deceive Eve (*Life of Adam and Eve* 9:1–3; *Apocalypse of Moses* 17:1), and the apostle could be alluding to these. Or it may simply be that Paul, as a result of his missionary experiences, came to recognize Satan's devices (cf. 2:11). Καὶ οὐ θαῦμα, "and no wonder!" Θαῦμα, nom. sg. neut. θαῦμα, -ατος, τό, "object of wonder." Αὐτός, nom. sg. masc. pron. in pred. position, "himself," emphasizes Σατανᾶς. Μετασχηματίζεται, 3rd sg. pres. mid. indic. of μετασχηματίζω, "disguise." Εἰς, prep. with acc. ἄγγελον, "as an angel." Ἄγγελον, acc. sg. masc. ἄγγελος, -ου, ὁ, "angel, messenger." Φωτός, gen. sg. neut. φῶς, φωτός, τό, "light." Prob. obj. gen. ("bringer of light"). Moule 175: "II Cor xi.14 ἄγγελον φωτός perhaps = ἄγγελον φωτεινόν."

VERSE 15

οὐ μέγα οὖν εἰ καὶ οἱ διάκονοι αὐτοῦ μετασχηματίζονται ὡς διάκονοι δικαιοσύνης·
So it is no great surprise if his servants also disguise themselves as servants of righteousness.

Μέγα, nom. sg. neut. subst. adj. μέγας, μεγάλη, μέγα, "great thing." Διάκονοι, nom. pl. masc. διάκονος, -ου, ὁ, "servant," subj. of μετασχηματίζονται. Μετασχηματίζονται,

3rd pl. pres. mid. indic. of μετασχηματίζω, "disguise." Ὡς, particle, "as." Διάκονοι δικαιοσύνης: Thrall 2:696–97 lists four main interpretations of this expression: (1) "upright servants of Christ." (2) They were "promoting his [Paul's] own gospel of righteousness, through faith, in competition with him." (3) "The opponents are Judaizers in the traditional sense." (4) "The phrase is an apostolic title, synonymous with ἀπόστολοι Χριστοῦ."

Δικαιοσύνης, descriptive gen. sg. fem. δικαιοσύνη, -ης, ἡ, "righteousness." Harris 775: "The genitive δικαιοσύνης could be adjectival 'righteous' or 'upright,' but more probably is objective, 'men in the service of righteousness' . . . Clearly, δικαιοσύνης does not carry its distinctive Pauline sense of a right standing before God that is graciously given by God and received by faith. Nor will it refer to a righteousness that depends on works of Torah obedience . . . there may be here in v. 15 an implicit contrast between Paul's rivals who are self-styled 'servants of righteousness' working under disguise as agents of Satan, and Paul himself, a true servant of righteousness working openly under a commission from God."

ὧν τὸ τέλος ἔσται κατὰ τὰ ἔργα αὐτῶν.
Their end will be according to their works.

Ὧν, gen. pl. masc. rel. pron. ὅς, ἥ, ὅ, "whose." Τέλος, nom. sg. neut. τέλος, -ους, τό, "end." Ἔσται, 3rd sg. fut. indic. εἰμί, "be." ESV: "correspond to." Κατά, prep. with acc. τὰ ἔργα, "according to (their) works." Ἔργα, acc. pl. neut. ἔργον, -ου, τό, "work, deeds."

FOR FURTHER STUDY

96. Paul's Appeal and the Betrothal Image (11:2–3)

Batey, R. "Paul's Bride Image: A Symbol of Realistic Eschatology." *Int* 17 (1963): 176–82.

Bieringer, R. "Paul's Divine Jealousy: The Apostle and His Communities in Relationship." *LouvStud* 17 (1992): 197–231.

Böttrich, C. "2 Cor 11,1 als Programmwort der 'Narrenrede.'" *Bib* 88 (1997): 135–39.

John, M. P. "The Jealousy of God—2 Cor 11:2." *BT* 30 (1979): 447–48.

Leivestad. R. "'The Meekness and Gentleness of Christ.' II Cor. x.1." *NTS* 12 (1966): 156–64.

Ortlund, R. C. *God's Unfaithful Wife: A Biblical Theology of Spiritual Adultery*. Downers Grove, IL: InterVarsity, 1999.

97. Another Jesus, a Different Spirit, and Another Gospel (11:4)

Fee, G. D. "'Another Gospel Which You Did Not Embrace': 2 Corinthians 11.4 and the Theology of 1 and 2 Corinthians. In *Gospel in Paul: Studies on Corinthians, Galatians and Romans for Richard N. Longenecker*, edited by L. A. Jervis and P. Richardson, 111–33. JSNTSup 108. Sheffield: Sheffield Academic, 1996.

Holsten, C. "Zur Erklärung von 2 Kor 11,4-6." *ZWT* 16 (1873): 1–56.

Murphy-O'Connor, J. "Another Jesus (2 Cor. 11:4)." *RB* 97 (1990): 238–51.

Oostendorp, D. W. *Another Jesus: A Gospel of Jewish-Christian Superiority in II Corinthians.* Kampen, Neth.: Kok, 1967.

98. Boasting and Foolishness (11:5–6)

Travis, S. H. "Paul's Boasting in 2 Corinthians 10–12." *Texte und Untersuchungen* 112 (1973): 527–32.

Wong K. H. *Boasting and Foolishness: A Study of 2 Cor 10,12–18 and 11,1a.* Hong Kong: Alliance Bible Seminary, 1998.

99. Paul's Financial Policy (11:7–12)

Hock, R. F. "Paul's Tentmaking and the Problem of His Social Class." *JBL* 97 (1978): 555–64.

Stowers, S. K. "Περὶ μὲν γάρ and the Integrity of 2 Corinthians 8 and 9." *NovT* 32 (1980): 340–48.

Talbert, C. H. "Money Management in Early Mediterranean Christianity: 2 Corinthians 8–9." *RevExp* 86 (1989): 359–70.

100. False Apostles, Servants of Satan (11:13–15)

Barrett, C. K. "Paul's Opponents in 2 Corinthians." In *Essays on Paul*, 60–86. London: SPCK, 1982.

———. "ΨΕΥΔΑΠΟΣΤΟΛΟΙ (2 Cor. 11.13)." In *Essays on Paul*, 87–107. London: SPCK, 1982.

Kee, D. "Who Were the Super-Apostles of 2 Corinthians 10–13?" *RestQ* 23 (1980): 65–76.

McClelland, S. E. "'Super-Apostles, Servants of Christ, Servants of Satan': A Response." *JSNT* 14 (1982): 82–87.

Sumney, J. L. *"Servants of Satan," "False Brothers" and Other Opponents of Paul.* JSNTSup 188. Sheffield: Sheffield Academic, 1999.

Thrall, M. E. "Super-Apostles, Servants of Christ, and Servants of Satan." *JSNT* 6 (1980): 42–57.

HOMILETICAL SUGGESTIONS

Concern for Converts (11:1–6)

1. Acting against one's better judgment for the sake of the ministry (v. 1)
2. Protecting people's devotion to Christ against Satanic attack (vv. 2–3)
3. The importance of exposing dangerous distortions of the gospel message (v. 4)
4. Sometimes self-defense is necessary for the sake of the ministry (vv. 5–6)

Responding to Criticism (11:5–11)

1. Preaching "free of charge" to silence criticism of moneygrubbing (vv. 7–9)
2. Rebutting false accusations can be necessary to protect the integrity of ministry (vv. 10–11)

Straight Talk (11:12–15)
1. Removing the grounds employed for criticism (v. 12)
2. Exposing the true nature of false teachers (vv. 13–15)

C. THE FOOL'S SPEECH (11:16–12:13)

Because of concern for his converts and their susceptibility to deception, Paul exposed the false apostles' true nature as servants of Satan (11:13–15). And against his better judgment, here in 11:16–12:13 he demonstrates that, even using his opponents' criteria, he is a better servant of Christ than they are. So in the extended "fool's speech" of 11:16–12:13, he boasts of his credentials, apostolic trials, visionary experiences, and the mighty works he has performed. He knows such worldly boasting is foolish, but under the circumstances, where his converts have been swayed by the boasting of others, he feels compelled to boast a little himself. But in the end he turns this boasting match on its head and boasts not of his strengths but of his weaknesses, for God's strength is made perfect in human weakness.

1. Accept Me as a Fool (11:16–21a)

In this opening section of the "fool's speech," Paul asks his audience to bear with him and makes clear that what he is about to say is not said with the Lord's authority. Then with biting irony he asks them to bear with him, seeing that they have been ready enough to bear with other fools, being wise themselves! These others have acted in the most highhanded and pretentious fashion, but, Paul says ironically, "we have been too weak for that!"

STRUCTURE

16 Πάλιν λέγω,
   μή τίς με δόξῃ ἄφρονα εἶναι·
      εἰ δὲ μή γε,
   κἂν ὡς ἄφρονα δέξασθέ με,
      ἵνα κἀγὼ μικρόν τι καυχήσωμαι.
17   ὃ λαλῶ,
   οὐ κατὰ κύριον λαλῶ
      ἀλλ᾽ ὡς ἐν ἀφροσύνῃ,
      ἐν ταύτῃ τῇ ὑποστάσει τῆς καυχήσεως.
18 ἐπεὶ πολλοὶ καυχῶνται κατὰ σάρκα,
   κἀγὼ καυχήσομαι.
19 ἡδέως γὰρ ἀνέχεσθε τῶν ἀφρόνων
               φρόνιμοι ὄντες·
20 ἀνέχεσθε γὰρ
      εἴ τις ὑμᾶς καταδουλοῖ,
      εἴ τις κατεσθίει,
      εἴ τις λαμβάνει,
      εἴ τις ἐπαίρεται,
      εἴ τις εἰς πρόσωπον ὑμᾶς δέρει.
21a κατὰ ἀτιμίαν λέγω,
      ὡς ὅτι ἡμεῖς ἠσθενήκαμεν.

VERSE 16

Πάλιν λέγω, μή τίς με δόξῃ ἄφρονα εἶναι·
I repeat: Let no one consider me a fool.

Πάλιν, adv., "again." Λέγω, 1st sg. pres. act. indic., "say." Μή τίς με δόξῃ, "let no one get the idea. . . ." BDF (§495[3]): "Paul knows how to change his tone in an astonishing way and uses *prodiorthosis* (an anticipatory correction) when he feels he is about to give offense (e.g. 2 C 11:1ff.)." μή δόξῃ is cited in R 933 as an example of a "volitive subjunctive." Harris 779: "μή . . . with a third person subject . . . expresses an intense wish (a hortatory subjunctive) . . . μή . . . δόξῃ forbids a future action and is ingressive, 'let no one get the idea.'" Τίς, nom. sg. masc. indef. pron. τίς, τί, "one," subj. of δόξῃ. Με, acc. 1st sg. pron. ἐγώ, "me," obj. of δόξῃ. Δόξῃ, 3rd sg. aor. act. subjunc. of δοκέω, "consider." Ἄφρονα, acc. sg. masc. subst. adj. ἄφρων, -ον, "foolish person." Εἶναι, pres. inf. of εἰμί, "be."

εἰ δὲ μή γε, κἂν ὡς ἄφρονα δέξασθέ με, ἵνα κἀγὼ μικρόν τι καυχήσωμαι.
But if you do, at least accept me as a fool so that I can also boast a little.

R 1025: "In 2 Cor. 11:16 we have both εἰ δὲ μή γε and κἂν (δέξησθε) to be supplied," cited as an example of ellipsis. Εἰ δὲ μή γε, "But if you do." ZG: "otherwise." Harris 779: "(literally) 'but if not,' 'but otherwise' = 'but if (you think) otherwise' = 'but if you do think me a fool.'" Γε, BDAG 190b: "enclit. particle, appended to the word or words it refers to . . . it serves to 'focus the attention upon a single idea, and place it, as it were, in the limelight." ZG 558: "particle emphasizing the forgoing word.'" Κἂν = καὶ ἐάν, "and if." Κἂν ὡς ἄφρονα δέξασθέ με, BDAG 507b: "*accept me at least as a fool.*" Ὡς, comp. particle "as." Ἄφρονα, acc. sg. masc. subst. adj. ἄφρων, -ον, "foolish person."

Ἵνα, with subjunc. καυχήσωμαι, "so that I can boast." Κἀγώ = καὶ ἐγώ, "I also." Μικρόν τι, BDAG 651b: "subst. neut. *a little.*" R 743: τι with adjectives: "the effect is rhetorical. There is 'a double adjectival sense.'" Καυχήσωμαι, 1st sg. aor. mid. subjunc. of καυχάομαι, "boast."

VERSE 17

ὃ λαλῶ . . . ἐν ταύτῃ τῇ ὑποστάσει τῆς καυχήσεως.
What I am saying in this matter of boasting,

Ὃ λαλῶ, Harris 780: "refers specifically to what Paul is about to utter in his foolish boasting, not to whatever he says at any time . . . the emphasis is on the content of what Paul says (ὃ λαλῶ), not on the fact of his speaking." Ὅ, acc. sg. neut. rel. pron. ὅς, ἥ, ὅ, "what," dir. obj. of λαλῶ. Λαλῶ, 1st sg. pres. act. indic. of λαλέω, "say." Ἐν, prep. with dat. ταύτῃ τῇ ὑποστάσει, "in this matter." Ὑποστάσει, dat. sg. fem. ὑπόστασις, -εως, ἡ, "matter." BDAG 1040d: "a plan that one devises for action, *plan, project, undertaking, endeavour.*" Καυχήσεως, gen. sg. fem. καύχησις, -εως, ἡ, "boasting," qualifies ὑποστάσει.

οὐ κατὰ κύριον λαλῶ ἀλλ᾽ ὡς ἐν ἀφροσύνῃ,
I don't speak as the Lord would, but as it were, foolishly.

Κατά, prep. with acc. κύριον, "according to the Lord." BDAG 512c: "marker of norm of similarity or homogeneity, *according to, in accordance with, in conformity with, according to.*" CSB, "as the Lord would;" NRSV, "with the Lord's authority." Thrall 2:713: "The preposition κατά, followed by the accusative of the person, indicates that something is done, or occurs, in accordance with the 'will, pleasure, or manner' of that person. Hence the present phrase could mean, '(not) according to the Lord's will', i.e., 'not on the Lord's authority.'" Λαλῶ, 1st sg. pres. act. indic. of λαλέω, "say." Ὡς, particle, "as." Ἐν, prep with dat. ἀφροσύνῃ, lit. "in/with foolishness," contrasts κατὰ κύριον. Ἀφροσύνη, dat. sg. fem. ἀφροσύνη, -ης, ἡ, "foolishness." Seifrid 421–22: "The term . . . may connote insanity, in contrast with the alternative term for 'foolishness,' *mōria*, which suggests stupidity. The former connotation is surely present in this context . . . His earlier description of his having been 'beside himself' . . . finds its counterpart here."

VERSE 18

ἐπεὶ πολλοὶ καυχῶνται κατὰ σάρκα, κἀγὼ καυχήσομαι.
Since many boast according to the flesh, I will also boast.

Ἐπεί, conj., "since." Πολλοί, nom. pl. masc. subst. adj., "many (people)," subj. of καυχῶνται. Καυχῶνται, 3rd pl. pres. mid. indic. of καυχάομαι, "boast." Κατά, prep. with acc. σάρκα, "according to the flesh." NRSV, "according to human standards," i.e., according to standards of human achievement, power and prestige, and even spiritual experiences, in terms that do not take into account what is pleasing to God. Σάρκα, acc. sg. fem. σάρξ, σαρκός, ἡ, "flesh." Κἀγώ = καὶ ἐγώ, "I also." Καυχήσομαι, 1st sg. fut. mid. indic. of καυχάομαι, "boast."

VERSE 19

ἡδέως γὰρ ἀνέχεσθε τῶν ἀφρόνων φρόνιμοι ὄντες·
For you, being so wise, gladly put up with fools!

BDF (§495[2]): "Paul also occasionally makes use of irony . . . of the sharpest kind: 2 C 11:19f.: ἡδέως γὰρ ἀνέχεσθε τῶν ἀφρόνων φρόνιμοι ὄντες·ἀνέχεσθε γὰρ etc." Cf. R 1199. Ἡδέως, adv., "gladly." Harris 783: γάρ "introduces a reason that justifies, not only Paul's plea for acceptance as a fool (v. 16), but also his prospective venture into foolish boasting (vv. 17–18)." Ἀνέχεσθε, 2nd pl. pres. mid. indic. of ἀνέχω, "put up with, endure." Ἀφρόνων, gen. pl. masc. subst. adj. ἄφρων, -ον, "foolish (person)," dir.

obj. of ἀνέχεσθε, a reference to the Corinthians' willing acceptance of the false apostles. Φρόνιμοι ὄντες, "being so wise," a cutting allusion to the Corinthians' tendency
to pride themselves on their own wisdom (cf. 1 Cor 3:18–20; 4:10; 6:5; 8:1–7; 13:2).
Φρόνιμοι, nom. pl. masc. adj. φρόνιμος, -ον, "wise." Barnett 532, n.14: "The combination here of ἀφρόνων [foolish] and φρόνιμοι [wise] adds to the rhetorical impact."
Ὄντες, nom. pl. masc. of pres. ptc. of εἰμί, "be." ZG 558: "(ironically) causal, *seeing
that you are ...*"

VERSE 20

ἀνέχεσθε γὰρ εἴ τις ὑμᾶς καταδουλοῖ, εἴ τις κατεσθίει, εἴ τις λαμβάνει,
In fact, you put up with it if someone enslaves you, if someone exploits you, if someone takes advantage of you,

Unlike Paul, who saw his role as working with people for their joy and not lording
it over their faith (1:24), the intruders brought those they influenced under their "lordship." In v. 20 Paul exposes the despicable authoritarianism of his opponents, as well
as the misplaced forbearance of the Corinthians.

Ἀνέχεσθε, 2nd pl. pres. mid. indic. of ἀνέχω, "put up with, endure." Ὑμᾶς, acc.
2nd pl. pron. "you," dir. obj. of καταδουλοῖ. Καταδουλοῖ, 3rd sg. pres. act. indic. of
καταδουλόω, "enslave." R 606 cites this as an example of κατά, in composition occurring "with 'perfective' force." Κατεσθίει, 3rd sg. pres. act. indic. of κατεσθίω, "devour,
exploit, prey upon," prob. refers to the intruders' greedy demands for remuneration.
Λαμβάνει, 3rd sg. pres. act. indic. of λαμβάνω, "prey upon, take advantage of." Paul
uses λαμβάνω again in 12:16, where he writes, "Now granted, I did not burden you;
yet sly as I am, I took you in [ἔλαβον] by deceit!" This illuminates the unusual use of
the verb λαμβάνω in the present context: the Corinthians were "taken in" or "fleeced"
by Paul's opponents.

εἴ τις ἐπαίρεται, εἴ τις εἰς πρόσωπον ὑμᾶς δέρει.
if someone is arrogant toward you, if someone slaps you in the face.

Ἐπαίρεται, 3rd sg. pres. mid. indic. of ἐπαίρω, "be arrogant." BDAG 357c–d: "to
suggest that one is better than one really is, *be presumptuous, put on airs.*" Εἰς, prep.
with acc. πρόσωπον, "to the face," indicates direction of the action of verb δέρει.
Πρόσωπον, acc. sg. neut. πρόσωπον, -ου, τό, "face." Ὑμᾶς, acc. 2nd pl. pron. "you," dir.
obj. of δέρει. Δέρει, 3rd sg. pres. act. indic. of δέρω, "slap, strike." To slap the face was a
way of humiliating a person. Paul may be using the expression literally, in which case
it would mean the false apostles had become so authoritarian in their dealings with
the Corinthians that they would actually slap the faces of those who questioned their
authority. Alternatively, Paul could be using the expression metaphorically to mean his
opponents were acting in a way that humiliated the Corinthians.

Harris 784: "In the five examples of this abuse that Paul proceeds to document, the
reader or hearer is struck by the fivefold repetition of εἴ τις ('if someone'). . . . This has

the effect of letting each item stand on its own, thus increasing the paradox step by step and hammering home the message."

VERSE 21a

κατὰ ἀτιμίαν λέγω, ὡς ὅτι ἡμεῖς ἠσθενήκαμεν.
I say this to our shame: We have been too weak for that!

Paul concludes this paragraph with another statement filled with biting sarcasm. The Corinthians had entertained the criticisms of Paul's opponents that he was weak (10:10). Paul now throws that back at them, saying in effect, "Yes, I admit, we were too weak to make such a despicable display of overbearing authoritarianism as that practiced by those intruders!"

Κατὰ ἀτιμίαν λέγω, ZG 558: "*to my shame I confess.*" Κατά, prep. with acc. ἀτιμίαν, "to (our) shame." Ἀτιμίαν, acc. sg. fem. ἀτιμία, -ας, ἡ, "shame." Ὡς ὅτι, Thrall 2:719–20: "we took ὡς to mean 'as,' assumed an ellipsis of a verb of saying between ὡς and ὅτι, and interpreted ὅτι as recitative. . . . The force of v. 21a would then be: 'I can say it to my shame. As you say: we have been weak.'" Barnett 533, n. 23: "The phrase ὡς ὅτι introduces a quotation (of theirs!), as in 5:19." Ἡμεῖς, nom. 1st pl. pron. ἐγώ, "we," emphatic. Ἠσθενήκαμεν, 1st pl. pf. act. indic. of ἀσθενέω, "be weak." Harris 788: "he had been too 'weak' to dominate and exploit the Corinthians as his rivals had been doing (11:20)."

2. Paul's Jewish Ancestry (11:21b–22)

In this brief section Paul responds to his opponents' claims to impeccable Jewish ancestry, asserting that his own Jewish credentials are just as good.

STRUCTURE

21b   ἐν ᾧ δ᾽ ἄν τις τολμᾷ,
          ἐν ἀφροσύνῃ λέγω,
     τολμῶ κἀγώ.
22   Ἑβραῖοί εἰσιν;
          κἀγώ.
     Ἰσραηλῖταί εἰσιν;
          κἀγώ.
     σπέρμα Ἀβραάμ εἰσιν;
          κἀγώ.

VERSE 21b

ἐν ᾧ δ᾽ ἄν τις τολμᾷ, ἐν ἀφροσύνῃ λέγω, τολμῶ κἀγώ.
But in whatever anyone dares to boast—I am talking foolishly—I also dare:

Ἐν ᾧ . . . ἄν, "in whatever. . . ." Ἐν, prep. with dat. ᾧ, "in what." Ὧ, dat. sg. neut. pron., "what." Ἄν, BDAG 56b: "A particle peculiar to Gk . . . denoting aspect of contingency, incapable of translation by a single English word; it denotes that the action of the verb is dependent on some circumstance or condition . . . *ever*." Τις, nom. sg. masc. pron.: τις, τι, "anyone, someone." Τολμᾷ, 3rd sg. pres. act. subjunc. of τολμάω, "dare." Ἐν ἀφροσύνῃ λέγω, "I am talking foolishly." ZG 558: "a parenthesis." Cf. R. 1199: "The rhetoricians call it a *prodiorthosis*" (a statement intended to prepare one's audience for something shocking or offensive). Ἐν, prep. with dat. ἀφροσύνῃ, "with foolishness." Ἀφροσύνη, dat. sg. fem. ἀφροσύνη, -ης, ἡ, "foolishness." Τολμῶ, 1st sg. pres. act. indic. of τολμάω, "dare." Κἀγώ = καὶ ἐγώ, "I also."

VERSE 22

Ἑβραῖοί εἰσιν; κἀγώ. Ἰσραηλῖταί εἰσιν; κἀγώ. σπέρμα Ἀβραάμ εἰσιν; κἀγώ.
Are they Hebrews? So am I. Are they Israelites? So am I. Are they the descendants of Abraham? So am I.

In this verse Paul employs rhetorical questions: BDF (§496[2]) "to express . . . astonishment or indignation."

Ἑβραῖοι, nom. pl. masc. Ἑβραῖος, -ου, ὁ, "Hebrew." The designation "Hebrews" may be understood in a couple of ways: (1) to denote ethnic purity, as in the expression "a Hebrew born of Hebrews" (Phil 3:5), distinguishing Jews by birth from proselytes; (2) to distinguish Aramaic-speaking Jews, who generally lived in Palestine (Hebrews), from Greek-speaking Jews generally of the dispersion (Hellenists) (cf. Acts 6:1). However, this distinction is not as clear-cut as it might seem, for as the inscription "Synagogue of the Hebr[ews]," found in Corinth, shows, even Jews of the dispersion referred to themselves as "Hebrews." In the present context it is best to see Paul claiming that he has the same pure Jewish ancestry as that claimed by his opponents. Whether they were Palestinian or Hellenistic Jews cannot be determined from these verses.

Εἰσιν, 3rd pl. pres. indic. of εἰμί, "are." Κἀγώ = καὶ ἐγώ, "I also."

Ἰσραηλῖται, nom. pl. masc. Ἰσραηλίτης, -ου, ὁ, "Israelite." It is difficult to know whether in Paul's mind Israelites were distinguished from Hebrews. However, seeing that proselytes were admitted into Israel but could never, of course, claim to be Hebrews (born of Hebrews), the term "Israelite" prob. denotes the religious and social aspects of being a Jew.

Σπέρμα, nom. sg. neut. σπέρμα, -ατος, τό, "seed, descendent." Ἀβραάμ, gen. sg. masc. Ἀβραάμ, ὁ (indecl.), "Abraham." If "Hebrews" is to be understood ethnically, and "Israelites" religiously and socially, then "descendants of Abraham" could be understood theologically and related to God's call and promises to Abraham's offspring, which includes believing Gentiles (cf. Gal 3:5–9, 29).

3. A Better Servant of Christ (11:23–33)

Paul concedes for the sake of argument that his opponents are servants of Christ but claims he is a better one (vv. 21b–23a). To reinforce his claim he provides a list of his apostolic trials (vv. 23b–29), which may be divided into four sections: (a) vv. 23b–25, which speak of imprisonments, beatings, and being near death, incl. a detailed explanation of what these involved; (b) v. 26, which speaks of frequent journeys, with a description of the dangers of travel; (c) v. 27, which speaks of toil and hardship, with an account of the privations involved in these; and (d) vv. 28–29, which speak of concern for all the churches, with an example of what caused it. Finally he narrates the story of his ignominious flight from Damascus as a further illustration of his "weakness" as an apostle (vv. 30–33).

STRUCTURE

```
23   διάκονοι Χριστοῦ εἰσιν;
     παραφρονῶν λαλῶ,
     ὑπὲρ ἐγώ·
          ἐν κόποις περισσοτέρως,
          ἐν φυλακαῖς περισσοτέρως,
          ἐν πληγαῖς ὑπερβαλλόντως,
          ἐν θανάτοις πολλάκις.
24             ὑπὸ Ἰουδαίων
          πεντάκις τεσσεράκοντα παρὰ μίαν ἔλαβον,
25        τρὶς ἐρραβδίσθην,
          ἅπαξ ἐλιθάσθην,
          τρὶς ἐναυάγησα,
          νυχθήμερον ἐν τῷ βυθῷ πεποίηκα·
26        ὁδοιπορίαις πολλάκις,
          κινδύνοις ποταμῶν,
          κινδύνοις λῃστῶν,
          κινδύνοις ἐκ γένους,
          κινδύνοις ἐξ ἐθνῶν,
          κινδύνοις ἐν πόλει,
          κινδύνοις ἐν ἐρημίᾳ,
          κινδύνοις ἐν θαλάσσῃ,
          κινδύνοις ἐν ψευδαδέλφοις,
27        κόπῳ καὶ μόχθῳ,
          ἐν ἀγρυπνίαις πολλάκις,
          ἐν λιμῷ καὶ δίψει,
          ἐν νηστείαις πολλάκις,
          ἐν ψύχει καὶ γυμνότητι·
28        χωρὶς τῶν παρεκτὸς
     ἡ ἐπίστασίς μοι ἡ καθ᾽ ἡμέραν,
     ἡ μέριμνα πασῶν τῶν ἐκκλησιῶν.
```

29 τίς ἀσθενεῖ
    καὶ οὐκ ἀσθενῶ;
    τίς σκανδαλίζεται
    καὶ οὐκ ἐγὼ πυροῦμαι;
30   Εἰ καυχᾶσθαι δεῖ,
    τὰ τῆς ἀσθενείας μου καυχήσομαι.
31 ὁ θεὸς καὶ πατὴρ τοῦ κυρίου Ἰησοῦ οἶδεν,

    ὁ ὢν εὐλογητὸς εἰς τοὺς αἰῶνας,
         ὅτι οὐ ψεύδομαι.
32   ἐν Δαμασκῷ
    ὁ ἐθνάρχης Ἁρέτα τοῦ βασιλέως ἐφρούρει τὴν πόλιν Δαμασκηνῶν
         πιάσαι με,
33 καὶ   διὰ θυρίδος
         ἐν σαργάνῃ
    ἐχαλάσθην
         διὰ τοῦ τείχους
    καὶ ἐξέφυγον τὰς χεῖρας αὐτοῦ.

VERSE 23

διάκονοι Χριστοῦ εἰσιν; παραφρονῶν λαλῶ, ὑπὲρ ἐγώ· ἐν κόποις περισσοτέρως,
Are they servants of Christ? I'm talking like a madman—I'm a better one: with far
more labors,

Παραφρονῶν, nom. sg. masc. of pres. act. ptc. of παραφρονέω, "be out of one's
mind, like a madman." Λαλῶ, 1st sg. pres. act. indic. of λαλέω, "talk." Ὑπὲρ ἐγώ, R
558: "Sometimes indeed the preposition is used alone (ellipsis) and the verb has to be
supplied, as in . . . ὑπὲρ ἐγώ in 2 Cor. 11:23."
Ὑπέρ, adv., "more." BDAG 1031c: "The adv. use of ὑπέρ is, so far, almost unknown
outside the NT . . . διάκονοι Χριστοῦ εἰσιν; ὑπὲρ ἐγώ *are they assistants of Christ? I am
so even more* (than they)." Moule 64: "cf. *adverbial* use in II Cor.xi. 23, ὑπὲρ ἐγώ, *I am
even more so*"; Z §78. Cf. Harris, *Prepositions*, 208: "Most grammarians . . . assume
ὑπέρ is here used adverbially, 'to a higher degree'. . . . But unambiguous evidence for
an adverbial use of ὑπέρ is lacking . . . , so it is preferable to supply αὐτούς after ὑπέρ
. . . as well as διάκονος Χριστοῦ εἰμί, 'I beyond them' = 'I am a better servant of Christ
than they are.'" Cf. R 450.
Ἐν, prep. with dat. κόποις, "with labors." Κόποις, dat. pl. masc. κόπος, -ου, ὁ, "labor."
Περισσοτέρως, comp. adv., "even more, greater."

ἐν φυλακαῖς περισσοτέρως, ἐν πληγαῖς ὑπερβαλλόντως, ἐν θανάτοις πολλάκις.
many more imprisonments, far worse beatings, many times near death.

Φυλακαῖς, dat. pl. fem. φυλακή, -ῆς, ἡ, "prison, imprisonment." Περισσοτέρως, comp. adv. "even more, greater." Πληγαῖς, dat. pl. fem. πληγή, -ῆς, ἡ, "blow, beating." Ὑπερβαλλόντως, adv. far worse, more severe." R 551: "Some participles come to be used adverbially." Cf. R 1109. Θανάτοις, dat. pl. masc. θάνατος, -ου, ὁ, "death." Πολλάκις, adv. "many times, often."

VERSE 24

ὑπὸ Ἰουδαίων πεντάκις τεσσεράκοντα παρὰ μίαν ἔλαβον,
Five times I received the forty lashes minus one from the Jews.

Ὑπό, prep. with gen. Ἰουδαίων, "from (the) Jews." Ἰουδαίων, gen. pl. masc. adj., Ἰουδαῖος, -αία, -αῖον, "Jewish," subst. "the Jews." Πεντάκις, adv., "five times." Τεσσεράκοντα, acc. pl. fem. adj., "forty (lashes)." Παρά, prep. with acc. μίαν, "minus one." Deut 25:1–3 specifies that punishment by beating must not exceed forty strokes, and as a hedge around the law, the Jews of Paul's day limited the number to forty minus one, lest by an error in counting, the prescribed number be exceeded and the law be broken by an impetuous executioner, and the offender permanently disgraced. Μίαν, acc. sg. fem. adj. εἷς, μία, ἕν, "one." Ἔλαβον, 1st sg. aor. act. indic. of λαμβάνω, "receive." Z §253: "the action expressed by the aorist may have occupied a long time, or the reference may be to an act frequently repeated; the aorist will be used so long as the writer wishes simply to record the fact of the act or acts, and not to represent the action as in progress or habitual, i.e. so long as the whole activity expressed by the verb is regarded globally . . . e.g. 'five times did I receive (ἔλαβον) from the Jews forty stripes save one. . . .'"

VERSE 25

τρὶς ἐρραβδίσθην, ἅπαξ ἐλιθάσθην,
Three times I was beaten with rods. Once I received a stoning.

Τρίς, adv., "three times." Ἐρραβδίσθην, 1st sg. aor. pass. indic. of ῥαβδίζω, "beat with a rod." BDF (§332[2]): "Repeated actions may also take the aorist provided the repetition is summed up and has a terminus: τρὶς ἐρραβδίσθην 2 C 11:25. –R. 831–34." Ἅπαξ, adv., "once." Ἐλιθάσθην, 1st sg. aor. pass. indic. of λιθάζω, "stone."

τρὶς ἐναυάγησα, νυχθήμερον ἐν τῷ βυθῷ πεποίηκα·
Three times I was shipwrecked. I have spent a night and a day in the open sea.

Τρίς, adv., "three times." Ἐναυάγησα, 1st sg. aor. act. indic. of ναυαγέω, "suffer shipwreck." Νυχθήμερον, acc. sg. neut. νυχθήμερον, -ου, τό, "a night and a day." Ἐν, prep. with dat. τῷ βυθῷ, "in the open sea." Βυθῷ, dat. sg. masc. βυθός, -οῦ, ὁ, "open/deep sea." Πεποίηκα, 1st sg. pf. act. indic. of ποιέω, "make," in this context "spend." BDF (§343): "use of the perfect in narrative."

Acts records only one shipwreck in which Paul was involved, and that took place after this letter was written. However, Acts records nine sea voyages the apostle made before this time, and there were almost certainly others. There were, then, plenty of voyages during which Paul could have suffered shipwreck. Spending a night and a day in the open sea must have brought the apostle face-to-face with death, as had his stoning at Lystra.

VERSE 26

ὁδοιπορίαις πολλάκις, κινδύνοις ποταμῶν, κινδύνοις λῃστῶν,
On frequent journeys, I faced dangers from rivers, dangers from robbers,

Ὁδοιπορίαις, dat. pl. fem. ὁδοιπορία, -ας, ἡ, "journey." Πολλάκις, adv., "many times, often." Κινδύνοις, dat. pl. masc. κίνδυνος, -ου, ὁ, "danger." Ποταμῶν, gen. pl. masc. ποταμός, -οῦ, ὁ, "river." Λῃστῶν, gen. pl. masc. λῃστής, -οῦ, ὁ, "robber."

κινδύνοις ἐκ γένους, κινδύνοις ἐξ ἐθνῶν, κινδύνοις ἐν πόλει,
dangers from my own people, dangers from Gentiles, dangers in the city,

Ἐκ, prep. with gen. γένους, "from my own people." Γένους, gen. sg. neut. γένος, -ους, τό, "family, race." BDAG 194d: "my compatriots, fellow-Israelites." Ἐξ, prep. with gen. ἐθνῶν, "from Gentiles." Ἐθνῶν, gen. pl. neut. ἔθνος, -ους, τό, "Gentile." Ἐν, prep. with dat. πόλει "in (the) city." Πόλει, dat. sg. fem. πόλις, -εως, ἡ, "city."

κινδύνοις ἐν ἐρημίᾳ, κινδύνοις ἐν θαλάσσῃ, κινδύνοις ἐν ψευδαδέλφοις,
dangers in the wilderness, dangers at sea, and dangers among false brothers;

Ἐν, prep. with dat. ἐρημίᾳ, "in the wilderness." Ἐρημίᾳ, dat. sg. fem. ἐρημία, -ας, ἡ, "wilderness." Ἐν, prep. with dat. θαλάσσῃ, "at sea." Θαλάσσῃ, dat. sg. fem. θάλασσα, -ης, ἡ, "sea." Ἐν, prep. with dat. ψευδαδέλφοις, "among false brothers." Ψευδαδέλφοις, dat. pl. masc. ψευδάδελφος, -ου, ὁ, "false brother."

VERSE 27

κόπῳ καὶ μόχθῳ, ἐν ἀγρυπνίαις πολλάκις, ἐν λιμῷ καὶ δίψει,
toil and hardship, many sleepless nights, hunger and thirst,

Κόπῳ, dat. sg. masc. κόπος, -ου, ὁ, "toil." Μόχθῳ, dat. sg. masc. μόχθος, -ου, ὁ, "hardship." Ἐν, prep. with dat. ἀγρυπνίαις, "in sleeplessness/nights." This prob. does not refer to sleeplessness because of anxiety, as that would be better included in v. 28, where Paul speaks of the pressure of his concern over the churches. But included as it is here among examples of labor and toil, the sleepless nights were prob. due either to his preaching and teaching into the early hours (cf. Acts 20:7–12, 31), when those who had to labor during the day would be free to listen, or to the occasions when he had to ply his trade at night so as to support himself when he used the daylight hours for missionary activity (2 Thess 3:7–8). Ἀγρυπνίαις, dat. pl. fem. ἀγρυπνία, -ας, ἡ, "sleepless night." Πολλάκις, adv., "many times, often." Ἐν, prep. with dat. λιμῷ καὶ δίψει, "in hunger and thirst." Λιμῷ, dat. sg. masc. λιμός, -οῦ, ὁ, "hunger." Δίψει, dat. sg. neut. δίψος, -ους, τό, "thirst."

ἐν νηστείαις πολλάκις, ἐν ψύχει καὶ γυμνότητι·
often without food, cold, and without clothing.

Ἐν, prep. with dat. νηστείαις, "in fasting, without food." Νηστείαις, dat. pl. fem. νηστεία, -ας, ἡ, "fasting." πολλάκις, adv., "many times, often." Ἐν, prep. with dat. ψύχει καὶ γυμνότητι, "in cold and nakedness." Ψύχει, dat. sg. neut. ψῦχος, -ους, τό, "coldness." Γυμνότητι, dat. sg. fem. γυμνότης, -ητος, ἡ, "nakedness."

VERSE 28

χωρὶς τῶν παρεκτὸς ἡ ἐπίστασίς μοι ἡ καθ᾽ ἡμέραν, ἡ μέριμνα πασῶν τῶν ἐκκλησιῶν.
Not to mention other things, there is the daily pressure on me: my concern for all the churches.

χωρίς, prep. with gen. τῶν παρεκτός, "not to mention other things." Παρεκτός, adv. BDAG 774d: "besides, outside, abs. χωρὶς τῶν π. (sc. γινομένων) apart from what I leave unmentioned or what is external." R 547: "a striking instance of the adverb treated as substantive appears in χωρὶς τῶν παρεκτὸς (2 Cor. 11:28)." Ἐπίστασις, nom. sg. fem. ἐπίστασις, -εως, ἡ, "pressure." BDAG 380d: "pressure, in the sense of anxiety caused by a heavy sense of responsibility is prob.: the daily pressure on me. Alternatives include: attention or care daily required of me." Μοι, dat. 1st sg. pron., ἐγώ, "on me." Καθ᾽, prep. with acc. ἡμέραν, "daily." Harris, Prepositions, 156: "'every day' . . . or, more colloquially, 'on a daily basis, day in and day out.'" Ἡμέραν, acc. sg. fem. ἡμέρα, -ας, ἡ, "day." Μέριμνα, nom. sg. fem. μέριμνα, -ης, ἡ, "concern, anxiety." Πασῶν τῶν ἐκκλησιῶν, descriptive gen. "(concern) for all the churches." Ἐκκλησιῶν, gen. pl. fem. ἐκκλησία, -ας, ἡ "church."

Harris 798: "Each of the twenty-six items in the catalogue contributes to the evidence for Paul's 'superiority,' so the meaning is not substantially altered whether we render the four instances of ἐν by 'in (the midst of)' (local ἐν cf. 6:4b-5; 11:26), 'with' (circumstantial or causal), 'with respect to' (referential), or 'because of' (causal)."

VERSE 29

τίς ἀσθενεῖ καὶ οὐκ ἀσθενῶ; τίς σκανδαλίζεται καὶ οὐκ ἐγὼ πυροῦμαι;
Who is weak, and I am not weak? Who is made to stumble, and I do not burn with indignation?

Ἀσθενεῖ, 3rd sg. pres. act. indic. of ἀσθενέω, "be weak." Ἀσθενῶ, 1st sg. pres. act. indic. of ἀσθενέω, "be weak." Σκανδαλίζεται, 3rd sg. pres. pass. indic. of σκανδαλίζω, "to cause to stumble." Harris 814: "Against the backdrop of 1 Cor 8:7–13, τίς σκανδαλίζεται; is more likely to mean 'Who is led into sin?' than 'Who is offended?' especially if 'offend' is given a psychological sense of 'cause resentment' or 'make angry.'" Πυροῦμαι, 1st sg. pres. mid. indic. of πυρόω, "burn with indignation." BDAG 899d: *"burn, be inflamed* w. sympathy, readiness to aid, or indignation." Hafemann 442: "The counterpart to Paul's weakness is his strong anger over the thought of someone falling away from Christ (11:29bc). The reference to his 'burning' in verse 29 is therefore an apt metaphor for the intense passion he experiences over those who are led astray (cf. 1 Cor. 7:9)."

VERSE 30

Εἰ καυχᾶσθαι δεῖ, τὰ τῆς ἀσθενείας μου καυχήσομαι.
If boasting is necessary, I will boast about my weaknesses.

Καυχᾶσθαι, pres. mid. inf. of καυχάομαι, "boast." Δεῖ, 3rd sg. pres. act. indic. of δεῖ, "be necessary." Τὰ τῆς ἀσθενείας μου, lit. "the things of my weakness." Τῆς ἀσθενείας μου, gen. phrase, qualifies τά. Ἀσθενείας, gen. pl. fem. ἀσθένεια, -ας, ἡ, "weakness." Καυχήσομαι, 1st sg. fut. mid. indic. of καυχάομαι, "boast."

VERSE 31

ὁ θεὸς καὶ πατὴρ τοῦ κυρίου Ἰησοῦ οἶδεν, ὁ ὢν εὐλογητὸς εἰς τοὺς αἰῶνας, ὅτι οὐ ψεύδομαι.
The God and Father of the Lord Jesus, who is blessed forever, knows I am not lying.

Thrall 2:761: "Paul here combines elements of doxological and oath formulas to make a very powerful statement." Ὁ θεὸς καὶ πατὴρ τοῦ κυρίου Ἰησοῦ, Harris 818: "standing under the nexus of a single article, θεός and πατήρ have a single referent; 'God' is none other than 'the Father of the Lord Jesus.'" Οἶδεν, 3rd sg. pf. act. indic. of οἶδα, "know."
Ὁ ὢν εὐλογητὸς εἰς τοὺς αἰῶνας, "who being blessed forever," descriptive phrase qualifies ὁ θεὸς καὶ πατὴρ τοῦ κυρίου Ἰησοῦ. BDF (§413[3]): "the participle ὢν can only be used when there are other adjuncts to the predicate." Ὤν, nom. sg. masc. of pres. ptc. of εἰμί, "be." Εὐλογητός, nom. sg. masc. adj. εὐλογητός, -ή, -όν, "blessed." Εἰς, prep. with acc. τοὺς αἰῶνας, "forever." Ὅτι οὐ ψεύδομαι, "that I am not lying," expresses the content of what ὁ θεὸς καὶ πατὴρ τοῦ κυρίου Ἰησοῦ knows. Ψεύδομαι, 1st sg. pres. mid. indic. of ψεύδομαι, "lie."

VERSE 32

ἐν Δαμασκῷ ὁ ἐθνάρχης Ἀρέτα τοῦ βασιλέως ἐφρούρει τὴν πόλιν Δαμασκηνῶν πιάσαι με,
In Damascus, a ruler under King Aretas guarded the city of Damascus in order to
arrest me.

’Εν, prep. with dat. Δαμασκῷ, "in Damascus." Δαμασκῷ, dat. sg. fem. Δαμασκός, -οῦ,
ἡ, "Damascus." Ἐθνάρχης, nom. sg. masc. ἐθνάρχης, -ου, ὁ, "ruler, governor, ethnarch."
Ἀρέτα τοῦ βασιλέως, gen. phrase qualifying ὁ ἐθνάρχης, "(the ruler) under King Aretas."
Ἀρέτα, gen. sg. masc. proper noun Ἀρέτας, -α, ὁ, "Aretas." King Aretas IV (9 BC–
AD 39) was ruler of the Nabataeans, an Arabian nation whose kingdom had once
included the city of Damascus (the daughter of Aretas IV was the first wife of Herod
Antipas, and whom the latter divorced to marry Herodias, the wife of his half brother,
Philip; cf. Matt 14:3–4). By NT times the city had been incorporated into the Roman
province of Syria. However, it seems that during the reign of the emperor Caligula
(AD 37–41), when a policy of reinstating eastern states of the empire as client king-
doms was followed, Aretas was given control over Damascus and thus would have
been able to appoint a governor there. If so, Paul's escape from Damascus must have
occurred between AD 37 and 39.
Βασιλέως, gen. sg. masc. βασιλεύς, -έως, ὁ, "king." Ἐφρούρει, 3rd sg. impf. act.
indic. of φρουρέω, "guard." Πόλιν, acc. sg. fem. πόλις, -εως, ἡ, "city." Δαμασκηνῶν, gen.
pl. masc. Δαμασκός, -οῦ, ἡ, "Damascus." Πιάσαι, aor. act. inf. of πιάζω, "arrest, seize."
Με, acc. 1st sg. masc. ἐγώ, "me," dir. obj. of πιάσαι.

VERSE 33

καὶ διὰ θυρίδος ἐν σαργάνῃ ἐχαλάσθην διὰ τοῦ τείχους καὶ ἐξέφυγον τὰς χεῖρας αὐτοῦ.
So I was let down in a basket through a window in the wall and escaped from his hands.

Διά, prep. with gen, θυρίδος, "through a window." Θυρίδος, gen. sg. fem. θυρίς,
-ίδος, ἡ, "window." ’Εν, prep. with dat. σαργάνῃ, "in a basket." Σαργάνῃ, dat. sg. fem.
σαργάνη,- ης, ἡ, "basket." Ἐχαλάσθην, 1st sg. aor. pass. indic. of χαλάω, "let down."
Διά, prep. with gen. τοῦ τείχους, "in the wall." BDAG 224a: *"through an opening in the
wall."* BDF (§223[5]): "in a spatial sense . . . 'along the wall' [Harris 823: "a dubious
rendering"]." Τείχους, gen. sg. neut. τεῖχος, -ους, τό, "wall." Ἐξέφυγον, 1st sg. aor. act.
indic. of ἐκφεύγω, "escape." Τὰς χεῖρας αὐτοῦ, "from his hands." Χεῖρας, acc. sg. fem.
χείρ, χειρός, ἡ, "hand."
This was prob. Paul's first taste of the ignominy of persecution, and it must have left
an indelible imprint upon him. It was a humiliating experience, and its inclusion here
seems to constitute a parody of the whole purpose of boasting. Thrall 2:766 regards
the report of this incident as "an example of Paul's weakness. Had it been intended to
illustrate not weakness but daring he would surely have emphasized his own initiative

in engineering his escape, whereas the implication of ἐχαλάσθην is that it was facilitated by fellow Christians in the city."

FOR FURTHER STUDY

101. Boasting and Foolishness (11:1–20)

Fahy, T. "St. Paul's 'Boasting' and 'Weakness.'" *ITQ* 31 (1964): 214–27.
Glancy, Jennifer A. "Boasting of Beatings (2 Corinthians 11:23–25)." *JBL* 123 (2004): 99–135.
Judge, E. A. "Paul's Boasting in Relation to Contemporary Professional Practice." *ABR* 16 (1968): 37–50.
Lambrecht, J. "Strength in Weakness. A Reply to Scott B. Andrews' Exegesis of 2 Cor 11.23b–33." *NTS* 43 (1997): 285–90.
Roetzel, C. J. "The Language of War (2 Cor. 10:1–6) and the Language of Weakness (2 Cor. 11:21b–13:10)." *BibInt* 17 (2009): 77–99.
Travis, S. H. "Paul's Boasting in 2 Corinthians 10–12." *Texte und Untersuchungen* 112 (1973): 527–32.
Wong, K. H. *Boasting and Foolishness: A Study of 2 Cor 10,12–18 and 11,1a.* Hong Kong: Alliance Bible Seminary, 1998.

102. False Apostles, Servants of Satan (11:20)

Barrett, C. K. "Paul's Opponents in 2 Corinthians." In *Essays on Paul*, 60–86. London: SPCK, 1982.
———. "ΨΕΥΔΑΠΟΣΤΟΛΟΙ (2 Cor. 11.13)." In *Essays on Paul*, 87–107. London: SPCK, 1982.
Kee, D. "Who Were the Super-Apostles of 2 Corinthians 10–13?" *ResQ* 23 (1980): 65–76.
McClelland, S. E. "'Super-Apostles, Servants of Christ, Servants of Satan': A Response." *JSNT* 14 (1982): 82–87.
Sumney, J. L. *"Servants of Satan," "False Brothers" and Other Opponents of Paul.* JSNTSup 188. Sheffield: Sheffield Academic, 1999.
Thrall, M. E. "Super-Apostles, Servants of Christ, and Servants of Satan." *JSNT* 6 (1980): 42–57.
Welborn, L. L. "Paul's Caricature of his Chief Rival as a Pompous Parasite in 2 Corinthians 11.20." *JSNT* 32 (2009): 39–56.

103. Hardships (11:23–29)

Bishop, E. F. F. "The 'Why' of Sleepless Nights." *EvQ* (1965) 28–31.
Fitzgerald, J. T. *Cracks in an Earthen Vessel: An Examination of the Catalogues of Hardship in the Corinthian Correspondence.* SLDS 99. Atlanta: Scholars, 1988.
Fridrichsen, A. "Zum Stil des Paulinischen Peristasenkatalogs. 2 Cor. 11, 23ff." *SO* 7 (1928): 25–29.
Kruse, C. G. *DNTB* 775–78.
Murphy-O'Connor, J. "On the Road and on the Sea with St. Paul: Traveling Conditions in the First Century." *BRev* 1 (1985): 38–47.
Welborn, L. L. "The Runaway Paul." *HTR* 92 (1999): 115–63.

104. Ethnarch of Aretas (11:32)

Campbell, D. A. "An Anchor for Pauline Chronology: Paul's Flight from 'the Ethnarch of King Aretas' (2 Corinthians 11:32–33)." *JBL* 121 (2002): 279–302.

Knauf, E. A. "Zum Ethnarchen des Aretas 2 Kor 11:32." *ZNW* 74 (1983): 145–47.

Lawlor, J. I. *The Nabataens in Historical Perspective.* Grand Rapids: Baker, 1973.

Negev. A. "The Nabataeans and the Provincia Arabia." *ANRW* II/1549–635.

Schürer, E. "Der Ethnarch des Königs Aretas, 2 Kor. 11,32." *TSK* 72 (1899): 95–99.

Starcky, J. "The Nabateans: A Historical Sketch." *BA* 18 (1955): 84–106.

Steinmann, A. "Aretas IV, König der Nabatäer." *BZ* 7 (1909): 174–84, 312–41.

Taylor, J. "The Ethnarch of King Aretas at Damascus: A Note on 2 Cor 11.32–33." *RB* 99 (1992): 719–28.

HOMILETICAL SUGGESTIONS

Speaking Foolishly (11:16–21a)

1. Speaking against one's better judgment for the sake of the ministry (vv. 16–18)
2. Exposing spiritual abuse (vv. 19–21a)

Speaking Foolishly of Ancestral Pride (11:21b–22)

1. A Hebrew, an Israelite, and a descendant of Abraham (v. 22)

Speaking Foolishly of External Sources of Suffering (11:23–26)

1. Imprisonments, beatings, and being near death (vv. 23–25)
2. The perils of missionary travel (v. 26)

Speaking Foolishly of Self-Imposed Privation and Anxiety (11:27–29)

1. Toil and hardship, sleepless nights, hunger and thirst (v. 27)
2. Paul's anxiety over all his churches (vv. 28–29)

Speaking Foolishly of the Ignominy of His First Experience of Persecution (11:30–33)

1. The inversion of boasting: of weakness, not strength (v. 30)
2. Speaking under oath (v. 31)
3. The humiliating escape from Damascus (vv. 32–33)

4. Visions and Revelations (12:1–10)

Paul's boasting now moves from apostolic trials to visions and revelations. He recounts, in the third person, an experience in which he was caught up to the third heaven, to paradise, where he heard things about which he was not permitted to speak. But rather than make mileage out of this disclosure, he speaks instead of a thorn in the flesh given to him so that he would not exalt himself. He tells how he sought God in prayer repeatedly for its removal, but in response was told that God's grace is sufficient for him. Through this revelation he learned of the simultaneity of weakness and God's power. Paul's emphasis on the coincidence of weakness and power was almost certainly intended to undermine triumphalist ideas about power and authority held by his opponents, and to support his own claim to apostolic authority, despite his imprisonments, persecutions, and rejection, which may seem to be inconsistent with that claim.

STRUCTURE

1 Καυχᾶσθαι δεῖ,
    οὐ συμφέρον μέν,
    ἐλεύσομαι δὲ εἰς ὀπτασίας καὶ ἀποκαλύψεις κυρίου.
2 οἶδα ἄνθρωπον
        ἐν Χριστῷ
        πρὸ ἐτῶν δεκατεσσάρων,
            εἴτε ἐν σώματι οὐκ οἶδα,
            εἴτε ἐκτὸς τοῦ σώματος οὐκ οἶδα,
                ὁ θεὸς οἶδεν,
                    ἁρπαγέντα τὸν τοιοῦτον
                        ἕως τρίτου οὐρανοῦ.
3 καὶ οἶδα τὸν τοιοῦτον ἄνθρωπον,
            εἴτε ἐν σώματι
            εἴτε χωρὶς τοῦ σώματος οὐκ οἶδα,
                ὁ θεὸς οἶδεν,
4   ὅτι ἡρπάγη εἰς τὸν παράδεισον
                    καὶ ἤκουσεν ἄρρητα ῥήματα
                        ἃ οὐκ ἐξὸν ἀνθρώπῳ λαλῆσαι.
5   ὑπὲρ τοῦ τοιούτου
    καυχήσομαι,
        ὑπὲρ δὲ ἐμαυτοῦ
    οὐ καυχήσομαι
        εἰ μὴ ἐν ταῖς ἀσθενείαις.
6   ἐὰν γὰρ θελήσω καυχήσασθαι,
    οὐκ ἔσομαι ἄφρων,
    ἀλήθειαν γὰρ ἐρῶ·
    φείδομαι δέ,
        μή τις εἰς ἐμὲ λογίσηται
            ὑπὲρ ὃ βλέπει με

ἢ ἀκούει [τι] ἐξ ἐμοῦ

7   καὶ τῇ ὑπερβολῇ τῶν ἀποκαλύψεων.
      διὸ ἵνα μὴ ὑπεραίρωμαι,
    ἐδόθη μοι σκόλοψ τῇ σαρκί,
              ἄγγελος Σατανᾶ,
      ἵνα με κολαφίζῃ,
      ἵνα μὴ ὑπεραίρωμαι.
8   ὑπὲρ τούτου τρὶς τὸν κύριον παρεκάλεσα
      ἵνα ἀποστῇ ἀπ' ἐμοῦ.
9   καὶ εἴρηκέν μοι,
      Ἀρκεῖ σοι ἡ χάρις μου,
      ἡ γὰρ δύναμις ἐν ἀσθενείᾳ τελεῖται.
    ἥδιστα οὖν μᾶλλον καυχήσομαι ἐν ταῖς ἀσθενείαις μου,
      ἵνα ἐπισκηνώσῃ ἐπ' ἐμὲ ἡ δύναμις τοῦ Χριστοῦ.
10 διὸ εὐδοκῶ ἐν ἀσθενείαις,
              ἐν ὕβρεσιν,
              ἐν ἀνάγκαις,
              ἐν διωγμοῖς καὶ στενοχωρίαις,
              ὑπὲρ Χριστοῦ·
          ὅταν γὰρ ἀσθενῶ,
    τότε δυνατός εἰμι.

VERSE 1

Καυχᾶσθαι δεῖ, οὐ συμφέρον μέν, ἐλεύσομαι δὲ εἰς ὀπτασίας καὶ ἀποκαλύψεις κυρίου.
Boasting is necessary. It is not profitable, but I will move on to visions and revelations
of the Lord.

While the apostle was convinced that there was nothing to be gained by boasting,
he recognized that in the present situation there was much to be lost if he did not. His
opponents had drawn up an agenda, it had been adopted by his converts, and he must
now respond to each item therein.

Καυχᾶσθαι, pres. mid. inf. of καυχάομαι, "boast." Δεῖ, 3rd sg. pres. act. indic. of δεῖ,
"it is necessary." Οὐ συμφέρον, Harris 831: "it is better to supply ἐστίν. . . . In that case,
οὐ συμφέρον ἐστίν is equivalent to οὐ συμφέρον, the reading of numerous witnesses . . .
meaning 'there is nothing to be gained by it.'" Συμφέρον, nom. sg. neut. of pres. act.
ptc. of συμφέρω, "be profitable."

Ἐλεύσομαι, 1st sg. fut. mid. indic. of ἔρχομαι, "go, move on." Εἰς, prep. with acc.
ὀπτασίας καὶ ἀποκαλύψεις, "to visions and revelations." Ὀπτασίας, acc. pl. fem.
ὀπτασία, -ας, ἡ, "vision." Seifrid 435–36: "The noun optasia, which is generally translated in English as 'vision' . . . should be rendered instead 'appearance' or 'appari-
tion.' The term signifies the appearance of an object or person. In contrast, a 'vision'
(expressed in Greek by horasis or horama) implies a mental image or perception. It is

orientated to the subject who receives the revelation, rather than the object revealed." Ἀποκαλύψεις, acc. pl. fem. ἀποκάλυψις, -εως, ἡ, "revelation." Κυρίου, gen. sg. masc. κύριος, -ου, ὁ, "Lord," either subj. gen. "given by the Lord," or obj. gen. "(a vision) of the Lord." Barnett 558: "The view we have taken is the 'visions and revelations' are *from* the Lord' because (1) 'Lord' is more likely to be subject than object since both nouns are connected to it, because (2) in vv. 2–4 no appearing of the Lord to Paul is involved, and because (3) given the centrality of Paul's Damascus road call (Gal 1:16, 18; 2:1), we would have expected a different form of words; 'revelation' would have been singular, and it would have preceded 'visions.'"

VERSE 2

οἶδα ἄνθρωπον ἐν Χριστῷ πρὸ ἐτῶν δεκατεσσάρων . . . ἁρπαγέντα τὸν τοιοῦτον ἕως τρίτου οὐρανοῦ.
I know a man in Christ who was caught up to the third heaven fourteen years ago.

Paul describes the experience in the third person, perhaps as a way of indicating its sacred character for him, or alternatively because he wanted to maintain a distinction between the Paul who was granted this superlative experience in the past and the Paul whose behavior people may see and whose words they may hear in the present (cf. 12:6). In fact, the account is so consistently cast in the third person that the reader may even wonder whether the apostle is relating the experience of another person, rather than his own. However, a careful rdg. and appreciation of the thrust of vv. 1, 5, 7 confirms that Paul is speaking of his own experience. It is possible that the apostle was using a rhetorical technique whereby a story is told as a third-person narration but into which a first-person narration is intruded, by one speaking on his own authority (cf. Anna Marmodoro, Jonathan Hill, eds., *The Author's Voice in Classical and Late Antiquity*. Oxford: Oxford University Press, 2013).

Of the many visions and revelations experienced, Paul singles out one that took place fourteen years ago. His dating of the experience underlines its historical reality. Barnett 561 comments, "Paul's 'fourteen years ago' must be calculated (by internal reckoning) from the time of writing this letter (c. AD 55), suggesting that this vision/ revelation occurred c. AD 42, at which time Paul would have been in his native Syria-Cilicia (Gal 1:18, 21; 2:1; Acts 9:29–30; 11:25)." This places the experience several years after his conversion, and thus it cannot be equated with the revelation of Christ to Paul on the Damascus Road.

Οἶδα, 1st sg. pf. act. indic. of οἶδα, "know." Ἄνθρωπον, acc. sg. masc. ἄνθρωπος, -ου, ὁ, "man," dir. obj. of οἶδα. Ἐν, prep. with dat. Χριστῷ, "in Christ." This expression has been variously interpreted: to belong to Christ; to live in the sphere of Christ's power; to be united to Christ; and to be a member of the Christian community through baptism. It is difficult to explain precisely what Paul intended by the expression here, and each of these options is feasible. At a minimum to be "in Christ" means to belong to him through faith, but that can also mean living in the sphere of his power, being united with him through the Spirit, and to have become a part of the Christian community by baptism.

Πρό, prep. with gen. ἐτῶν δεκατεσσάρων, "fourteen years ago." Harris, *Prepositions*, 186: "Clearly means 'fourteen years ago,' although the construction is unusual." Cf. BDF §213. Πρό, prep. "before, ago." Ἐτῶν, gen. pl. neut. ἔτος, -ους, τό, "year." Δεκατεσσάρων, gen. neut. pl. adj. δεκατέσσαρες, "fourteen."

Ἁρπαγέντα, acc. sg. masc. of aor. (divine) pass. ptc. of ἁρπάζω, "caught up." He used the same verb in 1 Thess 4:17 when speaking of Christians who are alive and remain until the coming of the Lord and will then be "caught up" to meet the Lord in the air. In both Jewish (e.g. *1 Enoch* 39:3f.) and Gentile (e.g. Plato, *Rep.* 10:614–21) literature, there are accounts sim. to that of the apostle's account of his experience. In the Babylonian Talmud (*Hag.* 14b) there is a story of four rabbis who were temporarily taken up into Paradise, but so awesome was their experience that only one, Rabbi Akiba, returned unharmed. The story postdates Paul (R. Akiba died c. AD 135) but indicates nevertheless the sort of accounts that were circulating in the first and second centuries of the Christian era. Τοιοῦτον, acc. sg. masc. pron. τοιοῦτος, -αύτη, -οῦτον, "such a one," i.e., "the man in Christ." Ἕως, prep. with gen. τρίτου οὐρανοῦ, "up to the third heaven." Τρίτου, gen. sg. masc. adj. τρίτος, -η, -ον, "third." Οὐρανοῦ, gen. sg. masc. οὐρανός, -οῦ, ὁ, "heaven."

εἴτε ἐν σώματι οὐκ οἶδα, εἴτε ἐκτὸς τοῦ σώματος οὐκ οἶδα, ὁ θεὸς οἶδεν.
Whether he was in the body or out of the body, I don't know; God knows.

Εἴτε, conj., "if, whether." Ἐν, prep. with dat. σώματι, "in the body." Σώματι, dat. sg. neut. σῶμα, -ατος, τό, "body." Οἶδα, 1st sg. pf. act. indic. of οἶδα, "know." Ἐκτός, prep. with gen. τοῦ σώματος, "out of the body." Οἶδεν, 3rd sg. pf. act. indic. of οἶδα, "know." Harris 839: "It is purely coincidental that the 'proper' preposition ἐν here modifies an anarthrous noun (ἐν σώματι), while the 'improper' preposition ἐκτός is followed by an articular noun (ἐκτὸς τοῦ σώματος) . . . for 'proper' prepositions often govern articular nouns, and 'improper' prepositions can be used with anarthrous nouns."

VERSE 3

καὶ οἶδα τὸν τοιοῦτον ἄνθρωπον, εἴτε ἐν σώματι εἴτε χωρὶς τοῦ σώματος οὐκ οἶδα, ὁ θεὸς οἶδεν,
I know that this man—whether in the body or out of the body I don't know; God knows—

Οἶδα, 1st sg. pf. act. indic. of οἶδα, "know." Τὸν τοιοῦτον ἄνθρωπον, acc. phrase, "such a man," dir. obj. of οἶδα. Τοιοῦτον, acc. sg. masc. dem. pron. τοιοῦτος, -αύτη, -οῦτον, "such a man, this man." Εἴτε ἐν σώματι, see notes on v. 2. Χωρίς, prep. with gen. τοῦ σώματος, "out of the body." Οὐκ οἶδα, ὁ θεὸς οἶδεν, see notes on v. 2.

VERSE 4

ὅτι ἡρπάγη εἰς τὸν παράδεισον καὶ ἤκουσεν ἄρρητα ῥήματα ἃ οὐκ ἐξὸν ἀνθρώπῳ λαλῆσαι.
was caught up into paradise and heard inexpressible words, which a human being is not allowed to speak.

Ἡρπάγη, 3rd sg. aor. pass. indic. of ἁρπάζω, "catch up." Εἰς, prep. with acc. τὸν παράδεισον, "to paradise." Παράδεισον, acc. sg. masc. παράδεισος, -ου, ὁ, "paradise." ZG 560: "Persian word, garden; paradise, home of the blessed."

Ἤκουσεν, 3rd sg. aor. act. indic. of ἀκούω, "hear." Ἄρρητα ῥήματα, "inexpressible words." Cf. Seifrid 442: "As his immediate elaboration of his report makes clear, the 'utterances' that he heard were not 'inexpressible' but 'unutterable.' The words (rhēmata) that he heard must remain secret. They were matters 'which are not permitted for a person to speak.' The visit to paradise and encounter with God was not a pre- or supra-linguistic experience but a speech event. Verbal communication took place." Ἄρρητα, acc. pl. neut. adj. ἄρρητος, -ον, "inexpressible, unutterable," qualifies ῥήματα. The word ἄρρητος is found only here in the NT but is common in ancient inscriptions. It is associated with the mystery religions and describes things too sacred to be divulged. Such secrecy concerning things that had been revealed was commonplace among devotees of the mystery religions in Paul's day, but quite unusual in Christian circles. Paul did speak of the "mystery" of the gospel, but that was something that, though previously hidden, had now been made known to the apostles and prophets through the Spirit for the express purpose that they should proclaim it to all people (cf. 1 Cor 2:1 mg.; Eph 3:1–9; 6:19–20; Col 1:25–27; 4:3). It is only in the present context that Paul speaks of something revealed to him which he could not speak about, presumably because it was so sacred and intended for him alone. Ῥήματα, acc. pl. neut. ῥῆμα, -ατος, τό, "word, thing."

Ἃ οὐκ ἐξὸν ἀνθρώπῳ λαλῆσαι, "which a human being is not allowed to speak," descriptive clause qualifies ῥήματα. Ἐξόν, nom. sg. neut. of pres. act. ptc. of ἔξεστιν, "be allowed." Ἀνθρώπῳ, dat. sg. masc. ἄνθρωπος, -ου, ὁ, "human being," dat. of respect. Λαλῆσαι, aor. act. inf. of λαλέω, "speak."

VERSE 5

ὑπὲρ τοῦ τοιούτου καυχήσομαι, ὑπὲρ δὲ ἐμαυτοῦ οὐ καυχήσομαι εἰ μὴ ἐν ταῖς ἀσθενείαις.
I will boast about this person, but not about myself, except of my weaknesses.

Ὑπέρ, prep. with gen. τοῦ τοιούτου, "about this person such a one." Z §96: "ὑπέρ is found where one might have expected περί." Καυχήσομαι, 1st sg. fut. mid. indic. of καυχάομαι. Ὑπέρ, prep. with gen. ἐμαυτοῦ, "about myself." Ἐμαυτοῦ, gen. 1st sg. masc. reflex. pron. ἐμαυτοῦ, -ῆς, "myself." Εἰ μή, "except." BDAG 278d: "except, if not." Ἐν, prep. with dat. ταῖς ἀσθενείαις, "in my weaknesses." Ἀσθενείαις, dat. pl. fem. ἀσθένεια, -ας, ἡ, "weakness."

VERSE 6

ἐὰν γὰρ θελήσω καυχήσασθαι, οὐκ ἔσομαι ἄφρων, ἀλήθειαν γὰρ ἐρῶ·
For if I want to boast, I wouldn't be a fool, because I would be telling the truth.

Θελήσω, 1st sg. aor. act. subjunc. of θέλω, "want, wish." Καυχήσασθαι, aor. mid. inf. of καυχάομαι, "boast." Ἔσομαι, 1st sg. fut. indic. of εἰμί, "be." Ἄφρων, nom. sg. masc. adj. ἄφρων, -ον, "foolish." Ἀλήθειαν, acc. sg. fem. ἀλήθεια, -ας, ἡ, "truth," dir. obj. of ἐρῶ. Ἐρῶ, 1st sg. fut. act. indic. of λέγω, "speak."

φείδομαι δέ, μή τις εἰς ἐμὲ λογίσηται ὑπὲρ ὃ βλέπει με ἢ ἀκούει [τι] ἐξ ἐμοῦ
But I will spare you, so that no one can credit me with something beyond what he sees in me or hears from me,

Harris 850 comments: "Seeing and hearing encompass the two primary ways in which an evaluation of a person can be undertaken—by observing conduct and listening to what is said. In Paul's case the reference would be to all his behavior as a person and as a missionary-pastor, and to all his preaching and teaching." Paul wanted people's evaluation of him as an apostle to be based on these things, not upon his past revelatory and visionary experiences.

Φείδομαι, 1st sg. pres. mid. indic. of φείδομαι, "spare" (obj. "you" to be understood). Εἰς, prep. with acc. ἐμέ, "to me." Λογίσηται, 3rd sg. aor. mid. subjunc. of λογίζομαι, "count, credit." Ὑπέρ, prep. with acc. phrase ὃ βλέπει με, "beyond what he sees in me." Βλέπει, 3rd sg. pres. act. indic. of βλέπω, "see." Ἀκούει, 3rd sg. pres. act. indic. of ἀκούω, "hear." Ἐξ, prep. with gen. ἐμοῦ, "from me."

VERSE 7

καὶ τῇ ὑπερβολῇ τῶν ἀποκαλύψεων.
especially because of the extraordinary revelations.

Ὑπερβολῇ, dat. sg. fem. ὑπερβολή, -ῆς, ἡ, "greatness, exceptional character." Τῶν ἀποκαλύψεων, gen. phrase "of the revelations," qualifies ὑπερβολῇ. Ἀποκαλύψεων, gen. pl. fem. ἀποκάλυψις, -εως, ἡ, "revelation."

διὸ ἵνα μὴ ὑπεραίρωμαι, ἐδόθη μοι σκόλοψ τῇ σαρκί,
Therefore, so that I would not exalt myself, a thorn in the flesh was given to me,

Διό, conj., "therefore." Ἵνα μὴ ὑπεραίρωμαι, purpose clause (ἵνα with subjunc.), "so that I would not exalt myself." Ὑπεραίρωμαι, 1st sg. pres. mid. subjunc. of ὑπεραίρω, "exalt." BDAG 1031d: "to have an undue sense of one's self-importance, *rise up, exalt oneself, be elated.*" R 538: "In 2 Cor 12:7, ἐδόθη μοι σκόλοψ τῇ σαρκί, the μοι is indirect object and σαρκί may be either dative of advantage or locative."

Ἐδόθη, 3rd sg. aor. pass. indic. of δίδωμι, "give." Μοι, dat. 1st sg. pron. ἐγώ, "me," indir. obj. of ἐδόθη. Σκόλοψ, nom. sg. masc. σκόλοψ, -οπος, ὁ, "thorn," dir. obj. of ἐδόθη. BDAG 930d: "'anything pointed' such as a '(pointed) stake,' then someth. that causes serious annoyance *thorn, splinter,* etc., specif. of an injurious foreign body." In the LXX σκόλοψ is used figuratively in Num 33:55, Ezek 28:24, and Hos 2:8. In each case it is used to denote something that frustrates and causes trouble in the lives of those afflicted. That Paul's "thorn" was a trouble and frustration to him is evident from his thrice-repeated prayer for its removal (v. 8). Many suggestions have been made concerning the nature of Paul's "thorn in the flesh": (a) some form of spiritual harassment, e.g., the limitations of a nature corrupted by sin, the torments of temptation, or oppression by a demon; (b) persecution, e.g., that instigated by Jewish opposition or by Paul's Christian opponents; (c) some physical or mental ailment, e.g., eye trouble, attacks of fever, stammering speech, epilepsy, headaches, or a neurological disturbance; and (d) the Corinthian church's rejection of his apostleship. However, there is insufficient data to decide the matter. Most modern interpreters prefer to see it as some sort of physical ailment, and the fact that Paul calls it a thorn in the *flesh* offers some support for this. Gal 4:15 is appealed to by those who want to identify it as an eye problem. Τῇ σαρκί, dat. phrase "in the flesh," locat. dat. Σαρκί, dat. sg. fem. σάρξ, σαρκός, ἡ, "flesh."

ἄγγελος Σατανᾶ, ἵνα με κολαφίζῃ, ἵνα μὴ ὑπεραίρωμαι.
a messenger of Satan to torment me so that I would not exalt myself.

Ἄγγελος, nom. sg. masc. ἄγγελος, -ου, ὁ, "messenger." Σατανᾶ, gen. sg. masc. σατάν, ὁ (indecl.), "Satan," qualifies ἄγγελος, either subj. gen. "sent by Satan," or poss. gen. "Satan's messenger." In 1 Thess 2:17–18 Paul tells his readers how he longed to revisit them after he was forced to leave Thessalonica (cf. Acts 17:1–10), but he could not do so because Satan blocked his way. And in the present context Satan is allowed to torment the apostle by means of a thorn in the flesh. However, in both cases the actions of Satan, while in themselves bad things, are made to serve God's purposes. In the first case, having his way blocked kept him on the move, and that meant the gospel came to Berea, Athens, and Corinth. In the second case, the torment served to keep Paul spiritually well-balanced. It was a weight upon his spirit, preventing him exalting himself. It is important to recognize that in both the OT and NT Satan has no power other than that allowed him by God.

Ἵνα με κολαφίζῃ, purpose clause (ἵνα with subjunc. κολαφίζῃ), "to torment me." Κολαφίζῃ, 3rd sg. pres. act. subjunc. of κολαφίζω, "torment." Ἵνα μὴ ὑπεραίρωμαι, purpose clause (ἵνα with subjunc. ὑπεραίρωμαι), "so that I would not exalt myself." Ὑπεραίρωμαι, 1st sg. pres. mid. subjunc. of ὑπεραίρω, "exalt." BDAG 1031d: "to have an undue sense of one's self-importance, *rise up, exalt oneself, be elated.*"

VERSE 8

ὑπὲρ τούτου τρὶς τὸν κύριον παρεκάλεσα ἵνα ἀποστῇ ἀπ' ἐμοῦ.
Concerning this, I pleaded with the Lord three times that it would leave me.

Ὑπέρ, prep. with gen. τούτου, "concerning this." BDF (§231[1]): "because of that." Τρίς, adv., "three times." Κύριον, acc. sg. masc. κύριος, -ου, ὁ, "Lord," dir. obj. of παρεκάλεσα. Παρεκάλεσα, 1st sg. aor. act. indic. of παρακαλέω, "plead, beseech." Ἵνα ἀποστῇ ἀπ' ἐμοῦ, purpose clause (ἵνα with subjunc. ἀποστῇ), "that it would leave me." Ἀποστῇ, 3rd sg. aor. act subjunc. of ἀφίστημι, "leave, withdraw from." Ἀπ', prep. with gen. ἐμοῦ, "from me."

VERSE 9

καὶ εἴρηκέν μοι, Ἀρκεῖ σοι ἡ χάρις μου, ἡ γὰρ δύναμις ἐν ἀσθενείᾳ τελεῖται.
But he said to me, "My grace is sufficient for you, for my power is perfected in weakness."

Εἴρηκέν, 3rd sg. perf. act. indic. of λέγω, "say." Μοι, dat. 1st sg. pron. ἐγώ, "me," indir. obj. of εἴρηκέν. Ἀρκεῖ, 3rd sg. pres. act. indic. of ἀρκέω, "be sufficient." Σοι, dat. 2nd sg. pron. σύ, "you," indir. obj. of ἀρκεῖ. Δύναμις, nom. sg. fem. δύναμις, -εως, ἡ, "power," subj. of τελεῖται. Some mss. add μου, reflected in the CSB translation "my power"; cf. discussion in Metzger 517. Harris 863: "In the present context it seems impossible to posit a precise distinction between δύναμις and χάρις: here they are essentially synonymous. Both denote divine gifts of enablement, the power for Paul to fulfill his apostolic calling." Ἐν, prep. with dat. ἀσθενείᾳ, "in weakness," locat. dat. Τελεῖται, 3rd sg. pres. pass. indic. of τελέω, "reach perfection, complete."

ἥδιστα οὖν μᾶλλον καυχήσομαι ἐν ταῖς ἀσθενείαις μου,
Therefore, I will most gladly boast all the more about my weaknesses,

Ἥδιστα, adv., "gladly." BDF (§60[2]): "very gladly." Μᾶλλον, adv., "all the more." Cf. BDF (§246): "ἥδιστα μᾶλλον 2 C 12:9 do not go together: 'gladly (stereotyped elative superl.) will I boast rather. . . .'" Cf. R 664. Καυχήσομαι, 1st sg. fut. mid. indic. of καυχάομαι, "boast." Ἐν, prep. with dat. ταῖς ἀσθενείαις, "in weaknesses." Moule 79: "perhaps *boast about*. . . ."

ἵνα ἐπισκηνώσῃ ἐπ' ἐμὲ ἡ δύναμις τοῦ Χριστοῦ.
so that Christ's power may reside in me.

Ἵνα with subjunc. ἐπισκηνώσῃ, "so that (Christ's power) may reside (in me)." Harris 865: "the acknowledgment of 'weakness' is a precondition for the exercise of Christ's power." Ἐπισκηνώσῃ, 3rd sg. aor. act. subjunc. of ἐπισκηνόω, "reside, rest upon." This verb is found only here in the NT, not at all in the LXX or the papyri. Before Paul, its only known use is by Polybius, the Greek historian (c. 201–120 BC) who used it twice of the billeting of soldiers. It may, therefore, be better to translate the verb as "dwell in" or "reside" rather than "rest upon." Either way it is the experience of Christ's power in his weakness that enables Paul to boast. Ἐπ', prep. with acc. ἐμέ, "upon/in me." Δύναμις, nom. sg. fem. δύναμις, -εως, ἡ, "power," subj. of ἐπισκηνώσῃ. Τοῦ Χριστοῦ, either subj. gen. "(power) bestowed by Christ," or poss. gen. "Christ's (power)."

VERSE 10

διὸ εὐδοκῶ ἐν ἀσθενείαις, ἐν ὕβρεσιν, ἐν ἀνάγκαις, ἐν διωγμοῖς καὶ στενοχωρίαις, ὑπὲρ
    Χριστοῦ·
So I take pleasure in weaknesses, insults, hardships, persecutions, and in difficulties, for the sake of Christ.

Διό, conj., "therefore." Εὐδοκῶ, 1st sg. pres. act. indic. of εὐδοκέω, "take pleasure, be well pleased." Harris 866: "It was precisely because (διό, 'that is why') Paul's weaknesses provided him with the opportunity to experience Christ's power (v. 9b) that he could even take pleasure in them." Ἐν, prep. with dat. ἀσθενείαις, "in weaknesses." Ἀσθενείαις, dat. pl. fem. ἀσθένεια, -ας, ἡ, "weakness." Ἐν, prep. with dat. ὕβρεσιν, "in insults." Ὕβρεσιν, dat. pl. fem. ὕβρις, -εως, ἡ, "insult." Ἐν, prep. with dat. ἀνάγκαις, "in hardships." Ἀνάγκαις, dat. pl. fem. ἀνάγκη, -ης, ἡ, "hardship." Ἐν, prep. with dat. διωγμοῖς, "in persecutions." Διωγμοῖς, dat. pl. masc. διωγμός, -οῦ, ὁ, "persecution." (Ἐν), prep. with dat. στενοχωρίαις, "in difficulties." Στενοχωρίαις, dat. pl. fem. στενοχωρία, -ας, ἡ, "difficulties." Ὑπέρ, prep. with gen. Χριστοῦ, "for the sake of Christ."

ὅταν γὰρ ἀσθενῶ, τότε δυνατός εἰμι.
For when I am weak, then I am strong.

Ὅταν, conj., "when, whenever." Ἀσθενῶ 1st sg. pres. act. subjunc. of ἀσθενέω, "be weak." Τότε, adv. "then." Δυνατός, nom. sg. masc. adj. δυνατός, -ή, -όν, "strong."

5. Signs of an Apostle (12:11–13)

With these verses Paul brings his "fool's speech" to an end. He says that the whole exercise was an act of folly, but one he was forced into by the failure of his converts to speak up on his behalf. They ought to have commended him, rather than he having to indulge in the folly of boasting on his own behalf, for in fact he was in no way inferior to the so-called super-apostles. The Corinthians had been favored by the performance of apostolic signs, the only thing they had missed out on was being burdened financially by Paul. He concludes ironically by asking their forgiveness for this wrong!

STRUCTURE

11 Γέγονα ἄφρων,
    ὑμεῖς με ἠναγκάσατε.
    ἐγὼ γὰρ ὤφειλον ὑφ᾽ ὑμῶν συνίστασθαι·
    οὐδὲν γὰρ ὑστέρησα τῶν ὑπερλίαν ἀποστόλων
        εἰ καὶ οὐδέν εἰμι.
12 τὰ μὲν σημεῖα τοῦ ἀποστόλου κατειργάσθη
                        ἐν ὑμῖν
                        ἐν πάσῃ ὑπομονῇ,
                        σημείοις τε
                        καὶ τέρασιν
                        καὶ δυνάμεσιν.
13 τί γὰρ ἐστιν ὃ ἡσσώθητε
        ὑπὲρ τὰς λοιπὰς ἐκκλησίας,
        εἰ μὴ ὅτι αὐτὸς ἐγὼ οὐ κατενάρκησα ὑμῶν;
    χαρίσασθέ μοι τὴν ἀδικίαν ταύτην.

VERSE 11

Γέγονα ἄφρων, ὑμεῖς με ἠναγκάσατε. ἐγὼ γὰρ ὤφειλον ὑφ᾽ ὑμῶν συνίστασθαι·
I have been a fool; you forced it on me. You ought to have commended me,

If, instead of accepting the criticisms made by his opponents, the Corinthians had spoken up on Paul's behalf, testifying that it was through his preaching they had been converted (cf. 1 Cor 9:1b–2), that God had confirmed his preaching with signs and wonders, and that his behavior among them had been exemplary, then he would have had no need to boast on his own behalf.

Γέγονα, 1st sg. perf. act. indic. of γίνομαι, "be, become." Ἄφρων, nom. sg. masc. adj. ἄφρων, -ον, "foolish." BDF (§495[3]): "Paul knows how to change his tone in an astonishing way and uses *prodiorthosis* (an anticipatory correction) when he feels he is about to give offense (e.g. 2 C 11:1ff., 16ff., 21) . . . or *epidiorthosis* (a subsequent correction of a previous impression) when he feels that he has offended e.g. 12:11 γέγονα ἄφρων . . .)."

Ὑμεῖς . . . ἐγώ, prons. used for emphasis: "In effect Paul says, 'You Corinthians forced me to indulge in self-commendation when in fact *I* ought to have been commended by you.'" Ὑμεῖς, emphatic subj. of ἠναγκάσατε. Ἠναγκάσατε, 2nd pl. aor. act. indic. of ἀναγκάζω, "compel, force." R 920: "in 2 Cor. 12:11, ἐγὼ ὤφειλον ὑφ᾽ ὑμῶν συνίστασθαι, we have a simple past obligation." Ἐγώ, emphatic subj. of ὤφειλον . . . συνίστασθαι, "*I* ought to have been commended (by you)." Cf. BDAG 743c. Ὤφειλον 1st sg. impf. act. indic. of ὀφείλω, "ought, be obligated." Ὑφ᾽, prep. with gen. ὑμῶν, "by you," expresses agency. Συνίστασθαι, pres. mid. inf. of συνίστημι, "commend."

οὐδὲν γὰρ ὑστέρησα τῶν ὑπερλίαν ἀποστόλων εἰ καὶ οὐδέν εἰμι.
since I am not in any way inferior to those "super-apostles," even though I am nothing.

Οὐδέν, acc. sg. neut. οὐδείς, οὐδεμία, οὐδέν, "nothing." Ὑστέρησα, 1st sg. aor. act. indic. of ὑστερέω, "be inferior, lack." Τῶν ὑπερλίαν ἀποστόλων, gen. of comp. "(when compared) to those 'super-apostles,'" referring to his opponents in Corinth. Ὑπερλίαν, adv., "outstanding, special," used sarcastically. Ἀποστόλων, gen. pl. masc. ἀπόστολος, -ου, ὁ, "apostle." Εἰ καί, "even if/though." Οὐδέν εἰμι, "I am nothing,"

VERSE 12

τὰ μὲν σημεῖα τοῦ ἀποστόλου κατειργάσθη ἐν ὑμῖν ἐν πάσῃ ὑπομονῇ,
The signs of an apostle were performed with unfailing endurance among you,

Harris 873: "v. 12 supplies the evidence for Paul's being 'in no way inferior' to the superlative apostles (v. 11b) and the reason why the Corinthians should have been rallying to support him (v. 11a)." Σημεῖα, nom. pl. neut. σημεῖον, -ου, τό, "sign." Τοῦ ἀποστόλου, gen. phrase qualifying σημεῖα, prob. subj. gen. "performed by an apostle." Κατειργάσθη, 3rd sg. aor. pass. indic. of κατεργάζομαι, "perform, work." Ἐν prep. with locat. dat. ὑμῖν, "among you." Ἐν, prep. with dat. πάσῃ ὑπομονῇ, "with all endurance," expresses the manner in which the signs of an apostle were performed by Paul. Ὑπομονῇ, dat. sg. fem. ὑπομονή, -ῆς, ἡ, "endurance, perseverance."

σημείοις τε καὶ τέρασιν καὶ δυνάμεσιν.
including signs and wonders and miracles.

This phrase stands in apposition to τὰ σημεῖα τοῦ ἀποστόλου, and it is a common expression used in the LXX, especially in relation to the events associated with the Exodus. Harris 876 lists four ways the dat. case of σημείοις τε καὶ τέρασιν καὶ δυνάμεσιν has been understood: (1) *locative* (the signs of an apostle were shown in signs and wonders), (2) *instrumental* (the signs of an apostle were shown by signs and wonders), (3) *epexegetical* (the signs of an apostle consisted of signs and wonders), and (4) *sociative* (the signs of an apostle were accompanied by signs and wonders). He concludes: "Our preference is for view (2)."

Σημείοις, dat. pl. neut. σημεῖον, -ου, τό, "sign." Τέρασιν, dat. pl. neut. τέρας, -ατος, τό, "wonder." Δυνάμεσιν, dat. pl. fem. δύναμις, -εως, ἡ, "miracles, mighty works."

In Romans (written shortly after these chapters) Paul speaks of his ministry in terms of "what Christ has accomplished through me by word and deed for the obedience of the Gentiles, by the power of miraculous signs and wonders, and by the power of God's Spirit" (Rom 15:18–19). Clearly the performance of "the signs of an apostle" was a normal accompaniment to Paul's ministry, and in this respect the Corinthian church had been no less favored than others.

VERSE 13

τί γάρ ἐστιν ὃ ἡσσώθητε ὑπὲρ τὰς λοιπὰς ἐκκλησίας,
So in what way are you worse off than the other churches,

BDAG 397b: *"in what respect, then, are you being made to feel less important than the other congregations?"* Τί γάρ ἐστιν ὃ ἡσσώθητε, Moule: "the mng. must be what is there in regard to which *you came off worse . . .* ?" Τί γάρ ἐστιν ὃ, "in what way." Ἡσσώθητε, 2nd pl. aor. pass. indic. of ἑσσόομαι, "treat worse." Ὑπέρ, prep. with acc. τὰς λοιπὰς ἐκκλησίας, "more than the other churches." Λοιπάς, acc. pl. fem. adj. λοιπός, -ή, -όν, "other, rest of." Ἐκκλησίας, acc. pl. fem. ἐκκλησία, -ας, ἡ, "church."

εἰ μὴ ὅτι αὐτὸς ἐγὼ οὐ κατενάρκησα ὑμῶν; χαρίσασθέ μοι τὴν ἀδικίαν ταύτην.
except that I personally did not burden you? Forgive me for this wrong!

Εἰ μή, "except." Αὐτός, nom. sg. masc. emphatic pron. with ἐγώ, "I *myself.*" Κατενάρκησα, 1st sg. aor. act. indic. of καταναρκάω, "burden," takes gen. of one burdened. Ὑμῶν, gen. 2nd pl. pron. "you," gen. after κατενάρκησα. Χαρίσασθέ, 2nd pl. aor. mid. impv. of χαρίζομαι, "forgive," here perhaps expresses sarcasm. Μοι, dat. 1st sg. pron. ἐγώ, "me," indir. obj. of χαρίσασθέ. Τὴν ἀδικίαν ταύτην, "this wrong," dir. obj. of χαρίσασθέ. Ἀδικίαν, acc. sg. fem. ἀδικία, -ας, ἡ, "wrongdoing."

Perhaps the Corinthians felt offended that Paul had refused to accept support from them while accepting it from other churches. If this was the case, then Paul asks them ironically, *forgive me this wrong,* implying it would seem strange indeed that they should object to being not burdened and not exploited by him, as they had been by his opponents (cf. 11:20).

FOR FURTHER STUDY

105. Visions and Revelation (12:1–4)

Baird, W. "Visions, Revelation, and Ministry: Reflections on 2 Cor 12:1–5 and Gal 1:11–17." *JBL* 104 (1985): 651–62.

Goulder, M. D. "Vision and Knowledge." *JSNT* 56 (1994): 53–71.

Litwa, M. D. "Paul's Mosaic Ascent: An Interpretation of 2 Corinthians 12.7–9." *NTS* 57 (2011): 238–57.

Mare, W. H. "The New Testament Concept regarding the Regions of Heaven with Emphasis on 2 Corinthians 12:1–4." *GJ* 11 (1970): 3–12.

Marmodoro, A., and J. Hill, eds. *The Author's Voice in Classical and Late Antiquity.* Oxford: Oxford University Press, 2013.

Morray-Jones, C. R. A. "Paradise Revisited (2 Cor 12:1–12): The Jewish Mystical Background of Paul's Apostolate. Part 1: The Jewish Sources." *HTR* 86 (1993): 177–217.

Thrall, M. E. "Paul's Journey to Paradise: Some Exegetical Issues in 2 Cor 12,2–4." In *The Corinthian Correspondence*, edited by R. Bieringer, 347–63. Leuven: Leuven University, 1996.

106. Human Weakness and the Power of God (12:5, 9–10)

Black, D. A. *DPL* 966–67.

Rauer, M. *Die "Schwachen" in Korinth und Rom.* Freiburg: Herder, 1923.

Ortlund, D."'Power Is Made Perfect in Weakness' (2 Cor. 12:9): A Biblical Theology of Strength through Weakness." *Presbyterion* 36 (2010): 86–108.

Roetzel, C. J. "The Language of War (2 Cor. 10:1–6) and the Language of Weakness (2 Cor. 11:21b–13:10)." *BibInt* 17 (2009): 77–99.

107. Paul's Thorn in the Flesh (12:7–8)

Heckel. U. "Der Dorn im Fleisch. Die Krankheit des Paulus in 2 Kor 12,7 und Gal 4,13f." *ZNW* 84 (1993): 65–92.

Hood, J. B. "The Temple and the Thorn: 2 Corinthians 12 and Paul's Heavenly Ecclesiology." *BBR* 21 (2011): 357–70.

Leary, T. J. "'A Thorn in the Flesh'– 2 Corinthians 12:7." *JTS* n.s. 43 (1992): 520–22.

McCant, J. W. "Paul's Thorn of Rejected Apostleship." *NTS* 34 (1988): 550–72.

Russell, R. "Redemptive Suffering and Paul's Thorn in the Flesh." *JETS* 39 (1996): 559–70.

Woods, L. "Opposition to a Man and His Message: Paul's 'Thorn in the Flesh' (2 Cor 12:7)." *ABR* 39 (1991): 44–53.

108. The Signs of an Apostle (12:11–13)

Jervell, J. "The Signs of an Apostle: Paul's Miracles." In *The Unknown God: Essays on Luke-Acts and Early Christian History*, 77–95. Minneapolis: Augsburg, 1984.

Käsemann, E. "Die Legitimität des Apostels. Eine Untersuchung zu II Korinther 10–13." *ZNW* 41 (1942): 33–71.

Twelftree, G. H. *DPL* 875–77.

109. False Apostles, Servants of Satan (12:11)

Barrett, C. K. "Paul's Opponents in 2 Corinthians" In *Essays on Paul*, 60–86. London: SPCK, 1982.

Barrier, J. W. "Visions of Weakness: Apocalyptic Genre and the Identification of Paul's Opponents in 2 Corinthians 12:1–6." *ResQ* 47 (2005): 33–42.

Kee, D. "Who Were the Super-Apostles of 2 Corinthians 10–13?" *ResQ* 23 (1980): 65–76.

McClelland, S. E. "'Super-Apostles, Servants of Christ, Servants of Satan': A Response." *JSNT* 14 (1982): 82–87.

Sumney, J. L. *"Servants of Satan," "False Brothers" and Other Opponents of Paul.* JSNTSup 188. Sheffield: Sheffield Academic, 1999.

Thrall, M. E. "Super-Apostles, Servants of Christ, and Servants of Satan." *JSNT* 6 (1980): 42–57.

HOMILETICAL SUGGESTIONS

Boasting about Visions and Revelations (12:1–6)

1. Boasting necessitated by the agenda set by Paul's opponents (v. 1)
2. Paul speaks in the 3rd person to minimize attention upon himself (vv. 2–6)

Paul's Thorn in the Flesh (12:7–10)

1. A thorn in the flesh keeps one from being too elated (v 7)
2. God's grace is sufficient—his power is perfected in weakness (v. 9–10)

Paul Is in No Way Inferior to the "Super Apostles" (12:11–13)

1. Speaking against one's better judgment for the sake of the ministry (v. 11)
2. The signs of an apostle (v. 12)
3. Paul's practice of not burdening people financially while working among them (v. 13)

D. PAUL'S PLANNED THIRD VISIT (12:14–13:10)

Having been forced to "boast" about his apostolic credentials in the "fool's speech" to demonstrate to the Corinthians that he was in no way inferior to the false apostles, in this section Paul addresses other matters that cried out for attention: he defends his financial integrity (12:14–18), insists he has his readers' best interests in mind (12:19–21), deals with charges brought against him (13:1–4), and exhorts his readers to examine themselves (13:5–10).

1. Paul Refuses to Burden the Corinthians (12:14–18)

In vv. 14–18 Paul defends his financial integrity, assuring the Corinthians that he is willing to spend his resources and to be spent himself for their benefit, and neither he nor those whom he sent intended to exploit them (12:14–18).

STRUCTURE

14 Ἰδοὺ τρίτον τοῦτο ἑτοίμως ἔχω ἐλθεῖν πρὸς ὑμᾶς,
    καὶ οὐ καταναρκήσω·
    οὐ γὰρ ζητῶ τὰ ὑμῶν ἀλλ᾽ ὑμᾶς.
    οὐ γὰρ ὀφείλει τὰ τέκνα τοῖς γονεῦσιν θησαυρίζειν
    ἀλλ᾽ οἱ γονεῖς τοῖς τέκνοις.
15 ἐγὼ δὲ ἥδιστα δαπανήσω
                καὶ ἐκδαπανηθήσομαι
                        ὑπὲρ τῶν ψυχῶν ὑμῶν.
                εἰ περισσοτέρως ὑμᾶς ἀγαπῶ[ν],
    ἧσσον ἀγαπῶμαι;
16 ἔστω δέ,
    ἐγὼ οὐ κατεβάρησα ὑμᾶς·
                ἀλλ᾽ ὑπάρχων πανοῦργος
    δόλῳ ὑμᾶς ἔλαβον.
17 μή τινα ὧν ἀπέσταλκα πρὸς ὑμᾶς,
        δι᾽ αὐτοῦ ἐπλεονέκτησα ὑμᾶς;
18 παρεκάλεσα Τίτον
    καὶ συναπέστειλα τὸν ἀδελφόν·
    μήτι ἐπλεονέκτησεν ὑμᾶς Τίτος;
    οὐ τῷ αὐτῷ πνεύματι περιεπατήσαμεν;
    οὐ τοῖς αὐτοῖς ἴχνεσιν;

VERSE 14

Ἰδοὺ τρίτον τοῦτο ἑτοίμως ἔχω ἐλθεῖν πρὸς ὑμᾶς,
Look, I am ready to come to you this third time.

This statement is ambiguous both in the original and in the CSB translation. It could mean either that this is the third time Paul has been ready to make a visit (without indicating whether he actually made all the visits for which he was ready), or that he is now ready to make his third visit. Fortunately, 13:1 resolves the question, confirming that he is about to embark on his third visit. The two previous ones were the pioneer missionary visit and the "painful visit." Paul's intended third visit is mentioned in several other places in this letter (10:2; 12:20–21; 13:1, 10), and from these references it is clear that the apostle was ready for a showdown, though he still hoped it would not come to that.

᾽Ιδού, particle, "behold." BDAG 468b: "demonstrative or presentative particle that draws attention to what follows. . . . It is actually the aor. mid. impv. of εἶδον, ἰδοῦ, except that it is accented w. the acute when used as a particle . . . '(you) see, look, behold.'" Τρίτον, adv., "a third time." Barnett 584, n. 6: "By its position at the head of the sentence, τρίτον is emphatic. τρίτον τοῦτο is preferably taken with (1) ἐλθεῖν rather than with (2) ἐτοίμως ἔχω. The emphasis is on the visit rather than the preparation for the visit." Ἑτοίμως, adv., "readily." Ἑτοίμως ἔχω, "be ready." Moule 161: "adverbs tend to be used instead of adjectives of states of health; but whereas English uses the verb *to be*, the Greek idiom curiously uses ἔχω. . . . ἐτοίμως ἔχω occurs in Acts xxi.13, II Cor. xii. 14, I Pet. iv.5." Cf. BDF §154. Ἐλθεῖν, aor. act. inf. of ἔρχομαι, "come." Πρός, prep. with acc. ὑμᾶς, "to you."

καὶ οὐ καταναρκήσω·οὐ γὰρ ζητῶ τὰ ὑμῶν ἀλλ᾽ ὑμᾶς.
I will not burden you, since I am not seeking what is yours, but you.

Καταναρκήσω, 1st sg. fut. act. indic. of καταναρκάω, "be a burden." Ζητῶ, 1st sg. pres. act. indic. of ζητέω, "seek." Τὰ ὑμῶν, "what is yours." Ἀλλ᾽, advers. conj., "but, on the contrary." Ὑμᾶς, acc. 2nd pl. pron., "you," dir. obj. of ζητῶ.

οὐ γὰρ ὀφείλει τὰ τέκνα τοῖς γονεῦσιν θησαυρίζειν ἀλλ᾽ οἱ γονεῖς τοῖς τέκνοις.
For children ought not save up for their parents, but parents for their children.

This is a second use of a parenthood metaphor (cf. 6:13). Ὀφείλει, 3rd sg. pres. act. indic. of ὀφείλω, "be obligated," sg. num. with neut. pl. subj. τέκνα. Τέκνα, nom. pl. neut. τέκνον, -ου, τό, "children." Γονεῦσιν, dat. pl. masc. γονεύς, -έως, ὁ, "parent," indir. obj. of ὀφείλει . . . θησαυρίζειν. Barnett 583: "Paul was their father-provider . . . who will spend himself for them . . . not their 'client,' to 'be patronized' in the conventions of that culture."

Θησαυρίζειν, pres. act. inf. of θησαυρίζω, "save up." Paul uses this verb in his advice concerning the collection: "On the first day of the week, each of you is to set something aside and *save* [θησαυρίζων] in keeping with how he is prospering, so that no collections will need to be made when I come" (1 Cor 16:2). This advice may have been falsely construed by his opponents to mean that he wanted his spiritual children to save up money for him. Paul denies such accusations by saying that it is parents who should lay up for their children and not vice versa.

Ἀλλ᾿, advers. conj., "but, on the contrary." Γονεῖς, nom. pl. masc. γονεύς, -έως, ὁ, "parent," subj. of ὀφείλει . . . θησαυρίζειν. Τέκνοις, dat. pl. neut. τέκνον, -ου, τό, "child," indir. obj. of ὀφείλει . . . θησαυρίζειν.

VERSE 15

ἐγὼ δὲ ἥδιστα δαπανήσω καὶ ἐκδαπανηθήσομαι ὑπὲρ τῶν ψυχῶν ὑμῶν.
I will most gladly spend and be spent for you.

Ἐγὼ δέ, emphatic. Ἥδιστα, adv., "very gladly." Δαπανήσω, 1st sg. fut. act. indic. of δαπανάω, "spend." Ἐκδαπανηθήσομαι, 1st sg. fut. pass. indic. of ἐκδαπανάω, "spend, exhaust." BDAG 300b: "in our lit. only fig. in pass. *be spent* of the sacrifice of one's own life ὑπέρ τινος *for someone*." Ὑπέρ, prep. with gen. τῶν ψυχῶν ὑμῶν, "for you," lit. "for your souls." Ψυχῶν, gen. pl. fem. ψυχή, -ῆς, ἡ, "soul."

εἰ περισσοτέρως ὑμᾶς ἀγαπῶ[ν], ἧσσον ἀγαπῶμαι;
If I love you more, am I to be loved less?

Εἰ περισσοτέρως ὑμᾶς ἀγαπῶν, Harris 886: "there are two ways of construing these words. 1. As the *protasis* of a conditional sentence in which v. 15a is the apodosis . . . 2. As the first part of a *rhetorical question* that is separate from v. 15a." Some MSS omit εἰ and others add καί (see Metzger 517). Περισσοτέρως, comp. adv., "more, even more so." Ἀγαπῶ, 1st sg. pres. act. indic. of ἀγαπάω, "love." Ἀγαπῶ[ν], nom. sg. masc. of pres. act. ptc. of ἀγαπάω, "love." Ἧσσον, adv., "less." Ἀγαπῶμαι, 1st sg. pres. pass. indic. of ἀγαπάω, "love."

VERSE 16

ἔστω δέ, ἐγὼ οὐ κατεβάρησα ὑμᾶς· ἀλλ᾿ ὑπάρχων πανοῦργος δόλῳ ὑμᾶς ἔλαβον.
Now granted, I did not burden you; yet sly as I am, I took you in by deceit!

Ἔστω, 3rd sg. pres. impv. of εἰμί, "granted," lit. "let it be." R 948: "ἔστω δέ is like our 'Let it be so' or 'Granted.'" Barnett 586 n. 16: "The idiom is used to express a point on which writer and readers are in at least provisional agreement." Ἐγώ, emphatic. Κατεβάρησα, 1st sg. aor. act. indic. of καταβαρέω, "burden." BDAG 514d: "*burden, be a burden to* τινά *someone*." Barnett 587: "The verb 'weigh down' [καταβαρέω], referring to ships' ballast (cf. 1:8), is even more definite than the verb 'burdened' [καταναρκά] in vv. 13 and 14." Ὑμᾶς, acc. 2nd pl. σύ, "you," dir. obj. of κατεβάρησα.

Ὑπάρχων πανοῦργος, Moule 103: "*villain as I was.* . . ." Ὑπάρχων, nom. sg. masc. of pres. act. ptc. of ὑπάρχω, "be." BDAG 1029d: "to be in a state or circumstance, *be* as a widely used substitute in H. Gk. for εἶναι." Barnett 587 n. 21: "a participle of causal meaning, 'since,' 'being,' which, when taken with πανοῦργος, means 'being by constitution crafty' (Hughes, 464)." Πανοῦργος, nom. sg. masc. adj., πανοῦργος, -ον, "sly, crafty." Cf. 11:3: "as the serpent deceived Eve by his cunning (πανουργίᾳ)." Δόλῳ, dat.

sing. masc. δόλος, -ου, ὁ, "deceit, cunning," dat. of means. Ὑμᾶς, acc. 2nd pl. σύ, "you,"
dir. obj. of ἔλαβον. Ἔλαβον, 1st sg. aor. act. indic. of λαμβάνω, "take."

VERSE 17

μή τινα ὧν ἀπέσταλκα πρὸς ὑμᾶς, δι' αὐτοῦ ἐπλεονέκτησα ὑμᾶς;
Did I take advantage of you by any of those [lit. "through him"] I sent you?

Z §29: "2 Cor 12,17 μή τινα ὧν ἀπέσταλκα πρὸς ὑμᾶς, δι' αὐτοῦ ἐπλεονέκτησα ὑμᾶς,
where the accusative of τινα is determined by the accusative latent in ὧν standing for
ἐκείνων οὕς." Cf. BDF §466[1]; R 436. Moule 176: "μή τινα . . . δι' αὐτοῦ ἐπλεονέκτησα,
is a well-known anacolouthon, and may possibly be due to the . . . Semitic way of
handling pronouns, as it were retrospectively." A question, introduced by μή, expects
a neg. response. Τινα, acc. sg. masc. indef. pron. τις, τι, "one, any one." Ὧν, gen. pl.
masc. pron. ὅς, ἥ, ὅ, "whom." Ἀπέσταλκα, 1st sg. pf. act. indic. of ἀποστέλλω, "send."
BDF (§343[2]) cited as an example of "the late use of the perfect in narrative." Πρός,
prep. with acc. ὑμᾶς, "to you."

Δι', prep. with gen. αὐτοῦ, "through him." Thrall 2:852: "an example of a suspended
noun or pronoun (i.e., a noun or pronoun unrelated grammatically to the main sentence) which is resumed (in effect repeated) by a pronoun in another case (correctly
related to the main sentence)." Ἐπλεονέκτησα, 1st sg. aor. act. indic. of πλεονεκτέω,
"take advantage of, exploit." Ὑμᾶς, acc. 2nd pl. σύ, "you," dir. obj. of ἐπλεονέκτησα.
Barnett 588: "Paul's reply evidently mirrors the charge some are making. 'True, he
does not receive money from us directly. But what about the money he receives from
us indirectly, *through* his envoys who have come here?'"

VERSE 18

παρεκάλεσα Τίτον καὶ συναπέστειλα τὸν ἀδελφόν· μήτι ἐπλεονέκτησεν ὑμᾶς Τίτος;
I urged Titus to go, and I sent the brother with him. Titus didn't take advantage of you,
did he?

Cf. earlier reference (8:16–18) to Paul sending Titus with the brother to Corinth.
Παρεκάλεσα, 1st sg. aor. act. indic. of παρακαλέω, "urge, exhort." Συναπέστειλα, 1st
sg. aor. act. indic. of συναποστέλλω, "send with." Ἀδελφόν, acc. sg. masc. ἀδελφός,
-οῦ, ὁ, "brother." Μήτι, interrog. particle. ZG 561: "a strengthened form of μή," introduces a question expecting a neg. response. Ἐπλεονέκτησεν, 3rd sg. aor. act. indic.
of πλεονεκτέω, "take advantage of, exploit." Ὑμᾶς, acc. 2nd pl. σύ, "you," dir. obj. of
ἐπλεονέκτησεν. Τίτος, subj. of ἐπλεονέκτησεν.

οὐ τῷ αὐτῷ πνεύματι περιεπατήσαμεν; οὐ τοῖς αὐτοῖς ἴχνεσιν;
Didn't we walk in the same spirit and in the same footsteps?

Οὐ, neg. particle introduces a question expecting a positive response. Τῷ αὐτῷ πνεύματι, dat. phrase expresses the manner in which Paul walked. Harris, *Prepositions*, 78: "περιπατεῖν is usually followed by κατά . . . the simple dative (2Co 12:18 . . .), or an adverb or adverbial phrase . . . when the manner, means, or time of the περιπατεῖν is designated." Αὐτῷ, standing in attrib. position, denotes "the same (spirit)." Πνεύματι, dat. sg. neut. πνεῦμα, -ατος, τό, "spirit." Περιεπατήσαμεν, 1st pl. aor. act. indic. of περιπατέω, "walk"; the pl. subject refers to Paul and Titus. Barnett 590, n. 43: "'the same spirit,' is to be understood anthropologically ('the same mind') because of the parallel in the balancing question ('the same steps'), as argued by Furnish, 560."

Τοῖς αὐτοῖς ἴχνεσιν, dat. phrase "the same footsteps (in which Paul walked)." Αὐτοῖς standing in attrib. position denotes "the same (footsteps)." Ἴχνεσιν, dat. pl. neut. ἴχνος, -ους, τό, "footstep." Moule 156: "In questions . . . μή expects the answer 'No' and οὐ 'yes': II Cor. xii.18 μήτι ἐπλεονέκτησεν ὑμᾶς Τίτος; (answer 'No'); οὐ τῷ αὐτῷ πνεύματι περιεπατήσαμεν; (answer 'Yes')."

2. The Real Purpose of Paul's Fool's Speech (12:19–21)

In these verses Paul seeks to clarify the underlying motive of his boasting. He felt forced into it because his audience had been influenced adversely by the boasting of his opponents, and he needed to show that he was in no way inferior to them. But underlining that, his real aim was to strengthen his converts (v. 19). And this he did because he was afraid that when he came on his third visit, both he and they would find in one another not what they would desire. They might find Paul acting with bold authority against them, and he might find that many of them were still caught up in the sins of the past (vv. 20–21).

STRUCTURE

19   Πάλαι δοκεῖτε
      ὅτι ὑμῖν ἀπολογούμεθα.
      κατέναντι θεοῦ
      ἐν Χριστῷ
  λαλοῦμεν·
      τὰ δὲ πάντα, ἀγαπητοί,
      ὑπὲρ τῆς ὑμῶν οἰκοδομῆς.
20   φοβοῦμαι γὰρ
          μή πως ἐλθὼν
          οὐχ οἵους θέλω
          εὕρω ὑμᾶς
          κἀγὼ εὑρεθῶ ὑμῖν
          οἷον οὐ θέλετε·
          μή πως ἔρις,
             ζῆλος,
             θυμοί,
             ἐριθεῖαι,

κατασαλιαί,
ψιθυρισμοί,
φυσιώσεις,
ἀκαταστασίαι·
21   μὴ πάλιν ἐλθόντος μου
ταπεινώσῃ με ὁ θεός μου
πρὸς ὑμᾶς
καὶ πενθήσω πολλοὺς
τῶν προημαρτηκότων
καὶ μὴ μετανοησάντων
ἐπὶ τῇ ἀκαθαρσίᾳ
καὶ πορνείᾳ
καὶ ἀσελγείᾳ
ᾗ ἔπραξαν.

VERSE 19

Πάλαι δοκεῖτε ὅτι ὑμῖν ἀπολογούμεθα.
Have you been thinking all along that we were defending ourselves to you?

This has been translated in the CSB (and also in the NIV and NRSV) as a question. It could also be translated as a statement: "You have been thinking all along that we have been defending ourselves to you." But either way Paul's point is the same. He wants to correct a view of his boasting, which interprets it as an effort to defend himself.

Πάλαι, adv., "all along." Δοκεῖτε, 2nd pl. pres. act. indic. of δοκέω, "think." Ὅτι, conj., introduces the content of what was thought. Ὑμῖν, dat. 2nd pl. pron., "you," indir. obj. of ἀπολογούμεθα. Ἀπολογούμεθα, 1st pl. mid. pres. indic. of ἀπολογέομαι, "defend oneself."

κατέναντι θεοῦ ἐν Χριστῷ λαλοῦμεν· τὰ δὲ πάντα, ἀγαπητοί, ὑπὲρ τῆς ὑμῶν οἰκοδομῆς.
No, in the sight of God we are speaking in Christ, and everything, dear friends, is for building you up.

Κατέναντι θεοῦ ἐν Χριστῷ λαλοῦμεν appears to be an oath formula. Κατέναντι, adv. used as a prep. with gen. θεοῦ, "before/in the sight of God." Ἐν, prep. with dat. Χριστῷ, "in Christ." Harris 895: "'in Christ' may be shorthand for 'in the name of Christ,' referring to Paul's role as a person commissioned and empowered by Christ and representing him." Λαλοῦμεν, 1st pl. pres. act. indic. of λαλέω, "speak."

Τὰ . . . πάντα, "everything, all things." Ἀγαπητοί, masc. pl. voc. subst. adj. ἀγαπητός, -ή, -όν, "beloved, dear friends." Ὑπέρ, prep. with gen. οἰκοδομῆς, "for building up." When Paul says "everything . . . is for building you up," he refers, most likely, to all that he has said, done, and written (particularly in the present letter) that they might have mistakenly construed as mere self-defense. Οἰκοδομῆς, gen. sg. fem. οἰκοδομή,

-ῆς, ἡ, "building up, edification." Τῆς ὑμῶν, gen. phrase qualifies οἰκοδομῆς, "your (building up)."

VERSE 20

φοβοῦμαι γὰρ μή πως ἐλθὼν οὐχ οἵους θέλω εὕρω ὑμᾶς κἀγὼ εὑρεθῶ ὑμῖν οἷον οὐ θέλετε·
For I fear that perhaps when I come I will not find you to be what I want, and you may not find me to be what you want.

Φοβοῦμαι, 1st sg. pres. mid. indic. φοβέω, "fear." Μή πως, "perhaps, lest." BDAG 901d: "as conj.: in the form μή πως . . . marker of a negative perspective expressing misgiving, frequently rendered *lest*." BDF (§428[6]): "After μή (πως) expressing apprehension . . . οὐ must be used even before a subjunctive if the verb itself is to be negated." Ἐλθών, nom. sg. masc. of aor. act. ptc. of ἔρχομαι, "come." Οἵους, acc. pl. masc. pron. οἷος, -α, -ον, "what, such as." BDAG 701c: "relative pron . . . pert. to being similar to someth. or belonging to a class, *of what sort (such)*." Θέλω, 1st sg. pres. act. indic., "wish, want." Εὕρω, 1st sg. aor. act. subjunc. of εὑρίσκω, "find." Ὑμᾶς, acc. 2nd pl. pron. σύ, 'you,' dir. obj. of εὕρω. Κἀγώ = καὶ ἐγώ. Εὑρεθῶ, 1st sg. aor. pass. subjunc. of εὑρίσκω, "find." Ὑμῖν, dat. 2nd pl. pron. σύ, "you," dat. of respect. Οἷον, acc. sg. masc. pron. οἷος, -α, -ον, "what, such as." Θέλετε, 2nd pl. pres. act. indic. of θέλω, "wish, want."

Harris 898: "Note the instance of chiasmus (A B C C´ B´ A´) in θέλω εὕρω ὑμᾶς κἀγὼ εὑρεθῶ . . . θέλετε, which has the effect of highlighting the essentially personal character of Paul's relationship to the Corinthian congregation."

μή πως ἔρις, ζῆλος, θυμοί, ἐριθείαι, καταλαλιαί, ψιθυρισμοί, φυσιώσεις, ἀκαταστασίαι·
Perhaps there will be quarreling, jealousy, angry outbursts, selfish ambitions, slander, gossip, arrogance, and disorder.

Cf. the vice list in Gal 5:19–21. Μή πως, "perhaps, lest." BDAG 901d: "as conj.: in the form μή πως . . . marker of a negative perspective expressing misgiving, frequently rendered *lest*." Ἔρις, nom. sg. fem. ἔρις, -ιδος, ἡ, "quarreling, discord." Ζῆλος, nom. sg. masc. ζῆλος, -ου, ὁ, "jealousy." Θυμοί, nom. pl. masc. θυμός, -οῦ, ὁ, "angry outbursts." Ἐριθείαι, nom. pl. fem. ἐριθεία, -ας, ἡ, "selfish ambitions." Καταλαλιαί, nom. pl. fem. καταλαλιά, -ᾶς, ἡ, "slander." Ψιθυρισμοί, nom. pl. masc. ψιθυρισμός, οῦ, ὁ, "gossip." Φυσιώσεις, nom. pl. fem. φυσίωσις, -εως, ἡ, "arrogance." Ἀκαταστασίαι, nom. pl. fem. ἀκαταστασία, -ας, ἡ, "disorder." ZG 562 "If deemed necessary, the pls. of these abstract nouns may be rendered by 'occasions of . . . , acts of. . . .'"

VERSE 21

μὴ πάλιν ἐλθόντος μου ταπεινώσῃ με ὁ θεός μου πρὸς ὑμᾶς
I fear that when I come my God will again humiliate me in your presence,

Πάλιν, adv., "again." Ἐλθόντος μου, gen. abs. depicting circumstances in force at the time of the main verb: "my God will again humiliate me," "when I come." Ἐλθόντος, gen. sg. masc. of aor. act. ptc. of ἔρχομαι, "come." Ταπεινώσῃ, 3rd sg. aor. act. subjunc. of ταπεινόω, "humiliate." The subjunc. mood (negated by μή) expresses doubtful assertion. Με, acc. 1st sg. pron. ἐγώ, "me," dir. obj. of ταπεινώσῃ. Ὁ θεός μου, subj. of ταπεινώσῃ. Πρός, prep with acc. ὑμᾶς, "in your presence."

καὶ πενθήσω πολλοὺς τῶν προημαρτηκότων καὶ μὴ μετανοησάντων
and I will grieve for many who sinned before and have not repented

Πενθήσω, 1st sg. aor. act. subjunc. of πενθέω, "grieve"; the subjunc. mood expresses doubtful assertion. Πολλούς, acc. pl. masc. adj. πολύς, πολλή, πολύ, "many." Τῶν προημαρτηκότων, partitive gen. phrase qualifying πολλούς: "(many) of those who sinned." Προημαρτηκότων, gen. pl. masc. of pf. act. ptc. of προαμαρτάνω, "sin beforehand." Μετανοησάντων, gen. pl. masc. of aor. act. ptc. of μετανοέω, "repent." Barnett 597 n. 16: "The perfect προημαρτηκότων suggests persistence in sexual sin going back to some point subsequent to their baptism . . . whereas the aorists μετανοησάντων and ἔπραξαν suggest that they did not repent during Paul's second visit, or, perhaps, even as a result of the 'Severe Letter.'"

ἐπὶ τῇ ἀκαθαρσίᾳ καὶ πορνείᾳ καὶ ἀσελγείᾳ ᾗ ἔπραξαν.
of the moral impurity, sexual immorality, and sensuality they practiced.

Ἐπί, with dat. ἀκαθαρσίᾳ, πορνείᾳ, ἀσελγείᾳ, expanatory clause specifies the sins for which the Corinthians may not have repented. Ἀκαθαρσίᾳ, dat. sg. fem. ἀκαθαρσία, -ας, ἡ, "moral impurity, uncleanness." BDAG 34a: "fig. a state of moral corruption." Πορνείᾳ, dat. sg. fem. πορνεία, -ας, ἡ, "sexual immorality." BDAG 854a: "unlawful sexual intercourse, *prostitution, unchastity, fornication.*" Ἀσελγείᾳ, dat. sg. fem. ἀσέλγεια, -ας, ἡ, "sensuality." BDAG 141d: "lack of self-constraint which involves one in conduct that violates all bounds of what is socially acceptable, *self-abandonment.*" Ἔπραξαν, 3rd pl. aor. act. indic. of πράσσω, "practice."

FOR FURTHER STUDY

110. Paul's Self-Understanding (12:14–15)

Gutierrez, P. *La Paternité Spirituelle Selon Saint Paul.* Ébib. Paris: Gabalda, 1968.
Peterson. B. K. "Conquest, Control, and the Cross: Paul's Self-Portrayal in 2 Corinthians 10–13." *Int* 52 (1998): 258–70.

111. Paul's Opponents and the Corinthian Church (12:14–17)

Barrett, C. K. "Paul's Opponents in 2 Corinthians." In *Essays on Paul*, 60–86. London: SPCK, 1982.
Court, J. N. "The Controversy with the Adversaries of Paul's Apostolate in the Context of His Relations to the Corinthian Congregation (2 Corinthians 12,14–13:13)." Pages

87–105 in *Verteidigung und Begründung des apostolischen Amtes (2 Kor 10–13)*. Edited by E. Lohse. Benedictina 11. Rome: Abbrazia San Paolo fuori le mura, 1992.

112. Paul's Financial Integrity (12:14–18)

Everts, J. M. *DPL* 295–300
Hurtado, L. W, "The Jerusalem Collection and the Book of Galatians." *JSNT* 5 (1979): 46–62.
McKnight, S. *DPL* 143–47.
Nickle, K. F. *The Collection: A Study in Paul's Strategy*. Naperville: Allenson, 1966.

113. Paul's Fellow Workers (12:17–18)

Barrett, C. K. "Titus," In *Essays on Paul*, 118–31. London: SPCK, 1982.
Best, E. *Paul and His Converts*. Edinburgh: Clark, 1986.
Ellis, E. E. *DPL* 183–89.
Ollrog, W. H. *Paulus und seiner Mitarbeiter*. Neukirchen-Vluyn, Ger.: Neukirchener, 1979.

HOMILETICAL SUGGESTIONS

Financial Integrity (12:14–18)

1. Putting personal relationships ahead of money (v. 14)
2. Willingness to outlay one's own resources in ministry (v. 15)
3. Defending one's integrity for the sake of ministry (vv. 16–18)

Building Up People Is the Goal of Ministry (12:19–21)

1. Ministry is not all about us (v. 19)
2. Deep disappointment experienced when those we serve fall into sin (vv. 20–21)

3. Paul Threatens Strong Action on His Third Visit (13:1–10)

The apostle speaks here in threatening terms of his third visit to Corinth. He informs his audience that when he comes again, any charges they want to bring against him must be supported by two or three witness (v. 1), and that he will not spare offenders (v. 2). If they want proof that Christ is speaking through him, then they shall get it! (v. 3). He tells them that just as Christ was crucified in weakness but now lives by the power of God, so too he (Paul), though sharing the weakness and suffering of Christ, will act with the power of God when he deals with them (v. 4). Alluding again to their demands for proof, Paul responds by challenging his audience to test themselves to see whether they are holding to the faith. He assures his audience that for his part he could never act contrary to the truth (vv. 5–8).

STRUCTURE

1   Τρίτον τοῦτο ἔρχομαι πρὸς ὑμᾶς·
         ἐπὶ στόματος δύο μαρτύρων καὶ τριῶν
     σταθήσεται πᾶν ῥῆμα.
2   προείρηκα καὶ προλέγω,
         ὡς παρὼν τὸ δεύτερον καὶ ἀπὼν νῦν,
         τοῖς προημαρτηκόσιν καὶ τοῖς λοιποῖς πᾶσιν,
         ὅτι ἐὰν ἔλθω εἰς τὸ πάλιν οὐ φείσομαι,
3   ἐπεὶ δοκιμὴν ζητεῖτε
         τοῦ ἐν ἐμοὶ λαλοῦντος Χριστοῦ,

                              ὃς εἰς ὑμᾶς οὐκ ἀσθενεῖ
                                  ἀλλὰ δυνατεῖ ἐν ὑμῖν.

4   καὶ γὰρ ἐσταυρώθη
             ἐξ ἀσθενείας,
         ἀλλὰ ζῇ
             ἐκ δυνάμεως θεοῦ.
     καὶ γὰρ ἡμεῖς ἀσθενοῦμεν
             ἐν αὐτῷ,
         ἀλλὰ ζήσομεν
             σὺν αὐτῷ
             ἐκ δυνάμεως θεοῦ
             εἰς ὑμᾶς.
5   Ἑαυτοὺς πειράζετε
             εἰ ἐστὲ ἐν τῇ πίστει,
     ἑαυτοὺς δοκιμάζετε·
     ἢ οὐκ ἐπιγινώσκετε ἑαυτοὺς
             ὅτι Ἰησοῦς Χριστὸς ἐν ὑμῖν;
             εἰ μήτι ἀδόκιμοί ἐστε.
6   ἐλπίζω δὲ
         ὅτι γνώσεσθε

ὅτι ἡμεῖς οὐκ ἐσμὲν ἀδόκιμοι.
7 εὐχόμεθα δὲ πρὸς τὸν θεὸν
    μὴ ποιῆσαι ὑμᾶς κακὸν μηδέν,
    οὐχ ἵνα ἡμεῖς δόκιμοι φανῶμεν,
    ἀλλ' ἵνα ὑμεῖς τὸ καλὸν ποιῆτε,
    ἡμεῖς δὲ ὡς ἀδόκιμοι ὦμεν.
8 οὐ γὰρ δυνάμεθά τι
        κατὰ τῆς ἀληθείας
        ἀλλ' ὑπὲρ τῆς ἀληθείας.
9 χαίρομεν γὰρ
    ὅταν ἡμεῖς ἀσθενῶμεν,
    ὑμεῖς δὲ δυνατοὶ ἦτε·
τοῦτο καὶ εὐχόμεθα,

τὴν ὑμῶν κατάρτισιν.
10 διὰ τοῦτο ταῦτα ἀπὼν γράφω,
    ἵνα παρὼν μὴ ἀποτόμως χρήσωμαι
            κατὰ τὴν ἐξουσίαν
            ἣν ὁ κύριος ἔδωκέν μοι
                εἰς οἰκοδομὴν
                καὶ οὐκ εἰς καθαίρεσιν.

VERSE 1

Τρίτον τοῦτο ἔρχομαι πρὸς ὑμᾶς·
This is the third time I am coming to you.

Τρίτον τοῦτο, R 674: "is merely an instance of the adjective used absolutely without a substantive." Τρίτον, adj. τρίτος, -η, -ον, used as adv., "a third time." Ἔρχομαι, 1st sg. pres. mid. indic., "come." Harris 906: "Since there is no evidence that the present letter was written en route to Corinth, ἔρχομαι must be a futuristic present ('I shall be coming.' . . .), denoting a present intention regarding future action." Πρός, prep. with acc. ὑμᾶς, "to you."

ἐπὶ στόματος δύο μαρτύρων καὶ τριῶν σταθήσεται πᾶν ῥῆμα.
Every matter must be established by the testimony of two or three witnesses.

Paul here introduces a slightly abbreviated version of Deut 19:15 (LXX). Ἐπί, prep. with gen. στόματος; BDF (§234[4]): "with persons 'before' [i.e., before two witnesses]." ZG 562: "Hebr. Idiom, on the evidence." Harris 907: "ἐπί here means 'on the basis of' . . . so that ἐπὶ στόματος means 'on the basis of the testimony.'" Στόματος, gen. sg. neut. στόμα, -ατος, τό, "mouth." Δύο, gen. pl. masc. adj., "two." Μαρτύρων, gen. pl. masc. μάρτυς, μάρτυρος, ὁ, "witness." Τριῶν, gen. pl. masc. adj. τρεῖς, τρία, "three." Σταθήσεται, 3rd sg. fut. pass. indic. of ἵστημι, "establish." Ῥῆμα, nom. sg. neut. ῥῆμα, -ατος, τό, "matter."

Thrall 2:876 opts for the view that "Paul's quotation from Deuteronomy refers to his two past visits to Corinth and to the third which is imminent. It is difficult to deny a connection between the τρίτον of v. 1a and the τριῶν of v. 1b, and since the first refers to a visit it is at least very likely that the second has identical reference." Cf. Seifrid 476: "The 'two witnesses and three' may be understood to refer not only to Paul's three visits but also to three persons. The first of these is Paul himself. The second is Christ, who speaks in the apostle . . . This third witness will be the Corinthians themselves, in whom Jesus Christ dwells . . ." Harris 908: "they are both visits and warnings, or, rather, warnings that are associated with visits."

VERSE 2

προείρηκα καὶ προλέγω, ὡς παρὼν τὸ δεύτερον καὶ ἀπὼν νῦν,
I gave a warning when I was present the second time, and now I give a warning while I am absent,

Προείρηκα, 1st sg. pf. act. indic. of προλέγω, "say beforehand." Προλέγω, 1st sg. pres. act. indic., "say beforehand." Ὡς, adv. used as comp. particle, "as, while." Παρών, nom. sg. masc. of pres. ptc. of πάρειμι, "be present." Τὸ δεύτερον, BDAG 221a: "neut . . . used as adv. *for the second time*." Δεύτερον, acc. sg. neut. adj. δεύτερος, -α, -ον, "second." Ἀπών, nom. sg. masc. of pres. ptc. of ἄπειμι, "be absent." Νῦν, adv., "now."

τοῖς προημαρτηκόσιν καὶ τοῖς λοιποῖς πᾶσιν, ὅτι ἐὰν ἔλθω εἰς τὸ πάλιν οὐ φείσομαι,
to those who sinned before and to all the rest: If I come again, I will not be lenient,

Τοῖς προημαρτηκόσιν καὶ τοῖς λοιποῖς πᾶσιν, dat. phrase indir obj. of προείρηκα καὶ προλέγω. Τοῖς προημαρτηκόσιν, "those who sinned before." Προημαρτηκόσιν, dat. pl. masc. of pf. act. ptc. of προαμαρτάνω, "sin beforehand/previously." Τοῖς λοιποῖς πᾶσιν, "all the rest." Λοιποῖς, dat. pl. masc. adj. λοιπός, -ή, -όν, as subst. "the others, the rest." Πᾶσιν, dat. pl. masc. adj. πᾶς, πᾶσα, πᾶν, "all."

Barnett 600 n. 38: "The ὅτι recitative suggests that Paul's words ἐὰν . . . οὐ φείσομαι, 'When I come I will not spare . . . ,' are verbatim, i.e., what he said during his second visit (cf. 2:1)." Ἐάν with subjunc. ἔλθω, "if I come." Ἔλθω, 1st sg. aor. act. subjunc. of ἔρχομαι, "come." BDAG 752d: "εἰς τὸ πάλιν = πάλιν." ZG 562: "another time." Moule 69: "again, for another visit." Εἰς used metaphorically in a temporal sense (BDF §206[1]). Πάλιν, adv., "again." Φείσομαι, 1st sg. fut. mid. indic. of φείδομαι, "be lenient, spare."

VERSE 3

ἐπεὶ δοκιμὴν ζητεῖτε τοῦ ἐν ἐμοὶ λαλοῦντος Χριστοῦ,
since you seek proof of Christ speaking in me.

Ἐπεί, conj., "since, because." Δοκιμήν, acc. sg. fem. δοκιμή, -ῆς, ἡ, "proof." Ζητεῖτε, 2nd pl. pres. act. indic. of ζητέω, "seek." Τοῦ . . . λαλοῦντος Χριστοῦ, "of Christ speaking." Barnett 601 n. 44: "Note that the present tense is used, pointing to the Christ's continuing to speak through his apostle." Λαλοῦντος, gen. sg. masc. of pres. act. ptc. of λαλέω, "speak." Ἐν, prep. with instr. dat. ἐμοί, "in me" (CSB), "through me" (NIV). Thrall 2:879: "Paul is not referring, and neither are the Corinthians, to a purely inward experience of verbal communion with Christ. The question is whether, through Paul's words to the Corinthians, the authentic voice of Christ himself is heard."

Influenced by his opponents, the Corinthians had adopted various criteria for testing the validity of apostolic claims. One of these was that through a true apostle the word of Christ should be heard, and there should be evidence to prove that this was so, evidence incl. an impressive presence and powerful speaking ability (10:10), and the performance of signs and wonders (12:11–13). Paul would not have objected to the view that through true apostles Christ speaks, but would have taken strong exception to the proofs of this demanded by his opponents and the Corinthians. He had learned that the power of Christ rested upon the weak, and that Christ spoke through his servants when they proclaimed the gospel, not because of their impressive personal presence, high-sounding words, or accompanying supernatural signs.

ὃς εἰς ὑμᾶς οὐκ ἀσθενεῖ ἀλλὰ δυνατεῖ ἐν ὑμῖν.
He is not weak in dealing with you, but powerful among you.

Harris 912: "εἰς ὑμᾶς (A) οὐκ ἀσθενεῖ (B) ἀλλὰ δυνατεῖ (B´) ἐν ὑμῖν (A´) forms a chiasmus that has the effect of highlighting items A and A´, that is, the personal relationship of Christ to the Corinthians, just as at the end of the next verse (v. 4) εἰς ὑμᾶς focuses attention on Paul's relation to them." Ὅς, nom. sg. masc. rel. pron. ὅς, ἥ, ὅ, "who." Εἰς, prep. with acc. ὑμᾶς, "towards you." CSB: "in dealing with you." Ἀσθενεῖ, 3rd sg. pres. act indic. of ἀσθενέω, "be weak." Δυνατεῖ, 3rd sg. pres. act indic. of δυνατέω, "be powerful." Ἐν, prep. with dat. ὑμῖν, "among you."

VERSE 4

καὶ γὰρ ἐσταυρώθη ἐξ ἀσθενείας, ἀλλὰ ζῇ ἐκ δυνάμεως θεοῦ.
For he was crucified in weakness, but he lives by the power of God.

Καὶ γάρ, ZG 562: "for in fact." Ἐσταυρώθη, 3rd sg. aor. pass. indic. of σταυρόω, "crucify." Ἐξ, prep. with gen. ἀσθενείας, "in/through weakness." R 598: "cause or occasion . . . conveyed by ἐκ." Ἀσθενείας, gen. sg. fem. ἀσθένεια, -ας, ἡ, "weakness."

Ζῆ, 3rd sg. pres. act. indic. of ζάω, "live." Ἐκ, prep. with gen. δυνάμεως, "by/through (the) power (of God)." Δυνάμεως, gen. sg. fem. δύναμις, -εως, ἡ, "power."

καὶ γὰρ ἡμεῖς ἀσθενοῦμεν ἐν αὐτῷ, ἀλλὰ ζήσομεν σὺν αὐτῷ ἐκ δυνάμεως θεοῦ εἰς ὑμᾶς.
For we also are weak in him, but in dealing with you we will live with him by God's power.

Ἡμεῖς, emphatic. Ἀσθενοῦμεν, 1st pl. pres. act. indic. of ἀσθενέω, "be weak." Ἐν, prep. with dat. αὐτῷ, "in him." Harris, *Prepositions*, 202: "The apostle is speaking of his imminent visit to Corinth when in unison with Christ (σὺν αὐτῷ) and with God's power, he will act decisively and vigorously (ζήσομεν) against unrepentant evildoers within the congregation." Ζήσομεν, 1st pl. fut. act. ind. of ζάω, "live." ZG 562: "future with intensive force, *we shall show ourselves very much alive.*" Σύν, prep. with dat. αὐτῷ, "with him." Ἐκ, prep. with gen. δυνάμεως, "by/through (the) power (of God)." Εἰς, prep. with acc. ὑμᾶς, "towards you." CSB: "in dealing with you."

VERSE 5

Ἑαυτοὺς πειράζετε εἰ ἐστὲ ἐν τῇ πίστει, ἑαυτοὺς δοκιμάζετε·
Test yourselves to see if you are in the faith. Examine yourselves.

Ἑαυτούς, acc. 3rd pl. masc. reflex. pron. ἑαυτοῦ, -ῆς, -οῦ, "yourselves." Moule 120: "*Third Person Plural.* This tends to extend itself so as to do duty also for the 1st and 2nd plural—a use not unknown in the Classics." Πειράζετε, 2nd pl. pres. act. impv. of πειράζω, "test." Harris 919: "After πειράζετε, the interrogative particle εἰ could introduce a direct question: 'Examine yourselves: are you living the life of faith?'" Ἐστέ, 2nd pl. pres. indic. of εἰμί, "be." Ἐν, prep. with. dat. τῇ πίστει, "in the faith." Barnett 608: "The article in the phrase, 'in *the* faith' . . . implies the propositional and theological content of that message about Jesus which is the object of 'faith.' The opponents preach 'another' Jesus, a gospel 'different' from that brought to the Corinthians by Paul (11:4); his is the true faith." Harris 920: "the most satisfactory option is to take ἡ πίστις in a broad sense as referring to Christian conduct that accords with Christian doctrine. That is, 'being in the faith' means continuing true to the faith in conduct as well as in belief." Πίστει, dat. sg. fem. πίστις, -εως, ἡ, "faith."

Δοκιμάζετε, 2nd pl. pres. act. impv. of δοκιμάζω, "examine." The positioning of the repeated refl. pron., ἑαυτούς, emphasizes that the Corinthians should be examining themselves rather than Paul.

ἢ οὐκ ἐπιγινώσκετε ἑαυτοὺς ὅτι Ἰησοῦς Χριστὸς ἐν ὑμῖν; εἰ μήτι ἀδόκιμοί ἐστε.
Or do you yourselves not recognize that Jesus Christ is in you?—unless you fail the test.

Ἤ, particle, "or," introduces a rhetorical question—with οὐκ, expects a positive answer. Ἐπιγινώσκετε, 2nd pl. pres. act. indic. of ἐπιγινώσκω, "know, realize." Ὅτι, conj., "that," introduces what Paul doubts the Corinthians realize: "that Jesus Christ is in you." Harris, *Prepositions*, 125: "the direct relation between two individuals is to the fore; reciprocity of fellowship between the believer and Christ is implied."

Εἰ μήτι ἀδόκιμοί ἐστε, BDF (§376): "unless it were so." Εἰ μήτι, "unless." Ἀδόκιμοί, nom. pl. masc. adj. ἀδόκιμος, -ον, "unacceptable." CSB: "fail the test." ZG 562: *not up to standard.*" Ἐστέ, 2nd pl. pres. indic. of εἰμί, "be."

When Paul urged the Corinthians to test themselves, was he implying that they might find they were not true believers? What he says next reveals this was not the case, as does the way he addresses them throughout the letter. The result Paul expected from their self-examination was that they were certainly "in the faith," and his purpose in urging them to do so was that they would conclude that the one who led them to faith in Christ must be a true apostle (cf. v. 6).

VERSE 6

ἐλπίζω δὲ ὅτι γνώσεσθε ὅτι ἡμεῖς οὐκ ἐσμὲν ἀδόκιμοι.
And I hope you will recognize that we ourselves do not fail the test.

Ἐλπίζω, 1st sg. pres. act. indic., "hope." Ὅτι, conj., introduces what Paul hopes: γνώσεσθε ὅτι ἡμεῖς οὐκ ἐσμὲν ἀδόκιμοι γνώσεσθε, "you will recognize that we ourselves do not fail the test." Γνώσεσθε, 2nd pl. fut. mid. indic. of γινώσκω, "know, recognize." Ἡμεῖς, emphatic. Ἀδόκιμοι, nom. pl. masc. adj. ἀδόκιμος, -ον, "unqualified, failed the test."

VERSE 7

εὐχόμεθα δὲ πρὸς τὸν θεὸν μὴ ποιῆσαι ὑμᾶς κακὸν μηδέν, οὐχ ἵνα ἡμεῖς δόκιμοι φανῶμεν,
But we pray to God that you do nothing wrong—not that we may appear to pass the test,

Εὐχόμεθα, 1st pl. pres. mid. indic. of εὔχομαι, "pray." Πρός, prep. with acc. τὸν θεόν, "to God." Μὴ ποιῆσαι ὑμᾶς κακὸν μηδέν, the content of Paul's prayer: "that you do nothing wrong." Ποιῆσαι, aor. act. inf. of ποιέω, "do." Ὑμᾶς, acc. subj. of inf. ποιῆσαι. Κακόν, acc. sg. neut. subst. adj. κακός, -ή, -όν, "wrong, evil." Μηδέν, acc. sg. neut. subst. adj. μηδείς, μηδεμία, μηδέν, "nothing." R 1163: "οὐχ is clearly an *addendum*." Ἵνα with subjunc. φανῶμεν expresses purpose, "(not) that we may appear." Ἡμεῖς, emphatic. Φανῶμεν, 1st pl. aor. pass. subjunc. of φαίνω, "appear." Δόκιμοι, nom. pl. masc. adj. δόκιμος, -ον, "approved, passed the test." R 656: An example of the "predicate adjective."

ἀλλ᾽ ἵνα ὑμεῖς τὸ καλὸν ποιῆτε, ἡμεῖς δὲ ὡς ἀδόκιμοι ὦμεν.
but that you may do what is right, even though we may appear to fail.

Ἵνα with subjunc. ποιῆτε expresses purpose, "that you may do." Cf. Z §415: "ἵνα can in the NT be used absolutely with the sense of an imperative." ποιῆτε, 2nd pl. pres. act. subjunc. of ποιέω, "do." Ὑμεῖς, emphatic complementing emphatic ἡμεῖς. Τὸ καλόν. R 763: an example of the art. occurring with the adj. alone. Καλόν, acc. sg. neut. subst. adj. καλός, -ή, -όν, "right, good."

Ἡμεῖς, emphatic. Ὡς, particle "as." Ἀδόκιμοι, nom. pl. masc. adj. ἀδόκιμος, -ον, "unqualified, failed the test." Ὦμεν, 1st pl. pres. subjunc. of εἰμί, "be." Harris 924: "both ἵνα clauses should be seen as telic, defining first negatively (οὐχ ἵνα), then positively (ἀλλ᾽ ἵνα) the purpose of the prayer."

VERSE 8

οὐ γὰρ δυνάμεθά τι κατὰ τῆς ἀληθείας ἀλλ᾽ ὑπὲρ τῆς ἀληθείας.
For we can't do anything against the truth, but only for the truth.

Δυνάμεθά, 1st pl. pres. mid. indic. of δύναμαι, "be able." Τί, acc. sg. neut. indef. pron. τις, τι, "anything." Κατά, prep. with gen. τῆς ἀληθείας, "against the truth." Ἀληθείας, gen. sg. fem. ἀλήθεια, -ας, ἡ, "truth," here mng. the truth of the gospel. Ὑπέρ, prep. with gen. τῆς ἀληθείας, "for the truth." Barnett 611: "Paul's claim to live 'on behalf of' . . . the truth is probably pointed at those who are 'pseudo,' 'false apostles' . . . they live against the truth."

VERSE 9

χαίρομεν γὰρ ὅταν ἡμεῖς ἀσθενῶμεν, ὑμεῖς δὲ δυνατοὶ ἦτε·
We rejoice when we are weak and you are strong.

Χαίρομεν, 1st pl. pres. act. indic. of χαίρω, "rejoice." Ὅταν, temporal particle "when, whenever." Ἡμεῖς, emphatic. Ἀσθενῶμεν, 1st pl. pres. act. subjunc. of ἀσθενέω, "be weak." Ὑμεῖς, emphatic complementing emphatic ἡμεῖς. Δυνατοί, nom. pl. masc. adj. δυνατός, -ή, -όν, "strong." Ἦτε, 2nd pl. pres. subjunc. of εἰμί, "be." Harris 927: "But it is not the case that Paul's weakness produced their strength, unless the 'weakness' were taken to be his self-expenditure for the Corinthians' welfare (cf. 12:15). Rather, his weakness resulted from their strength, for if the Corinthians were strong in Christ, reformed in attitude and conduct, Paul would have no occasion to use his apostolic power."

τοῦτο καὶ εὐχόμεθα, τὴν ὑμῶν κατάρτισιν.
We also pray that you become fully mature.

Τοῦτο, acc. sg. neut. pron. οὗτος, αὕτη, τοῦτο, "this," dir. obj. of εὐχόμεθα. Εὐχόμεθα, 1st pl. pres. mid. act. indic. of εὔχομαι, "pray." Τὴν ὑμῶν κατάρτισιν stands in appos. to τοῦτο. Cf. R 698. Κατάρτισιν, acc. sg. fem. κατάρτισις, -εως, ἡ, "maturation." BDAG

526c: "the process of perfecting." ZG 563: "*restoration to perfection.*" Thrall 2:899: "spiritual and moral rectification."

VERSE 10

διὰ τοῦτο ταῦτα ἀπὼν γράφω,
This is why I am writing these things while absent,

Διά, prep. with acc. τοῦτο, "on account of this," looking forward to what he will say next. Ταῦτα, acc. pl. neut. pron. "these things," dir. obj. of γράφω. Ἀπών, nom. sg. masc. of pres. ptc. of ἄπειμι, "be absent." Γράφω, 1st sg. pres. act. indic. "write."

ἵνα παρὼν μὴ ἀποτόμως χρήσωμαι κατὰ τὴν ἐξουσίαν
so that when I am there I may not have to deal harshly with you, in keeping with the authority

Ἵνα . . . with subjunc. χρήσωμαι expresses purpose, "that I may (not) need. . . ." Παρών, nom. sg. masc. of pres. ptc. of πάρειμι, "be present." Ἀποτόμως, adv., "severely, harshly," implying some sort of discipline. Χρήσωμαι, 1st sg. aor. mid. subjunc. of χράομαι, "act, use." BDAG 1088b: "*act, proceed* . . . w. adv. . . . ἀποτόμως 2 Cor 13:10." Κατά, prep. with acc. τὴν ἐξουσίαν "in keeping with/according to the authority." Ἐξουσίαν, acc. sg. fem. ἐξουσία, -ας, ἡ, "authority."

ἣν ὁ κύριος ἔδωκέν μοι εἰς οἰκοδομὴν καὶ οὐκ εἰς καθαίρεσιν.
the Lord gave me for building up and not for tearing down.

Hafemann 494 notes that this is another (cf. 10:8) allusion to Jer. 24:6, allusions that bracket chs. 10–13. Ἥν, acc. sg. fem. rel. pron. ὅς, ἥ, ὅ, "which," antecedent τὴν ἐξουσίαν, dir. obj. of ἔδωκέν. Ἔδωκεν, 3rd sg. aor. act. indic. of δίδωμι, "give." Μοί, dat. sg. masc. pron. ἐγώ, "me," indir. obj. of ἔδωκεν. Εἰς, prep. with acc. οἰκοδομήν, "for building up." Οἰκοδομήν, acc. sg. fem. οἰκοδομή, -ῆς, ἡ, "building up, edification." Εἰς, prep with acc. καθαίρεσιν, "for tearing down." Καθαίρεσιν, acc. sg. fem. καθαίρεσις, -εως, ἡ, "tearing down, destruction."

E. CONCLUSION (13:11–13)

Typical of ancient letters, this one concludes with some final words of exhortation and encouragement, followed by a benediction invoking God's blessing upon the readers.

1. Final Exhortations (13:11–12)

STRUCTURE

11 Λοιπόν, ἀδελφοί, χαίρετε,
            καταρτίζεσθε,
            παρακαλεῖσθε,
            τὸ αὐτὸ φρονεῖτε,
            εἰρηνεύετε,
    καὶ ὁ θεὸς τῆς ἀγάπης καὶ εἰρήνης ἔσται μεθ᾽ ὑμῶν.
12 ἀσπάσασθε ἀλλήλους
            ἐν ἁγίῳ φιλήματι.
    ἀσπάζονται ὑμᾶς οἱ ἅγιοι πάντες.

VERSE 11

λοιπόν, ἀδελφοί, χαίρετε, καταρτίζεσθε, παρακαλεῖσθε,
Finally, brothers and sisters, rejoice. Become mature, be encouraged,

Λοιπόν, adv., "finally." Harris 931–32: "The adverbial expression (τὸ) λοιπόν is an accusative of respect, 'with respect to what remains,' 'as far as the rest is concerned,' and has a variety of meanings. Here it points to concluding comments and means 'finally.'" Ἀδελφοί, voc. pl. masc. ἀδελφός, -οῦ, ὁ, "brother." Χαίρετε, 2nd pl. pres. act. impv. of χαίρω, "rejoice." Καταρτίζεσθε, 2nd pl. pres. mid. impv. of καταρτίζω, "be mature." BDAG 526b: *restore to a former condition, put to rights . . . mend your ways.*" Seifrid 488: "'Be restored!' or, as one might render it, 'Be made whole!'" Παρακαλεῖσθε, 2nd pl. pres. pass. impv. of παρακαλέω, "be encouraged." Harris 933: "We prefer the passive sense, 'be exhorted,' that is, 'heed my appeals,' or 'accept admonition.'"

τὸ αὐτὸ φρονεῖτε, εἰρηνεύετε, καὶ ὁ θεὸς τῆς ἀγάπης καὶ εἰρήνης ἔσται μεθ᾽ ὑμῶν.
be of the same mind, be at peace, and the God of love and peace will be with you.

Τὸ αὐτό, lit. "the same thing," standing in the attributive position, αὐτό means "the same." Φρονεῖτε, 2nd pl. pres. act. impv. of φρονέω, "think, hold an opinion." Εἰρηνεύετε, 2nd pl. pres. act. impv. of εἰρηνεύω, live at peace." Τῆς ἀγάπης καὶ εἰρήνης, attrib. gen. "(the God) of love and peace." Ἔσται, 3rd sg. fut. indic. of εἰμί, "be." Μεθ᾽, prep. with gen. ὑμῶν, "with you." Thrall 2:911: "we prefer to understand v. 11b as a promise, somewhat loosely connected in thought with v. 11a." Seifrid 491: "In all these instances, the condition to be fulfilled is not a mere act of the human being (which might then be thought to secure divine favor). It is rather an entrance into the reality and gift of salvation already given." Harris 935: "Since the verb in v.11b is an indicative (ἔσται), not an optative (εἴη), the statement Paul makes is in effect a promise."

VERSE 12

ἀσπάσασθε ἀλλήλους ἐν ἁγίῳ φιλήματι. ἀσπάζονται ὑμᾶς οἱ ἅγιοι πάντες.
Greet one another with a holy kiss. All the saints send you greetings.

Ἀσπάσασθε, 2nd pl. aor. mid. impv. of ἀσπάζομαι, "greet." Ἀλλήλους, acc. pl. masc. reciprocal pron., "one another." Ἐν, with dat. ἁγίῳ φιλήματι, "with a holy kiss." Ἁγίῳ, dat. sg. neut. adj. ἅγιος, -ία, -ον, "holy." Φιλήματι, dat. sg. neut. φίλημα, -ατος, τό, "kiss." In the NT the kiss was a sign of greeting and respect. Paul repeatedly exhorted members of the churches to greet one another with a holy kiss (cf. Rom 16:16; 1 Cor 16:20; 1 Thess 5:26; cf. 1 Pet 5:14). The fact that the kiss was described as "holy" indicates that erotic overtones were excluded; the kiss was a greeting, a sign of peace and Christian love. Harris 936: "As well as expressing love and unity, the 'holy kiss' signified reconciliation (cf. Gen. 33:4; 45:15; Luke 15:20) and forgiveness, and so naturally came to be associated in the post-NT period with the celebration of the Lord's Supper, possibly under the influence of Jesus' word in Matt. 5:23–24."

Ἀσπάζονται ὑμᾶς οἱ ἅγιοι πάντες. Harris 936–37: "in many EVV . . . this sentence is v. 13 and the final benediction is v. 14. . . . The division of 2 Corinthians 13 into fourteen verses seems to have begun with the second folio edition of the 'Bishops' Bible' (1572)." Ἀσπάζονται, 3rd pl. pres. mid. indic. of ἀσπάζομαι, "greet, send greetings." Ὑμᾶς, acc. 2nd pl. pron. σύ, "you." Ἅγιοι, nom. pl. neut. subst. adj. ἅγιος, -ία, -ον, "holy ones, saints." Πάντες, nom. pl. masc. adj. πᾶς, πᾶσα, πᾶν, "all."

FOR FURTHER STUDY

114. Two or Three Witnesses (13:1)

Jackson, B. S. "'Two or Three Witnesses.'" In *Essays in Jewish and Christian Legal History*. Studies in Judaism in Late Antiquity 10:153–71. Leiden: Brill, 1975.
Trites, A. A. *DPL* 973–75.
van Vliet, H. *No Single Testimony: A Study on the Adoption of the Law of Deut. 19:15 par. into the New Testament*. Studia Theologica Rheno-Traiectina 4. Utrecht: Kemink and Zoon, 1958.

115. Weakness and Power (13:3–4)

Beasley-Murray, G. *Power for God's Sake: The Use and Abuse of Power in the Local Church*. Carlisle, UK: Paternoster, 1998.
Black, D. A. *DPL* 966–67.

Gräbe, P. J. *The Power of God in Paul's Letters.* Tübingen: Mohr, 2000.

Heckel, U. *Kraft in Schwachheit: Untersuchung zu 2. Kor 10-13.* Tübingen: Mohr, 1993.

Kennedy, H. A. A. "'Weakness and Power': 2 Corinthians XIII.3, 4." *ExpTim* 13 (1901–02): 349–50.

Lambrecht, J. "Philological and Exegetical Notes on 2 Cor 13, 4." *Bijdragen* 46 (1985): 261–69.

116. Perseverance (13:5)

Brown, P. C. "What Is the Meaning of 'Examine Yourselves' in 2 Corinthians 13:5?" *BibSac* 154 (1997): 175–88.

Carson, D. A. "Reflections on Christian Assurance." *WJT* 54 (1992): 1–29.

Gundry Volf, J. M. *Paul and Perseverance: Staying In and Falling Away.* Tübingen: Mohr, 1990.

Marshall, I. H. *Kept by the Power of God: A Study of Perseverance and Falling Away.* London: Epworth, 1969.

HOMILETICAL SUGGESTIONS

Responding to Criticisms (13:1–4)

1. The importance of witnesses when bringing charges of wrongdoing (v. 1)
2. Pastoral warnings are sometimes necessary (v. 2)
3. The simultaneity of Christ's power and weakness (vv. 3–4)

Testing Oneself to Ensure the Authenticity of Christian Experience (13:5–8)

1. Self-examination to be done, remembering that "Christ is in you" (v. 5)
2. Praying that believers will do nothing wrong, but do what is right (v. 7–8)
3. Being ready to be regarded as "weak" if that means others become mature (v. 9)
4. Doing all we can to avoid "tearing down," and instead be "building up" (v. 10)

Exhortations and Encouragements (13:11–12)

1. The importance of exhortation, and the promise of God's presence (v. 11)
2. The "holy kiss" of affection and reconciliation (v. 12)

2. Benediction (13:13)

STRUCTURE

13 Ἡ χάρις
    τοῦ κυρίου Ἰησοῦ Χριστοῦ
  καὶ ἡ ἀγάπη
    τοῦ θεοῦ
  καὶ ἡ κοινωνία
    τοῦ ἁγίου πνεύματος
      μετὰ πάντων ὑμῶν.

VERSE 13

Ἡ χάρις τοῦ κυρίου Ἰησοῦ Χριστοῦ καὶ ἡ ἀγάπη τοῦ θεοῦ καὶ ἡ κοινωνία τοῦ ἁγίου πνεύματος μετὰ πάντων ὑμῶν.
The grace of the Lord Jesus Christ, and the love of God, and the fellowship of the Holy Spirit be with you all.

The closing invocation of God's blessing is especially significant because of its triadic formulation. It is the only place in the NT where God the Father, Son, and Holy Spirit are explicitly mentioned together in such a benediction.

Χάρις, nom. sg. fem. χάρις, -ιτος, ἡ, "grace." Τοῦ κυρίου Ἰησοῦ Χριστοῦ, subj. gen. "grace provided by the Lord Jesus Christ." Ἀγάπη, nom. sg. fem. ἀγάπη, -ης, ἡ, "love." Τοῦ θεοῦ, subj. gen., "love shown by God." Κοινωνία, nom. sg. fem. κοινωνία, -ας, ἡ, "fellowship."

Τοῦ ἁγίου πνεύματος, subj. gen. "fellowship engendered by the Holy Spirit." Cf. Harris, *Prepositions*, 166–67: "Τοῦ ἁγίου πνεύματος could be a subjective genitive in parallelism with the two preceding genitives ('the fellowship with one another engendered by the Holy Spirit' or 'the sense of community created by the Holy Spirit'; cf. Eph 4:3), but it could also be an objective genitive ('participation in the Holy Spirit'). . . . On this view, Paul is expressing a wish (εἴη is to be understood with μετά) that the Corinthians should continue (cf. 2Co 1:7; 12:13) in their common participation in the Spirit's life, power and gifts (cf. 1Co 12:7; 14:1)."

Μετά, prep. with gen. πάντων ὑμῶν, "(be) with you all." Harris, *Prepositions*, 166: "As he does in all his letters, Paul uses the preposition μετά in expressing his benedictory wish that a divine person or quality should be 'present with' or 'experienced by' his addressees and so should constantly fortify them. This contrasts starkly with contemporary letters that often conclude with a generalized wish such as ἐρρῶσθαι ὑμᾶς εὔχομαι, 'I pray you may fare well.'"

FOR FURTHER STUDY

117. Benedictions and Doxologies (13:13)

Champion, L. G. *Benedictions and Doxologies in the Epistles of Paul.* Oxford: Kemp Hall, 1934.

Depasse-Livet, J. "L'existence chrétienne. Participation à la Vie Trinitaire, 2 Cor 13,11–13." *Assemblées du Seigneur* 31 (1973): 10–13.

Klassen, W. *ABD* IV, 91.

Maleparampil, J. *The "Trinitarian" Formulae in St. Paul: An Exegetical Investigation into the Meaning and Function of Those Pauline Sayings Which Compositely Make Mention of God, Christ and the Holy Spirit.* Frankfurt am Main/New York: Lang, 1998.

O' Brien, P. *DPL* 68–71.

Wainwright, A. W. *The Trinity in the New Testament.* London: SPCK, 1962.

118. Fellowship (13:13)

Campbell, J. Y. "KOINΩNIA and Its Cognates in the New Testament." *JBL* 51 (1932): 352–80.

Martin. R. P. "The Spirit in 2 Corinthians in the Light of 'The Fellowship of the Spirit' in 2 Corinthians 13:14." In *Eschatology and the New Testament Eschatology and the New Testament: Essays in Honor of George Raymond Beasley-Murray*, edited by W. Hulitt Gloer, 113–28. Peabody, MA, 1988.

McDermott, J. M. "The Biblical Doctrine of KOINΩNIA." *BZ* 19 (1975): 64–77, 219–33.

Panikulam, G. *Koinōnia in the New Testament: A Dynamic Expression of Christian Life.* Rome: Biblical Institute, 1979.

HOMILETICAL SUGGESTIONS

A Trinitarian Benediction, Invoking Grace, Love, and Fellowship (13:13)

1. The grace of our Lord Jesus Christ (v. 13a)
2. The love of God (v. 13b)
3. The fellowship of the Holy Spirit (v. 13c)

Exegetical Outline

I. Paul's Response to a Crisis Resolved (1:1–9:15)
   A. Preface (1:1–11)
      1. The Address and Greeting (1:1–2)
      2. The Benediction (1:3–11)
         a. Paul Blesses God and Expresses His Hope for His Readers (1:3–7)
         b. Paul's Troubles in Asia (1:8–11)
   B. The Body of the Response (1:12–7:16)
      1. Personal Defense (1:12–24)
         a. General Defense of Integrity (1:12–14)
         b. Defense of Changed Travel Plans (1:15–22)
         c. Paul Calls upon God as His Witness (1:23–25)
      2. The "Severe Letter": Its Purpose and Aftermath (2:1–13)
         a. The Purpose of the "Severe Letter" (2:1–4)
         b. Forgiveness for the Offender (2:5–11)
         c. Waiting for Titus (2:12–13)
      3. Competency in Ministry (2:14–4:6)
         a. Led in Triumph (2:14–17)
         b. Letters of Recommendation (3:1–3)
         c. Ministers of the New Covenant (3:4–6)
         d. The Greater Glory of New Covenant Ministry (3:7–11)
         e. The Greater Boldness of New Covenant Ministers (3:12–18)
         f. The Conduct of Paul's Ministry (4:1–6)
      4. Present Suffering and Future Glory (4:7–5:10)
         a. Treasure in Jars of Clay (4:7–15)
         b. We Do Not Give Up (4:16–18)
         c. The Heavenly Dwelling (5:1–10)
      5. The Ministry of Reconciliation (5:11–21)
         a. Defense of His Ministry (5:11–15)
         b. God's Reconciling Act in Christ (5:16–21)
      6. Reconciliation Practiced (6:1–7:4)
         a. An Appeal for Reconciliation (6:1–13)

          b. A Call for Holy Living (6:14–7:1)

          c. A Further Appeal for Reconciliation (7:2–4)

      7. Paul's Joy after a Crisis Resolved (7:5–16)

          a. Paul's Relief When Titus Arrived (7:5–7)

          b. The "Severe Letter" and Its Effects (7:8–13a)

          c. Titus's Happiness and Affection for the Corinthians (7:13b–16)

  C. The Matter of the Collection (8:1–9:15)

      1. The Example of the Macedonians (8:1–6)

      2. Paul Exhorts the Corinthians to Finish What They Began (8:7–15)

      3. Commendation of Those Who Will Receive the Collection (8:16–24)

      4. Be Prepared and Avoid Humiliation (9:1–5)

      5. An Exhortation to Be Generous (9:6–15)

II. Paul Responds to a New Crisis (10:1–13:14)

  A. Paul's Exercise of Apostolic Authority (10:1–18)

      1. Paul Responds to Criticisms (10:1–11)

      2. Boasting within Proper Limits (10:12–18)

  B. A Plea for Tolerance and Condemnation of the Opponents (11:1–15)

      1. The Corinthians' Gullibility (11:1–6)

      2. The Matter of Financial Remuneration (11:7–15)

  C. The Fool's Speech (11:16–12:13)

      1. Accept Me as a Fool (11:16–21a)

      2. Paul's Jewish Ancestry (11:21b–22)

      3. A Better Servant of Christ (11:23–33)

      4. Visions and Revelations (12:1–10)

      5. Signs of an Apostle (12:11–13)

  D. Paul's Planned Third Visit (12:14–13:10)

      1. Paul Refuses to Burden the Corinthians (12:14–18)

      2. The Real Purpose of Paul's Fool's Speech (12:19–21)

      3. Paul Threatens Strong Action on His Third Visit (13:1–10)

  E. Conclusion (13:11–13)

      1. Final Exhortations (13:11–12)

      2. Benediction (13:13)

Grammar Index

A

accusative
  adv. acc. *216*
  of appos. *217*
  denotes movement *15, 68*
  direct obj. *148, 150, 152, 164*
  double acc. *86*
  pred. acc. *140*
  of respect (reference) *21, 220*
  subj. of inf. *18–19, 111, 130, 148, 164, 185*
adjective
  abs. adj. *269*
  comp. adj. *44–45, 96, 173, 176, 183*
  subst. adj. *82, 85, 99, 111, 120–22, 131, 133, 137–40, 148, 163, 167, 171, 174–75, 177, 181, 188–89, 211, 226, 231–32, 264, 273–74, 277*
  verbal adj. *12, 152*
adverb
  comp. adv. *26, 43, 148, 157, 238, 261, 270*
  dem. adv. *17, 157*
  temp. adv. (time) *75–76, 182*
agency
  efficient agency *47, 108, 123, 174, 254*
  implied agency *45, 74, 76, 98*
alliteration *189*
anacoluthon *191*
aorist
  constative *68, 176*
  epistolary *183*
  gnomic *189*
  inceptive (ingressive) *74, 151*
  timeless *82*

apodosis *70, 98*
apposition *13, 32, 40, 48, 105, 108, 117, 140, 153, 167, 177, 217, 255, 274*
article. *See* Granville-Sharpe rule
  anaphoric *109, 153*
  anarthrous *248*
  substantive *44*
aspect *21, 32, 37, 75*

C

chiasm *265, 271*
clause
  causal *87*
  purpose *20, 42, 46–47, 96, 108, 169, 171, 251*
  result *21, 45, 68, 175*
  subord. *42*
conditional sentence *69, 98, 204, 261*
  first-class cond. *43–44, 68, 84, 150, 203, 218–19*
  third-class cond. *104–5, 204*
conjunction
  adversative *20, 36, 44, 55–56, 119, 121, 260–61*
  ascensive *19, 153, 191, 204*
  causal *82*
  comp. *17, 27*
  conditional *110, 176*
  coord. *27, 36, 55, 104*
  explanatory *86, 151*
  inferential *30, 72, 154*
  temp. *75*
  transitonal *91*

D

dative
  of advantage *54, 116, 163, 201, 250*

of cause *29, 192*
of content *143*
of indir. obj. *45, 123–24, 137, 148, 154, 157, 161, 164, 168, 173, 182, 190–91, 217, 222, 224, 251–52, 256, 260–61, 264, 275*
of location *68*
of manner *77, 143, 263*
of means (instr. dat.) *37, 60, 68, 72, 262*
of respect *249, 265*
of time *98*

E

ellipsis *45, 176, 187–88, 231, 234, 237*
emphasis *32, 108, 189, 209, 254*

F

future
  gnomic *187*
  imperatival (command) *87*

G

genitive
  abs. *21, 124, 146, 157, 193, 266*
  of appos. *9, 35*
  attrib. gen. *26, 78, 99, 122, 130, 152, 161–62, 205, 276*
  of comp. *44, 220, 255*
  of content *85, 124*
  of description *48, 60, 68, 83, 86, 91, 95, 122, 138, 140, 190, 202, 210, 217, 224, 227, 240*
  epex. gen. *108, 161, 191–92*

obj. gen.   *13, 16, 36, 68, 70,*
   83–84, 88, 115, 117, 141,
   167, 201–2, 223, 226, 247
of poss.   *8, 36, 60, 69, 85,*
   88, 123, 130–31, 134,
   138–39, 161, 167, 176,
   183, 192–93, 198, 203,
   210, 222, 224, 226, 251,
   253
of separation   *218*
of source   *9, 60, 63, 85, 88,*
   91, 105, 122, 130, 151,
   161, 167, 224
subj. gen.   *8, 16, 54, 60,*
   84, 117, 164, 183, 198,
   224, 226, 247, 251, 253,
   255, 279
of subord.   *13*
Granville-Sharpe rule   *13*

H

hapax legomenon   *19, 30,*
   136, 198
hendiadys   *163, 198*

I

imperative
   aor. impv.   *125, 130, 134,*
      139, 142, 169, 256, 260,
      277
   pres. impv.   *139*
imperfect   *29, 41, 123, 150,*
   183, 216, 242, 254
implied verb   *86, 91*
infinitive
   complementary infin.   *18,*
      41, 188, 220
   explanatory (epex.) in-
      fin.   *169*
   purpose infin.   *14, 73, 85,*
      164, 169, 211
   result infin.   *19, 45, 68, 85,*
      142, 148, 155, 164, 185

M

metaphor   *20, 46, 52, 60, 106,*
   132, 200, 202, 241, 260

N

nominative
   of appos.   *8, 13, 32, 147,*
      174, 177
   nom. abs.   *8, 9*
   pred. nom.   *25, 54, 126,*
      139, 157

O

optative   *9, 188*

P

paronomasia   *64, 92, 152, 189*
participle
   adv. ptc.   *17, 30*
   attrib. ptc.   *8, 9, 14, 70,*
      122, 125, 174–75
   causal ptc.   *17, 96, 261*
   concessive ptc.   *168, 200*
   periph. ptc.   *20, 55, 123,*
      137, 184, 191, 205
   subst.   *73, 108, 116, 190,*
      211
   subst. ptc.   *208*
prepostion(al) (phrase)   *8, 14,*
   20, 25, 54, 151, 155
   location (locative)   *54, 143,*
      161
   means (instr.)   *164*
   origin   *106*
   reason   *116*
present
   futuristic   *269*
   gnomic   *64, 188*
   perfective   *233*
pronoun

dem.   *20, 46, 140, 166, 168,*
   174, 185, 192, 203, 224,
   226, 248
indef.   *46, 204, 262, 274*
interr.   *137*
pers.   *41, 217*
reciprocal   *277*
refl.   *19, 39, 59, 83, 86,*
   203, 272
protasis   *68, 261*

S

Semitic influence   *140, 190,*
   262
subject
   neut. pl. with sg. vb.   *260*
subjunctive
   hortatory   *140*
   purpose   *14, 20, 29, 41–42,*
      44, 46, 91, 93–94, 96,
      108, 111, 116, 119, 126,
      131, 155, 164–65, 171,
      183, 185, 188, 222, 225,
      250–52, 273–75
   result   *151, 184*

T

tautology   *107*
telic   *164, 167, 274*

V

verbs
   impers.   *168*
   implied   *12, 52, 170–71,*
      173
vocative   *18, 134, 140, 264,*
   276
voice
   divine pass   *161, 248*

Scripture Index

Genesis

1:26   *85*
3   *226*
27:1–40   *152*
33:4   *277*
45:15   *277*

Exodus

4:10   *55, 62*
28:41   *34*
31:18   *61*
34:29–32   *67*
34:33–35   *67, 71, 77*
34:34   *76*

Leviticus

4:24   *125*
5:12   *125*
19:19   *137*
26:11–12   *139*

Numbers

33:55   *251*

Deuteronomy

15:10   *188*
19:15   *269*
25:1–3   *238*
29:4   *74*

Joshua

3:10   *60*

1 Samuel

15:1   *34*
17:26   *60*
17:36   *60*

2 Samuel

7:8   *140*
7:14   *140*

12:13   *152*

1 Kings

19:16   *34*

2 Chronicles

25:4   *75*

Nehemiah

9:19   *13*
13:1   *75*

Psalms

32:2   *123*
51:1   *13*
51:1–11   *152*
95:8   *74*
112:9   *189*
115:1   *95*
116:10   *95*

Proverbs

3:4   *175*
12:25   *159*
14   *259*
15:30   *159*
18   *259*
21:22   *201*
22:8   *187–88*

Isaiah

1:22   *55*
9:2   *87*
28:16   *212*
40:1   *147*
49:8   *130*
49:13   *147*
51:3   *147*
51:12   *147*
51:19   *147*
52:9   *147*
52:11   *139*

53:4–6   *126*
53:12   *126*
55:10   *190*
61:2   *147*
63:7   *13*
65:17–25   *121*
66:13   *147*
66:22   *121*

Jeremiah

9:23–24   *211*
10:10   *60*
23:15   *140*
24:6   *275*
31:31   *61, 63*
31:31–34   *61, 64*

Ezekiel

28:24   *251*
36:24–32   *61*
36:25–27   *64*

Daniel

9:9   *13*

Hosea

2:8   *251*
10:12   *190*

Matthew

4:15–16   *87*
5:2   *133*
5:23–24   *277*
10:2   *8*
10:32–33   *100*
13:35   *133*
14:3–4   *242*
24   *99*
26:46   *93*
27:3–5   *152*
27:4   *125*
27:24   *125*

285

27:46 *13*

Mark

9:31 *94*
10:33 *94*
12:26 *75*
13:3–8 *99*
13:17–20 *99*
13:24–27 *99*
14:72 *152*
16:20 *34*

Luke

1:79 *87*
2:25 *13, 148*
4:18 *34*
8:12 *85*
10:17–20 *212*
12:42–48 *111*
15:20 *277*
18:1 *82*
21 *99*
22:20 *63*
23:47 *125*

John

1:1 *110*
1:2 *110*
8:46 *125*
14:9 *77*
20:17 *13*
20:29 *109*

Acts

1:2 *8*
2:38 *34*
4:27 *34*
6:1 *235*
9:1–22 *152*
9:3–6 *87*
9:4–5 *15*
9:29–30 *247*
10:38 *34*
11:25 *247*
11:27–30 *160*
11:29 *188*
13:44–45 *84*
14:15 *60*
15 *206*
15:21 *75*
15:23 *9*
17:1–10 *251*
17:5–9 *84*
17:5–14 *147*
18:1–4 *221*

18:2 *3*
18:5–6 *84*
18:9 *147*
18:12–17 *3*
18:12–31 *84*
18:18 *4*
18:23 *4*
19:8–9 *84*
19:23–41 *18*
20:7–12 *239*
20:31 *239*
21:13 *260*
22:6–11 *87*
23:26 *9*
24:4 *198*
24:15 *41*
26:12–18 *87*
27 *206*

Romans

1:4 *141*
1:5 *209*
1:9 *36*
1:13–14 *209*
1:16 *201*
1:18 *54*
1:18–32 *124*
1:25 *33*
1–11 *13*
2:5–11 *124*
3:25 *125*
4:8 *123*
4:15 *77*
5:10 *122*
5:11 *122*
5:12 *118*
5:16 *111*
5:18 *111*
5:18a *118*
5:19a *118*
5:20 *77*
6:9–10 *94*
6:15–23 *152*
7:4 *64*
7:6 *64*
7:8 *115*
7:10 *64*
7:12 *64*
7:14 *64*
7:17–18 *26*
7:23 *26*
7:25 *26*
8:1 *111*
8:2 *94*
8:2–4 *64*
8:3 *64, 125*

8:9 *76, 224*
8:10 *76*
8:17–18 *99*
8:17–23 *99*
8:18–24 *104, 104–6*
8:18–25 *121*
8:19–22 *123*
8:19–23 *121*
8:23 *104, 107*
8:24–25 *100*
8:31–39 *11*
8:32 *9*
9:5 *33*
9:33 *212*
10:11 *212*
10:12 *168*
10:14–17 *32*
11:12 *168*
11:15 *122*
11:36 *33*
12 *162*
12:1 *13*
12:3 *209*
14:10 *111*
15:6 *13*
15:16 *170*
15:17–19 *25, 61–62*
15:18–19 *209, 255*
15:31 *170*
15:32 *164*
15:33 *33*
16:3 *177*
16:7 *8*
16:9 *177*
16:10 *212*
16:16 *277*
16:21 *177*
16:27 *33*

1 Corinthians

1:1 *164*
1:5 *166*
1:6 *34*
1:8 *34*
1:17–25 *201*
1:18 *26*
1:18–2:5 *62*
1:18–25 *84*
1:26–31 *11*
1:31 *211*
1–2 *26*
2:1 *249*
2:1–5 *201*
2:4–5 *61*
3:3 *26*
3:10–15 *111*

3:13 *212*
3:15 *151*
3:16–17 *138*
3:17 *142*
3:18–20 *233*
4:2–5 *25*
4:5 *111–12*
4:10 *233*
5:7 *125*
6:1 *154*
6:5 *233*
6:16–20 *138*
7:6 *167*
7:9 *241*
7:11 *122*
7:25 *168*
7:29 *187*
8:1–7 *233*
8:7–13 *241*
9:1 *8, 254*
9:14 *222*
11:25 *63, 74*
12:7 *279*
13:2 *233*
14:1 *279*
14:2 *116*
14:37–38 *168*
15:7 *8*
15:9–10 *82*
15:15 *187*
15:20 *96*
15:23 *96, 110*
15:32 *18*
15:33 *142*
15:35–38 *98*
15:42–44 *110*
15:52 *110*
16:1–4 *160, 169*
16:2 *169, 260*
16:20 *277*

2 Corinthians

1 *141*
1:1 *8, 164, 177*
1:1–9:15 *4*
1:1–11 *4*
1:2 *9*
1:3 *12, 15*
1:3–4 *12*
1:3–11 *24*
1:4 *14*
1:5 *14*
1:6 *15*
1:6–7 *12, 17*
1:7 *17, 279*
1:8 *18, 92, 261*

1:8–9a *17*
1:9 *19, 92*
1:9b *17*
1:10 *17, 20*
1:11 *17, 21, 25*
1:12 *24, 27, 115*
1:12–7:16 *4*
1:12–14 *24, 28*
1:12–24 *4*
1:13 *26–27, 34*
1:14 *27, 96*
1:14a *27*
1:15 *29–30*
1:15–2:3 *205*
1:15–2:4 *24*
1:15–16 *30*
1:15–17 *31*
1:15–22 *24*
1:16 *29–30*
1:17 *30*
1:17a *31*
1:17b *31*
1:17–18 *32*
1:18 *31, 190*
1:18–22 *31*
1:19 *32*
1:20 *33*
1:21 *33–34*
1:21–22 *35*
1:22 *34*
1:23 *35–36*
1:23–24 *24, 31*
1:24 *36, 62, 87, 233*
2 *141*
2:1 *4, 39, 270*
2:1–4 *39*
2:1–13 *4*
2:2 *40*
2:3 *41–42, 154*
2:4 *42, 154*
2:5 *43, 129, 153, 196*
2:5–8 *39*
2:5–11 *196*
2:6 *44, 153*
2:6–7 *45*
2:7 *44*
2:8 *45*
2:9 *46, 154*
2:10 *39, 46*
2:11 *39, 47, 218*
2:12 *48*
2:12–13 *39*
2:13 *48, 146*
2:13a *48*
2:14 *52, 54*
2:14–4:6 *51*

2:14–7:4 *146*
2:14–17 *51–52*
2:15 *53–54*
2:16 *54, 61–62, 224*
2:17 *55, 59, 62, 83*
3 *62, 76*
3:1 *59, 84*
3:1–3 *51*
3:8–18 *64*
3:1–4:7 *90*
3:2 *26, 59*
3:3 *60–61, 77*
3:4 *61*
3:4–6 *51, 61*
3:5 *62, 64*
3:5–10 *64*
3:6 *63, 67, 74, 77, 94*
3:7 *63, 68–69*
3:7–8 *68–69*
3:7–11 *67, 72*
3:7–18 *51, 61, 67, 81*
3:8 *63, 69*
3:9 *69*
3:9a *70*
3:10 *70*
3:11 *69, 71–72*
3:12 *72, 74*
3:12–18 *67, 71*
3:13 *69, 71, 73–74*
3:14 *73–74, 218*
3:14–16 *84*
3:15 *74–75*
3:16 *76–77*
3:17 *76–77*
3:17a *78*
3:18 *74, 77–78, 98*
3:18b *77*
3:18c *78*
4 *85*
4:1 *67, 73, 82, 98*
4:1–6 *51, 81, 201*
4:2 *55, 59, 82–84*
4:3 *84, 86*
4:4 *84–85, 218*
4:4b *86*
4:5 *86*
4:6 *87, 90–91, 97*
4:7 *90–91*
4:7–12 *16–17*
4:7–5:10 *90*
4:8 *91*
4:8–9 *90–91*
4:9 *92*
4:10 *93–94*
4:10a *94*
4:10b *94*

4:10–11   *94*
4:10–12   *90*
4:11   *94*
4:12   *94–95*
4:13   *95*
4:13–15   *90*
4:14   *28, 95, 107*
4:14–15   *97–98*
4:15   *96–97*
4:15a   *95*
4:16   *82, 97, 103*
4:16–5:10   *103–5*
4:16–17   *95*
4:16–18   *97, 104*
4:17   *99–100, 103*
4:18   *100*
4:30   *34*
5   *105*
5:1   *103–4*
5:1a   *105*
5:1b   *105*
5:1–5   *98*
5:1–10   *97, 103–4, 107*
5:2   *106*
5:2–3   *107*
5:3   *106–7*
5:4   *107–9*
5:5   *108*
5:6   *108–9*
5:7   *109–10*
5:8   *109–10*
5:9   *110, 114*
5:10   *28, 107, 111, 114*
5:11   *114*
5:11–15   *114*
5:12   *59, 115–16, 131*
5:13   *116*
5:14   *117–18, 124*
5:14–15   *118, 121, 123*
5:15   *118*
5:16   *120*
5:16–21   *114*
5:17   *98, 121*
5:18   *122*
5:18a   *122*
5:18b   *122*
5:19   *118, 122–23*
5:19a   *123*
5:20   *122, 124, 129*
5:21   *123, 125, 168, 190*
5:21a   *126*
5:21b   *125*
5:23   *104*
5:23–24   *106*
6   *208*
6:1   *129–30, 136*

6:1–2   *128*
6:1–7:4   *128*
6:1–13   *141*
6:2   *130, 170*
6:3   *131*
6:3–10   *128*
6:4   *59*
6:4a   *131*
6:4–5   *131*
6:4b–5   *131–32, 240*
6:4–10   *133*
6:6   *132*
6:6–7   *132*
6:6–7a   *132*
6:6c–18   *136*
6:7   *132*
6:8–10   *132*
6:8a   *133*
6:8b–10   *133*
6:10   *168*
6:11   *133, 141*
6:11–13   *128, 133, 136*
6:12   *134*
6:12a   *134*
6:12b   *134*
6:13   *134*
6:14   *137*
6:14–7:1   *3, 128, 136, 141*
6:14a–16a   *136*
6:15   *138*
6:16   *138*
6:16–17   *140*
6:16b   *136*
6:17   *139*
6:18   *140*
7:1   *136, 140*
7:2   *47, 142*
7:2–4   *128, 136, 141, 196*
7:3   *141–42*
7:4   *141, 143, 162*
7:5   *49, 51, 146*
7:5–7   *146*
7:6   *147*
7:7   *141, 148*
7:8   *149–50*
7:8–13a   *146*
7:9   *150–51, 154*
7:10   *151, 153*
7:11   *59, 152–53*
7:11a   *154*
7:12   *129, 153–55, 196*
7:12–13a   *154*
7:13   *141, 156*
7:13b   *156*
7:13b–16   *146*
7:14   *156–57*

7:15   *157*
7:16   *158*
8:1   *161*
8:1–2   *147*
8:1–7   *160*
8:1–9:15   *4*
8:2   *161, 183*
8:3   *162–63*
8:4   *141, 163*
8:5   *163–64*
8:6   *164*
8:7   *166*
8:8   *167*
8:9   *9, 167*
8:10   *164, 168–69*
8:11   *169*
8:12   *169*
8:13   *170*
8:14   *170*
8:15   *171*
8:16   *173*
8:16–17   *171*
8:16–18   *262*
8:17   *173*
8:17–18   *8*
8:18   *174*
8:18–19   *171*
8:19   *174–75, 177*
8:20   *175*
8:20–21   *171*
8:21   *175*
8:22   *171, 176, 212*
8:23   *171, 176*
8:24   *171, 177*
8–9   *4*
9:1   *181*
9:1–5   *186*
9:2   *164, 182–83*
9:2–15   *182*
9:3   *183*
9:3a   *184*
9:3b   *184*
9:4   *184*
9:5   *184–85*
9:6   *187–88*
9:7   *187*
9:8   *188*
9:8–10   *185*
9:9   *189*
9:10   *189–90*
9:11   *162, 190–91*
9:11–13   *185*
9:12   *185, 191*
9:12–14   *185*
9:13   *162, 187, 191–92*
9:14   *192*

9:15 *193*
10 *206, 220*
10:1 *198–99, 208*
10:1–2 *197, 205*
10:1b–2 *200*
10:1–11 *196, 220*
10:1–13:13 *4*
10:1–18 *4*
10:2 *199–200, 260*
10:2b–3 *200*
10:3 *200*
10:3b *202*
10:3–5 *197*
10:3–6 *200*
10:4 *200–3*
10:5 *200–3, 218*
10:6 *197, 200, 202–3, 220*
10:7 *203*
10:7–8 *197*
10:8 *203–4*
10:9 *204–5*
10:9–11 *196–97*
10:10 *205, 208, 271*
10:11 *205*
10:12 *19, 59, 207–8*
10:12–18 *196, 206*
10:13 *209*
10:13–18 *59*
10:14 *209–10*
10:15 *210*
10:16 *211*
10:17 *211*
10:18 *59, 212*
10–13 *4, 196, 203, 275*
11:1 *4, 216, 254*
11:1–6 *196*
11:1–15 *4*
11:2 *28, 217*
11:2–3 *215*
11:3 *83, 147, 218, 261*
11:4 *215, 218–19*
11:4a–b *218*
11:4c *218*
11:5 *219–20*
11:5–6 *215*
11:6 *220*
11:7 *221*
11:7–8 *215*
11:7–9 *215*
11:7–11 *208*
11:8 *222*
11:9 *223*
11:10 *224*
11:11 *215, 224*
11:12 *115, 215, 225–26*
11:13 *4, 225*

11:13–15 *215, 230*
11:14 *226–27*
11:14–15 *202*
11:15 *226*
11:16 *231–32, 254*
11:16–12:10 *117*
11:16–12:13 *4, 196, 215–16, 230*
11:17 *117, 231*
11:18 *232*
11:19 *232*
11:19–20 *208*
11:20 *233–34, 256*
11:20–21 *208*
11:21 *234, 254*
11:21a *234*
11:21b–22 *208*
11:21b–23a *236*
11:22 *235*
11:23 *203, 237*
11:23–29 *16–17*
11:23b–25 *236*
11:23b–29 *236*
11:24 *238*
11:25 *18, 238*
11:26 *236, 239–40*
11:27 *236, 239*
11:28 *239–40*
11:28–29 *236*
11:29 *240–41*
11:29bc *241*
11:30 *241*
11:30–33 *236*
11:31 *13, 241*
11:32 *242*
11:33 *242*
12 *262*
12:1 *208, 247*
12:1–10 *117*
12:2 *218, 248*
12:2–4 *247*
12:4 *249*
12:5 *247, 249*
12:6 *247, 250*
12:7 *247, 250*
12:8 *252*
12:9 *252*
12:10 *253*
12:11 *216, 254*
12:11a *255*
12:11b *255*
12:11–13 *271*
12:12 *208, 255*
12:13 *256, 261, 279*
12:14 *259–61*
12:14–13:10 *4*

12:14–18 *259*
12:15 *261, 274*
12:15a *261*
12:16 *233, 261*
12:16–18 *83, 142*
12:17 *47, 262*
12:17–18 *164*
12:18 *47, 262–63*
12:19 *263–64*
12:19–21 *259*
12:20 *265*
12:20–21 *260, 263*
12:21 *205, 265*
13 *277*
13:1 *260, 268–69*
13:1a *270*
13:1–4 *259*
13:2 *205, 268, 270*
13:3 *208, 224, 268, 271*
13:4 *268, 271*
13:5 *272*
13:5–8 *268*
13:5–10 *259*
13:6 *273*
13:7 *273*
13:8 *274*
13:9 *274*
13:10 *260, 275*
13:11 *276*
13:11–13 *4*
13:11a *276*
13:12 *277*
13:13 *277*
13:14 *277*

Galatians

1:5 *33*
1:6–7 *219*
1:16 *88, 247*
1:18 *247*
1:19 *8*
1:21 *247*
2:1 *247*
2:7–8 *209*
2:10 *160*
3:5–9 *235*
3:13 *118, 125*
3:15 *45*
3:21 *64*
3:23–25 *77*
3:29 *235*
4:4 *13*
4:15 *251*
5:13 *115*
5:15–26 *121*
5:19–21 *265*

6:4 *212*
6:8 *64*
6:9 *82*

Ephesians

1:1 *164*
1:3 *12*
2:1 *54*
2:13–18 *9*
2:16 *122*
2:20 *11*
3:1–9 *249*
3:13 *82*
3:21 *33*
4:3 *279*
4:22 *142*
5:3–6 *124*
5:27 *217*
6:5 *158*
6:11–17 *201*
6:19–20 *249*

Philippians

1:8 *36*
1:23–24 *117*
1:29–30 *17*
2 *168*
2:6 *86*
2:12 *158*
2:13 *164*
2:16 *96*
2:25 *8, 177*
3:2 *147*
3:5 *235*
4:3 *177*
4:20 *33*

Colossians

1:1 *164*
1:15 *86*
1:19 *123*
1:20 *122–23*
1:22 *122, 217*
1:24–25 *15*
1:25–27 *249*
2:9 *123*
2:15 *52–53*
3:1–4 *100*
3:5–6 *124*
4:3 *249*
4:11 *177*

1 Thessalonians

1:9 *60*
2:5 *36*
2:10 *36*
2:17–18 *251*
2:19 *96*
3:2 *177*
3:13 *141*
4:6 *47*
4:14 *96*
4:17 *248*
5:2 *28*
5:12 *121*
5:26 *277*

2 Thessalonians

3:7–8 *240*
3:13 *82*

1 Timothy

1:12–16 *82*
1:17 *33*
1:19 *25*
5:14 *115*
6:16 *33*

2 Timothy

1:1 *164*
2:11–12 *100*
2:15 *212*
2:23 *147*
4:10 *92*
4:16 *93*
4:18 *33*

Titus

3:9 *147*

Philemon

1 *177*
8 *72*
24 *177*

Hebrews

1:9 *34*
3:8 *74*
3:15 *74*
4:7 *74*
4:15 *125*
9:15–28 *63*

11:1–3 *100*
12:15–17 *152*
13:21 *33*

James

1:1 *9*
4:1 *147*

1 Peter

1:3 *12*
1:19 *125*
2:22 *125*
4:5 *260*
4:11 *33*
5:11 *33*
5:14 *277*

2 Peter

3:10 *28*
3:12 *28*
3:18 *33*

1 John

2:2 *124*
2:20 *34*
2:27 *34*
4:19 *117*

2 John

11 *9*

Jude

25 *33*

Revelation

1:6 *33*
7:3–8 *34*
7:12 *33*
21:1 *121*